Contemporary Canadian Composers

Contemporary Canadian Composers

Edited by

Keith MacMillan and John Beckwith

Toronto
London
New York
OXFORD UNIVERSITY PRESS
1975

THIS BOOK
HAS BEEN PUBLISHED WITH THE HELP OF A GRANT
FROM THE HUMANITIES RESEARCH COUNCIL OF CANADA,
USING FUNDS PROVIDED BY THE CANADA COUNCIL

ISBN 19-540244-8

1 2 3 4 5 - 9 8 7 6 5

Printed in Canada by
THE BRYANT PRESS LIMITED

Preface

This volume is intended as a source of information about Canadian composers of the twentieth century and their works. 'Of the twentieth century' has needed to be defined: composers included are those who have produced all or most of their works since 1920. Prominent earlier composers are covered in other sources.

The book is a project sponsored by the Canadian Music Centre. It is the latest in a succession of similar guides whose titles and terms of reference may be interesting to recall. *A List of Canadian Music* was compiled for (and, it seems, by) the Canadian Federation of Music Teachers' Associations and published in 1946 by the Canadian Branch of the Oxford University Press; it lists music by 122 Canadian composers (including only 16 of French Canada), although giving no biographical detail. The first *Catalogue of Canadian Composers* (1947), published in mimeographed form by the Canadian Broadcasting Corporation and edited by J.-J. Gagnier and Jean-Marie Beaudet, listed 238 then-living composers and their works. The same publication, in its revised (second) edition, appeared in printed form in 1952 under Helmut Kallmann's editorship, and contained a historical foreword and a first-time compilation of biographical and bibliographical information on a number of composers from earlier periods (beginning with the mid-seventeenth century); there were full entries for a total of 356 composers (290 then living) and a short list naming 116 others. The Canadian League of Composers in 1957 added to the literature with their *Catalogue of Orchestral Music*, 'including works for small orchestra and band, concertos, vocal-orchestral and choral-orchestral music' – some 234 works of the 35 composer-members of the League. Different in intention, and indicative in that sense of the greater use made of Canadian composers' works by those involved in concert and broadcast programming, was the *34 Biographies of Canadian Composers/34 Biographies de Compositeurs Canadiens* (1964) edited for the CBC International Service by Helmut Blume and Gilles Potvin. This was a handbook of more fully written biographical entries for some of the most prominent living Canadian composers. The five catalogues (orchestral, keyboard, vocal, choral, and chamber music) issued since 1963 by the Canadian Music Centre comprise those works, mostly written after 1945, contained in the Centre's lending library of published and unpublished Canadian scores; the orchestral and chamber music catalogues also give thumbnail biographical sketches of the 85-odd composers listed.

Our book deals with 144 composers. The names represent in our view the most active and prominent professional composers from all parts of the country in the period covered. We have not included composers or arrangers primarily of popular or commercial music and we have included only two or three of the more prominent composers of serious jazz; similarly, band music is represented by only two or three outstanding figures, as is church music. Comparatively few younger composers are mentioned, since such entries become so quickly outdated, but we have included perhaps enough of those who have already attracted public attention to suggest something of the talent and vigour of the coming generation.

The previous catalogues or guides have either tried to include (almost indiscriminately) all activities, amateur and professional, or have narrowed themselves to a few of the most frequently performed composers: our approach aims midway between these two. Though not attempting to evaluate the music in any final sense, we have tried to serve the need, especially felt by those outside Canada, for a compilation that would give a full picture of activities in our creative music, and also a glimpse of styles and trends.

Most of the biographies and listings of works have been checked in their factual aspects by the composers. The biographies incorporate brief critical and stylistic comments prepared for the book by various contributors. Lists of works are given in considerable detail in most cases, but it has not been possible to do so in all. The material was prepared with the active assistance of the Canadian Music Centre staff, and is up-to-date as of January 1973. Some biographical information up to publication has been added past that date, but it would have been impossible to update each of the lists of works. We have resigned ourselves (as most reference-work editors must) to the fact that the music world has not stood still during the editing and publishing process of this book. Consolation comes from the knowledge that, however out-of-date the book may be at birth, it will be a decade more up-to-date than its 'latest' predecessor, and over two decades more than the prior (and more comprehensive) ones.

The volume will, we hope, afford a guide to students and musicians and a practical tool to assist their work. It will give incidentally, to anyone interested, a sense of the extent and proportions of the Canadian musical repertoire since 1920. For amplification, and for various evaluative or critical aids to study, users are referred to the sources in various articles and books listed in the bibliographies. Two general bibliographies will also be found useful: Ian L. Bradley, *A Selected Bibliography of Musical Canadiana* (Vancouver: Versatile Publishing Co., 1974) and George A. Proctor, 'Sources in Canadian Music: a Bibliography of Bibliographies', *Journal of the Canadian Association of University Schools of Music (CAUSM)*, Vol. IV, Nos 1–2, Autumn 1974 (44–73).

In its depth of detail this book is the most comprehensive yet published on the subject. Much of the information has therefore been compiled for the first time. Although the checking and cross-checking have been carefully done, undoubtedly errors and unintentional omissions have occurred. The editors will welcome corrections.

Acknowledgements are due to the composers who have co-operated with the project closely; to the writers of biographies (especially Clifford Ford, who wrote the largest number); to Eric Chafe, Dorith Cooper, John Fodi, Sharyn Hall, Carol Ip, Colleen Johnston, Tamara Nicholls, and Gordon Smith, who researched the lists of works and bibliographies; and the CMC staff particularly, for their patient assistance with the assembling, checking, and preparation of material.

JOHN BECKWITH
Chairman
Canadian Music Centre Publications Committee

KEITH MACMILLAN
Executive Secretary
Canadian Music Centre

January 1975

Illustrations

BETWEEN PAGES 104 AND 105

Abbreviations

BIBLIOGRAPHICAL REFERENCES

Aum — Austin, William. *Music in the Twentieth Century*. New York: W. W. Norton & Co., 1966.

B-B — *Bio-Bibliographical Finding List of Canadian Musicians*. Compiled by the Canadian Music Library Association, 1960–1.

B58 — *Baker's Biographical Dictionary of Musicians*, 5th ed. (Nicolas Slonimsky, ed.). New York: G. Schirmer, 1958.

B65 — *Baker's Supplement*. New York: G. Schirmer, 1965.

B71 — *Baker's Supplement*. New York: G. Schirmer, 1971.

Bec56 — Beckwith, John. 'Composers in Toronto and Montreal', *University of Toronto Quarterly*, Vol. XXVI, no. 1, 1956 (47–69).

Bec57 — ———. 'Music', *The Culture of Contemporary Canada* (Julian Park, ed.). Ithaca: Cornell University Press, 1957.

Bec58 ——. 'Music', *The Arts in Canada* (Malcolm Ross, ed.). Toronto: Macmillan Canada, 1958 (44–51).

Bec70 ——. 'What Every U.S. Musician Should Know About Contemporary Canadian Music', *Musicanada*, No. 29, 1970 (5–7, 12–13, 18).

Bt Blume, Helmut and Gilles Potvin (eds). *Thirty-Four Biographies of Canadian Composers/Trente-quatre biographies de compositeurs canadiens*. Montreal: Canadian Broadcasting Corporation, 1964. Repr. St Clair Shores Mich.: Scholarly Press, 1972.

C48 *Canadian Who's Who*, Vol. IV. Toronto: Trans-Canada Press, 1948.

C63 *Canadian Who's Who*, Vol. IX. Toronto: Trans-Canada Press, 1961–3.

C66 *Canadian Who's Who*, Vol. X. Toronto: Trans-Canada Press, 1964–6.

C69 *Canadian Who's Who*, Vol. XI. Toronto: Trans-Canada Press, 1967–9.

C72 *Canadian Who's Who*, Vol. XII. Toronto: Trans-Canada Press, 1970–2.

CanCo *The Canadian Composer/Le Compositeur canadien* (Richard Flohil, ed.). Toronto: CAPAC, May 1965–.

Cb *Catalogue of Canadian Composers* (Canadian Broadcasting Corporation, J.-J. Gagnier, ed.). Ottawa, 1947.

CMB *The Canada Music Book/Les Cahiers canadiens de musique*. Montreal: Canadian Music Council, 1970–.

CMJ *Canadian Music Journal*. Sackville, N.B., and Toronto: Canadian Music Council, 1956–62.

Cr *Canadian Radio and Television Annual*. Toronto: (n.p.), 1950.

CrC(I) and (II) *Creative Canada* (Macpherson Library, University of Victoria, B.C.). Toronto: University of Toronto Press, Vol. I, 1971; Vol. II, 1972.

D157 Dufourcq, Norbert, ed. *Larousse de la Musique*. Paris: Larousse, 1957.

D165 —— (ed.). *La Musique; les hommes; les instruments*. Paris: Larousse, 1965.

Ef *Encyclopédie de la musique* (François Michel, ed.). Paris: Fasquelle, 1958–61.

Esc Espinosa, Guillermo (ed.). *Composers of the Americas/Compositores de América*. Washington, D.C.: Pan American Union, 1959–.

Gf Gillespie, John. *Five Centuries of Keyboard Music*. New York: Dover, 1965.

Gmu Gatti, Guido, ed. *La Musica*. Torino, 1966.

Ip Illing, Robert (ed.). *Pergamon Dictionary of Music and Musicians*. Oxford: Pergamon Press Ltd, 1964.

JMC *Journal musical canadien*. Montreal: Les Jeunesses Musicales du Canada, 1955–68.

K	Kallmann, Helmut. *Catalogue of Canadian Composers.* Toronto: Canadian Broadcasting Corporation, 1952. Repr. St Clair Shores, Mich.: Scholarly Press, 1972.
Kh	——. *A History of Music in Canada, 1534–1914.* Toronto: University of Toronto Press, 1960.
Lv	Lasalle-Leduc, Annette. *La Vie Musicale au Canada Français.* Quebec: Ministère des Affaires Culturelles, 1964.
MAC	*Music Across Canada.* Toronto: Canadian Music Centre, Feb.-Aug. 1963.
Mce	*Enciclopedia di Musica* (Argia Bertini et al., eds). Milan: Ricordi & Co., 1964.
MGG	*Die Musik in Geschichte und Gegenwart* (Freidrich Blume, ed.). Kassell & Basel: Bärenreiter-Verlag, 1949–68.
Mm	MacMillan, Sir Ernest (ed.). *Music in Canada.* Toronto: University of Toronto Press, 1955.
MQ	*Musical Quarterly.* New York: G. Schirmer Inc., 1918–.
Mu	*Musicanada* (Canadian Music Centre; Keith MacMillan, ed.). Toronto, 1967–70.
MuSc	*The Music Scene* (Nancy Gyokeres, ed.). Don Mills: BMI Canada, 1967–. (French edition: *La Scène Musicale.*)
PAC	*Performing Arts in Canada* (Stephen Mezei, ed.). Toronto, 1961–.
R12	*Riemann Musik-Lexicon,* 12th ed. (W. Gurlitt, ed.), 1959, 1961. *Supplement,* Vol. I (Carl Dahlhaus, ed.), 1972.
S	Soeurs de Sainte-Anne. *Dictionnaire Biographique des Musiciens Canadiens.* Lachine, P.Q.: Mont-Saint-Anne, 1935.
Smh	Smoldon, W. L. *A History of Music.* London: H. Jenkins, 1965.
T	Thompson, Oscar (ed.). *International Cyclopedia of Music and Musicians.* New York: Dodd, Mead, 1956. 8th ed., 1958 (Nicolas Slonimsky, ed.); 9th ed., 1964 (Robert Sabin, ed.).
W41	*Who's Who in Music* (J.T.H. Mize, ed.). Chicago: (n.p.), 1941.
W51	*Who's Who in Music,* 1951.
Wa	Walter, Arnold (ed.). *Aspects of Music in Canada.* Toronto: University of Toronto Press, 1969. (French edition: *Aspects de la musique au Canada,* Maryvonne Kendergi and Gilles Potvin, eds. Montreal: Centre de Psychologie et de Pédagogie, 1970.)
Ww62	*Who's Who in Music.* London: Burke's Peerage, 4th ed., 1962.
Ww69	*Who's Who in Music.* London: Burke's Peerage, 5th ed., 1969.
Ww72	*Who's Who in Music.* London: Burke's Peerage, 6th ed., 1972.

GENERAL

accomp	accompanist
Amer	American
arr	arrangement
ass'n	association
aud	auditorium
bal	ballet
Bar	Baroque
Can	Canada (if after place), Canadian
chamb	chamber
Ch O	Chamber Orchestra
civ	civic
class	classical
Co	Company
Coll	College
Conc	Concert
cond	conductor
Cons	Conservatory
Counc	Council
dir	director
docum	documentary
elec	electronic
Eng	England (if after place), English
ens	ensemble
Fest	Festival
Gp	group
inst	instrument
Inst	Institute
int	international
Jr	Junior
Latv	Latvian
Libr	Library
Luth	Lutheran
Man	Manitoba
Mon	Mono
mov't	movement
Mtl	Montreal
mus	music
narr	narrator
Nat	National
no	number
O, orch	orchestra
op	opus
orch'd	orchestrated
orch'n	orchestration
perc	percussion
perf	performer
Phil	Philharmonic
Plyrs	Players
PO	Philharmonic Orchestra
Pop Conc	Pop Concerts
Prom Conc	Promenade Concerts
Qnt	Quintet
Qt	Quartet
repr	reprinted
Sask	Saskatchewan
SATB	full choir (soprano, alto, tenor, bass)
schl	school
Sgrs	Singers
SO	Symphony Orchestra
Soc	Society
Ster	Stereo
S'tn	Saskatoon
str	string(s)
Str Qt	String Quartet
symph	symphony, symphonique
sympos	symposium
Th	Theatre
Tor	Toronto

TV	television
unis	unison
U or Univ	University
Vanc	Vancouver
Vic	Victoria
voc	vocal
Wpg	Winnipeg

INSTRUMENTS & VOICES

accord	accordion
alt	contralto
bar	baritone
b cl	bass clarinet
BD	bass drum
bs	bass
bs-bar	bass-baritone
bsn	bassoon
cast	castanets
cb	contrabass
c bsn	contrabassoon
cel	celesta
cl	clarinet
cym	cymbals
EH	English horn
fl	flute
flhn	Flügelhorn
glock	glockenspiel
guit	guitar
hn	French horn
hp	harp
hpschd	harpsichord
mand	mandolin
mar	marimba
mezz	mezzo-soprano
narr	narrator
ob	oboe
orch	orchestra
org	organ
picc	piccolo
pno	piano
prep pno	prepared piano
pro-harm	pro-harmonium
qnt	quintet
qt	quartet
rec	recorder
SATB	full choir (sop, alt, ten, bs)
SD	snare drum
sop	soprano
spkr	speaker
str	string(s)
tamb	tambourine
tba	tuba
ten	tenor
timp	timpani
tpt	trumpet
trb	trombone
tri	triangle
unis	unison
vc(s)	voice(s)
vib	vibraphone
vla	viola
vlc	violoncello
vln	violin
WB	woodblock
ww	woodwind
xyl	xylophone
xylor	xylorimba

ORGANIZATIONS

ASCAP	American Society of Composers, Authors and Publishers
BMI	BMI Canada Limited
CAMMAC	Canadian Amateur Musicians/Musiciens amateurs du Canada
Can Ccl	The Canada Council
CAPAC	Composers, Authors and Publishers Association of Canada, Limited
CAUSM	Canadian Association of University Schools of Music
CBA	Canadian Band Directors Association
CBC	Canadian Broadcasting Corporation
CFMS	Canadian Folk Music Society
CFMTA	Canadian Federation of Music Teachers Associations
CLC	Canadian League of Composers
CMC	Canadian Music Centre
CMEA	Canadian Music Educators Association
CMLA	Canadian Music Library Association (later Canadian Association of Music Libraries)
CMPA	Canadian Music Publishers Association
FCMF	Federation of Canadian Music Festivals
GEMA	Gesellschaft für musikalische Aufführungs – und mechanische Vervielfältigungsrechte
JMC	Les Jeunesses Musicales du Canada
NAC	National Arts Centre (Ottawa)
NFB	National Film Board of Canada
ORTF	Office de radiodiffusion-télévision française
RCCO	Royal Canadian College of Organists
RCO	Royal College of Organists
RSCM	Royal School of Church Music
SMCQ	La Société de musique contemporaine du Québec
TCC	Ten Centuries Concerts
TPML	Toronto Public Music Library (later Music Division, Metropolitan Toronto Public Libraries)

PERFORMING & CONCERT GROUPS (See also GENERAL)

Arthur Romano Qt	Arthur Romano Quartet (Montreal)
ASO	Atlantic Symphony Orchestra (Halifax)
Bar Trio Mtl	Montreal Baroque Trio
BBC O	BBC Orchestra
Bristol Madrigal Soc	Bristol Madrigal Society (England)
Calg PO	Calgary Philharmonic Orchestra
Can Str Qt	Canadian String Quartet (Toronto)
Cassenti Plyrs	Cassenti Players (Vancouver)
CBC Ch O	a CBC Chamber Orchestra
CBC ens	a CBC ensemble
CBC Fest O	CBC Festival Orchestra
CBC O	a CBC Orchestra
CBCSO	CBC Symphony Orchestra (Toronto)
CBC Str O	a CBC String Orchestra
CBC wind gp	a CBC wind group
Cecilia Sgrs	Cecilia Singers (England)
Civ O of Minneapolis	Civic Orchestra of Minneapolis (when in Minneapolis)
COC	Canadian Opera Company (Toronto)
Corydon Str Trio	Corydon String Trio (Winnipeg)
Da Camera Sgrs	Da Camera Singers (Edmonton)
Dallas SO	Dallas Symphony Orchestra
Desser Str Trio	Desser String Trio (Toronto)
Dirk Keetbaas Plyrs	Dirk Keetbaas Players (Winnipeg)
East York Community Orch	East York Community Orchestra (Toronto)
Elizabethan Sgrs	Elizabethan Singers (London, Eng.)
England, York Univ Choir	England, York University Choir
Ens Pierre Roland	Ensemble Pierre Roland (Montreal)
ESO	Edmonton Symphony Orchestra
Fest Sgrs	Festival Singers of Canada
Grünfarb Qt	Grünfarb Quartet (Stockholm)

HHGC	Hart House Glee Club (University of Toronto)
HHO	Hart House Orchestra
HH Qt	Hart House Quartet
HPO	Hamilton Philharmonic Orchestra
Jacob Groob Qt	Jacob Groob Quartet (Toronto)
Janet Baldwin Co	Janet Baldwin School of Dance
Kingston, NY, SO	Kingston (New York) Symphony Orchestra
Kingston, Ont, SO	Kingston (Ontario) Symphony Orchestra
KYO	Kingston Youth Orchestra (Ontario)
LAT	Lyric Arts Trio (Toronto)
London, Eng, LSO	London (England) Symphony Orchestra
London, Ont, LSO	London (Ontario) Symphony Orchestra
Masella Wind Qnt	Masella Wind Quintet (Montreal)
Minneapolis Civ O	Civic Orchestra of Minneapolis (when outside Minneapolis)
MJSO	Montreal Junior Symphony Orchestra
MSO	Montreal Symphony Orchestra
NACO	National Arts Centre Orchestra (Ottawa)
Naruns Qt	Naruns Quartet (New York)
NatBalCo	National Ballet Company (Toronto)
New Dance Gp of Canada	New Dance Group of Canada (renamed Toronto Dance Theatre in 1968)
NYO	National Youth Orchestra of Canada
Okla City SO	Oklahoma City Symphony Orchestra
Orch da Camera	Orchestre da Camera (Montreal)
Orch de RTF	Orchestre de radiodiffusion-télévision française
Orford Qt	Orford Quartet (Toronto)
Ottawa PO	L'Orchestre Symphonique d'Ottawa (1940s), also Ottawa Philharmonic Orchestra
Parlow Qt	Parlow Quartet (Toronto)
Phila SO	Philadelphia Symphony Orchestra
Pro Arte O	Pro Arte Orchestra (Toronto)
Purcell Sgrs	Purcell Singers (Britain)
Purcell Str Qt	Purcell String Quartet (Vancouver)

QSO	Quebec Symphony Orchestra
RCAF Band	Royal Canadian Air Force Band
RCMP Band	Royal Canadian Mounted Police Band
RWB	Royal Winnipeg Ballet
Santa Cecilia O	Santa Cecilia Orchestra (Rome, Italy)
Scarborough Ch O	Scarborough Chamber Orchestra (Ontario)
SMCQ	La Société de musique contemporaine du Québec (Montreal)
Soli of the Cons	Soloists of the Conservatory
Spivak Qt	Spivak Quartet (Toronto)
SSO	Saskatoon Symphony Orchestra
St C SO	St Catharines Symphony Orchestra (Ontario)
S'tn Mus Fest O	Saskatoon Music Festival Orchestra
Stratford Fest O	Stratford Festival Orchestra (Ontario)
TCC	Ten Centuries Concerts
Thames Chamb Choir	Thames Chamber Choir (England)
T Mend	Toronto Mendelsohn Choir
TNM	Théâtre du Nouveau-Monde (Montreal)
Tor Dance Th	Toronto Dance Theatre
TRE	Toronto Repertory Ensemble (until 1967)
TRO	Toronto Repertory Orchestra (from 1967)
TS(O)	Toronto Symphony (Orchestra)
Tudor Sgrs	Tudor Singers (Montreal)
TWQ	Toronto Woodwind Quintet
TYS	Toronto Youth Symphony
U of Okla Faculty Trio	University of Oklahoma Faculty Trio
Vanc YO	Vancouver Youth Orchestra
VSO	Vancouver Symphony Orchestra
WLU Choir	Waterloo Lutheran University Choir (Ontario)
Wpg Bal Club	Winnipeg Ballet Club
WSO	Winnipeg Symphony Orchestra

PLACES OR EVENTS (See also GENERAL)

Can Mus Associates conc	Canadian Music Associates concert
Carnegie Hall	Carnegie Hall (New York City)
CLC conc	Canadian League of Composers concert
Concours Int de Mtl	Concours International de Montreal
Eaton Aud	Eaton Auditorium (Toronto)
EJB	Edward Johnson Building (University of Toronto)
Expo '67	Expo '67 World Festival (Montreal)
Fest of Arts	Festival of the Arts (Halifax)
Fest of the Sea	Festival of the Sea (Vancouver)
Guelph Spring Fest	Guelph Spring Festival (Ontario)
Int Pno Competition	International Piano Competition (Montreal)
ISCM	International Society for Contemporary Music
JMC Mus Camp	Les Jeunesses Musicales du Canada Music Camp, Mount Orford, Quebec
Lansdowne Th	Lansdowne Theatre (Toronto)
MacM Planetarium	MacMillan Planetarium (Vancouver)
MacM Th	MacMillan Theatre (University of Toronto)
Massey Coll	Massey College (University of Toronto)
New England Cons	New England Conservatory (Boston)
Otter Lake Mus Centre	Otter Lake Music Centre, CAMMAC (Quebec)
St Andrew's Luth Church	St Andrew's Lutheran Church (Toronto)
TPML	Toronto Public Music Library
Vanc Hotel Aud	Vancouver Hotel Auditorium
Women's Mus Club	Women's Music Club (Toronto)

PUBLISHERS

Abn	Abingdon Press
AMP	Associated Music Publishers, Inc.
Arch	Ed. Archambault, Inc.
AV	Avant Music
B&B	Barger & Barclay
B & H	Boosey and Hawkes (Canada) Limited
Ber	Berandol Music Limited (administers former BMI Canada publications)
Birchard	Summy-Birchard Co.
Chap	Chappell & Co., Limited
CMC	Canadian Music Centre
CMR	Church Music Review
CMS	Canadian Music Sales Corporation Limited
Ditson	Oliver Ditson Company
Durand	Editions Durand & Cie
E Arnold	Edward Arnold & Co.
FH	The Frederick Harris Music Co. Limited (includes Harmuse Publications)
Fischer	Carl Fischer Inc.
Gray	The H.W. Gray Company, Inc.
Greg	The Gregorian Association (Canada)
GVT	Gordon V. Thompson Limited (includes Chanteclair Music)
Jarman	Jarman Publications Limited
Jay	Jaymar Music Limited (includes Huron and Iroquois Presses)
Kalnajs	Alfred Kalnajs' Printing Co.
Kerby	E.C. Kerby Ltd (includes Caveat Music Publishers)
L'AC	L'Action catholique
Leslie	Leslie Music Supply
MCA	MCA Canada Ltd (includes Leeds Canada and Manitou Music)
MEC	Max Eschig, Paris
MPH	Music Publishers Holdings
Nord	A & S Nordheimer Ltd (no longer exists)
Novl	Novello and Company Ltd

Abbreviations: Publishers

NSB	N. Simrock, Berlin
NVMP	New Valley Music Press
ÖBV	Österreichischer Bundesverlag, Vienna
OUP	Oxford University Press
Peer	Peer International Corporation (Peer-Southern Organization (Canada) Ltd)
Peters	C.F. Peters Corporation
Presser	Theodore Presser Company
Ric	G. Ricordi & Co. (Canada) Limited
Rob	Robertson Publications
Rou	Roudanez, Paris
RSCM	Royal School of Church Music (England)
Sala or Salabert	Editions Salabert
E C Schirm	E.C. Schirmer Music Company
G Schirm	G. Schirmer Inc.
S H & M	Schmitt, Hall & McCreary
South	Southern Music Publishing Inc.
Summit	Summit Music Ltd
Tenuto	Tritone-Tenuto Publications
UE	Universal Edition
Wat	Waterloo Music Company (includes Peter McKee Music Co.)
WBM	Warner Bros Music
West or Western	Western Music Co. Ltd.
WIM	Western International Music
WLSM	World Library of Sacred Music
WR	Whaley, Royce & Co. Limited (now Algord Music Limited)

RECORDING LABELS

Acd	Acadia
Alm	Almitra Music Co. Inc.
Bar or BAR	Baroque Canada
Cap	Capitol
CBC BR	CBC Broadcasting Recording
CCM	Contemporary Canadian Music (BMI Canada Limited)
Col	Columbia
Conc	Concordia
Cor	Coronet
CRI	Composers Recordings, Inc.
CTL	Canadian Talent Library
Dec	Decca
Dom	Dominion
Folk	Folkways
LAB	Labyrinth (CAPAC)
Laur	Laurentian
Lou or Louis	Louisville, First Edition Records
Mad	Madrigal
Melb	Melbourne
Merc	Mercury
MMI or Marathon	Marathon Music Inc.
Poly	Polydor
RCA	RCA Victor
RCI	Radio-Canada International
Sel	Select
Victrola	RCA Victor (re-release label)
Vng	Vanguard
WST	Westminster

UNIVERSITIES & SCHOOLS OF MUSIC

Acadia	Acadia University (Wolfville, N.S.)
Banff	Banff School of Fine Arts (Alberta)
Brand Coll	Brandon College (Brandon, Man.)
Dal	Dalhousie University (Halifax, N.S.)
HCM	Hamilton Conservatory of Music (Royal Hamilton College of Music after 1959)
JSM	Juilliard School of Music (New York)
Laval	Laval University (Quebec, P.Q.)
McGill	McGill University (Montreal, P.Q.)
McMaster	McMaster University (Hamilton, Ont.)
Mt A	Mount Allison University (Sackville, N.B.)
Mtl-Cons	Conservatoire de musique de la Province de Québec (Montreal, P.Q.)
Que-Cons	Conservatoire de musique de la Province de Québec (Quebec, P.Q.)
RCMT	Royal Conservatory of Music of Toronto (formerly Toronto Conservatory of Music)
SFU	Simon Fraser University (Burnaby, B.C.)
St Fr Xav	St Francis Xavier University (Antigonish, N.S.)
Trois Riv-Cons	Conservatoire de musique de la Province de Québec (Trois Rivières, P.Q.)
U of Alta	University of Alberta (Edmonton, Alta)
U of BC	University of British Columbia (Vancouver, B.C.)
U of Calg	University of Calgary (Alberta)
U of Man	University of Manitoba (Winnipeg, Man.)
U of Mtl	Université de Montréal (Montreal, P.Q.)
U of Sask(Reg)	University of Saskatchewan (Regina Campus, now University of Regina)
U of Sask(S'tn)	University of Saskatchewan (Saskatoon Campus)
U of T	University of Toronto (Toronto, Ont.)
U Vic	University of Victoria (Victoria, B.C.)
U of Wat	University of Waterloo (Waterloo, Ont.)
UWO	University of Western Ontario (London, Ont.)
WLU	Waterloo Lutheran University (Waterloo, Ont.)

A

ADASKIN, MURRAY (b. Toronto, Ont., 28 Mar. 1906). Murray Adaskin is one of three brothers with distinguished careers in Canadian music. His family cultivated an early musical interest and he began violin studies with his older brother Harry. Thereafter his principal teachers were Luigi von Kunits in Toronto, Kathleen Parlow in New York, and Marcel Chailley in Paris. During the years 1926–36 Adaskin was a member of the Toronto Symphony Orchestra. In the 1930s and early 1940s he performed regularly with the Royal York Trio. Turning to composition in 1944, he studied first with John WEINZWEIG in Toronto and subsequently in the U.S. with Darius Milhaud and Charles Jones. In 1952 he became head of the Department of Music, University of Saskatchewan, Saskatoon, and was appointed composer-in-residence there in 1966, eventually retiring in 1973.

Throughout his career Murray Adaskin's contribution to Canadian music has been amply recognized. He was given a Canada Council Senior Arts Fellowship in 1960 and from 1966 to 1969 he served as a member of the Council. In March 1971 the CBC honoured him in a two-hour broadcast entitled 'A Portrait of an Artist'. Numerous CBC commissions include: *March No. 1 for Orchestra* (1950); *March No. 2 for Orchestra* (1953); *Coronation Overture* (1953); *Algonquin Symphony* (1957–8); *Rondino for Nine Instruments* (1961); and the opera *Grant, Warden of the Plains* (1967). The Golden Jubilee Committee of the University of Saskatchewan commissioned *Saskatchewan Legend* in 1959, and for its inaugural concert, October 7, 1969, the National Arts Centre Orchestra commissioned *Diversion for Orchestra (an entertainment)*. Adaskin holds two honorary degrees: an LL.D. from the University of Lethbridge (1970) and a Doctor of Music from the University of Brandon (1972).

What strikes one directly about Adaskin's music is its optimistic tone – a humane aspect that, as with Haydn, is never far from cheerfulness. This basic characteristic is reflected in his relaxed attitude towards the question of polarization in contemporary styles: essentially a conservative, Adaskin welcomes experimental ferment, only regretting that he cannot be part of it. And it is as a conservative that he is an immediately appealing composer. His music is generously lyrical, clearly crafted, rhythmically vital, witty, and, curiously enough, recognizably Canadian in content.

The lyrical amplitude in many of the works is a natural result of his early professional life as a violinist. That the 'tunes' should be so memorable without sounding like clichés is evidence of the composer's structuring ear. The opening theme of the *Serenade Concertante* (1954) is a typical example, with its discreetly smiling 'opportunity knocks' motif and clear tonal underpinning. This excellent work also shows Adaskin's concern with craft: an ingenious contrapuntal texture pervades, in which everything is clearly audible and the form-at-large easily articulates recapitulations that avoid any fatal symmetry.

The rhythms of Murray Adaskin, who still bears some affection for the bar-line, are energetic; in their irregular groupings and revolving or repeated chord patterns, they are reminiscent of Stravinsky. His marches and occasional pieces, of course, appropriately declare extroverted, toe-tapping rhythms, as in *Fanfare* (1970). A conservative is distinguished by what he wants to conserve, and Adaskin's continuation of the idea of music as entertainment finds expression in a deft use of syncopation, perhaps most urbanely in evidence in the *Serenade Concertante* and the *Diversion for Orchestra*. But his musical humour can be puckish as well: in the *Divertimento No. 4* (1970) a cleverly scored Canada bird is transmogrified into an insinuating bigband trumpeter. (This latter thematic fragment tails off with something very close to Hindemith's three-chord cadential formula, a perhaps unconscious but nonetheless funny touch.)

Murray Adaskin's one essay in opera is not an unqualified success. *Grant, Warden of the Plains* contains many fine passages, notably Maria's 'Autumn Song' for soprano and bassoon alone, and the exuberant governor's-ball scene; but the composer is hampered by a libretto that lacks carrying power – the dramatic situation is artificially conveyed through virtually untouchable lines like '... for sad remembering pays tribute to old evil and remembered sin'. The opera winds down in the end too, with a sentimental chorus culminating in the tonic chord with the third on top.

More recent works signal an expansion of emotional range and, paradoxically, are connected with Canadian folkloristic materials. As Canadian poets are anxious to escape the restricting 'regionalist' label, so Adaskin is concerned to establish his work on non-programmatic grounds. He writes: 'I didn't think that Canadian folklore played such an important part in my composing life, but I do find that because I have attempted the use of folk material in several of my works, I am often referred to as a specialist in that field – which of course I am not. I merely happen to like the basic material, and am interested in Canadiana as far as the arts are concerned – but the bulk of my music is not based on folk material.' Nevertheless the more commanding large-scale orchestral works are rooted in evocations of the country and its folk history. Chief among them is the *Algonquin Symphony*, an elegy on the death of Taylor Statten (a pioneering figure in the development of Canadian summer camps for children), which, in the finale, characteristically emerges as a nature celebration encompassing sounds of the wildlife of Algonquin Park. But it is with two more recent works that the elegiac tone is deepened: *Qalala and Nilaula of the North* (1969) and *There Is My People Sleeping* (1970). The former incorporates songs Adaskin collected from two Rankin Inlet Eskimos, the Qalala and Nilaula of the title. This symphonic 'poem' includes an amusing Eskimo women's game that accumulates contrapuntally what the composer calls 'throat rhythms'. But it is the more austere episodes and the conclusion of this work that leave the strongest impression – one of bleak space and a vanishing culture. The latter work evokes the atmosphere of an Indian prayer with its chant-like lyricism and sombre oscillations between two harmonies. Adaskin's music has always been refreshingly affirmative, springing as it does from a celebratory sensibility. This more recent elegiac strain will contribute to an interesting synthesis in future works.

Murray Adaskin is a member of the Canadian League of Composers and of CAPAC.

WILLIAM AIDE

MUSICAL WORKS

STAGE

Grant, Warden of the Plains (chamber opera). 1967. 58'30". sop, 4 ten, bar, bs-bar, SATB, med orch. CMC. Libretto: Mary Elizabeth Bayer. July 18, 1967, Wpg, CBC, Victor Feldbrill.

ORCHESTRA

Suite for Orchestra. 1948. 12'35". full orch. CMC. 1949, Tor, CBC O, Geoffrey Waddington.

March No 1. 1950. 3'. med orch. CMC. 1950, Tor, CBC O, John Adaskin.

Ballet Symphony. 1951. 24'25". full orch. CMC. RCI-71. Mar 26, 1952, Tor, CLC conc, TS, Geoffrey Waddington.

Coronation Overture. 1953. 6'55". full orch. CMC. 1953, Tor, Coronation Day broadcast, CBCSO, Geoffrey Waddington.

March No 2. 1953 (rev 1962). 3'45". full orch. CMC. 1953, Tor, CBC O, John Adaskin.

Serenade Concertante. 1954. 6'40". med orch. Ric, 1956. Col ML-5685; MS-6285; RCI-129. 1954, Vanc, Vanc CBC Ch O, John Avison.

Algonquin Symphony. 1958. 23'40". full orch. Ric, 1962. Dom 1372 (3rd mov't only). 1958, Tor, CBCSO, Geoffrey Waddington.

Saskatchewan Legend. 1959. 12'50". full orch. Ric, 1961. 1959, S'tn, SSO, Murray Adaskin.

Rondino. 1964. 5'30". full orch. CMC. 1965, Tor, Lawrence Park Collegiate O, Jim Coles.

Diversion for Orchestra (an entertainment). 1969. 8'. med orch. CMC. Oct 7, 1969, Ottawa, Inaugural conc of the NACO, Mario Bernardi.

Qalala and Nilaula of the North. 1969. 17'25". small orch. CMC. June 4, 1969, Tor, CBC Fest, CBC Wpg O, Murray Adaskin.

Fanfare. 1970. 4'45". full orch. CMC. CBC BR SM-163. 1970, Reg, Opening of the Sask Centre of the Arts, Reg SO, Howard Leyton-Brown.

There Is My People Sleeping. 1970. 12'.

med orch. CMC. Mar 30, 1971, Wpg, CBC O, Murray Adaskin.

BAND

Night Is No Longer Summer Soft. 1970. 2'50". CMC.

STRING ORCHESTRA

Suite for Strings. 1949. ms.

Essay for Strings. 1972. 5'30". CMC. 1972, Vic, Oak Bay Junior-Senior High Schl O, Bernard Rain(cond).

SOLOIST(S) WITH ORCHESTRA

Concerto for Violin and Orchestra. 1956. 17'15". CMC. 1956, Tor, CBCSO, Murray Adaskin(cond), Roman Totenberg(vln).

Concerto for Bassoon and Orchestra. 1960. 18'. CMC. CBC BR SM-143. Feb 5, 1961, Vanc, VSO, Irwin Hoffman(cond), George Zukerman(bsn).

Capriccio for Piano and Orchestra. 1961. 18'10". CMC. 1963, Tor, CBCSO, John Avison (cond), Kendall Taylor(pno).

Divertimento No 4. 1970. 12'45". solo tpt, picc, tpt, orch. CMC. 1970, SSO, Murray Adaskin(cond), Lawrence House(tpt).

CHOIR

Hymn of Thanks. 1953. unis. B & H, 1954. Text: A Eustace Haydon.

VOICE

The Shepherd. 1934. 1'40". high vc, pno. ms. Text: William Blake.

Epitaph. 1948. 1'57". vc, pno. CMC. Text: Guillaume Apollinaire; trans: Bertha Ten Eyck James.

The Prairie Lily. 1967. 2'. vc, pno. CMC. Text: Hugh Blakeney.

VOICE WITH INSTRUMENTAL ENSEMBLE

Of Man and the Universe. 1967. 10'. vc, vln, pno. CMC. Text: Alexander Pope. Aug 13, 1967, Mtl, Expo '67, Joan Maxwell (mezz), Arthur Polson(vln), Ross Pratt (pno).

INSTRUMENTAL ENSEMBLE

Sonata. 1946. 15'. vln, pno. CMC. RCI-73. June 22, 1949, Tor, CBC, Murray Adaskin (vln), Louis Crerar(pno).

Canzona and Rondo. 1949. 7'30". vln, pno. CMC. RCA CC/CCS-1015; RCI-221.

Andante from Concerto for Violin and Orchestra. 1955 (rescored 1957). 7'10". solo vln, fl, cl, b cl, str qnt. CMC.

Divertimento No 1. 1956. 10'35". 2vln, pno. CMC. Nov 20, 1956, Vanc Art Gallery, Harry Adaskin(vln), Murray Adaskin(vln), Frances Marr(pno).

Introduction and Rondo. 1957. 9'25". vln, vla, vlc, pno. CMC. 1959, U Sask (S'tn), Rafael Druian(vln), Albert Falkove(vla), Robert Jamieson(vlc), John Simms(pno).

Rondino for Nine Instruments. 1961. 4'50". fl, ob, cl, bsn, hn, str qt. CMC. RCA CC/CCS-1009; RCI-215. 1962, Tor, CBC ens, Mario Bernardi.

Cassenti Concertante. 1963. 9'15". ob, cl, bsn, vln, pno. CMC. 1964, U Sask (S'tn), Cassenti Plyrs.

Dance. 1963. 2'15". vln, pno. CMC. 1963, U Sask (S'tn), Roman Totenberg(vln), Boyd McDonald(pno).

Dedication. 1963. 3'10". vln, pno. CMC. 1963, U Sask (S'tn), Roman Totenberg (vln), Boyd McDonald(pno).

Quiet Song. 1963. 2'40". vln, pno. MCA, 1964. 1963, U Sask (S'tn), Roman Totenberg(vln), Boyd McDonald(pno).

String Quartet No 1. 1963. 19'50". CMC. 1963, Tor, Can Str Qt.

Divertimento No 2. 1964. 4'22". vln, hp. CMC. 1965, Tor, Unitarian Church, Hyman Goodman(vln), Erica Goodman(hp).

Divertimento No 3. 1965. 15'. vln, hn, bsn. CMC. 1965, U Sask (Reg), Howard Leyton-Brown(vln), Mel Carey(hn), Thomas Schudel(bsn).

Calisthenics. 1968. 3'10". vln, pno. CMC.

Daydreams. 1968. 3'. vln or sax or cl, pno. CMC.

Legato and Ricochet. 1968. 3'10". vln, pno. CMC.

Trio. 1970. 17'30". fl, vlc, pno. CMC. Apr 29, 1971, CBC, Alta Chamb Trio, Werner van Sweeden(fl), Talmon Herz(vlc), Gloria Saarinen(pno).

PIANO

Sonata. 1950. 9'25". CMC.

INSTRUMENTAL SOLO

Sonatine Baroque. 1952. 9'40". vln. Ric, 1961. RCI-73. 1952, Tor, Eugene Kash(vln).

Two Pieces for Solo Viola da Gamba. 1972. 9'10". CMC. 1972, Tor, York U, Peggie Sampson.

BIBLIOGRAPHY

See B-B; Bt; C69; CrC(I); Esc; Ip; K; Mm; Wa.

Brandhagen, W.L. 'Asking Adaskin', *PAC.*

Spring 1963 (31–3).
'CAPAC composers in the news', *CanCo.* No. 48, Mar. 1970 (44–5).
'Murray Adaskin – a portrait', *Mu.* No. 1, May 1967 (8–9).
Savage, Richard. 'Murray Adaskin: Composer, Professor, Gentleman', *CanCo.* No. 10, Sept. 1966 (4–5, 44–5).

LITERARY WORKS

ARTICLES

'Igor Stravinsky', *Architects of Modern Thought.* Series IV, CBC Radio Talks (95–107).
'Script of Analysis by Murray Adaskin to accompany his recording of "Serenade Concertante" ', Toronto, CMC, 1961 (8 pp.).

AITKEN, ROBERT (b. Kentville, N.S., 28 Aug. 1939). He began flute lessons at the age of nine in Pennsylvania, and then in Toronto studied with Nicholas Fiore. At nineteen he became principal flutist of the Vancouver Symphony Orchestra. He studied composition with Barbara PENTLAND at the University of British Columbia in Vancouver (1958–9). He returned to Toronto where he received the Mary Osler Boyd Award from the Women's Musical Club (1960) and completed his Bachelor of Music degree at the University of Toronto (1961). In 1961 he began studying composition with John WEINZWEIG and electronic music with Myron Schaeffer at the University of Toronto, receiving his Master of Music degree in 1964. He was awarded a Canada Council grant in 1964 to study flute in Europe with Jean-Pierre Rampal, Severino Gazzelloni, André Jaunet, and Hubert Barwahser. Also in 1964 he formed the Lyric Arts Trio with Mary Morrison, soprano, and his wife Marion Ross, piano. He was a member of the CBC Symphony Orchestra from 1959 until its demise in 1964 and has been co-principal flutist with the Toronto Symphony (1965–70) and the Stratford Festival Orchestra (1962–4). He served on the staff of the Marlboro Music Festival in Vermont (1959–61 and 1966), where he first came under the influence of Marcel Moyse, who became his principal teacher. In 1970 he left the Toronto Symphony to concentrate on solo and chamber playing and teaching. In 1972 he was appointed associate professor in the University of Toronto Faculty of Music.

As musical director of the Shaw Festival's 'Music of Today' concert series (summers of 1970 to 1972) and as musical director of New Music Concerts in Toronto, Aitken has been dealing with the latest experimental or avant-garde music, which doubtless accounts for his changes in style evident in the three works *Concerto for Twelve Soloists and Orchestra* (1968), *Spectra* (1969), and *Kebyar* (1971). The *Concerto* exhibits a conservative neo-classical style with a constant forward-moving, highly energetic quality. With *Spectra*, Aitken introduced mass-structure, as found in the music of leading Japanese composers (for example, Takemitsu and Mayuzumi). In *Kebyar* he has made a further change in style, the score containing not only traditional notation but also drawings and designs in the improvised sections, along the same lines as R. Murray SCHAFER's *Divan i Shams i Tabriz* (1970). *Kebyar* means 'a sudden release of forces such as an explosion, the crash of cymbals or the bursting open of a flower'. Aitken says it is a 'festival piece . . . with an emphasis on virtuosic playing and new and surprising effects'. This work deals in timbral exploitation with a changing mood and with subtle use of electronic music. The development in Aitken's style has embodied a change in emphasis from formal considerations to free experimentation in instrumental and electro-acoustical colour.

In 1969 Aitken was awarded the Canadian League of Composers' Canada Music Citation for outstanding service to the music of Canadian composers. He was a prize winner at the 1971 Concours International de Flûte de Paris. He has received commissions from the Toronto Repertory Orchestra (*Spectra*), the CBC (*Kebyar*, 1971), and the National Youth Orchestra (*Nekuia*, 1971).

Aitken is a member of the Canadian League of Composers and is affiliated with BMI Canada.

MUSICAL WORKS

ORCHESTRA

Rhapsody. 1961.
Concerto for Twelve Soloists and Orchestra. 1968; Kerby, 1974.

Spectra. 1969; Ric, 1973. 4 mixed chamb gps.
Nekuia. 1971.

INSTRUMENTAL ENSEMBLE
Suite for Violin and Piano. 1960.
Quartet. 1961. fl, vla, ob, cb.
Kebyar. 1971; Sala, 1973. fl, cl, tbn, 2cb, perc, elec tape.
Shadows (Part II), 'Lalitá'. 1972. fl, 3vlc, 2hp, 2perc.

INSTRUMENTAL SOLO
Music for Flute and Electronic Tape. 1963.

ELECTRONIC MUSIC
Noësis. 1963. Folk FM-3436.
Music for 'Hamlet'. 1964.

BIBLIOGRAPHY

'Canada Music Citation, 1969', *Mu.* No. 24, Nov. 1969 (5–6).

ANDERSON, WILLIAM HENRY (b. London, England, 21 Apr. 1882; d. Winnipeg, Man., 1955). He studied voice and composition with private teachers before winning two scholarships to attend the Guildhall School of Music, London. He studied voice in Italy with Garcia and Battistini and was tenor soloist in London at St Stephen's Walbrooke Church and St Paul's Cathedral. In 1910 he settled in Winnipeg where he was choir leader and soloist at the Central Congregational Church until 1934, then at St Andrew's United Church, River Heights (1934–54). He was founder and conductor of the Apollo Male Voice Choir, the CNR Mixed Choir and the Oriana Singers as well as conductor of the CBC Choristers (1940–55). He taught singing for many years in Winnipeg; his pupils included Gladys Whitehead, principal of the Royal Hamilton Conservatory, and Morley Meredith, leading baritone of the Metropolitan Opera Company. Anderson's compositions are mainly for voice, both chorus and solo voice. He also arranged a number of Ukrainian folk songs under the name of Michael Bilencko and composed ballads under the name of Hugh Garland. His estate is a member of CAPAC.

MUSICAL WORKS

RADIO
Everyman. 1949. Text: Old Mystery Play.

CHOIR
Mary. c1935; E Arnold, 1935. SSA/unis. Text: Vera V Robertson.
To Immortality. c1935; E Arnold, 1937. SSA. Text: Constance Barbour Holbein.
Fairyland. c1936; B & H 1936. SSA. Text: Mary S Morrison.
Moon Baby. c1936; B & H 1936. unis. Text: N Emerson.
The Birth Night. 1938; Western, 1938. SA/unis. Text: Myrtle J Broley.
Born of Marie. 1938; Western, 1938. SATB. Text: Old English words.
A Child's Prayer. 1938; Western, 1938. unis. Text: Constance Barbour Holbein.
Come I Pray Thee. 1938; Western, 1938. SATB. Text: Richard Rolle, Bishop of Hampole.
The Ivy Green. 1938; Western, 1938. unis. Text: Charles Dickens.
Lady May. 1938; Western, 1938. unis. Text: Sinclair Dunlop.
Marjory Maketh the Tea. 1938; Western, 1938. unis, pno. Text: Wilfred Campbell.
Sing Ivy. 1938; Western, 1938. unis. Text: nursery rhyme.
Sleep Little Jesus. 1938; Western, 1938. SSA/unis, pno (org). Text: Noreen Moore.
The Spider Hunter. 1938; Western, 1938. unis. Text: Lawrence Phillips.
Sweet Afton. 1938; Western, 1938. SA/unis, pno. Text: Robert Burns.
Meadows and Maidens. 1939; Western, 1939. unis. Text: Rose Fyleman.
The Bird in the Nest. 1940; Western, 1940. SSA. Text: Frank Dempster Sherman.
The Children's Friend. 1940; Western, 1940. SSA. Text: Eleanor Halbrook Zimmerman.
The Fairy Ring. 1940; Western, 1940. SA/unis. Text: anon.
In Brittany. c1940. SATB. Text: E V Lucas.
The Loveliest Picture. 1940; Fischer, 1940. SATB/SSA. Text: Constance Barbour Holbein.
Let All Around. 1940; Western, 1940. SATB. Text: Old Carol words.
My Master Hath a Garden. 1940; Fischer, 1940. SSA. Text: anon.
Two Christmas Carols. 1941; Western, 1941. SATB. Text: Isaac Watts, anon.
Two Christmas Songs. 1941; Western, 1946. SATB/SA. Text: Noreen Moore, Catherine Winkworth.
A Memory. 1941; Western, 1941. SSA. Text: Arthur L Salmon.

The Piper Wind. 1941; Western, 1941. SSA. Text: Norah Holland.
O Little Children Lead us Now. c1942; Western, c1942. SATB/SSA. Text: Constance Barbour Holbein.
Pease-Porridge Tawney. c1942; OUP, 1942. SS/TT, pno. Text: Frances Russell.
Sea Blue Gardens. c1942; OUP, 1942. SSA, pno. Text: Rose Cooper.
Autumn. c1943. SATB. Text: Ellen Gilbert.
Lullay My Liking. c1943; Western, 1948. SSAA. Text: 15th cent words.
Spring is Here. c1943; Western, 1943. SA. Text: Ruth Stirling Bauer.
Twilight. c1943; Western, c1943. SSA, pno. Text: Duncan Campbell Scott.
The White Dove. c1943; Western, 1943. SSA, pno. Text: old words.
Ane Song of the Birth of Christ. c1944; Western, 1944. SATB. Text: Medieval poem.
Give Ear to my Words O Lord. c1944; Western, 1944. SATB. Text: Anne Tripp.
Joy Fills our inmost Heart today. c1944; Western, 1944. SATB. Text: William Chatterton Dix.
A Load of Turnips. c1944; Western, 1944. unis. Text: M Murray.
Song For a Baby Sister. c1944; Western, 1944. unis. Text: R H Grenville.
To a Baby Brother. c1944; Western, 1944. unis. Text: R H Grenville.
Christmas Gifs. c1945; Western, 1945. SSA. Text: Catherine Cate Coblentz.
The Captain's Farewell to His Ship. c1945. Text: W H Anderson.
In the Morning, Oh Lord. c1945; Fischer, 1948. SATB. Text: Mozarabic Prayer.
In Autumn. c1945. Text: Ellen Gilbert.
Long Long Ago. c1945; Western, 1945. SSA/unis (pno). Text: anon.
Oh Brother Man. c1945, TTBB. Text: J G Whittier.
O Men From the Fields. c1945. SATB. Text: Padraic Colum.
Soldier's Song. c1945; Western, 1945, TBB. Text: Richard B Glaenzer.
The Two Nests. c1945; Western, 1945. unis, pno. Text: Francis Carlin.
Theme (Apollo Choir). c1945. SATB. Text: W H Anderson.
Theme (Choristers). c1945. SATB. Text: W H Anderson.
Wind in the Lilacs. c1945; Western, 1945. SSA. Text: R H Grenville.
In the Fall of the Year. c1946; Western, 1946. SA. Text: Sheila Barbour.
As I Walked in Bethlehem. c1947; Western, 1947. SATB. Text: Audrey Alexandra Brown.
As Mary Sings. c1947; Western, 1947. SSA. Text: Jean Paul Talbot.
Bread of the World. c1947; Western, 1947. SATB. Text: Bishop H Heber.
Cradle Carol. c1947; Western, 1947.
Five Introits and Vespers. c1947; Western, 1947. SATB. Text: Liturgical.
Hark All Around the Welkin Rings. c1947; Western, 1947. SATB/SSA. Text: Constance Barbour Holbein.
I Know a Bank. c1947; Western, 1947. SSA. Text: Shakespeare.
Liberty. c1947; Western, 1947. SATB/SSA/unis. Text: Kathleen Blanchard.
Music When Soft Voices Die. c1947; Western, 1947. SSA. Text: Percy B Shelley.
Popping Corn. c1947; Western, 1947. unis. Text: R H Grenville.
Fire Birds. c1948; Western, 1948. unis. Text: Catherine Cate Coblentz.
The Holy Child. c1948; Birchard, 1948. SATB. Text: Constance Barbour Holbein.
Indian Lullaby. c1948; Western, 1948. unis. Text: Duncan McKellar.
Madonna's Prayer. c1948; Birchard, 1948. SATB/SSA. Text: Lope de Vega.
Steal Away Little Birds. c1948; Western, 1948. SA, pno. Text: Noreen Moore.
The Sweet Nightingale. c1948; Western, 1948. unis. Text: trad.
The Torchbearers. c1948; Western, 1948. unis, pno. Text: Blanche Pownall Garrett.
'Twas in the Silent Night He Came. c1948; Western, 1948. unis, pno. Text: Kathleen Blanchard.
Two Christmas Carols. c1948; Western, 1948. SATB. Text: John of Damascus, anon. Trans: Phillip Schaaf.
Come Ye Children and Hearken. c1950. SSA. Text: Biblical.
Holy Spirit Truth Divine. c1950. Text: Samuel Longfellow.
Lullaby of the Little Angels. c1950; GVT, 1968. SSA. Text: Audrey Alexandra Brown.
Behold the Beauty of The Lord. c1952; Birchard, 1952. SATB. Text: anon.
The Beatitudes. c1953; GVT. SATB. Text: Biblical.
Come Holy Ghost our Souls Inspire. c1953; Fischer, 1953. SATB. Text: John Cosin.
If Thou but suffer God to Guide Thee. c1953; Fischer, 1953. SATB. Text: Georg

Neumark. Trans: Catherine Winkworth.
Night Song. c1955. Text: Constance Barbour Holbein.
Cradle Song. c1955; GVT, 1962. unis. Text: Kathleen Conyningham Greene.

Undated
At the Manger (G Schirm). SSATBB. Text: W H Anderson.
A Carol (Gray). SATB/SSA.
Cradle Song (GVT). unis.
Christmas Blessing (E Arnold). SSA. Text: W H Anderson.
Christmas Questionings (Western). SATB. Text: Father Andrew SDC.
The Christmas Rose (Gray). SATB. Text: old words.
Come Holy Ghost and with Thy Sacred Fire (Birchard). SATB. Text: old words.
Carol for Easter. Text: W H Anderson.
Christmas in Heaven. SSAATTBB. Text: I E Eccleston McKay.
Easter Joy (G Schirm). SATB. Text: W H Anderson.
Gentle Mary Laid Her Child. SATB. Text: J S Cook.
Glory, Laud and Honour.
Heart of Gold.
Holy Night (Gray). SATB. Text: old words.
Husheen Lo! SSA. Text: Norah Holland.
In Praise of Christmas (Birchard). SATB. Text: old words.
In the Barnyard's Southerly Corner (GVT). unis. Text: Charles G D Roberts.
Jesous Ahatonhia (Gray). SATB. Text: Jean de Brébeuf.
Lord in the Hollow of Thy Hand. TTBB. Text: G W Briggs.
Mary the Mother Sits on a Hill (Gray). SATB.
The Mother and Child (G Schirm). SATB. Text: old words.
Oh for a Closer Walk with God (G Schirm). SATB. Text: William Cowper.
Oh Brother Man (Birchard). SATB. Text: J G Whittier.
The Piper and the Chiming Peas (GVT). unis. Text: Charles G D Roberts.
Prayer For Our Home (Birchard). SATB. Text: Nancy Bird Turner.
Remembrance. SATB. Text: Allan Cameron.
Sing Loud, Sing Low (Fischer). SSA. Text: Elizabeth Harrison.
Skipping Song (Stainer & Bell). unis. Text: I E Eccleston McKay.
Swallow Song (Fischer). SSA.
Slumbering Deep the Ocean Lies.
Song of the Magi. TTB. Text: Felicia Wylie.
To A Blue Bell (Stainer & Bell). SSA/unis. Text: R H Grenville.
The Word of Light (Gray). SATB. Text: W H Anderson.
The World's Desire (Gray). SATB. Text: G K Chesterton.
Ye Mountains Praise The Lord. SSAA/TTBB. Text: K E Roberts.
Also, sometimes under the pseudonym of Hugh Garland, more than ninety arrangements of folk songs, mostly British, Canadian, and European (many Ukrainian, under pseudonym of Michael Bilencko).

VOICE
The Old Shepherd's Prayer. 1938; Western, 1938. vc, pno. Text: Helen Shackleton.
Sleep Little Jesus. 1938; Western, 1938. vc, pno. Text: Noreen Moore.
Last Year. 1940; Western, 1940. vc, pno. Text: Duncan Campbell Scott.
A Litany. 1940; Western, 1940. vc, pno. Text: Robert Herrick.
The Little Jesus Came to Town. 1941; Westtern, 1941. vc, pno. Text: Lizette Woodworth Reese.
A Memory. 1941; Western, 1941. vc, pno. Text: Arthur L Salmon.
Spring Magic. 1941; Western, 1941. vc, pno. Text: Katherine Rowlette.
To A Baby Brother. c1944; Western, 1944. vc, pno. Text: R H Grenville.
Fond Memories. c1948; Western, 1948. vc, pno. Trans: Allan Cameron.
Hospitality. c1948; Western, 1948. vc, pno. Text: old Scottish.
Indian Lullaby. c1948; Western, 1948. vc, pno. Text: Duncan McKellar.
Song of Mary. c1948; Western, 1948. vc, pno. Text: Constance Barbour Holbein.
To a Girl on Her Birthday. c1949; Western, 1949. vc, pno. Text: Blanche Pownall Garrett.
The Fairy Cobbler (Western). vc, pno. Text: A Neil Lyons.
Farewell. vc, pno. Text: Noreen Moore.
May You Walk in Peace. vc, pno. Text: Mabelle Mornington.
An Old Fashioned Song. vc, pno. Text: Gay Little.

BIBLIOGRAPHY
C48; Cb; CrC(II); Ef; K; Kh; Wa.

ANHALT, ISTVÁN (b. Budapest, Hungary, 12 Apr. 1919). Anhalt is the heavyweight among Canadian composers. No matter for what kind of performer or ensemble he writes – a soloist, chamber group, or full symphony orchestra – Anhalt always provides a substantial score of intense melodic lines, complex harmonies, intricate rhythmic juxtapositions, tightly packed, mostly dark sonorities, and brooding, unresolved densities. No matter what his chosen form, Anhalt always thinks big. His musical vocabulary, grammar, and syntax have the same thought-outness, complexity, and involvement in his smaller solo and chamber works as they have in his large symphonic and choral pieces, and his musical declamation retains its grand gesture and richness no matter which performance medium Anhalt uses – vocal, instrumental, electronic, or their various combinations.

Anhalt was born in Hungary and spent his youth in the culturally lush between-the-wars Budapest. In 1941 he graduated from the Royal Hungarian Academy, but combined circumstances of the war and his Jewish family background prevented him from immediately launching a professional career. In 1945 he worked for a brief period as assistant conductor at the Hungarian National Opera House. The following year he moved to Paris in order to continue his studies. He remained there until 1949 when a Lady Davis Foundation Fellowship enabled him to immigrate to Canada.

In Budapest his composition teacher had been Zoltan Kodaly; in Paris he chose to study with Nadia Boulanger. Whatever influence these two personalities may have had on the young composer during his student years, no trace of it is noticeable in that part of Anhalt's work that is publicly known. There are no echoes of folk music in his pieces, and his thick, subjective chromatic style is a far cry from the lean objectivity of most of Boulanger's disciples.

The foundations of Anhalt's personal style are firmly rooted in Schoenberg's twelve-tone-composition theories and practices. In fact, based on his music of the 1950s and early 1960s, Anhalt can be considered the most orthodox follower of Schoenberg's principles among Canadian dodecaphonists. Particularly in his earlier works, Anhalt adhered uncompromisingly to Schoenberg's dicta regarding avoidance of octave doublings and quasi-tonal interval constellations.

Upon his arrival in Canada, Anhalt was appointed to the Faculty of Music of McGill University and thus made Montreal his permanent home. It was there that the first performances of many of his earlier works took place and where in 1954 he presented an all-Anhalt program. This program included some of the major achievements of his early dodecaphonic period, such as *Fantasia* (1954) for solo piano and *Comments* (1954) for contralto, violin, cello, and piano.

Fantasia is a perfect example of athematic twelve-tone writing where continual transformation rather than development of thematic ideas is the main form-giving process used by the composer. There are no recurring melodic or rhythmic motifs, no distinguishable separations of individual sections, no sudden tempo changes. Instead Anhalt takes his tone-row through as many variations as there are reappearances of the row or its derivations, cleverly avoids any metric connotations (the piece is notated in 4/4 time, but the bar lines are there merely to facilitate reading, not to indicate up- and downbeats), and prescribes with great precision – sometimes from measure to measure – gradual tempo alterations.

While *Fantasia* is a piece of purely abstract music, *Comments* leans upon a verbal program. It is based on clippings from the *Montreal Star* dealing with such dramatic or prosaic items as a slaying and a weather report. The scope of Anhalt's imagination and craft becomes evident in this work as he manages to combine the rigidity of serialism with colouristic tone-painting such as quasi-imitations of gamelan orchestras, street cries of news vendors, or the tranquillity of motionless air.

The climax of Anhalt's creative work during the 1950s is his first large orchestral opus, the *Symphony No. 1* (1958). It took Anhalt four years to complete this 26-minute composition. It is an emotionally powerful work, solidly structured in its broad outline and meticulously organized. The structural foundation of this work is, to use the composer's own terminology, a 'density scale'. The composer interprets various combinations of pitches, rhythms, dynamics, instrumental ensembles, and tempi as corresponding with certain degrees on this scale, and arranges the balances of the work according to these data. This symphony, which was dedicated to the Bicentenary of Canadian Jewry, was at the time of its appearance considered not only a highlight in Anhalt's own creative career, but also a landmark on the Canadian symphonic landscape.

Having fulfilled his first symphonic ambitions, Anhalt was looking for new challenges. He found them in the medium that was gaining increasing prominence in the 1950s – electronic music. He confronted this challenge with his typical thoroughness and single-mindedness. Whatever time he had beyond his teaching duties at McGill he spent exploring and experimenting at various electronic studios, including the Electronic Music Laboratory of the National Research Council in Ottawa and the Columbia-Princeton Electronic Music Center. The tangible results of these excursions between 1959 and 1962 appear in the form of four tape compositions (*Electronic Compositions*, 1 to 4), each of them an essay on a different aspect of synthesized sound-production.

Although electronic laboratory music suited Anhalt's intellect and temperament well, he did not find ultimate satisfaction in it. Human voices and mechanical instruments had not lost their magnetism for him. Also, underneath Anhalt's cerebral surface lurked a romantic with an urge to express himself on a large scale. The answer was to bring together live and technological media and let them complement each other.

Anhalt did so in three sizeable works: *Symphony of Modules* (1967), *Cento on Eldon Grier's 'An Ecstasy' (Cantata Urbana)* (1967), and *Foci* (1969). The word sizeable does not necessarily mean in this case large performing forces or long duration. *Cento*, for instance, is scored for a twelve-voice mixed chorus and tapes, and lasts only eleven minutes. Yet this score is laden with musical intensity and richness of texture that reach far beyond normal chamber chorus fare. The basic musical materials of *Cento* are normal and exaggerated speech sounds. Anhalt makes the most of the intricate cadences and modulations of human speech and the rhythmic variations of words. He took a portion of Eldon Grier's poem 'An Ecstasy' and used its text now in the given sequence, now in a shuffled order, its words alternately straight and scrambled beyond recognition. He creates unique blends and interactions between live and taped voices, providing the listener with new insight into the most intimate of musical instruments, the human voice.

In *Cento* the external dimensions are small. Not so in the *Symphony of Modules* and *Foci*. The former employs a large orchestra with fourfold woodwinds, six horns, seven percussionists, harp, piano, harpsichord, guitar, accordion, and mixed chorus. As with its instrumentation, the musical materials of the work are of the most varied nature, ranging from tightly controlled dodecaphony to literal quotations from works of the classical era. It is a most complex score – so demanding, in fact, that at the time of this writing it had not yet been performed.

Foci does not call for large performing forces, but in content and scope it is just as complex and monumental as the *Symphony of Modules*. Scored for ten instrumentalists, soprano voice, three tape-recorder operators, and an off-stage percussionist, this half-hour piece is in essence a summary of all Anhalt's recent musical and extramusical experiences. Again speech-sounds are much in evidence throughout the score, but this time they stem from a variety of languages – English, French, Italian, German, Yiddish, Aramaic, Greek, Hungarian, and Creole. The texts come from sources as diverse as a dictionary of psychology, the New Testament, legal formulae, voodoo words, the Odyssey, and many others. The musical language encompasses everything from modality/tonality to formations of non-defined pitches, from rigid structures to aleatoric passages, from recorded and manipulated speech-sounds to live and amplified singing lines. It is the most varied of Anhalt's scores, one where the composer finally 'lets go' as much as his disciplined and conscientious personality allows. More than in any of his other works Anhalt reaches in *Foci* for extramusical elements. Not only are the individual sections of the piece heavy with many kinds of symbolism, but the whole performance is set up as a theatrical ritual (embracing a scenario of entrances and exits for the performers, as well as slide projections), the most fully developed so far of Anhalt's media mixes.

The number of Anhalt's compositions is not very large, primarily for two reasons. First, all his recent works are of a kind and scope that demand long preparation before the actual scoring can begin, and, once that stage has been reached, the sheer physical job of notating the performers' parts and preparing the tapes is so gigantic that only a person with Anhalt's determination and patience can carry it out. Second, the time that Anhalt can devote to composition has always had its limitations owing to the other half of his professional career – university teaching. During his years at McGill, various administrative duties were added to his quite heavy teaching load. In 1963 he installed an Electronic Music Studio as part of the Faculty of Music, and was named its director. Following that he was for several years the chairman of the theory department and a member of the university Senate. In 1969 he was offered the Slee Visiting Professorship at the State University of New York at Buffalo, a post that he filled by commuting between there and Montreal so as not to neglect his commitments at McGill.

In 1971 Anhalt left Montreal to become head of the Music Department of Queen's University, Kingston, Ont. He is a member of the Canadian League of Composers and an affiliate of BMI Canada. UDO KASEMETS

MUSICAL WORKS

STAGE

Arc en Ciel (ballet). 1951. 25′. 2pno. ms. 1952, Mtl, McGill, Dorothy Morton, Luba Sluzar.

ORCHESTRA

Symphony. 1958. 26′. full orch. Ber, 1963. Nov 1959, Mtl, Bicentenary of Can Jewry, István Anhalt.

SMALL ORCHESTRA

Concerto in stilo di Handel. 1946. 20′. 2ob, 2hn, str. ms.

Interludium. 1950. 7′. str orch, pno, timp. ms.

Funeral Music. 1951. 7′. fl, cl, bsn, hn, 2vln, 2vla, 2vlc. CMC. 1954, Mtl, McGill Orch, István Anhalt.

VOICE(S) WITH ORCHESTRA

Symphony of Modules. 1967. 28′. full orch, elec tape. CMC.

CHOIR

Seu Scheorim. 1951. 2′. SATB, org. ms.

Three Songs of Love. 1951. 8′. SSA. CMC. Text: Walter de la Mare, anon folk song.

Three Songs of Death. 1954. 14′. SATB. CMC. Text: Sir William Davenant, Robert Herrick. 1954.

Cento (Cantata Urbana). 1967. 10′45″. 12 spkrs (SATB), elec tape. Ber, 1968. RCI-357. Text: from 'An Ecstasy' by Eldon Grier. Feb 9, 1967, U of BC Chamb Sgrs, Cortland Hultberg.

VOICE

Six Songs from Na Conxy Pan. 1941–7. 14′. bar, pno. CMC. Text: Sandor Weöres. 1948, ORTF, D Conrad(bar), István Anhalt(pno).

Psalm XIX (a benediction). 1951. 3′. bar, pno. ms. Text: A M Klein.

Journey of the Magi. 1952. 7′. bar, pno. CMC. Text: T S Eliot. 1952, Mtl, McGill, Fadlou Shehadi(bar), István Anhalt(pno).

VOICE WITH INSTRUMENTAL ENSEMBLE

Comments. 1954. 12′. alto, vln, vlc, pno. CMC. Text: clippings from *Mtl Star*. 1954, Mtl, McGill, Maureen Forrester(alto), Eugene Kash(vln), Walter Joachim(vlc), Charles Reiner(pno).

Chansons d'Aurore. 1955. 9′. sop, fl, pno. CMC. Text: André Verdet. 1955, Mtl, Marguerite Lavergne(sop), Mario Duschenes(fl), Jeanne Landry(pno).

Foci. 1969. 31′. sop, fl, cl, b cl, trb, vln, vlc, cb, pno, elec org, cel, elec hpschd (opt), perc, 3 2-channel tape systems, mouth org. Ber, 1972. RCI-357. Dec 13, 1969, Buffalo, NY, Albright-Knox Art Gallery Aud, István Anhalt.

INSTRUMENTAL ENSEMBLE

Trio. 1953. vln, vlc, pno. CMC. RCA CC/CCS-1023; RCI-229. 1954, Mtl, McGill, Eugene Kash(vln), Walter Joachim(vlc), Charles Reiner(pno).

Sonata. 1954. 11′30″. vln, pno. CMC. RCA CC/CCS-1014; RCI-220. 1957, Mtl, CBC, François D'Albert(vln), Samuel Levitan(pno).

PIANO

Sonata. 1951. 12′. 1952, Mtl, McGill, Charles Reiner.

Fantasia. 1954. 11′. Ber, 1972. Col 32110045/46. 1954, Mtl, McGill, István Anhalt.

ELECTRONIC

Electronic Composition No 1; 'Sine Nomine I'. 1959. 8′. 1959, CBC.

Electronic Composition No 2; 'Sine Nomine II'. 1959. 9′30″. 1959, CBC.

Electronic Composition No 3; 'Birds and Bells'. 1960. 11′30″. MMI MS2111. 1960, CBC.

Electronic Composition No 4. 1962. 13′30″. MMI MS2111. 1962, CBC.

BIBLIOGRAPHY

See B-B; B65,71; Bec56,70; Bt; CrC(II); Esc; K; Lv; R12; Wa.

Beckwith, John. 'Recent Orchestral Works by Champagne, Morel and Anhalt', *CMJ.* Vol. IV, no. 4, Summer 1960 (44).

'István Anhalt', pamphlet, BMI Canada Ltd, 1970.

'István Anhalt – a portrait', *Mu.* No. 15, Nov. 1968 (8–9).

Rivard, Yolande. 'L'Enseignement de la composition à l'Université McGill', *Vie Musicale.* No. 8, May 1968 (5–12).

Schallenberg, Robert. 'Anhalt's Symphony No. 1', *Notes.* Vol. XXI, no. 4, Fall 1964 (625).

Stone, Kurt. 'Review of Records', *MQ.* Vol. VIII, no. 3, July 1967 (440–52). (Piano Trio, 1953).

LITERARY WORKS

ARTICLES

'Foci', *Artscanada.* Vol. XXVIII, Apr.-May 1971 (57–8).

'Luciano Berio's *Sequenza III*', *CMB.* Vol. VII, Autumn-Winter 1973 (23–60).

'The Making of "Cento" ', *CMB.* Spring-Summer 1970 (81–9).

'La Musique electronique', *Musiques du Kébèk* (R. Duguay, ed.). Montreal: Editions du Jour, 1971 (13–17).

REVIEWS

Boatwright, H. *Introduction to the Theory of Music, CMJ.* Vol. III, no. 4, Summer 1959 (83–5).

Hiller, L.A. and L.M. Isaacson. *Experimental Music: Composition with an Electronic Computer, CMJ.* Vol. V, no. 2, 1960–1 (61).

Messiaen, O. *The Technique of My Musical Language, CMJ.* Vol. II, no. 1, Autumn 1957 (67-71).

'New Records', *CMJ.* Vol. V, no. 2, Winter 1961 (34–9).

APPLEBAUM, LOUIS (b. Toronto, Ont., 3 Apr. 1918). Applebaum studied with Boris Berlin, Healey WILLAN, Leo SMITH, and Sir Ernest MAC MILLAN at the Toronto Conservatory and the Faculty of Music, University of Toronto, receiving his Bachelor of Music degree in 1940. He was awarded a scholarship to study composition with Bernard Wagenaar and Roy Harris in New York (1940–1). He was a staff composer (1941–2), musical director (1943–6), and consultant (1949-53) for the National Film Board of Canada and, from 1946 to 1949, in New York, was musical director of World Today, Inc., and a member of the Advisory Committee of the National Film Council. He has written incidental music for Stratford Shakespearean Festival productions since 1953, and in 1955 founded the Stratford Music Festival and was its director until 1960. He initiated the idea for the International Conference of Composers at Stratford (1960), sponsored by the Canadian League of Composers. From 1960 to 1963 he was a television consultant for the CBC (Toronto) and since 1963 has been a free-lance composer for television series and feature films. Many of his several-hundred film scores have won awards, including the Hollywood Writers Mobilization Award (*Tomorrow the World,* 1945), the Flaherty Award (*And Now Miguel,* 1946), an 'Etrog' award (*Athabasca,* 1968), and a nomination for an Academy Award (*The Story of G I Joe,* 1946). He has also received awards from the Canadian Performing Right Society (1938 and 1939). In 1967 he was given a Canada Centennial Medal.

Applebaum has composed works on commission from the Canadian Jewish Congress (*Cry of the Prophet,* 1951), and from the CBC for the Festival Singers of Toronto (*Two Newfoundland Songs,* 1958). For the Janet Baldwin Ballet Company he wrote *Legend of the North* in 1957 and for the Elizabethan Singers of Stratford *Two Maritime Carols* in 1958. In 1967 the Edmonton Symphony Orchestra commissioned *Concertante for Small Orchestra.* He has been a member of the boards of directors of the National Ballet School and of CAPAC (1956–68) and chairman of the Music, Opera, and Ballet Advisory Committee of the National Arts Centre (1963–6). He was musical executive of CAPAC (1968–71); a director of the Canadian Music Centre; and has been a member of the Canadian Conference of the Arts Advisory Committee since 1967. In 1971 he was appointed Executive Director of the Ontario Arts Council. He is a founding member of the Canadian League of Composers and a member of CAPAC.

MUSICAL WORKS

STAGE, FILM, RADIO, AND TELEVISION

Ride a Pink Horse (musical comedy). Text: Jack Gray.

Incidental music for plays, including: *Hamlet* (CBC radio production) (1951) Text: Shakespeare; *Le Médecin malgré lui* (CBC radio production) (1952) Text: Molière; *Antigone* (CBC radio production) (1953) Text: Jean Anouilh; *Oedipus* (CBC radio production) (1954) Text: Sophocles; *Tambourlaine* (Theatre production) (1956) Text: Christopher Marlowe; *Peer Gynt* (CBC TV production) (1957) Text: Henrik Ibsen; *Andorra* (NY Broadway production) (1963) Text: Max Frisch; and for many Stratford Festival productions of Shakespearean plays.

Incidental music for film, including: *And Now Miguel*; *Dreams that Money Can Buy*; *The Story of G I Joe*; *Walk East on Beacon Street*; *Paddle to the Sea*; *Teresa*; *Tomorrow the World*; *Lost Boundaries*; *Whistle at Eaton Falls*; for some 400 documentaries.

3 ballet scores: *Dark of the Moon* (1954); *Legend of the North* (1957); *Homage* (1969).

INSTRUMENTAL

Works for orchestra, including: *East by North* (1947); *Piece for Orchestra* (1951); *Suite of Miniature Dances* (1953, arr 1958); *Three Greek Dances* (1958); *Action Stations* (1962); *Concertante for Small Orchestra* (1967); *Fanfare and Anthem* (1969).

Suite of Miniature Dances. 1953 (arr 1964). band. Kerby, 1972. RCA PC/PCS-1004.

Works for instrumental ensembles, including: *Moments from 'Romeo and Juliet'* (1961); *Essay* (c1971). MCA, 1971. Dom S-69006.

Works for piano solo, including: *Four Thumbs and Sixteen Fingers* (1948); *Grande Valse à l'Envers* (1967); *Touch Wood* (1969) GVT, 1969. Dom S-69002.

Several fanfares, including: *Three Stratford Fanfares* (1953) brass, perc. MCA, 1966. RCA PC/PCS-1004; *Fanfare to Welcome a Queen* (1958); *Fanfare – Royal Ceremonial* (1967); *Terre des Hommes/Man and his World* (1967).

CHORAL

Carols of French Canada. 1951. SATB, orch (arr for SSA, pno, 1953).

Four English Carols. 1951. SATB, orch.

Song for the National Arts Centre. 1967. SSA, band. Text: Earle Birney.

Chorale 'Canada'. 1967. SATB, fl. Text: Robert Finch.

Two Maritime Carols. 1958. SATB. MCA, 1971.

Two Newfoundland Songs. 1958. SATB.

VOCAL

Cry of the Prophet. 1951 (rev 1952). bar, pno. RCA LSC-3092.

Two Shakespeare Songs. 1959. bar (mezz), orch.

Five Shakespeare Songs. 1959. sop, pno.

BIBLIOGRAPHY

See B-B; B65,71; Bt; C63,66,69,72;CrC(I); Esc; K; W41; Wa.

Abel, E. 'He Makes Movie Music', *Maclean's*. Vol. LIX, May 1946 (22, 44).

LITERARY WORKS

ARTICLES

'Film Music', in *Mm*.

'Introduction' to *The Modern Composer and His World* (Beckwith, Kasemets, eds). Toronto: University of Toronto Press, 1961.

'Musical Creation in an Age of Technology; with Discography', *Proceedings and Transactions, Royal Society of Canada.* Vol. IV, Series 7 (Transactions), 1961 (39–48).

'The Music Festival', *The Stratford Scene.* Toronto: Clarke, Irwin Ltd, 1969.

ARCHER, VIOLET (b. Montreal, Que., 24 Apr. 1913). Industry, discipline, and determination – galvanized but not governed by an Italianate intensity – have made Violet

Archer a particular and abiding force among Canadian composers. Her commitment to music was made early and passionately and never withdrawn. From her first formal lessons, when she was almost ten years old, her career has had the appearance of a single-minded plan for achievement. She assembled the tools and skills of a formidable craft in a way that might have seemed dryly academic had not her choices of guide been at once so practical and so discriminating. Douglas CLARKE and Claude CHAMPAGNE may have seemed obvious, since Miss Archer was a Montrealer and they were at McGill. But Bela Bartok was in New York and Paul Hindemith at Yale. Archer's work with all four distinguished men (Clarke and Champagne in the early thirties; Bartok in 1942; Hindemith in 1948–9) showed her determination to challenge herself at the highest level, a determination all the more evident when one considers that to study with Bartok, who normally chose not to give composition lessons, she commuted every two or three weeks to New York. The degrees of Bachelor of Music from McGill (1936) and the Master of Music from Yale (1949) were the trappings of a serious musical quest, and scholarships at McGill, the Charles Ditson Fellowship (1949), the Bradley-Keeler Memorial Scholarship (1948), and the Woods-Chandler composition prize (1949) at Yale were the trophies – as were, later, a Canada Council Senior Fellowship (1958–9), the Yale Alumni Citation for Distinguished Service in Music (1968), and an honorary doctorate from McGill (1971). Like all good Hindemith students, Archer took instrumentation seriously enough to study instruments, and to her proficiencies on piano and organ she added two years of clarinet study and significant amounts of time studying strings (at the Juilliard) and brass. She also taught: at McGill (1944–7); at North Texas State College, where she was also composer-in-residence (1950–3); at the University of Oklahoma (1953–61); and at the University of Alberta (since 1962), where she is a professor and chairman of the division of theory and composition.

The extensive body of Archer's acknowledged work as a composer begins in 1938 with a set of orchestral variations on 'A la claire fontaine', and it is interesting to note the range and enterprise of her intent even in the formative years stretching from then until the late forties. Choral music, orchestral works, songs, various chamber pieces including two string quartets, works for piano, two pianos, organ – all were undertaken with great energy and some success, though even as late as 1946 the orchestral *Fantasy on a Ground* used the orchestra somewhat turgidly and the *Concertino for Clarinet and Orchestra* demonstrated a pedestrian approach to rhythm even in the perky finale. The *Sonatina No. 2* for piano, dating from the same year, is much freer and finer, probably because the piano idiom was more naturally assumed at that time by the composer. The dark sonorities attempted in the *Fantasy* are more effectively achieved in the slow movement of the *Sonatina*, and the muscular little jig that serves so well as the *Sonatina*'s finale easily outclasses the *Concertino*'s, and is characteristic of the resourceful use she was to make again and again of jig rhythms and patterns (for example, in *Prelude & Allegro* for piano and violin, 1954, and in *Trio No. 2* for piano, violin, and cello, 1956–7).

The *Fanfare and Passacaglia* of 1948-9 shows immediately the bracing and emancipating effect of Archer's studies with Hindemith. The *Fanfare* is clean and bold, if a bit Max-Steinerish (does one expect to see Sheriff Randolph Scott and his posse gathering on the brow of the hill while Sitting Bull and his braves assemble in the valley?); and the *Passacaglia* – its ground rhythmically identical to that of the great C-minor Passacaglia of Bach – is Hindemithian, not only harmonically but also in orchestral clarity and articulateness.

The same influence is not so telling in the major choral-orchestral cantata, *The Bell* (1949), which, though an imposing and obviously major work, perpetuates chorally some of the unrelieved textures that had marred the earlier orchestral works. Consequently some of the marvellous words of Donne go for nothing. The third movement, with its opening bassoon solo over a bass of plucked strings and its ensuing Hindemithian allegro, fares best.

In a newspaper interview with Elaine Byron and Keith Ashwell in 1972, Archer commented that she was not stylistically affected by Hindemith. Her remark would seem to represent the mature composer's unwillingness to admit any influence by another composer, as if such influence were somehow a detraction, a slight on the individuality of the one compared. But while one can sympathize with such a denial, and while no one would dream of implying that Violet Archer is not her own considerable person, the influence in this instance is too obvious, too important, and too beneficial to be ignored. Since she is an estimable composer, the comparison is a compliment rather than otherwise, and to see how large a compliment we need only revisit the 'Marienleben', the 'Trauermusik', the 'Nobilissima Visione' or 'Mathis der Maler'. If it is true that with Archer, as with the master himself, the Hindemithian work ethic occasionally served instead of white-hot inspiration, it is also true that when inspiration came, the muscle of craft was in top trim to accommodate it.

The choral *Landscapes* of 1950 is an advance over *The Bell*; the setting for alto voice and piano of the *23rd Psalm* (1952) is handsome and moving. The first of the piano trios (1954) is crisp, fresh, humorous, and authoritative; the second is less likeable – brusque, scrubbed, dour, and rather deliberately imposing – still an admirable work, redeemed for pleasure by the aforementioned buoyant and glinting jig of its finale. The *Sonata for Cello and Pianoforte* (1956) is a fine, full-scale, idiomatic piece that should be heard oftener. It has a particularly good first movement – plain, broad, neo-Handelian, with a thoughtful and effective use of the cello's contrasting registers.

The 1956 *Concerto for Piano and Orchestra* is Archer in very top form. It is possibly the best concerto by a Canadian (though the WEINZWEIG *Harp Concerto*, the PENTLAND *Piano Concerto* and the ECKHARDT-GRAMATTÉ *Triple Concerto* make strong claims of their own); in any case it is a masterpiece and a genuine concerto in terms of display and dynamics. In the propulsive opening movement both piano and orchestra are used with real ease and virtuosity, exploiting their differences through an elegant co-ordination of contrasting weights, textures, and rhythms. The middle movement is pensive and lyrical, warmer and lovelier than Archer usually permits in a serious movement of this kind. The finale is vigorous and free and leaves the listener mildly appalled that a work of this calibre should be played so seldom.

The *Concerto for Violin and Orchestra* (1959) is by contrast a big, severe, impressive work, with all the hallmarks of vigorous Archer manufacture; but it is short on charm. Its second movement is like a pastorale without trees. It is, however, a favourite of the composer – rather as Bartok's similarly daunting voilin concerto was a favourite of his. The *String Trio No. 2* (1961) is another valuable work, laid out in four movements, with a rich quartet-like texture in its first movement and an uncharacteristically tender Siciliano for its third.

With the *Prelude-Incantation* for orchestra (1964) a new element enters the world of this methodical composer: expressionism. Not that there had been no forewarnings. As early as *Fantasy on a Ground*, and certainly the *The Bell* and *Landscapes*, hints of less-formalized impulses and more emotional procedures had been dropped. But with *Prelude-Incantation*, the composer – though still highly organized – gave way to effects that frankly evoke moods, pictures, a sense of strange events taking place in a dramatically heightened time continuum. Expressionism continues, though in less homogeneous terms, in the 1966 *Cantata Sacra* – a CBC Canadian centennial commission – based on medieval carols and poems assembled and prepared by John Reeves. This time Archer uses expressionism not so much to mystify or fascinate as to communicate simply and directly – perhaps too directly, one thinks on hearing the sore-thumb role of the piano in the score. Nevertheless Hindemith is nowhere to be heard: a changed Violet Archer is very much present. All of which leaves Miss Archer's 1973 opera – *Sganarelle*, to a libretto taken from Molière – an enticing prospect.

Violet Archer is a member of the Canadian League of Composers and an affiliate of BMI Canada. KENNETH WINTERS

MUSICAL WORKS

STAGE

Sganarelle (a one-act comic opera). 1973.

53′. 9 soli, sm orch. Ber. Text: Molière, Eng adaptation Samuel A Eliot, Jr. Feb 5, 1974, Ed'tn, U of Alta opera gp, orch, Alfred Strombergs.

ORCHESTRA

Scherzo Sinfonico. 1940. 4′. full orch. Ber. 1940, Mtl, MSO, Douglas Clarke.

Poem for Orchestra. 1940. 7′. full orch. Ber. 1960, Okla City, Okla City SO, Guy Fraser Harrison.

Britannia – A Joyful Overture. 1941. 6′. full orch. ms.

Symphony. 1946. 25′. full orch. ms.

Fantasy on a Ground. 1946 (rev 1956). 8′. full orch. Ber. 1956, Austin, Texas, Guy Fraser Harrison.

Fanfare and Passacaglia. 1949. 9′. full orch. Ber, 1964. RCI-130. 1948, New Haven SO, Robert Donovan.

Divertimento. 1957. 8′. full orch. Ber, 1968. 1958, Okla City, Okla City SO, Guy Fraser Harrison.

Three Sketches. 1961. 7′. full orch. Ber, 1966. CBC BR SM-119. 1961,Mtl, Mtl Jr SO, Lewis Elvin.

Prelude-Incantation. 1964. 10′40″. full orch. CMC. Nov 28, 1964, Ed'tn, ESO, Brian Priestman.

Sinfonietta. 1968. 15′. full orch. Ber. Mar 2, 1969, SSO, David Kaplan.

Sinfonia. 1969. 13′. full orch. Ber. 1970, Ed'tn, ESO, Lawrence Leonard.

SOLOIST(S) WITH ORCHESTRA

Concerto for Hand Timpani and Orchestra. 1939. ms.

Fantasy for Clarinet and Strings. 1942. 6′. CMC. 1942, Mtl, McG Cons O, R De Haviland-Tupper(cond), R Frank(cl).

Concertino for Clarinet and Orchestra. 1946 (rev 1956). 18′. Ber. 1972, Wpg, CBC O, Eric Wild(cond), Leslie Mann(cl).

Concerto No 1 for Piano and Orchestra. 1956. 17′. Ber. 1958, Tor, CBCSO, Victor Feldbrill(cond), William Stevens(pno).

Concerto for Violin and Orchestra. 1959. 27′. Ber. 1960, Mtl, CBC, 'Les Petites Symphonies', Roland Leduc(cond), Hyman Bress(vln).

CHOIR WITH ORCHESTRA

Choruses from 'The Bacchae'. 1938. SSAA, orch. ms. Text: Euripides.

Leaves of Grass. 1940. SATB, orch. ms. Text: Walt Whitman.

Lamentations of Jeremy. 1947. SATB, orch. ms.

The Bell. 1949. 21′. SATB, orch. CMC. RCI-130. Text: John Donne 'Sermons' & 'Devotions'. 1953, Mtl Bach Choir, George Little.

Apocalypse. 1958. 13′. sop, SATB, brass, timp. CMC. Text: 'Revelations'. 1959, Mtl Bach Choir, George Little(cond), Belva Boroditsky(sop).

Cantata Sacra. 1966. 31′. 5 soli, small orch. CMC. Text: Violet Archer, John Reeves (based on late mediaeval dialogues). Mar 14, 1967, Wpg, CBC, Phyllis Thompson(sop), Joan Maxwell(alto), John Masters(ten), Orville Derrough(bar), Glen Harder(bs).

CHOIR

Psalm 150. 1941. 4′. SATB, org. Wat, 1965.

Landscapes. 1950. 9′. SATB. CMC. RCI-10. Text: T S Eliot.

Proud Horses. 1953. 3′. SATB. CMC. RCI-189.

Songs of Prayer and Praise. 1953. 14′. SATB. CMC. Text: John Donne.

Three French-Canadian Folk Songs. 1953. 8′30″. SATB. Ber, 1962. Trans: Carolyn Osborne.

Two Songs for Women's Voices. 1955. 5′. SSAA, ob, pno (hp). GVT, 1972. Text: Althea Bass.

The Souls of the Righteous. 1960. 4′. SATB. CMC. Text: Wisdom of Solomon, III: 1–3.

Introit and Choral Prayer. 1961. 5′. SATB, org. Ber, 1963. Text: Eng Hymnal.

In Nomine Jesu (Introits and Anthems). 1962. 5′. SATB. CMC. Text: Eng Hymnal No 729.

Sing, The Muse. 1964. 17′. SATB. CMC. Text: Shakespeare, Raleigh, Drummond, Marston.

Paul Bunyan. 1966. 6′. SATB, pno. CMC. Text: Arthur S Bourinot. Feb 15, 1967, Ed'tn, Da Camera Sgrs, Sandra Munn (cond), John Butler(pno).

Centennial Springtime. 1967. 3′. unis or SATB, pno. CMC. Text: Jessie Alexander.

Harvest (arr). 1967. 3′. unis, pno. CMC. Text: Jessie Louise Hetherington. Melody: S Ferretti (1817–74).

I Will Lift Up Mine Eyes. 1967. 6′. SATB, org. Wat, 1969. Text: Psalm 121.

Sweet Jesu, King of Bliss. 3′. SATB (SA). Jay, 1967. Text: 13th cent Eng, anon.

A la claire fontaine (arr). 1968. 2′. SA, pno. Ber, 1970. Melody: Marius Barbeau 'Folk Songs of Old Quebec'; trans by John Osborne.

Amens for Church Use. 1968. 2′. SATB, org. CMC.
O Lord, Thou Hast Searched Me and Known Me. 1968. 6′30″. SATB, org. Wat, 1969. Text: from Psalm 139.
O Sing Unto the Lord. 1968. 3′30″. SA, 2tpt (org). Wat, 1969. Text: Psalm 96.
Où vas-tu, mon petit garçon (arr). 1968. 3′. SA, pno. CMC. Melody & text: Marius Barbeau 'Alouette' collection.
A Simple Anthem (Old 100th). 1969. 4′. SATB, org. CMC.
The Glory of God. 1971. SSAA. CMC. Text: Old Testament.

VOICE(S)
Moon Songs. 1942–4. bar, pno. ms. Text: Vachel Lindsay.
Snow Shadows. 1949. alto, pno. ms. Text: Arthur S Bourinot.
Under the Sun. 1949. 5′. sop, pno. CMC. Text: Arthur S Bourinot.
Some One. 1949 (rev 1959). 1′. unis, pno. CMC. Text: Walter de la Mare.
April Weather. 1950. 1′. med vc, pno. CMC. RCI-108. Text: Amy Bissett England.
Cradle Song. 1950. 1′30″. mezz, pno. FH, 1959. RCI-108. Text: Amy Bissett England.
Three Biblical Songs. 1950. 8′. med vc, pno. CMC.
The Twenty-third Psalm. 1952. 4′. med vc, pno. Ber, 1954. RCI-108.
The Gulls. 1955. 2′50″. med vc, pno. CMC. Text: John Gould Fletcher.
Irradiations. 1955. 4′. mezz, pno. CMC. Text: John Gould Fletcher.
The Storm. 1955. mezz, pno. ms. Text: Wildah Morris.
Four Canadian Folk Songs (arr). 1958. 3′. vc, pno. CMC. Melodies: from Marius Barbeau's collections, 'Alouette' and 'Folk Songs of Old Quebec'.
Two Songs. 1958. sop, cl. Text: William Blake.
The Forty-second Psalm. 1959. med vc, pno. ms.
Life in a Prairie Shack (arr). 1966. 2′. vc, pno. CMC. Text: 'Alberta Historical Review', Winter 1966. Melody: 'A Life on the Ocean Wave', mid 19th cent Eng popular tune.
Three Folk Songs of Old Manitoba (arr). 1966. 4′. med vc, pno. CMC. Text: A H Murray, L Riel, P Falcon. Melody: 'Songs of Old Manitoba'.
Gold Sun. 1971. 3′. alto, pno. CMC. Text: Dorothy Livesay.
Green Rain. 1971. 4′20″. mezz, pno. CMC. Text: Dorothy Livesay.
My Hands. 1972. 2′10″. med vc, pno. CMC. Text: Dorothy Livesay.
The Daffodils. 1972. 4′. med vc, pno. CMC. Text: William Wordsworth.

INSTRUMENTAL ENSEMBLE
Six Pieces for Piano and Timpani. 1939. ms.
String Quartet No 2. 1940. 22′. ms. 1954, Mtl, McG Str Qt.
Theme and Variations. 1942. str qt. ms.
Sonata. 1944. 21′. fl, cl, pno. CMC.
Quartet. 1945. fl, ob, cl, bsn. ms.
String Quartet No 1. 1949. 22′. CMC.
Divertimento. 1949. 9′35″. ob, cl, bsn, CMC. RCI-192. 1949, Boston, Int Student Sympos, New England Cons, Allan Williams(ob), Robert Barker(cl), Irvin Mitchniek(bsn).
Fugue Fantasy. 1949. str qt. ms.
Fantasy in the form of a Passacaglia. 1951. 6′. 4hn, 3tpt, 3trb, bar, tba, timp. CMC. 1951, Denton, Texas, North Texas State Coll Brass Ens.
String Trio No 1. 1953. 11′15″. vln, vla, vlc. CMC. 1953, Otter Lake Mus Centre, PQ; Hyman Bress(vln), Otto Joachim(vla), Walter Joachim(vlc).
Trio No 1. 1954. 14′. vln, vlc, pno. CMC. RCI-112. 1954, Mtl, Musica Antica e Nuova; Hyman Bress(vln), Walter Joachim(vlc), John Newmark(pno).
Prelude and Allegro. 1954. 7′40″. vln, pno. Ber, 1958. RCI-136. 1954, Otter Lake Mus Centre, PQ; Arthur LeBlanc(vln), Herbert Ruff(pno).
Three Duets for Two Violins. 1955. 5′30″. Peer, 1960. 1956, Norman, Okla, U of Okla; Charles Joseph, Donald Hatch.
Sonata for Cello and Pianoforte. 1956. 19′23″. CMC. RCI-139. 1957, Mtl, Ladies' Morning Mus Club; Walter Joachim(vlc), John Newmark(pno).
Sonata No. 1. 1956. 14′30″. vln, pno. CMC. RCI-196. 1958, Norman, Okla; Charles Joseph(vln), Digby Bell(pno).
Trio No. 2. 1957. 15′. vln, vlc, pno. CMC. RCI-196 & 241; CBC BR SM-5. 1958, Washington, DC, Inter-Amer Mus Fest; Walter Balsam(pno), Marc Gottlieb(vln), Irving Klein(vlc).
Divertimento No 2. 1957. 8′. ob, vln, vlc. CMC. 1960, U of Okla, Faculty Trio, Catherine Paula(ob), Michael Avsharian

(vln), David Vanderkooi(vlc).
String Trio No 2. 1961. 18'20". vln, vla, vlc. CMC. 1961, Wpg, Corydon Trio, Lea Foli (vln), Gerald Stanick(vla), Peggie Sampson (vlc).
Divertimento for Brass Quintet. 1963 . 20'. ms. 1963, Mtl, 100th conc Sarah Fischer Series, MBQ.
Sonata. 1965. 12'30". hn, pno. CMC. 1965, Reg, U Sask Fest of Mus, Mel Carey(hn), Gordon McLean(pno).
Sonata. 1970. cl, pno. CMC.
Three Little Studies. 1970. 3'. vln, pno. CMC.
Suite for Four Violins. 1971. 8'. CMC.
Fantasy for Violin and Pianoforte. 14'30". CMC.
Sonata for Alto Saxophone and Piano. 1972. 15'35". CMC.

PIANO

Variations on Canadian Folk Tune, 'Isabeau s'y promène'. 1941. ms.
Sonatina No. 1. 1945. ms.
Sonata for Pianoforte. 1945 (rev 1957). 6'30". CMC.
Birthday Fugue à la Weinberger. 1946. 3'. 2pno.
Sonatina No 2. 1946. 8'40". B & H, 1948. RCI-132.
Three Sketches for Two Pianos. 1947. 5'. CMC.
Six Preludes. 1947. 15'40". CMC.
Fantasy. 1947. ms.
Suite for Pianoforte. 1947. 7'05". CMC.
Three Two-Part Inventions. 1948. ms.
Ten Folk Songs for Four Hands. 1953. 7'55". Ber, 1955. RCI-113.
Rondo for Pianoforte. 1955. 3'10". Peer.
Minute Music for Small Hands. 1957. 3'. Peer.
Eleven Short Pieces. 1960. 10'. Peer, 1964. CCM-1.
Theme and Variations for Piano. 1963. 3'45". Wat, 1964.
Four Little Studies for Piano. 1963. 3'. Wat, 1964.
Three Miniatures for Piano. 1963. 4'. Wat, 1965. CCM-1.
Improvisations for Piano. 1968. 5'30". CMC.
Two Miniatures. 1970. 3'. CMC. Wat ('Little March').
Black and White. 1971. 20". CMC.
Holiday. 1971. 30". CMC.
Lydian Mood. 1971. 3'. CMC.
A Quiet Chat. 1971. 45". CMC.

INSTRUMENTAL SOLO

Two Pieces for Flute Solo. 1947. ms.

ORGAN

Sonatina. 1944. 8'. GVT, 1971.
Eight Chorale Preludes. 1940-8. ms.
Chorale Prelude: 'Dominus Regit Me'. 1948 (rev 1960). 2'20". CMC.
Chorale Prelude: 'Henlein'. 1948 (rev 1960). 4'. CMC.
Prelude and Allegro. 1955. ms.
Chorale Improvisation on 'O Worship the King'. 1967. 5'. CMC. July 28, 1967, Mtl, Expo '67, Can Pavilion, Hugh Bancroft.

BIBLIOGRAPHY

See B-B; B65,71; Bt; C63,66,69,72; CrC(I); K; Lv; Wa.
Crandell, Ev. 'Violet Archer', *MuSc.* May-June 1968.
'Violet Archer', pamphlet, BMI Canada Ltd, 1970.
'Violet Archer – a portrait', *Mu.* No. 13, Aug.-Sept. 1968 (8–9).

LITERARY WORKS

ARTICLES

'Alberta and its Folklore', *Canadian Folk Music Society Bulletin.* Vol. II, no. 1, July 1967 (45–66).

B

BANCROFT, HUGH (b. Cleethorpes, England, 29 Feb. 1904). Bancroft received his FRCO diploma in 1925 and his Bachelor of Music degree from Durham University in 1936. He came to Canada in 1929, becoming organist and choirmaster at St Matthew's Church (1929–37) and All Saints' Church (1938–46) in Winnipeg and at Christ Church Cathedral in Vancouver (1946–8). He was also conductor of the Vancouver

Bach Choir and teacher at the British Columbia Institute of Music and Drama (1946–8). In 1948 he moved to Australia where he was organist and master of the choristers at St Andrew's Cathedral in Sydney until 1952, when he returned to Canada and was again organist and choirmaster at All Saints' Church in Winnipeg (1953–7). During 1957 he was organist and choirmaster at Christ Church Cathedral in Nassau, Bahamas. In 1958 he moved to Edmonton, where he is organist and choirmaster at All Saints' Cathedral and a teacher at the University of Alberta. Most of Bancroft's compositions are either for choir or organ, although an early work for strings, *Intermezzo and Marching Tune* (1938), was premièred by Dmitri Mitropoulos with the Minneapolis Symphony Orchestra. Among his many works for mixed choir (usually with organ accompaniment) are *Love of the Father* (1938, SATB, organ), *Until the Shadows Lengthen* (1938, SATB, organ), *Good Christians Now Let All Rejoice* (1938, SATB), *I Sing of a Maiden* (1954, SATB, organ), *O Thou not Made with Hands* (1955, SATB, organ), *Bread of the World* (1971, SATB, organ), and *Ye Holy Angels Bright* (1971, SATB, organ). Bancroft is a member of the RCCO, the RCO, and of CAPAC.

BIBLIOGRAPHY

See B-B; CrC(I); Wa.

BARNES, MILTON (b. Toronto, Ont., 16 Dec. 1931). At the Royal Conservatory in Toronto Barnes studied composition with John WEINZWEIG (1952–5) and Ernst Krenek (summer 1955). From 1950 to 1958 he was a jazz and popular-music performer on drums. He studied conducting in Toronto with Victor Feldbrill, Boyd Neel, and Walter Susskind, and received scholarships to study conducting at the Berkshire Music Center in 1958 and 1961. In 1961 he graduated from the Vienna Academy of Music in orchestral and operatic conducting. He has been conductor of the University of Toronto Orchestra (1962–3), the Toronto Repertory Ensemble (1964–70), and the St Catharines Symphony Orchestra and Chorus (1964–70), and was musical director of the Crest Theatre (1964–6) in Toronto. He is the conductor of the Philharmonic Orchestra of Niagara Falls, New York (1966–) and musical director of the Toronto Dance Theatre (1968–). His composition style, exemplified in *Amber Garden*, a commission from the Toronto Dance Theatre on a grant from the Canada Council (1972), employs dissonant tonality in a generally romantic idiom. He has received commissions from the St Catharines Symphony Orchestra on a grant from the Canada Council (*Psalms of David*, a cantata, 1972), the French Club of the University of Toronto (*Thespis*, 1956), Robert AITKEN (*Sonata*, 1965), and the Ontario Federation of Symphony Orchestras (*Pinocchio*, 1967). He is a member of CAPAC.

MUSICAL WORKS

STAGE

Several background scores for theatre and television.

6 ballet scores, including: *Masque of the Red Death* (1971) ob, vln, vlc, hpschd, perc; *Three-Sided Room* (1972) vln, cl, vlc, pno; *Amber Garden* (1972) str qt, ww qnt, pno.

INSTRUMENTAL

4 works for full orchestra, including: *Symphony No 1* (1964); *Pinocchio, Symphonic Tone Poem* (1966).

Variations for String Orchestra. 1958.

Variations for Clarinet and Full Orchestra. 1968.

Sonata for Flute and String Orchestra. 1970.

4 works for chamber ensemble: *Three Folk Dances* (1953) vln, pno; *Burletta* (1957–8) str qt; *Sonata* (1965) fl, pno; *Rhapsody on a Late Afternoon* (1971) str qt.

3 solo piano works: *Fantasia* (1958); *Portraits* (1964); *Masque of the Red Death* (1971).

3 works for instrumental solo: *Lamentations of Jeremiah* (1959) vlc; *Seven Easy Pieces for Solo Guitar* (1968); *Variations for Solo Violin* (1972).

CHORAL

4 works for choir and instruments: *Thespis* (1956) ten, SATB, 2pno; *Third Choral Ode from 'Antigone'* (1966) SATB, orch; *In Our Time* (1968) SATB, brass; *Gloria* (1968) SATB, ww, brass; *Psalms of David* (1972) sop, bar, SATB, orch.

Two Eskimo Poems. 1968. bass, male choir.

VOCAL

2 works for voice and piano: *The Vision* (1953); *A Spirit Pass'd Before Me* (1958).

2 works for voice and flute: *Nocturne* (1961); *Poems for Voice and Flute, No 2: 'The New Year'* (1964).

BIBLIOGRAPHY

Wa.

Goddard, Peter. 'A Conductor Goes through Changes', *CanCo.* No. 67, Feb. 1967 (4–11).

Schrank, D. 'Most Conductors of Our Smaller Orchestras Have No Idea of What Canadian Music They Can Programme for Their Orchestra', *CanCo.* No. 36, Jan. 1969 (30–1).

LITERARY WORKS

ARTICLES

'And Now, According to Milton Barnes', *CanCo.* No. 38, Mar. 1969 (28–31).

BECKWITH, JOHN (b. Victoria, B.C., 9 Mar. 1927). Beckwith is an unusually versatile musician who, in addition to his compositional activities, has performed publicly as pianist (before 1953) and served as music critic (*Toronto Star* 1952–62, 1963–5), as program annotator (Toronto Symphony, 1966–70), and as radio script writer (the important weekly CBC series, 'Music in our Time' and 'The World of Music'). His writings on music include articles for the *University of Toronto Quarterly*, the *Canadian Music Journal*, and the *Canadian Forum*, and he co-edited (with Udo KASEMETS) *The Modern Composer and His World* (1961). Since 1952 he has been a teaching member of the University of Toronto and in 1970 was appointed Dean of its Faculty of Music. In this capacity he has shown himself to be a most influential teacher and administrator. He is active in Canadian musical life and has served or is serving on the boards of the Canadian League of Composers, Ten Centuries Concerts and New Music Concerts, the Canadian Music Centre, and the Canadian Opera Company.

Beckwith's principal musical education spans the period 1945–50 when he studied piano with Alberto Guerrero at the Royal Conservatory of Music and attended the University of Toronto (Bachelor of Music, 1947). He is one of a select group of Canadian composers (others are ANHALT, BLACKBURN, JONES, and PAPINEAU-COUTURE) who have studied with Nadia Boulanger (Paris, 1950–2) and, as with other students of this noted teacher, Beckwith shares their common concern for meticulous craftsmanship and an attitude of respect and understanding for the music of the past; his knowledge of repertoire of all musical ages is rivalled by few Canadian composers. In 1960–1 he returned briefly to student life to receive a Master's degree and in 1974 he was awarded an honorary doctorate from Mount Allison University.

Without denying the inevitable creative maturation that has taken place over the period of thirty years or his assimilation of new techniques and styles as they emerged, one can say that Beckwith's compositional outlook has remained remarkably consistent from the earliest pieces (mid-1940s) to the present day. The essence of this unity can only be generalized, but at least three tendencies can be observed throughout the entire output.

Beckwith is foremost a 'North American' composer – his music has an ambiance that is unmistakably 'American', specifically Canadian, possibly even Southern-Ontarian. Obviously this can be attributed in part to the regional subject material in the pieces with supporting texts. But at the level of raw sound, despite the influence of Stravinsky, one hears prominently the sound environments of Charles Ives, Aaron Copland, Virgil Thomson, Henry Brant and, to a less degree perhaps, John WEINZWEIG.

Although Beckwith writes with assurance for instruments, many of his important compositions feature voices speaking and/or singing. (In terms of duration, at least two-thirds of his output employs the voice.) He has a keen ear for the English language, for the appropriate musical representation of its prosody and for the aptness of the supporting music. The texts he has used are often a result of direct collaboration with Canadian poets: Margaret Atwood, Dennis Lee, and in particular James Reaney. His collaboration with Reaney has been so successful that it is difficult to read or hear other Reaney works without imagining Beckwith's music.

There is also an element of 'theatre'

underlying not only Beckwith's vocal but his instrumental pieces as well – musical gestures can operate at extra-musical levels, creating 'dramatic' situations and continuities. Some works – like the brass quintet, *Taking a Stand* (1972) – are obviously theatrical and the score is just as much a script or scenario; but in less obvious corners of his music, the concertato textures in particular evoke the drama of a Mozart operatic ensemble-finale. His long-standing interest in the theatre, and the influence of his wife Pamela Terry, the stage director, might conceivably account for this quality in some of his music.

Beckwith has contributed works to all sections of the musical repertory with a few noteworthy exceptions – he has never written a symphony in its commonly accepted sense, nor has he composed a string quartet. Otherwise he has found time in his very active life to compose many short occasional pieces or extended works, in response to commissions or just for the sheer joy of writing. The works themselves can be conveniently examined in groups according to genre: songs, collage, choral music, opera, piano music, chamber music, and orchestral music.

SONGS: Beckwith's approach to writing songs does not necessarily conform to the commonly accepted norm of vocal soloist with piano accompaniment. *Five Lyrics of the T'ang Dynasty* (1947) and *Four Songs to Poems by e. e. cummings* (1950) are for solo voice and piano. But *A Chaucer Suite* (1962) employs unaccompanied alto, tenor, and baritone soloists, the *Four Songs from Ben Jonson's Volpone* (1961) are accompanied by guitar, while the *Great Lakes Suite* (1949) requires soprano and baritone soloists along with clarinet, cello, and piano accompaniment. The melodic writing is always 'vocal' and considerate of the singer; when the accompanying instruments are specified, they are equal partners in the musical action.

Of the earlier songs, the *Great Lakes Suite* (the first of his many collaborations with Reaney) is most characteristic and stands up well after many years. From a later period, *A Chaucer Suite* shows Beckwith's expert handling of the difficult texts. The melodic lines of the Chaucer songs are developed serially with a continuous 'spinning out' reminiscent of Ockeghem; his awareness of older music is also found at the end of the first and fourth songs, where all three voices combine in a polyphony suggestive of a Dunstable motet.

COLLAGE: Among Beckwith's most original works is a series of collaborations with Reaney from the 1960s, intended for radio, which they called 'collages'. Beginning with *A Message to Winnipeg* (1960) and culminating in *Canada Dash, Canada Dot* (1965–7), they evolved a format of great flexibility where disparate musical and poetic ideas are juxtaposed and superimposed, operating in 'real' time yet traversing freely along a continuum that includes past and present. The resulting mosaics are more than just sound experiences – they are also eloquent and compassionate interrogations of the Canadian identity. To single out a representative section from these pieces is unfair to both Beckwith and Reaney, but in the second section of *Canada Dash, Canada Dot* ('The line up and down') there exists a remarkable 'trip' up Toronto's Yonge Street, out to the suburbs, and finishing at the village of Sharon. For this writer the Sharon section might be one of the most eloquent moments in Canadian music.

The collages are scored for speakers and singers accompanied by a small group of instrumentalists, who present musically independent ideas according to stop-start cues. Beckwith adopted aspects of this 'chance' technique in later instrumental pieces (e.g. *Circle, with Tangents*, 1967).

CHORAL MUSIC: The choral compositions of the 1960s are considered by many of his colleagues to be Beckwith's finest pieces. These highly original works defy brief summations; not only do they comprise the major portion of his complete works, but they also encompass the entire range of his social and artistic attitudes. A reading of the texts themselves (further collaborations with distinguished Canadian poets or of Beckwith's own choosing) gives us a partial insight into this complex man.

Jonah (1963), a cantata for chorus, strings, and a few solo instruments, employs poetry by Jay Macpherson and biblical quotations to relate the well-known story. The work begins with a hymn and concludes with a chorale that is undoubtedly an allusion to the Bach cantatas. A less obvious reference to Bach's cantata practice is Beckwith's use of solo obbligato instruments (horn and clarinet), here used to support the narrative.

To commemorate the anniversary of Shakespeare's birth, Beckwith collaborated with Margaret Atwood on *The Trumpets of Summer* (1964), a six-movement suite for narrator, vocal soloists, and a small group of instruments. Atwood's text, through transformations and parodies of Shakespeare's own language, satirizes Canadian life in Shakespearean terms and consequently the Canadian-Stratford syndrome. The musical techniques include those of the collage he had been developing over the three previous years. Two different but interrelated tone rows, as is often the case in his music, are the source of his thematic material for the entire suite.

For *Place of Meeting* (1967) Beckwith again reverts to his collage technique, but this time for larger forces – a speaker, tenor soloist, blues singer, chorus, and large orchestra. Dennis Lee's text, a disturbing commentary on the Canadian urban life style, flows along three simultaneous streams and is appropriately conveyed by Beckwith in multi-layered textures in the manner of Ives. Because of its textural complexity and ironic texts, it asks more of the listener than do his other works.

Shorter, contrasting, but easily accessible choral pieces of the 1960s are *Sharon Fragments* (1966) for a cappella chorus and *Gas!* (1969) for twenty speaking voices. *Sharon Fragments* uses texts from David Willson (d. 1866), founder of the Children of Peace sect in Sharon, Ont., and can be considered ancillary to the *Canada Dot* trilogy. The thematic material is based on two nineteenth-century hymn tunes transcribed from the early Ontario barrel organ at Sharon. *Gas!* is a collage, with the texts borrowed from street signs in Ontario: 'Right lane must exit', etc.

OPERA: A work deserving of greater acceptance is Beckwith's rarely performed chamber opera, *Night Blooming Cereus* (1953–8). The libretto by Reaney sets the action in a small Ontario town and reveals the character of its simple people through their reactions to the singular once-per-century blooming of the cereus plant. The musical continuity alternates recitative-like sections with arias, duets, and trios, and the general approach is somewhat reminiscent of Virgil Thomson, whose operas Beckwith admires. Certainly the use of quasi-nineteenth-century hymn tunes (e.g. for the celebration of the flowering) is indebted to Thomson.

PIANO MUSIC: Considering that he himself is a competent pianist, Beckwith has written surprisingly little solo keyboard music, his major contributions to this repertory being the quasi-concertos *Concerto Fantasy* (1959) and *Circle, with Tangents* (1967). The early piano duet, *Music for Dancing* (1948), is the work of a gifted young man who has embraced the North American style of neo-classicism, a style that combines elements of Stravinsky and Copland. The remaining solo piano pieces are primarily pedagogic in intent.

CHAMBER MUSIC: From Boulanger, Beckwith learned the value of writing preliminary studies for extended pieces: *Five Pieces for Flute Duet* (1951) and *Four Pieces for Bassoon Duet* (1951) can be considered 'warm-ups' for the *Woodwind Quartet* of 1951. Also from the 1950s are the *Three Studies for String Trio* (1956). The last of the *Studies* shows Beckwith turning to serial procedures for the first time. In this and succeeding works, the classic twelve-tone technique is employed rather freely, more in the manner of Stravinsky's serial pieces of the 1950s. Though Beckwith has considerable admiration for the music of Schoenberg and Webern, their styles rarely infiltrate his own music.

Coming after the collages (and choral music) of the 1960s, the remaining chamber pieces, *Circle, with Tangents* and *Taking a Stand*, might be considered spin-offs from the previous works, i.e. instrumental collages without texts or correlative musical quotations. *Circle, with Tangents* is a miniature concerto for harpsichord and thirteen string soloists. Its rich polyphonic texture operates at two levels, the counterpoint of recurring pitch and rhythmic patterns and what Stockhausen calls the points of 'contact' arising from the respective articulations and timbres of the harpsichord and string instruments. Under actual performance conditions, the work seems to anticipate the theatrical and spatial qualities particularized by the composer in *Taking a Stand*. This work, for '5 players, 8 brass instruments, 14 music stands and 1 platform', localizes the musical action in three areas – the stage or platform, backstage, and within the audience – and calls upon the players to move and play in and through these locations.

These two works invite other comparisons: both are reminiscent of Ives and Brant; both employ multiple tone-rows; and both have inflections from jazz. Though both pieces have also been described as 'chance' compositions, pitch location and durations are for the most part specified strictly; only in certain details – synchronization and relative metronome markings – is there the freedom of choice usually associated with chance.

ORCHESTRAL MUSIC: Compositions conceived directly for orchestra, with or without soloists, form a small but significant part of Beckwith's catalogue. *Fall Scene and Fair Dance* (1956) and *Flower Variations and Wheels* (1962) are programmatic pieces in the North American style and could easily be transformed into ballets. Of the remaining works, the *Concerto Fantasy* (1959) for piano and large orchestra is the composer's most successful piece in the neo-classic manner. (In its last movement we detect for the first time the influence of Weinzweig.) These works, devoid of texts and the counterpoint of the collage, allow us to see another side of Beckwith, the composer-craftsman searching for solutions to diverse technical problems: orchestration, variation technique, rondo form (*Wheels*), concerto form, cadenzas, fugue form, the 'all-interval' row (the last movement of *Concerto Fantasy*), and so forth.

Beckwith's orchestration is functional and represents the best of twentieth-century practices. Unusual colours arise from specific doublings (or triplings) and from the use of exotic instruments (the celeste in the second movement of *Concerto Fantasy*) or the unexpected assignments of thematic material to 'wrong' instruments. The writing for instruments is idiomatic, especially for strings.

In 1972 Beckwith was awarded the Canadian Music Council medal. He is a founding member of the Canadian League of Composers, a member of the Board of Directors of the Canadian Music Centre, and an affiliate of BMI Canada.

GUSTAV CIAMAGA

MUSICAL WORKS

STAGE

Night Blooming Cereus (chamber opera). 1953–8. 60′. 3sop, 2mezz, alto, bar, bs-bar, small orch. Ric. Libretto: James Reaney. 1959, Tor, CBC, Ettore Mazzoleni.

The Killdeer (incidental music). 1959. prepared pno. ms. Text: James Reaney.

The Shivaree (chamber opera). 1965 (still in progress). Libretto: James Reaney.

ORCHESTRA

Montage. 1953 (rescored 1955). 4′30″. med orch. CMC. 1953, Tor, CBC O, John Adaskin.

Music for Dancing. 1948 (for pno duet; orch'd 1959). 18′. med orch. Ber, 1961. CBC BR SM-47. 1959, Nat Bal O, George Crum.

Flower Variations and Wheels. 1962. 13′20″. med orch. Ber. Apr, 1963, Vic, Vic SO, Hans Gruber.

SOLOIST(S) WITH ORCHESTRA

Fall Scene and Fair Dance. 1956. 7′. vln, cl, str. Ber, 1957. 1957, Tor, U of T SO, Robert Rosevear(cond), Ivan Kowaliw(vln), Terence Bailey(cl).

Concerto Fantasy. 1959. 23′10″. pno, full orch. Ber, 1962, Mtl, MSO, Roland Leduc (cond), Mario Bernardi(pno).

Concertino. 1963. 13′40″. hn, full orch. Ber. Mar 17, 1964, Tor, CBCSO, Sir Ernest MacMillan.

CHOIR WITH ORCHESTRA

Jonah (chamber cantata). 1963. 33′40″. alto, ten, bar, bs-bar, SATB, cl, hn, timp, str. Ber, 1969. 1963, Tor, Fest Sgrs, instr ens, Elmer Iseler.

The Trumpets of Summer. 1964. 36′. sop, alto, ten, bs-bar, SATB, narr, fl, bsn, tpt, hp, vlc, perc. Ber. Cap Ster: ST-6323. Text: Margaret Atwood. Nov 29, 1964, Mtl, Mtl Bach Choir, Le Petit Ens Vocal, George Little.

Place of Meeting. 1967. 25′. spkr, ten solo, blues sgr with guit, SATB, full orch. CMC. Text: Dennis Lee. Nov 15, 1967, Tor, T Mend, TS, Elmer Iseler and John Beckwith (conds), Jacob Barkin(ten), Phil Maude (blues sgr), Al Harris(guit), Colin Fox(spkr).

CHOIR

Sharon Fragments. 1966. 7′30″. SATB. Wat, 1966. Cap T/ST-6258. Text: David Willson.

1967, Waterloo, Ont, WLU Choir, Walter Kemp.
The Sun Dance. 1968. 17'15". SATB, 6voc solos, spkr, org, perc. CMC. Oct 26, 1969, Tor, St George's Church Choirs, Lloyd Bradshaw(cond), George Brough(org).
Three Blessings. 1968. 3'. SATB (instr accompaniment opt). Ber, 1968. Cap ST-6323; CBC BR SM-81. Text: A S T Fisher, Robert Burns, John Wesley.
Gas! 1969. 4'. 20 spkrs. CMC. Text: John Beckwith.
1838. 1970. 2'15". SATB. Novl, 1970. Text: Dennis Lee.

VOICE(S)
Five Lyrics of the T'ang Dynasty. 1947. 7'. high vc, pno. Ber, 1949. RCI-148. Text: Li Po, Wang Wei, Li Shang-Yin; trans by Witter Bynner.
Serenade. 1949. 2'7". med vc, pno. CMC. Text: Colleen Thibaudeau.
The Formal Garden of the Heart. 1950. med vc, pno. CMC. Text: Colleen Thibaudeau.
Four Songs to Poems by e. e. cummings. 1950. 8'30". sop, pno. CMC.
A Chaucer Suite. 1962. 11'. alto, ten, bar. CMC. 1963, Otter Lake, PQ, Otter Lake Fest, Le Petit Ens Vocal.
Ten English Rhymes. 1964. 12'. young vcs, pno opt. Ber, 1964.
Four Songs from Ben Jonson's 'Volpone'. 1961. 3'45". bar, guit. Ber, 1967.
Four Love Songs (arr). 1969. 10'. bar, pno. Ber, 1970. CBC BR SM-111(Nos 1, 3, and 4 only). Text: from Can Folk Collections.
Five Songs (arr). 1970. 15'. alto, pno. Wat, 1971. Select CC-15073; CBC BR SM-77. Text: from Can Folk Collections.

VOICES WITH INSTRUMENTAL ENSEMBLE
The Great Lakes Suite. 1949. 15'. sop, bar, cl, vlc, pno. CMC. Text: James Reaney. 1950, Tor, CBC, Lois Marshall(sop), Bernard Johnson(bar), Leslie Mann(cl), Cornelius Ysselstyn(vlc), John Beckwith(pno).

INSTRUMENTAL ENSEMBLE
Five Pieces for Brass Trio. 1951. 12'. tpt, hn, trb. CMC. 1955, Mtl, CBC.
Five Pieces for Flute Duet. 1951. 12'. Ber, 1962. 1951, Paris, Cercle Interaliée.
Four Pieces for Bassoon Duet. 1951. 8'. CMC.
Quartet for Woodwind Instruments. 1951. 11'. fl, ob, EH, bsn. CMC. 1953, Tor, CLC conc, Dirk Keetbaas(fl), Perry Bauman(ob), Harry Freedman(EH), Elver Wahlberg(bsn).
Three Studies for String Trio. 1956. 9'. CMC. 1959, Tor, Isidor Desser(vln), Eugene Hudson(vla), George Horvath(vlc).
Circle, with Tangents. 1967. 14'. hpschd, 13 str. Ber, 1968. July 16, 1967, Vanc, George Malcolm(hpschd).
Taking a Stand. 1972. 5 plyrs, 8 brass instr, 14 music stands, 1 platform. Aug 25, 1972, Stratford Fest, Can Brass.

PIANO
Four Conceits 1945–48. 1945–8. 6'35". CMC. RCA CC/CCS-1022, RCI-228. 1948, Vanc, John Beckwith.
Music for Dancing. 1948. 21'5". pno 4 hands. CMC. CBC BR SM-47, RCI-113. 1949, Tor, Raymond Dudley and John Beckwith.
The Music Room. 1951. 2'35". FH, 1955. RCI-134. 1953, Tor, John Beckwith.
Novelette. 1951. 5'. Ber, 1954. 1951, Paris, Eugene Gash.
Six Mobiles. 1959. 7'. Ber, 1960. CCM-2.
Interval Studies. 1962. 3'. Ber, 1962.
Suite on Old Tunes (arr). 1966. 5'. Ber, 1967. CCM-2.
Variation Piquant sur la 'Toronto Opera House Waltz'. 1967. 2pno. CMC. Dec 9, 1967, Tor, opening of TPML.
New Mobiles. 1971. CMC.

COLLAGE
A Message to Winnipeg. 1960. 23'. 4spkrs, vln, vlc, pno, perc. ms. Text: James Reaney. CBC BR.
Twelve Letters to a Small Town. 1961. 32'. 4spkrs, fl, ob, guit, pno-harm. ms. Text: James Reaney. CBC BR.
Wednesday's Child. 1962. 30'. 3spkrs, sop, ten, fl, vla, pno, perc. ms. Text: James Reaney. CBC BR.
Canada Dash – Canada Dot (a centennial collage-trilogy). 1965–7. 4sgrs, 4spkrs, fl, cl, trb, tba, perc, pno, cel, reed org, vln, vla, cb. ms. Text: James Reaney. Nov 28, 1967, Tor, John Beckwith.
The Journals of Susanna Moodie (incidental music for a CBC radio reading of the poem-cycle by Margaret Atwood). 2 keyboard plyrs (org, harm, cel, 2pno, elec hpschd), perc. Mar 1973, CBC.

BIBLIOGRAPHY

See B-B; B65,71; Bec70; Bt; CrC(I); D165;

Esc; K; R12; Wa.
'John Beckwith', pamphlet, BMI Canada Ltd, 1970.
'John Beckwith – a portrait', *Mu.* No. 6, Nov. 1967 (8–9).
Read, Gardner. 'Circle with Tangents', *Notes.* Vol. XXVI, no. 4, June 1970 (841).
Reaney, James. 'An Evening with Babble and Doodle', *Canadian Literature.* No. 12, Spring 1962 (37–43).
Such, Peter. *Soundprints.* Toronto: Clarke, Irwin Ltd, 1972 (54–77).
Wilson, M. 'John Beckwith's New Cantata "Jonah" ', *Alphabet.* No. 7, Dec. 1963 (92).

LITERARY WORKS

BOOKS

The Modern Composer and His World (co-editor with Udo Kasemets). Toronto: University of Toronto Press, 1961.

ARTICLES

'Alberto Guerrero, 1886–1959', *CMJ.* Vol. IV, no. 2, Winter 1963 (33–5).
'The Bernstein Experiment', *Canadian Forum.* Vol. XLIV, Apr. 1964 (1–3).
'Canadian Music', *Dictionary of Contemporary Music* (Vinton, ed.), New York: Dutton, 1974 (119–24).
'Canadian Music', *Encyclopedia Americana.* Vol. V, Toronto, Encyclopedia Americana, Canadian Office, 1963 (439–43).
'About Canadian Music: The P. R. Failure', *Mu.* No. 21, July-Aug. 1969 (4–7, 10–13). Reprinted with a postscript in *Music: The AGO-RCCO Magazine,* Mar. 1971 (33–7, 56).
'Aims and Methods for a Music-Theory Program', *CAUSM Journal.* Vol. I, no. 1, Spring 1971 (27–30).
'Composers in Toronto and Montreal', *University of Toronto Quarterly.* Vol. XXVI, no. 1, Oct. 1956 (47–9).
'Healey Willan', *Canadian Forum.* Vol. LII, Dec. 1972 (32–4).
'Jean Papineau-Couture', *CMJ.* Vol. III, no. 2, Winter 1959 (4–20).
'Music', *The Arts in Canada* (Malcolm Ross, ed.). Toronto: Macmillan Co. of Canada, 1958 (44–51).
'Music', *Canadian Annual Review for 1961.* Toronto: University of Toronto Press, 1962 (396–407).
'Music' (with R. Murray Schafer), *Canadian Annual Review for 1962.* Toronto: University of Toronto Press, 1963 (400–14).
'Music', *Canadian Annual Review for 1963.* Toronto: University of Toronto Press, 1964 (514–24).
'Music', *The Culture of Contemporary Canada* (Julian Park, ed.). Ithaca: Cornell University Press, 1957 (143–62).
'Music in Canada', *Musical Times.* Vol. CXI, Dec. 1970.
'Musical Education', *Encyclopedia Canadiana* (Grolier Society, eds). Ottawa, 1958 (228–31).
'Musical Instrument Building' (with Helmut Kallmann), *Encyclopedia Canadiana.* Ottawa, 1958 (213–17).
'Notes on "Jonah" ', *Alphabet.* No. 8, June 1964 (2–3, 6–18).
'Recordings', *Mm* (158–66).
'A Stravinsky Triptych', *CMJ.* Vol. VI, no. 4, Summer 1962 (5–22).
'Teaching New Music: What? How? Why?', *MuSc.* No. 270, Mar.–Apr. 1973 (8–9).
'Trying to Define Music', *Royal Conservatory Bulletin,* Christmas 1970 (2–3).
'What Every U.S. Musician Should Know About Contemporary Canadian Music', *Mu.* No. 29, 1970 (5–7, 12–13, 18).

REVIEWS

'CBC International Service Transcriptions', *CMJ.* Vol. I, no. 4, Summer 1957 (48–55).
'A "Complete" Schoenberg', *Canadian Forum.* Vol. XLVI, Jan. 1967 (229–32).
George, Graham. *Tonality and Musical Structure, Music: The AGO-RCCO Magazine,* Dec. 1971 (27, 47).
'Iannis Xenakis', *CMB.* Spring-Summer 1971 (32–4).
Kallmann, Helmut. *A History of Music in Canada, 1534–1914, University of Toronto Quarterly.* Vol. XXX, no. 4, July 1961 (433–8).
Landowska, Wanda. *Landowska on Music, Tamarack Review.* No. 34, Winter 1965 (98–106).
McCarthy, Pearl. *Leo Smith: A Biographical Sketch, University of Toronto Quarterly.* Vol. XXVI, no. 3, Apr. 1957 (329–30).
'Music in Toronto, 1964–65', *Canadian Forum.* Vol. XLV, July 1965 (83–5); Correction, Aug. 1965 (101).
'Notes on a Recording Career', (Glenn Gould) *Canadian Forum.* Vol. XL, Jan. 1961.
'Notes on Some New Music Heard on CBC

Radio', *CMJ*. Vol. IV, no. 2, Winter 1960 (37–9).
'Recent Orchestral Works by Champagne, Morel and Anhalt', *CMJ*. Vol. IV, no. 4, Summer 1960 (44–8).
Rowland, D.B. *Mannerism – Style and Mood, Alphabet*. No. 10, July 1965.
Schafer, R. Murray (ed.). *British Composers in Interview, University of Toronto Quarterly*. Vol. XXXIII, no. 4, July 1964 (426–8).
'Schoenberg Ten Years After', *Canadian Forum*. Vol. LXI, Nov. 1961 (180–2).
Stravinsky, Igor and Robert Craft. *Conversations with Igor Stravinsky, Canadian Forum*. Vol. XXXIX, Nov. 1959 (183–4).
Stravinsky, Igor and Robert Craft. *Dialogues and a Diary, Canadian Forum*. Vol. LXIV, July 1964 (91–2).
'The Summer Season: Stratford', *CMJ*. Vol. VI, no. 1, Autumn 1961(21–4).
'The Toronto Bach Society', *CMJ*. Vol. IV, no. 1, Autumn 1959 (34–7).

BEECROFT, NORMA (b. Oshawa, Ont., 11 Apr. 1934). At the Royal Conservatory of Music in Toronto, Beecroft studied piano with Aladar Ecsedy, Gordon Hallett, and Weldon Kilburn (1950–8), flute with Keith Girard (1957–8), and composition with John WEINZWEIG (1952–8), receiving a scholarship for the year 1957–8. In the summer of 1958 she studied composition with Lukas Foss and Aaron Copland on a scholarship from the Berkshire Music Center. In 1959 she entered the 'Corso di Perfezionamento' at the Academy of St Cecilia in Rome, where she studied composition with Goffredo Petrassi and flute with Severino Gazzeloni, graduating in 1961. In the summer of 1960 she studied composition with Bruno Maderna in Darmstadt, Germany, and at the Dartington School of Music in Devon, England. In 1961 she received both a Canada Council Arts Scholarship and a grant from the Italian Ministry of Foreign Affairs. Her work during this period, exemplified by *Improvvisazioni Concertanti* (1961) and *Contrasts for Six Performers* (1962), calls on the twelve-tone technique. In the *Improvvisazioni* the flute plays a fantasy-like line over a basically static chordal texture (strings), interjected with short, loud percussion or brass sections. This structural device of contrasting areas of high energy with areas of low energy typifies *Contrasts for Six Performers* as well, the texture being mainly pointillistic, with one instrument usually having a more legato line. Her style in these two pieces exhibits the detachment of the post-Webern period when, throughout Europe and North America, composers were experimenting with timbral composition.

Beecroft studied electronic music with Myron Schaeffer at the University of Toronto from 1962 to 1963 and with Mario Davidovsky at Columbia University, New York, during the summer of 1964. On staff at the CBC in Toronto she was script assistant for television music programs (1954–7, 1958–9, 1962–3), talent booking officer for television and radio (1963–4), program organizer and producer for the National Music Department (1964–9), and, since 1969, has been free-lance commentator for the CBC-FM series 'Music of Today'. In 1967 she completed works for Waterloo Lutheran University (*Living Flame of Love*), the Velleman puppeteers (*Undersea Fantasy*), and Ten Centuries Concerts (*Elegy* and *Two Went to Sleep*). She also received commissions from the Charlottetown Festival (*Pièce Concertante No. 1*, 1966) and the Société de Musique Contemporaine du Québec (*Rasas*, 1968).

Living Flame of Love for unaccompanied chorus is conservative in style, using soft dissonances, the effect being quite airy and well suited to the erotic, religious mysticism of the words of St John of the Cross. Concerning the song *Elegy*, Beecroft mentions that she 'inadvertently wrote [it] in E-flat major'. In *Two Went to Sleep* she uses contemporary techniques (including electronic tape), yet the result is similar in mood to *Elegy*, both being subdued. A change in her style can be seen in the development of a more personal means of expression, exemplified by *Improvvisazioni Concertanti No. 2* (1971), a commission from the National Arts Centre Orchestra. This work appears to alternate soft, static chords with pointillistic interjections from the woodwinds, brass, and percussion – the same device found in her earlier compositions; however, this piece has retained the introverted, subdued quality of the vocal works.

In 1969 Norma Beecroft received a Canada Council Senior Arts Fellowship.

She has been president of the board of directors of Ten Centuries Concerts (1965–73) and of New Music Concerts (1971–). She is a member of the Canadian League of Composers and of the board of directors of CAPAC.

MUSICAL WORKS

STAGE

Undersea Fantasy (puppet show). 1967. elec tape.

ORCHESTRA

Two Movements for Orchestra. 1957–8.
Fantasy for Strings. 1958.
Pièce Concertante No 1. 1966.
Improvvisazioni Concertanti No 2. 1971. MCA.

SOLOIST WITH ORCHESTRA

Improvvisazioni Concertanti No 1. 1961; MCA, 1973. fl, med orch. Audat 477-4001.

CHOIR WITH ORCHESTRA

From Dreams of Brass. 1963–4. sop, narr, SATB, orch, elec tape. MCA RCA CC/CCS-1008, RCI-214. Text: Jane Beecroft.

CHOIR

The Hollow Men. 1956. Text: T S Eliot.
The Living Flame of Love. 1968; Wat, 1969. Text: St John of the Cross. Trans: Norma Beecroft.

VOICE WITH INSTRUMENTAL ENSEMBLE

Elegy and *Two Went to Sleep.* 1967. sop, fl, perc or pno, elec tape. Text: Leonard Cohen.
Rasas II. 1972–3. alto, fl, guit, hp, pno/org, 2perc, elec tape. Text: Ecclesiastes, Kevin Flynn, Onitsura, Ransetsu, Jagdip Maraj, Sokan, Jane Beecroft.

INSTRUMENTAL ENSEMBLE

Tre Pezzi Brevi. 1960–1. UE, 1962. fl, hp (or guit or pno). Dom s-69006.
Contrasts for Six Performers. 1962. ob, vla, xylor, vib, perc, hp.
Rasas. 1968. fl, hp, vln, vla, vlc, perc, pno.

BIBLIOGRAPHY

C69,72; Esc; Wa.
'A Conversation with Norma Beecroft: The New World of Electronic Music', *CanCo.* No. 22, Oct. 1967 (34–7).
'From Dreams of Brass', *CBC Times.* Feb. 19–25, 1966 (15).
'Miss Norma Beecroft: Well-Travelled Composer', *CanCo.* No. 9, May 1966 (4–5, 40–1, 44–5).
'Norma Beecroft – a portrait', *Mu.* No. 19, May 1969 (10–11).
Stone, Kurt. 'Review of Records', *MQ.* Vol. LIII, no. 3, July 1967 (440–52).
Such, Peter. *Soundprints.* Toronto: Clarke, Irwin Ltd, 1972 (78–101).
Winters, Kenneth. 'A Composer Who Doesn't Wear Music Like a Straitjacket', *CanCo.* No. 64, Nov. 1971 (4–9).
———. 'Eight Composers Speak About Their Works for the Future', *CanCo.* No. 56, Jan. 1971 (32, 34, 36).

LITERARY WORKS

ARTICLES

'Two Musical Adventures in Italy: A Canadian Composer Reports Back', *CanCo.* No. 76, Jan. 1973 (18–21, 45).

BELLAVANCE, GINETTE (b. Lévis, Que., 30 June 1946). Since receiving her Master of Music degree in composition, studying with Serge GARANT at the University of Montreal, Bellavance has pursued three fields of interest: 'perception', her subject of instruction both at the University of Montreal and at the University of Quebec in Montreal; 'the song', via a pop-music research group, *Yul,* which she has directed since September 1970; and 'music of the theatre'. Since October 1971 the Nouvelle Compagnie théâtrale, the Théâtre populaire du Québec, the Théâtre du Nouveau Monde, the Théâtre des Pissenlits, and the Sun Valley Summer Theatre have invited her to compose music for twelve of their productions, including *Le timide au palais* (Tirso de Molina, 1971), *Bobby Boom* (Jean Apostolidès, 1972), *Don Juan* (Molière, 1972), and *Julien, Julien* (Marcel Godin, 1973). To do this she uses mainly the Moog synthesizer in conjunction with traditional instrumental sonorities, adapting the whole to the spirit of the theatrical work while illuminating it with original sonorities. She has also written *Match en coordonnées* (1971) for two percussionists, two guitars, and electronic tape; *CLAC* (1972) for electronic tape; as well as scores for twenty-two films between 1971 and 1972. She is a member of CAPAC.

BETTS, LORNE (b. Winnipeg, Man., 2 Aug. 1918). He studied in Winnipeg with Filmer Hubble (piano and organ), W.H. ANDERSON (voice), and Hunter Johnston (composition), later studying composition with John WEINZWEIG (1947–53) in Toronto and in summer courses at the Royal Conservatory of Toronto with Ernst Krenek, Alan Rawsthorne, and Roy Harris (1950–3). He holds the ACCO and LRSM diplomas and is a Fellow of the Royal Hamilton College of Music. From 1952 to 1959 he was principal of the Hamilton Conservatory of Music (later the Royal Hamilton College of Music), and has been the director of music at St Paul's Presbyterian Church and at Melrose United Church in Hamilton. In 1965 he became the music critic for the Hamilton *Spectator*.

His *Music for Orchestra* (1963), commissioned by Lee Hepner for the Hamilton Philharmonic Orchestra, uses a twelve-tone series, which Betts exploits through rhythmic variation. The structure is not complex; in fact Betts prefers the clearest statement of the row and its variations. This is not typical of Betts' style, however, which usually combines tonal writing with dissonant interjections for colouristic effect. *Three Songs* (1948), in which he calls on chromatic material, is dark and dramatic; the *Five Songs* (1950) are polytonal and lighter than the earlier set. The vocal writing in *Festival Psalm* (1968) is quite traditional and again the material is tonal.

Betts is a member of the Provincial Council of the Ontario Registered Music Teachers' Association, the Canadian Association of Music Festival Adjudicators, the Canadian Federation of Registered Music Teachers' Associations, and of CAPAC.

MUSICAL WORKS

STAGE

Music for Theatre. 1950. ob, 2cl, hn, tpt, pno, cb.

Riders to the Sea (opera). 1955. Libretto: J M Synge.

Music for a Ballet. 1960. pno.

The Woodcarver's Wife (opera). 1960. Libretto: Marjorie L C Pickthall.

Music for a Modern Dance. 1961. pno.

ORCHESTRA

Suite for Strings. 1948.

Sonata for Orchestra. 1949.

Two Dances for Orchestra. 1950.

Sinfonietta. 1952.

Suite da Chiesa. 1952.

Suite for Small Orchestra. 1954.

Symphony No 1. 1954.

Fantasia Canadiana. 1955.

Five Portraits from Robert Burns. 1958.

Divertimento. 1959.

Symphony No 2. 1961.

Two Abstracts for Orchestra. 1961.

Music for Orchestra. 1963.

Kanadario; 'Music for a Festival Occasion'. 1966.

Variants for Orchestra. 1969.

SOLOIST WITH ORCHESTRA

Five Songs for High Voice and String Orchestra. 1949. Text: Ezra Pound.

Elegy. 1949. EH, str.

Concertino. c1950. hpschd, orch.

Concerto for Piano and Orchestra No 1. 1955.

Six Songs. 1956. alto, orch. Text: Robert Louis Stevenson.

Concerto for Piano and Orchestra No 2. 1957.

Music for Violin and Orchestra. 1960.

A Cycle of the Earth. 1962–7. vc, orch. Text: Bliss Carman.

CHOIR WITH ORCHESTRA

David. 1949. Text: Earle Birney.

Joe Harris, 1913–42. 1951. Text: Earle Birney.

CHOIR

A Carol. 1952. Text: anon.

The Seasons. 1952. Text: Arthur S Bourinot.

Build Well the Peace. 1953. Text: Arthur S Bourinot.

The Christmas Promise. 1954. Text: Christmas carols.

The Apostles' Creed. 1956. Text: Liturgical.

Psalm 67. 1956.

And It Came to Pass. 1957. Text: Scripture and Christmas carols.

The Souls of the Righteous. 1957. Wat, 1960. Text: The Book of Wisdom.

God So Loved the World. 1958. Text: Bible.

Te Deum Laudamus. 1958. Text: liturgical.

Four Hymn Anthems. 1958–9.

Child in a Manger (arr). 1959. Text: Gaelic Christmas carol.

An Easter Prayer. 1959. Text: anon.
Psalm Tune 'Coleshill' (arr). 1959.
Swedish Christmas Carol (arr). 1959.
A Mighty Fortress. 1960. Text: Martin Luther.
Prayer. 1960. Text: C Wesley.
A St Paul Requiem. 1960. Text: various sources.
Antiphon for Palm Sunday. 1961. Text: Liturgical.
Three Sonnets for Mixed Voices. 1963. Text: John Donne.
Vespers. 1966. Text: Scriptures, The Common Service Book of the Lutheran Church in America.
Festival Psalm. 1968. Text: Te Deum.
Come Bless the Lord. 1969. Text: Psalms 90, 134.
He Came All so Still. 1970. Text: anon.
Psalm Triptych. 1970. Text: Psalms 150, 121, 148.
Thank You Canada. 1970. Text: Barbara Gaasenbeek.

VOICE AND PIANO

Three Songs. 1949. Text: James Joyce.
Five Songs. 1950. Text: James Joyce.
Three Songs of the Highlands. 1950. Text: Murdoch McLean.
Six Songs. 1951. Text: James Joyce.
Five Songs. 1952. Text: James Joyce.
Songs of the Grass. 1954. Text: Bliss Carman.
Six Songs. 1956. Text: Robert Louis Stevenson.
Five Epitaphs. 1957. Text: Robert Burns.
Five Songs. 1957. Text: Paul Verlaine.
Five Canadian Folk Songs (arr). 1958.
Two Songs. 1958. Text: William Shakespeare.
Three Scottish Folksongs (arr). 1959.

VOICE AND ORGAN

Behold! Thy King. 1957. Wat. Text: H H Milman.
Hosanna!. 1959. Text: J Threlfall.
Nowell!. 1959. Text: anon.
Six Sacred Songs. 1959–70. Text: anon, Hofgesangbuch, Psalm 23, Boris Pasternak.
Psalm 100. 1960.
A Christmas Song. 1960. Text: L Jonas.

VOICE(S) WITH INSTRUMENTAL ENSEMBLE

Prelude for Spring. 1951. mezz, bar, fl, hp, str qt. Text: Dorothy Livesay.
Nocturne. 1955. alto, str qt. Text: William Shakespeare.

INSTRUMENTAL ENSEMBLE

Sonata for Violin and Piano. 1948.
Prelude, Pastoral and Dance. 1949. fl, EH, bsn.
Sonata for Clarinet and Piano. 1949.
Suite. c1950. fl, cl.
String Quartet No 1. 1950.
String Quartet No 2. 1951.
String Trio. 1959.
Quartet. 1960. fl, cl, b cl, cel.
Sonata for Violin and Piano. 1970.
String Quartet No 3. 1970.

PIANO

Miniature Suite for Piano. 1948.
Piano Sonata. 1950.
Suite for Piano. 1950. FH (#3), 1955.
8 Recital Pieces for Young Pianists. 1959. MCA, 1963. Dom s-69002 (3 only).
Short Pieces for Piano (2 sets). 1959.
Suite Brève. 1967. MCA.
Sonatina for Piano. 1969.

ORGAN

Prelude on 'Rockingham'. 1960.
Three Hymn Preludes. 1960.
Improvisations on B-A-C-H. 1969.

BIBLIOGRAPHY

See B-B; B65,71; CrC(II); Esc; K.
'Lorne Betts – a portrait', *Mu.* No. 28, Apr. 1970 (8–9).

BISSELL, KEITH (b. Meaford, Ont., 12 Feb. 1912). Although often asked to write for professional musicians, Bissell's main interest is writing for amateurs – school children and choirs – and his work has given him ample opportunity. After receiving his Bachelor of Music degree from the University of Toronto in 1942, he graduated from Toronto Teachers' College and in 1948 was appointed supervisor of music for the Edmonton schools. While in Edmonton he was organist at Christ Church and formed the Edmonton Junior Symphony Orchestra. In 1955 he was appointed chief supervisor of music for the public schools in the Metropolitan Toronto borough of Scarborough. After a period of study in Munich with Gunild Keetman and Carl Orff in 1960, he introduced the Orff method of elementary music education into the Scarborough schools. He organized and conducted the Scarborough Orff Ensemble and the Scarborough Teachers' Chorus. With the late John Adaskin of the Canadian Music Centre, Bissell organized the first Canadian composers' seminar in music education (1963). In an article by Michael Schulman in *The Music Scene* (Nov.-Dec. 1972), he is quoted as saying: 'I think of my music chiefly as *Gebrauchsmusik*,' the term first used by Hindemith to describe 'useful' or 'work-a-day' music. Bissell considers writing for amateurs to be more challenging and rewarding for a composer than writing for professionals.

His style is only mildly dissonant and still holds quite firmly to diatonic harmony. Occasionally he moves into polytonality, but generally this occurs only in his works for professional performers. His *Sonata for Organ* (1963) is an excellent example of his more complex writing. In a basically polyphonic style, Bissell achieves a tight structure employing polytonal material and creating a dissonant character that is completely convincing. Nevertheless he is never far from diatonicism, each main section being completed with a diatonic chord. In his works for young performers and for choir, Bissell has achieved a simplicity of style that marks him as a traditionalist, a title he readily accepts. *Three Pieces* for strings (1960) – fairly simple pieces for a school orchestra – employ dissonant but still diatonic harmonies that have a bitter-sweet quality. *Little Suite for Trumpet and Strings* (1963) was originally written for children. 'It was originally for voice and percussion, with the children vocalizing and accompanying themselves on drums and sundry percussion. All my own children's groups performed it. The strange thing was, after I rescored it for trumpet and strings, the professionals who performed it did it note-perfect but they never performed with the freedom, the complete naturalness that the youngsters did originally.' (*Music Scene*, Nov.-Dec. 1972.)

Bissell's choral works are reminiscent of Healey WILLAN, a number of them being arrangements of traditional folk songs. He has received commissions from Memorial University in Newfoundland (*Newfoundland*, 1964), the Hart House Orchestra (*Divertimento for Strings*, 1964), the Fathers of Confederation Centre in Charlottetown (*Christmas in Canada*, 1967), and the St Catharines Symphony Orchestra (*A Bluebird in March*, 1969). He has also written works for Charles Peaker (*Organ Sonata, No. 1*, 1963, and *Passion According to St Luke*, 1971) and for Lois Marshall (*Six Maritime Folk Songs*, 1970).

Formerly a member of the board of directors of the Toronto Symphony, Bissell is a director of the Canadian Music Council and the Canadian Music Centre and in 1970–1 was the president of the National Youth Orchestra Association of Canada. He is an affiliate of BMI Canada.

MUSICAL WORKS

STAGE

Rumpelstiltzkin (operetta). 1947. 60′. schl vcs. ms.

His Majesty's Pie (an operetta for young people). SSA, pno. Wat, 1966. Text: Keith Bissell.

Incidental Music to 'The Centennial Play'. 1967. ms. Text: Robertson Davies, W O Mitchell, Dr A Murphy, Eric Nicol, Yves Thériault. Jan 1967, Ottawa.

ORCHESTRA

Canada 1967. 1967. 5′30″. med orch. CMC.

SMALL ORCHESTRA

Adagio for Small Orchestra. 1963. 5′30″. Ber.

Five Dances for Small Orchestra. 1963. 6′.

Andante e Scherzo. 1971. 7′. chamb orch. Kerby, 1972. May 1971, Quebec, Can Mus Counc Conf, Scarborough Schl Ch O, Donald Coakley.

STRING ORCHESTRA

Three Pieces. 1960. 7′30″. Kerby, 1972. 1961, CFRB, HHO, Boyd Neel.

Divertimento. 1964. 10′40″. Kerby, 1972. June 6, 1965, Halifax, CBC Str, Gordon Macpherson.

Variations on a Canadian Folk Song. 1972. 8′15″. CMC. Feb 24, 1973, Tor, Chamb Plyrs of Tor, Victor Martin.

SOLOIST WITH ORCHESTRA

Under the Apple Boughs. 1961. 4′. hn, str. Ber.

Concertino for Piano and Strings. 1962. 9′30″. Ber.

Little Suite for Trumpet & Strings. 1963. 6′. Ber, 1968. Tor, Student Conc, TS, Keith Bissell.

CHOIR WITH ORCHESTRA

A Bluebird in March. 1967. 7'10". SATB, orch or pno. Wat, 1969 (pno version). Text: Bliss Carman. Apr 9, 1967, St Catharines SO and Chorus, Milton Barnes.

Christmas in Canada. 1968. 55'. narr, soli, SATB, orch. CMC. Text: Ernest Buckler. Dec 10, 1967, Charlottetown, PEI, Confederation Centre, Keith Bissell.

Passion According to St Luke. 1971. 60'. soli, SATB, orch. Wat.

CHOIR

O Starry Night. 1948. SSA. West, 1950. Text: Keith Bissell.

Christmas Cantata. 1949. 30'. solo vc, SATB, org. ms.

Now that the Morning. 1950. 4'. SATB. ms.

The Earth is the Lord's. 3'. SATB, org. Ber, 1957. Text: Psalm 24.

Lullaby. unis. GVT, 1957. Text: Christina Rossetti.

Two Christmas Songs. SA, pno (org). GVT, 1957. Text: anon.

Christ Being Raised From the Dead. SATB, org (pno). GVT, 1958. Text: Romans 6:9.

Cindy (arr). SATB, pno. Wat, 1958. Text: Amer folk song.

The Dark Hills. 1'30". SATB. Ber, 1958. Text: E A Robinson.

Hear Thou My Prayer, O Lord. SATB, org. GVT, 1958. Text: Psalm 39.

In April. SSA, pno. Wat, 1958. Text: Ethelwyn Wetherald.

Sunday, Sunday (arr). TTBB. Wat, 1958. Text: French folk song.

Cape St Mary's (arr). 2'30". SATB. Wat, 1959. Text: Otto P Kelland.

Christ, Whose Glory Fills The Skies. SATB. GVT, 1959. Text: Charles Wesley.

Dream River. 2'. SA, pno. Ber, 1959. Text: Marjorie Pickthall.

God Save the Queen (arr). SAB, pno. Wat, 1959. Text: Third verse by Robert Murray.

I Was Glad When They Said Unto Me. SATB, org. Wat, 1959. Text: from Psalms 122 and 135.

The Plowman. 1'30". SA, pno. Ber, 1959. Text: Ethelwyn Wetherald.

Lord, Dismiss Us With Thy Blessing. SATB. GVT, 1960. Text: John Fawcett (1740–1817).

Rejoice Today With One Accord. unis. FH, 1960. Text: Rev Sir Henry W Baker (1861).

Shepherds in the Field Abiding (arr). SSA. Wat, 1960.

Six Songs for SA (arr). SA, pno. South, 1960.

Christ Is Risen From The Dead. SATB, org. Wat, 1961. Text: I Corinthians 15:20.

God Be Merciful Unto Us; 'Deus Misereatur'. SATB. Wat, 1961. Text: Psalm 67.

Lo! He Comes With Clouds Descending (arr). SAB. Wat, 1961. Text: Charles Wesley.

Puer Nobis Nascitur (arr). SAB. Wat, 1961.

Two Canadian Folk Songs. 4'. SATB. GVT, 1961.

Ah, Holy Jesu. 2'30". SATB, pno (org). Wat, 1962. Trans from German by Robert Bridges (1899).

Click! Go the Shears (arr). TTBB. Wat, 1962. Text: Australian ballad.

Laudate Dominum. SATB, org. Wat, 1962. Text: Psalm 65.

O Holy Spirit. SATB. Wat, 1962. Text: trans from Latin by Rev J Chandler (1857).

Old Adam, the Carrion Crow. SATB. Wat, 1962. Text: T L Beddoes.

Summer's Queen (arr). SA, pno. Wat, 1962. Melody: Danish folk tune; text: Keith Bissell.

The Three Princes. SATB, pno (org). Wat, 1962.

None Other Lamb. SATB, org. Wat, 1964. Text: Christina Rossetti.

A Maid I am in Love (arr). SATB. GVT, 1965. Text: N S folk song.

The SAB Choir (arr only). SAB. B & H, 1965.

Two Songs from Shakespeare. 4'5". SATB. Ber, 1965.

Baloo, Baleerie (arr). SSA. Wat, 1966.

Canada, Dear Home. SATB (SAB), pno or orch or band. Wat, 1966. Text: Keith Bissell.

Go and Leave Me If You Wish, Love (arr). SATB. GVT, 1966. Text: Nfld folk song.

A Bluebird in March. 1967. 7'10". SATB, pno or orch. Wat, 1969. Text: Bliss Carman. Apr 9, 1967 (orch version), St Catharines SO and Chorus, Milton Barnes.

Requiem. SSA. Wat, 1967. Text: Robert Louis Stevenson.

A Summer Evening. SSA, pno. Wat, 1967. Text: Archibald Lampman (1861–99).

Adieu de la Mariée à ses Parents (arr). 3'45". SATB. GVT, 1968. Text: Sask Métis songs.

Gloria in Excelsis Deo. ten solo, TBB. Wat, 1968.

Nous Etions Trois Capitaines (arr). 2'. SATB. GVT, 1968. Text: French Can folk song.

Singing and Playing/Chantons et Jouons. unis, perc. Wat, 1968.

Sweet Nightingale (arr). SAAB. Wat, 1968. Text: Eng folk song.
The Turtle Dove (arr). SAAB. Wat, 1968. Text: Eng folk song.
Behold The Tabernacle of God. SATB, org. Wat, 1969. Text: Rev S D Abraham.

VOICE
Three Songs. 1948. 10′. mezz, pno. ms. Text: William Blake.
Two Songs of Farewell. vc, pno. Wat, 1963. Text: Claude Bissell.
Hymns of the Chinese Kings. high vc, pno. Wat, 1968. Text: Claude Bissell.
Quatre Chansons sur des Poèmes du Vieux Français. vc, pno. MCA, 1970. Text: J du Bellay, P de Ronsard, C d'Orleans.
Six Folk Songs from Eastern Canada (arr). 1970. med vc, pno. B & H, 1971. CBC BR SM-144. 1971, Tor, CBC Fest, Maureen Forrester.
Six Maritime Folk Songs – set one – (arr). 10′. med vc, pno. Ber, 1970. CBC BR SM-168 (nos 1–4, 6).
Six Maritime Folk Songs – set two – (arr). 10′. med vc, pno. Ber, 1970. CBC BR SM-168 (nos 1 and 2).
Five Canadian Folk Songs (arr). 1972. 12′. high vc, pno. CMC.
Four Songs for High Voice and Harp. 1972. 12′. CMC.
Ten Folk Songs of Canada (arr). 1972. 20′. med vc, pno. Wat, 1972. CBC BR SM-168.

VOICE(S) WITH INSTRUMENTAL ENSEMBLE
Wabanaki song. 1950. 7′. sop, fl, str qt. ms.
Newfoundland. 1964. 8′45″. SATB, narr, brass. CMC. Text: E J Pratt.
People, Look East (An Advent Cantata). 1965. 14′45″. soli, SATB, org, brass, timp. Wat, 1966. Text: Eleanor Farjeon.
Ten Short Pieces. 8′. SSA, perc. Ber, 1965.
Let There Be Joy (a cantata). 1965. 10′15″. SATB, org, fl, vlc, glock, xyl. GVT, 1968. Text: Gaelic sun dances.
How the Loon Got Its Necklace. 1971. 7′ (music only), narr, str qnt, perc. CMC.
From Heaven On High. 1972. 14′. soli, SATB, 2vln, vlc, org. CMC. Text: Luther; trans: Winkworth-Macpherson.
The Gracious Time. 1972. 18′. soli, SATB, fl, vla, vlc, pno. CMC.
Overheard on a Saltmarsh. 5′30″. mezz, fl, pno. Kerby, 1972. Text: Harold Monro.
Three Songs in Praise of Spring. 7′30″. SSAA, pno, perc. Kerby, 1972. Text: Robert Bridges, A E Housman, Thomas Nash.

INSTRUMENTAL ENSEMBLE
Sonata. 1948. 16′. vln, pno. ms.
Ballad. 1949. 5′. vln, pno. Ber, 1950.
A Folk Song Suite for Woodwinds. 1960. 3′45″. 2fl, 2cl, b cl, bsn. B & H, 1963.
Little Suite. 1962. 6′20″. tpt, pno. Ber, 1968.
Suite for String Quartet. 1968. 4′. CMC.
Serenade for Five Winds. 1972. 12′. 2ob, 2hn, bsn. CMC.
Three Etudes. 1972. alto sax, pno. CMC.

PIANO
Sonata. 1947. 15′. ms.
Etude. 1949. 4′. ms.
Rondo. 1′. Wat, 1968.
Variations on a Folk Song. 5′. Wat, 1970.

ORGAN
Sonata for Organ. 1963. 13′. Ber, 1964.
Trio Suite for Organ. 4′. Wat, 1963.
Two Preludes for Organ. 3′. Wat, 1963.

BIBLIOGRAPHY

See B-B; CrC(I); K.
Schulman, Michael. 'Keith Bissell', *MuSc.* No. 268, Nov.-Dec. 1972 (4).

LITERARY WORKS

BOOKS
Choral Music in Ontario (with Ezra Schabas). Toronto: Province of Ontario Council for the Arts, 1970.

ARTICLES
'Canadian Composer and the Public', *PAC.* Vol. I, 1961 (58–9).
'R. M. Schafer's Books', *CMB.* Spring-Summer 1971 (192–4).
'School Music Today and Tomorrow', *MuSc.* Nov.-Dec. 1967 (5).
'What's Wrong with Music Educators?', *MAC.* Vol. I, 1963 (22–4).

BLACKBURN, MAURICE (b. Quebec City, Que., 22 May 1914). He began his musical studies at the School of Music of Laval University with Jean-Marie Beaudet (piano and composition), Henri Gagnon (organ), and Georges-Emile TANGUAY (harmony). While studying composition with Claude CHAMPAGNE in Montreal, he won second prize in the Jean Lallemand National Competition (*Les petites rues du vieux Québec*, 1938). In 1939 he won a scholarship from the Quebec government to study in Europe, but because of the war he went to Boston instead, where he studied with Quincy Porter (counterpoint) and Francis Findlay (orchestration and conducting) at the New England Conservatory. His *Sonatine pour piano* won the George Allan Prize of the Conservatory (1940). Since 1942 Blackburn has been a staff composer with the National Film Board of Canada. His music for Norman McLaren's film *Blinkity Blank* won the Palme d'Or Prize at the International Film Festival at Cannes (1953). In 1954–5, on a fellowship from the Canadian Arts Council, he studied composition, counterpoint, harmony, and fugue with Nadia Boulanger in Paris.

Blackburn's compositions, exemplified in *Concertino for Piano, Woodwinds and Brass* (1948), have some of the characteristics, including the rhythmic vigour, of French music of the early part of this century (Honegger and Poulenc, for example). In 1960 he received commissions from the Hart House Orchestra (*Suite for Strings*) and the Jeunesses Musicales du Canada (*Pirouette*). He is a member of the Canadian League of Composers and of CAPAC.

MUSICAL WORKS

STAGE

Rose La Tulippe (ballet). 1953.

Une Mesure de silence (chamb opera). 1954. Libretto: Marthe Morisset Blackburn.

Pirouette (chamb opera). 1960. Libretto: Marthe Morisset Blackburn.

La Chasse au corbeau (comedy). Text: E Labiche. Chansons: Maurice Blackburn.

Hymenée (television). 1964. vcs, balalaika, accord, pno. Text: Nicolai Gogol.

INCIDENTAL MUSIC

Midsummer Night's Dream. c1950. Text: William Shakespeare.

La Mercière assassinée. 1958. vc alone. Text: Anne Hébert.

Le Mariage de Barillon. 1960. Text: G Feydeau. Chansons: Maurice Blackburn.

FILM

Kleewick. 1947. NFB.

A Phantasy. 1952. NFB.

Blinkity Blank. 1955. NFB.

Je. 1960. NFB.

Lignes verticales. 1960. NFB.

Anna la bonne. 1961. Film: Les Films du Carrosse.

Jour après jour. 1962. NFB.

Over 100 other films for NFB. 1942–72.

ORCHESTRA

Les petites rues du vieux Québec. 1938.

Fantaisie en mocassins. 1940.

Symphonie en un mouvement. 1942.

Mazurka (arr of Henri Gagnon). 1949.

Suite from Le Gros Bill. 1949.

Charpente. c1950.

Petite Suite. c1950.

Overture for a Puppet Show. 1951.

Promenade. 1951.

STRING ORCHESTRA

Bal à l'Huile. c1950.

Marine. c1950. str, hp.

Pantomime. c1950.

Suite pour cordes. 1960.

SOLOIST WITH ORCHESTRA

Concertino en do majeur pour piano et instruments à vent. 1948.

Rigaudon. 1949. vln, chamb orch.

Nocturne. c1950. fl, str.

CHOIR

Messe. 1949. children's vcs.

Notre Père (arr). c1950. SATB. Text: trad.

Mon Oncle a bien mal à sa tête (arr). 1954. SATB. Text: trad.

La Rose blanche (arr). 1954. SATB. Text: trad.

VOICE(S)

La Haut sur ces montagnes (arr). 1949. Text: trad.

J'ai cueilli la belle rose (arr). 1949. Text: trad.

Jeannette revient du marché. 1949. Text: trad.

Je me lève à l'aurore du jour (arr). 1949. Text: trad.

Le Marchand de Velours (arr). 1949. Text: trad.

La Mariée s'baigne (arr). 1949. Text: trad.

Mon p'tit garçon (arr). 1949. Text: trad.

Pour charmer mon attente. 1949. Text: J Bobet.

Trois Poèmes d'Emile Nelligan. 1949. Text: Emile Nelligan.

Voici le printemps (arr). 1949. Text: trad.

Chant de mariage. c1950.

Clôches du soir. c1950. Text: Aime Plamondon.

Epithalame. c1950. Text: Roger Brien.

Nanette (arr). c1950. Text: trad.
Le petit canard. c1950. Text: Maurice Blackburn.
Le petit zoo. c1950.
Tant Mieux. c1950.
Le petit chaperon rouge. 1952. 3vcs, pno. Text: Aime Plamondon.
Chanson du gars perdu. 1955. Text: Eloi de Grandmont.
Chanson des jeunes amoureux. 1957. Text: Eloi de Grandmont.
Garde notre amour. 1957; Jacques Labrecque, 1957. Text: Eloi de Grandmont.
Le Piano robot. 1957. Text: Eloi de Grandmont.
Ramenez-moi chez-moi. 1957; Arch, 1958. Text: Eloi de Grandmont.
Les Vacances du pendu. 1957. Text: Ginette Letondal.
La Vie me prend. 1957. Text: Eloi de Grandmont.
Musique originale. 1958. Text: Eloi de Grandmont.
Le Chien du charcutier. 1958. Text: Maurice Blackburn.
Dans mon île. 1958. Text: L Thériault.
Belle au bois dormant (Pirouette). 1962. Text: Marthe Morisset Blackburn.

VOICE WITH INSTRUMENTAL ENSEMBLE
Six Musical Forms. 1967, narr, ww qt, str trio, pno, org. JMC CD-6. Text: Marthe Morisset Blackburn.

PIANO
Cinq digitales. 1940; FH (2 & 5), 1955.
Sonatine. 1940.
Trois danses. 1949.
Etude. c1950.
Polka. c1950.
Marionettes. c1950.
Valse ivre. c1950.

BIBLIOGRAPHY

See B-B; Bt; CrC(II); D157; K; Lv; Wa.
'Fugue', *Arts/Canada.* Vol. XXV, June 1968 (12).
Kraglund, John. 'Two Canadian Operas', *CMJ.* Vol. I, no. 2, 1957 (42–3).
'Maurice Blackburn', *CanCo.* No. 38, Mar. 1969 (4–7).

BOTTENBERG, WOLFGANG (b. Frankfurt-am-Main, Germany, 9 May 1930). He came to Canada in 1958 and pursued his composition studies with R.A. Stangeland at the University of Alberta, where he received his Bachelor of Music degree in 1961. Then, at the College-Conservatory of Music, University of Cincinnati, he studied composition with T. Scott Huston, receiving his Master of Music degree in 1962. He taught in Calgary (1963–4) and in Alberni, B.C. (1964–5), and in 1965 was appointed lecturer and later assistant professor of music at Acadia University, Wolfville, N.S. He continued with his studies in composition at the University of Cincinnati with Huston, Paul Cooper, and Jenö Takasz, receiving his Doctor of Musical Arts degree in 1970. His works are highly dissonant yet still based on tonal harmony. This is particularly true of his work for children, *The World is a Rainbow*, a secular cantata for choir and orchestra (1968). Bottenberg is a member of CAPAC.

MUSICAL WORKS

INSTRUMENTAL

5 works for orch: *Passacaglia* (1961, rev 1971); *Sinfonietta* (1961, rev 1969–70); *A Suite of Carols* (1963–7); *Fantasia* (1966) tpt, small orch; *Fantasia Serena* (1973).

13 works for chamber ensemble: *Sonata with Variations on a South-German Folk Song* (1959, rev 1972) 2alto rec, pno; *Quartet* (1960) fl, 2cl, bsn; *Sonata* (1960) fl, cl; *Trio for Flute, Clarinet and Bassoon* (1963); *Trio* (1963–4) fl, cl, pno; *Trio for Three Recorders* (1964; Apogee, 1970); *Divertimento for Flute Quartet* (1968); *First String Quartet* (1968); *All mein Gedanken* (1969) vln, vlc, pno; *Variables* (1969) rec, ww qt, str qnt; *Dialogue* (1971, rev 1972) alto rec (fl), hpschd (pno); *Octet* (1972) fl (picc), ob, cl, bsn, tpt, 2hn, trb; *Fa So La Ti Do Re* (1972) sop sax (cl), str qt.

5 works for piano: *Sonata for Piano Duet* (1961, rev 1967); *Three English Carols* (arr) (1963) pno 4 hands; *Deck the Hall* (arr) (1967) pno 4 hands; *Moods of the Modes* (c1967); *Fantasia Serena* (arr) (1973) pno 4 hands.

7 works for organ: *Chorale Prelude on 'Geneva'* (1963; WLSM, 1963); *Chorale Prelude on 'Lobe den Herren'* (1963; WLSM, 1963); *In Dulci Jubilo* (c1967; WLSM, c1967); *Intrada* (1968; WLSM, 1968); *Meditation* (1968; WLSM, 1968);

Fughetta (1969; WLSM, 1969); *Lenten Interlude* (1969; WLSM, 1969).

CHORAL

2 works for choir and orch: *Duino Cantata* (1962) bar, SATB, orch Text: Rainer Maria Rilke; *Ritual* (1970) SATB, orch Text: Wolfgang Bottenberg.

4 works for choir and instruments: *Fairest Lord Jesus* (arr) (1963; WLSM, 1963) SATB, 2vln, org Text: German crusaders hymn; *When Morning Fills the Sky* (arr of Louis Boureois) (1963; WLSM, 1963) SATB, 2rec (fl), org Text: E Caswall; *Praise We Our God* (arr of Johann Crüger) (c1966) SATB, 2tpt, 2trb; *The World is a Rainbow* (1968) sop, ten, SATB, ww qnt Text: Henry Beissel.

3 works for choir (and org): *The Lord is My True Shepherd* (arr of Russell Woolen) (1964; WLSM, 1964) SATB (3 equal vcs) Text: Paul Francis; *The Law of Love* (1969; Apogee, 1969) 2 equal (mixed) vcs, org Text: J Clifford Evers; *The Power of Prayer* (1969; Apogee, 1969) 2 equal (mixed) vcs, org Text: J Clifford Evers.

VOCAL

4 works for vcs and instruments: *Three Amerindian Songs* (1961, rev 1968) ten, alto rec, ten rec, guit (med vc, fl, cl, hpschd (pno)) Text: Eskimo, Peruvian, Hopi Indian Trans: W E Calvert, Margot Astrov; *Four Emily Dickinson Songs* (c1967) high vc, pno Text: Emily Dickinson; *Those Passions . . . Which Yet Survive* (1968) bs, fl, cl, str trio, xyl, perc Text: Percy B Shelley; *My Funny Little Clock* (1969) vc, alto rec (fl), hpschd/(mezz (bar), cl, pno) Text: Henry Beissel.

LITERARY WORKS

ARTICLES

'Music and Creativity in School', *Journal of Education*. Vol. XVII, no. 3 (Halifax, N.S.), Feb. 1968 (32–8).

BRASSARD, FRANÇOIS (b. Métabetchouan, Que., 6 Oct. 1908). He studied composition with Claude CHAMPAGNE (Montreal), Albert Bertelin (Paris), and Ralph Vaughan Williams (London). He received his Bachelor of Arts degree from Laval University (1928), where he also received an honorary doctorate in 1961. He was awarded a Canada Council grant in 1962 to do research in Europe and in 1964 a grant from the Quebec government to compose *Matapédienne*. In 1967 he was commissioned by CAMMAC to write *Poème d'Amour et de Joie*. He was organist at Saint-Dominique in Jonquière, Que., from 1930 to 1971 and in 1946 was appointed professor in the School of Music, Laval University. Since 1971 he has worked in the Archives de Folklore of that university, collecting traditional songs from different provinces of Canada, and in New England, Illinois, and Louisiana. Many of these songs he arranged in a five-volume collection, *Chansons populaires de l'Amérique française*; he also presented some of them in a series of broadcasts over the CBC French radio network (1959–61 and 1965–7). Besides arranging folk songs, Brassard has written instrumental works employing folk material (for example, *Suite villageoise*, 1948, and *Orléanaises*, 1945). He is a member of the International Folk Music Council and of CAPAC.

MUSICAL WORKS

INSTRUMENTAL

3 works for org: *Sonatine* (1936) Arch 1938; *Basilicale No 1* (1962); *Basilicale No 2* (1969).

2 works for pno: *Luminures* (1938) MCA 1969; *Orléanaises* (1939) Ber 1953 RCI-134.

Suite villageoise. 1948. vln, pno.

3 works for orch: *Marche fantasque et Festival* (1949); *Vigile* (1973); *Matapédienne* (Symphonie avec poème).

Poème d'amour et de joie. 1967. bar, orch Text: Hervé Dumont.

CHORAL

4 works for choir: *Chansons populaires de l'Amérique française II, IV* and *V*: *No II* (1947) SATB MCA 1973 Vox PL-11.860 Text: trad; *No IV* (1959) SATB MCA 1969 Vox PL-11.860, ATPL-511.860 Text: trad; *No V* (1959) SATB, pno Text: trad; *Petites chansons populaires de l'Amérique* (1972) 2 & 3 equal vcs Text: trad.

VOCAL

3 works for accompanied vc: *Panis angelicus* (1942) Edition Procure Générale de Musique 1942 vc, org; *Chansons populaires de l'Amérique française I* (1946) and *III* (1956) vc, pno Text: trad.

BIBLIOGRAPHY

See B-B; CrC(I); D157; K; Lv.

LITERARY WORKS

ARTICLES

'Chansons d'accompagnement', *Journal of the International Folk Music Council.* Vol. II, Mar. 1950 (45–7).

'Une date pour la musique canadienne', *La Revue de l'Université Laval.* Vol. V, no. 8, Apr. 1951 (3–11).

'Une exposition Saint Bernard', *Culture.* Vol. XV, Dec. 1954 (442–4).

'French-Canadian Folk Music Studies: a Survey', *Ethnomusicology.* Vol. XVI, no. 3, Sept. 1972 (351–9).

'D'où viens-tu, bergère? (nouvelles versions d'un Noël ancien recueillies et annotées)', *Les Archives de Folklore.* Vol. III, 1948 (13–20).

'Recordeurs de chansons', *Les Archives de Folklore.* Vol. II, 1947 (191–202).

'Refrains canadiens de chansons de France', *Les Archives de Folklore.* Vol. I, 1946 (41–59).

'Le retour du soldat et le retour du voyageur,' *Journal of American Folklore.* Vol. LXIII, 1950 (147–57).

BROTT, ALEXANDER (b. Montreal, Que., 14 Mar. 1915). He studied violin, piano, and composition at the McGill Conservatorium (1928–35) and in 1935 won a scholarship to attend the Juilliard School of Music in New York, where he studied with Sascha Jacobsen, Willen Willeke, and Bernard Wagenaar, receiving his graduate diploma in 1939. At the Juilliard he won the Loeb Memorial Award for performance (1938 and 1939), the Elizabeth Sprague Coolidge Award for chamber music composition (1939 and 1940), and the Lord Strathcona Award to study in England. The war, however, prevented this, and in 1939 he returned to Montreal where he joined the staff of McGill University and founded the McGill Chamber Orchestra, of which he is still the conductor. He was concertmaster and assistant conductor of the Montreal Symphony Orchestra from 1945 to 1958. He has been active as a guest conductor with the CBC since 1948 and the BBC since 1950 and has made conducting tours in many parts of the world, including Scandinavia, Israel, and the USSR. From 1960 to 1966 he was musical director of the summer seasons of the Montreal Symphony Orchestra. Since 1963 he has also conducted the Kingston Symphony Orchestra in Kingston, Ont. He was awarded an honorary Doctor of Music degree from the Chicago Conservatory College in 1955.

Counterpoint is a basic component of Brott's style. In *From Sea to Sea* (1947), for example, folk-like melodies are varied by several contrapuntal means, including fragmentation. His *Concerto for Violin and Orchestra* (1950) shows motivic development in a polyphonic texture of chromatic material. The complexity of his counterpoint sometimes reaches such density that the impression is of a constantly moving mass-structure, as in *Three Astral Visions* (1959) and *Spheres in Orbit* (1960). Many of his works are tongue-in-cheek, for example, *Critic's Corner* (1950) and *Centennial Colloquy* (1965). In *Critic's Corner* Brott uses chromatic material with deliberately trite interjections by the percussion for satirical effect. In *Centennial Colloquy* he uses a mutilated *O Canada* as his main theme, which is dealt with by various satirical and, as always, contrapuntal means, often obscuring the familiar tune. For the Beethoven centennial in 1970 he wrote works based on Beethoven's music, for example *The Young Prometheus* (1969) – an orchestration of some small pieces by the student Beethoven – and *Paraphrase in Polyphony* (1967), in which Brott used a theme from a canon written by Beethoven in 1825 for the German-Canadian music teacher Theodore Molt. The opening of this work is orchestrated in Beethoven style; developing in variation form, it takes on a style closer to Brott's own. Throughout Brott's compositional career there has been little change in his musical style, which has always been governed by counterpoint and streaked with satire and humour.

Brott's many commissions include several works for the CBC, for example *From Sea to Sea* (1946) and *Royal Tribute* (1953). He has written works for the McGill Chamber Orchestra (*Critic's Corner*, and *7 Minuets, 6 Canons*, 1971) and McGill University (*Sept for Seven*, 1955, and *Martlet's Muse*, 1962). Several other Montreal organizations have commissioned works: the Montreal

Symphony Orchestra (*Spheres in Orbit*, 1960), the Montreal Brass Quintet (*Mutual Salvation Orgy*, 1962), the Montreal Little Symphony (*Violin Concerto*, 1950), the Lapitsky Foundation (*Three Astral Visions*; *Profundum Praedictum*, 1966), the Baroque Trio of Montreal (*Three on a Spree*, 1962), l'Ecole Normale de Musique (*Elie, Elie, Lama Sabachtani*, 1967; *Esperanto*, 1967; *Badinage*, 1968), and Les Grands Ballets Canadiens (*La Corriveau*, 1966). His compositions have won CAPAC awards (1941, 1942, and 1943) and Olympic Medals (1948 and 1952). In 1961 Brott won the Bax Society Prize. He is an honorary member of the Montreal Musicians' Guild (Montreal Branch of the American Federation of Musicians) and a member of the Canadian League of Composers and of CAPAC.

MUSICAL WORKS

STAGE

La Corriveau (ballet). 1966.

ORCHESTRA

Oracle. 1938.
War and Peace. 1944.
Concordia. 1946.
From Sea to Sea. 1947.
Delightful Delusions. 1950.
Prelude to Oblivion. 1951.
A Royal Tribute to Queen Elizabeth II. 1953.
Fancy and Folly. 1953.
Scherzo. 1954.
Analogy in Anagram. 1955.
Spheres in Orbit. 1960. Bar BC 1831/2831.
Martlet's Muse. 1962.
Centennial Colloquy. 1965. ww, brass.
Paraphrase in Polyphony. 1967. RCA CC/CCS-1029.
The Young Prometheus (arr of Beethoven). 1969. Sel CC 15.038.
Seven Minuets, Six Canons (arr of Beethoven). 1971.
Kinderscenen (arr of Schumann). 1972.

BAND

Laurentian Idyll. 1940.

SMALL ORCHESTRA

Cradle Song. 1943.

STRING ORCHESTRA

Lament. 1939.
Laurentian Idyll. 1940.
Lullaby and Procession of Toys. 1943.
Three Astral Visions. 1959; Ric, 1973.
Triangle, Circle, 4 Squares. 1963. RCA CC/CCS-1010, RCI-216.
Dirge.

SOLOIST(S) WITH ORCHESTRA

Characteristic Dance. 1940. vln, orch.
Ritual. 1942. str qt, str.
Songs of Contemplation. 1945. sop, str. Text: R M Lord Houghton, Alfred Lord Tennyson, anon, Christina Rossetti.
Concerto for Violin and Chamber Orchestra. 1950.
Arabesque. 1957. vlc, chamb orch.
The Vision of Dry Bones. 1958. bar, pno, str. Text: Ezekiel 37: 1–14.
From the Hazel Bough. 1959. sop, str. Text: Earle Birney.
Profundum Praedictum. 1964, cb (or vln or vlc), str. RCA LSC-3128.
Accent. 1970, narr, str. Text: Lawrence Lande.
The Emperor's New Clothes. 1970, narr, orch. Text: George Whalley from Hans Christian Andersen.

CHOIR WITH ORCHESTRA

Israel. 1956. SATB, str. Text: Alexander Brott.
Centennial Cerebration. 1967. narr, SSAA, str. Text: Alexander Brott.

CHOIR

Israel. 1952. SATB. Text: Alexander Brott.
Canadiana. 1955. SATB.
Elie, Elie, lama sabachtani. 1964. SSAA, pno (or org). Text: Scriptures.
Esperanto. 1967. SSA, pno.
Badinage. 1968. SATB, pno.
Fun-Ethic-S. 1968. SA, pno. Text: Alexander Brott.

VOICES

The Prophet. 1960. sop, ten, pno. Text: Kahlil Gibran.

VOICE WITH INSTRUMENTAL ENSEMBLE

Sept for Seven. 1954. narr, cl, alto sax, str trio, pno. Text: Earle Birney, E J Pratt, G Douglas, Marjorie Pickthall, Arthur S Bourinot.
World Sophisticate. 1962. sop, brass qnt, perc. Text: Alexander Brott.
How Thunder and Lightning Came to Be. 1972. narr, perc, pno, cb ens. Text: Eskimo Legend.

INSTRUMENTAL ENSEMBLE

Quintet for Recorder and Strings. 1940. rec, str qt.
Invocation and Dance. 1941. vln, pno.
String Quartet. 1941.
Critic's Corner. 1950. str qt, perc.
Five Miniatures for Eight Players. 1950. cl, hn, bsn, str qnt.
Arabesque. 1957. vlc, pno.
Three Acts for Four Sinners. 1961. sax qt.
Berceuse. 1962. sax qt.
Mutual Salvation Orgy. 1962. brass qnt.
Three On a Spree. 1963. fl, ob, hp (or 2vln, pno, or fl, vln, hpschd, or vln, ob, pno).
Mini-Minus. 1968; MCA, 1971. cl, bsn, tpt, trb, vln, cb, perc.
Spasms for Six. 1971. 6perc.
Saxi-foni-Saties. 1972. sax qt.
Saties-Faction. 1972. str qt.

PIANO

Suite for Piano. 1941; FH, 1955 ('Sacrilege').
Vignettes en Caricature. 1952.

INSTRUMENTAL SOLO

Pristine Prisms in Polychrome. 1966. vln.
Tout de Suite. 1970. vlc.

BIBLIOGRAPHY

See B-B; B58,65,71; Bec57; Bt; C63,66,69, 72; CrC(II); D157; Esc; K; Lv; R12; T; Wa.
'Alexander Brott Follows Some Very Good Advice', *CanCo.* No. 28, Apr. 1968 (4–5, 44–5).
'Alexander Brott – a portrait', *Mu.* No. 17, Mar. 1969 (10–11).
Cowell, Henry. 'Current Chronicle: New York', *MQ.* Vol. XL, no. 1, Jan. 1954 (60–1).
'Europe Hears Canadian Music', *CBC Times.* Oct. 16, 1949 (1).
Heller, Zelda. 'The Alexander Brott Family: Music, Rare Instruments, and the Sound of the Telephone', *CanCo.* No. 12, Nov. 1966 (32–3, 42–3).

LITERARY WORKS

ARTICLES

'My Most Successful Work: "Spheres in Orbit"', *CanCo.* No. 24, Dec. 24, 1967 (20–1).

BUCZYNSKI, WALTER (b. Toronto, Ont., 17 Dec. 1933). He studied at the Royal Conservatory of Music in Toronto with Earle Moss (piano) and Godfrey RIDOUT (theory). His *Piano Trio* (1954) won a CAPAC-sponsored composition competition in 1954. He made his orchestral début with the Toronto Symphony Orchestra in 1955, playing the Chopin 'F minor Concerto'. In 1956 he spent the summer studying with Darius Milhaud and in the same year his *Woodwind Quintet* won a Fromm Foundation award. In 1957 he toured Canada with the Canadian soprano Marguerite Gignac. He studied piano in New York (1958–60) and with Zbigniew Drzewiecki in Warsaw (1959–60; 1961–2). In 1960 and 1962 he received Canada Council grants to study composition with Nadia Boulanger in Paris.

Buczynski's early works of the 1950s develop from a tonal or polytonal to a free atonal style. His *Suite for Woodwind Quintet* (1955) and *Divertimento for Four Soloists* (1957) incorporate chromatic polytonality with a rhythmic drive reminiscent of Stravinsky. Even through his numerous style-changes, Buczynski habitually holds to this rhythmic characteristic.

His more esoteric works of the early 1960s, employing the twelve-tone technique, include *Suite for String Trio* (1959), *Three Thoughts for Orchestra* (1964), and *Trio '67* (1967), which reveal a marked change in emphasis from the emotionally charged extended lines of the earlier works to a more pointillistic polyphony. Most of the compositions of this period do not employ strict serialism but rather some serial operations (for example, in *Two and a Half Squares in a Circle*, 1967; *Triptych*, 1964; *Two French Love Poems*, 1967). Although these works exhibit a rhythmic randomness at times, they are generally characterized by a more driving rhythm, especially in the fast sections, with longer melodic lines.

Buczynski's experimental period begins with the song *Milosc* (1967), in which an energetic or nervous quality is achieved by quick changes in mood or emotion. In *Iskry* (1968) the experimentation with clusters and indeterminacy results in a playful yet emotionally disturbing work for orchestra. His *Zeroing In* series (for various instrumental combinations) employs theatrical techniques.

Buczynski is an accomplished concert pianist, performing and recording a number of works by Canadian composers, including Barbara PENTLAND, Oskar MORAWETZ, John WEINZWEIG, and himself. Not surprisingly he has written a large number of piano works, and it is the study of these pieces that affords the most complete view of his style. *Three Romantic Pieces* (1957–8) and *Aria and Toccata* (1963) are atonal, having emotionally charged melodic lines with organically developed short motifs. In *Amorphous* (1964), a twelve-tone piece, Buczynski employs pointillism and rhythmic randomness, creating the ethereal quality suggested by the title. His *Sonata* (1967) has this same quality in the slow middle section, with stormy and energetic outer sections. The turbulence in his *Sonata* appears again in *Four Movements for Piano and Strings* (1969), where the pianist plays clusters and plucks or hits the strings of the piano with various types of mallets, the string orchestra providing background only. Beginning in 1970, Buczynski introduced theatrical devices into his compositions; for example, *Burlesque* (1970), which is really an exposé of a performer's thoughts during a performance, includes electronic tape and requires the pianist to vocalize. The work is in three main sections: the pianist practising, giving a lesson, and doing some original composing. The newly composed music of this last section becomes the opening material for *Zeroing In No. 1* (1971). Again using the pianist's voice and an electronic tape, Buczynski has divided this work into five sections: 'Overture', 'Aria', 'Debate (schizophrenia)', 'The Piano Is Alive and Well and Living in Toronto', and 'A Dark Dark'. This work was shown on the CBC television program 'Music to See' using the split-screen technique, a method necessary to convey precisely the composer's intentions, for in the final section, a duet, Buczynski played both parts. The visual element would also enhance the performance of *Zeroing In No. 5* (sub-titled 'A Dictionary of Mannerisms', 1972). The work is in two sections: Book I, performance mannerisms; Book II, stylistic mannerisms. In Book I, in a series of short pieces with such titles as 'The Attacker', 'The Eye-brow Specialist', and 'The Intellectual', Buczynski mimics some common affectations of pianists by directing the performer to 'raise eye-brows' or 'shake head from left to right as if in true feeling of saying "How beautiful it is!" '. Book II is a series of pieces in the styles of many contemporary composers, including Boulez, Stockhausen, and Weinzweig. Buczynski is an experimenter and in the last three works mentioned above he has delved into the minds of both performer and composer.

From 1962 to 1970 Buczynski taught piano and theory at the Royal Conservatory of Music, Toronto, and from 1970 to 1972 divided his time between two divisions of the University of Toronto: the Faculty of Music and suburban Erindale College, where he was composer-in-residence. In 1972 he assumed full-time duties at the Faculty of Music. In 1967 he received commissions from William Kuinka (*Trio '67*), Jesse Kregal (*Two and a Half Squares in a Circle*), and Daryl Irvine (*Piano Sonata*). The CBC has commissioned two works: *Iskry* (1968) and *Zeroing In No. 2* (1971). Buczynski is a member of the Canadian League of Composers and of CAPAC.

CLIFFORD FORD

MUSICAL WORKS

STAGE

Do Re Mi. 19'30". sop, ten, bar, 2 actors, instr ens. ms. Libretto: Lilly Barnes. Dec 13, 1967, CBC.

Mr. Rhinoceros and His Musicians. 15'50". sop, bar, narr. ms. Libretto: Lilly Barnes. Dec 25, 1965, CBC.

From the Buczynski Book of the Living (chamber opera). 1972. 58'. sop, ten, cl, pno, perc. CMC. Libretto: Walter Buczynski.

ORCHESTRA

Three Thoughts for Orchestra. 1964. 11'15". full orch. CMC. Apr 13, 1967, Tor, CBC, TS, John Avison(cond).

Triptych for Orchestra. 1964. 6'30". full orch. CMC. July 20, 1967, Tor, CBC, CBC Fest O, John Avison(cond).

Iskry/Sparks. 1969. 5'20". full orch. ms. 1969, Tor, CBC, CBC Fest O, Alexander Brott (cond).

7 Miniatures for Orchestra. 1970. 9'. med orch. CMC. July 22, 1970, CBC Fest O, Boris Brott(cond).

Zeroing In #2; 'Distractions and Then'. 1971. 12'10". full orch. CMC. Mar 16, 1973, Tor, CBC, CBC Fest O, Lukas Foss(cond).

SMALL ORCHESTRA

A Work for Dance. 1970. 18'40". cl, perc, str. CMC.

STRING ORCHESTRA
The Open String. 1964. 1'30". CMC.
Index and Two. 1965. 1'20". CMC.
Introduction of Finger Three. 1965. 1'45". CMC.
Last and Not Least Finger Four. 1965. 1'25". CMC.

SOLOIST(S) WITH ORCHESTRA
Beztitula. 1964. 10'. pno, orch. CMC.
Four Arabesques and Dance. 1964. 14'50". fl, str. CMC. 1966, Tor, CBC Str, Eugene Kash(cond), Robert Aitken(fl).
Four Movements. 1969. 22'. pno, str. CMC. 1970, Tor, TRO, Milton Barnes(cond), Daryl Irvine(pno).
Zeroing In #4; 'Innards and Outards'. 1972. 22'45". sop, fl, pno, orch. CMC. May 26, 1973, Tor, LAT, TS, Alexander Brott(cond).

VOICE
Cycle of Three Songs. 1954. high vc, pno. CMC. Text: Hilaire Belloc, William Blake, Gilbert Keith Chesterton.
Four Poems of Walter de la Mare, Op 12. 1955. alto, pno. CMC.
How Some Things Look (13 songs for voice and piano). 1966. 16'30". CMC. 1967, CBC, Mary Morrison(sop), Walter Buczynski (pno).

VOICE WITH INSTRUMENTAL ENSEMBLE
How Some Things Look (13 songs for voice and chamb gp). 1966 (arr 1967). 16'30". sop, fl, cl, vlc, pno. CMC. 1967 (pno version), CBC, Mary Morrison(sop), Walter Buczynski (pno).
Milosc/Love. 1967. 7'15". sop, fl, pno. CMC. Text: Jane Beecroft. 1971, Tor, CBC, LAT.
Two French Love Poems. 1967. 7'15". sop, fl, pno. CMC. 1967, Tor.

INSTRUMENTAL ENSEMBLE
Trio for Violin, Cello and Piano, Op 4. 1954. 25'. CMC. 1954, Tor, RCMT, Walter Babiak(vln), Mary Oxley(vlc), Earle Moss (pno).
Suite for Woodwind Quintet, Op 13. 1955. 12'. CMC. 1955, Aspen, Colo.
Divertimento for Four Solo Instruments, Op 15. 1957. 13'. vln, vlc, cl, bsn. CMC. CBC BR SM-74. 1964, Tor, CBC.
Suite for String Trio, Op 20. 1959. 9'. CMC. 1967, Tor, CBC, Desser Str Trio.
Chorale and Five Variations for Mixed Chamber Ensembles. 1960. 13'. fl, ob, cl, 2bsn, 2hn, tpt, trb, str qnt. CMC.
Elegy for Violin and Piano; 'In Memoriam to Kathleen Parlow'. 1963. 5'45". CMC.
Six Miniatures for String Quartet. 1963. 15'. CMC.
Trio/67. 1967. 11'30". mand, cl, vlc (cb). CMC. 1968, Tor, CBC, Kuinka(mand), Morton(cl), Whitton(vlc).
Two and a Half Squares in a Circle. 1967. 11'50". timp, fl, vln, vlc. CMC. 1967, Stratford.

PIANO
Three Preludes, Op 14. 1956. 7'45". CMC.
Three Improvisations. 1957. 3'. CMC.
Three Romantic Pieces. 1957–8. 7'40". CMC. 1963, CBC, Walter Buczynski.
Aria & Toccata for Piano. 1963. 6'. CMC. CBC BR SM-162. 1966, CBC, Daryl Irvine.
Eight Preludes for Piano. 1963. 9'45". CMC. 1964, CBC, Walter Buczynski.
Le Temps du Jour avec Christophe. 1963. 9'55". CMC. 1964, CBC, Rudi Van Dijk.
Amorphus. 1964. 4'5". CMC. CBC BR SM-162. 1966, CBC, Ralph Elsaesser.
Sonatine pour le piano. 1964. 10'. CMC. 1965, CBC, Walter Buczynski.
Suite pour le piano. 1964. 9'15". CMC. 1965, CBC, William Aide.
Four Pieces for the Middle Grades. 1965. 4'. CMC. 1966, CBC.
Seven Pieces for Piano. 1965. B & H ('Dance', 'Swing', 'Canon'). Dom S-69002 ('Canon' only). 1966, CBC.
Suite de la radio pour le piano. 1965. 4'30". CMC.
Ten Piano Pieces for Children. 1965. 8'. CMC. Dom S-69002 ('Happy', 'Solitude'). 1966, CBC.
Sonata for Piano (Dzieki). 1967. 14'30". CMC. CBC BR SM-162. 1967, Tor, CBC, Daryl Irvine.
8 Epigrams for Young Pianists. B & H, 1969.
Burlesque. 1970. 12'30". 1 prep pno, speaking vc, tape. CMC. 1971, CBC, Walter Buczynski.
Three Piano Pieces. FH, 1970.
Zeroing In. 1971. 1 prep pno, speaking vc, tape. CMC. 1972, CBC, Walter Buczynski.
Zeroing In #5; 'Dictionary of Mannerisms'. 1972. 26'30". Jan 1973, Walter Buczynski.

INSTRUMENTAL SOLO
Four Corners of Gregory. 1966. guit. CMC.

ORGAN
Five Atmospheres. 1966. 8'. CMC. 1971, Tor, Convocation Hall, U of T, Don Gillies.

BIBLIOGRAPHY

Such, Peter. *Soundprints*. Toronto: Clarke, Irwin Ltd, 1972 (102–25).

'Walter Buczynski', *CanCo*. No. 33, Oct. 1968 (4, 44–5).

BURRITT, LLOYD (b. Vancouver, B.C., 7 June 1940). He began his musical studies with Jean COULTHARD and Cortland Hultberg at the University of British Columbia, where he received his Bachelor of Music (1963) and Master of Music (1968) degrees. In 1964 he studied composition with Gordon Jacob and Herbert Howells at the Royal College of Music, London. Scholarships enabled him to attend the Berkshire Music Center in Tanglewood during the summers of 1965 and 1966, where he studied with Gunther Schuller, Iva Dee Hiatt, Erich Leinsdorf, and Leonard Bernstein. During this period (1964–8) he also taught music in various schools in and around Vancouver.

At Tanglewood Burritt had been introduced to electronic music and immediately began to use the medium in composition and teaching. Most of his subsequent works have included electronic tape. He is mainly concerned with mood, resulting in a freely structured building-up and relaxation of tension. *Assassinations* (1968), for tape and orchestra, is colour-oriented, the electronic sounds taking on almost a solo importance, with the orchestra as a complementary sound source. The work evokes tension by subdued yet violent sounds on tape (scratches and thunder) that are imitated by the orchestra. The orchestral writing involves the overlaying of many repeated patterns that create a dense texture, a type of mass-structure. *Icon* (1970), for organ and tape, opens with a *sforzando* chord on the organ followed by quiet, electronic *glissandi*; the organ continues to interject with loud staccato chords before moving into sustained clusters.

Since 1968 Burritt has received many commissions for electronic works. *Electric Soul* (1969) was commissioned by Byron Gilliam and choreographed by him into a ballet; the Vancouver Symphony Orchestra commissioned *Assassinations* (1968), *Fanfare* (1970), and *Electric Tongue* (1970); and in 1972 the CBC commissioned both *Spectrum* and *Peer Gynt*. He also has written works on commission for the National Arts Centre Orchestra (*Overdose*, 1971), for Ken Dorn, San Diego (*Electric Chair*, 1971), and for the RCCO 1972 Spring Convention (*Memo to RCCO*). He is a member of CAPAC.

MUSICAL WORKS

ORCHESTRA

Symphony in One Movement. 1964.
Assassinations. 1968. orch, tape.
Electric Tongue (1). 1969. orch, tape.
Electric Tongue (2). 1969. orch, telephone, tape.
Cicada. 1970. orch, tape.
New York. 1970. orch, tape.
Overdose. 1971. orch, tape.
Spectrum. 1972. str orch, pno, tape.

SOLOIST(S) WITH ORCHESTRA

Song. 1963. mezz, orch. Text: Lloyd Burritt.
Three Autumn Songs. 1965. mezz, pno, orch. Text: Robert Frost, F R Scott, Archibald MacLeish.

CHOIR WITH ORCHESTRA/BAND

Hollow Men. 1968. SATB, orch, tape. Text: T S Eliot.
Rocky Mountain Grasshopper. 1971. SATB, band, 2 tapes. Text: Lloyd Burritt.

CHOIR

'In the Time of the Breaking of Nations'. 1963. Text: Thomas Hardy.
Kyrie. 1967. Text: trad.
'Once Again – Pop!'. 1969. SATB, tape. Text: Lloyd Burritt.

VOICE(S)

Landscapes. 1968. sop, alto, tape. Text: T S Eliot.
Haiku. 1969. bar, tape. Text: 17th cent Japanese Haiku.

INSTRUMENTAL ENSEMBLE

Sonata for Violin and Piano. 1963.

PIANO

Sonata for Piano. 1962.

ORGAN

Icon. 1970. org, 2 tapes.
Memo to - - -. 1972. org, typewriter, tape.
Memo to RCCO. 1972. org, tape.

ELECTRONIC/MULTI MEDIA

Acid Mass. 1969. SATB, dancers, film. Text: T S Eliot.

Electric Soul. 1969. tape.
Fanfare. 1970. brass, tape, film.
Electric Chair. 1971. alto sax, actress, tape.
Memo to FATC. 1972. keyboard, tape.

ELECTRONIC WITH STAGE PURPOSES (INCIDENTAL MUSIC)
Moby Dick – Rehearsed. 1969. Text: Orson Welles.
Tiny Alice. 1969. Text: Edward Albee.
Peer Gynt. 1972. sop, tape. Text: Henrik Ibsen.

BIBLIOGRAPHY

'Electronic... ? Baroque... ?', *CanCo.* No. 43, Oct. 1969 (39–40).
'Lloyd Burritt: Electronic Music', *CanCo.* No. 55, Dec. 1970 (4–9).

C

CHAMPAGNE, CLAUDE (b. Montreal, Que., 27 May 1891; d. Montreal, 21 Dec. 1965). To speak of Champagne is to make a page of Canada's musical history come alive. Alongside the work of preceding generations (represented by Calixa Lavallée and Guillaume Couture), Champagne seems like a bridge between old and new, between the nineteenth and twentieth centuries. His music has traits of a prolonged romanticism and his other activities show him presiding at the formation of many organizations working towards the establishment and conservation of our musical heritage.

Adonaï Desparois (later Claude) Champagne was born on Montreal's St Catherine Street, across from what used to be the home of the newspaper *La Patrie.* Until his departure for Europe in 1921, he benefited from a family setting propitious for the development of his musical talent. His grandfather, a fiddler ('violoneux') who was very highly regarded in the region of Repentigny, was a source of admiration for Champagne, who very early developed an ear for the rather raw and joyous modal sonorities of Quebec folk music.

This period was one of absorption of the milieu and an opening of the spirit to cultural manifestations which, we know from Champagne himself, were richer and more brilliant than at the time of his return to Montreal in 1929. At the beginning of the century, one should remember, poets of the Ecole Littéraire de Montréal were trying, in their quest for emancipation, to avail themselves of European culture. This was a time of great divergencies between ideas of universalism on the one hand, and those of regionalism, 'the soil', on the other. One should also recall the salon of Alfred LALIBERTÉ and the wave of composers who became followers of the various musical trends in Europe, with Laliberté and Morin as leaders – the one familiarizing himself with the music of the German and Russian schools, the other with the French. They heard Scriabin, Medtner, Debussy, and Fauré. The Montreal Opera Company (1910–13) was thriving at His Majesty's Theatre, its productions including one of *Louise* scarcely a decade after its Paris première. Champagne saw them all. In short, the years 1900–20 were particularly fruitful in cultural manifestations and Champagne discovered in that period an essential element that he developed throughout his life – dilettantism.

He was a dilettante from every point of view, as were most men to some degree in that generation. Champagne never finished his advanced education; his daughter speaks of him as always having a book in his hand – books that dealt with a wide variety of subjects, since Champagne was interested in virtually everything. His subtle spirit, linked to a gentle but firm character, never became partisan to any given system; to his students he was a master who knew how to develop their individual personalities.

The modal flavour of Champagne's music shows the Quebec roots of his musical heritage, the modality of which, through the old French melodies, is derived from that of plainsong. Did not Champagne study with R.-O. Pelletier, that fervent exponent of the new 'Niedermeyer' style of plainchant accompaniment? Modality was also one of the ingredients he encountered in France – others being impressionism and the spirit of the Diaghilev ballets.

On his arrival in Paris in 1921, Champagne was well prepared to receive the lessons that were to be lavished upon him by his French teachers. However, he was already thirty and still an amateur, familiar with musical matters without knowing them closely, a dilettante. Behind him were violin lessons with Albert Chamberland and piano lessons with R.-O. Pelletier. He had also tried his hand at composition: incidental music for a play by Father Marie-Victorin from the Collège du Varenne, where Champagne had taught a variety of instruments, *Ils sont un peuple sans histoire* (c1918); music for the Canadian Grenadier Guards Band of J.J. Gagnier (in which Champagne had played saxophone), *La Ballade des Lutins* (c1916); and above all there was *Hercule et Omphale* (1918), an attempt at a symphonic poem, the work that decided Laliberté to help the young Champagne, financially and with his moral support, to study in Europe.

Champagne's European sojourn lasted eight years, until 1929. He studied counterpoint and fugue with André Gédalge, and then, after Gédalge's death, with Charles Koechlin. In Raoul Laparra's class he rounded out his formal training as composer and orchestrator.

Champagne did not frequent only the Conservatoire milieu. Through his lessons with the great Russian violinist Jules Conus, one finds him at the Schola Cantorum, the Concert Babaïans, etc. His activities were numerous, although his temperament allowed him to benefit from life in Paris. (It was at this time that he married; he later became the father of two children.) *Hercule et Omphale* was performed by the Conservatoire Concerts in 1926, and his 1927 *Suite canadienne* (which won the Beatty competition organized by the Canadian Pacific Railway) by the Pasdeloup Orchestra in 1928.

Champagne had gone to Paris intending to pursue an education, to develop a craft. He wanted to absorb himself in a musical tradition that he could not find at home in Canada. Throughout his life he esteemed the value of work well done. One notes in his music a clarity and a conciseness that are often astonishing. His output is actually quite small; in all only some fifteen works attest to a reaction against the excesses of romanticism, such as extended developments and complication of style. His works from the years 1918–30 (*Suite canadienne*, *Prélude et Filigrane*, 1918; *Habanera*, 1924; and *Danse villageoise*, 1930) are but passing fragrances; it is his later mature works that bear the mark of conciseness.

On his return from Europe, Champagne became involved in many sectors of Canadian musical life, teaching in particular. He was attached to the Montreal Catholic School Commission as co-ordinator of solfège in elementary schools, and he was professor at the McGill Conservatorium as well as at various new religious musical institutions for women. In 1942 he became associate co-ordinator at the Conservatoire of Music and Dramatic Arts of Quebec in Montreal, which had just opened and in the founding of which he no doubt played a part. In his free time he composed. Between 1930 and 1963 he wrote a dozen pieces, mostly for orchestra. The catalogue of his music contains, besides his major works, a considerable number of vocal pieces – arrangements and adaptations of folk songs that, although minor, show skill and finesse.

This restricted production, however, sets into relief Champagne's wish to write for orchestra, as orchestral writing was a necessity of the time. Montreal had no permanent symphony orchestra until after 1934, but it was necessary to write for orchestra if one wanted to establish a tradition of promoting Canadian music. Among the major items in his output, the *Symphonie gaspésienne* (1945) is one of the most important examples of Canadian orchestral scene-painting based on a regional landscape – in this instance, the Gaspé region of east-coast Quebec. The work drew an immediate response from the public and in fact Champagne was one of the first Canadian composers to be played consistently in his own lifetime. It was partly because of this that he was recognized as the 'doyen' of Canadian composers.

With regard to the characteristics of

Champagne's music, his rapprochement with romanticism has been mentioned. To this one should add the stylistic traits of French music. His works certainly have a French accent, an elegance and a clear grasp of things, that would seem to be more significant than the influence of Quebec folklore with which some critics have tried to mythologize his music. Of course the influence of folklore should not be minimized, especially in the context of other ideas of the period, not the least of which arose through his encounters with the folklorist Marius Barbeau. However, folklore is important in Champagne's work only as a source of inspiration. For him it was not a means of creating a uniquely Canadian music. His rhythms, for example, do not conform to those of folk music. One finds with Champagne a sort of intimate union of melody and rhythm that serves to eliminate the rigidity of bar lines and creates a kind of unending song, where all characteristic rhythmic formulas are abandoned.

Although Champagne drew on themes from folk music, these did not undergo transformation. He used those that he enjoyed, dispersing them throughout the score in a sort of contrapuntal play (as in the *Suite canadienne*). His harmonies are classical and not folkloric, in the sense that his compositional craft uses procedures learned from his studies of modality. His principle of 'harmonie par le chant' owes some allegiance to principles developed by Fauré and Debussy; it is perhaps the intimate union of harmony and rhythm, both subordinate to the melodic line, that imparts to Champagne's music such a limpid and touching simplicity. Here and there one recognizes timbres like the open-string playing of a gigue, well stressed, but these are circumstantial and are used for special effect (*Danse villageoise*).

Newer trends are reflected in two later compositions, the *Quatuor à cordes* (1951) and *Altitude* (1959) – somewhat surprising in one of Champagne's generation and demonstrating his absorption of Schoenberg and Messiaen. *Altitude* was inspired by his first extended visit to the Canadian Rockies and employs forces both orchestral (including ondes Martenot) and choral for musical description and religious comment.

Thus the music is universal in conception throughout. The modality that seems to emanate from almost every page is centred on the Dorian and Hypodorian (D and A) modes which, more than any others, permeate the folk music of French-speaking Canada; it is the intermingling of these modes, with the more usual major-minor sonorities, that evokes an echo of familiarity in his music.

Claude Champagne was a man who neither pushed nor stumbled. His career was a slow and steady upward climb. In 1964 the man whom the Montreal critic Andrée Desautels has called 'Claude de Nouvelle-France' was honoured when the Ecole Vincent d'Indy named the Claude Champagne concert hall after him; thus were his life and work given recognition before his death. Appreciation of this kind has been bestowed on few of our composers. Also in 1964 a National Film Board film appeared, oddly entitled 'Bonsoir Claude Champagne'. He died as quietly as he lived, on Tuesday, December 21, 1965, at 11:30 a.m., while writing Christmas greetings.

Claude Champagne was a member of the Canadian Arts Council (honorary president, 1951) and an honorary member of the Académie de Musique du Québec and of the Canadian League of Composers; he received the Canada Council Medal in 1962. He was an affiliate of BMI Canada, of whose publication division he was editor-in-chief for many years. LOUISE BAIL-MILOT

MUSICAL WORKS

Many of these works (especially in the vocal categories) exist in several forms, making simple categorization difficult.

STAGE

Ils sont un peuple sans histoire (theatre music to a play by Rev Marie-Victorin). c1917. 40′. ms. Jan 31, 1918, Mtl, l'Orchestre des Concerts, J J Gagnier.

ORCHESTRA

Fantaisie 'J'ai du bon tabac' (arr). c1917. 1′30″. orch or chamb ens. ms. Jan 31, 1918, Mtl, l'Orchestre des Concerts, J-J Gagnier.
Hercule et Omphale. 1918. 12′. full orch. Ber. Mar 31, 1926, Paris, Orch Symph des Artistes du Conservatoire, Juan Manen.
La Laurentienne. 1937. ms.

Petit Jean. str, ww, hn. ms.
Scoutisme. 1937. 2'. ms.
Gaspesia. 1944. 10'. ms. Nov 3, 1944, Mtl PO, Wilfrid Pelletier.
Symphonie gaspésienne (expanded version of *Gaspesia*). 1945. 20'. full orch. Ber, 1956. RCI-213-A1; RCI-216; RCA CC/CCS-1010. autumn 1947, Mtl, CBC O, Jean-Marie Beaudet.
Danse villageoise (4th version, orch'd after 1954). 4'30". full orch. Ber. Dom 1372/s-1372. 1931, Quebec, QSO, Wilfrid Pelletier.

BAND

La Ballade des Lutins. 1914. 3'. ms. May 20, 1915, Band of His Majesty's Canadian Grenadier Guards, J-J Gagnier.
La Laurentienne. 1937. ms.
Scoutisme. 1937. ms.

SMALL ORCHESTRA

Berceuse. 1933. 2'30". Ber. Mtl, CBC O, J-J Gagnier.
Evocation. 1943. 4'. ms. Ottawa PO, Eugene Kash.
Paysanna. 1953. 6'30". med orch. Ber, RCI-90; CBC BR SM-214. May 27, 1953, Mtl, CBC O, Roland Leduc.

STRING ORCHESTRA

Danse villageoise (3rd version, orch'n date unknown). 3'30". str, pno, hp. Ber, 1961. CTL M1030, S5030. Mar 30, 1947, Mtl, CBC O, Jean-Marie Beaudet.
Concertino Grosso (arr of *Suite Miniature*). 1963. 7'30". CMC.

SOLOIST WITH ORCHESTRA

Concerto. 1948. 14'. pno, orch. Ber. RCI-17. May 30, 1950, Mtl, CBC Montreal Little Symphony, Roland Leduc(cond), Neil Chotem(pno).

CHOIR WITH ORCHESTRA

Suite canadienne. 1927. 8'. SATB, small orch. Durand (vc, pno version). RCI Alb I. Oct 20, 1928, Paris, l'Orchestre Symphonique des Concerts Pasdeloup, Rhené Bâton.
Noël Huron. 1'30". SATB, small orch. CMC. Mar 19, 1929, Mtl, Cédia Brault (vc, pno version).
La Laurentienne. 1937. choir, orch or vc(s), pno or band. Arch, 1938 (vc, pno version). Text: Adrien Plouffe. June 13, 1938, Mtl.
Scoutisme. 1937. choir, orch or band or pno. Arch (vc, pno). Text: Adrien Plouffe, June 13, 1938, Mtl.
Images du Canada français. 1943. 15'. SATB, orch. Ber. RCI-152. Mar 9, 1947, Mtl, 'La Cantoria' choir, Victor Brault, CBC O, Jean-Marie Beaudet.
Altitude. 1959. 20'. SATB, full orch. Ber, 1961. RCI-179. Text: St Francis of Assisi. trans: Harold Heiberg. Apr 22, 1960, Tor, CBCSO and chorus, Charles Houdret.

CHOIR OR SOLO VOICES

Ave Maria. 1924. 2'. TbarB (or SATB, vlc) (or SATB, recorders, vlc). Ber, 1954. RCI-206. Paris, Claude Champagne.
A St Malo beau port de mer (arr). c1939. TTBB. ms. Mtl, Orpheon Choir, Arthur Laurendeau.
Missa Brevis. 1951. 3vc, org (or SATB, 16 recorders, vlc). Ber, 1955. Oct 21, 1952, Mtl, student choir of L'Ecole Vincent d'Indy, Sr Marie Stéphane, Mtl Recorder Group, Mario Duchesnes.
Petit Jean (arr). unis, pno (vc, pno). Trans: Amy Bissett England. FH, 1959.
C'est la belle Françoise/Lovely Frances (arr). SSAA or TTBB. Wat, 1960. Trans: Amy Bissett England. c1933, Mtl, Orpheon Choir, Arthur Laurendeau.
Gai lon la, gai le rosier/The Rosebush (arr). SSAA or TTBB. Wat, 1960 (SSAA, TTBB). Trans: Amy Bissett England. c1933, Mtl, Orpheon Choir, Arthur Laurendeau.
Images du Canada français. 1943. 13'. vc, pno. ms.
Isabeau s'y promène/Isabel went walking (arr). SSAA or TTBB. Wat, 1960. Trans: Amy Bissett England. Mtl, Orpheon Choir, Arthur Laurendeau.
Dans Paris/In Paris (arr). vc, pno. FH, 1961. Trans: Amy Bissett England.
A qui marierons-nous? (arr). Wat, c1933, Mtl, Orpheon Choir, Arthur Laurendeau.
Au Bois du Rossignolet/In the Wood of the Nightingale (arr). TTBB(SSAA) (unis, pno) (vc or vcs, pno). Trans: Amy Bissett England. CMC.
Au clair de la lune. SATB. ms.
Cadet Roussel. SATB, 2pno (opt).
C'est une belle tourterelle (arr). vc, pno. ms.
(5) *Chants du Canada.* vc, pno. ms.
Chanson d'hiver. Text: Adrien Plouffe.
Easter. 1963. vc, pno. Peer. Trans: Amy Bissett England.
En roulant ma boule (arr). SATB. CMC.
For the Christ Child. med vc, pno. Peer, 1966. Text: Amy Bissett England.

Frost in the Air. unis (vc), pno. Peer (vc, pno) 1966. Text: Amy Bissett England.
Il y avait un petit bateau (children's song). Text: Adrien Plouffe. ms.
J'ai cueilli la belle rose (arr). SATB and soli. Arch (Solfège Pédagogique, Claude Champagne). c1933, Mtl, Orpheon Choir, Arthur Laurendeau.
J'ai du bon tabac.
Le bon lait de chez grand-mère. Text: Adrien Plouffe.
Ma Normandie (arr). SATB. ms.
Marianne s'en va-t-au moulin/Marianne went to the Mill (arr). unis, pno. FH, 1959. Trans: Amy Bissett England.
Monsieur le Curé. vc, pno. ms.
Noël Huron. 1'30". SATB, pno (orch) or vc, pno (2pno). ms.
Une Perdriole (arr). sop, ten, SATB, pno (sop, alto, ten, bs, pno). CMC.
La Petite Galiote (arr). unis (vc, pno). CMC.
Quand j'étais chez mon père (arr). SATB (2pno opt). CMC. Apr 20, 1927, Mtl, Société Pro-Musica.
Rondel. 1935. Text: Lucien Rainier. male vcs. ms.
Thanksgiving. vc, pno. Peer, 1966. Text: Amy Bissett England.
Time for Thanks. vc, pno. Text: Amy Bissett England.
V'la l'bon vent/Fair Wind. SSAA or TTBB. Wat, 1960. c1933, Mtl, Orpheon Choir, Arthur Laurendeau.
Vive la Canadienne. SATB. ms.
Vive Napoléon (arr). SATB. ms.
Voici le temps et la saison/This is the Time and Season. SA, guit (hp) (pno). Wat, 1962. Trans: Amy Bissett England.
Vos jolis yeux. vc, pno. ms.

VOICES WITH INSTRUMENTAL ENSEMBLE

Le Nez de Martin (arr). 1956. SA, guit (hp) (pno). Wat, 1962. Trans: Amy Bissett England.

INSTRUMENTAL ENSEMBLE

Habanera. 1929. 2'. vln, pno. CMC. Mar 19, 1929, Mtl, Annette Lasalle-Leduc(vln), Léo-Pol Morin(pno).
Danse villageoise. 1929. 3'30". vln, pno. Ber & Parnasse Musical, 1949. Acd 3000 CB. Mar 19, 1929, Mtl, Annette Lasalle-Leduc (vln), Léo-Pol Morin(pno).
Danse villageoise (2nd version). c1936. 3'30". str qt. Mar 30, 1936, Quatuor de Montréal.
Chanson du Roi Richard Coeur de Lion. 1941. str qt, hpschd, pno. c1930, Mtl.
Quatuor à cordes. 1954. 14'. Ber, 1974. RCI-143. Aug 23, 1954, Mtl, JMC Qt.
Suite Miniature. 1958. 14'. fl (vln), vlc (viola da gamba) hpschd (pno). CMC.

INSTRUMENTAL ENSEMBLE (UNCONFIRMED)

Chansons de Croisade du Chatelain de Coucy. str qt, pno, hp.
Chanson de Croisade de Paul le Flem.
Chanson d'Henri IV. str qt, pno, hp.
Par derrière chez ma tante.

PIANO

Odelie Valse. before 1918. Bélair.
Prélude et Filigrane. 1918. 3'. Ber, 1960. Dec 3, 1918, Mtl, Léo-Pol Morin.
Valse de Genre. 1920.
Quadrilha brasileira. 1942. 2'30". Ber, 1951. RCI-252. July 1, 1942, Rio de Janeiro, Brazil, Ernaldo Estrella.
Le Pas de la Muse. early work. ms.
Pas des Lutins. early work. ms.
Petite Berceuse; 'Twilight Lullaby'. early work. ms.
Petits Canons, 1 and 2. GVT, 1958.
Petit Scherzo. GVT, 1958.
Tocane pour un clown. 1962. ms.
Improvisation. 1963.
Cadet Roussel.
Practical Sight Reading Exercises for Piano Students (with Boris Berlin). GVT.
Several untitled pieces for piano. ms.

INSTRUMENTAL SOLO

Untitled piece for violin. 1929. ms.

ORGAN

Prière (à la mémoire d'Henri Gagnon). 1963. 3'. ms. RCI-254. André Mérineau.

BIBLIOGRAPHY

See B-B; Aum; Bec70; Bt; CrC(II); D157, 165; Esc; Gf; Gmu; Ip; K; Lv; R12; Wa.
Archer, Thomas. 'Claude Champagne', *CMJ.* Vol. II, no. 2, 1958 (3–15).
Bail-Milot, Louise. *Les Oeuvres de Claude Champagne.* Unpublished thesis, University of Montreal, 1972.
Beckwith, John. 'Recent Orchestral Works by Champagne, Morel and Anhalt', *CMJ.* Vol. IV, no. 4, Summer 1960.
Brassard, François. 'Une date pour la musique canadienne', *La Revue de l'Université Laval.* Vol. v, no. 8, Apr. 1951 (3–11).
Clopoys, Andrew. 'Claude Champagne, a

Distinguished Canadian Composer', *Canadian Review of Music and Art.* Vol. v, Dec.-Jan. 1947 (14).
Demombynes, J. G. 'Un compositeur montréalais', *Carnet Viatoriens.* Vol. XIII, July 1948 (209–10).
Duchow, Marvin. 'Claude Champagne', *MuSc*, Sept.-Oct. 1968 (7).
——. 'Inventory List of the Compositions of Claude Champagne', *CAUSM Journal.* Vol. II, no. 2, Fall 1972 (67–82).
Morin, Léo-Pol. *Musique.* Montreal: Beauchemin, 1955 (267–70).
——. *Papiers de musique.* Montreal: Librairie d'Action français, 1930 (98–104).
Pilote, Gilles. *L'enseignement du solfège dans les écoles élémentaires de la C.E.C.M.: Claude Champagne et ses contributions.* Unpublished thesis, University of Montreal, 1970.
Provost, Marie-Paule. *Claude Champagne, l'un des nôtres.* Unpublished thesis, University of Montreal, 1970.
Walsh, Sister Ann. *The Life and Works of Claude Adonai Champagne.* Unpublished dissertation, Catholic University, 1972.

CHARPENTIER, GABRIEL (b. Richmond, Que., 13 Sept. 1925). It was while studying classics (1940–4) at Brébeuf College, Montreal, that Charpentier's mind was opened to history, literature, theatre, films, and to the music of Debussy, Schoenberg, Stravinsky, Berg, and Webern. Then, at the monastery of Saint Benoît-du-Lac (1945–7), Charpentier steeped himself in Gregorian chant, aspects of which were later to influence his musical writing. From 1947 to 1953 he lived in France and studied with Nadia Boulanger, Annette Dieudonné, and Andrée Bonneville.

Charpentier joined the CBC in 1953 as program organizer and artistic adviser for television musical broadcasts, a post he still occupies and that led him to collaborate with Pierre MERCURE, Françoys Bernier, Pierre Morin, and others in the planning and production of several series of television broadcasts, such as 'Concert pour la jeunesse', 'L'Heure du concert', 'Musiques folles des années sages', and 'Les Beaux Dimanches'. He is remembered for productions of *Les Noces* (Stravinsky, 1956), *Wozzeck* (Berg, 1957), *Les Dialogues des Carmélites* (Poulenc, 1960), *Le Barbier de Séville* (Rossini, 1965) – the latter winning the Emmy Award for Charpentier and Pierre Morin – and *Messe pour le temps présent* (Henri, 1971), as well as for a number of Balanchine ballets and the Boulez *Sacre du printemps* concert in 1963. Charpentier is credited with the French text of *Toi (Loving)*, an opera by Murray SCHAFER (1966) designed for television and produced by a staff that included Pierre Mercure as producer, the choreographer Françoise Riopelle, and Charpentier himself.

Alongside these activities, Charpentier was lecturer in music history at McGill University French Summer School 1955–6 and taught rhythm and music-history classes at the National Theatre School, 1962–4. From 1966 to 1971 he was a member of the board of directors of the Canadian Conference of the Arts; since 1971 he has been on the arts advisory panel of the Canada Council.

As well as being composer, Charpentier has described himself as a 'theatre musician'. He has written more than fifty scores for theatre, especially for Le Théâtre du Nouveau Monde, of which he was musical director from 1959 to 1972, and for the Stratford Festival (Ontario) from 1964. For the TNM he wrote the scores of *Les Choéphores* (Aeschylus, 1961), *Richard II* (Shakespeare, 1962), *Klondike* (Languirand, 1965), *Le Soulier de satin* (Claudel, 1967). At Stratford he wrote the music for *The Merchant of Venice* (Shakespeare, 1970), *Cymbeline* (Shakespeare, 1970), *The Duchess of Malfi* (Webster, 1971), and *Pericles* (Shakespeare, 1973). In these productions he evolved his personal philosophy of the role of music for the theatre. For Charpentier, music is an integral dimension of theatre; it should be totally involved, constructed in the closest collaboration with the producer, the actors, the designer, the technicians – a new creation for each production.

Charpentier has been quoted as saying: 'Clinical analysis of the text reveals its backbone, its structure. You find a new world, you fly over it, encompass it, touch it. You hunt out its history. You transfer it to a given time. It becomes part of you. It explodes. Then little by little rhythms, sounds, movements take form. Instrumental colours start to smile. Dialogue is invented between director, designer, technicians. Breathing together is very fast and very slow, always exhilarating. The chronometer begins. Timing is specified. Each musical interjection is noted, in words, in figures or colours. These decisions become the foundation agreed on by the whole team, the Black Book. We have emerged from the maze. Bound to this team the composer now returns, alone, to his study and remains for several weeks master of time. "One feels it, in proportion to time," he says to himself.' (Noted by Hélène Beauchamp-Rank, in 'Enquête auprès des créateurs en théâtre', Archives v, *Théâtre canadien-français*, published by the Centre de Recherche en civilisation canadienne-française of the University of Ottawa.)

Charpentier's theatre scores reveal his instrumental and vocal musical style. A melodist and contrapuntist above all, he displays a penchant for Gregorian melismas and his extraordinary feeling for rhythm, always illuminated by a most fertile imagination. From *Trois poèmes de Saint-Jean de la Croix* (1955) to *Processional* (1973 – a work written for the broadcast 'Ecoute', included in the Beaux Dimanches series and recorded at the Abbaye de Saint-Benoît-du-Lac) – he reveals a deep attachment to Gregorian arabesques, broadened into atonality and supported by an orchestration of luminous and brilliant sonorities. Charpentier plays with time as he enjoys melody. *Permutation 1 2 3 4* (1962, written for the students of the National Theatre School) embodies for the first time a new exploitation of rhythm in his music. *Electra* (Euripides, 1973) and *Pericles* (Shakespeare, 1973), dramatic works in which voices and instruments are allotted to twelve actors, mark a high point in this line of development. These works offer extremely complicated rhythmic counterpoint, creating a mood that fosters better understanding of the inner meanings of the tragedies.

In Charpentier the poet is often grafted on to the composer. His poem 'Cantate pour une joie' blends marvelously with Pierre Mercure's music. His poetic imagination is expressed too in a work-in-progress called *A Night at the Opera*, comprising eight operas (seven comic operas and one dramatic opera) of a maximum length of fifteen minutes each and for which Charpentier is writing both scenario and music. Two of these operas are finished: the 'opera happening', *An English Lesson* (1968), and *A Tea Symphony* or *The Perils of Clara*, 'a kitsch opera in nine drinks' (1972). These recent works perhaps foretell a new direction for Gabriel Charpentier in which the poet and composer is served by fantasy in delirium.

Gabriel Charpentier is a member of the Executive Committee of the Canadian Conference of the Arts and of the Canadian League of Composers and CAPAC.

FRANCE MALOUIN-GÉLINAS

MUSICAL WORKS

STAGE (OPERA)

An English Lesson. 1968. 10'. Text: Gabriel Charpentier. Aug 3, 1968, Stratford Fest, Nat Fest Orch, Lawrence Smith(dir).

Orphée (Liturgy in 7 Parts). 1969 (revised version in Eng 1972 under title *Orpheus*). 70'. chorus of sgrs and dancers, hp, perc, pno, ondes Martenot. ms. Text: Gabriel Charpentier. Trans: Michael Bawtree. June 10, 1969 (French version), Ottawa, NAC opening, Serge Garant(mus dir).

STAGE (THEATRE MUSIC)

Music for some 38 stage productions, for theatres including Stratford, Théâtre du Rideau Vert, Théâtre du Nouveau Monde, St Lawrence Centre for the Arts, National Theatre School, and others, to texts by authors including Aeschylus, Shakespeare, Molière, Racine, Ionesco, Bertolt Brecht, Ben Jonson, Samuel Beckett, Jean Anouilh, F Garcia Lorca, Morvan Lebesque, Robert Thomas, Ugo Betti, Motokiyo, Sean O'Casey, P de Marivaux, Jacques Languirand, Alfred de Musset, Félix-Antoine Savard, Anne Hébert, Arthur Schnitzler, Jean-Louis Roux, Paul Claudel, Jacques Ferron, and Gabriel Charpentier.

FILM MUSIC

Lumières. 1953. Film by Jacques Giraldeau.

La Chute de la maison Usher. 1955. Silent film (1929) by Jean Epstein.

Histoires extraordinaires. 1961–2. Films at TNM. Texts: Balzac, Poe, Stevenson, Wilde, etc.

La courte échelle. 1964. Film by Jacques Giraldeau.

CHOIR

Messe I. 1952. 8'20". 3 equal vcs. CMC. Poly 2917009 (Gloria & Credo only), RCI-189. 1955.

Sept Chansons enfantines. 1952. 5'. SATB. ms. Text: Max Jacob, Raymond Radiguet, Robert Desnos, Gabriel Charpentier. 1955. Mtl, CBC, Mtl Bach Choir, George Little (cond).

L'Avenir. 1962. alto, SATB. ms. Text: Henri Michaux. National Theatre School.

Permutation 1 2 3 4. 1962. 5'20". SATB. ms. May 1962, Mtl, students of the National Theatre School.

Permutation 1 2 3 4 5. 1962. SATB. ms. National Theatre School.

VOICE

Jamais. 1963. voc trio. ms. Text: Gabriel Charpentier. Nov 1965, Mtl, CBC.

VOICE WITH INSTRUMENTAL ENSEMBLE

Trois Poèmes de St-Jean de la Croix. 1954. 30'. alto, vln, vlc. Trans: Armand Godoy. CMC. 1955, Mtl, CBC, Maureen Forrester (alto), Mildred Goodman(vln), Walter Joachim(vlc).

Trois Oraisons. 1971. 10'. sop, hp, pno, hpschd, perc. ms. 1971, Tor, Art Gallery of Ontario, Lynne Cantlon(sop), Judy Loman(hp), Walter Buczynski(pno), Carol Birtch(hpschd), Robin Engelman(perc).

A Tea Symphony; 'The Perils of Clara' (a stage work). 1972. 17'. sop, fl, vlc, pno. ms. Text: Gabriel Charpentier. May 5, 1972, Can Mus Counc Conference, Banff, Alta, LAT.

INSTRUMENTAL ENSEMBLE

Trois Ricercars. 1966. 15'. ob, hpschd. ms. July 1966, Mtl, McGill, Jacques Simard(ob), Kenneth Gilbert(hpschd).

PIANO/HARPSICHORD

O Guruma. 1960. 2pno. ms.

Suite d'après la musique de 'Le Bourgeois Gentilhomme'. 1964. 22'. hpschd. ms. 1964, Mtl, CBC, Hubert Bédard.

Grande Chaconne d'après la musique de 'Galileo Galilei'. 1971. 11'. hpschd. ms. Nov 23, 1971, Paris, Centre Culturel Canadien, Kenneth Gilbert.

ORGAN

Quinze Chorals. 1959. ms.

BIBLIOGRAPHY

Bec 56,57,70; CrC(II); Lv; Wa.

Campbell, Francean. 'Gabriel Charpentier is Shakespeare's Musical Composer', *CanCo.* No. 54, Nov. 1970 (4–7).

Desjardins, P. W. 'Orphée', *Vie des Arts.* No. 57, Winter 1969–70 (59, 81).

Doré, F. 'La musique n'est qu'un élément du grand tout', *Maclean's* (French ed.). Vol. VIII, Aug. 1968 (46).

'Gabriel Charpentier: Musique du Théâtre', *Musiques du Kébèk* (R. Duguay, ed.). Montreal: Editions du Jour, 1971 (33–8).

'Un petit Opéra from Stratford', *CBC Times.* Aug. 3–9, 1968 (8).

Thistle, Lauretta. 'Orphée – the Opera by Gabriel Charpentier', *CanCo.* No. 39, Apr. 1969 (10–12).

LITERARY WORKS

POETRY

'Poèmes', *Liberté.* Vol. LX, Nov.-Dec. 1960 (362–3).

CHERNEY, BRIAN (b. Peterborough, Ont., 4 Sept. 1942). Except for brief periods of study at Columbia University and the 'Ferienkürse für Neue Musik' in Darmstadt, Cherney received all his formal musical education at the Royal Conservatory of Music in Toronto and at the Faculty of Music, University of Toronto, where he completed his Bachelor of Music (1964) and Master of Music (1967) degrees in composition. He studied piano with Jacques Abram and Margaret Miller Brown and composition with Samuel DOLIN and John WEINZWEIG. He was awarded a Canada Council Doctoral Fellowship to continue work in Germany on his Ph.D. dissertation in musicology (1969–70). He has received commissions from the Toronto Repertory Ensemble (*Kontakion*, 1969), the Lyric Arts Trio (*Eclipse*, 1972), and the CBC (*Seven Images for Twenty-Two Players*, 1971).

Cherney's early student works (*Sonata for Violin and Piano*, 1961; *Quintet*, 1962, for alto saxophone and string quartet) are of a highly dissonant character, with a thick, polyphonic texture, showing the influence of Weinzweig's rhythmic vitality. These two works differ in that the second is subdued, a characteristic that reappears in later works. In *Kontakion*, subtitled 'Quiet Music for Eleven Players', the freedom afforded Cherney by the use of graphic rather than traditional notation has produced a more pointillistic style. This style appears again in his four *Mobiles* (1968–9), a form Cherney has developed from his observation of the visual mobile. In his analysis of his *String Quartet No. 2* (1970), he says: 'In these works [*Mobiles*], similar ideas are presented (both in the same work and from one work to another) in different perspectives, through variations in time and instrumentation.' The techniques here are experimental but carefully thought out to achieve a consistency of style. This formal idea is again used in his *String Quartet No. 2* where his earlier *Mobiles* are incorporated into the form of the quartet. This work, which was awarded a McMaster University Prize for Chamber Music in 1970, is a theatre piece in which the performers appear at times to be playing but without actually touching the strings. The composer says 'it is a work of sudden contrast, shifts in mood, half-uttered allusions and silent gestures'.

In 1971–2 Cherney was lecturer in theory and composition at the University of Victoria and in 1972 was appointed to the Faculty of Music, McGill University, Montreal. He is a member of the Canadian League of Composers and is affiliated with BMI Canada.

MUSICAL WORKS

ORCHESTRA

Variations for Orchestra. 1962.
Variations for Orchestra. 1967.

SMALL ORCHESTRA

Seven Images for 22 Players. 1971.

SOLOIST WITH ORCHESTRA

Two Songs for Soprano and Chamber Orchestra. 1963. Text: Rainer Maria Rilke.
Concerto for Violin and Orchestra. 1964.
Six Miniatures for Oboe and Strings. 1968.

VOICE WITH INSTRUMENTAL ENSEMBLE

Mobile IV. 1969; Jay, 1970. sop, chamb ens. Text: Tu Fu, Trans: Kenneth Rexroth.
Eclipse. 1972. sop, fl, pno. Text: Brian Henderson.

INSTRUMENTAL ENSEMBLE

Sonata for Violin and Piano. 1961.
Three Pieces for String Quartet. 1961.
Quintet. 1962. alto sax, str qt.
Interlude and Variations. 1965; Jay, 1970. ww qnt.
Suite for Viola and Piano. 1965.
Woodwind Quintet. 1965.
String Quartet No 1. 1966.
Kontakion (Quiet Music for Eleven Players). 1969. ww qnt, str qt, cb, pno.
String Quartet No 2. 1970.

PIANO

Fantasy for Piano. 1962.
Sonata for Piano. 1966.
Intervals, Shapes, Patterns. 1968; Wat, 1970.
Jest. 1968; Jay, 1971.
Pieces for Young Pianists (Bks I, II, III). 1968; Jay, 1972(I); Jay, 1971(II,III).
Six Miniatures for Piano. 1968; Jay, 1971.
Elegy for a Misty Afternoon. 1971; WBM, 1973.

INSTRUMENTAL SOLO

Suite for Solo Oboe. 1962.
Mobile II. 1968. vlc.
Mobile IIIa. 1970. ob.

BIBLIOGRAPHY

Morgan, Kit. 'Good Performance Means More than Acclaim to Cherney', *MuSc.* No. 264, Mar.-Apr. 1972 (4, 16).
'Stratford Music', *CBC Times.* July 26-Aug. 1, 1969 (11).

CHOTEM, NEIL (b. Saskatoon, Sask., 1920). He began studying piano at the Palmer School of Music at the age of five and later studied with Lyell Gustin in Saskatoon (1930–8). He made appearances as piano soloist with the Regina Symphony Orchestra and from 1938 to 1940 gave several radio recitals for the CBC in Winnipeg. He joined the Royal Canadian Air Force in 1941 and served overseas. After the war he settled in Montreal where he studied with Michel Hirvy (1946–50). He appeared with several orchestras, including the Montreal, Ottawa, and Toronto Symphony Orchestras, and the McGill Chamber Orchestra. In 1953 he toured Japan and Korea for the Canadian armed forces. Chotem was the regular conductor of the Montreal Symphony Orchestra's summer series from 1969 to 1972 and has been guest conductor of the Quebec Symphony Orchestra (1970–2) and the National Arts Centre Orchestra in Ottawa. He taught courses in arranging, composition, and orchestration at McGill University (1970–1), the University of Montreal (1969; 1970–1), and the Ecole Vincent d'Indy (1969; 1970–1). He is active as an arranger for the Montreal and Quebec Symphony Orchestras and as composer, conductor, and arranger for such singers as Maureen Forrester and Monique Leyrac; for various television and radio programs, including 'Music from Montreal'; for films and stage productions, including the Théâtre du Nouveau Monde's productions of *Klondike* (1967) at the Old Vic Theatre, London, and *Lysistrata*; for *Sound and Light* (1967), presented during the centennial year at Parliament Hill, Ottawa; and for the CBC film documentary *Camera on Canada*. Chotem adapts to whatever style in which he is asked to write, although he generally composes in a conservative, tonal idiom (*Fantasy for Orchestra*; *Earth and High Heaven*) and at times in a popular idiom (*Mayday Meets Frankenstein*, incidental music, 1966). He appeared as piano soloist, conductor, composer, and arranger in the CBC television production 'Centennial Concerto' (1967) and has toured extensively as pianist for Les Jeunesses Musicales of Canada. He is a member of the board of directors of CAPAC.

MUSICAL WORKS

STAGE

Incidental music for Théâtre du Nouveau Monde productions, including *Klondike* (1967); *Lysistrata*.

RADIO AND TELEVISION

Incidental music to radio programs, including: *The Song of Solomon* (1951); *So Long at the Fair* (1967); *Raven* (1971).

Incidental music for television programs, including: *Camera on Canada* (1967); *Opus* (c1968); *Musique folle des années sages* (1972).

INSTRUMENTAL

17 works for orchestra, including: *Dances out of the West* (1951); *Concerto* (1967); *Salute to Expo* (arr) (1967); *Sound and Light* (1967); *Narcisse* (1971).

2 works for string orchestra and 2 works for band.

4 works for soloist and orchestra, including: *Scherzo Tarantelle* (1936) pno, orch; *Rapsodie on El Vito* (arr) (1963) pno, timp, perc, orch.

13 works for chamber ensemble, many for jazz groups, including: *Slow Rock*; *Opus Minus*; *Bleuets Verts* (1970); *Narcisse* (1971); *Jazz et la Java*; *Snake Eyes*.

7 works for piano solo: 3 *Preludes*; 3 *Valses lentes* (1972); *Fuguey Wooguey*.

CHORAL

Song of Solomon. SATB, orch.

VOCAL

Song of the Maritimes (arr). vc, orch. Text: trad.

3 works for voice and instrumental ensemble: *Et Bye-Bye*. Text: Michel Conte; *Je resterai tout seul*. Text: Michel Conte; *Je veux*. Text: Michel Conte.

BIBLIOGRAPHY

See B-B; K; Lv; Mm; Wa.
Campbell, Francean. 'Neil Chotem', *CanCo*. No. 47, Feb. 1970 (4–9).

CIAMAGA, GUSTAV (b. London, Ont., 10 Apr. 1930). He began his musical studies at the University of Western Ontario in London, at the same time studying privately with Gordon DELAMONT. At the University of Toronto he studied composition with John WEINZWEIG and John BECKWITH (1953–6). From 1956 to 1963 he studied musicology and composition at Brandeis University in Waltham, Mass., with Arthur Berger, Harold Shapero, and Irving Fine. While there he organized the electronic music studio. In his compositions Ciamaga has concentrated on producing a series of short, contrapuntal electronic studies exploiting a singular technique or musical idea conceived under the generic title 'Invention'. In *One-Part Invention* (1965) – 'part' refers to the number of loudspeakers or channels employed in the sound transmission. The Serial Structure Generator (SSG) is used for the source material, modified by the envelope-shaper to produce a water-drop effect. The work is stereophonic, with the second channel echoing the first at constantly varying intervals. The SSG is used in a number of his two-part inventions. *Two-Part Invention No. 3* (1967) is based on a series of complex timbres resulting from the technique of frequency modulation; these timbres are arranged in a serial order, and, through the use of SSG, are developed according to the principles of serial technique. Ciamaga also calls on musique concrète, as in the *Two-Part Invention No. 1* (1965), which employs electronically manipulated piano and harpsichord sounds. In *Canon for Stravinsky* (1972) Ciamaga applies the computer to produce a short work with quotations from Stravinsky's *Orpheus*.

In 1963 Ciamaga joined the staff of the Faculty of Music, University of Toronto, and later became chairman of the theory and composition department and director of the electronic-music studio. He is a member of the American Society of University Composers, the Audio Engineering Society, the Canadian League of Composers, and of CAPAC.

MUSICAL WORKS

ELECTRONIC TAPE

One-Part Invention. 1965.
Two-Part Inventions Nos 1 (1965), *2* (1966), *3* (1966–7), *4* (1967), *5* (1967), *6A* (1967), *7* (1968), *8* (1970).
Scherzo (new version). 1966.
Four-Part Invention No 1. 1967.
Ragamuffin Nos 1 and 2. 1967. collab with Lowell Cross.

ELECTRONIC TAPE WITH STAGE PURPOSES

Ottawa 1967 (electronic sections for outdoor theatre production). 1966. collab with Louis Applebaum.
Curtain Raiser. 1969. collab with Louis Applebaum.

TELEVISION

Phone-phugue. (1965). collab with Lowell Cross.
Margaree. 1966. collab with Tony Gnazzo.

FILM

Mosaic. 1966. film: Jack Chambers.
Music for the film 'Dizziness'. 1968–9. collab with Talivaldis Kenins. Film: U of T Fac of Med.

COMPUTER

Fanfare for Computer. 1967.
Bach: Brandenburg Concerto No 1 (mov't 3). 1969.
Canon for Stravinsky. 1972.

INSTRUMENTAL ENSEMBLE

Solipsism While Dying. 1972. fl, vc, pno, tape. Text: Margaret Atwood.

Other non-electronic works include pieces for jazz or stage band, a Mass, string quartet, and short pieces for orchestra.

BIBLIOGRAPHY

Bec70; Wa.

LITERARY WORKS

ARTICLES

'Computer Control of Sound Apparatus for Electronic Music' (with A.J. Gabura), *Journal of the Audio-Engineering Society*. Vol. XVI, no. 1, 1967 (114–18).
'Digital Computer Control of Sound Generating Apparatus for the Production of Electronic Music' (with A.J. Gabura), *Electronic Music Review*. Vol. I, no. 1, 1967 (54–7).
'Initiation du compositeur aux nouveaux procédés technologiques', *La Revue Musicale*. Paris, 1970 (139–47).
'Kennwort – UTEMS', *MELOS, Zeitschrift für Neue Musik*. No. 12, Dec. 1971 (517–19).
'A Preliminary Report on the Serial Sound Structure Generator' (with Hugh LeCaine), *Perspectives of New Music*. Vol. VI, no. 1, Fall-Winter 1967 (114–18).
'Some Thoughts on the Teaching of Electronic Music', *Inter-American Institute for Musical Research Yearbook*. Vol. III, 1967 (69–74).
'The Sonde: A New Approach to Multiple Sine Wave Generation' (with Hugh LeCaine), *Journal of the Audio-Engineering Society*. Vol. XVIII, 1970 (536–9).

UNPUBLISHED PAPERS

'Analog and Digital Techniques for Producing and Controlling Randomness in Electronic Composition', paper delivered at the Canadian Computer Conference, Session 1972, June 1972.
'Computer Music', paper delivered at the Faculty of Music, University of Toronto, 1970.
'Electronic Music, 1948–1968 – a Retrospective View', paper delivered at the Royal Canadian Institute, Feb. 1, 1969.
'Sequencers in Electronic Music', paper delivered at the Audio-Engineering Society, Oct. 14, 1969.
'The Use of Sequencers in Electronic Music', paper delivered at the Convegno Internazionale Centri Sperimentali di Musica Electronica, May 1968.

CLARKE, DOUGLAS DEAN (b. Reading, England, 4 Apr. 1893; d. Warwick, England, 13 Nov. 1962). He studied composition with Sir Hugh Allen at Reading University College (1909–12), where he won the Tirbutt Memorial Prize and the College Prize. He studied composition privately with Gustav Holst, Ralph Vaughan Williams, and Charles Wood (1918–20), and obtained his FRCO diploma in 1920, receiving the Turpin Prize. He was organist at Christ's College, Cambridge, where he received his Bachelor of Music and Master of Arts degrees (1923–7), and later was organist at St Peter's, Eaton Square, London. In 1927 he came to Canada and became organist at Holy Trinity Church in Winnipeg and conductor of the Winnipeg Male Voice Choir and the Philharmonic Society (1927–9). In 1929 he was appointed Director of the McGill Conservatorium and was Dean of the Faculty of Music of McGill University from 1930 to 1955. He was also conductor of the Montreal Symphony Orchestra (1930–41). Clarke wrote extensively for choir, including *The Passion* (Stainer & Bell), *Communion Service in D*, and various liturgical works published by Stainer & Bell. He also wrote for orchestra (*Piece for Full Orchestra* and *Hunter's Moon*), for organ (*Fantasia on 'Lo, He Comes'*), and for chamber ensembles (*Buffoon* for violin and piano). On retirement from McGill he returned to Warwick, England where he was organist of St Mary's Church. He was a fellow of the Royal College of Music.

BIBLIOGRAPHY

See B-B; K; Lv; Wa.

CLARKE, FREDERICK R. C. (b. Vancouver, B.C., 7 Aug. 1931). He studied piano in Vancouver with Kenneth Ross until 1949, organ with Eric Rollinson at the Royal Conservatory in Toronto, and theory and composition with Healey WILLAN, Drummond Wolff, and George Laughlin at the University of Toronto (1949–53). He received his Bachelor of Music (1951) and his Doctor of Music (1954) degrees from the University of Toronto; his ARCT in organ (1951), winning the Gold Medal; and his ACCO (1951) and FCCO (1952). Most of Clarke's compositions, both choral and organ, are for use in church; his style is in the tradition of Healey Willan and Alfred WHITEHEAD. Clarke has been organist at Trinity Anglican Church (1950–1) and Wychwood Presbyterian Church (1951–3) in Toronto, and at Westminster United Church in St Catharines, Ont. (1954–8). He was also the conductor of the St Catharines Civic Symphony (1957–8) and taught at the Hamilton Conservatory (1956–8). In 1958 he moved to Kingston, where he is organist at Sydenham St United Church, conductor of the Kingston Choral Society, and (since 1964) on the music staff of Queen's University. His many years as a church musician have resulted in a large output of choral and organ works, such as the *Christmas Cantata* (1955) for soprano, tenor and bass solo, SATB and organ; numerous motets and anthems, including the Clarke Sacred Choral Series published by Waterloo Music; the *Sonata for Organ and Strings* (1956–8); *Six Hymn-tune Voluntaries* (1964); and *William Boyce Suite* (1970) for organ solo. He has also written for orchestra (*Mini-Suite*, 1971) and piano (*Five Easy Variations on a Theme, Ostinette*, and *Three Easy Pieces*, 1970, published by Waterloo for piano students).

Clarke won several CAPAC Student Composer Awards, an ORMTA Piano Composition Award (1956), and a CBC Choral Composition Prize (1967). He was chairman of the Music Sub-committee for the new Anglican-United Church Hymn Book. He is a member of the RCCO and of CAPAC.

CLEMENTS, PETER (b. Regina, Sask., 4 Dec. 1940). He received his early musical training at the Regina Conservatory of Music. He studied composition with Leslie Bassett and Ross Lee Finney (1959–65) at the University of Michigan in Ann Arbor, where he received his Bachelor of Music and Master of Music degrees. Since 1965 he has taught theory and composition at the Faculty of Music, University of Western Ontario, where he inaugurated a program in electronic music.

With a relatively small output, Clements has composed mainly for orchestra (*Sestina*, 1965), choir (*Let the People Praise Thee*, 1964; *Canadian Bronze*), and instrumental ensembles (*Quintet*, 1964). His compositions are characterized by a conservative polytonal style, as in *Fanfare and Chorale in F* (1966). His *Cloud of Unknowing* (1967), a commission from the University of Western Ontario Orchestra and Choir, similarly follows this polytonal style with the addition of electronic tape. He also received a commission from the London Symphony Orchestra for *Suite Grotesque* (1972).

COLLIER, RONALD (b. Coleman, Alta, 3 July 1930). He began his musical training on piano and trombone and played trombone in the Vancouver Kitsilano Boys' Band from 1943 to 1949. His interest in jazz composition stimulated a move in 1951 to Toronto, where he studied with Gordon DELAMONT. He was a free-lance trombonist with various orchestras, including the National Ballet Orchestra, the Toronto Symphony, CBC radio and TV orchestras, and local commercial orchestras. Collier led his own jazz group, which performed his music extensively in concert and on radio and television. His group was small and cultivated the cool style prevalent in the 1960s. Collier's works – such as *Aurora Borealis* (1967) and *The Carnival* (1969), both CBC commissions, and *Requiem for JFK* (1964) – exhibit a refined and subdued quality. The CBC also commissioned *The City* (1960) and entered it in the Italia Prize competition. In 1965 Collier was the first jazz composer to receive a Canada Council grant, which afforded him six months of study in New York City with George Russell and Hall Overton. In the early 70s he collaborated on a number of works with Duke Ellington. Since 1972 he has been the resident composer at Humber College, Toronto. He is a member of the Canadian League of Composers and of CAPAC.

MUSICAL WORKS

STAGE

The Mechanic (play). 1965. Text: Jack Winter.

Aurora Borealis (ballet). 1967. Alm, 1971. Dec DL-75069.

FILM

For Westminster Films: *Seven Criteria* (1967); *Bell Telephone Film* (1968); *Rye on the Rocks* (1968); *Life Lines* (1969); *You Take the Credit* (1969); *Your Money Matters* (1969); *A Place To....?* (1970); *Downstream* (1970); *Growing* (1970); *A Way Out* (1971); *Northwood* (1971); *Shebandowan* (1971); *The Shield Project* (1971).

Face Off (partial score). 1971. MCA, 1972. The Hub, Nepantha Blues, Reflection One & Two, Sweet and Tight. Film: George McCowan.

A Fan's Notes. 1972. Film: Eric Till.

Follow the North Star. 1972. Film: Eric Till.

Paperback Hero. 1973. Film: Peter Pearson.

RADIO DRAMA

Demirgian (1968) Text: John Sack; *The Dove, the Fish, the Cup, the Kiss, the Cross* (1971) Text: Gwen MacEwen; *Garden Variety* (1972) Text: Phyllis Gotlieb; *The Bacchic Women* (1973) Text: Euripides, John Pepper.

TELEVISION DRAMA

Silent Night, Lonely Night (1965; Alm, 1971) Text: Robert Anderson; *Talking to a Stranger* (1971) Text: John Hopkins.

ORCHESTRA (JAZZ)

Cambodian Suite (1959); *First Floor Fancy* (1960); *Midsummer* (1960); *Requiem for JFK* (1964; Alm, 1971); *Bonjour Canada Opening* (1967); *Humber Suite* (1973).

SOLO WITH ORCHESTRA/BAND (JAZZ)

The City. 1960. narr-sgr, orch. Text: John Reeves.

The Carnival. 1969. narr-sgr, flhn, orch. Text: Gwen MacEwen.

Lyric for Trumpet. 1970. Alm, 1971. tpt, concert band.

Celebration. 1972. pno, orch. Collab with Duke Ellington.

VOICE WITH INSTRUMENTAL ENSEMBLE (JAZZ)

Weary. 1958. vc, qnt. Text: Don Francks.

Elegy. 1964. vc, cb. Text: John Reeves.

Hear me Talkin' to Ya. 1964. narr, sgr, octet. Text: quotations from players and writers on jazz.

INSTRUMENTAL ENSEMBLE (JAZZ)

Pennies of Lennies (1953), tentet; *Dance No 1* (1955), qnt; *Invention No 1 & 2* (1955), qnt; *Opus for Quintet* (1956); *Opus for Saxophone and Trombone* (1956), octet; *Stratford Adventure* (1956), qnt (octet); *Tone Poem* (1956), octet; *Adagio* (1957);

Sextet (1957), pno, qnt; *Theme and Improvisation* (1957), qnt; *Four Moods* (1958), qnt & tentet; *Quintet* (1958), qnt & tentet; *Relax'n* (1958), qnt & tentet; *Blue Boy* (1959), qnt; *Blues on One Theme* (1959), qnt & tentet; *Just About Now* (1959), qnt & tentet; *Laredo* (1959), qnt; *Jazz Ballet* (1960), qnt; *Lee's Lament* (1960), qnt & tentet; *Myth of Marsyas* (1960), tentet; *Quintet Minus Five* (1960); *Solly's Saga* (1960); *Steve's Straight* (1960), qnt; *Meet Mr Nar* (1961), qnt; *Autumn Haze* (1962; Alm, 1971), septet; *Two Shades of Blue* (1962), sextet; *Impressions* (1963), tentet; *Ad Libitum* (1963), octet; *Walk'n Out* (1965; Alm, 1971), septet; *Waterfront, Night Thoughts* (1965; Alm, 1971), fl, pno. Dom s-69006.

BIBLIOGRAPHY

CrC(II).
'"The Duke" Plays Canadian Works on Latest Jazz LP Release', *CanCo.* No. 32, Sept. 1968 (12–42, 42–3).
Norris, John. 'Jazz Composing in Canada', *CanCo.* No. 4, Dec. 1965 (26–7).
'Ron Collier: A Serious Approach to Jazz', *CanCo.* No. 18, May 1967 (4–5, 44–5).

COULTHARD, JEAN (b. Vancouver, B.C., 10 Feb. 1908). She began her musical training in Vancouver, first with her mother, then with Frederick Chubb (theory) and Jan Cherniavsky (piano). She won a scholarship from the Vancouver Women's Musical Club in 1928 to study at the Royal College of Music in London, England, with Kathleen Long (piano), Ralph Vaughan Williams (composition), and R. O. Morris (theory), obtaining an LRSM diploma in composition. On returning to Vancouver in 1930 she became the head of the music departments of St Anthony's College and Queen's Hall School. She continued to broaden her compositional horizons through brief studies with Arthur Benjamin (1939), Bernard Wagenaar (1945 and 1949), and Gordon Jacob (1965–6), and through having her work appraised during lessons with Darius Milhaud (1942), Bela Bartok (1944), and Nadia Boulanger (1955). In 1947 she was appointed lecturer in music at the University of British Columbia and in 1957 became senior instructor.

In the composer's own words: 'I have written many kinds of musical compositions, from quite simple forms and combinations of instruments, to large forms of full orchestra, and in it all, my aim is simply to write music that is good. . . . I also think that a composer's musical language should be instructive, personal and natural to him, and not forced in any way as to specific style or technique of the moment. For if one becomes over-involved in the mechanics of one's thoughts, inspiration is easily lost.' (*Jean Coulthard*, pamphlet, BMI Canada.) On hearing Miss Coulthard's work, one is immediately aware of the influence of her teacher, Vaughan Williams. Her music is generally tonal with only occasional digressions into chromaticism or dissonant polyphony (*String Quartet No. 2*, 1953). She often chooses picturesque titles – *A Quiet Afternoon* (1964), *The Frisky Pony* (1964), *Legend of the Snows* (1970), *Song to the Sea* (1942), *Rider on the Sands* (1953) – descriptive of a style that involves tone-painting to a great extent, again a characteristic of English music of the early part of this century. She has an interest in writing for voice, both solo and choral, where perhaps her particular diatonic style is most at home. She has also written a large number of educational piano pieces.

Jean Coulthard has received many awards, commissions, and honours, including the McGill University Chamber Music Award (*Three Shakespeare Sonnets*, 1949), the Olympiad (London) Arts Section award (*Sonata for Oboe and Piano*, 1948), and CAPAC Awards (*Four Etudes for Piano*, 1945; *Sonata for Cello and Piano*, 1947). Besides a Canada Council grant to study with Dr Jacob, she was also awarded a Grant-in-Aid from the Committee for the Humanities of the Pacific Coast Branch of the American Learned Societies (1949) and a Royal Society Fellowship for one year of study in France (1955). In 1953 she was commissioned by the CBC to write music in honour of the coronation of Queen Elizabeth (*A Prayer for Elizabeth*, 1953). A song cycle for Maureen Forrester, *Spring Rhapsody* (1958), was commissioned by the Vancouver International Festival. The Vancouver Symphony Orchestra has commissioned two works: the *Violin Concerto* (1959) and the choral cantata *This Land*

(1967). She has also written works for several CBC Festivals, including *The Pines of Emily Carr* (1969) – based on the painter's journals and written for narrator, soprano, piano, string quartet, and timpani – and *The Birds of Lansdowne* (1972) for violin, cello, piano, and tape of bird songs. She is a member of the Canadian League of Composers and is affiliated with BMI Canada.

MUSICAL WORKS

STAGE

Excursion (ballet). 1940.

The Devil's Fanfare: Four Bizarre Dances (ballet). 1958. vln, pno, 3 dancers.

ORCHESTRA

Canadian Fantasy. 1939. Ber.

Excursion (arr). 1940.

Song to the Sea. 1942. CBC BR SM-215.

Symphony No 1. 1950–1.

Rider on the Sands. 1953.

Endymion. 1964.

STRING ORCHESTRA

Ballade (A Winter's Tale). 1940. Ber. CBC Album 2 PR 1081-2-3.

A Prayer for Elizabeth. 1953. Ber, 1961.

Music for Saint Cecilia. 1954 (rev 1969). str, org, elec tape.

Musenade (Meditation and Three Dances). 1961.

SOLOIST WITH ORCHESTRA

Love Song (from *Two Songs from the Haida Indians*) (arr by W M Miles). 1944. sop, orch. Text: trad. Trans: Constance L Skinner.

Music on a Quiet Song. 1946. fl, str.

Cycle of Three Love Songs (arr). 1948. vc, str. Text: L A McKay.

Night Wind (arr). 1952. low vc, orch. Text: Douglas LePan.

Spring Rhapsody (arr). 1958. alto, orch. Ber. Text: Bliss Carman, W E Marshall, L A McKay, Duncan Campbell Scott.

Concerto for Violin and Orchestra. 1955–9.

Fantasy. 1960–1. vln, pno, chamb orch. Ber.

The Bird of Dawning Singeth All Night Long. 1962. vln, str, hp.

Concerto for Piano and Orchestra. 1963 (rev 1967).

Symphonic Ode. 1965. vlc, orch.

Two Visionary Songs. 1970. sop, fl, str. Text: Harold Monro, Walter de la Mare.

CHOIR WITH ORCHESTRA

This Land (choral symphony). 1966–7. SATB, soli, orch, elec tape. Text: Canadian poets.

Pastorale Cantata. 1967. SATB, narr, brass qt, org. Text: Psalms of David.

CHOIR

Cradle Song (arr). 1928; Ber, 1960. SA, pno. RCA CC/CCS-1020. Text: Padraic Colum.

Threnody. 1935; Ber, 1961. SATB. Text: Robert Herrick.

Canadian Carol. 1941. SATB.

Quebec May. 1948. SATB, 2pno. Text: Earle Birney.

Sea Gulls. 1954; Jay, 1967. SA, pno. Text: E J Pratt.

Stopping By the Woods on a Snowy Evening. 1954. unis, pno. Text: Robert Frost.

More Lovely Grows the Earth. 1957. SATB. Text: Helena Coleman.

Soft Fall the February Snows. 1958. TTBB. RCA CC/CCS-1020. Text: Wilfred Campbell.

The Axe of the Pioneer. 1958. SATB. Text: Isabella Valancy Crawford.

The Signature of God. 1964; Ber, 1967. SA, pno. RCA CC/CCS-1020. Text: John Hall.

A Child's Evening Prayer. 1963–5; Jay, 1967. unis, pno. Text: Mary Landie Duncan.

Flower in the Crannied Wall. 1963–5; Jay, 1969. unis, pno. Text: Alfred Lord Tennyson.

Lullaby for Christmas. 1963–5; Jay, 1967. unis, pno. Text: trad.

On Easter. 1963–5; OUP, 1964. unis, pno. Text: Sharon Banigan.

The Star Shone Down. 1963–5; Jay, 1967. unis, pno. Text: Jean Coulthard.

Auguries of Innocence. 1965. SATB. RCA CC/CCS-1020. Text: William Blake.

Walk Softly in Springtime. 1967. unis, pno (org).

The White Lily Flower. 1967. unis, pno. Text: Jean Coulthard.

Romance. 1970. boys vcs, TB, pno.

VOICE(S)

Piping Down the Valleys Wild. 1917. sop, pno. Text: William Blake.

Cradle Song. 1927; Ber, 1960. mezz, pno. WST-17137. Text: Padraic Colum.

Two Songs of the Haida Indians. 1942. sop, pno. Text: trad. Trans: Constance L Skinner.

Three Songs. 1946. mezz, pno. Text: James Joyce.
Three Songs. 1946. low vc, pno. Text: L A McKay.
Two Songs. 1947. bar, pno. Text: James Joyce.
Gulf of Georgia. 1949.
Night Wind. 1951. sop, pno. Text: Douglas LePan.
Five Love Songs for Baritone. 1955. Text: Emily Dickinson.
Three Songs for Contralto and Piano. 1957. Text: Marjorie Pickthall.
Two French Songs for Baritone. 1957. Text: Emile Nelligan.
Spring Rhapsody. 1958; Ber, (#4) 1968. alto, pno. Text: Bliss Carman, W E Marshall, L A McKay, Duncan Campbell Scott.
Duets for Soprano and Tenor with Piano. 1960. Text: Robert Herrick.
To Blossoms. 1960. sop, alto, pno. Text: Robert Herrick.
Six Mediaeval Love Songs. 1962. bar, pno. Text: Latin. Trans: Helen Waddell.
Three Songs for Soprano and Piano. 1962. Text: Alfred Noyes, Christina Rossetti, Thomas Lowell Beddoes.
Five Irish Poems. 1958–64. alto, pno. Text: Boyle O'Reilly, Francis Ledwidge, Monk Gibbon.
First Song of Experience. 1968. vc, pno. Text: William Blake.
So Are You To My Thoughts As Food To Life. 1968. vc, pno. Text: William Shakespeare.
Ecstasy. 1969; Ber, 1969. vc, pno. Text: Duncan Campbell Scott.
Songs for Enchantment. 1972. bar, pno. Text: Percy B Shelley, Coventry Patmore, Richard Scrace, Bliss Carman, Anna Wickan.
Songs from the Distaff Muse. 1972. sop, alto, vlc. Text: Elizabeth I, Countess of Winchelsea, Katherine Mansfield, Sara Coleridge, Dorothy Farmiloe, Emily Dickinson.

VOICE(S) WITH INSTRUMENTAL ENSEMBLE

Three Shakespeare Sonnets. 1948. sop, str qt. Text: William Shakespeare.
Two Night Songs. 1960. bar, str qt, pno. Text: Harold Monro, Hilaire Belloc.
Two Visionary Songs. 1968. vc, fl, str qt. Text: Harold Monro, Walter de la Mare.
The Pines of Emily Carr. 1969. narr, alto, str qt, pno, timp. Text: Journals of Emily Carr arr by Dorothy Davies.
Three Shakespeare Sonnets (arr). 1970. sop, vlc solo, 8vlc. Text: William Shakespeare.
Two Songs for Midsummer. 1970. sop, vla, pno. Text: Percy B Shelley, Lascelles Abercrombie.

INSTRUMENTAL ENSEMBLE

Piano Quintet. 1932. str qt, pno.
Two Sonatinas for Violin and Piano. 1945.
Poem for Violin and Piano. 1947.
Sonata for Cello and Piano. 1947; Novl, 1970. Col ML-5942.
Sonata for Oboe and Piano. 1947.
String Quartet No 1. 1948.
Lively. 1948. str qt.
Duo Sonata for Violin and Piano. 1952; Ber, 1963.
String Quartet No 2 (Threnody). 1953 (rev 1969).
Piano Quartet (Lyric Suite: Sketches from a Mediaeval Town). 1957. str trio, pno.
The Bird of Dawning Singeth All Night Long (arr). 1962. vln solo, 9str, hp.
Sonata Rhapsody. 1962. vla, pno.
Sonata No 2 (Correspondence). 1964. vln, pno.
Day Dream. 1964. vln, pno.
The Frisky Pony. 1964. vln, pno.
Music on a Scottish Folk Song. 1964. vln, hp (guit).
On the March. 1964; Ber, 1965. vln, pno.
A Quiet Afternoon. 1964; Ber, 1965. vln, pno.
Ballade of the North (Theme and Variations). 1965–6. vln, pno.
Divertimento for Five Winds and Piano. 1968. ww qnt, pno.
Lyric Trio. 1968. vln, vlc, pno.
Lyric Sonatina for Bassoon and Piano. 1969; Wat, 1973.
When Music Sounds. 1970. vlc, pno.
Legend of the Snows. 1970–1. vln, vlc, pno.
Lyric Sonatina for Flute and Piano. 1971.
Octet (Twelve Essays on a Cantabile Theme). 1972. 2str qt.
The Birds of Lansdowne. 1972. vln, vlc, pno, elec tape.

PIANO

Ten Early Pieces. 1917–20 (rev 1960).
Four Variations on Good King Wenceslas. 1933–4.
Three Piano Pieces. 1938–9.
Four Etudes. 1945; Ber, 1952–4. Bar BC-

1837/2837 (No. 1 and No. 2), RCI-134 (No. 4).
Sonata for Piano. 1947–8; Ber, 1953.
Theme (Music on a Quiet Song) (arr). 1948.
Three Dances. 1950; FH, (#3), 1957.
Variations on B-A-C-H. 1951; Novl, 1972.
Four Pieces To Jane. 1952; Ber, 1955.
Three Dances for Piano. 1953–4; FH, (#1,2) 1955.
Rondo (White Caps). 1954; Ber, 1955.
Twelve Preludes for Piano. 1954–8; Ber, (#1–3) 1959.
Aegean Sketches. 1961; Ber, 1964.
12 Preludes. 1963–4.
Dare Devil. 1964; Ber, 1966.
Noon Siesta. 1964; Ber, 1966. CCM-1.
Requiem Piece (Threnody). 1968.
Sketches From the Western Woods. 1970.

BIBLIOGRAPHY

See B-B; B65,71; Bt; CrC(I); Esc; Gf; K; Wa.
Cluderay, Lawrence. 'Jean Coulthard', *MuSc.* Mar.-Apr. 1968.
'Jean Coulthard', pamphlet, BMI Canada Ltd, 1970.
Ridout, Godfrey. 'Two West Coast Composers', *Canadian Review of Music and Art.* Vol. III, no. 11–12, Dec.-Jan. 1945 (39–40).

D

DAUNAIS, (NOËL-FERDINAND) LIONEL (b. Montreal, Que., 31 Dec. 1902). He studied singing and solfège with Céline Marier and harmony and composition with Oscar O'Brien. In 1926 he won the Prix d'Europe for singing and went to Paris, staying four years. Auditioned by the conductor D.E. Inghelbrecht of the Concerts Pasdeloup, he was engaged as first baritone of the Algiers Opera, where he sang twenty-three roles. On his return to Montreal he made his début in 'Mireille' with the Canadian Operetta Society and took part in the Canadian Pacific Railway folk arts and crafts festival in Quebec in 1930. In 1932 he founded the Lyric Trio, for which he wrote many songs and several arrangements. In 1936, with Charles Goulet, he founded the Variétés Lyriques, a company that was active for twenty years. Daunais began to write songs for voice and piano in 1925; the first of these that he kept, *Les larmes,* was dated 1929. At this time he wrote some several hundred songs and tunes, usually humorous, often to his own text. Several won prizes and became quite the vogue, in Europe as well as Canada. Among them were song cycles, such as *Fantaisies sur tous les tons, Sept Epitaphes plaisantes,* and *Quatre Ballades de Paul Fort.* He is the composer also of choral works, religious and secular, and a work for string orchestra, *Propos piquants,* on a Canadian folk theme. Daunais was active as a stage director and teacher and adapted a number of operettas for radio and television. In the fall of 1971 the CBC devoted a series of broadcasts to his works. In 1972 the Canadian Music Council awarded him its medal for services to music in Canada. He is a member of CAPAC.

BIBLIOGRAPHY

See B-B; K; Lv; Wa.

DAVIES, VICTOR (b. Winnipeg, Man., 1 May 1939). He studied piano and violin until the age of thirteen, later attending music courses with Peggie Sampson and Ronald Gibson at the University of Manitoba. In 1964 he received his Bachelor of Music degree in composition from Indiana University. Works he composed while studying include *Three Songs on Poems by Walt Whitman* (1962), *Three Movements* (1964) for percussion and piano, *Variations 1* (1963) and *Variations 2* (1964) for orchestra, and *Sonata* (1964) for piano. He was organist and choirmaster at Wesley United Church and the Stoney Mountain Penitentiary in Manitoba (1959), musical director and composer for the Manitoba Theatre

Centre (1964), and conductor of the Greater Winnipeg Schools Junior Symphony, the River Heights School Orchestra, and the Churchill School Orchestra (1964–6). He composed, arranged, and conducted music for CBC radio and television (1966–70) and was musical director and conductor of the University of Manitoba Glee Club and Interfaith Harmony Theatre (1967–70). In the summer of 1969 he studied conducting with Pierre Boulez in Basel, Switzerland. He leads his own concert jazz ensemble. He has been commissioned to compose works for the Contemporary Dancers of Winnipeg (*The Colour of the Times*, 1966), for the commemoration of the one hundredth anniversary of St John's College (*The Egg that Laid the Eagle*, 1966), and for the Winnipeg Symphony Orchestra (*Celebrations for Orchestra*, 1969). In *The Beginning and End of the World* (1971), a multi-media theatre piece tailored for showing in a planetarium theatre, Davies employs orchestra, boys' choir, and electronic tape and jazz ensemble, using mainly 'third-stream' music. Also among his works for theatre are *Let Us Pay Tribute to Lord Gordon Gordon* (1970; libretto by Goldie Weatherhead) and *Reginald the Robot* (children's musical, 1970; libretto by the composer and Victor Cowie), as well as several incidental scores for theatre, radio, and television. He is a member of CAPAC.

DELA, MAURICE (b. Montreal, Que., 10 Sept. 1919). After obtaining his Bachelor of Arts degree from the University of Montreal (1940), Dela continued his studies there in Latin and literature (1941–2) and later in English at Notre Dame University in Indiana. He began his musical training with lessons on the organ and in harmony with Raoul Paquet (1940–3). In 1944 he began studies in composition with Claude CHAMPAGNE, and Sévérin Moisse (harmony and counterpoint) and J.-J. GAGNIER (orchestration) at the Conservatoire, later studying orchestration with Leo Sowerby in Chicago. In 1947 he received a CAPAC award for *Ballade* (1945) and for *Petite Suite Maritime* (1947), which was commissioned by the CBC. He was a prize winner in the song-composition contest sponsored by the CBC in 1950 (*Ronde*, 1949) and also won the Prix du Tricentenaire of Laval University in 1952 (*Les Fleurs de Glais*, 1951). In 1960 he was awarded first prize in the composition competition of CKVL radio station (*Adagio pour orchestre à cordes*, 1956) and first prize in the chamber music competition organized by the Canadian Federation of Music Teachers' Associations (*Quatuor à cordes*, 1956). Dela's early music is tonal; later works are more dissonant and more intense, with some of the rhythmic complexity characteristic of such composers as Milhaud and Honegger. Dela has received commissions from the Montreal Symphony Orchestra (*Projections*, 1967) and from the CBC, Vancouver (*Symphony No. 2 for chamber orchestra*, 1972). He is organist at the Church of Notre Dame des Sept-Douleurs in Verdun, Que., and is also a free-lance arranger and composer for radio and television in Montreal. Since 1965 he has been in charge of music teaching for the Chambly County School Board. He is a member of the Canadian League of Composers and is affiliated with BMI Canada.

MUSICAL WORKS

INSTRUMENTAL

7 works for orch, including: *Scherzo* (1953) Ber CBC BR SM-132; *Berceuse* (1954) Ber; *Deux Esquisses pour orchestre* (1962); *Projection* (1966); *Symphonie No 1* (1968); *Symphonie No 2 (Concertante)* (1972).

3 works for string orch, including: *Dans tous les Cantons!* (1949) Ber CTL Ster 477-65137; *Adagio* (1956) CTL Ster 477-65137.

6 works for soloists and orch, including: *Ballade* (1945) pno, orch Ber; *Concerto for Piano and Orchestra* (1946, rev 1950); *Concertino for Piano and Orchestra* (1961–2); *Le Chat, la Bélette et le petit Lapin* (1965) narr, orch Text: after fable by Lafontaine.

9 works for instrumental ensemble, including: *Petite Suite Maritime* (1946) Ber; *Suite pour Flûte, Cello et Piano* (1953–4); *2 String Quartets* (1960 & 1963); *Divertissement* (1962) brass qnt; *Dix Miniatures* (1968) 3rec Ber 1968; *Vingt Duos Faciles* (1969) Ber 1970.

3 works for piano solo: *Hommage* (1950) Ber 1950; *La Vieille Capitale* (1953) Ber 1953; *Deux Impromptus* (1964) Ber 1964.

CHORAL

4 works for choir: *La Belle Hirondelle*

(1957) SATB, orch Ber; *Dessus la Fougère* (1957) SATB, orch Ber; *Le Vaisseau d'or* (1967) SATB Text: Emile Nelligan; *Le Paysage* (1972) SATB Text: Gilles Vigneault.

VOCAL

7 works for vc and pno, including: *XAMI* (1945) Arch 1945; *Berceuse Béarnaise Passe-Temps* (1947) WST Ster 17137; *Ronde* (1949) Ber 1949 Text: Victor Hugo; *Spleen* (1949) Ber 1950 Text: Paul Verlaine; *La Lettre* (1958) Ber 1958.

BIBLIOGRAPHY

See B-B; Bec57; Bt; Esc; K; Lv.

DELAMONT, GORDON (b. Moose Jaw, Sask., 27 Oct. 1918). He studied trumpet and played in the Kitsilano Boys' Band of Vancouver, which his father conducted. He moved to Toronto in 1937 and played trumpet on CBC radio and in several dance orchestras. From 1945 to 1959 he led his own dance band and arranged music for it. After a short period in New York, in 1949 he opened his own music studio in Toronto where he teaches harmony, composition, and arranging. His many pupils have included Norman SYMONDS, Ron COLLIER, Gustav CIAMAGA, Lawrence House, Paul Hoffert, and Saul Chapman. Delamont concentrates on jazz not only as a performer and teacher but also as a composer. *Collage No. 3* (1966) uses tonal material in the cool, progressive jazz style of the 1950s and 1960s. In *Song and Dance* (1966) and *Ontario Suite* (1965), a commission from the Ontario Government for Expo 67, he enlarged the same kind of material by employing polytonal counterpoint.

For centennial year (1967) Delamont received a commission from Ten Centuries Concerts (*Centum*, 1966). The CBC has also commissioned works from him for television and concert series. He is a member of CAPAC.

MUSICAL WORKS

INSTRUMENTAL ENSEMBLE(S)

Allegro and Blues. 1964. stage band.

Ontario Suite. 1965; Kendor. stage band and concert band.

Centum. 1966; Kendor. stage band.

Song and Dance. 1969. stage band. Dec DL 75069.

Collage No 3. 1969. stage band. Dec DL 75069.

Three Entertainments for Saxophone Quartet. 1970; Kendor.

Moderato and Blues for Brass Quintet. 1972; Kendor.

BIBLIOGRAPHY

Bec70; CrC(II).

' "The Duke" Plays Canadian Works on Latest Jazz LP Release', *CanCo*. No. 32, Sept. 1968 (12–13, 42–3).

'Jazz in Concert', *MAC*. Feb. 1963 (18–21).

Wilkinson, Bryan. 'Gordon Delamont's Suite Unique Canadian Composition', *CanCo*. No. 15, Feb. 1967 (16–17).

LITERARY WORKS

BOOKS

Delamont, G. *Modern Arranging Techniques*. New York: Kendor Music, 1965.

Delamont, G. *Modern Harmonic Techniques* (2 vols). New York: Kendor Music, 1965.

ARTICLES

'Is it Music?', *Saturday Night*. Vol. LXV, Apr. 25, 1950 (30–1).

'Jazz at Stratford', *CMJ*. Vol. II, No. 1, 1957–8 (39).

'My Most Successful Work: "Ontario Suite" ', *CanCo*. No. 31, July-Aug. 1968 (18–19, 38–9).

'Remarkable Changes Evident in Jazz Composition', *CanCo*. No. 12, Nov. 1966 (3, 12–13, 43).

DETWEILER, ALAN (b. Toronto, Ont., 15 June 1926). He studied composition with Godfrey RIDOUT and Barbara PENTLAND (1945–6), winning several CAPAC prizes. In 1950 he received his Bachelor of Arts degree in philosophy from the University of Toronto and in 1952 his Bachelor of Literature degree from Trinity College, Dublin, for a thesis on the philosophies of Leibniz and Whitehead. On a grant from the Swedish government he spent 1952 in Stockholm doing research on the music of Franz Berwald. He studied composition with Lennox Berkeley and Howard Ferguson in London, where he completed his Ph.D. requirements in musical aesthetics at London University (1956). Detweiler calls on pentatonic or modal material, imparting to his music a folk-like character. He is particularly interested in writing for children, for example, *Beware of the Wolf* (1964), and his children's entertainments have been performed in schools and churches in Britain and broadcast by the BBC, the CBC, and the Australian Broadcasting Commission, as well as in Germany, France, Nigeria, Hong Kong, the United States, and other countries. His church opera *David and Goliath* was performed in Southwark Cathedral (1969) and, in 1970, in Ely Cathedral, where it was filmed by the Columbia Broadcasting System (USA) and broadcast on the CBS television network. He is a member of the Performing Right Society.

BIBLIOGRAPHY

'A Canadian Composer in London', *CanCo.* No. 44, Nov. 1969 (18–20).

LITERARY WORKS

ARTICLES

'Musical Criticism: Its Function and Limitations', *CMJ.* Vol. III, no. 4, 1958–9 (24).

DOLIN, SAMUEL (b. Montreal, Que., 22 Aug. 1917). He began his musical training in Montreal with Tania and Vladimir Elgart, Stanley Gardiner, and Vladimir Emenitov (piano and theory). In 1936 he began studying at the Toronto Conservatory and later at the Faculty of Music, University of Toronto, receiving his Bachelor of Music degree in 1942. From 1942 to 1945 he was music supervisor of schools in Durham and Northumberland, Ont., and visiting music master of Trinity College School, Port Hope, Ont. In 1945 he joined the teaching staff of the Royal Conservatory of Music in Toronto, continuing his own studies in piano with Reginald Godden and Weldon Kilburn and, in composition, with John WEINZWEIG. He has also studied with E. Robert Schmitz and Ernst Krenek. In 1958 he was awarded his Doctor of Music degree from the University of Toronto.

Dolin's style, as represented by *Serenade for Strings* (1951), is highly chromatic but has fairly traditional thematic development with extensive use of ostinato figures. In his *Symphony No. 2* (1957) Dolin uses a chromatic language again in a filmscore-like style with thematic development. He often employs lyrical diatonic themes in a cacophonous texture. A more recent work, *Concerto Grosso* (1971) for accordion, five percussionists, and computer, was commissioned by the CBC and performed extensively. Dolin has complete control over his compositional technique and uses instrumental colour to good effect, even though his language is on the whole fairly traditional. His output is not extensive, probably owing to his busy occupation as a teacher. He encourages his students to compose and has arranged public concerts of their works, from small chamber-music recitals to large-scale orchestral concerts. Among his former students are Ann SOUTHAM, Brian CHERNEY, and Steven GELLMAN.

In 1967 Dolin received commissions from the Toronto Repertory Ensemble (*Fantasy for Piano and Chamber Orchestra*) and from the Stratford Music Festival (*Casino*). In 1971, under the auspices of the Canada Council, he received a commission from the Royal Conservatory of Music of Toronto for *Marchbankantata.* From the CBC he received two commissions in 1972, *Mass* (CBC television) and *Drakkar* (CBC radio). He is a founding member and has served as president (1969–73) of the Canadian League of Composers and is chairman of the Canadian section of the ISCM and vice-president of the ISCM (1972–). He is affiliated with BMI Canada.

MUSICAL WORKS

DRAMATIC

Casino (Greed) (opera). 1966–7. Libretto: Ronald Hambleton.

Machina (film). 1970. Film: Choklakian-Schmidt.

The Meeting Point (television). 1971. 6vcs, synth, org. Film: Leo Rampen. Text: Scriptures.

Missionaries (radio drama). 1971. Text: Timothy Findlay.

Drakkar. 1972. mezz, 2bar, narr, 2dancers, chamb ens, 2synth, slides. Text: Samuel & Leslie Dolin.

ORCHESTRA

Sinfonietta. 1950. Ber.

Symphony 'Elk Falls'. 1956.

Symphony No. 2. 1957. Ber.

STRING ORCHESTRA

Serenade for Strings. 1951. Ber.

Sonata for String Orchestra. 1962.

SOLOIST WITH ORCHESTRA
Isometric Variables. 1957. bsn, str. Ber.
Fantasy for Piano and Chamber Orchestra. 1967. Ber.

CHOIR
The Hills of Hebron. 1954. SATB, pno. Text: Louis Model.

VOICE(S)
Three Songs. 1951. Text: Louis Model.
Chloris. 1951; Ber, 1961. Text: William Strode.
Julia. 1951. Text: Robert Herrick.
Ozymandias. 1951. Text: Percy Bysshe Shelley.
Mass. 1972. 6vcs, congregation, org. Text: trad.

VOICES WITH INSTRUMENTAL ENSEMBLE
Marchbankantata. 1971. bar, SATB, pno, synth. Text: Robertson Davies.

INSTRUMENTAL ENSEMBLE
Sonatina for Violin and Piano. 1954.
Sonata for Violin and Piano. 1960; Ber, 1968.
Portrait for String Quartet. 1961.
Barcarolle. 1962. vln, pno.
Little Sombrero. 1964. vln, pno. Ber.
Concerto Grosso; 'Georgian Bay'. 1970. perc, accord, elec tape.

PIANO
Four Miniatures. 1949.
Three Piano Preludes. 1949.
Sonata. 1950.
Little Suite. 1954; FH (Old Dance), 1955.
Dance of the Satellites. 1958.
Nocturne on White Note Triads. 1958.
Little Toccata. 1959; Ber, 1961.
Sonatina. 1959; Ber, 1960. CCM-2.
Slightly Square Round Dance. 1966. Ber.
Variation for Two Pianos. 1967.
If. 1972; Wat, 1972.

INSTRUMENTAL SOLO
Sonata. 1970; Wat, 1972. accord.

BIBLIOGRAPHY

See B-B; CrC(II); K.
'Samuel Dolin', pamphlet, BMI Canada Ltd, 1972.

LITERARY WORKS

ARTICLES
'Canada Returns to Play its Part in ISCM Festivals', *MuSc.* No. 262, Nov.-Dec. 1971 (4).
'1971 Festival of the ISCM in London', *CMB.* Vol. III, Autumn-Winter 1971 (131–4).

DOUGLAS, WILLIAM (b. London, Ont., 7 Nov. 1944). He received a Bachelor of Music degree from the University of Toronto (1966), where he studied bassoon with Nicholas Kilburn. In 1966 a Woodrow Wilson Fellowship enabled him to study with Robert Bloom (bassoon) and Mel Powell (composition) at Yale University, where he obtained his Master of Music (1968) and Master of Musical Arts (1969) degrees. In 1969 he received the Margaret M. Grant Award for the best student composition at Tanglewood (*String Quartet*, 1968). On a Canada Council Bursary he studied composition privately in London, England, with Cornelius Cardew (1969–70). He has been bassoonist with the Toronto Symphony (1964–5), the National Ballet Orchestra (1966–7), and principal bassoonist with the New Haven Symphony Orchestra (1968–9). Since 1970 he has been instructor in bassoon, piano, composition and improvisation at the California Institute of the Arts. He is a member of CAPAC.

MUSICAL WORKS

INSTRUMENTAL ENSEMBLE
Improvisations I. bsn, vlc.
Improvisations II. 1968. fl, pno.
String Quartet. 1968.
Improvisations III. 1969. cl, pno. Orion ORS 73125 RCI-358.
Intermezzo. 1969. ob, pno.
Vajra. 1972. any comb. Orion ORS 73125.
Xaruna. 1972. any comb.
Flower. 1973. any comb.
It's Here. 1973. any comb.
Playtime. 1973. any comb.
Warrior. 1973. any comb.

PIANO
Celebration. 1970.
Ten Improvisation Etudes. 1972.

E

ECKHARDT-GRAMATTÉ, S. C. (SOPHIE-CARMEN) (b. Moscow, USSR, 6 Jan. 1902; d. Stuttgart, Germany, 2 Dec. 1974). She received her early training in piano from her mother, a pupil of Anton Rubinstein, and continued piano as well as violin studies at the Conservatoire in Paris. At the age of eleven she made a double début on the violin and piano and by 1919 was performing concerti on both instruments. Living in Berlin from 1914, she pursued her violin studies with Bronislaw Huberman and for some time with Jacques Thibaud. In the early twenties she toured with Edwin Fischer as a two-piano team. In 1920 she married the painter Walter Gramatté and they lived from 1924 in Barcelona, Spain. In 1929, after the death of Gramatté, she embarked on an American tour, playing her own works with Stokowski (Philadelphia) and Stock (Chicago). In 1934 she returned to Germany and married the art historian Ferdinand Eckhardt. From 1936–42 she studied with Max Trapp at the Preussische Akademie in Berlin, giving up her concert career and turning almost exclusively to composition. In 1939 she moved with her husband to his native Vienna.

Eckhardt-Gramatté created a dense, aggressive style that was much closer to and dependent on late romanticism than on twentieth-century techniques. Her use of dissonance was a logical development from post-Wagnerianism, although it never reached the emotional atonality of the Viennese masters (Schoenberg, Berg, and Webern). Nevertheless one detects some characteristics, especially in the style of her early works, that hint at the expressionism of such composers as Kurt Weill and Hanns Eisler. Her *Suite VI* for solo piano consists of three pieces spanning three decades (1928–52), from which it is possible to obtain a capsule view of her style. All three pieces are similar in having a relentless forward drive with few breathing spaces and with a high degree of emotional intensity and excitement. Her *Concertino* (1947) is tonal with passages of dissonance suggesting music being twisted or deformed, a characteristic of expressionism. In *Concerto for Orchestra* (1953–4), a twelve-tone opening theme is used, although not the twelve-tone technique itself; occasionally touching on tonality, dissonance is treated more freely than in previous works. In *Trio* (1967) the composer returned to a less dissonant and more lyrical style, but still with density and aggressiveness. Her *Suite IV for Violin Solo* (1968) is a virtuoso piece exploiting the violin technique with as much vigour as piano technique is exploited in *Suite VI*.

Eckhardt-Gramatté won composition prizes from the Musikverein in Vienna (1938 and 1939), the Australian Section of the International Society for Contemporary Music (1951), and the Genossenschaft deutscher und oesterreichischer Kuenstlerinnen (GEDOK) in 1961 and 1966. Her *Triple Concerto* (1950) was awarded the Austrian State Prize. She received commissions from the Vienna Music Academy (*Bassoon Concerto*, 1949) and the Austrian Section of the ISCM (*Piano Suite No. 5*, 1951; *Second Violin Concerto*, 1952).

After settling in Winnipeg (1954), where her husband was appointed director of the Winnipeg Art Gallery, Eckhardt-Gramatté composed works on commission for such organizations as the Saskatoon Festival (*Cello-Piano Duo*, 1959), the CBC (*Woodwind Quintet*, 1963), and the Chamber Music Group of the University of Manitoba (*Third String Quartet*, 1964). In 1967 she received four Centennial commissions: *Piano Trio* for the Marta Hidy Trio, *Symphony-Concerto for Piano and Orchestra* for the CBC, *Suite for Flute, Clarinet and Bassoon* for the School of Music, University of Manitoba, and *Nonet* for the University of Saskatchewan (Regina) Chamber Players. The Winnipeg Symphony Orchestra commissioned her *Symphony No. 2* (called 'Manitoba') for the Provincial Centennial (1970). Also in 1970 she received an honorary doctorate in music from the University of Brandon and the same year received the title of professor from the

Minister of Education, Vienna, Austria. She died as a result of a street accident while visiting Europe with her husband.

She was a member of several musical organizations, including the Oesterreichische Gesellschaft für zeitgenössische Musik, the Canadian League of Composers, and CAPAC.

MUSICAL WORKS

ORCHESTRA

Ziganka (ballet suite). 1920.
Symphonie in C. 1939.
Capriccio Concertante. 1940.
Concertino for Strings. 1947.
Concerto for Orchestra. 1953–4.
Symphony No 2 ('Manitoba'). 1969–70.

SOLOIST(S) WITH ORCHESTRA

Concerto for Piano and Orchestra No 1. 1925.
Concerto for Piano and Orchestra No 2. 1946.
Tripel-Konzert. 1949; UE, 1952. tpt, cl, bsn, str, timp.
Markantes Stück. 1950. 2pno, orch.
Concerto for Bassoon and Orchestra. 1950.
Concerto for Violin, Concertante of Wind Instruments and Orchestra. 1950–1.
Concerto for Violin and Orchestra No 2. 1952.
Symphonie-Concerto for Piano and Orchestra. 1966–7. RCA LSC-3175.

CHOIR WITH SEVERAL INSTRUMENTS

4 Christmas Songs. 1953.

INSTRUMENTAL ENSEMBLE

4 Paganini Caprices with piano accomp (arr). 1922; NSB, 1922. vln, pno.
Berceuse and Presto in old Style. 1923. fl, pno.
String Quartet No 1 in C-sharp Minor. 1938.
String Quartet No 2 ('Hainburger'). 1943.
Duo for 2 Violins No 1. 1944.
Duo for 2 Violins No 2. 1944; ÖBV 1949.
Duo for Viola and Cello. 1944.
Duo for 2 Celli. 1944.
Wind Quartet. 1946.
Nicolas Trio. 1947. vln, vla, vlc.
Ruck-Ruck Sonata. 1947 (rev 1962). cl, pno.
Trio for Winds. 1947. ob, cl, bsn.
Triotino. 1947. vln, vla, vlc.
Duo Concertante. 1956. fl, vln.
Duo Concertante. 1959. vlc, pno. RCA CC/CCS-1018.
Woodwind Quintet. 1962–3.
String Quartet No 3. 1962–4.
Nonet. 1966. str qt, ww qnt.
Trio. 1967. vln, vlc, pno.
Woodwind Trio. 1967. fl, cl, bsn.
Concerto for Gamba and Harpsichord. 1971.
Fanfare for 8 Brass Instruments. 1971.

PIANO

Danse de Nègre. 1922; NSB, 1924.
Suite No 1 (Sonata). 1923; NSB, 1924.
Sonata No 2 (Biskaya Sonate). 1923–4.
Suite No 3. 1925.
Suite No 4. 1928.
6 Caprices. 1934–6.
Passacaglia and Fugue. 1937. 2pno.
Markantes Stück. 1946–50. 2pno.
Klavierstück (Sonate Nr 5). 1950.
3 Klavierstücke (Suite VI). 1928–51. RCA CC/CCS-1018.
Some piano arrangements of works by Paganini & Chopin.

INSTRUMENTAL SOLO

Suite for Violin Solo No 1 ('Sonata I'). 1922; NSB, 1924.
Suite for Violin Solo No 2 ('Partita II'). 1922; NSB, 1924.
Suite for Violin Solo No 3 ('Partita III, Mallorca'). 1924; MEC, 1929.
Concerto for Violin Solo. 1925. Odeon O-6973-6.
10 Caprices for Violin Solo. 1924–34; NSB, 1925.
Suite for Violin Solo No 4 ('Pacific'). 1968.

BIBLIOGRAPHY

See B-B; 65,71; CrC(1); Esc; T; Wa.
Anderson, Jeffrey. 'Winnipeg Composer Completes Four Centennial Commissions', *CanCo.* No. 25, Jan. 1968 (10).
'Eckhardt-Gramatté', *CanCo.* No. 42, Sept. 1969 (9–11).
'Manitoba Composers: a Collective Voice', *CanCo.* No. 52, Sept. 1970 (16, 18).
Sanguine, Jean. 'Sophie Carmen Eckhardt-Gramatté', *Chatelaine.* Sept. 1967 (43).
'Sophie Carmen Eckhardt-Gramatté – a portrait', *Mu.* No. 23, Oct. 1969 (8–9).
Stone, Kurt. 'Review of Records', *MQ.* Vol. LIII, no. 3, July 1967 (440–52). (Duo concertante for cello and piano, 1959; Suite No. 6).

EGGLESTON, ANNE (b. Ottawa, Ont., 6 Sept. 1934). She studied piano and composition with Robert FLEMING in Ottawa and later, from 1953, at the Royal Conservatory in Toronto with Pierre Souvairan (piano), Oskar MORAWETZ, Godfrey RIDOUT, and John WEINZWEIG (composition). In 1956 she received the Artist Diploma from the University of Toronto and the following year entered the Eastman School of Music in Rochester, N.Y., where she studied with Emily Davis, Orazio Frugoni (piano), and Bernard Rogers (composition), receiving her Master of Music degree in 1958.

Awards she has won include the Arthur Comeau scholarship for composition, the Canada Foundation Trophy of the Ottawa Music Festival, and two CAPAC prizes in composition (1953 and 1954). Her *String Quartet* (1956–7) and *Sonatine for Piano* (1964) were prize winners in the first Original Music Competition of CBC Ottawa radio (1964–5). She has received commissions from CAMMAC (*Three Songs: Night on the Ottawa River, Johnny, Song to the Four Seasons*, 1967, and *Five French Canadian Folk Songs*, arranged for SAT recorders, 1967), and from the Merivale High School Concert Band, Ottawa (*Suryanamaskar*, 1972). Since 1958 she has been teaching piano, theory, and composition privately in Ottawa. This has resulted in a number of works for young performers, including *On Citadel Hill* (1964, commissioned by the Canadian Music Centre) and *Sketches of Ottawa* (1962) for piano solo. Her compositions, embodying traditional forms, characteristically employ polytonal or modal harmonies.

Eggleston has also composed a folk opera, *The Wood Carver's Wife* (1961); several orchestral pieces, including *Three Pieces for Orchestra* (1956), *Fanfare for Orchestra* (1966), *Autumnal Clouds* (1958) for baritone and orchestra, and *Variations on a Theme by Bela Bartok* (1972) for violin and string orchestra; as well as many vocal works (for example, *To the Lute Player,* 1952; *Songs from Deep Wood,* 1955; *Five Lullabies of Eugene Fields,* 1960); and several chamber works, including *Rhapsody* (1954) for violin and piano, *Piano Quartet* (1955), and *Antique Suite* (1967) for two alto recorders and piano. She is a member of CAMMAC, the Musical Arts Club of Ottawa, the Canadian League of Composers, and CAPAC.

EVANGELISTA, JOSÉ (b. Valencia, Spain, 5 Aug. 1943). He had his early and professional musical training at the Conservatorio Superior de Música de Valencia from 1951 to 1967, when he received diplomas in harmony and composition. He also studied at the Faculty of Sciences, University of Valencia, from 1961 to 1967, and was awarded his Licence ès Sciences, having majored in physics. During the early 1960s he organized contemporary music events at the University of Valencia (1969–71) and was in charge of music at the Colegio Mayor Universitario 'Aquinas' in Madrid (1962–3); in 1967 he organized a series of lectures on music history for the Colegio Mayor Universitario 'San Juan de Ribera' in Valencia. He came to Canada in January 1969 and studied at the Faculty of Music, University of Montreal, from 1970 to 1973, when he was awarded a Master's degree in composition. Since 1970 he has been organizer of the student-composer concerts at the University of Montreal where, since 1972, he has also taught musical analysis.

Evangelista's acknowledged output includes some nine works for piano, including *Suite de cuatro piezas* (1961), *Sonata en un movimiento* (1964), and *Sonata en do* (1966–9); several works for voice, including settings of Spanish folk songs and *Tres recuerdos del cielo* (for voice and piano, 1968); a few chamber works, including a *Sonatine pour flûte et piano* (1971) and *Danses* for two pianos (1971). Of his four orchestral works, two are for solo voice and orchestra (one being *Deux poèmes d'Anne Hébert*, 1972–4, for strings, piano, harp and percussion), one is for choir and orchestra, and the fourth, *Danses* (1971), is for full orchestra.

LITERARY WORKS

'Une Analyse de "Madrigal III" de Bruce Mather', *CMB*. Vol. VI, Spring 1973 (81–109).

F

FIALA, GEORGE (b. Kiev, Ukraine, 31 Mar. 1922). He received his early musical training from K. Mikhailoff (piano) at the music school for gifted children in Kiev. In 1939 he entered the Tchaikovsky State Conservatory in Kiev where he studied with Lev Revutsky, Vladimir Groudin, Boris Liatoshinsky, and Andrew Olkhovsky. From 1942 to 1945 he studied with Hansmaria Dombrowski (composition) and Wilhelm Furtwängler (conducting) at the Akademische Hochschule für Musik in Berlin. He won a scholarship from the Vatican in 1946 and continued his composition and conducting studies with Leon Jongen at the Conservatoire Royal de Musique in Brussels. As a member of the Seminaire des Arts in Brussels, under the direction of the Belgian composer André Souris, Fiala participated in various musical events as composer, pianist, and conductor. Since his arrival in Montreal in 1949 he has been active as organist, pianist, teacher, and as music producer with the CBC's International Service. Fiala's *Chamber Music for Five Woodwind Instruments* (1948) is neoclassical and polytonal with canonic counterpoint alternating with simple melody and ostinato accompaniment. This music is light, reminiscent of the film scores of Eldon Rathburn. The same can be said of *Concertino for Piano, Trumpet, Timpani and Strings* (1950), although here the mood is heavier. In two later works (*Divertimento Concertante,* 1965; and *Sinfonietta Concertata,* 1971), Fiala's style is more dissonant, chromatic, and explosive.

Fiala is a member of the Canadian League of Composers and is affiliated with BMI Canada.

MUSICAL WORKS

INSTRUMENTAL

10 works for orchestra, including: *Autumn Music* (1949); *Orchestra Music #1* (1950); *Symphony in E minor* (1950); *Concertino,* Op 2 (1950) pno, tpt, timp, str Ber RCI-184; *Shadows of our Forgotten Ancestors* (1962); *Eulogy: 'In Memoriam of President J F Kennedy'* (1965); *Montreal* (1969) Ber 1969 RCI-291; *Ouverture Burlesque* (1972); *Symphony No 4 (Ukrainian)* (1973).

11 works for soloist and orchestra, including: *Suite Concertante* (1956) ob, str; *Introduction and Fugato* (1961) EH, str; *Capriccio for Piano and Orchestra* (1962); *Divertimento Concertante* (1965) vln, orch; *Serenade Concertante* (1968) vln, str; *Musique Concertante* (1968) pno, orch; *Sinfonietta Concertata* (1971) free-bass accord, hpschd, str Wat; *Concerto for Violin and Orchestra* (1973).

27 works for chamber ensemble, including: *Quartet No 2 for Saxophones* (1961) Ber 1970 RCA LSC-3141; *Cantilena and Rondo,* Op 3 (1963) sop rec, pno Ber 1963; *Pastorale and Allegretto,* Op 4 (1963) rec qt Ber 1963; *Wallaby's Lullaby,* Op 5 (1964) vln, pno Ber 1966; *Sonata for Cello and Piano* (1969); *Sonata for Violin and Piano* (1969); *Musique à Quatre* (1972) str qt; *Concertino Canadese* (1972) 4hp; *Sonata Breve* (1972) cl, hp.

16 works for piano solo, including: *Australian Suite* (1963) Ber CCM-2; *Ten Postludes,* Op 7 (1947, rev 1968) Wat 1969 CCM-2; *Trois Bagatelles,* Op 6 (1968) GVT 1968; *Sonate pour deux pianos* (1970).

CHORAL

Canadian Credo. 1966. SATB, orch.

VOCAL

Four Russian Poems. 1968. med vc, pno. Wat, 1972.

Five Ukrainian Songs. 1973. sop, orch.

BIBLIOGRAPHY

See B-B; B65,71; Bt; Lv.

'George Fiala', pamphlet, BMI Canada Ltd, 1970.

Levitan, Samuel. 'George Fiala: Montreal', *CMB.* Vol. II, Spring-Summer 1971 (177–8).

FLEMING, ROBERT (b. Prince Albert, Sask., 27 May 1921). In 1937 Fleming went to London, England, to study with Arthur Benjamin (piano), Percy Buck, Basil Alchin, and Herbert Howells at the Royal College of Music, where he won a piano scholarship for 1938–9. In 1939 he returned to Saskatchewan, where he continued piano studies with Lyell Gustin. In 1941 he won a Canadian Performing Right Society scholarship for a year's study at the Toronto Conservatory of Music, where his teachers included Healey WILLAN (composition), Norman Wilks (piano), Ettore Mazzoleni (conducting), and Frederick Silvester (organ). Fleming won a second CPRS scholarship for *Rondo for Two Pianos* in 1942, deferred until 1945, when he again studied at the Toronto Conservatory with Willan, Mazzoleni, and John Weatherseed (organ). In 1946 he joined the National Film Board in Ottawa (later in Montreal) as composer and conductor and was its musical director from 1958 to 1970. In 1959 he was appointed organist and choirmaster of St George's Anglican Church in Ste-Anne de Bellevue, a suburb of Montreal. In 1970 he moved to Ottawa again to join the Department of Music, Carleton University, and in 1972 was appointed organist and choirmaster of St Matthias Church.

Fleming is one of Canada's most prolific composers. His style is lyrical, incorporating dissonant tonality with emphasis on melodic writing (for example, *Recollections*, 1954; *Ballet Introduction*, 1961). Another trait is the use of ostinato accompaniment, as seen in *Three Contrasts* (1964) for school orchestra, a work that is more ethereal than the earlier pieces, particularly in sections of the slow movements, but that is still dominated by the melodic line. In *The Confession Stone* (1966), for low voice and piano, an ostinato figure is again used to accompany the modal line in the more lyrical sections, which alternate with recitative-like sections; open fifths, moving in contrary motion in the accompaniment, and dissonance, on the words 'Cold and icy is my bed', are used in setting mood. His choral writing, exemplified by *Heirs Through Hope* (1968), is reminiscent of Healey Willan in the use of modal material, typical of much early twentieth-century choral music.

In 1967 Fleming wrote three works for the puppeteers Dora and Leo Velleman: *Indian Legend*, *Square-dance* based on '*The Maple Leaf Forever*', and *Laurentian Parade*. He has received commissions from the Royal Winnipeg Ballet (*Shadow on the Prairie*, 1955), the Cosmopolitan Club for the Saskatoon Symphony Orchestra (*Summer Suite*, 1957), the Montreal Brass Quintet (*Three Miniatures*, 1962), the Baroque Trio of Montreal (*Go for Baroque*, 1963), Expo 67 (*Variations on a Timeless Theme* for organ, 1966), the Lakeshore Music Society of Ste-Anne de Bellevue (*String Quartet*, 1970), Deer Park United Church, Toronto (*Divertimento* for organ, oboes, and strings, 1970), and the National Arts Centre Orchestra (*Hexad*, 1972). He is a member of the Canadian League of Composers and of CAPAC.

MUSICAL WORKS

STAGE

Chapter 13 (ballet). 1950.
Shadow on the Prairie (ballet). 1952.
Romance (arr of Glazunov) (ballet). 1954. 2pno.
Why there are no Frogs on the Queen Charlotte Islands (puppet play). 1967. fl, ob, bsn, perc, pno.
Laurentian Parade (puppet play). 1967. 2 pno.
Square-dance ('The Maple Leaf Forever') (puppet play). 1967. vln, pno.
Over 250 films for NFB and others.

ORCHESTRA

Around the House Suite (1942); *Rondo* (arr) (1942); *Red River Country* (1953); *Ballet Suite (Shadow on the Prairie)* (1952); *Sea-Board Sketches* (1953); *Mestizo* (1954); *Summer Suite* (1957); *Plantation Song* (1958); *Going Going Gone* (1958); *Ragamuffin Band* (1958); *Autumn Day* (1958); *Regality* (1958); *Days of Grace* (1958); *Period Piece* (arr) (1958); *Something for Margot* (arr) (1958); *Black Mood* (1959); *Sparkler* (1959); *Solemn Occasion* (1959); *Ballet Introduction* (1960) Col ML-6163/MS-6763; *In Sorrow* (1961); *Prairie Song* (1961); *Introspection* (arr) (1961); *Three Contrasts* (1964); *Four Fantasias on Canadian Folk Themes* (1966); *Hexad* (1972).

BAND

Mestizo (1954); *Spit and Polish* (1954); *Fanfare* (for the RCMP) (1958); *By the Left* (1964); *Duffle Scuffle* (1964); *RCMP Opener* (1964); *Four Fantasias on Canadian Folk Themes* (1966); *Festival Suite* (1967); *Three Induction Fanfares* (1969).

SMALL ORCHESTRA

Tempo di Caprice (1946); *Kaleidoscope* (1949); *Country Fair* (1950); *Westland* (1950); *Winter Weekend* (1953); *The Son* (1953); *Lullaby* (arr) (1954); *Strolling* (arr) (1954); *Maritime Suite* (arr) (1963).

STRING ORCHESTRA

Suite for Strings (1942); *Six Variations on a Liturgical Theme* (1946); *Running Sprite* (arr) (1954); *Invocation* (1961); *A Little Ballad* (1961); *Vesper* (1961); *'You Name It' Suite* (1964; GVT, 1965).

SOLOIST WITH ORCHESTRA

Hymn to War. 1954. bar, str. Text: John Coulter.
Recollections. 1954. vln, str.
Suite Short and Simple. 1959. pno, str.
Concerto for Piano. 1963. pno, orch.
Concerto 64. 1964. pno, orch.
Concerto for Tuba. 1966. tba, orch.
Prairie Sailor (folk cantata). 1970. vc, orch. Text: Tom Kines.
Divertimento. 1970. org, 2ob, str.
Our Mind Was the Singer. 1972. bar, orch. Text: Robert Finch.

CHOIR

Shepherd's Song. 1936, SATB. Text: Norah Holland.
Dusk Lights. 1940. SSA. Text: Clara Hill.
Lynn Valley. 1940. SSA. Text: Clara Hill.
Praise Ye the Lord. 1942. SATB, org. Text: Psalm 150.
Would that I were there. 1942; OUP, 1949. SATB, pno. Text: Robert Fleming.
Missa Brevis in F minor. 1942. SATB.
Who is this Maid. 1950. SSA. Text: Robert Fleming.
God's Glory be by Man Extolled. 1953. SATB, org. Text: Introit.
Nunc Dimittis in D minor. 1953. SATB, pno (org).
A Kangaroo Sat on an Oak (arr). 1954; West, 1960. SATB. Text: trad.
Nunc Dimittis. 1954. SATB.
The Old Man (arr). 1954; West, 1960. SATB. Text: trad.
Show Me the Way to the Manger. 1954. SATB. Text: Margaret Fleming.
O Lord Support Us. 1956. SATB, org. Text: J H Newman.
Approaching the Manger. 1957. SATB. Text: Constance Barbour Holbein.
Sing Praise to the Christ Child. 1957. SATB. Text: Margaret Fleming.
Choral Eucharist in D. 1958. SATB, org.
O Taste and See. 1959. SATB. Text: Psalm 34.
Evensong in G. 1960. SATB.
O Saints in Glory Everlasting. 1960. SATB. Text: Margaret Fleming.
Choral Eucharist in E Flat. 1963. SATB, org.
Grandma's Advice (arr). 1964. SAB. Text: trad (Laura Boulton Collection).
King of Glory. 1964; OUP, 1969. SA, org (pno). Text: George Herbert.
Madrigal. 1964; Wat, 1965. SA (unis), pno. Text: William Shakespeare.
Three Eucharist Hymns. 1964. SAB. Text: Bishop Heber, T Parnell.
The 23rd Psalm. 1964; OUP. SA (unis), org (pno). Text: Old Irish paraphrase.
Horse Sense. 1966. SA. Text: anon.
Simple Eucharist in D. 1967. unis, org.
Heirs Through Hope. 1968. ten, SATB. Text: Margaret Fleming.
Awake, Sons of the Day. 1969. SATB. Text: Margaret Fleming.

VOICE

Cradle Song (1937) Text: William Blake; *Cradle Song* (1937) Text: Padraic Colum; *Fantasy* (1938) Text: Virginia Knight; *Starfall* (1939) Text: E H Visiak; *Midnight* (1940) Text: Michael Roberts; *The Night* (1940) Text: Hilaire Belloc; *Secrets* (1940; OUP, 1942) Text: W H Davies; *Winter Is Here* (1941) Text: John Freeman; *February Morning* (1942) Text: John Freeman; *Immortal Sails* (1942) Text: Alfred Noyes; *The Oxen* (1942; OUP, 1945) Text: Thomas Hardy; *Away* (1943) Text: Alfred Noyes; *Courage* (1943) Text: Walter de la Mare; *Two Songs for Children* (1943) Text: Walter de la Mare; *Absent* (1944) Text: Mary Matheson; *Dance My Dearies ('The Little Shepherdess to her Lambs')* (1944) Text: Rose Fyleman; *The Trusting Heart* (1944) Text: Dorothy Parker; *He is so Sweet and Small* (1945) Text: Gerald Bullett; *Song at Dusk* (1945) Text: Nancy Byrd Turner; *Reunion* (c1945) Text: Robert Fleming; *Coulter Songs* (1946–54) RCI-248 Text: John Coulter; *Summer Thunder* (1946) Text: Harold Applebaum; *Auvergnat* (1948) Text: Hilaire Belloc; *Came a Day* (1948) Text: Robert Fleming; *The Little Serving Maid* (1948) Text: Hilaire Belloc; *The Moon is Dead* (1948) Text: Hilaire Belloc; *The Night* (1948)

Text: Hilaire Belloc; *Two Art Songs* (1949) Text: Archibald Lampman; *A Bond is a Wonderful Buy* (1950) Text: Gordon Burwash; *Achill Girl's Song* (arr) (1950) Text: Padraic Colum; *Furrows* (1950) Text: Edward Rollins; *A Great Big Sea Hove in Long Beach* (arr) (1950) sop, alto, pno Text: trad; *I'm a Poor Stranger* (arr) (1950) Text: Ancient Irish music (Patrick Joyce); *The Lark in the Clear Air* (arr) (1950) Text: Sir Samuel Ferguson; *Let Us Leave It at That* (arr) (1950) Text: Ancient Irish music (Patrick Joyce); *The Blackbird and the Thrush* (arr) (1951) Text: Old Irish Croonawns (Honoria Galway); *High Flight* (1951; Armed Services Divine Service Bk) Text: John G McGee; *Jezebel Carol* (arr) (1951) Text: Keltic song book (A P Graves); *Folk Lullabies* (arr) (1952; MCA, 1973) Text: trad; *The Cursed Duck* (1952) Text: Paul Hiebert; *The Drunken Sailor* (arr) (1952) Text: trad; *The Genius* (1952) Text: Paul Hiebert; *Nell Flaherty's Drake* (arr) (1952) Text: Old Irish Croonawns (Honoria Galway); *Hi Sooky - Ho Sooky* (1953) Text: Paul Hiebert; *Summer Song* (1953) Text: Edward Rollins; *I Have No Time* (1954) Text: Paul Hiebert; *Love-Wonder* (1954) Text: Archibald Lampman; *For the Fallen* (1955) Text: Laurence Binyon; *Time* (1956) Text: Margaret Fleming; *Five for Five* (1957) Text: Margaret Fleming; *O Gladsome Hearts Remember* (1961) Text: Margaret Fleming; *He's Young But He's Daily A-Growing* (1964) Text: trad; *A Sea Dirge* (1964) Text: William Shakespeare; *The Confession Stone (Songs of Mary)* (1966; MCA, 1968) RCI-246 Text: Owen Dodson; *Four Songs* (1967) Text: Robert Finch; *Nova Scotia Folk Songs* (arr) (1972) Text: trad; *Afton Water* (arr) (1972) Text: Robert Burns.

VOICES WITH INSTRUMENTAL ENSEMBLE

The Wealden Trio (Song of the Women). 1940. SSA, str qt. Text: Thomas Hardy.

INSTRUMENTAL ENSEMBLE

Skip Caprice (1939) vln, pno; *Lullaby* (1940) vln, pno; *Bella Bella Sonatina* (1943) vln, pno; *Sonata* (1944) vln, pno; *Juguette* (1947) vln, pno; *A Musician in the Family* (1952) trb, pno; *Two Yukon Tunes* (1952) vln, pno; *Recollections* (arr) (1954) vln, pno; *A Two Piece Suite* (1958) ob, cl, bsn; *A Two Piece Suite* (arr) (1959; MCA, 1970) 2cl, b cl. Dom s-69004; *Five Graded Pieces* (1959) vln, pno. (1959; FH, 1959); *Berceuse* (1962) vln (vla or vlc), pno; *Colours of the Rainbow* (1962) ww qt, str qt, hp; *Maritime Suite* (1962) ww qt, str qt, hp; *Three Miniatures* (1962) brass qnt; *Suliram* (arr) (1963) mand, guit, rec, glock; *'Go For Baroque'* (1963) fl, ob, hpschd; *Three Dialogues for Flute or Oboe Solo* (1964) fl (ob), pno (hpschd); *Quintet for Brass* (1965); *Three Pieces* (1967) ob, hpschd; *Fanfare for a City* (1968) brass, perc; *A Quartet for Strings* (1969); *Almost Waltz* (1970; Jay, 1971) fl, pno. Dom s-69006; *Threo* (1972) sop sax, pno.

PIANO

Three Preludes of the Mediums (1938–40); *Five Duets for Children* (1940); *Caprice* (1941) 2pno; *Sonatina* (1941; OUP, 1943); *A Winter's Tale* (1942) 2pno; *Humoresque* (1943); *Rondo* (1943) 2pno; *Spanish Banks* (1943); *Five Modernistics* (1946; FH (Strolling), 1955); *Lullaby* (1946); *Rhythmpromptu No 1* (1946); *Rhythmpromptu No 2* (1946); *Waltz and Siesta* (1949); *Chapter 13* (arr) (1950) 2pno; *Postscript* (1950); *Tocattina for Young Pianists* (1951; Wat, 1968); *Ballerina* (1952; Wat, 1968); *Rigadoon* (1952); *Tocattina* (1952); *Saddle Song* (1953); *Shadow on the Prairie* (1952, arr 1953) 2pno; *Three Piano Pieces* (1954; FH, 1970) Dom s-69002; *Lilting* (1958; GVT, 1967) Dom s-69002; *Period Piece* (1958); *The Bluebird Ballet* (1959); *Bag O'Tricks* (1960; Wat, 1968) Dom s-69002; *Ballet Introduction* (arr) (1960) 2pno; *Introspection* (1960); *Study No 4* (1960; FH, 1966); *Jackie Visits the Zoo* (1963) 2pno; *Crazy Clock* (1965; GVT, 1967); *Trick March* (1967; GVT, 1967) Dom s-69002; *Laurentian Parade* (1967) 2pno; *Introduction, Nocturne, Finale* (1971); *Two Piano Pieces* (1973; FH, 1973).

ORGAN

Three Pieces for Organ (1962); *Variations on a Timeless Theme* (1966).

INSTRUMENTAL SOLO

Choreographic Sketches (1966) fl; *Explorations* (7 short pieces) (1970; Wat, 1970) accord.

BIBLIOGRAPHY

B65,71; Bt; CrC(I); Esc; K; Wa.
'The Composer who Commutes Between

his Church and the NFB', *CanCo.* No. 39, Apr. 1969 (4–9).
Smith, Leo. 'Competition Reveals Outstanding Talent', *Canadian Review of Music and Art.* Vol. II, no. 11-12, Dec.-Jan. 1944 (22).

LITERARY WORKS

ARTICLES

'Biographical Notes of Canadian Composers Featured on "Canadian Music in Wartime" Programme', *Canadian Review of Music and Art.* Vol. III, June-July, 1944 (34–5).
'Music for Films', *JMC Musical Chronicle.* Jan. 1963 (3).

FODI, JOHN (b. Nagyteval, Hungary, 22 Mar. 1944). He lived in West Germany from 1946 to 1951 before moving to Canada. He studied accordion at the age of nine, and theory with Lorne BETTS in Hamilton (1964). In 1966 he began studying at the Faculty of Music, University of Toronto, with John WEINZWEIG and John BECKWITH (composition), and Gustav CIAMAGA (electronic music), obtaining his Bachelor of Music (1970) and Master of Music (1972) degrees. He was awarded two Canadian League of Composers awards (1968 and 1970), the William St Clair Low Fellowship (1970), and a Woodrow Wilson Fellowship (1970). In Montreal he studied composition with István ANHALT at McGill University (1970–1). Since 1971 he has been actively involved in promoting Canadian contemporary music with the Array group of young composers. Fodi's music is characterized by thick textures in a twelve-tone idiom, although in some later works (*Trees*, 1970 and *Variations*, 1972) the texture has become much thinner, quieter, and less active. He is a member of CAPAC.

MUSICAL WORKS

INSTRUMENTAL

2 works for orch: *Symphony*, Op 6 (1964–6); *Symparanekromenoi*, Op 25 (1969–71).
5 str qts: Op 1 a&b (1963); Op 8 (1965); *Fantasia*, Op 10 (1967); *Ch'ien* (1969).
11 works for instr ens: *Movement*, Op 3 (1964) ww qt, str qt; *Chamber Symphony*, Op 14 (1967) fl, hn, pno, str qt; *Polyphony*, Op 15 (1967) 2ww, 2str; *Tettares*, Op 17 (1968) perc qt; *Pi*, Op 18 (1968) trb, pno; *Four for Four*, Op 20 (1968) cl qt; *Signals*, Op 22 (1969) sop sax, ten sax, trb, perc, pno; *Sui*, Op 27 (1969) fl, perc; *Divisions II*, Op 31 (1972) pno, hpschd; *Caligo*, Op 36 (1972) ob, bsn, vla, vlc; *Variations*, Op 37 (1972) fl, cl, perc, 3str.
4 works for solo instr: *Seven Fantasias for Flute Unaccompanied*, Op 13 (1968); *Sonata for Harpsichord*, Op 19 (1968); *Toccata for Harpsichord (Magic Strings)* (1968); *Divisions III for Viola Sola*, Op 34 (1971).
Concerto for Viola and Two Wind Ensembles, Op 35 (1972).
10 works for pno: *Parthie*, Op 4 (1964); *Sonata for Piano*, Op 5 and *Contrasts Four*, Op 9 (1964–6); *The Autumn Wastes*, Op 11, *Three Preludes for Piano*, Op 12 and *Five Results*, Op 16 (1967); *Five Extensions*, Op 21 (1968); *Three Perpl' Patches*, Op 24 (1969); *Divisions*, Op 29 (1970); *Segments for Piano*, Op 33 (1971).

CHORAL

Hamartia, Op 23. 1969. 4 SATB choirs. Text: St Columba, Tibullus, Angilbert.
7 vocal works for accompanied vc: *Spring*, Op 2 (1964) alto, pno Text: Patric Dickinson, Edward Thomas, Florence Wyle; *Two Songs on Han Dynasty Texts*, Op 7 (1965) sop, pno Text: 'Nineteen Poems', Trans: (ed) Robert Payne; *Farewells*, Op 26 (1969) ten, fl Text: Wang Wei, trans: Chang Yin-nan & Lewis C Walmsley; *Design for Alto and locked room* (1969) Text: various; *Sappho Fragments*, Op 28 (1969) sop, pno Text: Sappho, trans by Mary Barnard; *Symphonias*, Op 30 (1970) ten, pno Text: Catullus, trans by Peter Whigham; *Trees, Bk I*, Op 32 (1970) sop, pno Text: Tagore.

ELECTRONIC & MIXED MEDIA

Music Bockxd. 1969. 3 actors/dancers, 7 mus boxes, tape.
4 works for elec tape: *E.S. 1-141269* (*Can*). 1969; *E.S. 2-181170 (B.A.Z.I.M.)* (1970); *E.S. 3-022171 (Tricycle)* (1971); *E.S. 4-042871 (Noise)* (1971).

BIBLIOGRAPHY

'MacMillan-Low Fellowships Awarded to Student Composers by CAPAC', *CanCo.* No. 52, Sept. 1970 (28–9).

LITERARY WORKS

ARTICLES

'Travels into Several Remote Nations of the World', *ARRAY Newsletter*. Vol. I, no. 2, Winter 1973–4 (1–6).

FORD, CLIFFORD (b. Toronto, Ont., 30 May 1947). He studied voice, piano, and organ privately in Toronto with Eric Lewis (1957–62). A scholarship and several bursaries allowed him to study theory and composition with John BECKWITH at the Royal Conservatory, Toronto (1960–4). At the Faculty of Music, University of Toronto, he studied composition with John WEINZWEIG and Beckwith (1966–70), receiving a Bachelor of Music degree in 1970. He was awarded CAPAC's Sir Ernest MacMillan Fellowship in 1970, enabling him to study composition with István ANHALT at McGill University in Montreal (1970–1). Such works as the *String Quartet* (1970), *Epicycles* (1970), and the *Cantata* (1972), although twelve-tone and Webernesque in conception, do not hide Ford's preference for the dramatic. With *Thorybopoioumenoi* (1972) he took a new direction away from the sparse twelve-tone idiom towards a more delicate and refined polyphony. In 1971 he received a Canada Council Arts Bursary. His opera *Hypnos* (1972) was commissioned by the Young Canada Opera Theatre. He is a founding member of a Toronto concert-promoting group of young composers called Array and is a member of CAPAC.

MUSICAL WORKS

STAGE AND FILM

Incidental music for Bertolt Brecht's 'A Man's a Man'. 1969. vcs, chamb ens.

Hypnos (opera). 1972. SATB soli, SATB, spkr, mar (vib), pno, tape. Libretto: Kenneth Peglar.

3 films: 2 films by Clifford Ford: *White Dot on Black Velvet* (1971), *Opus II* (1971); *Valley of the Moon* (1972), film by Ron Webber.

INSTRUMENTAL

5 str qts. 1965, 1966, 1968, 1969, 1970.

Woodwind Quintet. 1968.

Three Pieces for Orchestra. 1969.

3 works for instr: *Telekinesis for Eight Instrumentalists* (1969) fl, cl, bsn, perc, pno, str trio; *Atman-Source* (1969) cl, vla, pno; *Trio 6'20"* (1970) vla, vlc, pno.

3 works for piano: *Epicycles No 1, 2 & 3*. 1970.

Variations for Guitar solo. 1971.

Piece for Organ No I. 1972.

CHORAL

Cantata. 1972. bar, SATB, chamb orch Text: Izumi, Tagore, Kazantzakis, Nietzsche.

2 works for unaccompanied chorus: *Three Haiku on Loneliness* (1968) SSAATTBB Text: Clifford Ford; *Gloria* (1969) SAB Text: liturgical.

VOCAL

From the Four Seasons. 1971. mezz, pno Text: Japanese poets, translated by Peter Beilenson.

2 works for vc and instr ens: *Journey* (1967) alto, str qt Text: Clifford Ford; *Thorybopoioumenoi* (1972) sop, fl, vla, tape Text: Clifford Ford.

ELECTRONIC TAPE

2 works: *Pulse* (1970); *Study* (1970).

BIBLIOGRAPHY

'MacMillan-Low Fellowships Awarded to Student Composers by CAPAC', *CanCo*, No. 52, Sept. 1970 (28–9).

LITERARY WORKS

ARTICLES

'ARRAY Visits the Gaudeamus Festival, 1973', *ARRAY Newsletter*. Vol. I, no. 2, Winter 1973–4 (17–18).

FORTIER, MARC (b. Jonquière, Que., 7 Dec. 1940). He began studies in harmony and composition at the age of seventeen with François BRASSARD. After obtaining his Bachelor of Arts degree from Laval University in 1961, he enrolled in the Conservatoire at Quebec and the following year in the Conservatoire at Montreal, where he studied cello with Walter Joachim and composition with Gilberte Martin, Gilles TREMBLAY, Clermont PÉPIN, and Sylvio Lacharité. After graduating in 1966 he studied conducting with Vladimir Golschmann and Franz-Paul Decker, participating in 1967 and 1968 in the international Dimitri Mitropoulos Competition for young conductors. Since 1963 he has pursued a strong interest in recording and arranging. In April 1969 his symphonic overture *Un Doigt de la lune* (1968) was awarded the first prize in the annual Ferdinando Ballo composition contest organized by the 'I Pomeriggi musicali di Milano' academy; the work received its première performance on April 26, 1969, at the Teatro Nuovo in Milan under the direction of Nino Sansogno and has been played many times since in Europe and Canada.

Among Fortier's other works are some eight for orchestra, including five overtures (two dedicated to Renée Claude) and three 'essays for chamber orchestra' (*Salambo*, 1963, rev. 1968; *Bessarah*, 1964, rev. 1968; and *Quand l'été revient*, 1967, rev. 1968). In 1968 he also revised his *19 Printemps* (1962) for brass quintet and *Tempo (Fantaisie)* (1965). Since 1968 he has written many songs. Although most of Fortier's works appear under his own publishing name, Emmef, his piano piece *Pirouettes* (1966, rev. 1968) is published by Jaymar Music.

Fortier is a member of CAPAC.

BIBLIOGRAPHY

'A Teacher Talks about Listening', *CanCo.* No. 69, Apr. 1972 (32–3).

FREEDMAN, HARRY (b. Lodz, Poland, 5 Apr. 1922). Freedman was brought to Canada by his parents at the age of three. Their destination was Medicine Hat, then a small community in Alberta, where his father engaged in the fur trade. (The composer still remembers the fur traders, among whom were many Indians, coming to sell their pelts.) In 1931 the Freedmans moved to Winnipeg, a prairie city noted even then for the vigour of its cultural life. Young Freedman began to draw at an early age and at fourteen enrolled at the Winnipeg School of Art to train for a career as a professional artist.

During the 1930s, broadcasts of big jazz bands awakened in the boy a keen interest in music and at eighteen he started lessons on the clarinet. Initially attracted to the instrument by jazz artists like Benny Goodman and Artie Shaw, Freedman was introduced to the repertoire of symphonic music by his teacher, Art Hart, who played in the Winnipeg Symphony Orchestra. Jazz and painting have since been prominent influences in his attitude towards music.

After service in the Royal Canadian Air Force, which included a memorable trip to the Canadian Arctic, Freedman went to the Royal Conservatory of Music, Toronto, in 1945. There he studied composition with John WEINZWEIG and oboe with Perry Bauman. Sir Ernest MACMILLAN, who was then conductor of the Toronto Symphony Orchestra, engaged Freedman as English horn player in 1946. Freedman remained with the orchestra for twenty-five years, spending his final year as its first, and so far only, composer-in-residence. From his first-hand experience in the orchestra, Freedman developed a fine sensitivity to instrumental techniques and orchestral sonorities. Continuing his studies with Weinzweig until 1951, he learned to use twelve-tone technique in a modified manner as a means of developing and extending motivic material. During the summer of 1950 he studied at Tanglewood with Messiaen.

Freedman's earliest works date from the late 1940s, commencing with the *Divertimento for Oboe and Strings* (1947), a work modelled on similar compositions by Weinzweig. He considers *Tableau* (1952) his first mature composition. Inspired by a painting depicting the Canadian Arctic that hung in the Winnipeg School of Art, it is one of several important compositions he has based on Canadian paintings, others being *Images* (1958) and *Klee Wyck* (the Indian name for Emily Carr, the painter of West Coast Indian scenes) (1970).

The first movement of Freedman's *Symphony* was composed during 1954 while the composer was taking a summer course with Ernst Krenek at the Royal Conservatory, Toronto. The *Symphony* marks a turning away from twelve-tone technique. In his own words: 'The obvious and immediate advantage of this system – namely, the built-in discipline – was in my case counterbalanced by several disadvantages, chiefly a feeling that the creation and manipulation of the tone row drew too much of my attention to notes and not enough to music.' The *Symphony* was completed in 1960 and first performed in 1961 at the Inter-American Festival in Washington, D.C. 'The influence of Bartok is strong,' wrote the *Washington Post* critic Paul Hume, who noted that 'Freedman handles a real allegro with easy ingenuity and has an unusual gift for expressive melodic contours.'

Images is one of the composer's best-known compositions. Each of the three movements of this neo-Impressionist work is based on a painting by a Canadian artist: 'Blue Mountain' by Lawren Harris, 'Structure at Dusk' by Kazuo Nakamura, and 'Landscape' by Jean-Paul Riopelle. Freedman states that he was 'not so much concerned with the content of the paintings as with their design – that is, in line, colour and mood.' A sensitive colourist, Freedman orchestrates with real finesse. Soft tints of vibraphone and harp, semitone trills in high string clusters, and bold dynamic contrasts are features of the work. He is able to produce motivic material of interest and to expand and develop his ideas with a good sense of musical logic. In an uncanny way he manages to translate the essence of the paintings into sound: the stark grandeur of Harris's 'Blue Mountain' by massive, dissonant chords on a two-note motive; Nakamura's pale criss-cross lines by running passages of heterophony; and Riopelle's bold splashes by dramatic sweeps of sound and sudden pianissimos.

Freedman returned to twelve-tone writing with *The Tokaido* (1964), which he has described as his most strictly serial work. The text consists of Japanese poems used to illustrate prints made by Hiroshige in 1834 depicting stopping places on the road called Tokaido (the way facing the eastern ocean) from Tokyo to Kyoto. The poems are arranged according to subject matter into four main sections and set for mixed chorus (SATB) and woodwind quintet. The poetic imagery of the text is reflected in the writing for the woodwind quintet in a manner reminiscent of renaissance madrigal polyphony, but in a twentieth-century context: rain or dew is suggested by a pointillistic patter of woodwind notes, wind by glissandos, rippling water by trills, endless time by long notes, and so forth.

A similar treatment is evident in *Anerca* (1966), a setting for soprano and piano of three Eskimo poems translated by Knud Rasmussen. The piano writing is lean, at times acerbic, in keeping with the brevity of the poetic scenario. The voice part has wide leaps of dissonant intervals on words like '*great* sea' and 'only one *great* thing'. Except for the rhythmic middle section, the third song is written without bar lines, a practice employed throughout *Soliloquy* (1970) for flute and piano and partially in other works such as *Tangents* (1967).

A lean texture is characteristic of *Variations* (1965), written for the Baroque Trio of Montreal, consisting of flute, oboe, and harpsichord. A set of variations based on a tone row, this work is part of a small but important segment of Freedman's writing in absolute forms that includes the *Symphony*, *Quintet for Winds* (1962), and *A Little Symphony* (1966). 'The Variations explore different timbral and textural manipulations,' wrote Kurt Stone in the *Musical Quarterly* (July 1967). 'It is an interesting and a very musical piece.'

The first of three ballets written for the Royal Winnipeg Ballet was *Rose Latulippe*, premièred by the group at the Stratford Festival of 1966. Based on a French-Canadian legend, the story concerns a pious girl who is captivated by a handsome stranger (the devil in disguise) at a barn dance on the north shore of the St Lawrence River around 1740. The girl is finally restored to her fiancé and family by the curé as dawn dispels the black winter night. The ballet is scored for a Mozart-size orchestra with added harp and percussion as well as electronic tape. The full-length score (written in sixty days) includes a twelve-tone square dance. The ballet *Five over Thirteen* was performed in Paris in 1970. From the same year dates *The Shining People of Leonard Cohen*, a ballet score made up of words of the poet arranged by Freedman and spoken by the RWB choreographer Brian Macdonald and Mary Morrison, the well-known Canadian soprano who has been married to Freedman since 1951.

Tangents, composed for the National Youth Orchestra, is one of Freedman's finest orchestral scores. Written in 1967, it is a set of continuous variations that are grouped according to mood and tempo so as to constitute a three-divisional work in one movement (fast-slow-fast). The variations are based on a tone row that gives prominence to a favourite melodic formula of Freedman's: an ascending fourth followed by a further ascending semitone. This module is a prominent feature of many Freedman works beginning with the early *Oboe Divertimento* (1947) and including

Tableau (1952), *Images, Rose Latulippe, Klee Wyck, A Little Symphony,* and *Graphic I* (1971). In addition to the tone row, Freedman makes use of groupings based on the numbers 2 and 3 to determine other parameters of *Tangents.* A rhythmic feature found in *Tangents* is typical of Freedman: repeated eighth notes are given additive rhythmic groupings resulting from changes of the time signature or accents reinforced by dissonance and melodic contour. Such usage derives no doubt from Stravinsky, but Freedman has internalized the effect, lacing it with timbral variations. Percussion instruments are utilized for the presentation of the music material as well as for colouristic purposes. Impressionistic elements and textural writing are a feature of the slow middle section of *Tangents.* The strings are divided into fifty-nine solo parts and there are aleatoric cadenzas in which six solo instruments (viola, cello, harp, tambourine, glockenspiel, and harp) are uncoordinated in tempo. They perform without conductor, rather like a sound mobile. The piece concludes with a noisy reference to rock-and-roll, where the tone row is replaced by the major chords of D and G – an affirmation of faith in jazz and youth.

The influence of jazz is apparent in most of Freedman's music. The accent is often thrown on different notes of a repeated phrase, and frequently melodic inflections similar to 'blue notes' are employed. In certain works (belonging to the 'third stream'), jazz elements become predominant, as in *Toccata* (1968), *Armana* (1967), and *Scenario* (1970). *Armana* makes use of jazz percussion instruments and Latin-American rhythms, while *Scenario* calls for alto saxophone (played in a jazz style), electric bass guitar, and jazz drummer.

In *Graphic I* and *II* (1972), aleatoric elements are prominent. *Graphic I,* written for the fiftieth anniversary season of the Toronto Symphony, makes use of prepared tape in addition to the orchestral instruments. The dynamic level is on the whole pianissimo, with only rare outbursts. Strings employ practice mutes in a freely structured improvisatory section resulting in shimmering clusters spanning five octaves. *Graphic II,* for string quartet, makes use of speech and humming by the players in addition to numerous instrumental effects that include microtones and glissandos of harmonics. *Tapestry* is a contemporary treatment of Baroque tunes for classical orchestra with winds in pairs. It was commissioned by the National Arts Centre Orchestra and completed in February 1973.

Freedman introduces theatrical elements in *Pan* (1972), a work written for the Lyric Arts Trio (soprano, flute, piano). The pianist shouts into the strings, strikes them with a wire brush, slides a bottle down their length, and strums them with a guitar pick. The flutist is instructed to slap his key pads without blowing on the instrument, to stamp his foot and whistle loudly, while the singer must whisper, speak, shout, clap her hands, and cluck her tongue. At one point the trio is stamping and clapping after a section in jazz style; at another the whole performance breaks down and must be resumed with some 'pretended' embarrassment.

In addition to works intended for concert performance, the composer has written music for films, television documentaries, and dramatic productions. The feature film, *An Act of the Heart* (1970), makes use of a cantata titled 'The Flame Within' that serves as a dramatic focal point and musical highlight.

Freedman may well be cited as an example of Canadianism in music. He is one of the first composers of national stature to have been trained almost exclusively in Canada, the creative stimulus for his music has been provided largely by the Canadian environment, and much of his work has been written for Canadian groups and artists.

Freedman is a member of the Canadian League of Composers and of CAPAC.

LEE HEPNER

MUSICAL WORKS

STAGE

Rose Latulippe (ballet in 3 acts). 1966. 90'. med orch, tape. ms. Aug 16, 1966, Stratford Fest, RWB, Carlos Rausch(cond), Brian MacDonald(choreog).

Five over Thirteen (ballet). 1969. small orch. ms. 1970, Ottawa, NAC, RWB.

The Shining People of Leonard Cohen (ballet). 1970. tape. ms. 1970, Paris, RWB.

FILMS

An Act of the Heart. ms. Decca DL-75244.

China; 'The Roots of Madness'. ms.
The Dark Will Not Conquer. ms.
Isabel. ms.
Let Me Count the Ways. ms.
Pale Horse, Pale Rider. ms.
Romeo and Jeannette. ms.
Seven Hundred Million. ms.
Spring Song. ms.
Twenty Million Shoes. ms.
Where Will They Go. ms.

ORCHESTRA

Symphonic Suite. 1948. 14'20". full orch. ms. RCI-19.

Nocturne. 1949. 5'25". med orch. CMC. RCI-71. 1952, Tor, CLC Conc, TS, Geoffrey Waddington.

Matinee Suite; 'Caricatures', 'March for Small Types', 'Harlem Hoedown'. 1951–5. small orch. ms. 1952 (*March for Small Types*) Tor, CBCSO, John Adaskin.

Images (Suite on Three Canadian Paintings). 1958. 17'. full orch. Ber, 1960. Col M2L-356 M2S-756; Odyssey Y31993. 1960, Tor, TS, Walter Susskind.

Symphony No. 1. 1961. 32'30". full orch. Ber. 1961, Washington, Inter-Amer Mus Fest, CBCSO, Geoffrey Waddington.

Chaconne. 1964. 5'45". full orch. CMC. Feb 16, 1964, Tor, CBCSO, Victor Feldbrill.

A Little Symphony. 1966. 17'. full orch. MCA. Feb 26, 1967, S'tn, SSO, David Kaplan.

Scales in Polytonality. 1966. schl orch or band. CMC.

Armana. 1967. 10'28". full orch. CMC. Feb 23, 1967, Tor, CBC, TS, Walter Susskind.

Tangents. 1967. 15'30". full orch. MCA, 1971. Audat 477-4001. July 21, 1967, Mtl, NYO, Brian Priestman.

Klee Wyck; 'The Laughing One'. 1970. 10'. full orch. CMC. 1971, Vic, First conc in BC Centennial Year, Vic SO, Laszlo Gati.

March? 1970. 5'. full orch. CMC. Jan 16, 1971, Tor, TS, Victor Feldbrill.

Graphic I; 'Out of silence...'. 1971. full orch, elec tape. CMC. Oct 26, 1971, Tor, TS, Karel Ancerl.

Preludes for Orchestra (orch'd from Debussy). 1971. full orch. ms. June 12, 1971, Tor, CBC Fest.

BAND

Laurentian Moods (Suite of French Canadian Songs). 1957. CMC.

STRING ORCHESTRA

Five Pieces for String Orchestra. 1949. 14'. CMC. RCI-43 (str qt version). 1953, Tor, Can Chamb Plyrs, Victor Feldbrill.

Tableau. 1952. 8'30". Ric 1960. Nov 29, 1952, Tor, Can Chamb Plyrs, Victor Feldbrill.

Images (Suite on Three Canadian Paintings). 1958. 17'. ms. RCI-187. Mar. 12, 1958, McG Ch O, Alexander Brott.

Fantasy and Allegro. 1962. 15'45". CMC. RCI-238. 1962, Brantford, HHO, Boyd Neel.

SOLOIST(S) WITH ORCHESTRA

Divertimento for Oboe and Strings. 1947. 10'. CMC. 1949, Tor, Students of the RCMT, Victor Feldbrill(cond), Harry Freedman (ob).

Fantasia and Dance. 1955 (rev 1959). 17'. vln, orch. CMC. 1956, Tor, RCMT O, Ettore Mazzoleni(cond), Jacob Groob(vln).

Trois Poèmes de Jacques Prévert. 1962. 13'25". sop, str. CMC.

Scenario. 1970. 14'35". alto sax, elec bs guit, orch. CMC. May 29, 1970, Tor, CBC Fest, TS, Meredith Davies(cond).

CHOIR

Three Vocalises. 1964. SATB. MCA, 1965.

Totem and Taboo. 1965. SATB, pno. ms.

Ookpik. 1969. SSA, pno. CMC. Text: Dennis Lee.

Keewaydin. 1971. SSA (tape opt). GVT. Poly Ster 2917 009.

VOICE

Anerca. 1966. 13'30". sop, pno. CMC. Text: 3 Eskimo poems. Trans: Knud Rasmussen. Oct, 1966, Mtl, Lois Marshall(sop), Weldon Kilburn(pno).

Poems of Young People. 1968. 10'25". low vc, pno. CMC. Sel CC-15.073. Text: B Snider, Ken Stickney, Elizabeth Park, Dave Mullin. Sept 6, 1969, Tor, St James Cathedral, Maureen Forrester(alto), John Newmark (pno).

VOICE(S) WITH INSTRUMENTAL ENSEMBLE

Two Vocalises. 1954. 5'. sop, cl, pno. CMC. 1954, Tor, CBC, Mary Morrison(sop), Abraham Galper(cl), Leo Barkin(pno).

The Tokaido. 1964. 18'30". SATB, ww qnt. CMC. Decca DL-75244. 1964, Tor, Fest Sgrs, TWQ, Elmer Iseler.

Toccata. 1968. 4'45". sop, fl. Kerby, 1972.

Tikki Tikki Tembo. 1971. 7'. narr, ww qnt. CMC.

Pan. 1972. fl, sop, pno. CMC. May 5, 1972, Banff, Alta, Banff Schl of FA, Can Mus

Counc Conf, LAT, Mary Morrison(sop), Robert Aitken(fl), Marion Ross(pno).

INSTRUMENTAL ENSEMBLE

Trio for Two Oboes and English Horn. 1948. ms.

Five Pieces for String Quartet. 1949. 14'. CMC. RCI-43. 1949, Tor, RCMT Str Qt, Morry Kernerman(vln), Victor Feldbrill(vln), Ross Lechow(vla), Donald Whitton(vlc).

Six French-Canadian Folk Songs (arr). 1950. vln, pno. ms.

March and Pastoral. 1951. 4'. ww qt. ms.

Quintet for Winds. 1962. 17'. ww qnt. Kerby, 1972. RCI-208. 1962, Tor, CBC, TWQ, Gordon Day(fl), Perry Bauman(ob), Stan McCartney(cl), Nicholas Kilburn(bsn), Eugene Rittich(hn). *Three Duets for String Basses (or Cellos).* 1965. MCA.

Trio for String Basses (or Cellos). 1965. MCA.

Variations. 1965. 15'30". ob, fl, hpschd. CMC. RCA CC/CCS-1013; RCI-219.

Soliloquy. 1970. 3'. fl, pno. MCA, 1971. Dom S-69005/S-69006.

Graphic II. 1972. 13'30". str qt. CMC. Aug 10, 1972, Courtenay Youth Mus Camp, Purcell Str Qt.

PIANO

Suite for Piano 1951. 10'. FH ('Scherzo'), 1955.

BIBLIOGRAPHY

See B-B; B65,71; Bec56,70; Bt; CrC(II); D165; Esc; K; Wa.

'Harry Freedman – a portrait', *Mu.* No. 8, Jan.-Feb. 1968 (8–9).

Stone, Kurt. 'Review of Records', *MQ.* Vol. VIII, no. 3, July 1967 (440–52).

'Standing Ovation for First Full-Length Canadian Ballet', *CanCo.* No. 11, Oct. 1966 (24–5, 29).

'Tangents', *CBC Times.* June 7–13, 1969 (7).

Wilkinson, Bryan. 'Harry Freedman: An Exciting Composer', *CanCo.* No. 17, Apr. 1967 (4–5, 36–7, 46).

FRIEDLANDER, ERNST (b. Vienna, Austria, 6 Oct. 1906; d. Vancouver, B.C., 1966). He studied at the Konservatorium für Musik, Vienna (1928–9) with Hans Pless (conducting) and Anton Walter (cello). From 1929 to 1930 he studied at the Hochschule für Musik with F. Buxbaum (cello) and Heinrich Schenker. He was cellist with the Popa Grama Quartet and the principal cellist with the Wiener Konzert Orchester (1935–7) in Vienna. When he went to the United States he became principal cellist with the Pittsburgh Symphony Orchestra (1937–8), the Kansas City Symphony Orchestra (1938–9), and the Indianapolis Symphony Orchestra (1939–42). After teaching cello at the Jordan Conservatory of Butler University, Indianapolis (1939–42), he moved in 1943 to Wisconsin where he was cellist with the Pro Arte String Quartet and was the head of the cello department, University of Wisconsin, until 1955. He also taught cello at the University of Wyoming during the summers of 1952, 1953, and 1954. In 1955 he moved to Chicago where he was cellist with the Chicago Symphony Orchestra and a teacher at the Cosmopolitan School of Music. From 1956–8 he was assistant professor at the University of Oklahoma. In 1958 he moved to Vancouver, where he was lecturer at the University of British Columbia (1958–66), principal cellist with the CBC Concert Orchestra and the Vancouver Symphony Orchestra (1958–66), and cellist of the Vancouver String Quartet (1960–6). Best known as a performer, Friedlander composed mainly for cello. Among his works are *Cello Concerto* (1959), *Rhapsody for Cello (or Bassoon) and Orchestra* (1964), and a number of solo cello pieces, including *Sonata for Violoncello Alone* (1963) and *Two Concert Etudes for Violoncello* (1942). He was affiliated with BMI Canada.

BIBLIOGRAPHY

See B-B; CrC(I); Wa.

G

GAGNIER, JEAN-JOSAPHAT (b. Montreal, Que., 2 Dec. 1885; d. Montreal, 16 Sept. 1949). At fourteen Gagnier was playing clarinet in several Montreal theatres and by eighteen was already conducting musical groups and choirs. Among his teachers were Alexis Contant, R.-O. Pelletier, and G.-E. TANGUAY. In 1910 he organized the Concordia band and from 1917 to 1920 he was leader of music for Sohmer Park of Montreal. In 1924 he reorganized the Montreal Symphony, of which he became conductor, at the same time continuing as conductor of the 'Petite Symphonie de Montréal'. As head of military music he directed the Canadian Grenadier Guards band from 1913 until his death. This band gave many series of concerts in Montreal as well as on numerous tours and radio broadcasts. Gagnier was regularly invited to conduct at important festivals in the U.S. In December 1934 he received a doctorate in music from the University of Montreal, his thesis being on orchestration; at the same time he was named the first music director of the CBC French Network, in whose music broadcasts he was active for a number of years; he co-edited with J.-M. Beaudet the first CBC catalogue of Canadian composers (1947). Gagnier's own output was considerable and of a great variety of style and inspiration; his *Journey*, for English horn and strings, is typical, with its lyrical and impressionistic accentuations, the entire work being based on an Indian song. His estate is a member of CAPAC.

MUSICAL WORKS

INCIDENTAL MUSIC

Le Bandit; *Cinq petits lapins*; *Coucher de soleil*; *Dans le marais*; *Le Faux Rossignol*; *La paix soit avec vous*; *Panache sur la neige*; *Le Rival.*

ORCHESTRA

Toronto Bay (Valse Scherzo) (c1935; Fischer, 1937); *Le Vent dans l'Erable effeuillé* (1939); *Pastiches Anciens* (1939); *Mélodie Brève* (c1939); *Pan aux Pieds de Chèvre* (c1943); *Croquis Madelinots* (c1946); *Currente Calamo*; *La Dame de Coeur*; *Divertissements*; *Forest Sketches*; *In the Olden Style*; *In the Shade of the Maples*; *Journey,* Cap ST 6261; *Marine Sketches*; *Tre Preludi a l'Eterna Comedia*; *Victoire (March).*

BAND

Hands Across the Border (c1935; Remick, 1938); *Skip Along* (c1935; Fischer, 1937); *Toronto Bay (Valse Scherzo)* (c1935; Fischer, 1937); *Palace Pier* (1939); *Le Vent dans l'Erable effeuillé* (1939); *Ca-Na-Ex* (c1941); *The Adjutant* (c1942); *Le Capitaine* (c1942); *Le Caporal* (c1942); *The Colonel* (c1942); *Le Conscript* (c1942); *Dans les airs* (c1942); *Fou du roi* (c1942); *The Lieutenant* (c1942); *Pan aux Pieds de Chèvre* (c1943); *The Major* (c1945); *La Soupe au Lard* (c1945); *Ace of Spades*; *Currente Calamo*; *La Dame de Coeur* (Fischer); *Here's to Tommy*; *In the Olden Style*; *Jack of Diamonds*; *Jeunesse Dorée*; *King of Clubs*; *Kiwanis March*; *Maple Leaves*; *Les Mont-Régiens*; *Safety First*; *The Sergeant*; *Suites of Fanfares*; *The Tanks*; *Trompettes*; *Victoire*; *Le Voyageur.*

STRING ORCHESTRA

Reflets (c1945; Parnasse, 1947); *Têtes d'Enfants* (c1945; Parnasse, 1947); *Apaisement*; *Clair obscur.*

SOLOIST(S) WITH ORCHESTRA

Suite for Harp. c1945; Fox, c1945. hp, orch.

Maman Bonne Fête. c1948. vc, SATB, orch. Text: M P Leduc.

Pyrame et Thisbé. soloists, SSAA, orch. Parnasse. Text: J-J Gagnier.

CHOIR WITH ORCHESTRA

Huit Plus Cinq. c1948. SATB, orch. Text: anon.

Tritons et Sirènes. SSAA, orch. Text: J-J Gagnier.

CHOIR

Noël Huron (arr). c1948. SATB. Text: Jean de Brébeuf.

As-Ke-Non-Don. SATB. Parnasse. Text: Iroquois.

Le Chant de l'ACJC. solo, SATB. ACJC. Text: H Lalande.
Cor Jesu. solo, SATB.
Danses Maléchites (arr). SATB. Text: Lorette.
Hamac dans les voiles. SSAA. Parnasse. Text: J-J Gagnier.
Homage au séminaire. SATB.
Hymne à mon collège. solo, SATB. Text: J-J Gagnier.
Kyrie. solo, SATB. Fr des EC.
Pisik (arr). SATB. Text: Eskimo.
Saint-Joseph. solo, SATB.
Three Quicumque. solo, SATB.

VOICE
Le Canada. c1935; Arch, 1935. Text: Octave Crémazie.
Hymne à la Patrie. 1939; Passe-Temps, c1945. Text: Albert Lozeau.
Regrets. 1939. Text: Jeannine Lavallée.
O toi. 1939. Text: Monise Robitaille.
Neseio. c1945. Text: J-J Gagnier.
Panis Angelicus. c1945.
Adeste Fidelis.
Cor Jesu.
Danse de la Decouvertes (arr).
Danses Maléchites (arr). Text: Lorette.
Filez, filez, o mon navire.
Hymne à mon collège. Text: J-J Gagnier.
Jesous Ahatonhia.
Kyrie. Fr des EC.
Pisik. Text: Eskimo.
Three Quicumque. Fr des EC.
Ressemblances (Romance). Parnasse. Text: Sully Prudhomme.
Le Sage. Text: Monise Robitaille.
Saint-Joseph.
Weather Incantation (arr). Text: Eskimo.

INSTRUMENTAL ENSEMBLE
Le Bandit. EH, bsn, timp.
Cinq petits lapins. 3ob, EH.
Coucher de soleil. EH, bsn, 3hn.
Le Faux Rossignol. ww qt.
In the Olden Style. str qnt.
Panache sur la neige. ob, bsn.
Petite Suite. ob, pno.

PIANO
Mélodie Brève (arr). 1939.
Ten Studies in Concert Form. c1939; Arch, 1939.
Trois esquisses musicales. c1945; Parnasse, 1947.
Apaisement (arr).
Soliloque.

INSTRUMENTAL SOLO
La Paix soit avec vous. hp.

ORGAN
Prélude (L'Eternelle Comédie) (arr). c1945; Parnasse, 1947.
Offertory (arr). c1945.
Air.

BIBLIOGRAPHY

See B-B; CrC(II); K; Lv; Wa.
Laurendeau, Arthur. 'Mort d'un artiste', *L'Action Nationale.* Vol. XXXIV, Oct. 1949 (121–5).

LITERARY WORKS

ARTICLES
'Peintres, sculpteurs, comédiens et musiciens: parents pauvres de chez nous', *L'Action Universitaire.* Vol. XV, Oct. 1948 (93–4).

GAGNON, ALAIN (b. Trois-Pistoles, Que., 22 May 1938). He received his early education in Rimouski, enrolling in Laval University where he was awarded his baccalaureate in music in 1963, the year he won the Lieutenant-Governor's Medal. The following year he was granted a licentiate in composition at Laval and won an award of the government of France. In 1965, having won a Prix d'Europe in composition, he went to Paris where he studied for a year under Henri Dutilleux and Olivier Alain. During 1966 and 1967 he spent some time at the electronic music studio in Utrecht, Holland, and subsequently studied composition with A.F. Marescotti in Geneva, Switzerland. Since 1967 he has been a member of the faculty of the Ecole de Musique of Laval University, teaching analysis and counterpoint.

Gagnon's output includes four sonatas, three suites, and five preludes for piano; two string quartets; two song cycles; *Esquisse* (1965) and *Prélude* (1969) for orchestra; and a choral work, *Rumeurs et Visions* (1966) for three soprano soloists and mixed chorus. Gagnon without hesitation identifies Debussy as his musical idol, although he is also especially interested in such other composers as Messiaen, Penderecki, Berg, and Webern; indeed, his music does have linear qualities not generally associated with Debussy – usually lyrical and with a certain Frenchness of sonority. Gagnon is a member of CAPAC.

LITERARY WORKS

ARTICLES

'Autour d'une Sonate', *Vie Musicale*. No. 9, Sept. 1968 (21–3).

GARANT, SERGE (b. Quebec City, Que., 22 Sept. 1929). If Serge Garant's music owes any allegiance to the past, it is only to the recent past – that of Schoenberg and Webern, or better still, Boulez and Stockhausen. Garant was spared the conventional historic approach to music learning. His first significant musical contacts were with music of his own time, and all his learning has zeroed in on matters of immediate importance rather than on traditions of bygone times.

Garant is to a great extent self-taught, or more accurately, self-educated: he is well read, knowledgeable in poetry, literature, and the visual arts, an expert collector of paintings, prints, and antiques. His formal schooling ended with grade 9. He 'flunked out' from the second year of a technical school and was expelled from a Catholic seminary for questioning the authorities. Although he was surrounded by music at home – both his parents played instruments, as did six of his seven brothers and sisters – his active involvement with it started when he was fifteen. At that time the Garant family moved from Quebec City to Sherbrooke and in the new environment, partly prompted by the example of his older brother, who had taken up trombone playing, young Serge started to practise the clarinet and saxophone. When their father bought a second-hand piano, Serge also set out to master the secrets of the keyboard.

His progress on the three instruments was so rapid that after a year and a half he was a regular with local dance bands and was accepted as a clarinetist into the ranks of the Sherbrooke Symphony. Although he eventually sought some instruction from various teachers (Sylvio Lacharité and Yvonne Hubert for piano and Claude CHAMPAGNE for composition), his main sources of information and inspiration remained the scores of new music that he picked up at the local music store and his practical involvement with the local bands. He discovered the music of Schoenberg and Webern and taught himself to play their piano pieces. He composed music for jazz bands and (at the suggestion of the bandmaster, Harry Long) a work for the Sherbrooke band, *Music for Alto Saxophone and Band* (1948). Although not serial in the Schoenbergian sense, it is nevertheless atonal and thus forecasts the direction in which Garant was to move in the years to come.

In the fall of 1951 Garant went to Paris where he attended the analysis classes of Olivier Messiaen and studied counterpoint with Mme Arthur Honegger. In Paris he was exposed to the music of Pierre Boulez and started to cultivate seriously a personal approach to dodecaphony – an approach that over the years may have undergone certain changes, primarily refinements, but that has nevertheless retained its basic characteristics to this day.

It is this consistency that makes Garant stand out among his contemporary colleagues. While so many of them zig-zag in search of new idioms and experiment with various methods, materials, and media, Garant walks a straight course. Not that he doesn't look left or right. He is as receptive as anyone to innovations of all kinds – be they open-ended forms, indeterminate performance procedures, notational devices or stereophonic sound distributions – but whatever he needs he always adopts to *his* firmly established style rather than letting his musical speech lose its identity among new mannerisms.

Garant's personal musical speech is notable for its precise organization on the one hand and its sonic sensitivity on the other. Garant is a confirmed subscriber to the principles of serialism. Not unlike his idol of student days, Pierre Boulez, he finds happiness in musical mathematics. Besides using twelve-tone series as the basic intervallic materials in most of his works, he frequently applies mathematical logic to such parameters of sound as duration and amplitude, or organizes the relative proportions of his compositions, the degrees of sonoric densities, or the choices of instrumental timbres according to pre-programmed numerical systems. Various manifestations of the concept of symmetry, including its antithesis, asymmetry, play a decisive role in many of his structures.

Yet for all its intellectuality, Garant's

music is first and foremost sound-oriented. For him, mathematical equations and arithmetical progressions serve one purpose: to establish relationships between sounds, their sequences and constellations, that express orderliness, uniqueness, and purpose. Vibrant sonorities, unhackneyed rhythms, balanced dynamics, and unerring timings are the characteristics that one first notices when encountering a Garant composition. The clever structural features unfold only after an intensive study of the score.

That Garant is capable of successfully combining the cerebral and the sensitive in his work is not so surprising when one remembers that he has never been an ivory-tower composer but rather a practising musician keenly involved with the realities of music-making, often on a quite mundane level. His activities as a budding jazz and band player and composer were mentioned earlier. On his return from Paris in 1952, and for almost a decade after, he earned his living by improvising for ballet classes, playing nightly engagements at bars and cocktail lounges, and eventually working as arranger and conductor for CBC French-network musical pop-shows.

All these realities of life notwithstanding, the same 1950s saw another side of Garant: a fighter in word and deed for the cause of new music – not just any new music, but music that would stand up when measured against the most exacting criteria. He polemicized and pamphleteered in the pages of various publications, from the left-wing *Totalité* to the house-organ of Les Jeunesses Musicales, feuded openly with fellow critics and composers, and spoke his mind regularly over the airwaves of CBC. The subject, with variations, was always the same: if there is to be a musical culture in Quebec, or for that matter in Canada, it must be modelled on examples and standards set by the best anywhere in the world. Mediocrity, provincialism, and parochialism have no place in the concert halls of a growing nation.

To put these words into practice Garant, together with several similarly thinking colleagues – Gilles TREMBLAY, François MOREL, Otto JOACHIM, and Jean Landry among them – organized a series of concerts featuring what they considered to be the best of the international repertoire, as well as new works of their own. Webern's 'Variations' and parts of Boulez' 'Second Piano Sonata', along with Garant's *Caprices* (1954) for voice and piano to words by Garcia Lorca, were featured in the first concert in 1954. A Webern memorial followed in 1955, and in 1957 and 1958 a series of concerts was given under the name 'Musique de notre temps', featuring Canadian premières of works by Berg, Webern, Stravinsky, Messiaen, Stockhausen, Joachim, Morel, and Garant himself. Although sporadic, these concerts helped to establish a climate for new music ventures of larger scope and far-reaching significance, for which Montreal became known in the 1960s. The first such event was the International Week of Today's Music, held in conjunction with the Montreal Festival in 1961. Garant's *Anerca* (1961, rev. 1963) for soprano and instrumental ensemble was the only Canadian piece of live music chosen to be performed during the festival, and its première at the opening concert in the illustrious company of Edgar Varèse, John Cage, Earle Brown, Morton Feldman, Mauricio Kagel, and Bruno Maderna was a personal triumph for a composer who for a decade had valiantly fought to establish international standards in Canadian music.

It was a significant turning-point in Garant's career. He began to receive commissions and conducting assignments. In 1963 there was a commission from the Quebec Symphony Orchestra and the next year another from the Sherbrooke Symphony; *Ouranos* (1963) and *Ennéade* (1964) were the two scores provided in response to these requests. In 1966 he was invited to conduct the television première of Murray SCHAFER's opera *Loving* (*Toi*) over the CBC-TV French network. When in December of the same year the Quebec Government instigated the foundation and guaranteed the funding of La Société de Musique Contemporaine du Québec, a new music-performing organization, Garant was named its music director. In this capacity he has since planned, prepared, and presided over fifty concerts featuring some 180 (mostly mid-twentieth-century) works, including about sixty Canadian premières.

All these practical activities, which also include frequent guest conducting and teaching a class of composition students at the University of Montreal, have unavoidably put certain quantitative limitations on Garant's creative work. At the same time such restrictions have prompted the composer to work with heightened concentration and intensely focused energies. Consequently every one of the ten scores Garant has produced since 1967 is a most thoroughly thought out and meticulously worked out musical statement, notable for the originality of its underlying ideas and structural complexities. These ten scores fall into two distinct groups, each resting on a common unifying concept. In the first one, comprising *Phrases I* (1967) and *II* (1968), *Amuya* (1968), and *Jeu à Quatre* (1968), Garant explores in depth the possibilities of aleatoric performance procedures and fragmentation and reassembling of ideas in order to create ever-shifting listening perspectives. Although the scoring of the two *Phrases* versions is of contrasting dimensions – *Phrases I* is a chamber work for three musicians; *Phrases II*, a Montreal Symphony Orchestra commission, is a composition for full orchestra – the similarities between the two scores are easily detectable. Both are constructed of flexible modules, the order of which is determined by the players in *Phrases I* and the two conductors who lead the divided orchestra in *Phrases II*. All modules and their sum totals are of precisely fixed durations, while inside this rigid framework there is plenty of 'breathing space' left for the players' individual gestures. The proportion 7/8 plays a magic role in both scores: the relative durations of individual modules are patterned on this formula, as are the comparative dimensions of the two orchestras in *Phrases II*. And in both works the composer makes use of sung and/or spoken texts: in *Phrases I* a singer intones, now *ad verbatim*, now in bits and pieces, a statement of Pierre Bourgault, while in *Phrases II* the whole orchestra utters fragmented pronouncements taken from Che Guevara's writings. *Amuya*, a CBC commission for small orchestra, falls chronologically between the two *Phrases* and serves as a further testing ground for Garant's modular and aleatoric structuring concepts, whereas the later *Jeu à Quatre*, a Stratford Festival commission, places the idea of indeterminate interactivity of separate instrumental groups into a quadraphonic setting with the sixteen musicians divided into four units and placed in four locations.

While the latest six Garant works – *Offrandes I* (1969), *II* (1970), and *III* (1971), and *Circuits I* (1972), *II* (1972), and *III* (1973) – maintain many of the structural and textural features of his earlier compositions, they stand out as a special group because they all draw their construction materials from the same germinal source – the theme of Bach's 'Musical Offering'. Not that Garant has written a series of variations on this famous theme – that for him would have been too primitive an approach. His sophisticated way was to translate the interval relationships of the theme into a numerical sequence, and then use it and its various permutations as serial cells for organizing pitches, durations, timbres, dynamics and other parameters and proportions of the compositions. Each of the *Offrandes* and *Circuits* is scored for an ensemble of a different size and make-up, ranging from full orchestra to smaller ensembles of mixed instruments. Scoring devices cover the whole gamut, from for the most part conventionally notated, linearly arranged structures with a few interspersed aleatoric sections, as in *Offrande III*, to purely numerical charts like those used by the six percussionists in *Circuit I*. While fragments of the original 'Musical Offering' theme may be recognized in *Offrande I* (a CBC commission) and are faintly recognizable in *Offrande II* (a National Youth Orchestra commission), in all the later works its presence becomes a total abstraction: an invisible and inaudible source of unifying energies.

Garant was awarded the Canadian Music Council medal in 1971. In 1973 he received an $18,000 Italian cultural fellowship and took a year-long creative sabbatical in Rome.

Garant is a member of the Canadian League of Composers and is affiliated with BMI Canada. UDO KASEMETS

MUSICAL WORKS

FILMS

Music for the film of the 'Man and the Polar Regions' Pavilion. ms. 1967, Mtl, Expo 67.

Vertiges (music for NFB documentary film).

1969. ms. 1969, Tor, Can Film Fest (most original music award).

ORCHESTRA

Musique pour Saxophone alto et Orchestre. 1948 (transcribed for orch 1950). 6'. ms.

Ouranos. 1963. 13'. full orch. ms. Nov 18, 1963, QSO, Françoys Bernier.

Ennéade. 1964. 11'. full orch. ms. Feb 18, 1964, Sherbrooke, Sherbrooke SO.

Phrases II. 1968. 14'15". 2 orch. ms. Text: Ernesto 'Che' Guevara. May 14, 1968, Mtl, MSO, Serge Garant – Franz-Paul Decker (conds).

Offrande II. 1970. 11'. full orch. CMC. July 29, 1970, Tor, NYO, Brian Priestman.

SMALL ORCHESTRA

Amuya. 1968. 19'. 20 musicians. CMC. July 12, 1968, Tor, CBC Summer Fest, Serge Garant.

Offrande I. 1969. 12'. 19 musicians, pre-recorded vc. CMC. RCI-368. Mar 6, 1970, Mtl, CBC, SMCQ ens, Serge Garant.

STRING ORCHESTRA

Ta forme monte comme la blessure du sang. 1950. 6'. ms. 1950, Sherbrooke, Que.

SOLOIST WITH ORCHESTRA

Musique pour la mort d'un poète. 1954. 15'. pno, str. ms.

VOICE

Un grand sommeil noir. 1949. 1'30". ms. Text: Paul Verlaine.

Concerts sur terre. 1951. 7'5". sop, pno. CMC. RCI-201. Text: Patrice de la Tour du Pin.

Et je prierai ta grâce. 1952. 2'30". sop, pno. ms. RCI-201. Text: St-Denys-Garneau.

Caprices. 1954. 4'30". sop, pno. CMC. RCI-201. Text: Garcia Lorca; trans: Pierre Darmangeat.

Cage d'oiseau. 1962. 8'. sop, pno. Ber, 1968. Text: St-Denys-Garneau. 1967, Mtl, Rencontres, Salle St Sulpice, Josèphe Colle (sop), Serge Garant(pno).

VOICE WITH INSTRUMENTAL ENSEMBLE

Anerca. 1961 (rev 1963). 9'. sop, fl, cl, bsn, vln, vla, vlc, hp, perc. Ber, 1967. RCA CC/CCS-1011; RCI-217. Text: Eskimo poems; trans, Knud Rasmussen. Aug 3, 1961, Mtl, La Semaine Internationale de Musique Actuelle, Mauricio Kagel(cond), Claire Grenon-Masella(sop).

Phrases I. 1967. 26'. mezz, pno, cel, perc. Ber, 1969. RCI-240. Text: Pierre Bourgault. Sept 9, 1967, Mtl, Expo 67, Pavillon de la Jeunesse, Serge Garant(cond, pno, cel), Fernande Chiocchio(mezz), Guy Lachapelle (perc).

INSTRUMENTAL ENSEMBLE

Adagio et Allegro pour piano et harmonie. 1948. ms.

Musique pour Saxophone alto et Fanfare. 1948. 6'. ms.

Pièces pour quatuor de saxophones. 1948. ms.

Fantasie. 1950. 5'30". cl, pno. ms. 1950, Sherbrooke, Que.

Nucléogame. 1955. 7'30". fl, ob, cl, tpt, hn, trb, pno, tape. ms. 1955, Mtl, Webern anniversary conc, Jean Vallerand(dir), Serge Garant(pno).

Canon VI. 1957. 10'. fl, cl, vlc, cel, xyl, vib, pno, 3perc. ms.

Pièces pour quatuor à cordes (study on chance). 1958. 5'. ms.

Asymétries No 2. 1959. 6'30"–8'. cl, pno. CMC. 1959, Hanover, NH, Dartmouth Coll Fest for Eng, Can and Amer Mus.

Jeu à Quatre. 1968. 4 instr Gps (16 plyrs), Gp 1: pno, cel, cb, perc; Gp 2: hp, ob, cl, tpt; Gp 3: perc, tpt, hn, trb; Gp 4: hn, fl, cl, bsn, perc. CMC. RCI-300. July 20, 1968, Stratford Fest, Serge Garant.

Offrande III. 1971. 3vlc, 2hp, pno, 2perc. Salabert, 1973. RCI-368. Mar 28, 1971, Mtl, CBC, SMCQ, Serge Garant.

Circuits I. 1972. 6 (12) percussionists. ms. Jan 24, 1972, Ottawa, NAC, Inaugural conc of the 'Percussions du Québec'.

Circuits II. 1972. 2fl, cl, tpt, hn, trb, 2pno, 3perc. ms. RCI-368. Mar 31, 1972, Royan, France, IXe Festival International d'Art Contemporain, ens of the SMCQ, Serge Garant.

PIANO

Sonatine. 1948. 8'30". ms. 1950, Sherbrooke, Que.

Pièce pour piano no 1. 1953. 5'. CMC.

Musique rituelle. 1954. 4'. ms.

Variations. 1954. 4'25". ms. RCI-135.

Asymétries No 1. 1958. 5'30". CMC. 1958, Mtl, Serge Garant.

Pièce pour piano no 2; 'Cage d'oiseau'. 1962. 8'. Ber, 1969. RCI-252. 1963, Mtl, Ballet Jeanne Renaud, Serge Garant.

BIBLIOGRAPHY

See B-B; B65,71; Bec70; Bt; CrC(II); D165; K; Lv; Wa.

Bisbrouck, Noël. 'Un musicien canadien: Serge Garant', *Ici Radio-Canada. Culture-Information.* Montreal, Vol. I, no. 2, May 20-June 20, 1966 (18–21).

Gingras, Claude. 'Serge Garant', *MuSc.* Jan.-Feb. 1971 (4–5).

McLean, Eric. 'Serge Garant', *MuSc.* Jan.-Feb. 1968 (8–9).

'Serge Garant – a portrait', *Mu.* No. 10, Apr. 1968 (8–9).

'Serge Garant: Le Structuralisme Ouvert', *Musiques du Kébèk* (R. Duguay, ed.). Montreal: Editions du Jour, 1971 (47–54, 64–70).

LITERARY WORKS

ARTICLES

'Un esprit de genèse', *Liberté.* Vol. LIX, Sept.-Oct. 1959 (284–6).

'Karlheinz Stockhausen à Montréal', *JMC.* Montreal, Mar. 1964 (7).

'Music in Montreal 1961–62', *Canadian Art.* Vol. XIX, July-Aug. 1962 (307, 309).

'Musique 1961', *Liberté.* Vol. III, Mar.-Apr. 1961 (514–16).

'Notes sur "Anerca"', *Musiques du Kébèk* (R. Duguay, ed.). Montreal: Editions du Jour, 1971 (55).

GAYFER, JAMES (b. Toronto, Ont., 26 Mar. 1916). He studied piano, theory, composition, and conducting at the Toronto Conservatory and the Faculty of Music, University of Toronto, receiving his Bachelor of Music degree in 1941. In 1943 he joined the Royal Canadian Corps of Signals Band as clarinetist and then was sent to the Royal Military School of Music in England for a bandmasters' course, also obtaining his Associate and Licentiate diplomas from the Royal College of Music. He returned to Canada in 1947 and gained his Doctor of Music degree from the University of Toronto in 1950. In 1951 he was appointed director of the First Canadian Infantry Battalion Band and, in 1954, director of the Canadian Guards Band. He has been conductor of the Pembroke Community Choir, musical instruction officer of the Royal Canadian Navy Band School, and director of the Gilbert and Sullivan Society, the Gayfer Singers, and the Arts Society Opera Group of Victoria, B.C. After his retirement from the army he taught music at Southwood Secondary School in Galt, Ont. (1966–72) and from 1972 to 1974 was with the department of music, Dalhousie University, Halifax.

Gayfer's *String Quartet in A Minor* (1943) won a Canadian Performing Right Society award in 1944 and his song cycle, *Six Translations from the Chinese* (1942), won a CAPAC award in 1947. In 1972 he received a commission from the Barrie Central Collegiate Band for *The Wells of Marah.* Gayfer's compositional style is traditional and tonal with light, playful melodies. He is a member of the Canadian Band Directors' Association, the National Band Association, the American Bandmasters' Association, and of CAPAC.

MUSICAL WORKS

INSTRUMENTAL

19 works for band, including: *Come On, Sigs* (1943); *Intermezzo* (1956); *'Canada, the Unknown'* (1956); *From Sea to Sea* (1957); *Royal Visit* (1957) B & H 1959, RCA PC/PCS-1004; *March of the Children* (1958); *The Royal Canadian Dental Corps* (1959) Wat; *Parliament Hill* (1960); *Red River Valley* (1961); *Canadian Landscape* (1963) B & H 1973; *Green Fields and White Hawthorne* (1970); *The Wells of Marah* (1972).

Pastorale. 1943. cl, small orch.

String Quartet in A Minor. 1943.

4 works for orchestra: *Suite for Orchestra* (1946–7); *Symphony in B♭* (1947); *Symphony in E♭* (1949–50); *Canadian Landscape* (1963) (also for band).

Suite for Woodwind Quintette. 1947. B & H 1950.

22 works for piano solo, including: *Nonchalance* (1947); *Mobiles* (1960); *Rhapsody in E minor* (1964); *Cave Pools* (1973).

Autumn Idyll. 1950. str orch.

CHORAL

10 works for choir, including: *This Happy Christmas Day* (1935) SATB; *And Did He Die?* (1937); *The Children's Prayer* (1957) SATB; *Melfa* (1958) SATB; *Psalm 150* (1967) SSAATTBB, tpt, tamb, cym, org; *Gloria* (1969) SATB; *Response: 'Write These Words'* (1969).

VOCAL

16 works for voice, including: *Six Translations from the Chinese* (1942) ten, fl, hp, str; *Song Cycle: 'Four Songs of Separation'* (1963) Trans: Arthur Waley (from Chinese); *Who are you, little i?* (1963) sop, ob, cl, pno Text: e e cummings; *Venite: 'O Come, Let Us Sing Unto the Lord'* (1967) B & H 1967; *King of Glory, King of Peace* (1967) Text: George Herbert; *Lord, who createdst Man* (1967) Text: George Herbert; *Three Songs for Medium Voice* (1970) B & H 1970 Text: Henry Howard, Robert Bridges.

BIBLIOGRAPHY

See B-B; CrC(I); K.
Meredith, Joan. 'James Gayfer Bandmaster in the Classroom', *CanCo.* No. 58, Mar. 1971 (8–13).

GELLMAN, STEVEN (b. Toronto, Ont., 16 Sept. 1948). He studied piano and composition with Samuel DOLIN at the Royal Conservatory in Toronto, performing with the CBC Symphony Orchestra as soloist at the age of sixteen in his own *Concerto for Piano and Orchestra* at the opening ceremonies of the Edward Johnson Music Building in Toronto. In 1964 he received a BMI Student Composer Award. From 1965 to 1968 he studied at the Juilliard School of Music in New York with Luciano Berio, Vincent Persichetti, and Roger Sessions. In the summers of 1965 and 1966 he studied with Darius Milhaud at Aspen, Colo, where he won first prize in composition in 1966.

Fantasy for Piano (1967) exhibits various influences, including the style of early Schoenberg or Berg, where Gellman's concern for colouristic treatment becomes an important characteristic in his music. In *Mythos II* (1968), a commission from the Stratford Music Festival, the influence of both Berio and some rock music idioms begins to appear; at the 1970 International UNESCO Rostrum of Composers in Paris, this work received a special commendation as the best work by a composer under twenty-five. The CBC has commissioned two works: *Symphony in Two Movements* (1971) and *Symphony II* (1972). The first movement of *Symphony in Two Movements,* in which the harp and piano are effectively used, is dark and brooding with constantly reiterated two- or three-note motifs; the second movement, a scherzo, is much lighter in character. The work is quite loosely constructed, the main emphasis being on mood and colouristic treatment. *Odyssey* was commissioned in 1971 by the Hamilton Philharmonic Orchestra and the rock group Tranquility Base and, Gellman says, 'was composed as an act of love and joy'. Various ideas for this piece, which stem from his work with a rock band, had been sketched during his travels through South America in the summer of 1969. He says he 'felt very fortunate in being asked to write a work combining [rock band and orchestra]. I have had first-hand experience in both worlds and also an appreciation of the merits of both' (*The Music Scene,* July-Aug. 1971). In 1972 Gellman received a commission from the National Arts Centre Orchestra for *Overture for Ottawa.* He is affiliated with BMI Canada.

MUSICAL WORKS

ORCHESTRA

Andante for Strings. 1963.
Mural for Orchestra. 1965.
Symphony in Two Movements. 1970–1; Ric, 1972.
Symphony II. 1972.
Encore (Mythos I Revisited). 1972.
Overture for Ottawa. 1972.

SOLOIST(S) WITH ORCHESTRA

Concerto for Piano and Orchestra. 1964.
Movement for Violin and Orchestra. 1967.
Odyssey. 1971; Ric, 1973. rock gp, pno, orch.

VOICE WITH INSTRUMENTAL ENSEMBLE

Quartets: Poems of G M Hopkins. 1966–7. vc, fl, vlc, hp. Text: Gerard Manley Hopkins.

INSTRUMENTAL ENSEMBLE

Two Movements for String Quartet. 1963.
'After Bethlehem'. 1966. str qt.
Mythos II. 1968. fl, str qt.

PIANO

Three Preludes and Fugues. 1962.
Sonata. 1964.
Fantasy. 1967.
Melodic Suite. 1971–2.

INSTRUMENTAL SOLO

Soliloquy. 1966. vlc.

LITERARY WORKS

ARTICLES

'Rock, Symphony Combined', *MuSc.* No. 260, July-Aug. 1971 (6, 9).

GEORGE, GRAHAM (b. Norwich, England, 11 Apr. 1912). He has lived in Canada since 1928. His teachers have included Alfred WHITEHEAD (organ and composition), Willem van Otterloo (orchestral conducting), and Paul Hindemith (composition). He received his Bachelor of Music (1936) and Doctor of Music (1939) degrees from the University of Toronto. Since 1932 he has been a church musician in Montreal, Sherbrooke, and Kingston and from 1938 to 1941 was a teacher of music in schools in Montreal and Sherbrooke. He founded and conducted the St Francis Madrigal Singers in Sherbrooke (1938), the New Symphony Orchestra of Kingston (1954), and the Kingston Choral Society (1953). He was appointed assistant professor of music and Resident Musician at Queen's University in 1946, becoming acting head of the department (1968–71) and professor from 1970. He won the Jean Lallemand prize for composition in 1938 and two Canadian Performing Right Society awards (1943 and 1947). He has received commissions from the Shakespeare Society of Montreal (incidental music to *King Lear*, 1945); the International Folk Music Council (*Songs of the Salish*, 1961); the Organ Fund Committee of St George's Cathedral, Kingston (*Passacaglia: Lobe den Herren*, 1963); the Kingston Musical Club (*Quintet for Piano and Strings*, 1967); the Canadian Government Pavilion at Expo 67 (*Sonatina for Organ*, 1967); the Royal Canadian College of Organists (*Song of Mary* and *Song of Simeon*, 1969); Paul Brodie (*Quartet for Saxophones* for the Third World Saxophone Congress, 1972); and the CBC (*Red River of the North*, 1970; *Figures in a Landscape*, 1972). Among George's invited works are the two ballets *Jabberwocky* (1947) and *Peter Pan* (1948) for Bettina Byers; *Concerto for Flute and Strings* (1963) for Wolfgang Kander; and a memorial anthem for John F. Kennedy, *In God's Commands* (1964), composed for Dr George Maybee and performed at Washington Cathedral.

Although George studied with Hindemith, his style and traditional formal structures owe more to his studies with Alfred Whitehead. In *A Hymn for Christmas Day* (1954) he reiterates the same motif, combining modal counterpoint with folk-like homophony. In both *Concerto for Flute and Strings* (1963) and *Introduction and Fugue* (1958) George has chromatic alterations of basically modal material that touch on polytonality. His choral writing forms a link with that of WILLAN and Whitehead of a generation earlier.

His musicological activities have included much work on the structural aspects of music, resulting in articles, papers, and the book *Tonality and Musical Structure* (1970). On a request from Marius Barbeau, George prepared an article on, and transcriptions of, songs of the Salish tribe of British Columbia. In a manual, *Twelve-Note Tonal Harmony and Species Counterpoint*, he set out a controversial method for the teaching of a twelve-note tonal idiom based on procedures of Bartok, Stravinsky, and Hindemith. Among his major research awards are a Canada Council Senior Arts Fellowship (1966–7), a grant from Queen's University (1970–3), and an exchange grant from the Canada Council and the Ministère des Affaires Etrangères of France (1972).

A member of the American Musicological Society and the Royal College of Organists, George is past president of the Canadian Folk Music Society (1965–8), president of the Royal Canadian College of Organists (1972), and since 1969 secretary-general of the International Folk Music Council. He is affiliated with BMI Canada.

MUSICAL WORKS

STAGE

Jabberwocky (ballet). 1947.

Evangeline (opera). 1948. Libretto: Paul Roddick, Don Warren.

Peter Pan (ballet). 1948.

The King, the Pigeon and the Hawk (ballet). 1949.

Way Out (opera). 1960. Libretto: Graham George.

INCIDENTAL MUSIC

King Lear (1946), *The Tempest* (1947), *Hamlet* (1960).

Songs for Much Ado About Nothing (1946), *Othello* (1950), *Midsummer Night's Dream* (1961).

Le Malade Imaginaire. 1964. Text: Molière.

FILM MUSIC

5 Stock pieces for the National Film Board. 1960.

RADIO DRAMA

Love is the Crooked Thing. 1955. 2ob, bsn, str qt, cb.

ORCHESTRA

Overture in C minor (1936); *Variations on an Original Theme* (1937); *Kingston Suite* (1940, rev 1968); *Prelude, Andante and Fugue* (1940); *Music for Cordelia (Variations on an Original Theme)* (1948); *Prelude for Orchestra* (1949); *Symphonic Study* (1950); *Symphony* (1951); *Experiences of a Self-made Theme* (1956); *Songs of the Salish* (1961).

SMALL ORCHESTRA

The Queen's Jig. 1950.

STRING ORCHESTRA

Dorian Fugue (1942, rev 1957); *Variations for Strings* (1942).

BAND

March for School Band (1958); *Music in Memory of C A Dunning, Chancellor of Queen's University* (1958); *Overture ('Run Smooth')* (1960).

SOLOIST WITH ORCHESTRA

Concerto for Flute and Strings. 1963.

CHOIR WITH ORCHESTRA

The Song of the Victory of Agincourt (1939) Text: Michael Drayton; *A Hymn for Christmas Day* (1954) Text: Jeremy Taylor; *Red River of the North* (1970) Text: Thomas Saunders.

CHOIR

Let Thy Merciful Ears (1934) Text: Collect for the 4th Sunday after Trinity; *The Strain Upraise (Troyte's Chant)* (1935) Text: B Notker. Trans: J M Neale; *Creator of the Starry Height* (1935) Text: Latin. Trans: J M Neale; *If Ye Love Me* (1936; Gray, 1937) Text: St John 14:15; *O Worship the King* (1936; Gray, 1946) Text: Robert Grant (Psalm 104); *O Lord, Support Us* (1936) Text: John Henry Newman; *Lord of all Power and Might* (1937; Gray, 1940) Text: Collect for the 7th Sunday after Trinity; *Eternal God, the Light of the Minds* (1937) Text: Gelasian Sacramentary; *Office of Holy Communion* (1937); *Office of Holy Communion (Missa Brevis)* (1937); *Good Christian Men, Rejoice (In dulci jubilo)* (1937) Text: J M Neale; *When the Sun had Sunk to Rest* (two versions) (1938) (1939); *Praise to the Lord (Lobe den Herren)* (1938) Text: J Neander. Trans: C Winkworth; *As I Sat on a Sunny Bank* (arr) (1938) Text: trad; *Benedictus es, Domine* (1938; Gray, 1940) Text: American Episcopalian Prayer Book; *Magnificat and Nunc dimittis* (1940) Text: St Luke 1:46–55, St Luke 2:29–32; *Ride On, Ride On In Majesty* (1940; Gray, 1941) Text: Henry H Milman; *Unto Us a Son Is Given* (1942; OUP, 1945) Text: Alice Meynell; *Blessed be the Lord God* (1942) Text: Psalm 72:20–1; *Thou art Worthy* (1957) Text: Epistle (Revelations 4) and Proper for Trinity Sunday; *O Mortal Man* (1958); *O Trinity, Most Blessed Light* (1958) Text: St Ambrose. Trans: J M Neale; *O Dearest God* (1960) Text: Jeremy Taylor; *O God, Wonderful art Thou* (1960; Ber, 1965) Text: Jeremy Taylor; *New Prince, New Pomp* (1962; Gray, 1962) Text: Robert Southwell; *Now Glad of Heart* (1962; Gray, 1962) Text: A H Fox-Strangways; *In God's Commands* (1964; Gray, 1964) Text: Robert Herrick; *Junior Choir Anthems for the Church Year* (1965–6; Aug, 1967); *The King of Love* (1965) Text: H W Baker; *Let All Mortal Flesh* (1965) Text: Liturgy of St James. Trans: Gerard Moultrie; *Father Most Holy* (1965) Text: Percy Dearwer; *Fight the Good Fight* (1966; Abn, 1966) Text: J S B Monsell; *Present-day Anthems for Junior Choirs* (1968–72); *Missa Brevis* (1969); *The Song of Mary* (1969) Text: St Luke 1:46–55; *The Song of Simeon* (1969) Text: St Luke 2: 29–42; *Brightest and Best* (1969) Text: R Heber; *My God, I Thank Thee* (1971) Text: St Luke 18:11, 13; *Glory be to God for Dappled Things* (1973) Text: Gerard Manley Hopkins; 11 *Hymn-tunes* (1939–65).

VOICES (PART-SONGS)

The Wonders of Heaven (1934) Text: Robert George; *Lay Daffodils Upon Sweet Flora's Grave* (1935); *O Surely Melody From Heaven Was Sent* (1935) Text: Kirke White; *The Miller of Dee* (1937) Text: trad; *She Comes Not When Noon is On the Roses*

(1939) Text: Herbert Trench; *Fear No More the Heat O' the Sun* (1940) Text: William Shakespeare; *Two Songs on Kingston Themes* (1950) Text: John Murray Gibbon; *Queen's University Songs* (1950).

VOICE

Often the Day Had a Most Joyful Morn (1935); *Song* (without words) (1937); *Blow Away the Morning Dew* (1947) Text: trad; *Margaret, Are You Grieving* (1949) Text: Gerard Manley Hopkins; *Upon the Heavenly Scarp* (1951) Text: A M Klein; *Seven Songs on Poems of Robert George* (1958) Text: Robert George; *Petit Bout d'Homme* (1959) Text: M A Allard.

VOICE(S) WITH INSTRUMENTAL ENSEMBLE

While I Long for My Love (1938) sop, ob, str qt Text: Graham George; *Robin Hood of Sherwood* (1970) SATB, str qt, cb Text: Audrey Alexandra Brown; *Figures in a Landscape* (1972) sop, str qt Text: David Helwig.

INSTRUMENTAL ENSEMBLE

String Quartet No 1 (1936); *Fugal Rhapsody for String Quartet* (1939); *String Quartet No 2* (1946); *String Quartet No 3* (1950); *Sonata for Oboe and Piano* (1950); *Duo for Violin and Cello* (1951); *Processional Fanfare for 3 Trumpets and Organ* (1951); *Sonata for Violin and Piano* (1951); *String Quartet No 4* (1951); *String Trio* (1951); *Fantasy for Violin and Piano* (1952); *Sonata for Flute and Piano* (1952); *Trumpet Tune* (1952) tpt, org; *Concerto for Violin, Recorders and Piano* (1958); *Introduction and Fugue* (arr) (1958); *Trio for Young Performers* (1958) vln, vlc, pno; *Six Flourishes for Academic Brass* (1961–71); *Quintet for Piano and Strings* (1967); *Quartet for Saxophones* (1972).

PIANO

Lullaby for Susan (1940); *Suite for Piano* (1952); *Suite for Children* (1958); *Elégie pour une jeune fille inconnue* (1970); *Eight Structured Minutiae* (1971).

ORGAN

A Pompous Fancy (1938); *Prelude No 1 on 'The King's Majesty'* (1946); *Three Fugues* (1951); *Introduction and Fugue* (1957); *Processional March No 1 & 2 for a Secular Occasion* (1957 & 1958); *Elegy* (1958; Gray, 1968); *Two Preludes on 'The King's Majesty'* (1959; Gray, 1963); *Three Fugues* (1964; Ber, 1970); *Suite on 'Grace Church, Gananoque'* (1965; Abn, 1972); *Suite on 'St Paul's Kingston'* (1966); *Sonatina* (1967); *Suite on 'Heart's Adoration'* (1969); *Prelude and Fugue Nos 1 & 2* (1971); *A Small Chaconne and Fugue* (1972).

BIBLIOGRAPHY

See B-B; C69,72; CrC(II); K; Smh; Wa.
'Folk Music in Opera', *Opera Canada*. Vol. VI, no. 3, Sept. 1965 (11, 86–7).
Hepner, Lee. ' "Tonality and Musical Structure" (Graham George)', *CMB*. Vol. III, Autumn-Winter 1971 (185–7).
Smith, Leo. 'Winner of 1943 Award', *Canadian Review of Music and Art*. Vol. III, no. 5–6, June-July 1944 (22).

LITERARY WORKS

BOOKS

Tonality and Musical Structure. London: Faber & Faber, 1970.

ARTICLES

'Alfred Whitehead: Doctor of Music', *AGO/RCCO Magazine*, 1971 (60, 66).
'Antics and Accomplishments by Mr. Gould', *Saturday Night*. Vol. LXXV, Sept. 3, 1960 (17–19).
'Back to the Drawing Board (Louis Riel)', *Saturday Night*. Vol. LXXXIII, Feb. 1968 (42).
'Ballet in Canada: a Critical Look', *Saturday Night*. Vol. LXXIX, Dec. 1964 (22–5).
'Canada's Music – 1955: an Attempt to Assess the Quality of Contemporary Canadian Composition', *Culture*. Vol. XVI, Mar. 1955 (51–65).
'Canada's New Concert Halls – a Survey', *Saturday Night*. Vol. LXXV, Jan. 9, 1960 (10–12).
'Folk-Singing or Just Folks', *Saturday Night*. Vol. LXVI, Sept. 30, 1961 (33–5).
'International Folk Music Council', *CMJ*. Vol. VI, no. 1, 1961–2 (36).
'Music at Stratford: Tail of a Comet', *CMJ*. Vol. III, no. 1, 1958–9 (24).
'Music at Stratford and Vancouver', *Saturday Night*. Vol. LXXIV, Sept. 12, 1959 (24–8, 32).
'Music Leads a Double Life', *Saturday Night*. Vol. LXXVI, Sept. 2, 1961 (13–15).
'Music Where the Wind Blows Free', *CMJ*. Vol. VI, no. 3, 1961–2 (12).
'Music: Winnipeg's Centennial Concert

Hall Opens With a Fine Flourish', *Saturday Night*. Vol. LXXXIII, June 1968 (41–3).
'Reports from the Festivals: Vancouver', *CMJ*. Vol. v, no. 1, 1960–1 (47).
'Songs of the Salish Indians of British Columbia', *Journal of the International Folk Music Council*. Vol. XIV, 1963 (22–9).
'Stratford', *Saturday Night*. Vol. LXXIV, May 23, 1959 (14–15).
' "The Structure of Dramatic Music", 1607–1909', *MQ*. Vol. 52, no. 4, Oct. 1966 (465–82).
'Three Canadian Concert Halls', *CMJ*. Vol. IV, no. 2, 1959–60 (4).
'Towards a Definition of Romanticism in Music', *Queen's Quarterly*. Vol. LXXII, Summer 1965 (253–69).
'Vernon Barford', *CMJ*. Vol. v, no. 2, 1960–1 (4–12).
'White Noise and Breaking Crockery', *Saturday Night*. Vol. LXXV, Sept. 17, 1960 (17–20).
' "Work-of-artness" of a Work of Art', *Queen's Quarterly*. Vol. LXXIV, Spring 1967 (119–39).

GLICK, SRUL IRVING (b. Toronto, Ont., 8 Sept. 1934). He began his serious compositional studies with John WEINZWEIG at the University of Toronto, where he received his Bachelor of Music (1955) and Master of Music (1958) degrees. He studied composition with Darius Milhaud for two summers in Aspen, Colo, and in Paris, and also studied composition in Paris with Louis Saguer and Max Deutsch.

In his early works Glick employs dark polytonal material with lyrical melodic writing, *Four Preludes for Piano* (1958) being an example of this brooding character. In *Sinfonia Concertante* (1961) a chromatic but tonal thematic language is used; the opening is again brooding and the melodic material is sustained to build thick chordal textures. In conjunction with a lyrical quality, this textural thickness becomes a characteristic trait in Glick's subsequent works, e.g. *Trio* (1964). In his dance-symphony *Heritage* (1967), a commission for the New Dance Group of Toronto, Glick reflects the life of a Jewish immigrant to Canada through references to Jewish folk material, employing tonal and lyrical melodies in a contrapuntal texture. On another Jewish subject, *... i never saw another butterfly ...* (1968, a CBC commission for Maureen Forrester), Glick uses a collection of poems by children, many of whom subsequently died in the death camps of Nazi Europe. The texts are so emotionally charged that Glick's uncomplicated setting, using lyrical, atonal material, is both sensitive and poignant. In *Gathering In* (1970), commissioned by the McGill Chamber Orchestra, Glick experiments with more contemporary formal ideas but the style, although more virtuosic than in previous works, has not changed significantly. *Lamentations* (1971) contains clusters and exotic colours achieved by extensive use of vibraphone, glockenspiel, tubular chimes, and glissandi harmonics in the strings. *Psalm for Orchestra* (1971), commissioned by the Hamilton Philharmonic Orchestra, is built on two Jewish Chassidic folk songs. With an effective marriage between the old lyrical tonal melodies and Glick's use of clusters, the work is, in effect, poly-sectional with the solo string octet acting as a concertante to the orchestra's role as ripieno.

Glick has written several orchestral works on commission, among them *Elegy for Orchestra* (1964) for the East York Community Orchestra; *Pan* (1966) for the Atlantic Symphony Orchestra; *Symphony No. 2* (1967) for the Toronto Chamber Orchestra; and *Lamentations (Sinfonia Concertante No. 2)* (1971) for the Kingston Symphony Orchestra. He is a producer of music programs for CBC Radio (Toronto) and conductor of the Beth Tikvah synagogue choir in Toronto, and was a teacher of theory and composition at the Royal Conservatory in Toronto (1963–9). He is a past president of the Canadian League of Composers and a member of CAPAC.

MUSICAL WORKS

STAGE

Heritage Dance Symphony. 1967.

ORCHESTRA

Two Essays. 1957.
Sinfonietta for Full Orchestra. 1958
Suite Hebraique. 1961 (rev 1964).
Elegy for Orchestra. 1964.
Pan. 1966.
Psalm for Orchestra. 1971.

SMALL ORCHESTRA

Dance Concertante No 1. 1963.

Symphony for Chamber Orchestra (Symphony No 1). 1966.
Symphony No 2. 1967.

STRING ORCHESTRA
Sonata for String Orchestra. 1957.
Sinfonia Concertante for String Orchestra. 1961; Ric, 1973. RCA LSC-3128.
Suite Hebraique (arr). 1965.
Gathering In (A Symphonic Concept for Strings). 1970; Ric, 1972.

SOLOIST WITH ORCHESTRA
Symphonic Dialogues for Piano and Orchestra. 1963.
... i never saw another butterfly.... 1968. alto, chamb orch. Text: Children's poems from the concentration camp at Terezin.
Lamentations (Sinfonia Concertante No 2). 1972. str qt, orch.
Four Songs of Peace and War. 1972. ten, orch. Text: Kenneth Patchen.

VOICE WITH INSTRUMENTAL ENSEMBLE
Deborah (Flaming Star). 1972. narr, brass qnt. Text: Donia Clenman.

VOICE
Suite from Snow White and Rose Red (7 songs). 1962. vc, pno. Text: Brothers Grimm.
Anthropos in Transit (Song Cycle). 1963. bar, pno. Text: Gerald Vise.
... i never saw another butterfly.... 1968; MCA, 1972. alto, pno. Select CC 15.073. Text: Children's poems from the concentration camp at Terezin.
Two Landscapes for Tenor and Piano (from 'Four Songs of Peace and War'). 1973. Text: Kenneth Patchen.

INSTRUMENTAL ENSEMBLE
Wedding Suite for String Quartet. 1957.
Divertimento Sextet. 1958. fl, cl, bsn, str trio.
Trio for Clarinet, Piano and Cello. 1958–9.
Suite Hebraique (arr). 1963; B & H, 1968. cl, pno. Dom s-69004.
Suite Hebraique (arr). 1963. sop sax, pno. Golden Crest RE 7049.
Trio for Violin, Viola and Cello. 1963.
Dance Concertante No. 2. 1964. fl, cl, tpt, vlc, pno.
Suite Hebraique (arr). 1964. str qt.
Sonata for Jazz Quintet. 1964. cl, vib, elec guit, cb, perc.
Sonatina for Jazz Sextet. 1965 (rev 1966). cl, vib, guit, vlc, cb, perc.
Divertissement for Seven Instruments and Conductor. 1968. cl, vib, guit, mand, vlc, cb, perc.
Suite Hebraique No 2. 1969. cl, str trio, pno.
Suite from Flaming Star. 1972. brass qnt.

PIANO
Four Preludes. 1958; GVT, 1968. London CTLS-5107.
Seven Preludes for Piano. 1958–9.
Ballade for Piano. 1959.
Song and Caprice. 1960; GVT, 1968. Dom s-69002 (Caprice).

INSTRUMENTAL SOLO
Petite Suite pour flûte. 1960; GVT, 1972.

BIBLIOGRAPHY

CrC(I); Wa.
'Srul Irving Glick: a Canadian Who Came Home', *CanCo*. No. 23, Nov. 1957 (20, 38–9).
'Srul Irving Glick – a portrait', *Mu*. No. 5, Oct. 1967 (8–9).

LITERARY WORKS

REVIEWS
'Sydney Hodkinson: "Caricatures" ', *CMB*. Vol. I, Spring-Summer 1970 (146–7).

GOLDBERG, THEO (b. Chemnitz, Germany, 29 Sept. 1921). In Berlin Goldberg studied at the Staatliche Hochschule für Musik (1945–50) and with the composer Boris Blacher. His *Robinson und Freitag* was commissioned by RIAS Berlin and the *Engel-Etude* by the Berliner Festwochen 1952. He came to Canada in 1954 and since then has been teaching in Vancouver and has also been a free-lance composer for radio dramas and stage productions. In 1972 he received his Doctor of Music degree in composition from the University of Toronto.

Goldberg's *Divertissement No. 3 in G* (1957) is neo-classical, with dissonant tonality and a Stravinsky-like rhythmic drive. *Sinfonia Concertante* (1967), a commission from the Vancouver Symphony Orchestra, was written 'to allow young people to see what it means and what it feels like to work with professional musicians in professional music-making', the student concertante group consisting of flute, clarinet, trumpet, violin, and cello; the work is propelled by a constant forward-moving rhythm. His opera *Galatea Elettronica* (1969) is based on the Pygmalion theme. Pygmalion is an eccentric inventor who creates an electronic prima donna, Galatea; the inventor's two sponsors seek to exploit Galatea for their own selfish purposes, but Pygmalion has fallen in love with his creation and jealously guards her. Using a twelve-tone row, Goldberg exploits the sound spectrum afforded him by the use of electronic organ and synthesizer.

Goldberg is a member of the Canadian League of Composers and of GEMA.

MUSICAL WORKS

STAGE

Nacht mit Kleopatra, Op 3 (opera/ballet). 1950. Libretto: Theo Goldberg.

Four Surrealistic short operas (Agamemnon's Death, Phedra, Judith, Odysseus and the Sirens), Op 4. 1949–50. Libretto: Johannes Huebner.

Robinson und Freitag, Op 6 (radio opera). 1951. Libretto: Heinz von Cramer.

Engel-Etude, Op 10 (chamb opera). 1952. Libretto: Heinz von Cramer.

Galatea Elettronica (opera). 1969. Libretto: Theo Goldberg and writings of Leonardo da Vinci.

Jeanne des Anges (chamb opera). 1972. Libretto: Theo Goldberg.

ORCHESTRA

La Femme Cent Têtes, Op 5. 1950.

Variations on a Theme by Strauss, Op 9. 1952; Bote & Bock.

Divertissement No 3 in G, Op 15. 1957.

SOLOIST(S) WITH ORCHESTRA

Double Concerto for Oboe and Bassoon, Op 11. 1952.

Cantata, Op 13. 1953. ten, SATB, orch. Text: Werner Bergengruen.

Sinfonia Concertante. 1967. fl, cl, tpt, vln, vlc, orch.

VOICE WITH INSTRUMENTAL ENSEMBLE

Samogonski-Trio, Op 8. 1951; Bote & Bock, 1952. bar, cl, vlc, pno. Text: Werner Bergengruen.

INSTRUMENTAL ENSEMBLE

String Quartet in D, Op 1. 1949.

Trio for Woodwinds, Op 2. 1949.

Clarinet Quintet, Op 7. 1952; Bote & Bock, 1952. cl, str qt.

Divertissement No 1, Op 12. 1953. vln, pno.

Divertissement No 2, Op 14. c1955. ww, pno, vln.

Quartet for Alto Flute, Viola, Violoncello and Harp. 1962.

Three Movements for Bassoon and Buchla. 1971. bsn, elec tape.

Calliope. 1973. bsn, trb, pno, vln, elec tape, sound-related images.

ELECTRONIC TAPE

Variations of a Mandala. 1973. elec tape, sound-related images.

Metachrosis. 1973. elec tape, computer. Collab with Ralph Dyck.

BIBLIOGRAPHY

See B-B; B65,71.

GRATTON, (J.-J.) HECTOR (b. Hull, Que., 13 Aug. 1900; d. Montreal, Que., 16 July 1970). He studied piano with Alphonse Martin and Alfred LALIBERTÉ, who introduced him to the works of Scriabin and Medtner. For harmony, counterpoint, and composition, his teachers were Oscar O'Brien, Alfred WHITEHEAD and Albertine Morin-Labrecque. O'Brien interested him in folk song, which influenced his later work. Gratton was touring accompanist for the entertainer Charles Marchand and took part with him in the Canadian Pacific Railway folk arts and crafts festivals in Quebec City from 1927 to 1930. As arranger and conductor, he was involved in early broadcasts of the CBC and composed the music for the well-known series 'Je me souviens', for which Félix Leclerc was writer. In 1937 Gratton's symphonic poem *Légende* won the Prix Jean-Lallemand in the second annual composition competition sponsored by the Société des Concerts Symphoniques de Montréal. The work was given its first performance in Plateau Hall on April 23 of that year under Wilfrid Pelletier, and repeated the following year by the Toronto Symphony Orchestra under Sir Ernest MAC MILLAN. Gratton also wrote five *Danses canadiennes*, the suite *Coucher de soleil* (1947) for string orchestra, and a sonata for piano and violin, as well as a large number of settings and arrangements of folk songs for various combinations. He is also remembered for the music he wrote for a Christmas story, *L'Imagerie*, to verses by

Cécile Chabot, broadcast by the CBC in 1945. He was affiliated with BMI Canada.

MUSICAL WORKS

STAGE

Les Feux follets (ballet). 1952.
La Légende de l'arbre sec (ballet).
Le Pommier (ballet).
Marie Madeleine (ballet).

RADIO

L'Imagerie (Pastorale de Noël). 1945. actors, soli, chorus, small orch. Text: Cécile Chabot.

ORCHESTRA

Légende. 1937.
Fantasia on Two French-Canadian Folk Songs. 1950.
Dansons le Carcaillou. 1952.
Fantasia sur V'la l'bon vent. 1952.
L'Ecossaise (arr).
Troisième Danse canadienne (arr).

SMALL ORCHESTRA

Crépuscule (Nocturne) (arr). 1952.
Danse rustique (arr).
Sous les Erables (fantaisie sur 'O Canada').
Troisième Danse canadienne (arr).

STRING ORCHESTRA

Deuxième Danse canadienne (arr). 1928.
Coucher de soleil. 1947. str, pno.
Variations libres sur 'Isabeau s'y promène'. 1954. str, pno, cel, hp.
Au Bois du rossignolet.
Berceuse sauvage (arr).
Chanson écossaise (arr).
Chanson intime.
Chanson pastorale (arr).
Cinquième Danse canadienne.
Danse rustique (arr).
L'Ecossaise (Clog Dance) (arr).
Filey Filey o mon navire.
Inquiétude (arr).
La Joie de vivre (arr).
Là-haut sur ces montagnes.
Nocturne from 'Maria Chapdelaine'.
Près de la fontaine.
Sixième Danse canadienne (arr).
Septième Danse canadienne.
Suite pastorale.
Tendresse (arr).

SOLOIST(S) WITH ORCHESTRA

A la veillée. accord (or vln or harmonica), orch.
Nocturne (Lune). sop, pno, str.
Le Violoneux. vc, orch. Text: Marcel Gagnon.
Les Sucres. vc, orch. Text: Marcel Gagnon.
L'Epluchette. vc, orch. Text: Marcel Gagnon.
D'où viens-tu bergère. vc, str.
Marie-Anne s'en va-t'au moulin (fantaisie). sop, ten, orch.
Complainte de la folle. alto, pno, orch.
Le Roi Dagobert. vc, orch.
19 French Canadian Folk Songs (arr). vc, orch.

CHOIR WITH ORCHESTRA

O Canada (arr). SATB, orch.

CHOIR

A St-Malo (arr). SATB, pno. Text: trad.
La Croix et le Drapeau. c1940; Arch, 1943. SATB, pno. Text: Marie-Thérèse Vaillancourt.
Ola Glomstula (arr). SATB, pno. Text: trad.
Vocero. SATB. Text: Rudyar.
180 Canadian folk songs (harmonized). TTB.

VOICE

Dollard t'appelle. c1940. vc, pno. Arch.
Blondinette. vc, pno. Text: Ernest Pallascio-Morin.

VOICES WITH INSTRUMENTAL ENSEMBLE

Complainte du Père Buteux. TTBB, str, pno.
Pique à la Pointe. TTBB, str, pno.

INSTRUMENTAL ENSEMBLE

Première Danse canadienne, Op 3. 1927; FH, 1930. vln, pno.
Deuxième Danse canadienne, Op 5, No 1. 1928; FH, 1930. vln, pno.
Reminiscence, Op 5, No 2. 1928; FH, 1930. vln, pno.
Troisième Danse canadienne. c1930. vln, pno.
Quatrième Danse canadienne. 1935; Ber, 1952. vln, pno.
Chanson écossaise. 1940; Ber, 1957. vln, pno.
Berceuse sauvage. fl (or vln), pno.
Chanson enfantine. vln, pno.
L'Ecossaise (Clog Dance). vln, pno.
Légende. vlc, pno.
Papillon, tu es volage. vlc, pno.
Rondo. str qnt, pno.
Sérénade. vlc, pno.

PIANO

Tendresse. c1940; Passe-Temps, 1946.

La Joie de vivre. c1940; Passe-Temps, 1945.
Crépuscule. 1952; Ber, 1956.
Conte (Fairy Tale). 1954; Ber, 1958.
Danse rustique.
Chanson intime (arr).
Chanson pastorale.
Etude sur le mouvement perpétuel de Weber.
Inquiétude.
Sixième Danse canadienne.
Sonate pour piano.

BIBLIOGRAPHY

See B-B; K; Lv; Mm; Wa.

LITERARY WORKS

ARTICLES

'Eminent Canadian Composers', *Canadian Review of Music and Art.* Jan. 1943 (3).

H

HANSON, JENS (b. Raton, N. Mex., 29 Nov. 1936). He studied piano from the sixth grade on with various teachers. After receiving his Bachelor of Science degree from the Massachusetts Institute of Technology (1954), he studied at the University of Denver, Colo, with Norman Lockwood (composition, 1961–3) and Fred Ruhof (viola, 1961–4), receiving a Master of Arts degree in 1963. In Aspen, Colo, he studied composition with Darius Milhaud and viola with John Garvey (summer 1964). From 1965 to 1968 he studied at Yale University with Allen Forte (theory) and David Schwarz (viola). In 1968 he joined the staff of the University of Windsor, where he is an associate professor. He received his Doctor of Philosophy degree from Yale in 1969.

MUSICAL WORKS

INSTRUMENTAL

Symphony in Four Movements. 1963. med orch.
4 works for chamber ensemble: *String Quartet* (1963); *Trio for Flute, Clarinet and Bassoon* (1963); *Suite for Three Clarinets – One Player* (1964); *A Small Entertainment with which to Enliven a Sunday Afternoon* (1971) cl, vln, pno.
Festival Sonata. 1965. org.
Incidental Music for Shakespeare's 'Romeo and Juliet'. 1970. 2cl, rec, brass, tamb, str qt.

CHORAL

2 works for a cappella mixed choir: *Psalm 46* (1963); *Discipline* (1964).
Incarnation. 1969. SSAATTBB, fl, cl, b cl, 2vln, vla, perc.
Expectations. 1970. alto, SATB, ww, brass, timp, perc, 2vln, vlc, org.

VOCAL

2 works for vc and pno: *Psalm 3* (1963) bar, pno; *Five from Dorothy* (1972) mezz, pno.
His Roses and Hers. 1972. 2 readers, pno, 2 tape rec, elec synthesizer.

HARTWELL, HUGH (b. Hamilton, Ont., 18 Jan. 1945). He studied composition with István ANHALT at McGill University, receiving his Bachelor of Music degree in 1967. At the University of Pennsylvania, where he received his Master of Arts degree in 1971, he studied composition with George Rochberg, R. Wernick, and George Crumb. He has won several awards, including a BMI Student Composer Award for *Alba* (1967), the Golden Jubilee Award of the Canadian Federation of University Women for which he composed *Kâmê'a* (1971), and he tied with John HAWKINS for first prize in the Second-Century-Week Composition Competition sponsored jointly by the Universities of Alberta and Calgary (*Matinée d'ivresse*, 1967).

Hartwell's *Septet* (1969) is twelve-tone with complex rhythmic counterpoint, the approach being intellectual with some exploitation of instrumental colour. In *Kâmê'a* he moved away from the clear lines of counterpoint of the earlier work to a fragmented pointillism, with complex rhythmic structures still an important characteristic. In 1972 Hartwell received a commission from the CBC to compose a work for the Lyric Arts Trio. He is an assistant professor of music at Kirkland College in Clinton, N.Y., and is affiliated with BMI Canada.

MUSICAL WORKS

CHOIR

ALBA from 'Langue d'Oc'. 1967. Text: Ezra Pound.

VOICE WITH INSTRUMENTAL ENSEMBLE

'How to Play Winning Bridge'. 1969. alto, fl, vla, tamb, BD. Text: Hugh Hartwell.

INSTRUMENTAL ENSEMBLE

Movements for Woodwind Quintet (withdrawn).
Rondo for Woodwind Trio. 1965.
Matinée d'ivresse (a.r., 1872). 1966; Jay, 1971. cl, vln, vlc, pno, perc.
Soul-Piece for 6 or 7 Players. 1967 (rev 1969); Ber, 1969.
3 x 3: An Epigram. 1968. cl, vib, vla.
Acitoré. 1968. 3ww, tba, pno, 2perc.
Septet. 1969; Jay, 1971. 3cl, hn, str trio.
Kâmê'a. 1971. alto fl (picc), tpt, hn, trb, hp, cb, 2perc.

PIANO

Four Piano Pieces for Children. 1966.
Piece for Piano. 1968.

BIBLIOGRAPHY

Rivard, Yolande. 'L'Enseignement de la composition à l'Université McGill', *Vie Musicale.* No. 8, May 1968 (5–12).

HAWKINS, JOHN (b. Montreal, Que., 26 July 1944). In spite of the mere seven works to his credit, John Hawkins in his thirtieth year has, through the remarkable quality and maturity of his works, become one of the foremost composers in Canada. In listening to his works or analysing them in detail one is struck by an intense musicality, an extraordinarily sensitive ear, and by a very high intelligence in the ordering of musical materials. No two of his works are alike. He is a true perfectionist, as a composer and as a performer.

Born in Montreal in 1944, he studied piano with Lubka Kolessa at the Conservatoire in Montreal, where he won the Premier Prix in piano (1967), and at McGill University where he obtained his Bachelor of Music degree (1967) and Concert Diploma (1968). He was subsequently awarded a Woodrow Wilson National Fellowship to study composition with István ANHALT at McGill, receiving his Master of Musical Arts degree in 1970 before leaving for Toronto to begin his duties as lecturer in theory and composition at the University of Toronto. In 1969 he attended Pierre Boulez' conducting course in Basel, along with Serge GARANT and Bruce MATHER.

Hawkins' *Eight Movements* for flute and clarinet won first prize (jointly with Hugh HARTWELL) in the Second-Century-Week Composition Competition of the University of Alberta (1967). In 1968 he wrote *Remembrances* in response to the John Adaskin Memorial Award of the Canadian Music Centre. In the same year he won a BMI Student Composer Award for *Sequences* and in 1965 and 1966 awards for performance excellence from the Foundation des Amis de l'Art. The Canada Council gave him Arts Bursaries for study in performance (1967–8) and in composition (1969–70). *Waves* (1971) was the result of a commission of the Société de Musique Contemporaine du Québec. An outstanding pianist, Hawkins has performed regularly with the SMCQ in Montreal and with New Music Concerts in Toronto.

The smallness of Hawkins' output is partially due to the demands of his teaching position and his activity as a performer. However, commenting in 1973 on a compositional silence of two years he said, 'I could probably write a lot more if I wanted to rehash older ideas, but I want to do something new to *me.* I simply haven't hit upon an idea which I think is different from the other pieces I've written.' (*Canadian Composer*, Sept. 1973)

There is very little in the way of improvisation, open form, or other aleatoric procedures in Hawkins' work. His own experience in performed aleatoric pieces has caused him to view the freedom of the performer with suspicion: 'I think in many cases the composer simply can't make up his mind what he wants to do and so he leaves it to the performer. A lot of pieces these days are only sound effects and are very weak in structure. The most satisfying pieces for me to play are those where everything is written out ... where I don't have to be the composer.' (Op. cit.)

Hawkins views his activity as a performer as a vital adjunct to his composing, in spite of the heavy demands in time that it imposes. 'I think the experience of performing is very important for a young composer. The practical experience is worth more than any lessons in composition. Other people's music has meant everything to me. I've learned what aspects of the language of contemporary music I like and which things I can develop myself, perhaps, in a small way. I have also learned what *not* to do, where the pitfalls lie, especially notation-wise.' (Op. cit.)

Among contemporary composers, Boulez, Ligeti, Carter, and Crumb are those who have perhaps most influenced Hawkins' musical thinking. He agrees that the Carter 'Piano Sonata', of which he has given superb performances, is an austere work, but 'I can't think of a single piano sonata written in this century that compares with it – a massive monumental work. I take music seriously. I don't like "pretty" pieces of music. I've never tried to write anything humorous. I like music that seems to be on edge, that disturbs. I like to be disturbed by things. What I like about Mahler's music is a kind of terror, of not knowing exactly where you're going. I find the same things in Carter too. I suppose this is indicative of my own musical approach. I'm trying to find something through music.' (Op. cit.)

Hawkins has made extensive use of musical quotation in only one work, *Remembrances* (1969). 'There's a lot of Mahler in *Remembrances.* I was going through a soul-searching period then and the music is sort of autobiographical, sad, nostalgic. It's certainly my most "successful" piece but I wouldn't write another piece like that. It's part of the past and the idea of quotation doesn't appeal as much to me now as it did then.' (Op. cit.) Quotations from Mahler, Beethoven, and Brahms are presented as distant memories of which only details – a melodic fragment, a chord, a figuration, or a sonority – remain of the original. The instrumental ensemble itself – harp, piano, and three brass instruments – heightens this sense of transmutation. The transitions between the various quotations are of extraordinary tonal subtlety.

Waves (1971) was inspired by the 'Four Quartets' of T.S. Eliot. As distinct from the sectional nature of many of Hawkins' other works, *Waves* is one great arch: 'I'm aiming at a control of musical time so that the piece will have some kind of higher unity, and that's very difficult for me to achieve. Musical ideas come to me in the form of small cells and to develop those into a long piece is very difficult.' (Op. cit.) Hawkins' harmonic mastery is apparent in the beautiful florid vocal writing and in the multi-dynamic piano part, in the magnificent variety of vertical sonorities, the spacing of chords, the handling of fixed and mobile pitches that give *Waves* an enormous sense of direction. The piano part is like an amplification of the wave motion of the vocal line. In the piano writing, the control of dynamics and of resonances yields an incredible variety of colours.

One of Hawkins' finest works, *Variations for Orchestra* (1970), had not been performed by a professional orchestra up to the time of writing.

John Hawkins is a member of the Canadian League of Composers and of CAPAC.

BRUCE MATHER

MUSICAL WORKS

ORCHESTRA

Two Pieces for Orchestra. 1970. 8′. full orch. CMC. Mar 27, 1971, (2nd mov't only) Mtl, Mtl-Cons, Seventh Annual Sympos for Student Composers, Sympos Orch, Serge Garant. June 4, 1975, (both mov'ts) Tor, TS, Lukas Foss.

VOICE

Waves. 1971. 11′. sop, pno. CMC. Nov 4, 1971, Mtl, SMCQ, Margo McKinnon(sop), Bruce Mather(pno).

VOICE WITH INSTRUMENTAL ENSEMBLE

Three Cavatinas. 1967. 7′. sop, vln, vlc, vib, cel. Ber, 1969. Text: Walt Whitman, W B Yeats, W S Burroughs. Nov 1, 1968, Ann Arbor, Mich.

INSTRUMENTAL ENSEMBLE

Eight Movements. 1966. 7′55″. fl, cl. CMC. Mar 6, 1967, Ed'tn.

Sequences (for two groups). 1968. 8′20″. 3fl, 3cl, 12str, 2 (3)perc plyrs. CMC. Nov. 4, 1972, Tor, EJB, John Hawkins and Robert Aitken(conds).

Remembrances. 1969. 11′15″. pno, hp, tpt,

hn, trb, xyl. Jay, 1971. July 19, 1969, Stratford Fest.

PIANO

Five Pieces for Piano. 1967. 7'. Jay, 1972. Jan 15, 1968, Tor, John Hawkins.

BIBLIOGRAPHY

Mather, Bruce. 'Le collage musical: "Remembrances" de John Hawkins', *CMB.* Vol. III, Autumn-Winter 1971 (98–102).

Morgan, Kit. 'Hawkins Believes Performance Integral Part of Composing', *MuSc.* No. 265, May-June 1972 (12, 25).

Schulman, Michael. 'For John Hawkins, composing isn't easy', *CanCo.* No. 83, Sept. 1973 (5–9).

HAWORTH, FRANK (b. Liverpool, England, 13 Jan. 1905). Haworth's early musical studies were largely by self-teaching, with guidance from local musicians. He began composing at the age of eleven. He received his Licentiate in Music from Trinity College, London (1927). He played cello and organ, founded and conducted several ensembles, and taught in schools during the 1930s. In 1940 he was sent to Bermuda for wartime service and later became Music Officer for the British Council in the West Indies. He was director of concert music for Radio Bermuda and music journalist for the *Royal Gazette.* He composed music for radio and dramatic productions, including a Bermuda Festival production of *Macbeth.* In Toronto from 1956, he became part-time art and music critic for the *Globe and Mail.* Besides being a free-lance critic, commentator, teacher, conductor, he was also a composer for CBC radio and television, writing music for two TV series: 'Mr. O' and 'Old Testament Tales'. He was traveling organizer-instructor for the Community Programs Branch of the Ontario Department of Education (1962–7) and has written much for community groups, especially for the recorder. In 1967 he was commissioned by the Sudbury Arts Guild for the ballet *Our Lady's Juggler,* a work scored for piano and adapted from a medieval legend and miracle play.

Haworth has composed several works for orchestra, including the three suites, *Holgrove* (1958), *Roycroft* (1968), and *Edenvale* (1969); *Calday Grange Suite* (1958) and *Dalegarth* (1958) for string orchestra; and *Cornucopia Suite* (1972) for horn and strings. He has also written works for choir, including *Euphrosyne* and *Mass of St. Michael* (1972); for organ, including *Oratorian Suite*; and for chamber ensembles, including *The Glory and the Dream* (1958) for recorder quartet, *Glenrose Suite* (1960) for woodwind quintet, *Gonfalon Suite* (1961) for brass quintet, and *Karnwood Suite* (1972) for saxophone quartet. Haworth is a member of CAPAC.

BIBLIOGRAPHY

'Frank Haworth: A Traditionalist Without Being Old-Fashioned', *CanCo.* No. 31, July-Aug. 1968 (4–5, 44–5).

LITERARY WORKS

ARTICLES

'Colas et Colinette: A Character Larger than Life', *CanCo.* No. 31, July-Aug. 1968 (28–9, 45–6).

'The Composer's Voice', *CanCo.* No. 33, Oct. 1968 (28–9, 34–7, 46).

'Music – Mirror of the Mind', *CanCo.* No. 32, Sept. 1968 (28–9, 34–5, 45–6).

'Teaching Composition in a Lakehead Classroom', *CanCo.* No. 53, Oct. 1970 (22–3).

'Terpsichore's Triumph in Toronto', *Saturday Night.* Vol. LXXVII, Feb. 17, 1962 (33–4).

HEALEY, DEREK (b. Wargrave, England, 2 May 1936). He studied at the Royal College of Music in 1953 with Harold Darke (organ), Herbert Howells (composition), John Francis (flute), and Harry Stubbs (piano). He was awarded the Sullivan, Cobbett, and Farrar prizes in composition. In 1961 he received his Bachelor of Music degree from the University of Durham. During the summers of 1961, 1962, 1963, and 1966 he studied at the Accademia Chigiana in Siena, Italy, with Vito Frazzi and Goffredo Petrassi (composition) and Sergio Celibidache (conducting), receiving the F.M. Napolitano Prize. He also studied composition with Boris Porena in Rome (1962–3) and with Luciano Berio at the Summer School in Durham (1967). He was organist at several churches in England, including the Cookham Parish Church

(1965–7), where he founded and directed the Cookham Festival (1967). He has been lecturer in the music department of the University of Victoria, B.C., (1969–71), and in Ontario part-time lecturer at both Waterloo Lutheran University and the University of Toronto (1971–2). In 1972 he was appointed assistant professor of music at the University of Guelph.

One of Healey's early works (*Concerto for Organ, Strings & Timpani*, Op. 8, 1960) employs contrapuntal, polytonal material that weaves in and out of tonality. Later in *Variants*, Op. 24 (1964) and *Discendi, Amor Santo*, Op. 28 (1967), this conservative style gives way to experimentation with mass-structure. *Variants* uses either sustained chords or ostinato figures under an atonal melody-line, all of which alternates with toccata-like passages. *Discendi, Amor Santo* opens with a speaking chorus, but the main feature of the work is the static clusters that are built up alternately by organ and chorus. In two works of 1971 – *Stinging*, Op. 38, and *Arctic Images*, Op. 40 – Healey has placed greater emphasis on instrumental colour. Containing fragments of melodic writing, the score of *Stinging* directs the performers to evoke moods in sections entitled 'Calm', 'Hesitant', 'Aggressive', 'Mysterious', etc. This work, which includes electronic tape, in effect requires the performers to imitate the electronic sounds on their instruments by making trills and squeaks. *Arctic Images* is dry, with fragmented explosive percussion sections: it is in five movements, each one an interpretation of an Eskimo print.

Healey has composed works for the organists Gordon Jeffery (*Concerto for Organ, Strings and Timpani*, 1960; *Variations on The Three Gypsies*, 1965) and Barrie Cabena (*O Praise the Lord*, 1960; *Sonata Opus* 10, 1961; *Variants*, 1964). In 1967 he completed *Maschere* for the Duo Notariello and *Discendi, Amor Santo* for the Royal Canadian College of Organists. He has also received commissions from the CBC (*Night Thoughts*, 1971), the CBC Vancouver Chamber Orchestra (*Arctic Images*, 1971), and Waterloo Lutheran University (*Clouds*, 1972). He is a member of the Royal Canadian College of Organists, the Canadian League of Composers, and is an affiliate of BMI Canada.

MUSICAL WORKS

STAGE

Il Carcerato, Op 24a (ballet). 1965.
The Three Thieves, Op 27 (ballet). 1967.
Mr. Punch, Op 33 (opera for children). 1969. Libretto: Collier & Hayhew adapted by Derek Healey.

ORCHESTRA

The Willow Pattern Plate, Op 4. 1957 (rev 1962); Chap, 1965. school orch.
Tre Movimenti Per Orchestra, Op 19. 1963.
Ruba'i, Op 34. 1968.
Arctic Images, Op 40. 1971.

STRING ORCHESTRA

Variations on The Three Gypsies, Op 22. 1965. with org.
Serenata, Op 24b. 1968.
The Raven, Op 37. 1971. Jay.

SOLOIST WITH ORCHESTRA

Concerto for Organ, Strings and Timpani, Op 8. 1960. CMC BR SM-143.
Lustra. 1966. vc, orch. Text: anon.
Butterflies, Op 36. 1970. Jay. Text: Basho, Buson, Moritake, Shiki, Shusen.

CHOIR WITH ORCHESTRA

Praise the Lord, Op 7. 1960. Text: Psalm 103.

CHOIR

The Shepherd Boy's Song. 1963; RSCM, 1965. Text: John Bunyan.
The Days of Man. 1966. Jay. Text: Psalm 103.
O God of Truth. 1966. Text: St Ambrose.
Discendi, Amor Santo, Op 28. 1967. Jay. Text: Bianco da Siena.
O King Enthroned On High. 1968. Jay. Text: Pentecostarion. Trans: J Browlie.
O Trinity of Blessed Light. 1968. Jay. Text: St Ambrose.
There is One Body. 1972. Text: Ephesians.
Clouds, Op 41. 1972; Wat, 1973. Text: Matsuo Basho.

VOICE

Six Greek Fragments, Op 11. 1961. Text: Plato, Leonidas, Maleagros, Palladas, Agathias.
Hardy Songs, Op 13. 1961. Text: Thomas Hardy.
Six American Songs, Op 14. 1961. Text: e e cummings, Edgar Allan Poe, Ogden Nash, Bret Harte, T S Eliot.
Six Irish Songs, Op 16. 1962. Text: Oscar

Wilde, James Joyce, Oliver St John Gogarty, W B Yeats.

INSTRUMENTAL ENSEMBLE

Prelude for Oboe and Piano, Op 2b. 1958.
String Quartet in A, Op 9. 1961.
Sonata for Cello and Piano, Op 12. 1961.
Partita Bizzara, Op 17a. 1962; Chap, 1964. ob, pno.
Bagatelles for Beginners, Op 17c. 1963; Chap, 1964. vlc, pno.
Divisions for Brass Quartet. 1963.
Five Cameos. 1963; B & H, 1966. sop rec, pno.
Mobile, Op 20a. 1963. fl, vib, cel, hp, 2perc, vlc.
Six Epigrams, Op 21. 1963. vln, pno.
Movement, Op 20b. 1965. fl, ob, cl, str trio.
Laudes, Op 26. 1966. fl, hn, perc, hp, 2vln, vlc.
Maschere, Op 29. 1967. vln, pno. Jay.
Stinging, Op 38. 1971. alto rec, vlc, hpschd, elec tape.

PIANO

Paeanistic Waltz, Op 3b. 1956.
October's Dream, Op 3a. 1957.
Odmesh Suite, Op 3c. 1958.
Partita Moderna, Op 5. 1959.
Twelve Preludes, Op 6. 1960; Jay, 1972.

INSTRUMENTAL SOLO

Three Pieces for Flute Solo, Op 2a. 1956.

ORGAN

Voluntaries Nos 1, 2, 3, Op 1a, b, c. 1956; Jay, 1971–2.
Sonata, Op 10. 1961.
Voluntaries Nos 4 & 5, Op 15a & b. 1962–3.
Voluntary No 6, Op 15c. 1962; Novl, 1965.
Three Preludes on French Hymn Tunes, Op 18. 1963; Novl, 1965.
Variants, Op 23. 1964; Novl, 1967.
Partita '65, Op 25. 1965; Novl, 1967.
Cookham Notebook, Op 30, 1967.
Festus, Op 32. 1968. Jay.
The Lost Traveller's Dream, Op 35. 1970; Jay, 1972.

ELECTRONIC TAPE

Incidental Music to 'Night Thoughts', Op 39. 1972.

BIBLIOGRAPHY

See Ww69, 72.
Schulman, Michael. 'Country of residence an influence on Healey's music', *Music Scene*. Nov.-Dec. 1973 (4).

HEARD, ALAN (b. Halifax, N.S., 7 Feb. 1942). He began studying violin, theory, and harmony in Montreal at the age of twelve. In 1958 he entered McGill University, studying composition with István ANHALT; he obtained his Bachelor of Music degree in 1962. In the same year he was awarded the Lieutenant-Governor's Bronze Medal and the Harold H. Helm scholarship to enter Princeton University, where he studied composition with Roger Sessions and Earl Kim; he received his Master of Fine Arts degree in 1964. In that year the Canada Council awarded him a grant to study composition with Boris Blacher at the Hochschule für Musik in Berlin. In 1967 he joined the staff of the Faculty of Music of McGill University and in 1971 resigned to take a position at Kirkland College in Clinton, N.Y. Heard's small output is devoted almost entirely to chamber works, exceptions being the *Symphonic Variations* and *Clarinet Concerto*. Among his works are *Rondos for Flute and Harp* (1965), *String Quartet*, *String Trio* (1965), *Sonata for Pianoforte* (1966), *Timai* ('A Cosmic March for Ten Instrumentalists', 1972–3, a commission from New Music Concerts), and two chamber works involving voice: *Song Cycle* (text by e. e. cummings) and *Voices* (1969, text by Shiki, Brian G. Segal, and L. Lévesque). The latter, a Canadian entry to the ISCM of 1972, is concerned mainly with tone-painting through the exploitation of instrumental colours. Heard is a member of CAPAC.

HENNINGER, RICHARD (b. Pasadena, Calif., 8 Dec. 1944). He studied composition with Karl Kohn at Pomona College in Claremont, Calif. (1963–6), receiving his Bachelor of Arts degree in music in 1966. He was awarded a Bracken Fellowship to study composition at Indiana University with Thomas Beversdorf (1966–7) and Roque Cordero (1967). In 1967 he received a University of Toronto Open Fellowship to study with John WEINZWEIG (composition) and Gustav CIAMAGA (electronic music), completing his Master of Music degree in 1968. Since 1968 he has lectured in theory and composition at the Faculty of Music, becoming assistant professor in 1972, and taught electronic music at the

Faculty of Education, both at the University of Toronto.

Henninger employs free atonal devices with some use of the twelve-tone technique. His main concern is the exploitation of instrumental colours in well-developed structures (*Catena*, 1968; *Evolutions*, 1971). While still writing for live instruments, Henninger has also been exploring electronic and computer music, his 1973 doctoral program at Stanford University centring on musical applications of the computer. *Visions of Outer Space* was commissioned by the McLaughlin Planetarium (Toronto) in 1969 and his *Catena* won the International Competition of the City of Birmingham Orchestra for its fiftieth anniversary in 1970.

Henninger's output, which is not extensive, includes the orchestral work *Catena*, *Variations for String Quartet* (1967), and *Evolutions* for solo alto saxophone. He has written for choir (*Music for the Order of Holy Communion*, 1966, for SSATB; *Nunc Dimittis*, 1967, for SATB); for voice (*Three Proverbs*, 1966, for low voice, flute, and oboe; *Two Songs*, 1968, for high voice and piano, text by Henninger; *Songs of Winter*, 1972, for voice, flute, piano, and tape, text by Henninger); and for electronic tape alone (*Piano Pieces*, 1968; *Visions from Outer Space*, 1969; *Marguerite Miniatures*, 1970). He is a member of CAPAC.

BIBLIOGRAPHY

'ARRAY in Conversation with Richard Henninger', *ARRAY Newsletter*. Vol. I, no. 1, Fall 1972 (3–7).

'Composer Wins Prize in Competition Honouring the City of Birmingham Symphony Orchestra', *CanCo*. No. 46, Jan. 1970 (42–3).

LITERARY WORKS

ARTICLES

'Introduction to a Weinzweig Sourcebook', *CMB*. Spring-Summer 1973 (15–17, 19, 39–40, 41, 45, 57, 63, 69, 73).

HÉTU, JACQUES (b. Trois-Rivières, Que., 8 Aug. 1938). Nothing in Hétu's background seems to have foreshadowed his musical career, neither in his family nor through attachment to any particular instrument. Having received a classical education at the Collège Jean-de-Brébeuf in Montreal (1950–5), he first began to consider a career in music at the age of fifteen; a sudden awareness of the world of sound and the discovery of symphony concerts had a great impact on him and within six months he decided to become a composer. Accepted in 1956 by the Conservatoire in Montreal, he studied composition with Clermont PÉPIN and acquired solid backgrounds in both piano and oboe, which stood him in good stead later in his career.

Hétu's efforts were crowned with success when he won the composition prize in 1961 awarded by the Conservatoire, as well as several other scholarships that same year (the composition prize from the Festival de Musique du Québec and the Prix d'Europe). A study scholarship from the Canada Council enabled him to go to Paris to further his musical education. There his professors were Henri Dutilleux for composition at the Ecole Normale de musique (1961–3) and Olivier Messiaen for analysis at the Conservatoire (1962–3). This period saw Hétu's first efforts at composing for piano and orchestra, as well as several larger projects: sketches for an opera, which was soon abandoned and the broad outlines for an oratorio that later became a symphonic poem (*L'Apocalypse*, 1967).

Returning to Canada in 1963, Hétu settled in Quebec City where he was appointed professor of music literature and analysis at the Ecole de Musique of Laval University, later becoming professor of composition, analysis, and orchestration. Among his young disciples are a number of promising talents such as Ginette Bertrand, Jean-Claude Paquet, and Antoine Padilla.

As a composer, Hétu has a predilection for the piano, solo or in concertante. So far he has written on commission for symphony orchestras and for smaller ensembles. His instrumental palette shows varying combinations: the *Trio* for flute, oboe, and harpsichord Op. 3 No. 2 (1960) is written in Baroque style, the *Wind Quintet*, Op. 13 (1967) in traditional form, and *Cycle*, Op. 16 (1969) was written for the Société de Musique Contemporaine du Québec. A small foray into the vocal genre is seen with *Pièce en miroir* (1964) and five songs written specially for Ginette Duplessis – Hétu's only contribution so far to music for voice. As requests or commissions generally involve works of short duration, usually not exceeding fifteen or twenty minutes, the possibilities of development much loved of composers are therefore limited. After 1972 however, Hétu concentrated on large scores, such as a fourth symphony.

Formally Hétu remains faithful to a classical esthetic firmly attached to structural forms of the past, often using the bithematicism of the sonata allegro, the ternary adagio, the scherzo, the rondo, and exploiting techniques deriving from the variation principle, as in *Variations*, Op. 8 (1964, piano), *Variations*, Op. 11 (1967, violin), and *Passacaille*, Op. 17 (1970, orchestra). If in his early works (*Toccata*, Op. 1 for piano, 1959; *Symphonie pour Cordes*, 1959) Hétu shows the influence of Bartok or Hindemith, he has also appeared as a fervent admirer of the Viennese school in strongly atonal compositions making use of serial techniques creating subtle play between the twelve notes of the scale. This was a period of learned calculation, with cells cyclically developed, retrograded, and dispersed throughout the movements of a composition, or carefully renewed from one work to another. One can examine the *Petite Suite*, Op. 7 (1962) and Variations II and III of Op. 8 to perceive the unity created by the motif B-A-C-H or the mood of *Quatre pièces* for flute (1965) and the *Wind Quintet* to see the preoccupations of Hétu as he approached his thirtieth year. He has a great admiration for Alban Berg, for a long time his favourite composer, but he also uses the modes catalogued by his teacher Messiaen, thus avoiding the exigencies imposed by a tone row. Incisive rhythms characterize his fast movements: clipped tuttis, percussive motifs, bouncing syncopations, shredded phrases of notes – such are the elements he uses to forge a dynamic musical language. Many pages gravitate around pedal points, tonal poles, insistent tremolos, or rocking figures, as in the *Interlude*, Op. 7, the two sets of *Variations*, Op. 8 and 11, and their successors, the *Passacaille* and the *Quatuor à cordes* (1972).

If we feel that in Hétu's dodecaphonic inspiration, the melody of timbres rests in dislocated intervals, we should not forget the large phrases in the symphonies, the warm arabesques in the concertos, or the lyrical cantilena of the flute 'Intermezzo' from the *Quatre pièces*, Op. 10 (1965). There is also the touching simplicity of the adagio of the wind quintet, the important viola solo in the andante of the string quartet, and above all the pathetic declamation of the five songs of Op. 20. Expressive or dramatic intensity is often enhanced by precise choice and delicate nuance; the two opening bars of the Impromptu section of the *Petite Suite* follow a dynamic gradation, *pp* – *mp* – *fff*, *p* to *ppp*, which reminds us of the 'Modes de valeur et d'intensité' of Messiaen.

Hétu's harmonic language comprises parallelisms and composites of serial, modal, or chromatic techniques. Solid counterpoint – evidence of which may be found tempering the works of his youth (*Symphonie No. 2*, Op. 4, 1961; Variation III of Op. 8 for piano, Variation IV of Op. 11 for violin) – becomes more consolidated in more recent works (*Passacaille*; the finale of *Symphonie No. 3*, 1971; and the last allegro of the string quartet).

Deeply classical in the structure of his scores, post-romantic for his time, on the point of abandoning Berg for Mahler whom he has recently discovered, knowing the various currents of the contemporary world and freeing himself from serial acquisition, Jacques Hétu has come into his own. His *Symphonie No. 3*, the *Quatuor à cordes*, and *Les Clartés de la nuit* (1972) represent a clear transformation towards a new lyricism, to which Mahler certainly was by no means alien. Perhaps in a few years he will complete a project dear to his heart since his student days at the Conservatoire: a large stage work with choirs. Or perhaps he will investigate the domain of electronic music, which also arouses his curiosity. However, it seems certain that Hétu, teacher and composer, has come to a decisive turning point in his musical evolution.

Jacques Hétu is a member of the Canadian League of Composers and an affiliate of BMI Canada. IRÈNE BRISSON

MUSICAL WORKS

ORCHESTRA

Prélude pour orchestre, Op 5. 1961. 7'25". ms.

Symphonie No 2, Op 4. 1961. 17′. full orch. CMC.

L'Apocalypse; 'Fresque Symphonique d'après St-Jean', Op 14. 1967. 14′. full orch. CMC. May 1968, Tor, CBC Fest, TS, Pierre Hétu.

Passacaille, Op 17. 1970. 10′. full orch. CMC. Apr 13, 1971, Mtl, Place des Arts, MSO, Franz-Paul Decker.

Symphonie No 3, Op 18. 1971. 17′. med orch. CMC.

STRING ORCHESTRA

Symphonie Pour Cordes, Op 2. 1959. 18′. CMC. RCI-293. 1959, Mtl, Orch da Camera, Remus Tzincoca.

Adagio et Rondo pour orchestre à cordes, Op 3 No 1B. 1960. 9′. CMC. 1970, PQ, Mount Orford Mus Camp, Paul Kuentz Chamb Orch.

SOLOIST(S) WITH ORCHESTRA

Rondo pour violoncelle et orchestre à cordes, Op 9. 1965. 10′. ms. 1965, Quebec, CBC, Quebec Ch O, Edwin Bélanger, Arpad Szomoru.

Double Concerto pour violin, piano et orchestre de chambre, Op 12. 1967. 16′. CMC. July 23, 1967, Charlottetown, PEI, Halifax Ch O, John Fenwick(cond), Joseph Pach (vln), Arlene Pach(pno).

Concerto pour piano, Op 15. 1969. 20′. pno, full orch. CMC. 1970, Quebec, QSO, Pierre Dervaux(cond), Robert Silverman(pno).

CHORAL

Pièce en Miroir. 1964. 2′40″. SATB. ms. 1964, Quebec, CBC TV, Ens Vocal, Chantal Masson.

VOICE

Les Clartés de la Nuit, Op 20. 1972. 15′. sop, pno. Text: Emile Nelligan.

INSTRUMENTAL ENSEMBLE

Adagio et Rondo pour quatuor à cordes, Op 3 No 1. 1960. 9′. CMC. 1970 (orch version), PQ, Mount Orford Mus Camp, Paul Kuentz Chamb Orch.

Trio pour flûte, hautbois et clavecin, Op 3 No 2. 1960. 13′. CMC. 1961, Mtl, CBC, Bar Trio Mtl.

Quatre pièces pour flûte et piano, Op 10. 1965. 11′53″. Editions Billaudot, 1969. Mad MA/MAS-402. 1965, Jean Morin(fl), André Sébastien Savoie(pno).

Quintette pour instruments à vent, Op 13. 1967. 12′ CMC.

Cycle pour piano et instruments à vent, Op 16. 1969. 10′. pno, fl, cl, b cl, bsn, hn, 2tpt 2trb. ms. Feb 5, 1970, Mtl, SMCQ conc Serge Garant.

Quatuor à Cordes, Op 19. 1972. 15′. July 27, 1972, Ottawa, NAC Studio, Orford Str Qt.

PIANO

Toccata, Op 1. 1959. 2′45″. CMC.

Petite Suite, Op 7. 1962. 9′. CMC. RCI-252.

Sonate pour deux pianos, Op 6. 1962. 14′ CMC. RCA CC/CCS-1021, RCI-227.

Variations, Op 8. 1964. 8′45″. Ber, 1970. CBS 32110045/0046, JMC 4, RCI-251.

INSTRUMENTAL SOLO

Variations pour violon seul (ou alto ou violoncelle), Op 11. 1967. CMC. June 1967, Vanc, JMC Str Competition.

BIBLIOGRAPHY

Bec70; CrC(I); Lv; Wa.

'Jacques Hétu – a portrait', *Mu.* No. 27 Mar. 1970 (8–9).

Samson, Marc. 'Hétu Airs his Opinions on Composing in Canada', *MuSc.* Nov.-Dec 1971 (5, 12).

LITERARY WORKS

ARTICLES

'Pour un style composite', *Vie Musicale* No. 11, Mar. 1969 (12–15).

HODKINSON, SYDNEY (b. Winnipeg, Man., 17 Jan. 1934). He studied composition with Louis Mennini and Bernard Rogers (1953–8) at the Eastman School of Music, receiving his Bachelor and Master of Music degrees. In 1960 he studied with Elliott Carter, Roger Sessions, and Milton Babbitt in the Seminar in Advanced Musical Studies, Princeton University, and from 1967 to 1968 with Ross Lee Finney, George Balch Wilson, Leslie Bassett, and Niccolo Castiglioni at the University of Michigan, where he received his Doctor of Musica Arts degree in 1968.

Hodkinson is also a professional clarinetist and conductor and was woodwind instructor in Rochester, N.Y., and in the public school system in Brighton, N.Y (1955–8), also conducting chamber ensembles and orchestra concerts throughou the U.S. and Canada, including the 'Contemporary Directions' series and Composer's Forums at the University of

Michigan (1966–8). He was assistant professor of music theory at the University of Virginia (1958–63) and at Ohio University (1963–8), giving lectures in twentieth-century music, electronic music, and music education on his conducting tours. He was appointed associate professor of music theory at the School of Music, University of Michigan, in 1968. In 1971 he was guest conductor of the St Paul Chamber Orchestra and the Minnesota Orchestra, continuing as conductor of the Contemporary Directions Ensemble in Ann Arbor. Also in 1971 he was composer-in-residence for Twin Cities, Minn., under a grant from the Contemporary Music Project of the Ford Foundation.

If a characteristic sound of the 1960s exists – a post-Webern, spatially arrayed, serial-implied, disjunct style – then Hodkinson's music represents that decade. In works such as *The Dissolution of the Serial* (1967), *Arc* (1969), and *Valence* (1970) Hodkinson handles the pointillism of this style with bursts of notes coloured by unconventional modes of playing of traditional instruments. The composer's program note for *The Dissolution of the Serial,* while providing some insight into the cerebral preoccupations that mark his style, at the same time reveals a tongue-in-cheek impatience with musical analysts and program annotators who take seriously this sort of description: '... the equivalent analogous sequences of formulable pre-determined elements and varying magnitudes based on differing quanta characterizes all of the permutational relationships; ergo, enabling the parametrical properties, coupled with interlocking rotational juxtaposition, to provide the maximal significant referential functionality of the interconstructival hierarchization. But then ...'.

Hodkinson has received numerous commissions, some of which were from the Hegyi Trio (*Stanzas,* 1959), the National Association of College Wind and Percussion Instruments (*Drawings, No. 3,* 1960), Bloomsberg, Pennsylvania State College (*Lyrics,* 1966), Upsala College (*Ritual,* 1970), Bertram Turetzky (*Interplay,* 1966; *One Man's Meat,* 1970), the CBC for the Lyric Arts Trio (*Arc,* 1969), the Civic Orchestra of Minneapolis (*Epigrams,* 1971), and the St Paul Chamber Orchestra (*Vox Populous, Valence, Stabile, another ... man's Poison,* 1970–2). Among his many composition awards are the 'Prince of Monaco' award for *Caricatures* (1966) and second prize in the 1967 International Federation of Jeunesses Musicales competition in Montreal for *Interplay* (1966). He is a member of the National Association for American Composers and Conductors, the Southeastern Composers' League, the American Society of University Composers, and is affiliated with BMI Canada.

MUSICAL WORKS

STAGE

Lament for Guitar and Two Lovers (a fable for actors, dancers, and musicians). 1962. Libretto: Lee Devin.

Armistice (a truce for dancers and musicians). 1966. 6′–12′. Any, preferably homogeneous, gp of instr. Ber. Nov 11, 1966, Ann Arbor, Michigan.

Taiwa (a myth for actors, dancers, and musicians). 1966. Choreog: F Coggan.

Scissors. 1967. elec tape. film by K Dewdney.

Vox Populous (a chamber oratorio). 1972. 45′.

ORCHESTRA

Lyric Impressions. 1956. full orch.

Diversions on a Chorale. 1957. full orch.

Threnody. 1957. full orch.

Dynamics (five miniatures for symphony orchestra). 1960.

Caricatures (five paintings for symphony orchestra). 1966. 8′. full orch. Ric. Apr 5, 1969, Dallas SO, D Johanos(cond).

Fresco (a mural for symphony orchestra). 1968. 19′–20′. full orch. Jobert, Paris, 1971.

Drawings, Set No 7. 1970. 4′. youth orch. Presser, Phila.

Drawings, Set No 8. 1970. 4′. youth orch. Presser, Phila.

Stabile. 1970. 7′30″. youth orch. Jobert, Paris. St Peter, Minnesota, Civic Orch of Minneapolis.

Valence. 1970. 7′. chamb orch. Jobert, Paris. CRI SD 292.

Epigrams. 1971. 10′.

Incentus. 1972. 6′.

BAND

Fanfares. 1961. symphonic band.

Festival Overture. 1963. symphonic band.

Blocks. 1972. 8′.

Contemporary Primer. 1972. 46′. Presser, Phila.

SMALL ORCHESTRA
Laments. 1957.

STRING ORCHESTRA
Diversions. 1964. young plyrs.

SOLOIST WITH ORCHESTRA
Dialogue (a concertino for piano and wind band). 1963.

CHOIR
Communion Service. 1954. SATB.
The Betrayal. 1958. SSATB.
Three Sixteenth Century Love Lyrics. 1964. SSAA.
Four Seventeenth Century Lyrics. 1966. SATB.
Ritual. 1970. SATB. 8′.
Menagerie Set No 1. 1971. 8′30″. young choral ens. Presser, Phila.
Sea Chanteys for mixed chorus a cappella. 1971. 7′30″. Presser, Phila.

VOICE
Two Canadian Songs. 1954. sop, pno.

VOICE(S) WITH INSTRUMENTAL ENSEMBLE
Four Songs. 1959. vocal trio, ww, perc. Text: 17th cent anon.
Arc (aria with interludes). 1969. 13′. sop, fl, picc, pno, 2perc. CMC. June 23, 1970, Tor, Eaton Aud, CBC Tor Fest, LAT, Robin Engelman(perc).

INSTRUMENTAL ENSEMBLE
Three Little Pieces. 1953. cl, pno.
Sketches, Set No 1. 1955. cl, b cl.
Sketches, Set No 2. 1955. cl, b cl.
Two Pieces. 1955. str qt.
Quartet. 1956. pno, str.
Structures. 1958. perc ens. Music for Perc, NY.
Two Studies. 1958. str qt.
Litigo. 1959. ww, perc.
Stanzas. 1959. vln, vlc, pno. Tritone.
Drawings, Set No 1. 1960. perc qt. Music for Perc, NY.
Drawings, Set No 2. 1960. perc qt.
Drawings, Set No 3. 1961. cl, drums. Music for Perc, NY.
Drawings, Set No 4. 1961. perc trio. Music for Perc, NY.
Drawings, Set No 5. 1962. fl, perc.
Five Absurdities from Lewis Carroll. 1964. 5 trb.
Mosaic. 1964. brass qnt.
Drawings, Set No 6. 1965. vln, 3cl.
Vignettes, Set No 1. 1965. trb, FH.
Interplay (a histrionic controversy for four musicians). 1966. 12′. alto fl (picc), cl (alto sax), perc, cb. CMC.
Dissolution of the Serial. 1967. pno, 1 instr. CRI SD 292.
Funks (an improvisation for seven jazzmen). 1967.
Homage to Ionesco. 1967. pno, others.
Imagind Quarter. 1967. 16′. 4perc. Ber.
Shifting Trek. 1967. 11 instr.
another . . . man's Poison. 1970. brass qnt.

PIANO
Four Character Pieces. 1956.
Refractions. 1965.

ELECTRONIC
Study No 1. 1960. mag tape.
Study No 2. 1962. mag tape.

INSTRUMENTAL SOLO
One Man's Meat (for live and recorded double bass solo). 1970. 7′. Presser, Phila. Los Angeles, UCLA, Bertram Turetsky.
Trinity (for solo treble instrument). 1972. 6′.

BIBLIOGRAPHY
Glick, Irving. 'Sydney Hodkinson: "Caricatures" ', *CMB*. Vol. I, Spring-Summer 1970 (146–7).

HOLT, PATRICIA BLOMFIELD (b. Lindsay, Ont., 15 Sept. 1910). She studied piano with Norah Drewett de Kresz, Norman Wilks, and B. H. Carman, and composition with Healey WILLAN. In 1938 her *Suite for Violin and Piano* won the Vogt Society award for the best Canadian composition. Her early works, of the 1930s and 1940s, exhibit in a lyrical way a pan-tonal style with an organic formal structure. She has since developed a simpler tonal style. She teaches piano, theory, and composition at the Royal Conservatory in Toronto. Many of her recent piano pieces are educational and can be found in the Royal Conservatory pianoforte examination books (for example, *Studies Nos. 1 and 2*, and *Sauntering Tune*). Mrs Holt's compositions are mainly for chamber groups, although there are some works for larger ensembles, for example *Songs of My Country* (1950) for baritone or alto, horn, harp, and strings. Among her works for chamber ensembles are *Three Songs of Contemplation* (1970) for high voice and piano; two *Lyric Pieces* (1937, 1938) for cello and piano; and *String Quartet No. 1* (1937) and *Suite No. 2* (1939) for violin or viola and piano. She is affiliated with BMI Canada.

BIBLIOGRAPHY

See B-B; K.

HUSE, PETER (b. Gadsby, Alta, 12 Mar. 1938). He began to study the clarinet at the age of eight and to compose at twelve. He studied architecture at the University of British Columbia (1956–60) before changing to music, studying composition with Cortland Hultberg and Barbara PENTLAND and receiving his Bachelor of Music degree in 1963. On fellowships from Princeton University and grants from the Koerner Foundation he studied composition at Princeton (1963–5) with Roger Sessions, Edward T. Cone, Milton Babbitt, J.K. Randall, and Earl Kim, and worked in the Columbia-Princeton Electronic Music Studio, obtaining his Master of Fine Arts degree in 1965. In 1964 he won a BMI Student Composer Award for three compositions: *String Quartet, Vanity of Vanities,* and *Sonata for Two Pianos.* In *Preludes* (1963–4) and *Recurrences* (1966) the influences of Webern and Babbitt can be seen in Huse's use of refined serialism and sparse pointillistic textures.

Huse has received doctoral fellowships from Princeton and from the Canada Council. After round-the-world studies and travels he joined the Centre for Communications and the Arts at Simon Fraser University in 1967 and later became co-director of its Sonic Research Studio. From 1969 to 1972 he taught music at the National Theatre School of Canada and McGill University in Montreal and with further assistance from the Canada Council continued his doctoral work at Princeton. His compositions include works for band, for choir, for piano, and for various instrumental ensembles (including *Antiphony for Two Ensembles,* 1962, for four woodwinds, three brass, piano, percussion, and twelve strings). He has written a number of works that include tape, including *Mass of Sins* (1967) for jazz ensemble, mime troupe, slide projections, and tape; *Ism* (1968) for four-track tape, twelve dancers, and lights; *Swan Song of Improvisations for Mary's Ism* (1968) for four-track tape; *Assembly Towards East* (1968) for four-track tape; *Space Play* (1968) for eight-track tape; and *Bricolage* (1971) for mezzo, poet, flute, clarinet, trombone, piano, two percussionists, three strings, and tape.

In 1972 Huse returned to Simon Fraser as assistant director of the World Soundscape Project and Instructor in Communication Studies. He is affiliated with BMI Canada.

LITERARY WORKS

ARTICLES

'Barbara Pentland', *MuSc.* July-Aug. 1968 (9).

J

JAQUE, RHENÉ (b. Beauharnois, Que., 4 Feb. 1918). Christened Marguerite Cartier, upon joining the Order of the Saints of the Holy Names of Jesus and Mary she took the name Sister Jacques-René, adopting the pen name Rhené Jaque for her compositions. She began her musical education in her native town and later at l'Ecole Vincent-d'Indy in Montreal with Claude CHAMPAGNE and François MOREL (composition) and with Jean VALLERAND (orchestration). She received her bachelor degree and licentiate diploma in music from the University of Montreal. In the summer of 1972 she studied composition with Tony Aubin in Nice, France. Many of Rhené Jaque's piano works are intended for young students and often have picturesque titles, revealing her interest in tone-painting. She calls on pentatonic or whole-tone scales for material in many of her earlier works (*Rustic Dance*, 1962; and *Two Two-Part Inventions*, 1963) but more recently she has turned to a free atonal style. She has also written extensively for voice, including *Le perroquet gris*, *Le petit éléphant*, and *Mon château* (published 1968); for chamber ensemble, including *Daussila* for violin and piano and *Un petit Air roumain* (published 1970) for violin and piano; and for orchestra, including *Suite* (published 1967) for string orchestra and *Symphony No. 1*. Although a number of her works remain unpublished, her principal publishers are Berandol, l'Ecole Vincent-d'Indy, and Gordon V. Thompson. Rhené Jaque teaches violin and cello at l'Ecole Vincent-d'Indy and is affiliated with BMI Canada.

BIBLIOGRAPHY

Thériault, Jacques. 'Composer's Works Reveal Devotion to Young Musicians', *MuSc.* No. 263, Jan.-Feb. 1972 (4).

JOACHIM, OTTO (b. Düsseldorf, Germany, 13 Oct. 1910). Otto Joachim became a Canadian almost by accident. Having fled his native Germany in 1934, a year after Hitler's ascent to power, he spent fifteen years in the Far East – first in Singapore, later in Shanghai. A stateless 'displaced person', in 1949 he was forced to move again. This time he obtained an immigrant's visa to Brazil and, in order to transfer from one ship to another, a one-month visitor's visa to Canada. Much impressed with life in this country and with the cosmopolitan atmosphere of the city of Montreal, he extended his stay, applied for landed-immigrant status, and became a valuable member of the Canadian musical community.

Music had been part of Joachim's life since his early childhood. His father was a professional singer – a member of the Düsseldorf Opera chorus – and music studies became part of Otto's education as soon as he was strong enough to hold up a violin. He entered the violin class of the Buths-Neitzel Conservatory at the age of six and continued to attend this institution throughout his elementary and high school years. In 1928 he became a student of Hermann Zitzmann at the Rheinische Musikschule in Cologne to prepare himself for a professional career as a violinist and violist, with a special interest in chamber music.

It was as a string player and teacher that Joachim first became involved in the musical life of Canada. He became a member, and later leader, of the viola section of the Montreal Symphony Orchestra, and acted in the same capacity with the McGill Chamber Orchestra. With his cellist brother Walter and the violinists Hyman Bress and Mildred Goodman, he founded the Montreal String Quartet. In 1956 he joined the teaching staffs of McGill University and the Conservatoire in Montreal. Eventually he abandoned his orchestral and quartet-playing activities and in 1964 resigned from the McGill faculty, but he continues to teach at the Conservatoire. His teaching specialty is music for antique instruments. He is founder and director of the Montreal Consort of Ancient Instruments and has built with his own hands replicas of a few old and otherwise unobtainable instruments.

Although Joachim had done some sporadic composing since his student days in Cologne, his real development as a composer with a personal style took place after he had settled in Montreal and taken a fresh approach to the practice of his art. Between 1928 and 1939 he had worked on a twenty-minute symphonic poem, *Asia*, a string quartet (the score of which is lost), and *Three Bagatelles* for piano. Romantic, somewhat modal, these works reflect the latent musicality and technical proficiency of a youth reared in the stimulating cultural environment of Germany before the rise of Hitler.

Once he had put down new roots in Montreal, Joachim set out to re-establish his contact with the music of the western world and lost no time in discovering the directions this music had moved in during his fifteen years in China. He acquainted himself with the work of Varèse, Schoenberg, and Webern, perused Ernst Krenek's twelve-tone *Studies in Counterpoint*, and thus soon found principles for ordering his musical materials in a manner that suited both his mind and his temperament.

Joachim made his Canadian début as a composer in 1953–4 when he introduced to the public four solo and duo works scored for strings, piano, and voice. In these pieces he not only came to grips with the mechanics of serial writing but also experimented with some original approaches to structure, time, and densities. For instance in *Music for Violin and Viola* (1953), the five movements decrease in length while the textural complexity increases from one movement to the next; in *L'Eclosion* (1954) for solo piano, lengths of sound-groups and durations of silences are arranged according to numerical patterns.

These initial exploratory scores were immediately followed by two more significant ones: *Concertante No. 1* for solo violin, string orchestra, and percussion (1955–7), and the *String Quartet* (1956). Both are works of substance, brilliance, drive, and virility. Written by a practising string player, they make use of a wide variety of string techniques and sonorities. Their main virtues are sonoric sensitivity and textural clarity, achieved through a selective balancing of melodic, harmonic, contrapuntal, and rhythmic elements.

Joachim's treatment of the tone-row is at once quite conventional and undogmatic. Since his writing is basically melody oriented, his rows are easily recognizable and tuneful. He follows the serial order of the rows very conscientiously, yet at the same time disregards such conventions of twelve-tone writing as the avoidance of octave doublings, literal repeats of sections, and sound-structures with tonal implications. Joachim frequently uses pedal-points, ostinati, and unorthodox tone-repeats which, though not tonal in the traditional sense, create temporary centres of gravity and an illusion of a harmonic framework. He may owe some debt to the first generation of dodecaphonists, but his textures are much leaner than Schoenberg's, his lines show greater continuity than Webern's, and his music is warmer and less cerebral than Krenek's. He never over-abstracts, over-structures, or over-orchestrates his ideas. Instead he brings joy and buoyancy to his music, both qualities not overly common among most twelve-toners' work.

The fact that the chronological listing of Joachim's compositions has no entries for several years after the completion of the *Concertante No. 1* and the *String Quartet* does not mean that the composer suddenly became idle or uncreative. On the contrary, once he had fulfilled his ambitions in his initially chosen idiom, he was off on explorations in several other areas of music-making.

A compleat musician, Joachim has always been interested not only in matters of musical composition and performance, but also in the physical construction of musical instruments. His skill as a builder of ancient instruments has been mentioned. While these were needed for teaching and performing purposes, as a composer he also required new tools of his own time. He found them in electronic oscillators, generators, filters, modulators, amplifiers and such, and in the mid-fifties set out to assemble, step by long step, a fully workable electronic music studio of his own.

It was not until a decade later that Joachim produced any large-scale works in his studio. But meanwhile he probed other areas of musical innovation: new approaches to notation and indeterminacy as part of musical form and performance. In the middle movement of his *Nonet* (premièred during the 1960 International Conference of Composers in Stratford, Ont.), the players decide independently of each other which sections to play at which time. His 1962 *Divertimento* for wind instruments contains sections where durations and tempi are determined by the performers. In *Expansions* for flute and piano (of the same year), Joachim takes a fresh look at the issue of time, abandons all implications of a regular metre, and drops the bar lines.

All these explorations and experiments during the late 1950s and the first half of the 1960s led to a new peak of creative achievement in Canada's centennial year, 1967. It was then that Joachim unveiled his major four-track tape composition, *Katimavik*, commissioned for the Canadian Pavilion of Expo 67, and fulfilled a centennial commission for the Toronto Symphony with *Contrastes*. In these works Joachim demonstrated how well he understood the electronic and orchestral media and that he knew how to use them most effectively. *Katimavik* is not just another abstract tape composition to be played at a concert or over the radio. It was conceived as an

1. Healey Willan

2. Rodolphe Mathieu

3. Sir Ernest MacMillan and Claude Champagne during a visit to Rio de Janiero, 1946.

4. John Weinzweig

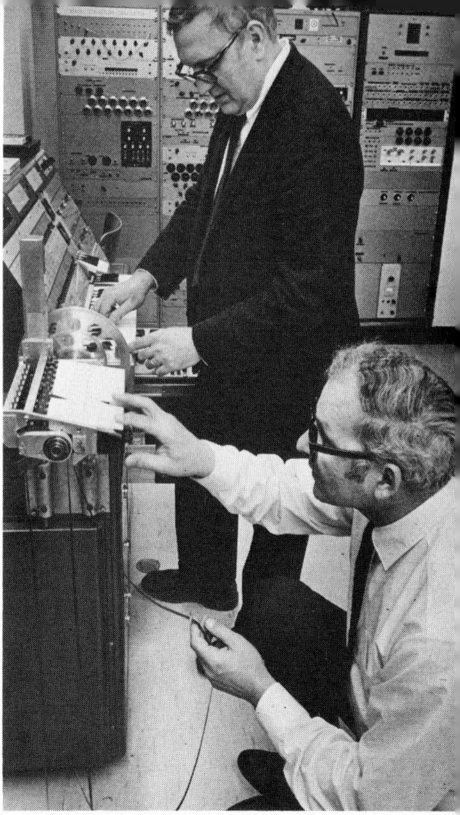

5. Gustav Ciamaga and Louis Applebaum in the Electronic Music Studio, University of Toronto.

6. Harry Freedman

7. John Hawkins

8. *L. to r.*, Jean Papineau-Couture, Jacques Hétu, Serge Garant, at a reception of the Société de musique contemporaine du Québec, 1970.

9. Serge Garant conducting a chamber choir and instrumental ensemble in rehearsal for a concert of the Société de musique contemporaine du Québec.

10. The twentieth-anniversary conference of the Canadian League of Composers at the University of Victoria (B.C.), 1971. *L. to r.*, George Fiala, Gabriel Charpentier, John Weinzweig, Maurice Dela, Eldon Rathburn, Charles Wilson, Morris Surdin, Norma Beecroft, Louis Applebaum, Anne Eggleston, Walter Buczynski, Paul McIntyre, Lothar Klein, Kelsey Jones, John Hawkins, Brian Cherney, Violet Archer, Rudi van Dijk, Robert Aitken, Samuel Dolin, Harry Freedman, William McCauley, Talivaldis Kenins, unknown, Kenneth Peacock, Otto Joachim, Ronald Tremain, Thomas Schudel, unknown, Barbara Pentland, John Roberts (CBC music department).

11. Pierre Mercure

12. Harry Somers during a performance of his *Improvisation* at Redpath Hall, McGill University, 1969.

13. Gilles Tremblay

14. R. Murray Schafer

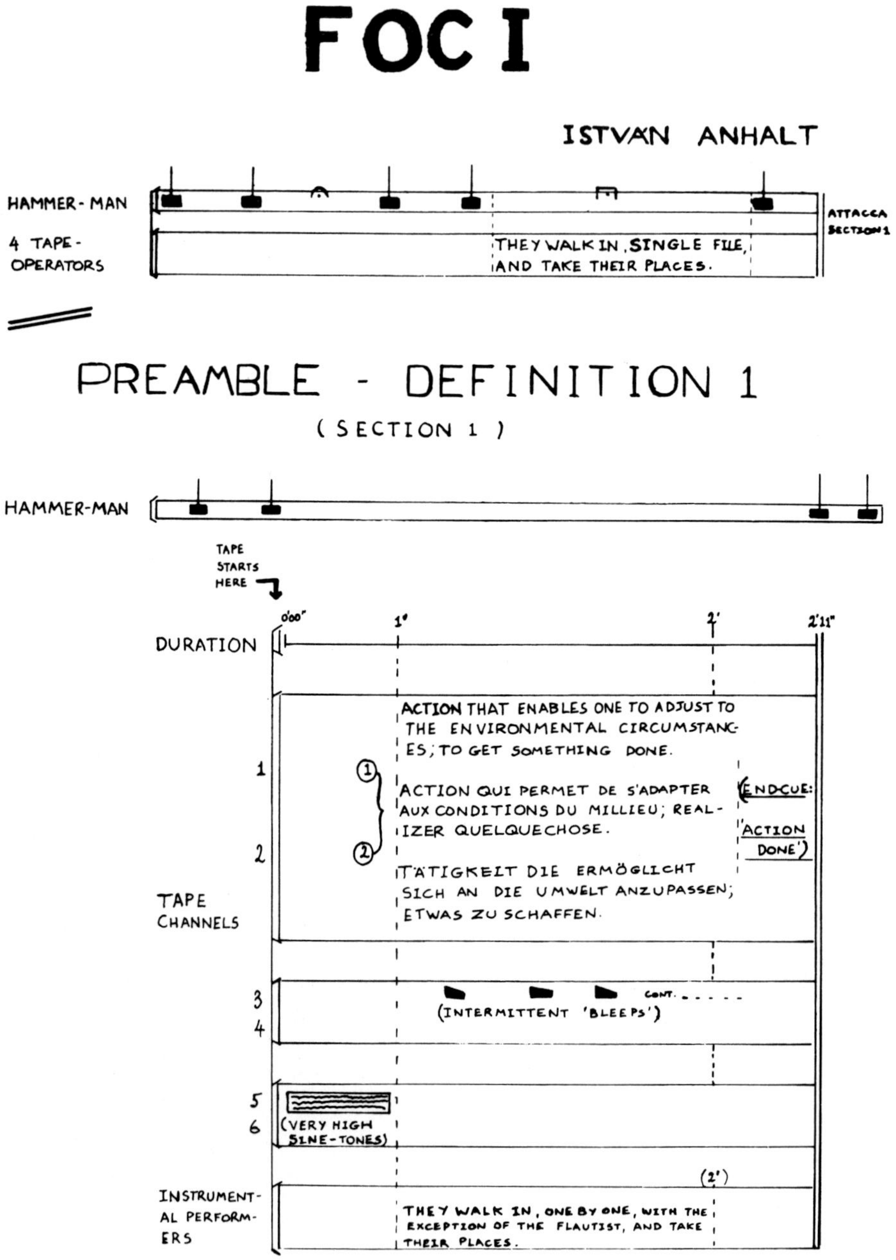

15. First page of the autograph score of *Foci* by István Anhalt, 1969.

16. From the autograph score of *Occasions* by Barbara Pentland, 1974.

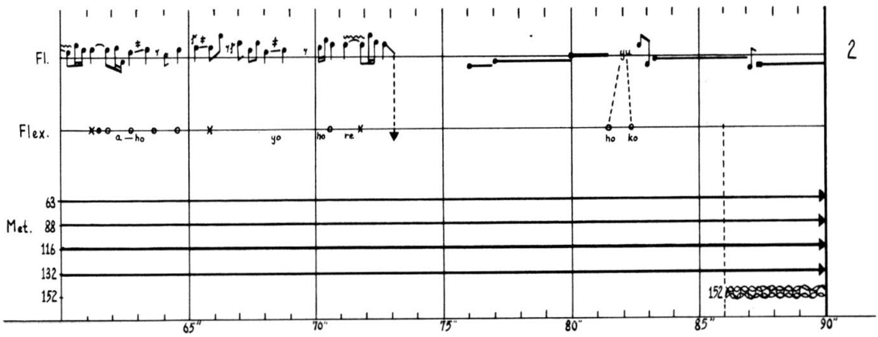

17. From the autograph score of *Sui* (for bamboo flute, flexiton, and five metronomes) by John Fodi, 1969.

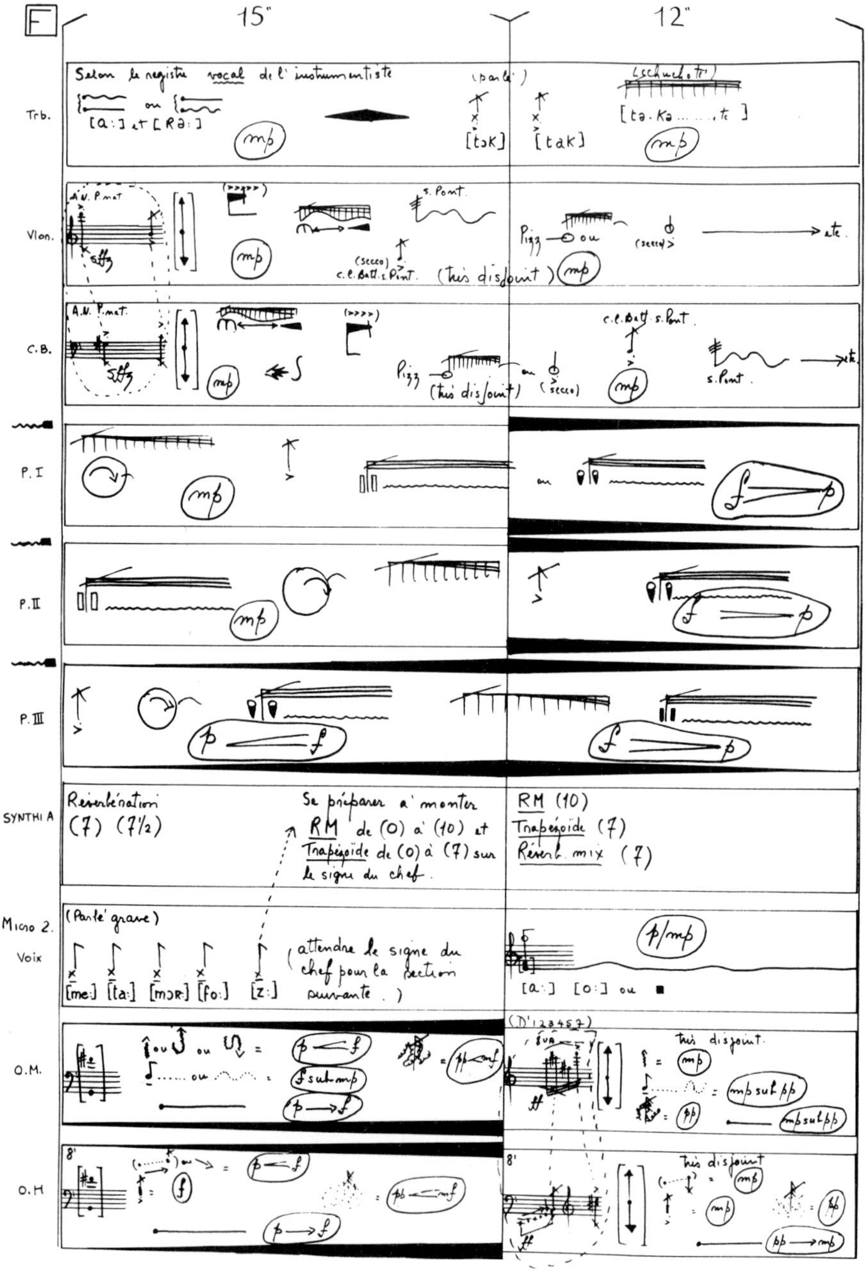

18. From the autograph score of *Ishuma* by Micheline Coulombe Saint-Marcoux, 1974.

integral component of the inverted pyramid-shape architectural space of the Canadian Pavilion. Few people could have done better justice to this acoustical setting than Joachim, whose muscular manner of music-making fitted such an environment like a glove. *Contrastes,* too, is a muscular score – instrumentally effective and formally sturdy. Here Joachim gives considerable leeway to the conductor and the players by providing them with various aleatoric materials and indeterminate notations. Yet he never loses control of the overall structure and energies of the piece. The timing and balancing of the free-form sections and those that are rigidly controlled are carried out with an uncanny musician's instinct.

In *Contrastes,* despite its open-endedness, Joachim still leaned on the legacy of the symphonic tradition, but in a series of mixed-media pieces, at which he has been working off and on since 1965, he throws away all conventional concepts of musical form and performance practice. All three – *Illuminations I* (1965) and *II* (1969) and *Mankind* (1972) – though scored for different instruments, voices, and electronic sound-sources, have one basic feature in common: they explore the relationships between the quantities and qualities of light and sound. In these pieces performers read from their individual parts, mostly carrying fragmentary information regarding textures, pitches, dynamics, etc., but doing so only when overhead spotlights beam directly on the score. These lights are controlled by the conductor who, by regulating the timing and intensity of each individual performer's light, takes charge of the overall direction of the performance. The performers' actions are triggered primarily by sensory stimulae: the dynamics, tempi, and durations of the players' gestures depend on what they see on the page, how clearly, and for how long. At the same time listeners not only hear, but also see lights in their one-to-one relationship with the sounds.

Although the basic optical triggering system is common to all three works, each has its own identity. *Illuminations I* is scored for four instrumentalists and a speaker and, being essentially an experiment in the manipulation of the fundamentals of audio-visual interactions, is relatively loose in content and structure. In *Illuminations II* Joachim considerably tightens up the concept, eliminates the live speaker in favour of a pre-recorded four-channel tape carrying a manipulated reading of a scientific text, and makes use of ten instrumentalists. This realization of the Joachim sight/sound concept was so successful that it won for him the Grand Prix Paul Gilson in 1969.

In the third piece in this cycle, *Mankind,* Joachim goes another step further in the choice and exploitation of performance media. His performing apparatus consists of four synthesizers (developed and marketed by himself as a viable alternative to the Moogs, Buchlas, Arps, and Putneys dominating the scene), a pianist, a timpanist, slides, incense, and four readers. The latter are to be no ordinary actors or singers but ordained clerics or their authorized deputies of four major world religions. Joachim, the imaginative orchestrator, not only mixes media but searches for vibrations common in diverse cults and cultures.

To sum up, Joachim is one of those fortunate personalities who have retained through many years and changing circumstances their liking of life and their curiosity about its many manifestations, and who exuberantly convey their experiences to people of different generations and backgrounds. Joachim talks to the young (he has published several study-works introducing twelve-tone music, chance performance practices, and mixed media to students), to the regular concert-goer, and to the man in the street such as an Expo visitor – no mean feat in a time of generation gaps and mass alienation.

Joachim is a member of the Canadian League of Composers and an affiliate of BMI Canada. UDO KASEMETS

MUSICAL WORKS

ORCHESTRA

Asia (symphonic poem for orchestra). 1928–39. 19′. full orch. Ber.

Contrastes. 1967. 15′–20′. full orch. Ric, 1968. May 6, 1967, Mtl, Expo '67, TS, Seiji Ozawa.

STRING ORCHESTRA

Concertante No. 2. 1961. 14′. str qt, str orch. Ber. 1962, McGill Chamb Ens, Alexander Brott.

SOLOIST WITH ORCHESTRA

Concertante. 1955. 12'. vln, str, perc. Ber, 1960. RCI-293. 1958, Paris, France, Théâtre des Champs-Elysées, Orchestre Radio-Symphonique de Paris, George Little (cond), Hyman Bress(vln).

CHOIR

Psalm. 1960. 7'. SATB. Ber, 1961. RCI-206. 1961, Mtl, McGill, Redpath Hall, Mtl Bach Choir, George Little.

VOICE

March. 1954. vc, pno. Text: Ian Clark.

VOICE WITH INSTRUMENTAL ENSEMBLE

Illumination I. 1965. dur'n indeterminate. spkr, fl, alto fl, bs &/or picc, guit, perc. Ber, 1968.

Kinderspiel (aleatoric music for children). 1969. dur'n at discretion of narr. narr, vln, vlc, pno. 1970, Mtl, Mtl-Cons.

INSTRUMENTAL ENSEMBLE

Music for Violin and Viola. 1953. 14'15". 1954, Mtl, CBC, Hyman Bress(vln), Otto Joachim(vla).

Sonata for cello and piano. 1954. 8'6". Ber, 1963. RCI-139, CBC BR SM-113. 1955, Mtl, Musica Antica e Nuova Conc, Walter Joachim(vlc), John Newmark(pno).

String Quartet. 1956. 18'30". AMP, 1959 & Ber, 1960. RCI-190. 1957, Mtl, 'Music of Our Times' Series, Mtl Str Qt, Hyman Bress (vln), Mildred Goodman(vln), Otto Joachim (vla), Walter Joachim(vlc).

Nonet. 1960. str, ww, pno. ms. 1960, Stratford, Fest Conc.

Interlude; 'Quartet for Four Saxophones'. 1960. 3'5". ms. Mtl, Moyse Hall, McGill, Arthur Romano Qt.

Expansion. 1962. 5'. fl, pno. Ber, 1967. 1963, Tor, 'Men, Minds and Music', Robert Aitken(fl), William Aide(pno).

Divertimento. 1962. 17'. ww qnt. Ber. 1963, Sainte-Anne-de-Bellevue, PQ, Masella Wind Qnt.

Music. 1962. 4 viols. ms.

Dialogue. 1964. 3½'–10' (variable). vla, pno. ms. 1964, Mtl, CBC, Otto Joachim(vla), John Newmark(pno).

Illumination II. 1969. 10 plyrs, 4 channel tape, spotlight control. Apr 2, 1970, Mtl, Théâtre Maisonneuve, SMCQ, Serge Garant.

Twelve 12-tone pieces for the young. 1970. vln, pno.

PIANO

Bagatelles (3). 1939.

L'Eclosion. 1954. 4'30". Ber, 1968. RCI-133. 1955, Mtl, McGill, Redpath Hall, Rose Goldblatt.

Twelve 12-tone pieces for children. 1961. Ber, 1961. CCM-2.

ORGAN

Fantasia. 1961. 6'35". org. Ber, 1967. RCA CC/CCS-1019, RCI-225. 1962, Mtl, Christ Church Cathedral, Gian Lyman.

INSTRUMENTAL SOLO

Six Guitar Pieces. 1971.

ELECTRONIC

Katimavik. 1967. 1967, Mtl, Expo '67, Can Pavilion.

5.9. 1971. 5'54". 4 channel. RCI-373.

6½. 1971. 6'30". 4 channel.

MULTI-MEDIA

Mankind. 1972. 4 spkrs, 4 synthesizers, org, timp, incense, slides.

BIBLIOGRAPHY

See B-B; B65,71; Bec56,70; Bt; CrC(I); Esc; Lv; Wa.

Campbell, Francean. 'Otto Joachim's Mastery Influences Son', *MuSc.* Sept.-Oct. 1970 (4–5).

'Otto Joachim – a portrait'. *Mu.* No. 20, June 1969 (10–11).

JOHNSTON, RICHARD (b. Chicago, Ill., 7 May 1917). He received his early training from Ruth Cazier Curtiss and John S. Fearis. After obtaining his baccalaureate in composition from Northwestern University (1942), he taught piano and theory at Luther College in Nebraska and studied with Nadia Boulanger in Madison, Wis. (1942–4). He received his Master of Music (1945) and Doctor of Philosophy (1951) degrees in composition from the Eastman School of Music, University of Rochester, where he was a teaching fellow from 1944 to 1947. From 1947 to 1968 he taught at the Faculty of Music, University of Toronto. From 1968 to 1973 he served as Dean of the Faculty of Fine Arts, University of Calgary, where he is also professor of music.

Johnston has been widely heard over the CBC networks as composer, arranger, conductor, and commentator. From the CBC he received commissions for his *March 'M. S.'* (1953) and *The Irish Book* (1972); in 1972 *Portraits*, for full orchestra, was commissioned by the Calgary Philharmonic Society under a grant from the Canada Council. He is much interested in the voice and even his instrumental works have the lyrical quality and soft textures characteristic of traditional vocal writing. He is co-founder of both the Canadian Music Educators' Association and (with Marius Barbeau) of the Canadian Folk Music Society, and is a past president of the Ontario Music Educators' Association. He is also editor-in-chief of *Horizons*, a Western Board of Music piano series devoted to new idioms. He is a member of the board of the Canadian Conference of the Arts, the Canadian Music Council, and the Calgary Philharmonic Society. He is a founding member and president of the Alberta Music Conference and is affiliated with BMI Canada.

MUSICAL WORKS

INSTRUMENTAL

4 works for orchestra: *Suite for Bassoon and Orchestra* (1946); *Symphony No 1* (1950); *March 'M. S.'* (1953); *Portraits* (1972).

Suite for Bassoon and Piano. 1946.

2 *Suites for Piano*. 1965; Ber 1965.

CHORAL

The Face of Night (1956) SATB Wat 1956; *Old Fiddler's Dream* (1959) SATB Wat 1959 Text: Marie Halbert King; *Canticle of the Sun* (1962) 2 soli, SATB, med orch; *A Christmas Garland* (1965) SSA Wat 1965 Text: Margaret Mackay; *Alleluia* (1966) SSA Wat 1966 Text: J M Neale; *The Owl and The Pussy-Cat* (1966) unis Wat 1966 Text: Edward Lear; *Nocturne* (1967) SATB Wat 1967 Text: Marie Halbert King.

c14 arrangements of folk songs.

Arranged and co-edited (with Edith Fowke) *Folk Songs of Canada, Chansons de Québec, More Folk Songs of Canada*. Wat 1954, 1958, 1967.

VOCAL

Bruce Country Ballad. Ber.

The Irish Book (A set of four songs). 1972.

BIBLIOGRAPHY

See B-B; K; Wa.

'Folk Songs of Canada', *CBC Times*. May 30–June 5, 1954 (3).

LITERARY WORKS

ARTICLES

'Canadian String Quartet', *MAC*. Feb. 1963 (17–22).

'North American Children's Folklore as it Relates to the *Schulwerk* of Carl Orff', Unpublished Paper delivered at the Conference on Elementary Music Education, July 26–8, 1965, University of Toronto.

'Western Board of Music Gathers', *CanCo*. No. 52, Sept. 1970 (32–3).

'Zoltan Kodaly: a True Citizen of the World', *PAC*, Vol. v, no. 1, 1967 (14–16).

JONES, KELSEY (b. South Norwalk, Conn., 17 June 1922). He came to Canada in 1939 and began his theoretical music studies with Harold Hamer at Mount Allison University, in Sackville, N.B., where he received his Bachelor of Music degree in 1945. He continued his compositional studies at the University of Toronto with Sir Ernest MACMILLAN, Healey WILLAN, and Leo SMITH, completing his doctorate in music in 1951. Later he studied composition with Nadia Boulanger in Paris. In 1950 he founded the Saint John Symphony Orchestra and was its conductor until 1954. Since 1954 he has been a member of the teaching staff of the Faculty of Music of McGill University in Montreal and harpsichordist with the Montreal Symphony Orchestra, the McGill Chamber Orchestra, and the Baroque Trio of Montreal.

Jones is a specialist in renaissance and baroque music, and in his own compositions his training in counterpoint shows clearly. His *Sonata da Chiesa* (1957) seems polytonal in the sense that there are highly chromatic single lines that can be felt in their own tonality. In *Sonata da Camera* (1967) he has adopted the baroque suite form and written a work with a contrapuntal texture using chromatic fugal subjects. His chosen style, which is basically tonal with a liberal use of chromaticism, works well both in the form and for the instrumentation (flute, oboe, and harpsichord). The *Sonata da Camera* does not hark back to the archaic style found in his *Sonata da Chiesa*, although the structure can be fitted loosely into the baroque suite form. Both these works were written for the Baroque Trio of Montreal.

In *Quintet for Winds* (1968) Jones employs chromatic themes in a polytonal and polyphonic texture, using contrapuntal techniques such as inversion and stretto. In *Miramichi Ballad* (1954) he developed a suite of New Brunswick folk songs and dealt with them tonally, the orchestration being frequently woodwind solos with string accompaniment. *Songs of Experience* for choir (1958) is essentially two-part writing with one voice holding a single pitch in a section while a counter-voice moves dissonantly against it, recalling a technique of the Middle Ages. *Sam Slick*, an opera written in 1967, although for radio, is an example of Jones' sense of theatre. (Sam Slick, the Yankee clockmaker, was the creation of Thomas Chandler Haliburton; the character first appeared in a series of sketches in a Halifax newspaper in 1836 that were reprinted in *The Clockmaker; or The Sayings and Doings of Sam Slick of Slickville* (1836), a book that became a bestseller in English-speaking countries.)

Jones has composed works for the Montreal Bach Choir (*Songs of Experience*, 1955; *The Prophecy of Micah*, 1963) and the Montreal Recorder Group (*Four pieces for recorder quartet*, 1955; *Mosaic*, 1956). He has also received commissions from the CBC (*Songs of Innocence*, 1961; *Sam Slick*, 1967; *Kishimaquac Suite*, 1971), from the Jeunesses Musicales of Canada (*Passacaglia*, 1961), from the Lakeshore Chamber Music Society (*Quintet for Winds*, 1968), and from the Tudor Singers of Montreal (*Hymn to Bacchus*, 1972). He is a member of the Canadian League of Composers and of CAPAC.

MUSICAL WORKS

STAGE

Sam Slick (chamber opera). 1967. 80′. 8 soli, med orch. CMC. Libretto: Rosabelle Jones. Sept 5, 1967, Halifax, CBC, Ettore Mazzoleni.

ORCHESTRA

Miramichi Ballad (a suite). 1954. 16′15″. full orch. B & H, 1972. CBC BR SM-163; RCI-291 (complete suite); Dom 1372 (The Jones Boys); RCI-152 (Peter Emberley). Text: based on folk songs of NB. 1956, Saint John SO, Kelsey Jones.

Jack and the Beanstalk. 1954. 12′. full orch or child's vc, SATB, pno 4 hands. ms. 1954, TS, Sir Ernest MacMillan.

SOLOIST WITH ORCHESTRA

A Suite for Flute and Strings. 1954. 20′. CMC. RCI-191. 1955, Mtl, CBC, Mario Duschenes(fl).

Songs of Innocence. 1961. 15′45″. sop, chamb orch. CMC. Text: William Blake. Sept 1963, Alexander Brott.

CHOIR WITH ORCHESTRA

Prophecy of Micah. 1963. 27′15″. SATB, orch. ms. RCI-355. Text: adapted by Rosabelle Jones. Feb 5, 1964, Mtl, Mtl Bach Choir, George Little.

CHOIR

Nonsense Songs. 1955. 8′. SATB. MCA, 1961. CBC BR SM-19. Text: Edward Lear. 1955, Mtl Bach Choir.

Songs of Time. 1955. 13′35″. SATB, pno 4 hands. CMC. RCI-144. Text: Robert Herrick, John Webster, Thomas Jordan, Francis Quarles. 1955, Mtl, Mtl Bach Choir.

Songs of Experience. 1958. 6′50″. SATB. ms. RCI-189. Text: William Blake. 1958, Edinburgh Fest, Mtl Bach Choir.

Kishimaquac Suite. 1971. 10′. SATB. CMC. Text: based on NB folk songs, adapted by Rosabelle Jones. Oct 1972, Tor, Fest Sgrs, Elmer Iseler.

Hymn to Bacchus. 1972. 16′. SATB, pno 4 hands. CMC. Text: Robert Herrick, adapted by Rosabelle Jones. 1972, Mtl, CBC, Mtl Tudor Sgrs.

VOICE(S)

Ole King Cole. 1954. 4′57″. child's vc, pno 4 hands. ms.

Jack and the Beanstalk. 1954. 12′. child's vc, SATB, pno 4 hands or full orch. ms.

To Music (song cycle). 1957. 17′. alto, pno. CMC. RCI-203. Text: Robert Herrick. Feb 1961, Mtl, Maureen Forrester(alto), John Newmark(pno).

Psalm Forty-Nine. 1962. 18′. bar, pno. CMC.

INSTRUMENTAL ENSEMBLE

Four Pieces for Recorder Quartet. 1955. 8′. CMC. Bar BC-1857. Apr 1955, Mtl, CBC, Mtl Rec Gp, Mario Duschenes.

Mosaic. 1956. 3′. fl, vla, hp. ms.

Sonata da Camera. 1957. 10′40″. fl, ob, hpschd. Peters, 1972. RCI-192. 1957, Mtl, Bar Trio Mtl.

Introduction and Fugue. 1959. 12′30″. vln,

pno. CMC. RCA CC/CCS-1014; RCI-220 & 244. 1959, Mtl CLC conc, Hyman Bress(vln), Charles Reiner(pno).
Prelude, Fughetta and Finale. 1963. 14′. vln, vlc, hpschd. CMC. 1964, Vanc, CBC, Hugh McLean Consort.
Sonata da Chiesa. 1967. 11′20″. fl, ob, hpschd. CMC. RCA LSC-3091; CBC BR SM-56. Oct 18, 1967, Ed'tn.
Quintet for Winds. 1968. 14′. fl, ob, cl, hn, bsn. Peters, 1972. RCI-355. 1968, Ste Anne de Bellevue, PQ, Lakeshore Chamb Mus Soc conc, Pro Arte Wind Qnt, Melvin Berman.

PIANO
Passacaglia. 1961. 11′25″. CMC. 1963, CBC, Charles Reiner.
Theme and Variations. 1961. 17′15″. pno 4 hands. CMC. 1961, CBC, Rosabelle and Kelsey Jones.
Five Pieces for Piano. 1964. 11′55″. CMC. June 27, 1965, Kelsey Jones.

INSTRUMENTAL SOLO
Rondo for Solo Flute. 1963. 5′15″. Wat. RCA CC/CCS-1013, RCI-219. Oct 1963, Mtl, Mario Duschenes.

BIBLIOGRAPHY

B65,71; Bt; CrC(I); Esc; Lv; Wa.
Bisbrouck, Noël. 'Kelsey Jones: A Sincere Musician', *CanCo.* No. 26, Feb. 1968 (4–5, 44–5).
'Marriage and Music', *CBC Times.* Feb. 10–16, 1952 (4).
'New Brunswick Youth Orchestra', *CanCo.* No. 36, Jan. 1969 (42–3).
'Sam Slick', *CBC Times.* Sept. 2–8, 1967 (12–13).
'Samuel Slick of Slickville: Hero of New Comic Opera', *CanCo.* No. 22, Oct. 1967 (6–7).

LITERARY WORKS

ARTICLES
'My Most Successful Work: "Prophecy of Micah" ', *CanCo.* No. 24, Dec. 1967 (20–1).

K

KALNINS, JANIS (b. Pernu, Estonia, 3 Nov. 1904). He studied composition and conducting at the Latvian State Conservatory in Riga with Erich Kleiber, Hermann Abendroth, and Leo Blech. He was conductor of the Latvian National Theatre (1923–33) and of the Latvian National Opera (1933–44) and guest conductor at the Royal Opera in Stockholm. He was decorated with the Three Star Order by the State of Latvia and with the Gustav Vasa Order by King Gustav of Sweden. He came to Canada in 1948 to be organist at St Paul's United Church in Fredericton, N.B. In 1951 he was appointed an instructor at the provincial Teachers' College in Fredericton as well as conductor of the Fredericton Civic Orchestra and of the New Brunswick Symphony Orchestra (1962–8).

Kalnins' work is romantic, using dissonant polytonal material with whole-tone and chromatic scales (*Trio,* 1967). Although following a more traditional style, his choral work *Bird's Lullaby* (1950) continues to incorporate rich chromatic harmonies.

He has received commissions from the Halifax Trio (*Trio for Piano, Violin and Cello,* 1967) and from the New Brunswick Symphony Orchestra (*A New Brunswick Rhapsody,* 1967). He is a member of CAPAC.

MUSICAL WORKS

STAGE
Lolita's Magic Bird (opera). 1936; Daina, 1936. Text: Anna Brigadere.
Hamlet (opera). Text: William Shakespeare.
In the Fire (opera). Text: Rudolf Blaumanis.
Unguni (opera). Text: Rudolf Blaumanis.

ORCHESTRA
Two Latvian Peasant Dances. 1936; UE, 1937.
Symphony in C minor. 1939–44.
Festal March. 1955.

Marching Through Fredericton. 1963.
Music for String Orchestra. 1965.
Irish Song (arr). 1966.
New Brunswick Rhapsody. 1967.
Festival Overture. 1969.
Symphony No. 3. 1972–3.
Latvian Rhapsody.
Lullaby.

SOLOIST(S) WITH ORCHESTRA
Violin Concerto in F♯ minor. 1945–6.
Theme and Variations for Clarinet, Horn and Orchestra. 1963.

CHOIR WITH ORCHESTRA
Symphony of the Beatitudes (Symphony No. 2). 1953. Text: St Matthew 5:1–12.
The Long Night. Text: Velta Toma.

CHOIR
Pirma Nakts. 1947.
The Bird's Lullaby. 1950; FH, 1951. Text: E Pauline Johnson.
The Lord's Prayer. 1954; FH, 1954. Text: Scriptures.
When Jesus Came to Birmingham. 1954; FH, 1954. Text: G A Studdert Kennedy.
Our Father. 1954. Text: Scriptures.
Which Bird Sings the Best (arr). 1955. Text: trad.
All That the Father Giveth Me. SATB, org. Text: Scriptures.
The Potter's Field. SATB, org. Text: Scriptures.
Let Not Your Heart Be Troubled. SATB, org. Text: Scriptures.
Song of Praise (arr). Text: trad.
Redz Kur Jaja Dir Bajari (arr). Text: trad.

VOICE
Whence Comest Thou Sorrow. 1957. Text: J Rainis.
So Seldom Open Souls. 1957. Text: V Strelerte.
Nunc Dimittis. 1957. Text: Scriptures.
Home. 1957. Text: J Rainis.
Davana. 1961. Text: Z Lagzda.
Apsnidzis Rozu Krums. 1961. Text: Z Lagzda.
Mocekli. 1963. Text: Karlis Skalbe.
Vakara Dziesma. 1967. Text: trad.
Gramata Ar Krustu. 1967. Text: trad.
Balta Puke. 1967. Text: trad.
Apsniegosa Pilseta. 1967. Text: J Sudrabkalns.
Pasaka par Pikamici. Text: J Sudrabkalns.
Petera Gailis. Text: J Sudrabkalns.

VOICE WITH INSTRUMENTAL ENSEMBLE
Two Shepherd Songs for Voice, Oboe and Piano. 1963. Text: trad.

INSTRUMENTAL ENSEMBLE
Sonata for Oboe and Piano. 1963.
Trio. 1966. vln, vlc, pno.
The Bells of Aberdovey (arr of Charles Dibdin). 1968. EH, pno.
Klusa Stunda. 1968. vln, pno.
Dance. vln, pno.
Meditation. vln, pno.
String Quartet in C♯ minor.

INSTRUMENTAL SOLO
Monologue. vln.

ORGAN
Variations on Tune 'St Andrew'. 1970.
Ten Chorale Preludes.

BIBLIOGRAPHY

See B-B; K.
'Janis Kalnins', *Atlantic Advocate.* Vol. XLVIII, May 1958 (99).
'Orchestra Conductor', *Atlantic Advocate.* Vol. LII, Aug. 1962 (87).
Sakss, Imants. 'Janis Kalnins', *Latvju muzika.* No. 3, May 1970 (210–31).

KASEMETS, UDO (b. Tallinn, Estonia, 19 Nov. 1919). He was educated at the Tallinn Conservatory and the State Music Academy, Stuttgart, and attended the Kranichstein Summer Courses in Contemporary Music in Darmstadt before immigrating to Canada in 1951. Dividing his activities between Hamilton, Ont., and Toronto, he has been at various periods a teacher of piano and theory, a vocal coach and recital accompanist, a church organist and choir director, a conductor and concert organizer for various series (such as those of 'Musica Viva', the Toronto Bach Society, 'Men, Minds, and Music', the Isaacs Gallery Mixed Media Ensemble, and the Toronto Synergetic Theatre), a newspaper critic (the Toronto *Star*), a publisher's editor (BMI Canada's *Canavangard* series, now handled by BMI's successor, Berandol), and a lecturer and commentator on, especially, new music.

Kasemets is one of the few Canadian composers steadily associated with the musical avant-garde in the United States. Through his efforts and enterprise, artists such as Ashley, Mumma, Caccioppo, Cage,

Turetzky, Lucier – and even (shortly before his death) Marcel Duchamp – have visited Toronto for public appearances. In return, Kasemets has published articles in U.S. journals such as *Source* and directed his own works in concerts in New York, California, Michigan, and other parts of the U.S.

A chronological listing of his works compiled by the composer is divided into three categories. The first contains twenty-one opus numbers dated 1941–50, covering 'works composed prior to the composer's contacts with the existing international trends in composition' and music exhibiting 'conventional tonality; few experiments with expanded tonality; traditional forms'. The second chronological grouping contains twenty-nine works with opus numbers and four without from the period 1950–60, 'following the stylistic and structural main stream of the time' – summarized as 'twelve-tone music; folk-music arrangements; traditional forms'. The third category constitutes the 'exploratory works' produced since 1960, embracing 'open forms, indeterminate performance forces, unconventional notation, mixed media and theatre pieces'. (In the list of works below, the first two categories are combined in Division I.)

None of the music before 1950 is in circulation. Twenty of the 1950–60 works are available for performance, the rest having been withdrawn. In effect Kasemets himself remains actively interested only in the works produced since 1960.

His assumption of open and indeterminate approaches and his fascination with the avant-garde mixing of various musical media and of music with other arts, especially literature, visual art, and theatre, broke into Kasemets' compositional development in the early 1960s with dramatic suddenness, suggesting an act of aesthetic conversion. Among his previous works, however, may be observed various signs foreshadowing his adoption of newer trends: the twelve-tone fugues, double-fugues, and chaconnes are schematic in a way that almost transcends physical sound, and some movements show a game-like patterning of compositional choices, going beyond conventional demands on the performer's creative imagination. Texts used (Lorca, Dylan Thomas, folk poetry) are also at times forward-looking in subject or style. On the other hand, the post-'conversion' works sometimes connect with broad musical traditions, or recall specific traits of the composer's earlier pieces – for example by emphasizing perfect intervals, or by exploiting familiar earthy qualities in deliberate borrowings from folk and popular sources.

Readily accessible examples of Kasemets' repertoire from the 1950s include the *Three Miniatures* (1956) on Shelley verses, for voice and piano; the *Six Preludes* (1952) for piano solo; and the *Recitative and Rondino* (1954) for orchestra, one of a handful of works by various Canadian composers based on songs of the Copper Eskimos. They show an assured grasp of form and a predilection for lines and intervals that are open in expression and easily retained. The larger products of the period include the *Poetic Suite* (1954) for soprano, piano, and string orchestra, on poems by the English poet Kathleen Raine; the *Sonata da camera* (1955) for cello alone; and an unusually large-scaled and highly successful *Violin Concerto* (1955–6).

The works of the 1960s and early 1970s reveal their newer and more avant-garde character in two general ways: by organizing sound-patterns informally (for example through the use of performance charts or other controlled-improvisation means) and by laying out schemes for performance-manifestations that will be acoustic only in part. Works from both types tend to spawn versions with new characteristics at each re-playing and are therefore sometimes retitled. Thus *Fifth Root of Five* (1962–3), for two pianos, provides quintuple choices (among its various musical parameters) to be made afresh by the players themselves at each performance, while *Trigon* (1962), for 1, 3, 9, or 27 participants on various media (musical and non-musical) up to eighty-one in number, can partake of the genre of the 'happening' in several of its allowable realizations. The most frequently performed of Kasemets' works, *Trigon*, has been realized by various solo instruments and also by various-sized chamber ensembles that have incorporated – among other elements – mobile sculpture, dance, and readings from cummings, Joyce,

Beckett, Cage, McLuhan, Fuller, and others. *Calceolaria* (1966) and the *Octagonal Octet and/or Ode* (1967) are closely related performance-schemes. In various executions, offshoots of the score of *Cascando* (1965) have been renamed 'Stereosonic Vocophony' (1969), 'Synersonic Octet' (1970), and 'Synersonophony: Vocosonic Poem; Sonophonic Interlude; Stereosonovocophony' (1971). Active audience involvement is called for in a number of Kasemets' compositions and realizations, including *Contactics* (1966) and *T* (subtitled 'Tribute to Buckminster Fuller, Marshall McLuhan, and John Cage', 1968). In the latter, audience-members decide various dimensions of the performance by punching cards, whose later mechanical processing forms the actual 'happening'.

In the early 1970s Kasemets moved through his compositions, writings, and teachings towards some larger creative concepts suggesting the influence of Cage in their character as participatory theatre and of Ives in their closeness to the latter's vision of a 'Universe Symphony'. The contemporaneous developments (in the U.S. especially) of happenings and earth-art are also brought to mind. Thus one partial realization of the *Quartet of Quartets* (1971–2) involves setting in motion tape-recorded readings of reference-volume entries selected according to a prescribed scheme and later superimposing these on further readings from other locales in other languages, gathered as the piece is in progress. With an open time-span for the presentation, phone or telegraph may be used to add to the accumulation of sound-materials. Musical values are inherent in the scheme by its implied appreciation of contrasting dynamic levels (called for by specific directions) and the distinctions between the various vocal timbres and inflections which may result. The piece has also a visual and quasi-ritualistic component, since the process of consulting the reference source and the lighting to be used are specified. Basic existential aspects are produced in a given realization of *Quartet of Quartets* by the fresh associations of the chosen verbal entries and by the human contacts which arise naturally from the process of superimposition.

Kasemets' late activities include articles and talks whose philosophic flavour incorporates instant illustration, either by typography or by sonorous or projective accompaniments, that bridge over into the main creative areas of his work. He sometimes calls these 'lecturessays' and 'quollages'. Their subjects are not solely aesthetic; on the contrary, they show strong humanistic considerations, for example by their anti-war, anti-pollution, or pro-sensitivity-training sentiments.

Since 1970 Kasemets has been associated, as a lecturer on music and mixed media, with the Ontario College of Art in Toronto. Various of his works have been commissioned by the CBC, the Saskatoon Symphony Orchestra, and other agencies. He is a former member of the Canadian League of Composers and is an affiliate of BMI Canada. JOHN BECKWITH

MUSICAL WORKS

Division I: 1941–60

STAGE

Story of the Three Sisters, Op 9. 1947. sop, mezz, SATB, cl, bsn, tpt, vln, vlc, cb, pno, perc. ms. Text: M Söödor.

Visions, Op 31. 1953. 35′. dancer, narr, small orch. CMC. Text: Karl Rumor.

ORCHESTRA

Preludio Sinfonico, Op 23. 1950. ms.

Variations on 'Jesus Christ en pauvre', Op 38. 1954. ms.

SMALL ORCHESTRA

Estonian Suite, Op 20, 1950. ms. 1954, Mtl, CBC, G Waddington(cond).

Sinfonietta. 1959. 15′. Ber. 1959, S'tn, Fest O, Udo Kasemets(cond).

STRING ORCHESTRA

Recitative and Rondino, Op 36 (based on songs of the Copper Eskimos). 1954. 8′. Ber. 1954, Vanc, CBC Vanc Ch O, John Avison (cond).

SOLOIST(S) WITH ORCHESTRA

Poetic Suite, Op 37. 1954. 20′. vc, pno, str orch. Ber. Text: Kathleen Raine. 1955, Tor, Massey Hall, TS, Sir Ernest MacMillan (cond), Irene Salemka(sop), George Brough (pno).

Concerto for Violin and Orchestra, Op 41. 1955–6. 35′. solo vln, full orch. Ber. 1967, Tor, CBC Fest O, John Avison(cond), Hyman Bress(vln).

Two Symphonic Songs, Op 43. 1956. 17′. bar (mezz), orch. CMC. Text: Dylan Thomas.
Passacaglia. 1959. 10′. fl, vln, orch. Ber. 1960, S'tn, SSO, Udo Kasemets(cond).

CHOIR WITH ORCHESTRA
Symphony 'B-A-C-H', Op 27. 1951–2. SATB, small orch. ms. Text: Rabindranath Tagore.
Serenata Dolorosa, Op 28. 1951–2. alto, SATB, pno, str orch. ms. Text: J Kork, K Lepik, K Rumor.

CHOIR
38 a cappella choruses for SATB, TTBB, SSA(A), (Op 1, Op 3, Op 13, Op 18 No 1a, Op 18 No 2). ms. Text: various.
Great Is, Lord, Your Might, Op 11. 1948. ten, SSAATB, org. ms. Text: F R Faehlman.
Little Requiem, Op 15. 1949. sop, alto, spkr, SSAA, org. ms. Text: Udo Kasemets.
Guardsman, Op 17. 1949. ten, SSAA, 2pno. ms. Text: H Visnapuu.
Hearth Songs, Op 21. 1950. vc, youth choir, pno. ms. Text: Estonian folk songs.
Four Canonic Settings of Estonian Folk-Songs, Op 25 No 1. 1951. SSA/TTB. ms. 1951, Tor.
Two Estonian Christmas Carols, Op 25 No 2. 1951. SSA/TTB. ms. 1951, Hamilton.
A Nativity of Carols, Op 34. 1953. SSA, SA, pno. ms. 1953, Hamilton.
Carmina Britannica, Op 35. 1953–4. SSA, pno. ms. Text: four folk songs from the British Isles. 1955, Hamilton.
Two Songs for Male Voices, Op 49. 1957. TTBB. CMC. Text: John Donne, anon.

VOICE(S)
10 songs (Op 4, Op 18 No 1b, Op 19). c1944–50. ms. Text: various.
Choreola Gaudiae, Op 32. 1952. 9′45″. sop, alto, ten, pno. CMC. Text: four old Christmas carols. 1952, Hamilton.
The Thousand Nights and One Night, Op 39. 1954. vc, pno. CMC. Text: anon Arab 13th-cent poetry. Trans: E Powys Mathers. 1956, Tor, Catharine Hindson(sop), Udo Kasemets(pno).
Two Symphonic Songs, Op 43 (arr). 1956. 17′. bar (mezz), pno. CMC. Text: Dylan Thomas.
Three Miniatures, Op 46. 1956. 6′. vc, pno. Ber, 1960. Text: Percy B Shelley. 1957, Tor, Catharine Hindson(sop), Udo Kasemets(pno).
Songs from the Atlantic Provinces. 1959. vc, pno. ms. Text: Folk songs. 1960, S'tn, Catharine Hindson(sop), Udo Kasemets (pno).
Hano, an Indian dirge. 1960. vc, pno. ms. Text: Cree Indian.
Five Songs for Children. 1964. vc, pno. Ber, 1964. Text: Laura E Richards, William Allingham, Christina Rossetti.

VOICE WITH INSTRUMENTAL ENSEMBLE
Canciones, Op 42. 1956. vc, fl, guit. CMC. Text: F Garcia Lorca. 1961, Mtl, Catharine Hindson(sop), Wolfgang Kander(fl), Stephen Fentak(guit).
To a Child Before Birth, Op 47. 1956. sop, fl, pno. ms.
Four for Four, Op 51. 1958. sop, str trio. Ber. Text: Carl Sandburg.

INSTRUMENTAL ENSEMBLE
Two Pieces for Cello and Piano, Op 5, 1945–7. ms.
Sonata in E, Op 10. 1949. vln, pno. ms.
Canzona, Op 12. 1949. vla, org. ms.
Trio in Classical Form, Op 16. 1949. vln, vlc, pno. ms. 1954, Hamilton, H Goodman (vln), W Grunsky(vlc), P Lewis(pno).
Duo for Flute and Clarinet, Op 22 No 1. 1950. ms.
Introduzione e Capriccio, Op 22 No 2. 1950. 11′. vln, pno. ms. 1956, Tor, Jacob Groob (vln), Udo Kasemets(pno).
Chaconne, Op 24 No 2. 1951. vla, pno. ms.
Capricious Pastorale, Op 29. 1952. cl, pno. ms.
String Trio, Op 33. 1953. 13′. vln, vla, vlc. CMC. 1956, Tor, Jacob Groob(vln), Walter Babiak(vla), George Horvath(vlc).
Recitative and Fugue, Op 40a. 1955. 9′. 2vlc. CMC.
Ecclesiastical Suite, Op 44. 1956. vla da gamba (vlc), hpschd (pno). ms. 1956, Hamilton, Wolfgang Grunsky(vla da gamba), Reginald Godden(pno).
String Quartet, Op 45. 1956–7. ms.
Quintet for Wind Instruments, Op 48. 1957. 7′45″. ww qnt. Ber. RCA-CC/CCS-1012, RCI-218. 1958, Mtl, Mario Duschenes(fl), Pietro Masella(ob), Rafael Masella(cl), Joseph Masella(hn), Rodolfo Masella(bsn).
Sonata Concertante, Op 50. 1957. str trio, pno. CMC.

PIANO

Three Piano Pieces, Op 2. 1941, 1946. ms.
Piano Pieces on Estonian Folktunes, Op 6. 1946–7. ms.
Two Impressions, Op 7. 1947. ms.
Sonatina No 1, Op 8. 1947. ms.
Concert Music for Piano (Sonatina No 2), Op 14 No 2. 1949. ms.
Sonata for Piano, Op 24 No 1. 1951. 16′. CMC. 1955, Mtl, CBC, Rose Goldblatt.
Six Preludes, Op 30. 1952. FH (No 2), 1955. 1953, Hamilton, Udo Kasemets.

INSTRUMENTAL SOLO

Concert Music for Solo Clarinet, Op 14 No 1. 1949. ms.
Sonata da Camera, Op 40. 1955. vlc. CMC. 1956, Tor, George Horvath.

ORGAN

Organ Chorale 'Father in Heaven', Op 26 No 1. 1951. ms.
Toccatina, Arietta and Fughetta, Op 26 No 2. 1956. ms. 1959, Tor, Lembit Avesson.

Division II: 1960–73

Open forms, indeterminate performance forces, unconventional notation, mixed media and theatre pieces. This Division is in three Sections, dealing with works written since 1960.
Section I comprises works of open form but fixed performance forces and a fixed score.
Section II comprises multi-purpose scores of open form and indeterminate instrumentation, and the various definitive realizations of these scores. The realizations are placed under the original title to show from which particular score they have been derived, but the ordering is still kept as in Division I, e.g., voice, instrumental ensemble, piano, etc. Also in Section II are Lecturessays, Quollages, and compositions in which elements of various multi-purpose scores or their definitive realizations are incorporated or combined.
Section III comprises theatre and participation pieces and 'Learningmusic'.

SECTION I:

19NooN61. 1961. vc, pno. ms. Text: Walter Hickling.
Haiku. 1961. 16′–20′. vc, fl, vlc, pno. Ber. 1963, LA, Janice Wheeler(sop), Patricia Garside(fl), Laurence Lesser(vlc), Karl Kohn(pno). Trans: Harold G. Henderson.
Communications – a non-composition to words by e e cummings. 1963. vcs, instr. Ber. Text: the complete works of e e cummings. 1966, Tor, The Isaacs Gallery Mixed Media Concerts, Catharine Hindson(sgr), William Kilbourn(spkr), Udo Kasemets (instr), The Isaacs Gallery Ensemble.
And M. D. Said. 1969. vc. ms. Text: Marcel Duchamp. 1969, Nashville, Tenn, Catharine Hindson.
Variations (on Variations [on Variations]). 1966. 12′. vc, instr, 4ch rec/playback system (or 4ch prep elec tape). Ber, 1967. Text: Charles Olson. 1968, Deep Springs, Calif, Catharine Hindson(vc), Udo Kasemets (pno).
Logos. 1960. 10′. fl, pno. ms. 1961, Mtl, Wolfgang Kander(fl), Udo Kasemets(pno).
Squares. 1962. 4′–20′. pno 4 hands. Ber, 1969. 1963, Tor, William Aide, Udo Kasemets.
$\sqrt[5]{5}$. 1962–3. 7′30″. 2pno. Ber, 1969. 1963, Chicago, Robert Ashley, Gordon Mumma.
La Crasse du Tympan. 1973. recordtapemix. 1973, Tor, OCA.

SECTION II

Trigon. 1963. 9′47″ or 17′09″. 1 or 3 or 9 or 27 perf. Ber, 1969. 1964, Tor.
Trigon – Trio Concertante (Triv and Quad). 1964. 17′09″. vc, fl (picc, alto), pno (hpschd, cel). Text: James Joyce. 1964, Tor, Catharine Hindson(vc), Anne Aitchison(fl), Udo Kasemets(pno).
Trigon – Solo for Voice. 1964. 9′47″. Text: James Joyce. 1965, Hamilton, Catharine Hindson(vc).
Trigon – Ensemble for Once. 1965. 17′09″. vc, 9spkrs, picc, fl, alto fl, sax, 2hn, tpt, 2trb, tuba, str trio, pno 6 hands, perc. Text: Samuel Beckett. 1965, Ann Arbor, Mich, Once Festival Ensemble, William Albright, Robert Ashley, Udo Kasemets(cond).
Trigon – Miniature Trio. 1965. 9′47″. vc, pno, perc. Text: Samuel Beckett. 1965, Hamilton, Catharine Hindson(vc), Paul Kilburn(pno), Udo Kasemets(perc).
Trigon – Nonet (Medium is the Message). 1965. 17′09″. vc, spkr, fl (cl, sax), pno 6 hands, painter, sculptor, collageist. Text: Marshall McLuhan, John Cage, Udo Kasemets. 1965, Tor, TCC, The Isaacs Gallery Ensemble.
Trigon – Nonet (Inferno). 1966. 17′09″. vc, 2spkrs, perc, artist, 4ch elec tape. Text:

Dante, LeRoi Jones. 1966, Tor, The Isaacs Gallery Mixed Media Concerts, The Isaacs Gallery Ensemble.

Trigon – Solo for Piano. 1965. 1965, Hamilton, Udo Kasemets.

Trigon – Solo for Keyboard Instruments. 1964, pno, hpschd, cel. ms.

Trigon – Solo for Oboe. 1964. 1964, Tucson, Ariz.

Trigon – Solo for Flutes. 1964. fl (picc, alto). ms.

Trigon – Solo for Double Bass. 1966. 1966, U of Indiana, Bertram Turetzky.

Cumulus. 1963–4. 13′30″. any solo or ens and 2 tape rec. ms. 1966, Tor.

Cumulus. 1966. 13′30″. spkr, pno, slides. Text: descriptions of clouds. 1966, Tor, The Isaacs Gallery Mixed Media Concerts, Catharine Hindson(spkr), Udo Kasemets (pno), Dennis Burton(slides).

Cumulus. 1968. 13′30″. spkr, 2ch elec tape. Text: Buckminster Fuller, Marshall McLuhan, John Cage. 1968, Tor, Sightsoundsystems, Festival of Art and Technology, Udo Kasemets(spkr).

In Memoriam Marcel Duchamp (Cumulus Realization). 1969. 30′. vc (autohp), prep pno (harmonicas), 3 tape rec, synth. Text: John Cage. 1969, Nashville, Tenn, Catharine Hindson(vc, autohp), Udo Kasemets (pno, harmonicas), Gilbert Trythall(synth).

Cumulus. 1963–4. tam-tam, 2 tape rec. 1966, Tor, The Isaacs Gallery Mixed Media Concerts, Max Neuhaus.

TT – Trigonic Tributes to Buckminster Fuller, Marshall McLuhan, John Cage (Cumulus Realization with Trigon and Tt). 1968. 2vc, 2ch elec tape. 1968, Oberlin, Ohio, Udo Kasemets, Catharine Hindson. Text: Buckminster Fuller, Marshall McLuhan, John Cage.

ABC – Aleabalanchange (Cumulus Realization). 1968. 2spkrs, 2ch elec tape. Text: Udo Kasemets. 1968, Mtl, Udo Kasemets, Catharine Hindson.

WWWW (#2) – A World Without War and Want (Cumulus Realization with Calceolaria and Octode). 1970. vc, spkr, 4ch elec tape, 3 slide proj, 16mm film with sound. Text: various. 1970, Tor, Toronto Synergetic Theatre.

Timepiece. 1964. any solo or ens. Ber, 1967. 1965, Vanc.

Timepiece – Ensemble (Breaking the Soundbarrier). 1965. vc, spkr, fl (cl, sax), pno, perc. Text: Udo Kasemets. 1966, U of T, Tor, The Isaacs Gallery Ensemble.

Timepiece – Quartet. 1965. fl, bsn, tpt, vlc. 1965, U of BC, Vanc, Paul Douglas(fl), Cortland Hultberg(bsn), Samuel Davies (tpt), Eugene Wilson(vlc), French Tickner (cond).

Timepiece – Duo. 1966. fl, pno. 1966, The Isaacs Gallery Mixed Media Concerts, Jean-Guy Brault(fl), Paul Kilburn(pno).

Timepiece – Solo for Piano. 1967, San Diego, Calif, Barney Childs.

Timepiece. 1966. hn, cybersonic circuitry. 1966, Waltham, Mass, Gordon Mumma.

Cascando. 1965. 1 to 128 perf. Text: Samuel Beckett. Ber, (Focus on Musicecology) 1970. 1965, Tor.

Cascando – Radio Piece. 1965. 24′. 2spkrs, fl. Text: Samuel Beckett. 1965, Tor, The Isaacs Gallery Mixed Media Concerts, Catharine Hindson, William Kilbourn (spkrs), Robert Aitken(fl).

Cascando – Poem. 1965. 6′30″. vc, fl/cl/sax. Text: Samuel Beckett. 1965, Tor, The Isaacs Gallery Mixed Media Concerts, Catharine Hindson(vc), Robert Aitken(fl).

Cascando – Radio Piece. 1968. spkr, 7ch elec tape. Text: Samuel Beckett. 1968, Oberlin, Ohio, Catharine Hindson.

Cascando – Stereosonic Vocophony. 1969. 6′30″. vc, 2ch elec tape. Text: Samuel Beckett. 1969, Nashville, Tenn, Catharine Hindson.

Cascando – Radio Piece. 1970. spkr, 2prep pno, Mono elec tape, spotlights. Text: Samuel Beckett. 1970, Tor, Catharine Hindson(spkr), Udo Kasemets, Gary Wilson (pno), Karol Rattray(spotlights).

Cascando – Synersonic Octet. 1970. 13′30″. 4vc, 2prep pno, 2ch elec tape, synersonic circuitry. Text: Samuel Beckett. 1970, Tor, Toronto Synergetic Theatre.

Cascando XXXII – Synersonophony: Vocosonic Poem: Sonophonic Interlude: Stereosonovocophony. 1971. 14vln, 4vla, 4vlc, 2cb, 2prep pno, 4vc, 8ch elec tape. Text: Samuel Beckett. 1971, Hamilton, HP Virtuosi, Boris Brott(cond), Toronto Synergetic Theatre.

Cascando – Quartet. 1965. 2fl, pno 4 hands. 1965, The Isaacs Gallery Mixed Media Concerts, Robert Aitken, Jean-Guy Brault (fl), Paul Kilburn, Udo Kasemets(pno).

Cascando – Duet. 1965. pno 4 hands. 1965, Tor, The Isaacs Gallery Mixed Media Con-

certs, Paul Kilburn, Udo Kasemets.
Cascando – Solo for Flute. 1965. 1965, Tor, The Isaacs Gallery Mixed Media Concerts, Robert Aitken.
Cascando – Solo for Saxophone. 1965. 1965, Tor, The Isaacs Gallery Mixed Media Concerts, Jean-Guy Brault.
Cascando – Phonographic Stereosonophony. 1969. 2ch elec tape or stereo recording. Marathon MS 2110.
Calceolaria (time/space variations on a floral theme). 1966. any number perf. Ber, 1967. 1967, Tor.
Calceolaria. 1967. 4ch elec tape. 1967, Brockport, NY.
Calce(olaria)/octode. 1970. 3 slide proj, 4ch elec tape. 1970, Tor, Toronto Synergetic Theatre.
Music of Here and Now (Calceolaria/Octode videotape realization with *Timepiece, Cascando – Stereosonophony* and *DDD*). 1970. 8perf, 3 cameras, synersonic soundsystem. 1970, Tor, Ont ETV, Channel 19.
Octagonal Octet and/or Ode (a Calceolaria variation). 1967. 1, 2, 4, 6 or 8 perf. Ber, 1968. Text: Ezra Pound. 1967, Tor, Catharine Hindson(sgr), William Kilbourn(spkr), Udo Kasemets(instr).
Octode – a Calceolaria variation. 1967. Mono elec tape. 1968, Deep Springs, Calif.
Octode/(calceo)laria. 1970. 16mm film with sound. 1970, Tor, Toronto Synergetic Theatre.
OO – Octagonal Oratory with Octode and Ode. 1967. lecturer, singer, elec tape, projections. 1968, Deep Springs, Calif, Udo Kasemets(lecturer), Catharine Hindson (sgr). Text: Udo Kasemets.
TEA – Technological Experiments and Art (Octagonal Ode/Cumulus). 1968. lecturer, 3ch elec tape, 8 radios, Maxfeed, projections. Text: Udo Kasemets. 1968, Tor, Udo Kasemets.
WWWW (#1) – A Workable World Without War (Octagonal Ode Realization). 1969. spkr, 8ch elec tape, slide and overhead projections, candles. 1969, Rochester, NY, Toronto Synergetic Theatre. Text: various quotations.
DDD – Deadly Deafening Decibels. 1970. 4spkrs, instr(s). ms. Text: various quotations. 1970, Tor, Toronto Synergetic Theatre.
S – The Subject is S (Octode). 1971. spkr, elec tape, incense. Text: Udo Kasemets. 1971, Tor, Udo Kasemets.
Colo(u)r is . . . (Octode). 1972. spkr, slide proj, 16mm film with sound. Text: Udo Kasemets. 1972, Tor.
J. C. – Without Saying Anything About John Cage That Hasn't Been Said By John Cage Himself. 1972. reader, tape-recorder, recordplayer, doors. ms. Text: John Cage. 1972, Tor.

SECTION III

5 PP–Five Performance Pieces (Painters X; SSS: Sight, Sound, Scent; Sound, Smell, Taste, Touch; Chance Dance with Tick of Consciousness; Bottlepiece). 1966. ms. 1966, Tor, The Isaacs Gallery Ensemble.
Contactics – a choreography for musicians and audience. 1966. Ber, 1967. 1967, Tor, The Isaacs Gallery Mixed Media Concerts.
Tt – Tribute to Buckminster Fuller, Marshall McLuhan, John Cage. 1968. readers, synths, projections, audience-controlled cybernetic systems. ms. Text: Buckminster Fuller, Marshall McLuhan, John Cage. 1968, Tor, Soundsightsystems, Festival of Art & Technology.
Bookmusic. 1971. 8 readers, audience-controlled cybernetic soundsystem. Text: any books by any eight authors or on any eight subjects.
Elaborations on Erratum Musical of Marcel Duchamp. 1971–2. any number of participants, any soundproducing media.
Quartets of Quartets. 1971–2.
Music for Nothing. 4 readers, 4 tape rec operators, pendulum-pushers. ms. Text: Samuel Beckett, John Cage, Norman O Brown. 1971, Tor, OCA.
Music for Anything (Wordmusic). 4 or more readers, 4 or more tape rec, calibrators. ms. Text: any dictionary. 1973, Tor.
Music for Something (Windmusic). windbells, windchimes, etc. windgenerators, 2 opaque projectors, 4 or more tape rec, pendulart calibrators. ms.
Music for Everything. 1 or 4 or 16 or 64 perf, any sound-producing media. ms. 1973, Tor, Gallery Z.
Son of Vexations. 1972. tape-loop, abacus. ms. 1972, Tor.
. . . Music(s) for John Cage. 1972.
Guitarmusic for John Cage. any number guit, projections, dimmers. ms.

Voicemusic for John Cage. any number vcs. ms. Text: Lankatavara Sutra.
Saladmusic for John Cage. any number of saladmakers. ms.
Walking/Talking. any number walkers-talkers. ms. Text: John Cage. 1972, Tor, OCA.
Time/Place Interface. 1970–1. ms.
Trans-Canada version. sound-collectors/recs at points across Canada, a coast-to-coast radio/TV network.
All-Ontario version. sound-collectors/recs at points across Ontario, sound-repro media.
Time/Space Interface. 1971–3. ms.
1971 OCA version ('In Search of Stillness'). any number participants, any media, a multi-roomed enclosed space. 1971, Tor, OCA.
1973 outdoor version ('In Search of Oneness'). any number participants, cassette-recs, videocorders, polaroid cameras, etc., open space.
Whole Earth Music. 1972-. . .in progress. a multi-dimensional acoustical/architectural cybernetic process.
Quadraphony (Music of the . . . Quarter of the . . . Moon of the Lunar Year). 1972–3. ms. an acoustical/architectural time/space exploration process.
1 + 1 (Twelve Easy Duets for Recorders). 1964. SS/SA rec. Ber, 1964.
1 + 1 (Twenty Exercises and Ten Easy Pieces on Well-known Songs). 1964. pno. Ber, 1964.
Eighteen Popular Christmas Carols. 1965. S rec, kybd. Ber, 1965.
1 + 1 (Eighteen Extremely Easy Elementary Ensemble Exercises for Potential Percussion Players). 1971. ms.
Musicgames. 1971. seven sound perception and conception group exercises. ms.
Mini/Midi/Maxi-Mix. 1971. tape-recorded sound-cognition exercises.
Minimix: timbre and soundsource cognition.
Midimix (Pixmix with Mixmatrix): pitch, duration and amplitude cognition.
Maximix: time and structure cognition.
Songbirdsong. 1971. tape-recorded bird-sound-cognition exercises.
Colourwalk. 1971. a colour-perception/notation exercise. ms.
Senslalom. 1972. a sight-sound-smell-taste-touch perception exercise. ms.

BIBLIOGRAPHY

See B-B; B65,71; Bec56,70; CrC(1); Esc; Mm; R12; Wa.
Beckwith, John. 'Kasemets – Torrents of Reaction', *MuSc.* No. 251, Jan.-Feb. 1970 (4–5).
Gregory, C. 'When is a Happening Not a Happening?', *Maclean's.* Vol. LXXIX, Apr. 1966 (20–1).
'Udo Kasemets', pamphlet, BMI Canada Ltd, 1972.
'Udo Kasemets – a portrait', *Mu.* No. 22, Sept. 1969 (8–9).

LITERARY WORKS

BOOKS

Canavangard (ed.). Don Mills: BMI Canada Ltd, 1968 (illustrated catalogue).
Focus on Musicecology (ed.). Toronto: Berandol Music Ltd, 1970.
The Modern Composer and His World (co-editor with John Beckwith). Toronto: University of Toronto Press, 1961.

ARTICLES

'Current Chronicle: Ann Arbor', *MQ,* Vol. L, no. 4 (515–19).
'Eight Edicts on Education with Eighteen Elaborations', *Source.* No. 4, University of California, July 1968 (37–43).
'John Weinzweig', *CMJ.* Vol. IV, no. 4, Summer 1960 (4–18).
'Nine Notes on Notation', *Artscanada.* June 1968 (24–6).
'Octode; Cascando', *Focus on Musicecology.* Toronto: Berandol Music Ltd, 1970 (26–49).
'Prologue to an Interlude and an Epilogue', *CMB.* Autumn-Winter 1972 (11–18).

REVIEWS

'Canadian Study Scores I', *CMJ.* Vol. V, no. 1, 1960–1 (62–7).
'Canadian Study Scores II', *CMJ.* Vol. V, no. 2, 1960–1 (48–53).
'Recent Works of Igor Stravinsky', *CMJ.* Vol. IV, no. 2, 1959–60 (63–73).
'The Saskatoon Summer Festival, 1959', *CMJ.* Vol. IV, no. 1, 1959–60 (14–23).
'Threnody', *CMB.* Autumn-Winter 1972 (205–8).

KENINS, TALIVALDIS (b. Liepaja, Latvia, 23 Apr. 1919). Music was much cultivated in the Latvian capital of Riga where Kenins' father was an important government official. The young Talivaldis began piano at five and at seven began composing music 'modelled on Waldteufel waltzes and intended as charming presents on family occasions'. By the age of ten he was an avid opera enthusiast, attending performances at the Riga State Opera where Richard Wagner had once been conductor. When he was fourteen his mother, a writer and journalist, enrolled him in the Lycée Champollion in Grenoble, France, to prepare for a diplomatic career. Piano lessons were continued. 'My piano teacher let me get away with the most untidy technique in Chopin Ballades and Beethoven Sonatas.' He graduated with the Bachelor of Literature degree in 1939.

Because of the outbreak of the Second World War Kenins returned home. In the midst of hostilities he turned seriously to music, from 1940 to 1944 studying with Joseph Wihtol, the founder of the Latvian State Conservatory. (Although a Latvian, Wihtol had taught composition at the St Petersburg Conservatory, succeeding Rimsky-Korsakov.) Forced to labour as a trench digger in Germany from 1944–5, he made his way to Paris. Russia had already taken possession of his homeland.

From 1945 to 1950 Kenins studied at the Paris Conservatoire. These were hard, often painful years. Food was scarce and coal unavailable. To earn the necessities of life he played the piano for dancing classes and in nightclubs. But Paris was an exciting musical centre. Composers like Bartok, Hindemith, Milhaud, Honegger, and Stravinsky were frequently performed and their scores carefully studied. Only Schoenberg's twelve-tone music was ignored; his 'system' was considered as contrived German expressionism that was not attractive to the French.

At the Paris Conservatoire Kenins received a rigorous, thorough musical education. He studied counterpoint with Simone Plé-Caussade, composition with Tony Aubin, and aesthetics with Olivier Messiaen. In a *concours* held in the Salle Gaveau in 1950, Kenins won the Premier Prix in Composition for his *Sonate pour violoncelle et piano* (1950); the jury of twelve composers included Honegger, Milhaud, Poulenc, Auric, Enesco, Ibert, and Nadia Boulanger. His *Septuor* (1949) for clarinet, bassoon, horn, violin, viola, cello, and bass was performed at the Ferienkurse für neue Musik in Darmstadt the same year with Hermann Scherchen conducting. He was awarded a UNESCO fellowship, which enabled him to continue his studies for a further year.

In 1951 Kenins came to Canada as organist-choirmaster at St Andrew's Lutheran Church in Toronto. Since 1952 he has been with the Faculty of Music at the University of Toronto, teaching composition, counterpoint and keyboard harmony. He became a full professor in 1973. Kenins is a dedicated educator. A number of his choral works were written for the University of Toronto Concert Choir and the now-defunct Hart House Glee Club; many of his keyboard pieces intended for younger students are performed in examinations and festivals throughout Canada. *Diversities* (1967), a set of twelve short piano pieces, introduces the young musician to elements such as unusual rhythms, irregular metres, dissonance, and free contrapuntal devices, as employed in twentieth-century music.

Kenins has been called a 'contemporary romanticist' and a 'conservative modern', but no exclusive definition can describe all of his works. He is the product of two musical traditions – one French, the other Russian. Baltic lyricism tinges the musical idea, and French classicism shapes the working out of the idea and the overall structure. Basic to Kenins' compositional technique is the use of a contrapuntal texture in which each voice or part has a distinctive role in the tonal fabric. 'The *concertante* style is the dominant part of my musical speech . . . After having studied and taught this technique for so many years, the canon and fugue techniques in all their forms were such a part of my musical expression that sometimes I wasn't even aware of their presence in my composing.'

Kenins' harmonic concept is pandiatonic, with elements of bitonality and polytonality. The minor and major third may appear together in a chordal combination, and likewise the altered tonic or fifth may appear together with the unaltered note. Chords are basically triadic with added notes, such as the sixth or ninth, but quartal harmony is also employed. The favoured melodic interval is the minor second and its inversion, the major seventh. The same note often appears in the same melodic module in varied chromatic alterations, somewhat in the style of Bartok. Melodies are freely conceived and are made up of unbalanced limbs rather than in 'antecedent-consequent' sequences of phrases. Triple and quadruple metre are the most frequently employed – usually throughout an entire movement – but Kenins has a predilection for septuple metre: seven-eight or seven-four. Additive rhythm is a feature of his writing, and the metrical organization of his music is more complex than is indicated by the metre. Typical of the larger works is a three-movement form, *fast-slow-fast*, with one or other of the fast movements preceded by a slow introduction.

The concertante style is evident in the early *Septuor*. The *Concertino à Cinque* (1968) written nearly twenty years later, has many similarities with the earlier work. It is more neo-classic in vein, however, and the organization of rhythm and melody is more advanced in concept. Each of the instruments emits 'chirps' and 'twitters' and occasionally short lyric bits to make up a lively texture in concertante style. The first movement (Alla Marcia in seven-four metre) is a five-way conversation, somewhat dominated by the flute and piano. The second movement (Nocturne) makes use of a twelve-tone row. At the *poco più mosso* the effect is similar to Messiaen's birds, and in several places in the movement there are pointillistic patches, similar in technique to the medieval hocket. After a slow introduction, the third movement is given over to a fugal *allegro con spirito* in seven-eight metre, a *mouvement perpetuel à sec.*

Of the four symphonies, only the third (1970) is scored for full symphony orchestra. The first (1959) is for chamber orchestra, while the second (1967) is a *Sinfonia Concertante* featuring flute, oboe, and clarinet. The fourth symphony requires an orchestra of only eleven players, although the strings (quartet) may be doubled or tripled. In it the composer has made use of aleatoric and textural elements together with written parts, as he has done also in the *Partita Brève* (1971), the *Serenade* (1973) for oboe and cello, and in the *Violin Concerto* (in progress). No experimentalist, Kenins declares that 'sound experiments of the type of piano-lid slamming, amplified gargling, or cello playing in the bath tub (however beautiful the lady may be) make me sick!' He has a high regard for technique and disparages dilettantism.

In the *Fantaisies Concertantes* (1971) for solo piano and orchestra, the concertante approach is effective in delineating the repartee between the soloist and the other instrumental forces. This one-movement work has a motoric, jabbing impact. The piano part is of virtuoso difficulty and makes unrelenting demands on the stamina of the solo performer. Short motoric kernels form the basic musical material. These are extended, bent, and twisted into a thick contrapuntal texture to which the percussion instruments contribute. The musical activity builds and erupts into a frenzy of activity, yielding occasionally to more lyrical contrasts. It is one of the most taut, dynamic, and contemporary compositions to come from Canada in recent decades.

In *Chants of Glory and Mercy* (1970) for soprano, contralto, tenor, and bass soloists, with mixed choir and symphony orchestra, the age-old Latin text of the Gloria from the Mass is the unifying element. Against this musical panorama sung by the choir, the soloists sing three twentieth-century texts in English. An exhortation of John XXIII is sung by the tenor, followed by a letter from a woman deported to Siberia sung by the contralto; the bass then sings words of Martin Luther King and the work is rounded off with an extended 'amen' for the soprano and choir. The texture is contrapuntal, but simple melodic contours, complementary rhythms, and the steady pacing of the music flow lend a monumental grandeur to the work. The personal utterances of the soloists are effectively projected against the ritualistic Gloria sung by the choir, replete with canonic and fugal segments. The most subjective outpouring of emotion is allotted to the contralto, who breaks into *sprechgesang* at the words 'I still live with the nightmare of that dreadful hour when we were dragged out of our home in the midst of the night to start that long fateful journey', while the soprano sings an exalted plea for mercy (the *miserere* section of the Gloria). This passage touches a deep, inextinguishable memory of the composer. Kenins' father was deported by the Russians in 1941 and never seen again.

Kenins retains a great love for the Latvia of his youth and a number of his compositions have been written for festivals of Latvian music. He has also sought inspiration from Canadian sources. *Lagalai* (1970) is a chamber drama for mixed choir, flute, horn, and percussion, concerning an evil witch who brings plague and death to the Indians of the West Coast until she is turned into stone. *Sawan-Oong, The Spirit of the Winds* (1973), a symphonic cantata for baritone, choir and orchestra, is based on an Ojibway-Cree legend.

Kenins has held executive positions with the Canadian League of Composers (president 1973–4) and is a member of CAPAC.

LEE HEPNER

MUSICAL WORKS

ORCHESTRA

Folk Dance, Variations and Fugue. 1964. 7'. schl orch. CMC. 1965, Tor, Eaton Aud, Kiwanis Mus Fest, North Tor Collegiate Orch, Douglas Couke(cond).

Symphony No 3. 1970. 19'50". full orch. CMC. July 5, 1970, Tor, Latv Song Fest, Ryerson P I, members of TS, Janis Kalnins.

SMALL ORCHESTRA

Scherzo Concertante. 1953. 4'10". CMC. 1953, Tor, CBC O, John Adaskin.

Symphony for Chamber Orchestra. 1959. 21'30". CMC. 1960, Indianapolis, Indianapolis Sinfonietta, V Ziedons.

4. Symphony. 1972. 20'. CMC.

STRING ORCHESTRA

Nocturne and Dance. 1963. 5'45". B & H, 1969. 1965, EJB, John Adaskin Project Conf, Northmount Jr High Schl Orch, Talivaldis Kenins.

SOLOIST(S) WITH ORCHESTRA

Piano Concerto. 1946. pno, med orch. ms.

Duo for Piano and Orchestra. 1951. pno, full orch. ms.

Concerto for Violin, Cello and String Orchestra. 1965. 27'30". CMC. 1965, Tor, Massey Hall, Latv Mus Fest, members of TS, Janis Kalnins(cond), Norma Auzin(vln), Ronald Leonard(vlc).

Second Symphony; 'Sinfonia Concertante'. 1967. 19'15". fl, ob, cl, orch. CMC. Mar 3, 1968, S'tn, SSO, David Kaplan(cond), William Egnatoff(fl), Alfred Dahl(ob), Jack Johnson(cl).

Fantaisies Concertantes. 1971. 15'15". pno, orch. CMC.

CHOIR WITH ORCHESTRA

Chants of Glory and Mercy; 'Gloria'. 1970. 23'. sop, alto, ten, bs, SATB, orch. CMC. May 3, 1970, Guelph, Bach-Elgar Choir, Guelph Oratorio Soc Chorus, Guelph Fest O, Charles Wilson(cond), Roxolana Roslak (sop), Patricia Rideout(alto), John Arab (ten), John Dodington(bs).

CHOIR

Christmas Chorale. 1948. 4'. SATB. Wat, 1953. 1954, Tor, Convocation Hall, U of T Chorus, B Labash.

Cantata 'To a Soldier'. 1953. 22'. mezz, bar, SATB, org. Kalnajs, 1953. Daina 1008-A. 1954, Tor, St Andrew's Luth Church, Talivaldis Kenins(cond), H Luse(mezz), P Geistauts(bar), E Timermane(org).

Daniel (A Biblical Scene). 1956. 20'. mezz, bar, SATB, org. private publication. Mar 14, 1957, Tor, Convocation Hall, U of T Chorus, Richard Johnston(cond), Ruth Ann Morse(mezz), Malcolm Russell(bar), Barbara Williams(org).

Bonhomme! Bonhomme! (arr). 1962. 2'45". SATB. FH, 1964. CBC BR SM-19. 1962, Tor, EJB, voc ens conducted by Richard Johnston.

Lyrical Suite. 1962. sop, bar, SATB, org. private publication, St Andrew's Luth Church of Tor. Text: Atis Kenins. 1962, Tor, St Andrew's Luth Church, A Purvs (cond), R Zaprauska(sop), J Ciruls(bar), R Thiman(org).

Ojibway Song (arr). 1962. SATB. FH, 1964. 1962, EJB, voc ens conducted by Richard Johnston.

The Carrion Crow (arr). 1967. 3'5". TTBB. GVT, 1967. Arc 260. 1967, Tor, U of T, HHGC, Walter Barnes.

Land of the Silver Birch (arr). 1967. 1'10". TTBB. GVT, 1967. Arc 260. 1967, Tor, U of T, HHGC, Walter Barnes.

The Maiden's Lament (arr). 1967. 3'. TTBB. GVT, 1967. Arc 260. 1967, Tor, U of T, HHGC, Walter Barnes.

Piae Cantiones Novae. 1968. 12'55". SSAATTBB. Wat, 1969. Text: 1582; trans: Warren Drake. Mar 15, 1970, Tor, U of T

Conc Choir, WLU Choir, Lloyd Bradshaw, Walter Kemp.
Lagalai – Legend of the Stone (chamb drama). 1970. 13'. SATB, fl, hn, perc. CMC. Text: Uldis Fogels. July 13, 1970, Tor, EJB, Fest Sgrs, Elmer Iseler.
Psalm 150. 1970. 3'7". SATB. Wat, 1970. Tor, Deer Park United Church, William Wright(cond).

INSTRUMENTAL ENSEMBLE

Quatuor pour cordes. 1948. 20'. CMC. 1949, Paris, RTF, Quatuor du Club d'Essai.
Prélude et Scherzo. 1949. 7'30". fl, cl, bsn. CMC. 1949, Paris, Salle du Conservatoire, soli of the Cons.
Septuor. 1949. 18'. cl, bsn, hn, vln, vla, vlc, cb. CMC. CBC BR SM-135 ster. 1950, Darmstadt, Germany, New Mus Fest, Hermann Scherchen.
Sonate pour violoncelle et piano. 1950. 20'. CMC. Christophorus-Schallplatte SCGLV-75980. 1950, Paris, Salle Gaveau, Maurice Gendron(vlc), Geneviève Joy(pno).
Trio. 1952. 19'. pno, vln, vlc. CMC. 1952, London, Eng, Wigmore Hall, Laveday Trio.
Sonata for Violin and Piano. 1955. 15'. CMC. 1956, Mtl, CBC 'Première', Arthur Davison(vln), John Newmark(pno).
Suite Concertante. 1955. 16'. vlc, pno. CMC. ALA. 1956, Boston, Jordan Hall, Baltic Conc Soc of New England, Ingus Naruns(vlc), A Berzkalns(pno).
Diversions on a Gypsy Song. 1958. 8'. vlc, pno. CMC. Latrec 2783. 1958, Kiel, Germany, Musikfreunde Soc Conc, Valdis Zakis(vlc), Rolf Albes(pno).
Quartet. 1958. 19'30". pno, vln, vla, vlc. CMC. 1958, New York, Town Hall, Latv Fest, Naruns Qt.
Divertimento. 1960. 9'30". cl (vln), pno. B & H, 1970. Dom S-69004. 1960, Tor, RCMT, Douglas Couke(cl), John Felice(pno).
Little Suite for String Quartet. 1965. 8'. CMC. 1966, Tor, Faculty of Mus, U of T.
Concertante for Flute and Piano. 1966. 13'. B & H, 1972. Dom S-69005. 1967, CBC, 'Distinguished Artists', Robert Aitken(fl), Marion Ross(pno).
Fantasy-Variations on an Eskimo Lullaby. 1967. 7'40". fl, vla. CMC. 1967, Tor, EJB, Suzanne Shulman(fl), Margot Burton(vla).
Concertino à Cinque. 1968. 17'35". fl, ob, vla, vlc, pno. CMC. 1968, Hannover, Germany, Stadthalle.
Two Dialogues. 1968. 2'30". vlc, pno. CMC. 1972, Vanc, Vanc Hotel Aud, George Kenins(vlc).
Partita Brève. 1971. 14'. vla, pno. CMC. 1971, Tor, EJB, Margot Burton(vla), Mary-Nan Dutka(pno).

PIANO

Rondine. 1955. GVT, 1956.
Concertino for Two Pianos Alone. 1956. 13'30". CMC. Vogt L-2258. 1956, Tor, Casa Loma, Can Mus Associates conc, Talivaldis Kenins, John Beckwith(pnos).
Horse Ride. 1956. GVT, 1957. Dom S-69002.
Indian Sun Dance. 1956. FH, 1956.
Little Romance. 1956. GVT, 1956.
Lullaby. 1956. FH, 1956.
Waltz. 1956. FH, 1956.
Two Little Pieces: 'Tenderness', 'Little March'. 1957. GVT, 1958. Dom S-69002.
Intermezzo in F. 1960. FH, 1971.
Dance of the Teddy Bears. 1961. FH, 1961.
Dreaming. 1961. FH, 1966.
Play. 1961. FH, 1961.
Sonata for Piano. 1961. 17'10". Kalnajs/FH, 1964. Cor 850C-3763, UR4M-3764, Daina T-54069, RCI-366. Sept 1961, Tor, Lansdowne Th, Latv-Amer Mus Fest, Talivaldis Kenins.
Folk Dance, Variations and Fugue. 1963. 10'. 2pno 8 hands. CMC. 1963, Tor, St Andrew's Luth Church, Dace, Aina, Tom and Peter Zvilna.
Canon. 1964. FH, 1964.
Fugue on 'The Toronto Opera House Waltz'. 1966. 2pno. CMC. Dec 9, 1967, Tor, Opening of TPML, Sheila Bluethner, Liesel Kohland(pnos).
Diversities. 1967. 10'25". MCA, 1968. Dom S-69002 (Nos 9, 12). 1968, Tor, EJB, Ruth Bishop.
The Juggler. 1969. B & H. Dom S-69002.
The Sad Clown. 1969. B & H. Dom S-69002.
Two Latvian Folk Dances. 1969. 2'30". CMC.
Toccata-Dance. 1971. FH, 1971.
Twilight. 1971. FH, 1971.

INSTRUMENTAL SOLO

Three Figures. accord. Wat, 1973.

ORGAN

Suite in D for Organ. 1967. 15'30". CMC. 1968, Caracas, Venezuela, Christian Grundman.

BIBLIOGRAPHY

See B-B; B65,71; Bec70; Esc; R12.
'Professor Talivaldis Kenins: From Diplomat to Composer', *CanCo.* No. 22, Oct. 1967 (4–5, 44–5).
'Talivaldis Kenins – a portrait', *Mu.* No. 18, Apr. 1969 (8–9).
Berzkalns, Valentins. 'Talivaldis Kenins', *Latvju muzika.* No. 3, May 1970 (232–61).

LITERARY WORKS

ARTICLES

'My Most Successful Work: "Symphony No. 1 for Chamber Orchestra"', *CanCo.* No. 31, July-Aug. 1968 (18–19).

KLEIN, LOTHAR (b. Hanover, Germany, 27 Jan. 1932). He moved to England in 1939 and to the United States in 1941. After studying composition with Paul Fetler at the University of Minnesota, where he received his Bachelor of Arts degree in music in 1954, he studied orchestration with Antal Dorati (1956–8) and composition with Goffredo Petrassi at the Berkshire Music Center in Tanglewood in the summer of 1956. He received the Golden Reel Award of the American Academy of Film Sciences for the best university-produced film score (*An Actor Prepares,* 1956). He was awarded a Fulbright Fellowship (1958–60) that enabled him to study in Berlin with Josef Rufer at the Free University, with Boris Blacher at the Hochschule für Musik and, during the summers, with Luigi Nono at the Ferienkurse für neue Musik in Darmstadt. During this period he was an assistant to Boris Blacher, teaching orchestration at the Hochschule für Musik. In 1961 he received his Doctor of Philosophy degree in music from the University of Minnesota. He has held teaching positions at the University of Minnesota (1962–4) and the University of Texas (1964–8), and in 1968 joined the staff of the Faculty of Music of the University of Toronto. In 1969 he was guest professor at the Hochschule für Musik, Berlin. In 1971 he was appointed chairman of the graduate department of music, University of Toronto.

Klein's *Appassionata for Orchestra* (1959) has pointillistic lines and clipped phrases and exhibits a Varèse-like use of percussion. Generally he utilizes a dry, sparse texture with fragmented phrases and ideas. *Musique à Go-Go* (1966) begins with fragments of jazz rhythms, harmonies, and idioms before moving into a longer passage of jazz material. In both *Symphony No. 2* (1965) and *Laments of Gondal* (1966) Klein has turned to longer, almost tonal, melodies in an atonal contrapuntal texture, but in *Design for Percussion and Orchestra* (1971) he has returned to the dry, fragmented style of his earlier works. His theatre scores were commissioned by theatre departments of the University of Minnesota, the University of Texas, and others. Other awards have included the Rockefeller New Music Prize in 1965 and 1967 and the Greenwood Choral Prize for his *Three Chinese Laments* (1968). He is a member of the Canadian League of Composers and of ASCAP.

MUSICAL WORKS

STAGE

Charades (ballet). 1950–6.
Lost Love (ballet). 1950–6.
La Ronde (ballet). 1950–6.
The Prodigal Son (dance drama). 1966.

INCIDENTAL MUSIC

Hamlet. 1950. Text: William Shakespeare.
A Comedy of Errors. 1951. Text: William Shakespeare.
Twelfth Night. 1951. Text: William Shakespeare.
Twin Menaechmi. 1951. Text: Plautus.
The Bluebird. 1952. Text: Maurice Maeterlinck.
Henry IV. 1953. Text: William Shakespeare.
Marco Millions. 1953. Text: Eugene O'Neill.
Richard III. 1954. Text: William Shakespeare.
The Theatre (film). 1958. Film: Ed div U of Minn.
The Bacchae. 1965. Text: Euripides.

ORCHESTRA

The Bluebird. 1952.
Symphony No 1. 1955.
Presto for Orchestra. 1958.
Symmetries for Large Orchestra. 1958; Presser, 1972.
Appassionata for Orchestra. 1959.
Epitaphs for Orchestra. 1963; Presser, 1965.
Rondo Giocoso for Orchestra. 1964.

Symphony No 2. 1966.
Charivari: Music for an Imaginary Comedy. 1966.
Musique à Go-Go (Symphonic Mêlée). 1966; Presser, 1972. Louis LS-672.
Symphonic Etudes (Symphony No 3). 1972.

BAND
Divertimento for Band. 1953.
Gloria for Band. 1961. S H & M.
Eroica: Variations on a Promethean Theme (Beethoven, Op 35). 1970.

SMALL ORCHESTRA
Sinfonia Concertante. 1956.
Janizary Music. 1970; Bote & Bock, 1971.

STRING ORCHESTRA
Passacaglia of the Zodiac. 1971.

SOLOIST(S) WITH ORCHESTRA
Concerto for Piano and Orchestra. 1954.
Eclogues for Horn and Strings. 1954.
Concerto for Woodwind Quartet, Brass, Timpani and Strings. 1956.
Trio Concertante. 1961. str trio, orch. Presser.
Paganini Collage for Violin and Orchestra. 1967.
Design for Percussion and Orchestra. 1971. 3perc, orch.
Music for Violin and Orchestra. 1972.
Le Trésor des Dieux (Suite). guit (hpschd), orch.

CHOIR WITH ORCHESTRA
Cantata. 1957. soli, SATB, ww. Text: Richard Rolle, Bishop of Hampole.

CHOIR
Eight Madrigals. 1957. SATB. Text: various Elizabethan poets.
Three Ancient Folksongs. 1959; MPH, 1963. Text: trad.
Exaltation. 1960; Wat, 1971. sop (ten), SATB, org. Text: Psalms 103, 148.
Two Christmas Madrigals. 1961; S H & M, 1963. SATB. Text: Elizabethan poets.
Choral Arrangements (Bach, Granados, Grieg, Mozart, Tchaikowsky). 1960–2. SATB. S H & M.
A Little Book of Hours. 1962; Lawson-Gould, 1964. SATB. Text: Phillip Murray.
Three Pastoral Songs. 1963; Wat, 1972. SSAA. Text: William Shakespeare.
Three Chinese Laments. 1968; Presser, 1968. SATB. Text: Chinese Book of Songs. Trans/ed: Robert Payne.
Good Night. 1970; Wat, 1970, SSA, pno. Text: trad.

VOICE
Pomes Penyeach. 1952. sop, pno. Text: James Joyce.
Six Scenes from 'The Old Man and the Sea'. 1964. bar, pno. Text: Ernest Hemingway.
Laments from Gondal. 1966. sop, vla. Text: Emily Brontë.
Three Melancholy Songs. 1966. sop, pno. Text: Emily Brontë.

VOICE(S)
Cantata II (On Epigrams of Sappho). 1958; Peters, 1964. actress, 6 solo instr. Text: Sappho. Trans: Mary Barnard.
Herbstlieder (Autumn Songs). 1958. sop, chamb orch. Text: Ricarda Huch, Friedrich Nietzsche, Rudolf Biending, Friedrich Hebbel, Rainer Maria Rilke, Johann Gottfried von Herder.
Meditations on Passyoun. 1958. ten, bar, ATB, ww, brass, hp. Text: Richard Rolle, Bishop of Hampole.

INSTRUMENTAL ENSEMBLE
Suite on Twelfth Night. 1951. ww octet, hp.
Quintet for Piano and Strings. 1953.
Woodwind Quintet. 1954.
Partita. 1955. fl, cl, hp.
Samba. 1956. vlc, pno.
Music for Violin and Piano. 1963.
Three Greek Rites. 1964; Music for Percussion, 1964. 8perc.
Dance Concerto. 1965. cl, stage band.
Arias for String Quartet. 1966.
Trio Sonata. 1969; Third Stream, 1970. cl, vlc, pno(hpschd), jazz perc.
Slices of Time. 1973. tpt, str qt.

PIANO
Three Sketches from 'Alice in Wonderland'. 1952.
Hommage à Satie. 1966.
Sonata for Piano. 1968; MCA, 1974.

INSTRUMENTAL SOLO
Variations and Epilogue. 1957; Modern Editions, 1965. vln.
4 for 1 (Suite for Contrabass Alone). 1970; Tenuto, 1972.
Eclogues for Solo Guitar. 1972; Bote & Bock, 1974.
A la Rossini. 1972. ob, opt pno.
Six Exchanges (da Capo). 1972; Tenuto, 1972. sax.

BIBLIOGRAPHY

R12. B65; B71.

LITERARY WORKS

ARTICLES

'History in Perspective: Another View', *Composer*. Autumn 1966 (13–18, 22).
'History, Tradition and Responsibility', *International Music Bulletin*. No. 42, July 1964 (40–51).
'The ISCM Festival at Hamburg', *CanCo*. No. 42, Sept. 1969 (12–14).
'Looking Backwards' (invited paper), *The American Society for Aesthetics*. Santa Fe, N. Mex., Oct. 26, 1966 (119–26).
'Music and Historical Necessity', *Review of History and Philosophy*. University of Texas, July 1965 (1–12).
'Reflections on Music and the Liberal Arts', *Music Educators Journal*. Vol. LIII, no. 4, Dec. 1966 (22–4).
'A Shaping Force in American Music', *Music Educators Journal*. Vol. LI, no. 2, Nov. 1964 (41–6).
'Standards, Suggestions and Stravinsky', *Music Educators Journal*. Vol. XLIX, no. 3, Jan. 1963 (33–40).
'Stravinsky's Oedipus: Perspectives and Meaning', *The Graduate Journal*. Austin: University of Texas Press (1–21).
'Stravinsky and the Theatre', *CMB*. Spring-Summer 1972 (65–72).
'The Twelve Tone Evolution 1930–60', *Essays in Honor of Paul Fisk*. Austin: University of Texas Press, 1965 (60–8).
'Twentieth Century Analysis: Essays in Miniature', *Music Educators Journal* (eleven essays). Dec. 1966–May 1968.

KOLINSKI, MIECZYSLAW (b. Warsaw, Poland, 5 Sept. 1901). He studied with Paul Juon (composition) and Leonid Kreutzer (piano) at the Hochschule für Musik in Berlin. At Berlin University he studied with Erich von Hornbostel, Curt Sachs, Arnold Schering, and Johannes Wolf (musicology) and Wolfgang Köhler (psychology), receiving his Doctor of Philosophy degree in 1930. From 1927 to 1933 he was assistant to Hornbostel at the Berlin Phonogrammarchiv, where much music of non-Western cultures was recorded. In 1933 he immigrated to Czechoslovakia, where he was an associate of the anthropologist Melville Herskovits and transcribed Suriname music and many songs from West Africa. He went to Belgium in 1938 to avoid Nazi persecution and remained there through the war years, part of the time in hiding. Later he immigrated to New York, where he was a music therapist and music editor of Hargail Music Press (1952–66). He came to Toronto in 1966, becoming special lecturer in ethnomusicology in the Faculty of Music, University of Toronto.

Kolinski's extensive research into non-western music has produced numerous transcriptions of traditional songs, a wealth of material from which he has arranged sets of songs and composed works using some folk idioms. His *Dahomey Suite* (1953), commissioned by the Hargail Music Press, is one of his most successful compositions, using material he had gathered through analysis of music from Dahomey in West Africa. His ballet, *Railroad Fantasy* (1935), was commissioned by the Mica Meyerova Dance Ensemble in Czechoslovakia. His *Encounterpoint* was commissioned for the inauguration of the Casavant organ in Walter Hall, University of Toronto, 1973.

Kolinski has done research on Canadian ethnomusicological topics for the Canadian Folk Music Society and the Centre for Folk Culture Studies of the National Museum of Man (Ottawa). He is co-founder and former president of the Society for Ethnomusicology, a member of the International Folk Music Council, and is affiliated with BMI Canada.

MUSICAL WORKS

STAGE

Bu Ru Bu (ballet). 1931. orch.
Railroad Fantasy (Expresszug-Phantasie) (ballet). 1935. 2pno.
Man and His Shadows (ballet). 1948. orch.

ORCHESTRA

Prelude. 1958. full orch.
Dance Fantasy (on *Man and His Shadows*). 1968. str orch.

SOLOIST WITH ORCHESTRA

Dahomey Suite (arr). 1953. fl, str.

VOICE

14 Songs. 1918. vc, pno.
5 Songs. 1922. sop, pno. Text: K Henckell, N Lenay, A van Lieber, F Stöber, E Geibel.
3 Songs. 1944. sop, pno.

4 Settings of American Folksongs. 1956. med vc, pno.
6 Settings of French Folksongs. 1957. high vc, pno.
6 Settings of German Folksongs. 1957. high vc, pno.
6 Settings of Yiddish Folksongs. 1957. high vc, pno.
7 Settings of Sephardic Folksongs. 1958. high vc, pno.

VOICE WITH INSTRUMENTAL ENSEMBLE

Lyric Sextet. 1929. sop, fl, str qt. Text: Rainer Maria Rilke, Herman Hesse, W von Schultz, E Lasker-Schüler, O J Bierbaum.
American Suite. 1949. med vc, str qt (pno). Text: Negro spirituals.
3 Three-part Inventions. 1950. sop, vla, vlc. Text: vocalise.
Concertino. 1956. sop (ob), str qt, pno. alt version, 1970. sop, fl, pno. Text: vocalise.
6 Settings of French Folksongs (arr). 1969. sop, fl, pno. Ber.

INSTRUMENTAL ENSEMBLE

Sonata (on a Russian Folksong). 1924. vln, pno.
Sonata. 1926. vlc, pno.
String Quartet. 1931.
Little Suite. 1933. vln, pno. FH.
Music on Open Strings (15 pieces). 1935. vln, pno.
Chamber Sonatina. 1937. str trio, pno.
16 Easy Duets. 1947. 2vln.
Dahomey Suite. 1951; Hargail, 1952. fl, pno. alt version, 1959. ob, pno. Folk FS-3855.
Music of the Hebrew People (20 Jewish folk songs). 1954; Hargail, 1955. 2rec.
Music Everywhere (75 folk and trad songs). 1955; Hargail, 1956. rec ens.
It's Still Christmas Around the World (21 carols). 1956; Hargail, 1967. 2rec.
French Christmas Suite. 1958; Hargail, 1960. rec trio.
Fun with Recorder Duets (20 pieces). 1958; Hargail, 1960. 2sop rec.
Fun with Recorder Duets (20 pieces). 1958; Hargail, 1960. sop & alto rec.
Fun with Recorder Trios (12 pieces). 1958; Hargail, 1961. SAT rec.
Hatikvah Variations. 1960. str qt.
Music of the Hebrew People (12 Jewish folk songs). 1960; Hargail, 1961. rec trio.
12 Settings of Christmas Carols. 1963. rec trio/qt.
First Book of Duets (13 folk songs). 1965; Hargail, 1966. 2sop rec.
20 Settings of Czech and Slovak Folksongs. 1966; Hargail, 1967. 2rec.
20 Settings of Dutch Folksongs. 1966. 2rec.
20 Settings of French Folksongs. 1966; Hargail, 1967. 2rec.
20 Settings of folksongs of the Crimean Tatars. 1966. 2rec.
20 Settings of Norwegian Folksongs. 1966. 2rec.
Casey Jones (16 folk songs). 1971; Hargail, 1972. 2alto rec.
Encounterpoint. 1973. str qt, org.

PIANO

Stimmungsbilder Suite. 1917.
Sonata. 1919.
First Suite. 1929.
Second Suite. 1934.
Third Suite. 1936.
A Day and its Seven Faces (Variations). 1938.
Four Dances in Etude Form. 1938.
Fourth Suite. 1946.
Sonata (Version 1). 1946.
Four-Hand Conversations (Divertimento). 1947. pno 4 hands.
Around the Maypole. 1952; Fischer, 1954. pno 4 hands.
At the Court of Old King Cole. 1952; Fischer, 1954. pno 4 hands.
By the Campfire. 1952; Fischer, 1954. pno 4 hands.
Little Fingers Sing and Dance (7 pieces). 1952; Hargail, 1953. pno 4 hands.
Dreamland. 1957; Fischer, 1960.
It's Spring Again. 1957; Fischer, 1960.
Merry Start. 1957; Boston, 1964.
Tin Soldier's Wedding March. 1957; MCA, 1958.
Music for Dance Rhythms (41 pieces). 1958. Folk FC-7673.
Introduction to Polyphonic Playing. 1963.
Snapshots (7 pieces). 1963.
The New Piano Method (3 vols). 1965.
Sonata (Version 2). 1966; Hargail, 1972.

INSTRUMENTAL SOLO

8 Preludes. 1939. carillon.
Merry-Go-Round (2 vols). 1970; Wat, 1970. accord.

BIBLIOGRAPHY

R12.
Handschin, Jacques. 'M. Kolinski und die Terz', *Der Toncharacter*. Zurich: Atlantis

Verlag, 1948 (89–91).
Kennedy, Raymond. 'A Bibliography of the Writings of Mieczyslaw Kolinski', *Current Musicology*. Spring 1966 (100–3).

LITERARY WORKS

(The works listed below are those not included in the Kennedy bibliography.)

ARTICLES

'An Apache Rabbit Dance Song Cycle as Sung by the Iroquois', *Ethnomusicology*. Vol. XVI, no. 3, Sept. 1972 (415–64).

'"Barbara Allen": Tonal versus Melodic Structure, Part I', *Ethnomusicology*. Vol. XII, May 1968 (208–18).

'"Barbara Allen": Tonal versus Melodic Structure, Part II', *Ethnomusicology*. Vol. XIII, Jan. 1969 (1–73).

'A Cross-Cultural Approach to Metro-Rhythmic Patterns', *Ethnomusicology*. Vol. XVII, Sept. 1973 (494–506).

'How about "Multisonance"?', *Ethnomusicology*. Vol. XVII, May 1973 (279).

'An Iroquois War Dance Song Cycle', *CAUSM Journal*. Vol. I, no. 2, Fall 1972 (415–64).

'Recent Trends in Ethnomusicology', *Ethnomusicology*. Vol. XI, Jan. 1967 (1–24).

REVIEWS

Hood, Mantle. *The Ethnomusicologist, Yearbook of the International Folk Music Council*. Vol. III, 1971 (146–60).

Merriam, Alan P. *Ethnomusicology of the Flathead Indians, Ethnomusicology*. Vol. XIV, Jan. 1970 (77–99).

Reinhard, Kurt. *Einführung in die Musikethnologie, Yearbook of the International Folk Music Council*. Vol. III, 1971 (161–2).

U.C.L.A. Institute of Ethnomusicology. *Selected Reports, Ethnomusicology*. Vol. XXI, May 1968 (277–83).

Wittrock, Wolfgang. *Die ältesten Melodietypen im ostdeutschen Volksgesang, Ethnomusicology*. Vol. XVII, Sept. 1973 (551–4).

KOMOROUS, RUDOLF (b. Prague, Czechoslovakia, 8 Dec. 1931). He began his formal musical studies on bassoon at the Prague Conservatory (1946–52), then studied composition with Pavel Borkovec and bassoon with Karel Pivonka at the Academy of Music in Prague (1952–9). In 1957 he won first prize in the Concours International d'Exécution Musicale in Geneva. The years from 1959 to 1961 were spent in Peking, China, where he was professor of bassoon and chamber music at the Central Conservatory of the University of Peking. Upon his return to Prague in 1961 he took the position of first bassoon of the Prague Opera Orchestra, which he held until 1968. In 1961 Komorous and Petr Kotik founded Musica Viva Pragensis, a society for the presentation of new music, whose reputation became known throughout Europe, although the society was given neither official recognition nor support in Czechoslovakia itself. After the Russian reentry into Czechoslovakia in 1968, Komorous left with his family, arriving in Toronto in January 1969. Finding it difficult to become established in a new country, he accepted a teaching post at Macalester College in Minnesota, although his family remained in Toronto; since 1971 he has been on the faculty of the Department of Music, University of Victoria, where he teaches analysis of twentieth-century music, composition, and theory. A composer of advanced tendencies, he has long been interested in electronic music, having first studied it in Russia and Poland in the summer of 1959 and having later issued the first recording of electronic music in Czechoslovakia. He is currently developing a studio at the University of Victoria.

Most of his compositions (many published by Universal, Vienna) are purely instrumental, characteristically being in the form of notated cells, and leave much to the discretion of the players within prescribed frameworks. He has received several commissions, for example *The Gloomy Grace* (1968) from the Donaueschinger Musiktage, *Bare and Dainty* (1970) from the Southwest German Radio in Baden-Baden, and *Dingy Yellow* (1972) from the Toronto saxophonist Paul Brodie under a grant from the Ontario Arts Council. His opera *Lady Whiterose* (1964–6; for voices alone) was premièred at the State University of New York at Buffalo in 1970.

Komorous is a member of CAPAC.

MUSICAL WORKS

STAGE

Lady Whiterose. 1964–6. chamb opera for voices alone. ms.

ORCHESTRA
Chamber music for bassoon and small orchestra. 1959. ms.
Bare and Dainty. 1970. UE.
Lethe. 1971. orch and tape. ms.

CHOIR
An Anna Blume. 1971. SATB. Text: Kurt Schwitters, trans from an English poem. ms.

INSTRUMENTAL ENSEMBLE
The Green Twig. 1960. Basset-hn, tri, harm, pno, vla, vlc. ms.
Flowers. 1961. 2cl, bsn, cymb, 3vla. ms.
Venus. 1963. str, perc. Experimental Music, London.
Olympia. 1964. flexatone, harmonica, nightingale, acolyte bells, sleigh bells, rattle. UE 14 407. Supraphon 1 10 0471.
Piccolomini. 1964. 4picc. ms.
Mignon. 1965. 4 four-str insts. UE 14 792. Supraphon.
Chanson. 1965. guit, clock-spring, vla. UE 14 793.
Minutenwalzer. 1965. harmonica, cowbell. catlg Smidra Group exhbtn, Ostrov, 1965.
York. 1967. fl, ob or tr, bsn, tri, pno, mand, cb. UE 15 173.
Dingy Yellow. 1972. sop sax, pno, tape. ms.

PIANO
The Devil's Trill. 1964. UE.

ELECTRONIC
Gone. 1969. UE.

BIBLIOGRAPHY

See R12.
Herzog, Eduard. 'Avantgarde aus der Tschechoslowakei', special issue of *Begegnung: Zeitschrift für Literatur, Bildende Kunst, Musik und Wissenschaft.* Donaueschinger Musiktage für zeitgenössische Tonkunst, Oct. 1968 (5–9).
Holzknecht, Václav. 'Běh za slávou', *Editio Supraphon.* Prague, 1971 (76–7).
Meyers Enzyklopädisches Lexikon. Bibliographisches Institut AG, Mannheim.
'Musik der neuen Generation', *Universal Edition Catalogue,* 1972 (87–8).

KUNZ, ALFRED (b. Neudorf, Sask., 26 May 1929). He studied theory and composition in Toronto (1949–55) with John WEINZWEIG, Gordon DELAMONT, and Heinz Unger. While teaching in Kitchener, he spent several summers in Europe studying composition with Karlheinz Stockhausen. In 1958 he organized and conducted the Kitchener-Waterloo Chamber Music Orchestra and Choir. From 1964 to 1965 he studied conducting in Mainz, Germany, on a scholarship from the West German government and successfully completed the West German State conducting examinations, while becoming assistant conductor of the Mainz City Opera Theatre. In 1965 he was appointed director of music of the University of Waterloo and principal of the Canadian Music Teachers' College in Burlington, Ont. (1965–7). He is conductor of the Kitchener Concordia Club Choirs. In 1964 he was commissioned by the Canadian Music Centre to compose two works for the John Adaskin Project in music education (*Fun for Two* and *Fun for Three*). Among his more ambitious works are *The Watchful Gods* (1962), an operetta for high school students; *Moses* (1965), a ballet in four acts; and *The Big Land* (1967), an oratorio for Canada's Centennial, which Kunz considers to be his most successful work. His early works exhibit both twelve-tone technique and experimentation with free timbral composition. Since about 1966 his attention has been drawn to choral writing and with this an interest has developed in a more conservative style. He is a member of CAPAC.

MUSICAL WORKS

STAGE
7 ballets, including *Moses.* 1965.
The Watchful Gods (operetta). 1962.
Let's Make a Carol (play with music). 1965; Wat, 1965.

INSTRUMENTAL
5 works for orchestra: *Sinfonietta Nos 1* (1952) and 2 (1962); *Excursion for Large Orchestra* (1964); *Five Night Scenes* (1971); *Concerto for Percussion and Orchestra* (1973).
3 sets of Fanfares for brass and percussion. 1964.
5 works for instrumental ensembles: *Sonata* (1959) vln, pno; *Emanation No 1* (1964) vln, hn, pno; *Emanation No 2* (1964) fl, cl, hn, bsn; *Fun for Two* (1964) 2bsn (2b cl); *Quintet* (1964) ww qnt.
3 works for piano solo: *Five Excursions* (1965); *Music to Do Things By,* Vols 1 and 2 (1969).

Three Excursions for Organ. 1964.
7 works for accordion solo.
4 works for accordion orchestra: *Prelude* (1963); *Miniature Suite* (1966); *Symphonic Movement No 1* (1966) and *No 2* (1967).

CHORAL
7 works for chorus and orchestra, including: *The Big Land* (1967); *The Creation* (1972).
Works for SATB and piano, including: *Will You Come* (1960, Wat 1966); *Eight Impressions on Japanese Haiku* (1969, Wat 1971); *The Rhinoceros* (Wat 1971).
11 a cappella choral works and 5 works for male chorus, many published by Wat.

VOCAL
18 songs for vc and pno in German and English.
The Song of the Clarinet. 1961. narr, fl, ob, cl, bsn, str qnt.
Love, Death and Full Moonnights. 1964. bar, ob, fl, cl, tpt, vln, pno.

BIBLIOGRAPHY

See B-B; K.

LITERARY WORKS

ARTICLES
'Composer's Corner', *CanCo.* No. 13, Dec. 1966 (32–3).
'My Most Successful Work: "The Big Land" ', *CanCo.* No. 25, Jan. 1968 (16–17).

L

LALIBERTÉ, (JOSEPH-FRANCOIS) ALFRED (b. Saint-Jean, Que., 10 Feb. 1882; d. Montreal, Que., 7 May 1952). He began his piano studies in Montreal with J.-B. Denys, R.O. Pelletier, and Dominique Ducharme. In 1900 he went to Berlin, where he stayed until 1905, studying piano with Paul Lutzenko, harmony with Ernst Baeker, and counterpoint and composition with Wilhelm Klatte; he was also heard in piano recitals. On his return to Canada he came to know the works of Scriabin and early in 1907 his enthusiasm for the Russian composer's works took him to New York, where he met Scriabin, becoming first his follower and then his pupil. He went once more to Europe, staying first in Berlin to work with Teresa Carreno before rejoining Scriabin in Brussels. After some recitals in Germany, Paris, and London (the latter under the sponsorship of Lord Strathcona and Emma Albani), he settled in Montreal in 1911. He opened studios in Montreal and New York, devoting himself to making known Scriabin's works through courses and lectures. In time Scriabin entrusted to him the manuscripts of the 'Poème de l'extase' and of his 'Sonata No. 5', both of which were donated by Madame Laliberté in 1972 to the Scriabin Museum in Moscow on the occasion of the one-hundredth anniversary of the composer's birth. Laliberté was also associated with Nicolas Medtner, who dedicated to him his 'Sonata minacciosa', Opus 53, No. 2, and his song 'The Captive', Opus 52, No. 7. To Laliberté also was dedicated 'Variations', Opus 22 for piano, by Marcel Dupré.

In Laliberté's output few works were completely finished. The most important – a three-act opera, *Soeur Béatrice,* on the text of the play by Maurice Maeterlinck – exists only in a version for voice and piano. A *Passacaille et choeur final* for piano, organ, orchestra, and chorus without words is unfinished. A song cycle on *La Chanson d'Eve,* to fifteen poems of Van Lerberghe, was nearly completed, but only three of the songs were published, in Paris by Eschig. In addition he wrote piano pieces, chamber music, and numerous arrangements of Canadian folk songs, Indian and Eskimo, some of which were published by Eschig and some in the journal *Le Passe-temps,* for which Laliberté also wrote a few articles. GILLES POTVIN

BIBLIOGRAPHY

See B-B; CrC(II); K; Lv; Mce; Wa.

LITERARY WORKS

ARTICLES

'Alexandre Scriabine', *Le Passe-Temps*. No. 898, May 1946.

'L'Art pour l'or', *Le Passe-Temps*. No. 909, Apr. 1947.

LAUFER, EDWARD (b. Switzerland, 25 Nov. 1938). He came to Halifax in 1939. In Toronto he studied piano with Lubka Kolessa and Alberto Guerrero and composition with John BECKWITH, Talivaldis KENINS, Oskar MORAWETZ, and John WEINZWEIG at the University of Toronto, where he received his Bachelor of Music (1957) and Master of Music (1960) degrees. From 1960 to 1962 he studied at the Juilliard School of Music with Edward Steuermann, William Bergsma, Norman Lloyd, and Vincent Persichetti, as well as taking private lessons in composition with Roger Sessions. A Canada Council Arts Scholarship (1961–2), the John Halsey Bonsall Fellowship (1962–3), and the University Wilson Fellowship (1963–4) enabled him to study composition with Milton Babbitt, Earl Kim, and Roger Sessions at Princeton University (1962–4), where he received his Master of Fine Arts degree in 1964. He is a doctoral candidate at Princeton. In 1968 he was awarded the Bennington Composers' Conference Fellowship. He was an instructor in music at Smith College (1969–71) and assistant professor at the State University of New York at Purchase (1972–3). He was awarded another Canada Council Arts Bursary in 1972.

Laufer's *Variations for Orchestra Part I* (1967), a commission from the Halifax Symphony Orchestra, has fragmented material in a highly dissonant idiom. *Nostos* (1972), also in a dissonant, atonal style, is dark and brooding. His *Divertimento* (1972) was commissioned by the CBC for the CBC Vancouver Chamber Orchestra.

Laufer is a member of the American Musicological Society, the Music Library Association, the Swedish Society for Musicology, the College Music Society, the American Society of University Composers, Beethoven-Haus-Bonn, and of CAPAC.

MUSICAL WORKS

ORCHESTRA

Composition. 1963–4.

Prelude. 1966.

Variations, Part I. 1967.

Variations, Part II. 1968.

Divertimento for Chamber Orchestra. 1972.

VOICE

Sonnet to Orpheus 19. 1964. Text: Rainer Maria Rilke.

Sonnet to Orpheus 22. 1965. Text: Rainer Maria Rilke.

VOICE WITH INSTRUMENTAL ENSEMBLE

Nostos. 1965 (rev 1967). sop, alto fl, b cl, vlc, pno. Text: Simonides, trans: J W MacKail.

INSTRUMENTAL ENSEMBLE

Sonata. 1961. fl, pno.

String Quartet. 1962 (rev 1963).

Septet. 1966.

Variations for Seven Instruments. 1967; NVMP 1972. fl (picc), cl, bsn, tpt, pno, vln, vlc.

BIBLIOGRAPHY

'Edward Laufer', *PAC*. Vol. v, no. 2, 1967 (21).

LE CAINE, HUGH (b. Port Arthur, Ont., 27 May 1914). He studied the piano in his youth but pursued a scientific career, receiving his Bachelor of Science (1938) and Master of Science (1939) degrees from Queen's University in Kingston, Ont. In 1948 he was awarded a National Research Council grant to study at the University of Birmingham in England, where he obtained his Doctorate of Philosophy in Science in 1952. Since 1952 he has worked at the National Research Council on the development of electronic music instruments and collaborated in the establishment of electronic music studies at the University of Toronto (1959), McGill University (1964), and the Hebrew University in Jerusalem (1961).

Le Caine's interest is directed almost exclusively towards electronic composition and his works are a result of his interest in designing electronic instruments. Many of these are short and exploit the electronic medium through a limited number of parameters. For example, *Ninety-nine Generators* (1956), in which he uses the NRC

Mk III touch-sensitive keyboard, was recorded in a 26-foot diameter radome (sphere) to produce long reverberation. In *Invocation* (1957) he employs just three sound objects, splicing being the only manipulative device used. *A Noisome Pestilence* (1958) uses an octave band filter controlled by the seven-octave touch-sensitive keyboard with white noise as the source material, without any splicing of tape. The development of instruments such as the touch-sensitive organ is an attempt to alleviate some of the tedious operations required in the electronic music studio (for example, splicing). Le Caine has continued to extend basic studio techniques through the use of both synthesizer and computer; *Paulution ('Charnel Number Five'*, 1970), for example, uses the Pauliphone synthesizer and *Mobile ('The Computer Laughed'*, 1970) the Pulfer computer system. Again both these works are short and call on few, but sophisticated, sound-sources and manipulative devices.

Since 1966 Le Caine has given occasional seminars and courses in electronic music at the University of Toronto and McGill University. In 1971 he was awarded an honorary Doctor of Music degree from McGill University and, in 1973, an honorary LL.D from the University of Toronto. In 1974 he received another honorary doctorate, this time with the musicologist Frank Harrison at his alma mater, Queen's, where the music department's new building was named the Harrison-LeCaine Building. He is a member of CAPAC.

MUSICAL WORKS

ELECTRONIC TAPE

Dripsody. 1955. Folk FM-34360.
Ninety-nine Generators. 1956.
Invocation. 1957.
The Burning Deck (electronic melodrama). 1958. Text: Dorthea Felicia Hemans.
A Noisome Pestilence. 1959.
Textures. 1959.
Sounds to forget. 1963.
Alchemy. 1964.
Nocturne. 1969.
Perpetual Motion. 1970.
Paulution ('Charnel Number Five'). 1970.

SOLO WITH ELECTRONIC TAPE

Study No 1 for Player Piano and Tape. 1969.

COMPUTER

Mobile ('The Computer Laughed'). 1970.

BIBLIOGRAPHY

Bec70; Wa.

LITERARY WORKS

ARTICLES

'Apparatus for Generating Serial Sound Structure', *Journal of the Audio Engineering Society*. Vol. XVII, no. 3, June 1969 (258–65).
'Electronic Music', *New Scientist*. Vol. XXVIII, Dec. 16, 1965 (814).
'Electronic Music', *Proceedings of the Institute of Radio Engineers*. Vol. XLVI, Apr. 1956 (457).
'A Preliminary Report on the Serial Sound Structure Generator' (with Gustav Ciamaga), *Perspectives of New Music*. Vol. VI, no. 1, Fall-Winter 1967 (114–18).
'Revised Specification for a Tape Recorder for use in Electronic Music Studios Developed by the National Research Council of Canada'. Ottawa: National Research Council of Canada, Radio and Electrical Engineering Division, ERB-581, May 1961.
'Some Applications of Electrical Level Controls', *Electronic Music Review*. No. 4, Oct. 1967 (25).
'The Sonde: A New Approach to Multiple Sine Wave Generation' (with Gustav Ciamaga), *Journal of the Audio Engineering Society*. Vol. XVIII, 1970 (536–9).
'Synthetic Means', *The Modern Composer and His World* (Beckwith and Kasemets, eds). Toronto: University of Toronto Press, 1961 (109–16).
'A Tape Recorder for use in Electronic Music Studios and Related Equipment', *Journal of Music Theory*. Vol. VII, no. 1, Spring 1963 (83).
'A Touch-Sensitive Keyboard for the Organ', *CMJ*. Vol. III, no. 3, Spring 1959 (26).
'Touch-Sensitive Organ Based on an Electroacoustic Coupling Device', *Journal of the Acoustical Society of America*. Vol. XXVII, no. 4, July 1955 (781).

LIDOV, DAVID (b. Portland, Oregon, 9 Jan. 1941). He studied composition with Otto Luening at Columbia University in New York, where he received his Bachelor of Arts (1962) and Master of Arts (1965) degrees in music and where he was awarded a Seilde Fellowship (1963–4). He was assistant conductor of the Columbia University orchestra in 1964. From 1968 to 1970 he was music specialist at Lower Canada College in Montreal and conductor of the Montreal Jewish Folk Choir. Since 1970 he has been lecturer in the Faculty of Fine Arts at York University, Toronto.

Lidov treats his material in a free atonal way. He has written a number of works for chamber groups, including *Sonatina* for violin and piano; *Istanpittas* (1968) for tenor saxophone, trombone, and cello; *Sonatina* (1969) for trumpet and piano; *Trio* (1969) for violin, cello, and piano; *Prelude* (1970) for violin and piano; and *Fantasie* (1972) for bassoon and piano. He has also written a piano sonata (1966), *Viola Fantasie* (1964), *Changes* (1970) for solo violin, and *Symphony* for full orchestra (1965). His works for voice include *Three Songs from Yeats* (1965) for tenor and woodwind quintet, *Crazy Jane's Songs* (1967–70; text by W.B. Yeats), and *I Have No Life but This . . .* (1970); and for chorus, *The Vision of Louis Riel* (1968; text by John Robert Colombo) and *The Lamb* (1970; text by William Blake). He has been engaged in research on musical applications of mathematical linguistics, 'a study which employs computer composition to discover how the logic of musical phrasing relates to the grammar of speech'. He is affiliated with BMI Canada.

LONGTIN, MICHEL (b. Montreal, Que., 20 May 1946). He studied composition and analysis with André PRÉVOST (1968–74), at the same time following a course in electronic music at the Royal Conservatory in Toronto (1971) with Samuel DOLIN. He pursued his studies in electronic music at McGill University with Paul PEDERSEN (1971–2) and Bengt Hambraeus (1972–3) In fifteen of his nineteen works he uses sounds of electronic origin, either alone or combined with traditional sonorities through which he seeks from the origin of his own experience to describe soul-states. Among his works for electronic tape are *Rituel II* (1971), *Mi E Meta* (1971), and *Requiem pour St-Charles Barromée* (1972). He has also written *Latitude 60° Nord* (1969) for ondes Martenot and orchestra; *Il était une fois* (1971) for choir, large orchestra, and electronic tape; a string quartet (1970); *Les immortels d'Agapia* (1972) for flute, clarinet, two percussionists, piano, and electronic tape; and *Deux rubans noirs II* (1972) for string quartet and electronic tape.

Imaginative, gifted with a sensitivity sharpened by his work in pantomime, Longtin describes and narrates more than he explains. In June 1973 three of his works – *Fedhibo, Embarque on ira pas vite,* and *Au Nord du lac Supérieur* – were chosen to represent Canada at the International Electronic Music Week in Madrid. He is affiliated with BMI Canada.

LORRAIN, DENIS (b. Ithaca, N.Y., 29 July 1948). He studied music in Montreal at the Faculty of Music, University of Montreal (1967–71), with André PRÉVOST and at the Faculty of Music, McGill University (1971–3), with Paul PEDERSEN and Bengt Hambraeus. In 1970 he joined the research team Informatique-musique (directed by Robert Dupuy) devoted to the exploration of possible usages of the computer in the creation and analysis of music. This collaboration led him to participate in the colloquium 'Arts and Music Computer Symposium' (Duluth, Minn.) in July 1971. During April and May 1972 he was assistant to Iannis Xenakis at the Center of Mathematics and Automatic Music (University of Indiana, Bloomington) and in the summer of the same year followed a course of study in 'information' at the Centre national d'étude des télécommunications (C.N.E.T.) in Paris. In the fall of 1972 he left the Informatique-musique group to become teaching assistant at McGill University, obtaining a Master of Music degree there in 1973.

Lorrain has written *ARC* (1969) for string orchestra, *P - A* (1971) for eight speaking voices, *L'Angelus* (1971) for clarinet and electronic tape, *Suite pour deux guitares* (1972), and *Séquence* (1972). He is affiliated with BMI Canada.

M

McCAULEY, WILLIAM (b. Tofield, Alta, 14 Feb. 1917). He had his early training on the piano and in 1936 moved to Toronto, where he played in the Conservatory Symphony Orchestra, the Harmony Symphony Orchestra, and the Horace Lapp Orchestra at the Royal York Hotel, and studied trombone with Harry Hawe. In 1940 he joined the Royal Canadian Air Force, becoming assistant bandmaster of the Toronto Manning Pool Band. In 1945 he began studies at the Royal Conservatory in Toronto with Margaret Parsons (piano) and Healey WILLAN (composition), obtaining his Bachelor of Music degree from the University of Toronto in 1947. He was appointed music director of the Ottawa Technical High School (1947–9) and joined the Ottawa Philharmonic Orchestra. In 1949 he joined Crawley Films, for which he composed and conducted music for many documentaries. He composed and conducted the music for the 1972 CBC television series *The Whiteoaks of Jalna*, the Twentieth Century Fox feature film *The Neptune Factor*, and has had many other film and television assignments.

Newfoundland Scene (1952) uses a tonal language, but in *Five Miniatures for Flute and Strings* (1958) McCauley turned to a dissonant, free-atonal style (using expressive titles: 'Adventurous', 'Dolorous', 'Dextrous', 'Languorous', and 'Capricious') in which, although dissonant, the writing is still lyrical. McCauley's style is structurally free and descriptive (for example, *Space Trip*, 1968), using fairly tonal material and occasionally moving into polytonal or atonal areas.

McCauley founded and conducted the William McCauley Choir in 1954, and in 1957 received a Canada Council senior fellowship to study for his doctorate at the Eastman School of Music in Rochester, N.Y. He studied piano with Harry Watts, choral conducting with Herman Genhart, and composition with Alan Hovhaness, Bernard Rogers, and Howard Hanson, receiving his Doctor of Musical Arts degree in 1960. He was appointed musical director of the O'Keefe Centre in Toronto (1960) and was Director of Music at York University (1961–9). In 1970 he became head of the music department of Seneca College, Toronto, continuing his activities as freelance composer, arranger, and conductor. In 1967 he received a commission from the Centennial Commission (*Fantasy on Canadian Folk Themes*) and that same year won the composition competition sponsored by the Alberta Centennial Commission. He is a member of the Canadian League of Composers and of CAPAC.

MUSICAL WORKS

STAGE, FILM AND TELEVISION

The Wilderness (television). 1964.
Beauty and the Beast (puppet play). 1967.
Incidental music for over 100 films and television programs.

ORCHESTRA

Newfoundland Scene. 1952. CTL M1043.
Quebec Lumber Camp. 1953. CTL M1043.
Saskatchewan Suite. 1956. CTL M1043.
Contrasts. 1958.
Theme and Deviations. 1960; MCA, 1961.

STRING ORCHESTRA

Two Nocturnes for Strings. 1968.
Sunday Morning at Wahanowin. 1968.

BAND

Day Dreams. 1942.
Canadian Ski Trail. 1948.
Centennial Suite. 1965.
Canadian Folk Song Fantasy. 1966; South, 1972.
Metropolis (Concert Suite for symphonic band). 1967; OUP, 1967.

SOLOIST(S) WITH ORCHESTRA

Five Miniatures for Flute and Strings. 1958; MCA, 1961. Merc 50277.
Concerto for Horn. 1959.
Five Miniatures for Bass Trombone, Harp and Strings. 1959.

CHOIR

Immanence. 1957. SATB. Text: Wilson MacDonald.
Les Anges dans nos campagnes (arr). c1958.
Canadian Folk Songs (arr). c1960. SATB. Col FL-226.

The Solitary Reaper. 1965. SSA. Text: William Wordsworth.
Ca, bergers, assemblons-nous (arr). 1968; Wat, 1970. SATB.
Dans une étable obscure (arr). 1968; Wat, 1970. SATB.
Dors, ma colombe (arr). 1968; Wat, 1970. SATB.
Il est né, le divin enfant (arr). 1968; Wat, 1970. SATB.
Le Sommeil de l'enfant-Jésus (arr). 1968; Wat, 1970. SATB.
Tout le ciel reluit (arr). 1968; Wat, 1970. SATB.
French Canadian Folk Songs (arr). 1968; Wat, 1970. SATB and SSA.
Canadian Counting Song. 1968. SATB. Text: William McCauley.
International Anthem. 1968. SSATB. Text: Wilson MacDonald.

VOICE
How Do I Love Thee. 1967. mezz, pno. Text: Elizabeth Barrett Browning.

VOICE WITH INSTRUMENTAL ENSEMBLE
He's Special. 1961. vc, fl, alto sax, tpt, 2trb, timp, perc, str. CTL M1043. Text: William McCauley.
I've Been Waiting for You. 1961. vc, fl, alto sax, tpt, 2trb, timp, perc, str. CTL M1043. Text: William McCauley.
Clear the Track, Here Comes Shack. 1966; South, 1966. vc, 2guit, cb, drums.
Warming the Bench. 1966; South, 1966. vc, 2guit, cb, drums.

INSTRUMENTAL ENSEMBLE
Fugitive from a Fugue Factory. c1958. tpt, alto sax, trb, pno, cb, guit, drums.
Five Miniatures for Six Percussionists. 1962; MCA, 1970.
Five Miniatures for Ten Winds. 1968. fl, ob, cl, bsn, 2hn, 2tpt, trb, tb.
Five Miniatures for Four Saxophones. 1972.

PIANO
Invention No 3. 1966; FH, 1966.
Mood Sketches. 1966; FH, 1966.
Space Trip. 1968; GVT, 1968.

INSTRUMENTAL SOLO
The Flute Family. c1972; McCauley, 1973.

BIBLIOGRAPHY

See B-B; K; Mm; Wa.
'Dr. William McCauley: Success in Many Directions', *CanCo*. No. 12, Nov. 1966 (4–5, 40–1).
'Dr. William McCauley: Wins Alberta Composition Contest', *CanCo*. No. 24, Dec. 1967 (32–3).

LITERARY WORKS

ARTICLES
'My Most Successful Work: "Five Miniatures for Flute and Strings" ', *CanCo*. No. 32, Sept. 1968 (8–9).

McINTYRE, PAUL (b. Peterborough, Ont., 7 Oct. 1931). He received his early training in Hamilton with Eileen MacManamy (piano) and Eric Rollinson (theory) and later studied composition with Arnold WALTER at the University of Toronto, where he received his Bachelor of Music degree in 1951. He continued his studies at the Paris Conservatoire and at the Mozarteum in Salzburg (1953–4). He received instruction in piano from Bela Boszormenyi-Nagy, Claudio Arrau, and Alexander Uninsky, in conducting from Igor Markevich, Sixten Ehrling, and Pierre Monteux, and in composition from Tony Aubin and Olivier Messiaen. He was assistant conductor of the Regina Symphony Orchestra (1952–3; 1954–5) and of the Canadian Opera Company (1959–60). In 1958 he received his doctorate in music from the University of Toronto and in the same year his dramatic cantata *Judith* won first prize in the Vancouver International Festival Competition. From 1961 to 1964 he was Carnegie Visiting Associate Professor and head of the music department of the University of Alaska, and conductor of the Fairbanks Symphony Orchestra. In 1963 he received a Resident Fellowship from the Huntington Hartford Foundation.

In *Judith* (1956–7) McIntyre builds up dramatic tension by setting the mood effectively with his use of dissonant intervals. In *Fantasy on an Eskimo Song* (1962), a commission from the Alaska Festival of Music, he derives his harmonic material from the pentatonic scale of the Eskimo song. Although *Out of the Cradle Endlessly Rocking* (1966) uses the twelve-tone technique, there is no extensive serial manipulation but rather a simple repetition of the row.

McIntyre was assistant professor in the

department of music, College of Liberal Arts, University of Minnesota (1964–7), and later associate professor and chairman of the music department at the College of Saint Catherine, St Paul, Minn. In 1970 he was appointed head of the music department of the University of Windsor, Ont. He is a member of the Canadian League of Composers and of CAPAC.

MUSICAL WORKS

STAGE

The Death of the Hired Man (chamb opera for TV). 1961. Text: Robert Frost.

This Is Not True (comic opera). 1966. Libretto: James Schevill.

STRING ORCHESTRA

Song of Autumn. 1958.

BAND

Pavan. 1961.

SOLOIST(S) WITH ORCHESTRA

Piano Concerto. 1952.

Judith (A Melodrama-Cantata). 1956–7 (rev 1959). Text: Genesis III, 14–15; Judith in Douay; trans (1609) anon.

Symphonia Sacra. 1958. ATB soli, SATB, orch. Text: Richard Crashaw.

Jean de Brébeuf (Dramatic Symphony). 1961. bs, orch. Text: Jean de Brébeuf.

CHOIR WITH INSTRUMENTAL ENSEMBLE

Gaudeamus Igitur. 1961. SATB, 11 instr/band. Text: anon.

CHOIR

Psalm 137. 1960. SATB. Text: Richard Crashaw.

Sighs and Grones. 1960. SATB. Text: George Herbert.

VOICE

Cradle Song. 1945. Text: Padraic Colum.

Four Poems of Walter de la Mare. 1950. Text: Walter de la Mare.

Suite of European Folksongs (arr). 1957. Text: trad. collab with Jan Rubes.

Amor Triumphans. 1958. Text: Arthur Symonds.

A Baker's Dozen of Well Assorted Limericks. 1961. Text: anon.

VOICE WITH INSTRUMENTAL ENSEMBLE

Out of the Cradle Endlessly Rocking. 1966. vc, fl, vla, vlc, hpschd. Text: Walt Whitman.

INSTRUMENTAL ENSEMBLE

Sonata for Violin and Piano. 1946.

Scherzo for Flute and Piano. 1948.

Trio-Serenade in E. 1949. vln, vlc, pno.

String Quartet in A minor. 1951.

Fantasy on an Eskimo Song. 1962. ww qnt.

Permutations on a Paganini Caprice. 1966. str qt.

Encounters. 1970. vlc, pno.

PIANO

Sonatina. 1950.

Theme and Variations. 1950.

Deux Etudes poétiques pour piano. 1954.

Holiday in Alaska. 1962; GIA, 1962.

INSTRUMENTAL SOLO

Abstract. 1963. fl.

ORGAN

Processional. 1960.

BIBLIOGRAPHY

See B-B; C63,66,69,72; K; Wa.

'The Cantata "Judith"', *CBC Times*. Aug. 10–16, 1958 (11).

MACLEAN, QUENTIN MORVAREN (b. London, England, 14 May 1896; d. Toronto, Ont., 9 July 1962). He began his musical education with Sir Richard Terry and in 1907 entered the Vienna Academy of Music to study organ. In 1912 he moved to Leipzig, where he studied with Karl Straube (organ) and Max Reger (composition), receiving a scholarship to continue his studies. In 1914 he was soloist at the Leipzig Bach Festival and in the same year, after the outbreak of war, was interned in the Ruhleben Prison Camp near Berlin, where he met Ernest MAC MILLAN. On his return to London in 1919 he became assistant organist at Westminster Cathedral and organist in several theatres, including the Regal Marble Arch and the Trocadero. He moved to Toronto in 1939 and was appointed organist and choirmaster of Holy Rosary Church and organist for the Victoria Theatre and Shea's Hippodrome. For many years he provided background music for CBC radio programs. He was a teacher at the St Michael's Choir School and at the Toronto Conservatory of Music.

Maclean's compositions are generally traditional, using modal or pentatonic material (*Rustic Rhapsody*, 1954). An earlier work, *String Quartet* (1936), is tonal in a romantic idiom with three movements: 'Preamble', 'Air with Variations', and 'Roundelay'. His estate is a member of CAPAC.

MUSICAL WORKS

FILM
The Vigil. c1930.
Petulance. c1955.
Mysterious Minuet. c1960.

ORCHESTRA
Babbling (arr). c1940. Prowse.
Parade of the Sunbeams. c1940. Prowse.
Rondelet. c1940. Prowse.
Variations on 'The Carman's Whistle' (Wm Byrd). 1943.
Prelude in the Form of a Ditty (Prelu-Ditty). 1950.
The Well Tempered Orchestra (Prelude and Fugue on a Tuning Formula). c1950.
Algonquin Legend (arr). 1952.
Flowers of the Forest (arr). c1953. str orch.
Rustic Rhapsody. 1954.
Mona.

SOLOIST WITH ORCHESTRA
Concert Piece for Organ and Orchestra. 1932.
Rhapsody on Two English Folk Tunes. 1938. hp, orch.
Stabat Mater. 1941. ten, SATB, orch. Text: Jacopone da Todi.
Algonquin Legend (arr). 1942. vln, str.
Concerto Grosso in Popular Style (Electric Concerto). 1942. solovox, elec org, elec guit, theremin, orch.
Concerto for Electric Organ. 1945. elec org, dance orch.
Concerto Romantico. 1953. pno, orch.
Theme and Variations. c1954. hpschd, orch.
Concerto Rococo. 1957. vln, orch.

CHOIR AND ORCHESTRA
Good Friday. SATB, orch. Text: John Masefield.

CHOIR
Festival Mass. c1935. SATB, org.
Figured Sections of Credo III. c1935. SATB, org.
Missa Brevis. c1940. SATB, org.
Missa in Honorem S S Innocentium. c1940. SATB.
Cognovi, Domine. 1942. SATB.
Christmas Mass. c1945. SATB, org.
Terra Tremuit. 1945. SATB, org. Text: Offertory for Easter Sunday.
Mass for Four Voices. 1946. SATB, org.
Easter Mass. 1947. SATB, org.
Missa 'Jesu Redemptor Omnium'. 1949. SATB, org.
Flowers of the Forest (arr). c1950. SATB. Text: Cockburn.
Easter Sunday Proper. c1953. SATB, org.
Missa Homophonica. c1957. SATB, org.
Cum Angelis. SATB. Text: Roman Missal.
Justorum Animae. SATB.
Lourdes Hymn. SATB.

VOICE
Just For Today. vc, org. Text: United Church hymnary.
Passionate Shepherd. sop (ten), pno. Text: Christopher Marlowe.
Standing at the Portal. vc, org. Text: Frances Ridley Havergal.
Eighteen Songs. vc, pno (org). Text: John Gerrard.
Fifteen Songs. vc, pno (org). Text: Kate Munro.
Thirteen Songs to Various Texts. vc, pno (org). Text: Rosemary Graham, Babs Brown, Quentin MacLean, John Bennett, Desmond Carter, Charles Kingsley.

INSTRUMENTAL ENSEMBLE
String Quartet. 1934.
Trio. 1937. vln, vlc, pno.
Trio. 1937. fl, vla, guit.
Algonquin Legend. 1942. vln, pno.
Trio 'Ricercare'. 1954. vln, vlc, pno.

PIANO
Twenty-one Short Pieces for Piano. c1940–61.

ORGAN
Sonata. 1932.
Concerto for Organ. 1935.
Victimae Paschali Laudes. 1944.
Laying the Scale for Organ (Prelude and Fugue). 1950.
Bridal Introit. c1960.
Regina Coeli. c1960.
Wedding Recessional. c1960.
Prelude (On a Tuning Formula). c1961.

BIBLIOGRAPHY

B65,71; CrC(II); K.
'"Background Music" Which Can Steal the Show', *CBC Times.* Vol. IV, no. 9, Sept. 16–22, 1951 (1–2).

MacMILLAN, (SIR) ERNEST (ALEXANDER CAMPBELL) (b. Mimico, Ont. (a suburb of Toronto). 18 Aug. 1893; d. Toronto, 6 May 1973). MacMillan was probably the best known and most widely influential Canadian musician of his generation. He studied organ under Arthur Blakeley in Toronto and in Edinburgh under Alfred Hollins and Frederick Niecks, and piano (briefly) with Thérèse Chaigneau in Paris, but in conducting and composition was largely self-taught. He was awarded the ARCO and FRCO diplomas and the Bachelor of Music degree at Oxford before he was eighteen, the Bachelor of Arts degree in modern history from the University of Toronto (1915, *in absentia*), and the Doctor of Music degree from Oxford (1918) on the basis of a major musical 'exercise', the choral-orchestral setting of Swinburne's *England*, submitted from a German prisoner-of-war camp. He was organist at Knox Church, Toronto (1908–10), at St Paul's Presbyterian Church, Hamilton, Ont. (1911–14), at Timothy Eaton Memorial Church, Toronto (1919–25), and was collaborative pianist with such artists as Emmy Heim, mezzo-soprano, and the Canadian Trio (Kathleen Parlow, violin, Zara Nelsova, cello). Conductor of the Toronto Symphony Orchestra (1931–56) and the Toronto Mendelssohn Choir (1942–57), he was guest conductor of orchestras in the U.S., England, Australia, and South America. He was principal of the Royal Conservatory of Music of Toronto (1926–42) and Dean of the Faculty of Music, University of Toronto (1927–52). He was president or chairman of many major musical and cultural bodies in Canada, including the Canadian College of Organists (1927–8), the Canadian Music Council (1947–66), Jeunesses Musicales du Canada (1961–3), the Arts and Letters Club (1930–2), and was President of the Canadian Music Centre (1959–70). He was editor of *Music in Canada* (1955) and the author of numerous essays and musical textbooks, as well as being a lecturer, teacher, and adjudicator.

Through his publications of educational books and anthologies and his travels, as adjudicator or Conservatory examiner, to many centres in Canada, he is credited with stimulating higher standards of taste and accomplishment among musical amateurs and professionals. During his tenure the Toronto Symphony Orchestra augmented its size and the duration of its season and made its first international tours and recordings. The annual performances of Bach's 'St Matthew Passion' under his direction were for thirty years an important fixture of the Toronto musical scene, and the later ones were broadcast nationally by the CBC. His writings and talks showed a shrewd sense of the country's musical needs. He was noted as a champion of young Canadian talent, assisting the soprano Lois Marshall, the tenor Jon Vickers, the conductor Victor Feldbrill, and others by his encouragement, and energetically directing, in his later years, the CBC's annual Talent Festival broadcasts. He programmed first performances of more Canadian orchestral compositions than any other conductor to date.

MacMillan was made a Fellow of the Royal College of Music in 1931, was knighted by King George V in 1935, and was made an honorary member of the Royal Academy of Music, London, in 1938. He received nine honorary doctorates from universities in Canada and the U.S., as well as the City of Toronto award of merit (1965), the Canada Council Medal (1964), and the medal of the Canadian Music Council (posthumously, 1973). In 1970 he was made a Companion of the Order of Canada.

Although composition was not MacMillan's main musical activity, a glance over his list of works reveals that in his youth he regarded composition as a normal activity of the complete musician. In these early years several works of serious scope show his contrapuntal skill (he was a lifelong student and exponent of Bach) and also his mastery of post-romantic harmonies and colours (e.g. *String Quartet in C minor,* 1914, rev. 1921; *Overture*, 1924), and these have benefited from revival. During the second half of the 1920s he made the acquaintance of the folklorist Marius Barbeau and – in collaboration with several other musicians also inspired by Barbeau's knowledge of and enthusiasm for the rich treasure of French-Canadian, Indian, and Nova Scotian folk music – initiated perhaps the first significant attempt to implant an indigenous element in Canadian musical literature. Some of his arrangements and settings, such as the *Two Sketches based on French Canadian Airs* (1927) for string orchestra or quartet and *Blanche comme la neige* (1928) for male or mixed choir, have become classics of that era of Canadian music. The *String Quartet* (1921) and the *Two Sketches* comprise the first recording devoted to one Canadian composer and distributed on a world-wide scale (Deutsche Grammophon, 1967). Broader indications of his imagination, improvisatory fluency, and sheer sense of fun are found in the many arrangements he made for some of the Toronto Symphony Orchestra's Pop Concerts (*Fantasy on Scottish Melodies,* 1946) and the celebrated 'Christmas Box' orchestra benefit concerts (medley of *Christmas Carols,* 1945; *There was an old woman,* 1946, with apologies to J.S. Bach).

MacMillan was a member of CAPAC, of which he was president from 1947 to 1969.

JOHN BECKWITH

MUSICAL WORKS

PRE-1914

A number of sacred and secular vocal and instrumental works dating from 1904 and including an early opera or masque (*Snow White,* 1907), at least ten songs and a dozen choral works, two or three works scored for small orchestra and a *Passacaglia* for organ (1907).

STAGE

Prince Charming (ballad opera on Scottish and French tunes). 1933. 7 solos, chorus, small orch. Text: J E Middleton.

ORCHESTRA

Overture 'Cinderella'. 1915. med orch. ms. 1915 Ruhleben prison camp, camp orch, Ernest MacMillan.

Overture. 1924. 12′35″. full orch. CMC. 1924, Tor, TS, Ernest MacMillan.

God Save the Queen (arr). c1934. full orch. FH, 1957.

Christmas Carols (medley-arr). 1945. full orch. CMC. 1945, Tor, Pop conc, TS, Ernest MacMillan.

Fantasy on Scottish Melodies (orig. *A St Andrew's Day Medley*). 1946. 7′5″. full orch. CMC. Nov 29, 1946, Tor, CBC, TS, Ernest MacMillan.

BAND

Fanfare for a Festival. 1959. 40″. brass, perc. CMC. 1959, Vanc, Opening of Queen Elizabeth Theatre, Ernest MacMillan.

Fanfare for a Centennial. 1967. 50″. brass, perc. CMC. July 3, 1967, Tor, CBC Fest Conc, Victor Feldbrill.

STRING ORCHESTRA

Two Sketches for String Orchestra, based on French Canadian airs. 1927. 7′6″. OUP, 1928. Odyssey Y31993. 1927 (str qt version), Quebec, HH Qt.

CHOIR WITH ORCHESTRA

Ode – 'England'. 1914–18. c60′. sop, bar, SSAATTBB, full orch. Novl. Text: Swinburne. Mar 17, 1921, Chorus & Orch Sheffield Musical Union, Henry Coward.

Te Deum Laudamus in E Minor. 1936. 7′45″. sop, alto, ten, bs, SATB, full orch. CMC. 1936, Tor, Tor Cons Choir, TS, Ernest MacMillan.

A Song of Deliverance. 1944. 5′30″. SATB, orch (org). OUP, 1945. Text: Old 124th – Scottish Psalter 1650. Tor, T Mend, TS, Ernest MacMillan.

CHOIR

I Heard a Voice from Heaven. c mid-1920s. SSAA. ms.

Au Cabaret/At the Inn. 1928. TTBB. Boston, 1928. Trans: John Murray Gibbon.

Blanche comme la neige/White as Cometh the Snowflake. 1928 (rev 1958). 7′. TTBB. Boston, 1928. SATB. GVT, 1968 (rev SATB version). Trans: John Murray Gibbon. RCA LSC-3154.

C'est la belle Françoise/The Fair Françoise. 1928. TTBB. Boston, 1928. Trans: John Murray Gibbon.

Dans tous les cantons/In all the Country Round. 1928. TTBB. Boston, 1928. Trans: John Murray Gibbon.

God Save the Queen (arr – 3 verses). 1934. SATB, full orch (pno). FH, 1934 (choral score only).

O Canada! (arr). SATB, full orch or str orch or band or pno. WR, 1930. Text: Adolphe Routhier. Trans: John W Garvin.

The King shall rejoice in Thy Strength. SATB, org. FH, 1935.

Land of the Maple Leaf (arr) c1943. SATB, pno. GVT, 1943. Text: Charles Venn Pilcher.

Recessional. 1928 (arr SATB 1951). SATB, pno. ms. Text: Rudyard Kipling.

VOICE(S)

Du bist wie eine Blume. 1913. vc, pno. ms. Text: Heinrich Heine.

O Mistress Mine. 1917. vc, pno. ms. Text: Shakespeare.

Three Songs for high baritone from 'The Countess Cathleen'. 1917. vc, pno. ms. Text: W B Yeats.

Songs from Sappho (only the first extant). 1920. vc, pno. ms. Text: Bliss Carman.

That Holy Thing. 1925. vc, pno. ms. Text: George McDonald.

Sonnet. 1928. vc, pno. FH, 1928. Text: Elizabeth Barrett Browning.

Three Indian Songs of the West Coast (arr). 1928. vc, pno. FH. Trans: Duncan Campbell Scott.

Vingt-et-une chansons canadiennes (arr of 9 songs). 1928. unis, pno. FH, 1928.

Recessional. 1928. vc, pno. Dent, 1929. Text: Rudyard Kipling.

Last Prayer. vc, pno. Boston, 1929. Text: Christina Rossetti.

Padded Footsteps. 1930s? vc, pno. ms. Text: Arthur Bourinot.

(16) *Northland Songs No 2* (arr). 1938. vc, pno. GVT, 1938. Text: John Murray Gibbon.

Canadian Boat Song (arr). vc, pno. GVT, 1941. Text: Thomas Moore.

(9) *Ballads of B.C.* (arr). vc, pno. GVT, 1947. Text: John Murray Gibbon.

Also a number of settings for vc and pno mostly of French-Canadian folk songs, including the 42 songs comprising 'Jongleur Songs of Old Quebec' (Rutgers, 1962), ed. Barbeau. 1958. ms.

VOICE(S) WITH INSTRUMENTAL ENSEMBLE

I Sing of a Maiden. 1925. 1'25". vc, str trio (pno). FH, 1927. 1926.

The Storke. 1925. 2'5". vc, str trio (pno). FH, 1927. 1926.

Six Bergerettes du bas Canada (arr). 1928. 18'. sop, alto, ten, 4 instr. OUP, 1935. Trans: Mrs Hugh Ross. 1928, Quebec.

Three French-Canadian Sea Songs (arr). 1930. 8'. med vc, str qt or str orch. CMC. 1930, Vanc, Fest of the Sea.

There was an old woman (style of J.S.B.). med vc, str. CMC. 1945, Tor, TS, Ernest MacMillan(cond), George Lambert.

INSTRUMENTAL ENSEMBLE

String Quartet in C Minor. 1914 (rev 1921). 25'. CMC. DGG-139 900 Ster. 1924, U of T, Hart House, Conc for British Ass'n for the Advancement of Science, HH Qt, Geza de Kresz and Harry Adaskin(vlns), Milton Blackstone(vla), Boris Hambourg(vlc).

Fugue for String Quartet. 1917. ms.

Fugue for String Quartet on a Theme of B. J. Dale. 1917. ms.

Two Sketches for String Quartet, based on French Canadian airs. 1927. 7'6". OUP, 1928. DGG-139 900 Ster. 1927, Quebec, HH Qt.

PIANO

D'où viens-tu bergère (arr). pno 4 hands. GVT, 1958.

ORGAN

Cortège Académique. 1953. 4'35". Novl, 1957.

BIBLIOGRAPHY

See B-B; B58,65,71; Bec57,70; Bt; C63,66, 69,72; Cr; CrC(I); D157,165; Esc; Ip; K; Lv; Mce; R12; Wa; Ww62,69,72.

Barbeau, Marius. 'The Thunder Bird of the Mountains', *University of Toronto Quarterly.* Vol. II, no. 1, Oct. 1932 (92–110).

Bryant, Giles. 'In practically every facet of the most spiritual of the arts we would be weaker in opportunity, tradition and environment, but for this man', *Music: AGO-RCCO Magazine.* Vol. III, no. 2, Feb. 1969 (22–3, 42).

Hamilton, H. C. 'Ernest Campbell MacMillan', *Musical Canada.* Oct. 1928.

Hannon, Leslie. 'The Elegant Enigma of Sir Ernest', *Mayfair Magazine.* Feb. 1953.

Kraglund, John. 'Sir Ernest's 75th: Special Musical Celebration', *CanCo.* No. 35, Dec. 1968 (12–13).

McCready, Louise G. *Famous Musicians: MacMillan, Johnson, Pelletier, Willan.* Toronto, Clarke, Irwin Ltd, 1957 (3–28).

MacKelcan, Fred R. 'Sir Ernest MacMillan', *Queen's Quarterly.* Vol. XLIII, Winter 1936–7 (408–14).

MacMillan, (Lady) Elsie. 'Life with Ernest', *TSO News.* Vol. III, no. 1, Oct. 1949 (5).

'MacMillan, Sir Ernest (Campbell)', *Current Biography.* Vol. XVI, no. 3, Mar. 1955 (391–3).

McStay, Angus. 'Prodigy's Progress', *Maclean's.* Vol. LIII, Oct. 1940 (16, 36–9).

Muir, Mary Dale. 'Music – Sir Ernest MacMillan resigns Conservatory Principalship', *University of Toronto monthly.* Oct. 1942 (10).

Peek, Elizabeth. 'Sir Ernest MacMillan', *The Canadian Red Cross Junior*. Vol. XXI, no. 6, June 1942 (6–7).

Ridout, Godfrey. 'Sir Ernest MacMillan: An Appraisal', *Canadian Music Educator*. Vol. VI, 1964–5 (39–48). Article reprinted from *MAC*. Vol. I, no. 6, July-Aug. 1963.

'Sir Ernest MacMillan 1893–1973', *CanCo*. No. 82, July 1973. (This issue is devoted entirely to Sir Ernest MacMillan, containing articles describing his various musical activities and achievements, written by Canadians such as: Robertson Davies, Kenneth Peacock, Charles Peaker, Godfrey Ridout, etc.; organized in the same format as *MAC*, July-Aug. 1963, containing some duplications of articles and contributors, etc.)

'Sir Ernest MacMillan', *CanCo*. No. 45, Dec. 1969 (26–7).

'Testimonial Dinner sponsored by CAPAC', *CanCo*. No. 42, Sept. 1969 (24–5).

'Thousands Pay Tribute to Sir Ernest in Massey Hall', *PAC*. Vol. VI, no. 2, 1969 (18–19).

'A Tribute to Sir Ernest MacMillan', *CBC Times*. Nov. 23–9, 1968 (4, 6).

'A Tribute to Sir Ernest MacMillan', *MAC*. Vol. I, no. 6, July-Aug. 1963. (This issue, like *CanCo*, no. 82, 1973, is devoted entirely to Sir Ernest MacMillan. Besides articles describing the various musical activities and achievements of MacMillan, there is a chronological survey of his life, as well as a bibliography listing some of his writings.)

LITERARY WORKS

BOOKS

Music in Canada (ed.). Toronto: University of Toronto Press, 1955.

On the Preparation of Ear Tests. Toronto: Frederick Harris, 1931.

Twenty Lessons in Ear Training – Grades I to VI (with Boris Berlin). Toronto: Frederick Harris, 1939.

ARTICLES

'After Edinburgh – Home Thoughts from Abroad', *Saturday Night*. Vol. LXVIII, Oct. 25, 1952 (28).

"Canada" in 'America', *Gmu* (43–6).

'Canada's Voice – The Canadian Music Centre', *PAC*. Vol. I, no. 1, Mar. 1961 (6–7).

'The Canadian Music Council', *CMJ*. Vol. I, no. 1, 1956 (3–6).

'Canadian Music and Its Place in the Music of the New World', Unpublished Paper delivered at the Institute of Inter-American Affairs, Columbia University, New York, Oct. 10, 1942.

'Canadian Musical Life', *Canadian Geographical Journal*. Vol. XIX, Dec. 1939 (330–9).

'Choral and Church Music', *Conservatory Quarterly Review*. Vol. XI, Winter 1929 (57, 59).

'Choral Music', *Mm* (79–91).

'Emmy Heim', *Royal Conservatory Bulletin*. Nov. 1954.

'Festival Report – Edinburgh's Varied Offerings', *Saturday Night*. Vol. LXVIII, Oct. 18, 1952 (23–5).

'A Few Aphorisms', *Conservatory Quarterly Review*. Vol. VII, no. 2, 1925.

'The Folk Song Festival at Quebec ... Some Impressions', *Conservatory Quarterly Review*. Vol. IX, Summer 1927 (130).

'Foreword' to *Kh* (v–vi).

'Healey Willan as I Have Known Him', *American Organist*. Aug. 1960.

'Hitler and Wagnerism', *Queen's Quarterly*. Vol. XLVIII, no. 2, 1941 (97–105).

'Hymns and Hymn Singing', *Diapason*. Oct. 1, 1929 (32–3).

'Impressions of the Lausanne Conference', *Conservatory Quarterly Review*. Vol. XIV, no. 1, 1931 (6).

'Marius Barbeau: His Work', *Canadian Author and Bookman*. Vol. XXXVIII, no. 2, Winter 1962 (10).

'Music in Canada', *Calendar of the Royal College of Organists*. 1936–7.

'Music in Canada', *Royal Commission on National Development in the Arts, Letters and Sciences, 1949–51*. Ottawa: Royal Commission Studies, 1951 (353–67).

'Music in Canadian Universities', *CMJ*. Vol. II, no. 3, 1958 (3–11).

'Music at the Education Conference', *Conservatory Quarterly Review*. Vol. VIII, Spring 1926 (85–7).

'Music and the Sea', *Imperial Oil Fleet News*. Spring 1956.

'Music and the Summer – Why not Canadian Festivals?', *Saturday Night*. Vol. LXVIII, Oct. 4, 1952 (10, 18).

'Music: Concert Performance', *Encyclopedia Canadiana*. Vol. VII, 1958 (222–8).

'Music in Wartime', *Music Bulletin*. No. 10, OUP, Oct. 15, 1942.

'The Music is Alive', *Saturday Review*. Oct. 24, 1959 (23).
'Musical Composition in Canada', *Culture*. Vol. III, 1942 (149–54).
'Musical Relations between Canada and the U.S.A.', *Proceedings of the Music Teachers' National Association*. 1931 (39–44).
'The Musical Season in Toronto', *Canadian Forum*. May 1928 (642–3).
'Orchestral and Choral Music in Canada', *Proceedings of the Music Teachers' National Association*. 1946 (87–117).
'Organ Accompaniments in Church Services (Part I)', *Conservatory Quarterly Review*. Vol. XIII, no. 2, 1931 (46).
'Organ Accompaniments in Church Services (Part II)', *Conservatory Quarterly Review*. Vol. XIII, no. 3, 1931 (109).
'The Organ was my First Love', *CMJ*. Vol. III, no. 3, 1959 (15–25).
'Our Musical Public', *Canadian Forum*. July 1924 (306–8).
'The Outlook for Canadian Music', *International Musician*. Oct. 1948.
'Problems of Music in Canada', *Yearbook of the Arts in Canada* (Bertram Brooker, ed.). Vol. II, 1936 (185–200).
'Reminiscences of Marius Barbeau', *Mu*. No. 18, Apr. 1969 (10, 11, 15).
'Sir Ernest and "Maple Leaf"', *Saturday Night*. Vol. LXVI, July 11, 1950 (4).
'Some Notes on Schubert', *The School*. Vol. XVI, no. 2, Oct. 1927 (120–5).
'Some Problems of the Canadian Composer', *Dalhousie Review*. Vol. XXXVI, 1956 (130–43).
'Three Notable British Composers', *Conservatory Quarterly Review*. Vol. XVI, Aug. 1934 (5–9).
'The University and Music', *University of Toronto Quarterly*. Mar. 1926 (263–4).
'We Need Music', *Chatelaine*. Vol. XV, Dec. 1942.
'What is Good Music?', *New York Herald Tribune Sunday Forum*. May 21, 1961, Section 2 (3).
'What Shall We Do With a Hundred Million?', *Crescendo*. Vol. II, no. 3, Apr. 1959 (3, 15).

REVIEWS

Barbeau, Marius and Edward Sapir. *Folk Songs of French Canada, Canadian Forum*. Dec. 1925 (79–82).
Barbeau, Marius. *Le Rossignol y Chante, Canadian Author and Bookman*. Vol. 38, no. 2, Winter 1962 (11, 13).
d'Harcourt, Marguérite and Raoul. *Chansons folkloriques françaises au Canada, CMJ*. Vol. I, no. 2, 1957 (77, 79).
Hutchings, Arthur. *Delius: A Critical Biography, University of Toronto Quarterly*. Jan. 1949 (210–12).
Myers, Robert Manson. *Handel's Messiah: A Touchstone of Taste, University of Toronto Quarterly*. Jan. 1949 (210–12).
Sharp, Cecil (ed.). *English Folk Songs, CMJ*. Vol. V, no. 1, Autumn 1960 (73–7).
Shaw, Watkins (ed.). *G. F. Handel: Messiah, CMJ*. Vol. IV, no. 2, Winter 1960 (57–60).
Vaughan Williams, R. and A. L. Lloyd (eds). *The Penguin Book of English Folk Songs, CMJ*. Vol. V, no. 1, Autumn 1960 (73–7).

MacNUTT, WALTER (b. Charlottetown, P.E.I., 2 June 1910). He studied at the Toronto Conservatory with Reginald Godden (piano) and Healey WILLAN (organ and composition). He was organist at Holy Trinity Church in Toronto until 1942 before serving in the Canadian Army (1942–6). He was organist at All Saints' Church in Winnipeg (1946–9), at All Saints' Church in Windsor (1949–53), and since 1953 at St Thomas' Church in Toronto. MacNutt has arranged and composed mainly for the church (choral, organ, and solo vocal pieces), his music being in a traditional, conservative style. His many choral works – including anthems, masses, and arrangements of folk songs (for example *Ride On! Ride On in Majesty!*, 1935; *Behold A Mighty Prelate*, 1968; *Missa Brevis in D Major*, 1962; *The Streets of Laredo*) – have been published by Berandol and by Waterloo Music Company, and his many songs, including *By Cool Siloam's Shady Rill* and *Two Songs of William Blake from 'Songs of Innocence'*, are published by Frederick Harris, Leeds, and Berandol. He is affiliated with BMI Canada.

BIBLIOGRAPHY

See B-B; K.

MANN, LESLIE (b. Edmonton, Alta, 13 Aug. 1923). He began to teach himself the clarinet at the age of thirteen and to compose at nineteen. At the end of the Second World War he was awarded a scholarship to study at the Royal Academy of Music in London, England, but returned to Canada instead. He studied in Toronto and later became a free-lance musician. In 1957 two concerts devoted entirely to his music were arranged at the Royal Conservatory of Music, Toronto. In 1958 he moved to Winnipeg as principal clarinetist of the Winnipeg Symphony Orchestra.

Mann's early style is similar to that of English music at the turn of the century (Vaughan Williams and Holst, for example). *Elegy for Strings* (1951) is tonal, with some chromatic alteration. However, his cantata *My Master Hath a Garden* (1963) uses dissonant tonality and his *Concerto for Clarinet and Orchestra* (1970) and *Orchestral Suite* from 'The Donkey's Tale' (1971) uses chromatic polytonal material, which becomes dissonant to the point of atonality.

In 1965 Mann received a commission from the Wednesday Morning Musicale (*Trio for Clarinet, Cello and Piano*). He is a former member of the Canadian League of Composers and a member of CAPAC.

MUSICAL WORKS

STAGE

The Donkey's Tale, Op 25 (chamb opera). 1971.

INSTRUMENTAL

8 works for orch: *Concertino in the Old Style*, Op 11 (1955) str orch; *Prelude and Fugue*, Op 12 (1955) sm orch; *Concerto for Flute and Orchestra*, Op 21 (1964); *Concerto for Clarinet and Orchestra*, Op 24 (1970); *Orchestral Suite from 'The Donkey's Tale'* (1971); *Sinfonia Concertante for Bassoon and Chamber Orchestra*, Op 27 (1971); *Concerto Grosso for Chamber Orchestra*, Op 30 (1972); *Meditation on a Chorale*, Op 31 (1972).

11 works for chamber ensemble: *Five Bagatelles*, Op 3 (1951) cl (vla), vlc; *Trio*, Op 6 (1952) fl, cl, vlc; *Sonata*, Op 5 (1953) vlc, pno; *Five Improvisations for Flute and Piano*, Op 10 (1954) RCA CC/CCS-1009; *Toccata alla Barocco*, Op 15 (1956) fl, cl, vlc; *Wind Quintet* (1961); *Sonata*, Op 17 (1962) cl (vla), pno; *Trio*, Op 22 (1967) cl, vlc, pno; *Four Studies in the Blues Idiom*, Op 23 (1969) ww qnt; *Music for Clarinet, Viola and Piano*, Op 26 (1971); *Partita for Violin and Bassoon*, Op. 28 (1972).

4 works for solo piano: *Five Lyrical Preludes*, Op 16 (1958); *Little Suite in the Old Style* (1963); *Preludes and Fugues*, Op 29 (1972); *Meditations on a Chorale*, Op 31 (1972).

2 suites: for cello solo, Op 20a (1963); for flute solo, Op 20b (1963).

VOCAL

Album of Songs, Op 9, Op 13. 1954–5. sop (ten), pno.

My Master Hath a Garden, Op 19 (cantata). 1963. sop (ten), chamb orch.

Three Songs to Poems of Shakespeare, Op 23a. 1967. mezz, cl.

BIBLIOGRAPHY

'Manitoba Composers: A Collective Voice', *CanCo.* No. 52, Sept. 1970 (16).

MATHER, BRUCE (b. Toronto, Ont., 9 May 1939). Though a contemplative artist and of a reticent manner, Bruce Mather may be reckoned as one of the strongest personalities in Canadian music, as composer, as teacher, and as one of Canada's leading keyboard practitioners of new music. He began playing the piano at six and composing at seven. As a more mature student he studied piano with Alberto Guerrero and composition with Godfrey RIDOUT, Oskar MORAWETZ, and John WEINZWEIG at the Royal Conservatory and the Faculty of Music, University of Toronto, receiving his Bachelor of Music degree in 1959. In the summers of 1957 and 1958 he attended the Aspen Music School in Colorado, studying piano with Alexander Uninsky, who introduced him to Darius Milhaud. A Canada Council Arts Scholarship (1959-60) enabled him to study at the Paris Conservatoire with Milhaud (composition), Simone Plé-Caussade (counterpoint and fugue), Lazare Lévy (piano), and Olivier Messiaen (analysis); in 1961–2 he received a French government scholarship for further study in Paris. He also spent brief periods of study with Leland Smith (1962–4) and Roy Harris (composition), Pierre Boulez (conducting, summer of 1969), and at the Darmstadt Festival and summer course in new music (1960). In 1964 he received a Master of Arts degree from Stanford University and in 1967 his doctorate in music from the University of Toronto. Besides numerous scholarships at the Royal Conservatory, he received a junior CAPAC composition award (1949) and two senior CAPAC awards. Other awards include a Women's Musical Club of Toronto award (1957), the Beta Sigma Phi International Sorority scholarship (1958), the Norma Capley Foundation (Chicago) award (1960), and the Kurt Weill Foundation award (1963).

As a professor full time at McGill University (since 1966) and part time at the Université de Montréal (since 1970), Mather has provided a musical link between the two Canadian cultures. He has been a leading spirit in the Société de musique contemporaine du Québec (SMCQ), where he has always supported a broad international outlook. As an excellent solo and ensemble pianist and as conductor he plays an important performing role in several concert organizations at the two universities as well as in the SMCQ, insisting on the highest standards of performance for the works of students and established composers alike. Thus all the various facets of his musical experience – composer, performer, teacher, and administrator – are fused into one personality.

Mather much prefers 'music to be listened to', rather than 'music to be looked at' (citing Cage) or 'music to be analysed', with its 'endless stream of pseudo-scientific jargon' (citing Babbitt). Listening to music ante-dating 1870 is to him 'an academic exercise', and although recognizing the great qualities of Beethoven, for example, he remains 'untouched by his music, as it is too far removed from the type of expression that interests me'. Few composers are admitted as his 'favourites', although Scriabin, Delius, and Szymanowski have been mentioned (all three having been as interested in French culture, be it noted, as is Mather himself). Beyond these three, however, he prefers to select individual works (or cycles) rather than any composer's general output – works of Messiaen, Boulez, or Berio for example. Nevertheless his judgements are categoric. When asked a question he will reflect carefully before giving a characteristically terse and clear answer. In describing a salient feature of his music, one may expand upon a phrase from his own notes to his *Music for Organ, Horn and Gongs* (1973): 'The image of inexorable waves, overlapping and engulfing, accounts for large sections of the work....' Waves overlapping, engulfing; transitions from one sound to another, from one instrument to another; the unbreakable continuity where new structures are born almost inaudibly. Suddenly the timpani emerge – but their sound was already there before we were aware of it in the slow beat-patterns of soft, low-pitched organ stops. Beats, rhythms, timbres, colours – one could easily associate them with the title of Messiaen's 'Chronochromie', which simply refers to time and colour.

A similar description could also apply to Mather's series of five *Madrigals* (1967–73). Usually for one or two female voices with various chamber ensembles, they provide the backbone of Mather's output to date. Again the transformation of timbre is a dominating feature – the almost imperceptible transitions, for example, in *Madrigal III* (1971) between marimba, harp, and piano.

The Madrigal series is lyric music, true chamber music for contemplation and meditation inspired by poems of the Canadian poet Saint-Denys-Garneau, whose texts are used in the first four of the five (in *Madrigal V*, 1973, the voices are used without text). *Madrigal IV* (1972, for flute, soprano, piano, and tape) is based exclusively on a sentence from Garneau's poetry: 'Et mon regard part en chasse effrénément de cette splendeur qui s'en va, qui s'échappe par les fissures du temps.' A short text, few words, a breath, in the spirit of an epigrammatic Japanese poem – Mather's music serves as a subtle ink drawing around the poem.

The same spirit also prevails in many of Mather's other solo or ensemble works. His *Sonata for Two Pianos* (written in 1970 for the Winnipeg duo-piano team, Boyd McDonald and Garth Beckett) is a refined conversation between the two instruments, where phrases are sometimes chain-linked to each other. This seems dense on paper, perhaps, but gives quite a different effect when the two instruments are spaced far apart, as the score indicates: the real tensions of the dialogue are thus revealed.

Describing his *a cappella* choral work *La Lune mince* (1965, text by Paul Valéry), Mather speaks of a 'basic harmonic network, consisting of four augmented triads separated by minor thirds'. This short technical description of the basic harmonic texture does little to anticipate the transparent, beautiful vocal music in the vibrating atmosphere that emerges from the poem. The very end of the composition almost becomes a musical interpretation of the words 'la lune mince' – a soft decay like the tapering ends of the crescent moon. This harmonic world, the basic harmonic network of augmented triads and minor thirds, is exploited with extensive use of *divisi*, a technique that is of course quite normal in choral music; contemporary *a cappella* works by Messiaen, Malec, or Xenakis, for instance, give the impression of being for many solo voices rather than chorally blended compositions in the traditional sense. However, the shifting densities of *La Lune mince* create a multidimensional perspective in a true choral sound.

The multidimensional effect is encountered also in *Madrigal IV*, where a prerecorded tape presents the same kind of sound as do the live performers on stage but directed through loudspeakers to provide a layered counterpoint on various dynamic levels, with or without reverberation, creating illusions of distance or nearness. Continuity is achieved by a basic harmonic network similar to that used in other works, in this case two consecutive minor sixths (D-sharp, B, G) that create an almost static, peaceful mood with rapid interpolated passages, like ripplings on the surface of a placid lake.

This attempt to catch a mood in a harmonic nucleus, though not yet elaborated into a 'basic network', is already apparent in a short piano piece written almost at the beginning of his career, *Smaragdin* (1960), a score for an abstract animated film of Jean Letarte. This piece remains Mather's only contribution to film. There is none for the stage.

However, inspiration from other arts is frequently seen in a number of works based on texts. In 1960 Mather composed another piano piece, *Like Snow*, 'A musical representation of a poem by Robert Graves'. He also set texts by the same poet in *Three Songs* for soprano and string orchestra (1957–8); *Sick Love* (1960–1, for soprano and large orchestra); *The Song of Blodeuwedd* (1961, for baritone, percussion, harp, piano, and strings), and the *Lament for Pasiphaë* (1962, for small mixed chorus, brass, percussion, celesta, harp, piano, and strings). In fact the latter three, from 1960–2, along with *Like Snow*, were originally conceived as parts of a cantata, *The White Goddess* (the title of Robert Graves' famous book on mythology).

In 1963 Mather composed *Orphée*, for soprano, percussion, and piano, based on the Paul Valéry poem. The first performance took place in December in San Francisco with the composer at the piano and John Chowning (a student colleague of Mather, later a well-known expert on computer and electronic music) as the percussionist.

Mather's absent-minded, somewhat nervous manner might be taken to reinforce his own contention that he is a 'disorganized person'. But beneath this façade he is very well organized indeed, whether in his teaching, in his administrative duties, or in his composition. His carefully methodical approach, coupled with his fine aural sensitivity, are well exemplified in a work written in 1971 at the request of the mandolinist William Kuinka. Although Mather would much rather have used the mandolin with guitar and harp, Kuinka insisted on the immiscible combination of mandolin and piano. In *Mandola* Mather has created a work with thoroughly idiomatic mandolin and piano parts that manage to blend into an indisputable whole.

When commissioned by the Faculty of Music, University of Toronto, to write a work for the inauguration of the Faculty's new organ, Mather wrote *Music for Organ, Horn and Gongs* (gongs here meaning a wide variety of metallic resonating instruments). As a one-time horn player he knows the horn well, but the organ was a new experience, although his long acquaintance with William Albright, William Bolcom, and Mireille Lagacé had given him some insight into its potentialities in inventive hands. Experimenting over a considerable period on a similar instrument in Montreal, and approaching the organ more as soundsource than as the traditional keyboard instrument that it is, he created a work, among the most interesting in the contemporary organ repertoire, that deserves acceptance.

Mather the composer should not be allowed completely to overshadow Mather the pianist. As solo performer of such composers as Albeniz, Scriabin, Crumb, or of his own works, or with his wife Pierrette Lepage in two-piano duo, his performances are outstanding. This writer will long remember the magic atmosphere felt in the small concert hall of the Mount Orford Music Centre in Quebec in the summer of 1972 with their playing of Mather's own *Sonata for Two Pianos*. Such moments are rare.

Bruce Mather is a member of the Canadian League of Composers and of CAPAC.

BENGT HAMBRAEUS

MUSICAL WORKS

FILM

Smaragdin (music for abstract animated film of Jean Letarte, Mtl). 1960. 4′. pno. CMC.

ORCHESTRA

Symphonic Ode; 'Catromjep 1964'. 1964. 7′40″. full orch. CMC. Mar 28, 1965, Tor, CBC, TS, Walter Susskind.

Orchestra Piece 1967. 1966 (rev 1969). 15′. full orch. CMC. Jan 11, 1967, Tor, TS, Jean Deslauriers.

Ombres. 1967. 5′30″. full orch. CMC. May 1, 1968, MSO, Pierre Hétu.

SMALL ORCHESTRA

Music for Vancouver. 1969. 11′. CMC. CBC BR SM-143. Sept 17, 1969, Vanc, CBC Fest, CBC Vanc Ch O, John Avison.

STRING ORCHESTRA

Musique pour Rouen. 1971. 10′. CMC. June 9, 1971, Rouen, France, Orchestre de Chambre de Rouen, J S Béreau.

SOLOIST(S) WITH ORCHESTRA

Two Songs for Bass-Baritone and Orchestra. 1956–9. 8′. ms. Text: Thomas Hardy. Apr 20, 1958, RCMT O, Ettore Mazzoleni(cond), James Whicher(bar).

Three Songs to Poems of Robert Graves. 1958. 13′. sop, str orch. CMC.

Concerto for Piano and Orchestra. 1958. 6′. pno, ww qnt, str qt. CMC. Aug 20, 1958, Aspen, Colo student ens, Bruce Mather (pno).

Elegy for Saxophone and Strings. 1959. 6′. Wat, 1965. Golden Crest RE7037. 1966, Quebec, L'Orchestre de Chambre de Québec, Sylvio Lacharité(cond), Pierre Bourque(sax).

Sick Love (part III of cantata 'The White Goddess'). 1961. 6′. sop, full orch. CMC. Text: Robert Graves.

The Song of Blodeuwedd (part II of cantata 'The White Goddess'). 1961. 6′. bar, perc, hp, pno, str. CMC. Text: Robert Graves.

CHOIR WITH ORCHESTRA

Lament for Pasiphaë (part IV of cantata 'The White Goddess'). 1962. 5′. small SATB choir, orch. CMC. Text: Robert Graves. Apr, 1963, Stanford, Cal The Stanford Chorale and Ch O, Bruce Mather.

CHOIR

La Lune mince. 1965. 7′. SATB. CMC. Poly 2917 009. Text: Paul Valéry. Apr 2, 1970, Mtl, Tudor Sgrs of Mtl, Wayne Riddell.

VOICE

Cycle Rilke. 1960. 8′30″. vc, guit. CMC. Text: Rainer Maria Rilke. Apr 20, 1960, Paris, RTF, Jeanne Héricard(sop), Jurgen Klatt(guit).

VOICE(S) WITH INSTRUMENTAL ENSEMBLE

Venice. 1957. 9′. sop, cl, vlc, pno. CMC. Text: Lord Byron. Aug 23, 1957, Aspen, Colo, Catherina Gayer(sop), William Kleinschmidt(cl), Robert Perry(vlc,) Bruce Mather(pno).

Orphée. 1963. 12′40″. sop, pno, perc. CMC. RCI-217, RCA CC/CCS-1011. Text: Paul Valéry. Dec 14, 1963, San Francisco, Anna Carol Dudley(sop), Bruce Mather(pno), John Chowning(perc).

Madrigal I. 1967. 5′. sop, alto, fl, mand, hp, vln, vlc. CMC. Text: St-Denys-Garneau. Apr 16, 1967, Tor, TCC, Mary Morrison (sop), Patricia Rideout(alto), Robert Aitken (fl), Judy Loman(hp), William Kuinka (mand), Andrew Benac(vln), Donald Whitton(vlc).

Madrigal II. 1968. 10′. sop, alto, fl, hp, vln, vla, vlc. Jobert, Paris. 1970. Text: St-Denys-Garneau. July 27, 1968, Stratford Fest, Margaret Zeidman(sop), Muriel Greenspon(alto).

Madrigal III. 1971. 20′. alto, hp, mar, pno. CMC. Text: St-Denys-Garneau. July 21,

1971, Toronto, EJB, MacM Th, CBC Fest, Patricia Rideout(alto), Judy Loman(hp), Robin Engelman(mar), Bruce Mather(pno).
Madrigal IV. 1972. 11'45". sop, fl, pno. CMC. Text: St-Denys-Garneau. Apr 13, 1973, Mtl, LAT, Robert Aitken(fl), Mary Morrison(sop), Marion Ross(pno).

INSTRUMENTAL ENSEMBLE

Sonata. 1956. 5'45". vln, pno. CMC.
Mandola. 1971. 9'. mand, pno. CMC. Feb 25, 1972, Tor, William Kuinka(mand), John Hawkins(pno).

PIANO

Like Snow. 1960. 4'. CMC. June 1, 1961, Paris, Bruce Mather.
Mystras. 1962. 6'45". CMC. June 1962, Paris, Bruce Mather.
Fantasy 1964. 1964 (rev 1967). 7'10". CMC. CBC BR SM-48. Nov 22, 1964, CBC, Bruce Mather.
Sonata for Two Pianos. 1970. 14'55". CMC. RCI-354. Oct 14, 1970, U of Man, Boyd McDonald, Garth Beckett.

INSTRUMENTAL SOLO

Etude pour clarinette seule. 1962. 5'29". CMC. CBC BR SM-184. Jan 1963, Stanford U.

BIBLIOGRAPHY

B65,71; Bec70; Esc; Wa.
'Bruce Mather', *Musiques du Kébèk* (R. Duguay, ed.). Montreal: Editions du Jour, 1971 (103–7).
'Bruce Mather – a portrait', *Mu*. No. 11, May 1968 (8–9).
'Bruce Mather: Teacher, Pianist, Secretary, Composer', *CanCo*. No. 49, Apr. 1970 (4–9).
Grenier, Albert. *Sonate pour deux pianos de Bruce Mather*. Unpublished thesis, University of Montreal, 1971.
Stone, Kurt. 'Review of Records', *MQ*. Vol. VIII, no. 3 (440–52).
'The 20th Century is Not Too Bad ...', *CanCo*. No. 2, Aug. 1965 (8, 38).

LITERARY WORKS

ARTICLES

'Le collage musical: "Remembrances" de John Hawkins', *CMB*. Vol. III, Autumn-Winter 1971 (98–102).
'Notes sur "Requiems for the Party-Girl" ', *CMB*. Vol. I, Spring-Summer 1970 (91–7).
'Pierre Boulez: "Structures pour deux pianos (2e livre)" ', *Musiques du Kébèc* (R. Duguay, ed.). Montreal: Editions du Jour, 1971 (108).
'La Société de musique contemporaine du Québec', *Mu*. No 25, Dec. 1969 (6–7).

MATHIEU, ANDRÉ (b. Montreal, Que., 18 Feb. 1929; d. Montreal, 2 June 1968). The son of Rodolphe MATHIEU, André showed a remarkable talent for piano and composition at an early age. In 1935 he gave his first recital in Montreal and the following year received a scholarship from the Quebec government. In Paris he studied composition with Jacques de la Presle and piano with Yves Nat and Mme Giraud-Latarse; he gave a recital at the Chopin-Pleyel Hall in December 1936. Sénart published six of his compositions for piano, and Mathieu recorded them himself (BAM 26). In March 1939 he gave a recital at Gaveau Hall at which time critics compared him to the young Mozart. On his return to Canada he performed in several cities and attracted the attention of New York critics after a recital in Town Hall in February 1940. He pursued his studies there in composition with Harold Morris. He participated in a concert for the League of Composers and in February 1942 was proclaimed winner of the first prize in a competition for young composers, organized by the New York Philharmonic on the occasion of its centennial celebration. He played his award-winning piece, the *Concertino No. 2 pour piano et orchestre,* at Carnegie Hall on February 21 under the direction of Rudolph Ganz (the preceding year he had performed it in Montreal under the baton of Sir Thomas Beecham). He gave numerous concerts in Canada and the United States and, in November 1945, when he was only sixteen, gave a concert in Windsor Hall in Montreal devoted entirely to his own compositions. A third concerto for piano and orchestra was composed in 1948 for a broadcast in France through the International Service of the CBC. A condensed version was used for a Canadian film and became popular under the title 'Concerto de Québec'. Mathieu returned to France and stayed there for the 1946–7 season, during which time he took lessons from Arthur Honegger. During the years that followed he was relatively less active and no work of importance dates from his last years.

André Mathieu's works comprise two concertinos for piano and orchestra, a concerto (no. 3), as well as another that remains in sketch form; a sonata for piano and violin; a trio for piano, violin, and cello, a quintet for piano and string quartet, as well as numerous works for piano solo: *Dans la nuit, Danse sauvage, Hommage à Mozart enfant, Les Gros Chars, Les Vagues, Les Mouettes, Saisons canadiennes, Bagatelles, Fantaisie, Laurentienne,* etc. There are also a few songs and some pieces for violin and piano: *Berceuse, Complainte, Fantaisie brésilienne* (the latter published by Parnasse). Taking into consideration the rich promise of Mathieu's youth, it is a matter of great regret that his talent did not flourish to greater advantage in more significant works. Unfortunately his star waned prematurely before he had given the best of himself. GILLES POTVIN

BIBLIOGRAPHY

See B-B; D165; K; Lv.

Corriveau, L. de B. 'André Mathieu', *Canadian Review of Music and Art*. Vol. II, no. 11–12, Dec.–Jan. 1944 (16).

MATHIEU, RODOLPHE (b. Grondines, Portneuf, Que., 10 July 1890; d. Montreal, Que., 29 June 1962). Known initially as the father of a piano and composition prodigy (see MATHIEU, André), Mathieu himself emerged only later as a composer of important and worthwhile works. Born into a cultivated family – his father was an amateur musician – at sixteen he went to live with his three sisters in Montreal, who taught him piano. The following year he was appointed organist of Saint-Jean-Berchmans church; he took singing lessons from Céline Marier and composition from Alexis Contant. In 1908 Céline Marier introduced him to the composer Alfred LALIBERTÉ, who brought him into the circle of Scriabin admirers. His first works followed in the Wagner and Debussy tradition. Between 1908 and 1920 he wrote *Le Poème de la Mer* (1908), a choral work dedicated to Céline Marier; *Chevauchée* (1911) and *Trois Préludes* (1912–15) for piano, played often by the Canadian pianist and critic, Léo-Pol Morin; *Les Yeux noirs* (1911), and *Un peu d'ombre* (1913) for tenor and chamber orchestra, in the Debussy style; and *Lied* (1915) for violin and piano, a chromatic and Wagnerian work but using Debussy techniques. It is not known whether the small orchestra transcription of the *Trois Préludes* dates from before 1920; the piano version is successful, the *Préludes* being brief and witty. The orchestra version demonstrates a remarkable knowledge and talent for orchestration.

On April 24, 1920 Mathieu sailed for France on the *Touraine*, a modest grant from the Saint-Jean-Baptiste Society enabling him to stay in Paris from 1920 to 1927. These years and those that followed were the most productive for the composer. He was stimulated by the musical life of Paris; the world of personalities like Honegger, Vincent d'Indy, Roland-Manuel, Louis Durey, Albert Roussel, and others led him into the musical currents of the day. Probably advised by Léo-Pol Morin, he went to Roussel for lessons. Roussel referred him to the Schola Cantorum, a school that he had founded himself. Mathieu's teachers at the Schola were Vincent d'Indy (composition) and Louis Aubert (orchestration).

During the autumn of 1920 he wrote a string quartet that was performed the following April 2 by the Krettly Quartet under the title of *Pièce pour quatuor à cordes*. The work employs two principal elements, a chromatic melodic line in counterpoint among different instruments, and trills in harmony. Following the Debussy style, it seeks subtle expression and plastic texture. The next work – the *Trio* (1922) for piano, violin, and cello – marks a departure. His previous works had been moving towards freedom from tonality; the *Trio* reveals an urge towards total chromatic organization, along the lines of the preserial experiments of Schoenberg – resolution of a melodic line or a harmonic progression by the exhaustion of the series of twelve sounds, a clearly serial outline of this melodic line. Favourite intervals are the tritone, the minor second, and the major seventh, all intervals designed to avoid an impression of tonality. The idea of consonance or dissonance is replaced by strong or weak intervals; treatment of the basic material is midway between traditional variation and continuous variation. Thematic material can be a cell, a germinal nucleus, giving place to a work of intervals with no clear thematic statement, supported by 'poles' stated at the meeting of sections, these sections having no clearly tonal implication. There is an occasional use of symmetrical modes, approaching those used later by Messiaen, this technique probably derived from Scriabin.

In the *Trio* Mathieu entered a more systematic chromaticism, in this new orientation veering towards serialism. Other works, especially instrumental ones, show the same tendencies. The *Douze Etudes modernes* or *Monologues* for solo violin and the *Vingt-deux Dialogues* for violin and cello (all composed before 1924) are in this vein. The vocal works *Harmonie du Soir* (1924, on the Baudelaire poem), *Saisons canadiennes* (before 1927), and *Symphonie-ballet avec choeurs* (1927) mark a return to the Debussy language and to the romantic Wagnerian esthetic. The one-movement *Sonate pour piano* (1927) is a return to the Scriabin-like writing of *Chevauchée*. More substantial, however, than the latter work, it is interesting for its liveliness, its lyrical quality, and for the craftsmanship that is evident from then on in Mathieu's writing. It is also one of Mathieu's rare works that exploit rhythm.

In 1927 Mathieu returned to Montreal. He taught at the teacher-training school of the Sisters of Sainte-Anne-de-Lachine (1928–33) and then founded the Institut Canadien de Musique which, in addition to teaching, organized concerts (the Soirées Mathieu) and made an annual grant to a student towards costs of studying in Paris. It was at this time that Mathieu began to set down his Tests d'Aptitudes Musicales, finished in 1950. He also organized the *Edition exclusive de Musique canadienne* (1934), which was to record on disc all published scores, although owing to shortage of funds the organization was unable to continue.

The first work written on his return was the *Sonate pour piano et violon* (1928), dedicated to his pupil, the violinist Mimi Gagnon, whom he married the following year. This long sonata, in one movement, is constructed on a single theme; it avoided monotony, however, for Mathieu was a master of his craft. Its atmosphere as much as its language approaches Berg of the years 1910–20. *Deux Poèmes pour chant et quatuor à cordes* (1928), a very chromatic and lyrical work, came next.

After the *Deux Poèmes* Mathieu wrote only one important work, the *Quintette pour piano et cordes* (1942). Probably because he felt so misunderstood by public and critics, he decided to direct his activities towards teaching, concentrating on the training of his son André. Recalling Franck and Fauré, the *Quintette* was an effort to cater to the tastes of audiences, being chromatic but tonal, gay, natural, without originality of structure or a search for new language. Other works of the period were short, vocal, recalling very little of the earlier Mathieu style. His last work, *Symphonie pour voix humaines* (1960), was not completed.

The output of Rodolphe Mathieu is a phenomenon unique in the history of Canadian music. Composed between 1910 and 1930, it is the wilful manifestation of a creative mind impelled to produce regardless of surrounding conditions, a natural talent rich in ideas, straightforward but always searching for new and personal means. His training had equipped him to follow in the French tradition – indeed his music often borrows from the grammar of Debussy. But the lyricism is German, stemming from Wagner via Berg. His art is essentially an art of becoming, without repetition, a mobile art realized through continual development, the atomization of a cell, a very sure sense of progression, an art not lending itself to schools of discipline but establishing rather its own rules in accordance with the work at hand. It involves an improvisatory character, an expression of spontaneity, exuberance, occasionally of abundance. All in all it is a form well suited to his musical temperament.

Mathieu is distinguished among composers before 1940 by his taste for a style oriented towards the new. In removing himself from tonal frameworks, he understood the need to organize new elements of language. Pushed to its limits, expanded tonality became a state of negative things in search of its own forms. This was Mathieu's stage of evolution in 1920, as with Schoenberg. Such an attitude inevitably detached him from musical life in Canada, his gifts not allowing him then to take his place among the pioneers of Canadian contemporary music. During the 1960's, when some of his works were heard again, the young Canadian school had already been born; Mathieu, in spite of his stature, had been unable even to preside at its birth.

Rodolphe Mathieu was a member of CAPAC. JULIETTE BOURASSA-TRÉPANIER

MUSICAL WORKS

ORCHESTRA

Trois Préludes. 1912–15 (arr c1930?). 6′45″. full orch (pno). Hérelle, Paris (pno version). RCI-135 (pno version). Apr 17, 1917, Léo-Pol Morin (pno version).

SOLOIST(S) WITH ORCHESTRA

Un peu d'ombre. 1913. 5′. vc, orch. CMC. Text: Pierre Newton. June 2, 1922, Paris, France, Salle Gaveau, Victor Brault.

Harmonie du soir. 1924. 6′. high vc, vln, orch. CMC. Text: Charles Baudelaire. Paris, France, Lamoureux Orch, Paul Paray (cond), Rodolphe Plamondon(sgr).

Concerto pour piano. 1955 (incomplete; no orchestral score).

Mélodies. 8′. vc, orch. ms.

CHOIR WITH ORCHESTRA

Symphonie-ballet avec choeurs. 1927 (incomplete; 2 mov'ts completed out of a projected 4 mov'ts). ms. Text: Rodolphe Mathieu.

Lève-toi, Canadien. 1934. 8′. SATB (vc), orch or band (opt). Edition de musique canadienne, 1934. Text & Trans: Rodolphe Mathieu. Oct 25, 1934, Mtl, Orpheon Choir, Arthur Laurendeau(dir).

CHOIR

Le Poème de la Mer. 1908. ms. Text: Rodolphe Mathieu.

Sanctus et Benedictus. 1931. SATB or 2part, org. Int Soc of Mus, 1931.

Prière: O Jésu vivant en Marie. 1932. unis, org. ms. Text: Rodolphe Mathieu.

VOICE

Les Yeux noirs. 1911. ten, pno. ms. Text: Jean-Eugène Marsoin. Apr 17, 1917, Mtl, Arthur Laurendeau(ten), Léo-Pol Morin (pno).

Saisons canadiennes. before 1927. 25′. bs vc, pno. ms. Text: Rodolphe Mathieu. 1928, Mtl, Ulysse Paguin.

Petite Main. 1955. sop, pno. ms. Text: Françoise Gaudet Smet. Mtl, Michelle Vilandré.

VOICE(S) WITH INSTRUMENTAL ENSEMBLE

Deux Poèmes pour chant et quatuor à cordes. 1928. 11′. ten, str qt. Text: Rodolphe Mathieu. Oct 28, 1930, Mtl, Windsor Hotel, Durieux Qt, Paul Trottier (ten).

Symphonie pour voix humaines. 1960 (incomplete; 4 parts, of which 1 part completed). 12vc, brass. ms. Text: Rodolphe Mathieu.

INSTRUMENTAL ENSEMBLE

Lied. 1915. 3′. vln, pno (org). Hérelle, Paris, 1921.

Quatuor no 1. 1920. 10′. ms. Apr 2, 1921, Paris, Krettly Qt.

Trio. 1921. 30′. pno, vln, vlc. ms. 1926, Paris Le Quatuor le Jeune.

Vingt-deux dialogues (8 extant). before 1924. vln, vlc. ms.

Sonate pour violon et piano. 1928. vln (vlc), pno. ms. Oct 28, 1930, Mtl, Windsor Hotel, Lucien Plamondon(vlc), Rodolphe Mathieu (pno).

Quintette pour piano et quatuor à cordes. 1942. 12′. CMC. RCI-123. 1956, CBC recording session, Mtl Str Qt, Charles Reiner(pno).

PIANO

Chevauchée. 1911. 6′. Int Soc of Mus.

Trois Préludes. 1912–15. 3′50″. Hérelle, Paris, 1921. RCI-135. Apr 17, 1917, Léo-Pol Morin.

Sonate pour piano. 1927. 12′5″. CMC. RCI-123. Oct 28, 1930, Mtl, Windsor Hotel, Hortense Lord.

INSTRUMENTAL SOLO

Douze Etudes Modernes/Douze Monologues. before 1924. vln. ms. RCI-243 (Nos 5, 6, and 8 only).

BIBLIOGRAPHY

See B-B; Bec70; CrC(II); K; Lv; S; Wa.

Bourassa-Trépanier, Juliette. 'La langue musicale de Rodolphe Mathieu', *CMB*. Vol. v, Autumn-Winter 1972 (19–30).

——. *Rodolphe Mathieu, Musicien Canadien (1890–1962)*. Unpublished doctoral thesis, Université Laval, 1972.

LITERARY WORKS

BOOKS

Parlons Musique. Montreal: Editions A. Lévesque, Libraire d'action canadienne-française, 1932.

MATTON, ROGER (b. Granby, Que., 18 May 1929). From his earliest childhood Roger Matton was destined for a career in music; each member of the family was an amateur instrumentalist, playing jazz and traditional repertoire alike. The classical-music radio fare of the 1930s intrigued the young boy, so that before he knew the alphabet he could understand the language of music. All these favourable circumstances, as well as a precocious interest in the world of sound, led to his study of the piano, and it was the nuns of his native city, particularly Sister Yvette Dufault, who gave him a basic training on the instrument. Thus prepared, Matton at thirteen was admitted to the Conservatoire in Montreal and the piano class of Arthur Letondal. Attracted to composition, he showed his early attempts to Claude CHAMPAGNE, then associate director, and in 1946 became one of Champagne's first students in the recently founded composition class. He spent three years there, working alongside others whose names have now become well known: François MOREL, Clermont PÉPIN and Pierre MERCURE. His early works date from this period: the *Berceuse* for piano (1945), *Danse brésilienne* for two pianos (1946), *Etude pour clarinette et piano* (1946), *Concerto pour saxophone et orchestre à cordes* (1948), and *Trois préludes* for piano (1947–9).

When Champagne had to leave his class, Matton, like his friend Mercure, decided to complete his studies in Paris. He studied advanced counterpoint with Andrée Vaurabourg-Honegger (1949-50), choral music, counterpoint, and composition with Nadia Boulanger (1952–5), and took Olivier Messiaen's class in analysis at the Conservatoire. During his years in Paris he worked on two new compositions, *Suite de Pâques* for organ (1950) and *Concerto pour deux pianos et percussion* (1955).

Matton returned to Canada in 1956 and spent several months in Montreal, which gave him the opportunity of writing music for CBC broadcasts. Then, at the end of the year, he settled permanently in Quebec City. A period of time with Marius Barbeau and a subsequent invitation to join the staff of the Archives de Folklore at Laval University constituted a new orientation for the young composer. The advancement of popular culture, initially suggested to Matton by Champagne, and the prospect of new discoveries in folklore, prompted Matton to follow this path. Thus it was that, as part of the group headed by Luc Lacourcière, Matton came to make studies, transcriptions, and recordings of the folk-song heritage of Quebec and Acadia. Besides this considerable task, the university assigned to him a class in history and contemporary music. After several years of teaching composition (Alain GAGNON was one of his students), Matton finally specialized in ethnomusicology. Today his teaching is generally in this area; it is divided between the faculties of Letters and Music.

This activity has limited the time available for composition, though Matton has produced large symphonic works (*Concerto pour deux pianos et orchestre,* 1964) and choral pieces (*l'Escaouette,* 1957; *Te Deum,* 1967). Since 1967, however, for health reasons, he has had to curtail considerably his musical production. A virtual silence of some seven years followed the *Te Deum*, but he has begun composing again and *Mouvement symphonique No. 3* (in progress, 1973) seems to be a point of departure for a new creative phase.

Matton is well known to his fellow Québécois. In 1962 the Montreal Symphony Orchestra on tour included his *Mouvement symphonique No. 2* (1962). In 1965 he carried off a prize for musical composition and he received a further distinction from the 7th Gala du Québec at Montreal for his choral suite, *l'Escaouette*. The following year he received the Prix du disque Pierre Mercure for his *Concerto pour deux pianos et orchestre*; in 1969 the Saint-Jean-Baptiste Society awarded him the *Prix Calixa-Lavallée* for his contribution to the renown of French Canada. Matton is known not only throughout Canada but also abroad. In 1960 the ballet *l'Horoscope* (1958) was presented in New York, thanks to Wilfrid Pelletier; *Mouvement symphonique No. 1* (1960) was played with success in Paris in 1963; likewise the *Te Deum* was given its European première and was recorded in the French capital in May 1969. *Mouvement symphonique No. 2* was again used in the program of the Montreal Symphony Orchestra on tour, this time in France and the Soviet Union. The (orchestral) double piano-concerto is much played by its dedicatees, Victor Bouchard and Renée Morisset, who have made it a popular part of their repertoire.

Matton now excludes certain works from his catalogue, particularly early student efforts. Since 1950 he has written essentially for large instrumental groups, revealing himself to be one of the country's most remarkable orchestrators. He has a special predilection for percussion, to the point of exploiting a formula previously used by Bartok (*Concerto pour deux pianos et percussion*) and giving them a particularly evocative role in the *Forge* episode of *l'Horoscope*.

Matton's output suggests three creative periods in his work. In his youth (1945–55) he was developing his musical language under the influence of Champagne and the French school. Of the twelve works written during these apprentice years one notes the *Berceuse*, which is both archaic and Debussyesque, and the *Trois préludes,* which are structured on modal lines with a Fauré-like simplicity and abundant chromaticism. With regard to rhythm, Matton, influenced by the vigour of Stravinsky and Bartok, seems to show a predilection for bouncing figures and ostinati; he also likes to impart to his more brilliant pieces the flair of the toccata or moto perpetuo (*Preludes* Nos 2 and 3). Many pages use chains of ninth and eleventh chords, such parallelism often contrasting with well-structured contrary motion. In several cases the composer makes use of well-known motifs such as South American rhythms (*Danse brésilienne*), the lumberman's song 'Les Raftsmen' in the finale of the *Concerto pour deux pianos et percussion,* and Gregorian melodies treated as cantus firmus or in fugato style, as in the organ *Suite de Pâques.*

The second period, 1955–65, coincides with Matton's appointment to Laval University. In contact with the authentic folklore of his country, he adopted a certain philosophy towards, and respect for, the spirit of ordinary people, reflected in a new 'genre' of creation. The shorter works of the preceding years were now followed by larger compositions for orchestra or choir: the ballet *l'Horoscope, l'Escaouette,* the two *Mouvements symphoniques,* and the double piano concerto of 1964. These works, employing a 'colouration' type of instrumentation, allowed Matton to develop a technique of timbral counterpoint, always original and tending to rejuvenate the presentation of certain motifs, for example in the *Mouvement symphonique No. 2* in which the principal theme, a chorale, unfolds in three episodes – first in the cellos, then in the brass – and provides a striking finale to the work. If Matton seems to prefer energetic pulsating rhythms, as in the vigorous motifs of the concerto for two pianos, he also makes use of new lyrical ideas deriving from simple music – the chorale, for example – or perhaps more often folklore. *L'Escaouette* is constructed around a succession of folk songs that in the course of the work are shared by four soloists, choir, and orchestra. Care for simplicity, straightforward rhythms accentuated by rigorous syllabic treatment of the text, and abundance of pedal points and elegant harmonization are all characteristics of this suite and prevent it from becoming a mere pot-pourri. In the same manner *l'Horoscope* has as its basis an Acadian legend revived by the specialists at the Archives; the five episodes are woven into a fabric of characteristic motifs of rich melodic interest.

The third and mature period begins in 1965–7 with the working out of the *Te Deum,* conceived originally for the inauguration of the Grand Théâtre in Quebec but (because construction of the Théâtre was delayed) not performed until 1967 in honour of the sixty-fifth anniversary of the Quebec Symphony Orchestra. This imposing work is one of the most original cantatas of recent years in Canada. It alternates verses of the Latin hymn with a French text by Mgr Félix-Antoine Savard and was a great success in both Quebec and Paris. Forsaking the conventional form, Matton constantly juxtaposes the two ideas, the Gregorian turns of the *Te Deum* and a simple melody sung by the baritone and commented upon by the chorus through Savard's poem on the Creation. As before in the works mentioned previously, the orchestra here also plays a leading role, being in turn descriptive or emotionally suggestive, masterfully handled in its detail and even using pre-recording techniques, unusual with Matton. We can see in this new approach a remarkable fusion between the aleatory symbolic element representing chaos and original sin and the symphonic precision that can be achieved by the composer. A particular feature is the meticulous transcription of the song of the thrush (as in Savard's text), which owes no allegiance to Messiaen. Finally, in an attractive use of the folk element, the composer uses the song 'Une Perdriole' in canon. All in all he has created in this work an artistic fusion between a feeling for nature and an element of picturesque and religious symbolism.

If, like many of his contemporaries, Matton was influenced in his youth by the harmonic language of the French school and by the rhythms of Stravinsky and Bartok, after nearly thirty years of composition he has developed a personal style that, though not reactionary, is solidly grounded in traditional structures. Through his knowledge of folklore, by the intelligent use he makes of folk themes from the roots of his heritage, through his expressive musical language, and as a sincere and independent composer, he is an authentic creator of contemporary Canadian music.

Matton is a member of the Canadian League of Composers and of CAPAC.

IRÈNE BRISSON

MUSICAL WORKS

STAGE

L'Horoscope (suite chorégraphique). 1958. 22′. full orch. CMC. RCI-185. 1959, CBC TV 'Heure du concert' series, Les Grands Ballets Canadiens, Mme L Chiriaeff(dir).

ORCHESTRA

Danse brésilienne. 1946. full orch (2 pno). ms. RCI-145 (pno version). 1947 (orchestral version), Mtl, Mtl CBC O, Jean Beaudet.

Pax (suite symphonique). 1950. 20′. full orch.

L'Horoscope (suite chorégraphique). 1958. 22′. full orch. CMC. RCI-185. Oct 12, 1958, Tor, CBCSO, Geoffrey Waddington.

Mouvement symphonique No. 1. 1960. 12′. full orch. CMC. Nov 14, 1960, Quebec, QSO, Françoys Bernier.

Mouvement symphonique No. 2 (musique pour un drame). 1962. 11′15″. full orch. CMC RCA LSC-2980. Apr 17, Mtl, MSO, Zubin Mehta.

SMALL ORCHESTRA

Danse lente (Gymnopédie). 1947. ms. 1948, Mtl, CBC O, Jean Beaudet.

SOLOIST(S) WITH ORCHESTRA

Concerto pour saxophone et orchestre à cordes. 1948. 14′. ms. Mtl, CBC O, Jean Beaudet.

Concerto pour deux pianos et orchestre. 1964. 23′10″. CMC. Cap W/SW-6123. Nov 30, 1964, Quebec, QSO, Pierre Dervaux (cond), Renée Morisset, Victor Bouchard (pnos).

CHOIR WITH ORCHESTRA

L'Escaouette. 1957. 10′. sop, mezz, ten, bar, SATB, full orch. CMC. Oct 13, 1957, Mtl, CBC O, Wilfrid Pelletier.

Te Deum. 1967. 38′50″. bar, SATB, orch, elec tape. CMC. Sel SSC-24.188. Text: Félix-Antoine Savard. Nov 27, 1967, Quebec, Le Choeur symphonique de Québec, Chantal Masson(cond), QSO, Françoys Bernier (cond), Gaston Germain(bar).

INSTRUMENTAL ENSEMBLE

Etude pour clarinette et piano. 1946. 5′.

Esquisse pour quatuor à cordes. 1949. 15′. ms.

Concerto pour deux pianos et percussion. 1955. 17′25″. ms. RCI-145. 1955, Mtl, CBC, CLC conc, Jeanne Landry, Josephte Dufresne(pnos), Louis Charbonneau, Guy Lachapelle(perc).

PIANO

Berceuse. 1945. 2′. ms. RCI-135.

Danse brésilienne. 1946. 4′25″. 2pno (orch). ms. RCI-145. 1947 (orchestral version), Mtl, CBC O, Jean Beaudet.

Trois Préludes. 1949. 4′8″. CMC. RCI-135.

ORGAN

Suite de Pâques. 1950. 14′. CMC.

Suite sur des thèmes grégoriens. 1952. 14′. ms.

BIBLIOGRAPHY

B58, Bt; CrC(I); K; Wa.

Bisbrouck, N. ' "A l'heure du concert", un compositeur canadien: Roger Matton', *La*

Semaine à Radio-Canada. Montreal, 1965, Vol. xv, no. 22 (1–3).
Grobin, Michael. 'Our Composers on Microgroove', *Mu*. Toronto, Mar. 1970, No. 27 (7, 10).
Kendergi, Maryvonne. 'Roger Matton: *Te Deum*', *CMB*. Montreal, Spring-Summer 1971 (200–5).
'Prix Calixa-Lavallée', *Vie Musicale*. Quebec, Sept. 1969, No. 13 (27–8).
'Roger Matton – a portrait', *Mu*. Toronto, Dec. 1968, No. 16 (8–9).
Weinzweig, Helen. 'The Creative Life of Roger Matton', *The Canadian Composer*. Oct. 1968 (16, 44).

LITERARY WORKS

ARTICLES
'J'étais l'élève de Claude Champagne', *Culture vivante*. No. 11, Dec. 1968 (19–20).
'Mouvement symphonique no. 2 de Roger Matton', *Vie Musicale*. Sept. 1970, No. 17 (16–20).

MERCURE, PIERRE (b. Montreal, Que., 21 Feb. 1927; d. near Avallon, France, 29 Jan. 1966). Pierre Mercure was one of the most ardent protagonists of contemporary music in Quebec during the 1960s. At a very early age he was taught by his mother and an aunt, both pianists, becoming a student at the Conservatoire in Montreal where he studied counterpoint and fugue as well as instrumental technique (organ, piano, flute, trumpet, bassoon, cello), with the aim of becoming an orchestra conductor. Introduced to harmony and composition by Claude CHAMPAGNE, Mercure very early demonstrated his creative talents, revealed in music for the theatre, some songs, a symphonic fantasy, *Kaléidoscope* (1948–9) and a *Pantomime* (1949).

Before leaving Montreal to study in Paris, Mercure took part in the creation of several modern ballets produced by Françoise Sullivan: *Dualité, Femme archaïque*, and *Lucrèce Borgia* (1949). This collaboration shows the first indication of a continuing preoccupation, the integration of different creative forms, fusing theatre, music, painting and the dance. This need was undoubtedly encouraged by a group of artists, writers, painters, actors, and dancers whose thinking was influenced by the painter Paul-Emile Borduas and who signed the manifesto *Refus global* (1948) that denounced the conservatism of bourgeois societies and demanded liberation for the artist.

On his arrival in Europe in the autumn of 1949, Mercure enrolled in the courses of Nadia Boulanger. However, as he was becoming more and more drawn towards new music, including aleatoric music and 'musique concrète', his association with the famous French pedagogue did not last more than a few months; he preferred to work assiduously on improvisations, superimposed forms, and collective works in collaboration with Gabriel CHARPENTIER, Jocelyne Binet and Clermont PÉPIN. At the same time he studied orchestration with Arthur Hoérée and conducting with Jean Fournet. While he was still in Europe, *Ils ont détruit la ville* (1950), for choir and orchestra on a poem by Gabriel Charpentier, won him first prize in a song competition sponsored by the CBC.

After an absence of a year, Mercure returned, resuming his position as bassoonist with the Montreal Symphony Orchestra (1947–9, 1950–2); also during 1951 he played with the Variétés Lyriques conducted by Lionel DAUNAIS and Charles Goulet. In the summer of 1951 a study scholarship from the Quebec government enabled him to study composition at Tanglewood with Luigi Dallapiccola. There Mercure encountered the principles of dodecaphony, which he almost immediately rejected. His lyrical nature found outlet in *Dissidence* (1955), three songs that, with *Ils ont détruit la ville*, constitute a large part of the *Cantate pour une joie* (1955) – seven movements for solo voice, choir, and orchestra on poems by Gabriel Charpentier. *Divertissement* (1957) for string quartet and orchestra and *Triptyque* (1959) for full orchestra constitute the culminating point of a somewhat hesitant development, one that was generously endowed with the traits of youth.

Throughout this first period (1948–59) Mercure was searching for new sonorities. Faced by the impossibility of achieving them, he allied himself not with tradition as such but with a form of spontaneous lyrical expression within the framework of traditional forms. His models were Stravinsky, Milhaud, and Honegger. He was not insensitive to the influence of American jazz and popular music; several themes are taken from songs popularized by the Glenn Miller orchestra. The rhythm is acknowledged, the orchestrations sparkling. All these elements are found in numerous stage works between 1950 and 1954, in radio plays for the CBC (Tagore's 'Amal', Gréban's 'Mystère de la Nativité') and in works performed by the Compagnons Saint-Laurent ('Bal des Voleurs') etc.

This association with the theatre, dance, and even painting and sculpture, was decisive. In January 1952 Mercure joined the music department of the CBC French television network and became its first producer of TV music broadcasts. From 1954 to 1959 he produced forty-one broadcasts of 'l'Heure du Concert' and several in the series 'Concerts pour la jeunesse', 'Jazz Workshop', 'Music-Hall', and 'Pays et Merveilles', among others. He commanded much attention for the quality of these broadcasts, always showing a quality of visual exploration and often of a certain audacity and even rashness. Among the most renowned were: 'Oedipus Rex', 'Jeanne d'Arc au bûcher', and 'Wozzeck'.

This continuous searching, this need to involve himself in the most contemporary forms of art, was hereafter the principal axis around which Mercure's work developed. During the years 1959–62 he searched for a new language in the electro-acoustic world of sound; this exploration began during his second period of study in Europe (1957–8), when he was in contact with Pierre Schaeffer and the Groupe de Recherches Musicales of the ORTF. *Répercussions, Structures métalliques I et II, Incandescence*, and *Improvisation*, all of 1961, are works that use electronically manipulated concrete sounds; they are sometimes accompanied by choreography and projected images.

This intense activity as composer coincided with the mounting of a festival of the avant-garde, of which Mercure was the guiding force. In organizing the 'Semaine internationale de musique actuelle' (International Contemporary Music Week, August 1961), Mercure was looking to the future: John Cage, Karlheinz Stockhausen, Mauricio Kagel, Christian Wolff, Iannis Xenakis, and Serge GARANT. Mercure sought to familiarize Montreal with contemporary manifestations in music: new sounds for a new audience. This unique event, which Mercure wanted to become annual, did open the way for the founding in 1966 of the 'Société de musique contemporaine du Québec', formed to present the most contemporary in music.

A third period of study in Paris, Darmstadt, and Dartington (summer 1962) allowed Mercure to become familiar with electronic music. His *Structures métalliques III*, composed during this period, was performed at the Fluxus Internationale Festspiele Neuester Musik at Wiesbaden on September 16, 1962.

Encouraged by these new experiences, in the autumn of 1962 Mercure undertook a cantata for radio, *Psaume pour abri* (1963), the first of three attempts to fuse electronic with traditional music. Using poems by Fernand Ouellette, this work calls upon an imposing array of sonorities: a singing chorus and a speaking chorus divided into two groups encircling seven instrumentalists and a narrator. Loudspeakers are placed around the ensemble, playing electronic music and pre-recorded transformed sounds of three brass quintets and four string quartets. *Psaume pour abri* is an 'outcry against barbarism, atrocity, and absurdity'. It is divided into seven sections, of which the three last are a (not literal) retrogradation of the first three; born of the human family, symbolically they return to it. This sort of pattern is also found in *Tétrachromie* (1963), a fresco in sound depicting the four ages of man, represented by four colours: green (spring), yellow (summer), red (autumn), and white (winter). Written for three wind instruments, four percussionists, and electronic sounds, this work was commissioned by Les Grands Ballets Canadiens for the inaugural festival at Place des Arts. A union dispute prevented the performance.

In September 1963 Mercure began *Lignes et points* (1964), a work for full orchestra, commissioned by the Montreal Symphony Orchestra. A suite of variations on a single theme, it acknowledges a writing style found in the two previous works mentioned. In fact the same three thematic cells (four- or five-note figures) are used as the basis for elaboration in these works; in the score most of the sequences are represented graphically by colours. In the previous two works sine-waves are transformed by filters, echo chambers, etc.; in *Lignes et points*, through the orchestra, the composer uses analogous procedures, trying to achieve from the orchestra colourations of timbre reminiscent of those from electronic techniques.

Two film scores in 1965, for *Formes des choses* and *Elément III*, by Jacques Giraldeau, are the last contributions by Mercure the composer. *H_2O per Severino* (1965), eight improvisations for flutes and/or clarinets, is derived from music tape-recorded by Severino Gazzelloni at Darmstadt in July 1965 for the film *Elément III*. Carrying as subtitles 'Notes soutenues, Notes liées, Notes brèves, Notes répétées, Notes variables, Traits rapides liés, Traits rapides non liés et mélanges' ('sustained notes, tied notes, short notes, repeated notes, variable notes, rapid shots joined, rapid shots unjoined, mixtures'), this work is constructed on a series of serially treated thematic sketches.

Before his accidental death near Avallon, France, Mercure had almost completed the production of a television opera on a libretto and score of R. Murray SCHAFER, 'Loving' (in French, 'Toi'), for the CBC French network. It was completed and broadcast not long after his death and stands as the most vibrant homage that could be rendered to his creative genius.

Mercure was a member of the Canadian League of Composers; his estate is an affiliate of BMI Canada.

LYSE RICHER-LORTIE

MUSICAL WORKS

BALLET

Dualité. 1949. 5′. tpt, pno. ms. May 8, 1949, Mtl, Théâtre des Compagnons, Françoise Sullivan.

La femme archaïque (pantomime). 1949. vla, pno, timp. ms. May 8, 1949, Mtl, Théâtre des Compagnons, Françoise Sullivan.

Lucrèce Borgia. 1949. 4′. tpt, pno, perc. ms. May 8, 1949, Mtl, Théâtre des Compagnons, Françoise Sullivan.

Emprise. 1950. 8′. cl, bsn, vlc, pno. ms. 1950, Paris, American Club, James Rosen (cl), Pierre Mercure(bsn), Monique Mercure (vlc), Gabriel Charpentier(pno).

Improvisation. 1961. prepared pno on elec tape. Dec 1961, Mtl, Studio Françoise Riopelle, Françoise Riopelle(choreog).

Incandescence. 1961. elec tape. ms. Aug 6, 1961, Mtl, Théâtre de la Comédie canadienne, Semaine internationale de musique actuelle, Françoise Riopelle(choreog).

Structures métalliques I. 1961. metallic sculptures, elec tape. ms. June 6, 1961, Mtl, Théâtre de l'Egrégore, Françoise Riopelle (choreog).

Structures métalliques II. 1961. metallic sculptures, elec tape. ms. Aug 6, 1961, Mtl, Théâtre de la Comédie canadienne, Semaine internationale de musique actuelle, Françoise Riopelle(choreog).

Manipulations. 1963. elec tape. May 8, 1964, Québec, Théâtre de l'Estoc, Françoise Riopelle and Jocelyne Renaud(choreogs).

Tétrachromie. 1963. 10′. cl, alto sax, b cl, perc, elec tape. CMC. Col MS-6763/ML-6163. 1965, Tor, Columbia recording session, instr ens under Walter Susskind & Pierre Mercure.

Surimpressions. 1964. prepared pno on elec tape. ms. Dec 16, 1964, Mtl, Studio Françoise Riopelle, Françoise Riopelle(choreog).

FILM MUSIC

Formes 64 or *La forme des choses*. 1965. brass qnt, concrete sounds. ms. MBQ, sculptors, Jacques Giraldeau(dir).

Elément III. 1965. fl. NFB film comm'd by UNESCO. Paris, Jacques Giraldeau(dir), Severino Gazzelloni(fl).

ORCHESTRA

Kaléidoscope. 1948. 11′. med orch (reduced orch version 1949). Ric, 1960. CBC BR SM-132. Mar 28, 1948, Mtl, CBC O, Jean-Marie Beaudet.

Triptyque. 1959. 10′20″. full orch. Ric, 1963. Col M2L-356/M2S-756, Odyssey Y-31993. July 1959, Vanc, VSO, Walter Susskind.

Lignes et points. 1964. 10′55″. full orch. Ric, 1970. RCA LSC-2980, RCI-230. Feb 16, 1965, Mtl, Place des Arts, MSO, Zubin Mehta.

SOLOISTS WITH ORCHESTRA

Divertissement. 1957 (rev 1958). 11′50″. str qt, str orch. Ric, 1970. CBC BR SM-6, RCI-154. Mar 26, 1957, Mtl, McGill Ch O, Alexander Brott(cond).

CHOIR WITH ORCHESTRA

Ils ont détruit la ville. 1950. 5'. SATB, 18 instr. ms. RCI-35. Text: Gabriel Charpentier. Mar 24, 1950, Mtl, CBC.

Cantate pour une joie. 1955. 19'. sop, SATB, orch. Ric, 1960. RCI-155. Text: Gabriel Charpentier; Trans: Harold Heiberg. Feb 1, 1956, Mtl, CLC Conc, Jean-Marie Beaudet (cond), Marguerite Lavergne(sop).

Psaume pour abri (cantata). 1963. narr, 2 choirs, brass qnt, str qt, hpschd, pno, hp, perc, elec tape. ms. Text: Fernand Ouellette. May 15, 1963, Mtl, CBC Wednesday Night Conc, Pierre Mercure(cond).

VOICE

Colloque. 1948. 3'. vc, pno. Ber, 1950. Text: Paul Valéry.

Dissidence. 1955. 7'30". sop (ten), pno. CMC. ARCLP-4; RCI-201. Text: Gabriel Charpentier. 1955, CBC Mtl, Marguerite Lavergne (sop), Colombe Pelletier(pno).

INSTRUMENTAL ENSEMBLE

Pantomime. 1949. 5'30". 18 ww, brass, perc (ww, str, perc version 1948; 14 ww, perc version 1949; vlc (vla), pno version 1949). Ric, 1971. RCI 2 & 117. Feb 13, 1948, Mtl, CBC O, Jean-Marie Beaudet.

H_2O per Severino. 1965. 4 to 10 instr. ms.

ELECTRONIC (see also BALLET above)

Répercussions. 1961. sounds of Japanese wind-chimes on elec tape. May 1961, Mtl, Studio Françoise Riopelle.

Jeu de Hockey. 1961. elec tape. ms. Dec 29, 1961, Mtl, CBC.

Structures métalliques III. 1962. elec tape. ms (incompl). Sept 16, 1962, Wiesbaden, Germany, Fluxus International Festival of New Music.

BIBLIOGRAPHY

See B-B; B65,71; Bec70; Bt; CrC(II); D165; Esc; K; Lv; Wa.

Bernier, Françoys. 'Pierre Mercure: "Lignes et Points; Divertissement" ', *CMB.* Vol. II, Spring-Summer 1971 (173–5).

Cowell, Henry. 'Current Chronicle: New York', *MQ.* Vol. XL, no. 1, Jan. 1954 (60).

Davidson, H. 'Pierre Mercure – 1927–1966', *Closed Circuit.* Feb. 14, 1966.

Kasemets, Udo. 'Pierre Mercure', *MuSc.* Mar.-Apr. 1969 (10–11).

'Pierre Mercure', *Dictionnaire de la musique* (Marc Honegger, ed.). Vol. II, France, Bordas, 1970.

'Pierre Mercure', *Musiques du Kébèk* (R. Duguay, ed.). Montreal, Editions du Jour, 1971 (115–28).

'A Tribute to Pierre Mercure', *CanCo.* No. 14, Jan. 1967 (10–11).

LITERARY WORKS

'Chronique musicale', *Revue des Arts et des Lettres.* Radio-Canada, Feb. 18, 1952.

'Commentaires', *Musiques du Kébèk.* Montreal, Editions du Jour, 1971.

'Lignes et points', typewritten notes signed by the composer, Jan. 26, 1965.

'Le mystère de la Nativité de notre Sauveur, de Gréban', *La semaine à Radio-Canada.* Vol. II, no. 2, Dec. 23–9, 1951.

'Opinions canadiennes sur la musique contemporaine', *Journal Musical Canadien.* Vol. II, no. 4, Feb. 1956.

'La semaine internationale de musique actuelle', *Programme des festivals de Montréal.* Festival musical et dramatique de Montréal, 26th season, Aug. 2 – Sept. 2, 1961.

MILLER, MICHAEL R. (b. Lisbon, Portugal, 24 July 1932). He received his Master of Arts (1956) and Doctor of Philosophy (1971) degrees in composition from the Eastman School of Music, University of Rochester. He taught music theory and composition at New York University (1961–5) and at Vassar College (1965–6). In 1967 he came to Canada and became assistant professor of composition and piano at Mount Allison University, New Brunswick. His music is generally chromatic and polytonal. He has written a chamber opera, *A Sunny Morning* (1962), as well as two orchestral works, *Strophe, Antistrophe* (1971) and *Capriccio on the Seven Ages of Man* (1972), and *Piano Variations* (1971) for solo piano. Also he has written works for chamber ensembles, including *Trio for Viola, Clarinet and Piano* (1969), *Four Canzonets for Brass Quintet* (1969), and *Interaction* (1971–2) for English horn, horn, cello, and harpsichord. His works for choir include three for mixed chorus a cappella: *Blake on Love* (1965), *Three French Carols* (arranged; Gregorian Institute 1964), and *Two Carols* (arranged; Gregorian Institute 1964); *Blake's Garden* (1965) for SSA and piano; *Blasphemies of Blake* (1965) for two baritones and tenor soloists, TTBB, piano and double bass; *Mass for Peace* (1962; Kalmus 1964) for SATB, soloists, brass quintet or organ; and *Haiku Set* (1964; translated by Harold Henderson) for six soloists. He is a member of CAPAC.

MILLS-COCKELL, JOHN (b. Toronto, Ont., 19 May 1943). He studied composition with Samuel DOLIN at the Royal Conservatory of Music in Toronto and electronic music with Gustav CIAMAGA at the Faculty of Music, University of Toronto. He has been active as technical assistant in the electronic music studio of the Royal Conservatory and as a member of the mixed-media organization 'Intersystems'. He was winner of a BMI Student Composer Award in 1967. From 1968 to 1969 he taught at the Royal Conservatory. Since 1968, deriving most of his compositional ideas from the electronic medium and more specifically on the Moog and Arp synthesizers, Mills-Cockell has produced a unique sound in rock music. Until 1972 he headed the three-man performing group 'Syrinx'. In 1972 he was commissioned by the Toronto Arts Foundation to compose a musical score for John Palmer's play 'Memories of my Brother, Part II: Guns of Silence'. He has also written and performed music for many radio, television, film, and theatre productions, including *The Effect of Gamma Rays on Man-in-the-Moon Marigolds* (St Lawrence Centre, 1970), *January Tree* and *For Internal Use Only* (National Ballet of Canada, 1971), *Starscape* (Toronto Dance Theatre, 1971), *Stringspace Suite* (1971), and *Icone* (film, 1970). He is an affiliate of BMI Canada.

BIBLIOGRAPHY

MacLaurin, Doug. 'Mills-Cockell's Music Expressed Electronically', *MuSc.* Mar.-Apr. 1971 (10).

MIRO, HENRI (ENRIQUE) (b. Tarrega, Spain, 13 Nov. 1879; d. Montreal, Que., 19 July 1950). He studied piano, organ, harmony, and composition in the Benedictine monastery of Montserrat with Padre Manuel de Guzman. At sixteen he was accepted at the Barcelona Conservatory, where his teacher was B. Socias. In 1898 he went to France as conductor of an opera company and in 1902 arrived in Montreal where his *Messe solennelle* was performed at the Monument National, establishing his reputation as a composer. He was musical director of the Berliner Talking Machine Company from 1916 to 1921. His operetta, *Le Roman de Suzon*, was premièred in the Princess Theatre in 1914 and repeated in 1925 by the Canadian Operetta Society. The cantata *Vox populi* for soloists, chorus, and orchestra was given in 1928 under the direction of Jean Goulet and repeated twice in 1929 at Holyoke, Mass., and a second time in Montreal under the composer's direction. His *Symphonie canadienne* was also played under his own direction in Montreal in 1931. In 1936 he won the Prix Jean-Lallemand for his *Scènes mauresques* in the first composition contest of the Montreal Symphony Orchestra, which premièred the work on April 3 of that year, under the direction of Wilfrid Pelletier. A second operetta, *Lolita,* with script by Armand Robi, was broadcast by the CBC on January 9, 1944. Miro also composed several works for orchestra, including two cello concertos, pieces for piano, for choir, and some twenty songs. Thirty of his works were published in the journal *La Lyre,* to which he also contributed as critic and essayist.

BIBLIOGRAPHY

See B-B; K; Lv.

MORAWETZ, OSKAR (b. Svetla, Czechoslovakia, 17 Jan. 1917). At the age of eight he moved with his parents to Prague, some eighty miles distant from his birthplace, and there received much of his musical training. He gained skill as a pianist and developed a remarkable ability to play full-orchestra scores on the keyboard. This ability, plus his knowledge of opera and his perfect pitch, brought Morawetz an offer of a conducting post at the Prague Opera.

Forced to flee the Nazi régime, Morawetz sojourned in several European countries before coming to Canada in 1940 to rejoin his parents who had taken up residence in Toronto.

Continuing with his musical education, Morawetz obtained a Bachelor of Music degree from the University of Toronto in 1944, and a Doctor of Music degree in

1953. He is currently a professor in the Faculty of Music at the University of Toronto. The *String Quartet No. 1* (1944), the earliest of his listed compositions, was written as a requirement for the Bachelor of Music degree. There was then, however, no instruction in composition *per se* offered at the university, and Morawetz views himself as a self-taught composer. The *Quartet* won a nation-wide competition sponsored by CAPAC in 1945. His *Sonata Tragica* (1945) for piano won the award for Morawetz again in 1946, and established him as one of Canada's leading composers.

Representative of his early style is the *Carnival Overture* (1946), which has received many performances throughout Europe, North America, and Australia. Bohemian in flavour, it is reminiscent of Dvorak in both its title and content. The composition combines bright orchestral garb, clear-cut structure, rhythmic vivacity, and melodic grace. In a similar vein are the *Divertimento for Strings* (1948, rev. 1954) and the *Overture to a Fairy Tale* (1956), the latter written to offer an alternative to the much-played *Carnival Overture* (1946). Morawetz's music does not always reflect the happy mood of the *Carnival Overture*: a number of later works are in a more serious vein. Nor has his style remained at the uncomplicated level of his early works. But his music is written for the large public of concert-goers rather than for a select circle of fellow composers.

'I still belong to the old school which believes that music which cannot be felt but needs explanation consists only of mathematical formulas,' declares the composer. Deeply felt musical experiences have a profound effect: 'Sometimes, if I really like a work, after the performance I just run out and don't want to speak to anybody for an hour or two.' Although Morawetz is clearly a neo-Romantic, a dreamer, perhaps a mystic, he also has a regard for the practicality of performance opportunities. The three movements of the *Symphony No. 1* (1951–3), for instance, have each been given titles to facilitate their performance as separate works. The published score of the *Passacaglia on a Bach Chorale* (1964), a work dedicated to the memory of John F. Kennedy, carries a tribute specially written by Lester B. Pearson, then Prime Minister of Canada, and a previously unpublished portrait by the Canadian photographer Yousuf Karsh. Mrs Rose Kennedy sent a letter of appreciation, much cherished by the composer. The work has received numerous performances.

Morawetz's piano music displays his remarkable ability to write keyboard showpieces that have attracted such outstanding pianists as Glenn Gould, Anton Kuerti, and Rudolf Firkusny. Works such as the *Suite for Piano* (1968) lie well under the fingers and the arms of the performer, who is often required to transfer quickly to the various ranges of the instrument for maximum sonority and effect. In more subtle moments, fresh colouristic effects of a quasi-impressionist character are achieved. In his orchestral writing, too, Morawetz is sensitive to problems of performance as well as to instrumental texture. Individual parts are rarely of excessive difficulty; yet even in the midst of a thickly scored passage, each instrumental *timbre* stands forth. The tam-tam, when introduced in a climactic pasage (a Morawetz device), contributes a monumental grandeur to the tonal fabric.

Melodic movement is conceived with regard to larger dimensions rather than to single phrases. Conjunct motion is frequent; a melodic capsule is repeated, extended, inverted, the intervals widened, a sequential treatment imposed, and a well-planned pinnacle of melodic contour eventually achieved. Harmonies verge on the atonal, although they are basically tonal in concept. Triads with added dissonant notes, the superimposition of triads, harmonies derived from the pentatonic or whole-tone scales, the use of consecutive fourths and fifths – all form the basis for his harmonic language. Rhythm, in vigorous passages, is made taut by means of syncopation and repetition, a rhythmic ostinato being characteristic of many of his works. In lyrical moments one finds longer, more evenly spaced notes, together with a homophonic rather than a polyphonic texture. The clear-cut phraseology of the early works is replaced by a more plastic moulding-together of the various parts of a work. Overlappings, elisions, and transitions create larger-dimensional units in a manner similar to Wagner's *unendliche Melodien.*

A work that blends these features is the *Piano Concerto No. 1* (1962). Premièred in Montreal by Anton Kuerti as soloist, with Zubin Mehta conducting, the work was awarded first prize in a competition sponsored by the Montreal Symphony Orchestra. The three movements, which are joined, contain music of symphonic thrust and biting lyricism, showing off both soloist and orchestra to great effect.

The *Sinfonietta for Winds,* written in 1965, won the Critic's Award at the International Composers Competition held in Cava dei Tirreni, Italy, in 1966. A companion piece to the *Sinfonietta for Strings* (1963, rev. 1968), it calls for a full symphonic complement of winds and percussion. Like other of Morawetz's larger works such as the *Symphony No. 1*, this is in three movements, the second of which is titled 'Elegy'. Of the chamber works, the *Quartet No. 2* (1952–5) is one of the finest. The second of the three movements has programmatic connotations. The muted atmospheric touches and the martial character of the middle section were suggested by filmed war scenes that affected the composer deeply.

Outstanding among the many songs are settings of poems by the Canadian writers Archibald Lampman and Bliss Carman. Morawetz displays a deft touch in reflecting the meaning and mood of the text in the piano writing. In *Four Songs* (1966), on poems by Bliss Carman, Morawetz utilizes impressionistic touches to denote the Dustman who puts the children to sleep (and will some day, with more potent dust, put us to sleep). 'The Juggler' is depicted by means of rhythm in perpetual motion. 'The Old Gray Wall' by a repeated B flat against changing harmonies, and the evocative 'Ships of Yule' is given an exotic high-register Chinese flavour in the manner of Ravel and Mahler.

The most deeply moving of Morawetz' vocal compositions is *From the Diary of Anne Frank* (1970) for soprano solo and orchestra. The text is taken from Anne's diary written when she was fourteen and in hiding from the Nazis. She thinks of her friend Lies who becomes a fleeting reality, clothed in rags, her face thin and worn. Anne imagines Lies looking reproachfully at her, her large eyes pleading for help – help that Anne is powerless to provide. She can only pray to God with heart-tearing anguish to help Lies, all Jews, and all those in need. Morawetz's setting blends characteristic aspects of Mahler and Berg in music ideally suited to the text, which is declaimed in a vocal line partly recitative and partly melody. Motivic fragments are combined and extended to achieve a lyrical line combining beauty and despair. The translucent orchestral score matches the pathos and despair of the text and there is one powerful extended passage for orchestra alone near the end of the work that concludes in a mood of quiet hope.

Morawetz is a member of the Canadian League of Composers and of CAPAC.

LEE HEPNER

MUSICAL WORKS

ORCHESTRA

Carnival Overture. 1946. 7′. full orch. MCA, 1970. RCI-41. July 1, 1947, Mtl, MSO, Sir Ernest MacMillan.

Dirge. 1951–3. 10′. full orch. CMC Study Score. 1956, Tor, CBCSO, Jean-Marie Beaudet.

Symphony No. 1. 1951–3. 32′. full orch. CMC. 1956, Tor, CBCSO, Jean-Marie Beaudet.

Fantasy for Orchestra. 1952. 11′. full orch. CMC. 1954, MSO, Geoffrey Waddington.

Symphonic Scherzo. 1952. 10′. full orch. CMC. Jan 19, 1956, Paris, Orch de RTF, Gaston Poulet.

Overture to a Fairy Tale. 1956. 12′30″. med orch. B & H, 1959. RCI-180. Feb 8, 1957, HSO, Thomas Mayer.

Symphony No. 2. 1959. 23′. full orch. CMC. CBC BR SM-4. Feb 2, 1960, TS, Walter Susskind.

Capriccio. 1960. 8′. full orch. CMC.

Passacaglia on a Bach Chorale. 1964. 6′15″. full orch. MCA, 1965. Nov 24, 1964, TS, Walter Susskind.

Reflections after a Tragedy. 1969. 11′50″. full orch. ms. June 17, 1969, Tor, CBC Fest O, Lawrence Leonard.

Symphonic Intermezzo. 1971. 9′. full orch. CMC. Apr 1971, Halifax, ASO, Klaro Mizerit.

SMALL ORCHESTRA

Sinfonietta for Winds and Percussion. 1965. 21′30″. MCA, 1967. RCI-292. Feb 22, 1966, MSO, Zubin Mehta.

STRING ORCHESTRA

Divertimento for Strings. 1948 (rev 1954). 9'30". Ric, 1959. July 14, 1955, Stratford, Ont, Fest Conc, CBC O, Boyd Neel.

Sinfonietta for Strings. 1963 (rev 1968). 15'. MCA, 1972. Nov 18, 1969, Tor, TS, Karel Ancerl.

Psalm for Strings. 1971. 13'. Apr 24, 1972, McG Ch O, Alexander Brott.

SOLOIST(S) WITH ORCHESTRA

Elegy; 'I am so tired'. 1947. 3'. med or high vc, orch or pno. ms. RCI-121 (pno version). Text: Anne Wilkinson. July 22, 1956, Phila, Phila SO, William Steinberg(cond), Dorothy Maynor(sop).

I Love the Jocund Dance. 1949. 2'. high vc, orch. GVT, 1953. CBC BR SM-8 (pno version). Text: William Blake. July 22, 1956, Phila SO, William Steinberg(cond), Dorothy Maynor(sop).

Land of Dreams. 1949. 5'. vc, orch. GVT, 1953. CBC BR SM-8 (pno version). Text: William Blake. 1960, Mtl, CBC TV, Sylvia Saurette(sop).

Grenadier. 1950. 5'. bar, orch. CMC. CBC BR SM-42; RCI-121 (pno version).

Piano Concerto No 1. 1962. 19'. MCA, 1966. Cap W/SW-6123; Pathé PAM/SPAM-68023; RCI-213-A. Apr 23, 1963, Mtl, MSO, Zubin Mehta(cond), Anton Kuerti(pno).

Two Preludes for Violin and Chamber Orchestra. 1965 (orch'd 1972). 9'. CMC.

Concerto for Brass Quintet and Orchestra. 1968. 23'10". MCA, 1972.

Memorial to Martin Luther King. 1968. 10'. vlc, orch. CMC.

From the Diary of Anne Frank. 1970. 19'. vc, orch. CMC. May 26, 1970, Tor, CBC Fest, TS, Lawrence Leonard(cond), Lois Marshall (sop).

A Child's Garden of Verses. 1971. 15'. alto or mezz, orch. CMC. Feb 10, 1973, Tor, CBC Fest, TS, Victor Feldbrill(cond), Maureen Forrester(alto).

CHOIR WITH ORCHESTRA

Keep Us Free. 1951. 5'. SSAATTBB, orch. GVT, 1952. 1951, CBC Chorus and Orch, Sir Ernest MacMillan(cond).

CHOIR

Two Contrasting Moods. 1966. SATB. CMC. Text: Archibald Lampman. June 26, 1969, Tor, CBC Fest Sgrs, Elmer Iseler(cond).

Crucifixion. 1968. 8'. SATB. MCA, 1971. Text: from a Negro Spiritual. Apr 18, 1970, Tor, Fest Sgrs, Elmer Iseler(cond).

Who has allowed us to suffer? 1970 (rev 1972). 8'. SATB. CMC. Text: Anne Frank. 1971, Tor, Mount Sinai Synagogue choir, Ben Steinberg.

VOICE(S)

The Fly. med vc, pno. CMC. Text: William Blake. 1947, CBC, Nicholas Goldschmidt (bar).

The Chimney-Sweeper. 1947. 3'50". med vc, pno. MCA, 1961. RCI-121. Text: William Blake. May 1953, CBC, James Milligan(bar), Oskar Morawetz(pno).

Mad Song. 1947. 3'30". med or high vc, pno. MCA, 1962. Text: William Blake. RCI-121. May 1953, CBC, James Milligan(bar), Oskar Morawetz(pno).

Piping Down the Valleys Wild. 1947. 3'. med or high vc, pno. GVT, 1953. CBC BR SM-8. Text: William Blake. Mar 14, 1954, CBC, Lois Marshall.

Elegy; 'I am so tired'. 1947. 3'. med or high vc, pno or orch. MCA, 1961. RCI-121. Text: Anne Wilkinson. Mar 24, 1949, Tor, Dorothy Maynor.

Cradle Song. 1949. 4'. med vc, pno. MCA, 1962. Text: William Blake. 1950, CBC, Elizabeth Benson-Guy(mezz), Oskar Morawetz(pno).

I Love the Jocund Dance. 1949. 1'30". high vc, pno. GVT, 1953. CBC BR SM-8. Text: William Blake. 1949, CBC, Elizabeth Benson-Guy.

Land of Dreams. 1949. 5'. vc, pno. GVT, 1953. CBC BR SM-8. Text: William Blake. 1949, Elizabeth Benson-Guy.

To the Ottawa River. 1949. 4'. med or low vc, pno. MCA, 1962. RCI-121. Text: Archibald Lampman. May 1953, CBC, James Milligan(bar), Oskar Morawetz(pno).

When We Two Parted. 1949. 5'. med (high) vc, pno. MCA, 1961. Text: Lord Byron. Oct 14, 1949, CBC, Elizabeth Benson-Guy.

Grenadier. 1950. 5'. bar (bs), pno or orch. MCA, 1962. CBC BR SM-42; RCI-121. Text: A E Housman. May 1953, CBC, James Milligan(bar), Oskar Morawetz(pno).

Mother, I Cannot Mind My Wheel. 1955. 2'. sop (mezz), pno. MCA, 1962. Text: Walter Savage Landor. May 14, 1957, CBC, Roma Butler(sop), Oskar Morawetz(pno).

My True Love Hath My Heart. 1955. 3'. sop (mezz), pno. MCA, 1962. Text: Sir Philip

Sidney. May 14, 1957, CBC, Roma Butler (sop), Oskar Morawetz(pno).
Sonnets from the Portuguese; 'Cycle of Four Songs'. 1955. 12'. sop, pno. CMC. Text: Elizabeth Barrett Browning. Sept 9, 1956, CBC, Ilona Kombrink(sop), Oskar Morawetz (pno).
Father William. 1957. 8'. sop (bar or bs), pno. CMC. Text: Lewis Carroll.
Four Songs. 1966. 19'30". vc, pno. CMC. Text: Bliss Carman. Feb 9, 1967, Tor, Donald Bell(bs).

INSTRUMENTAL ENSEMBLE

String Quartet No 1 in F. 1944. 28'. ms. Apr 1, 1944, RCMT Qt.
Duo for Violin and Piano. 1947. 8'30". Ric, 1961. CBC BR SM-28 & 135; RCI-124 & 244. Feb 3, 1948, Tor, Eugene Kash(vln), John Newmark(pno).
String Quartet No 2 in A Minor. 1952–5. 27'15". CMC. Mar 11, 1956, Tor, CBC, Parlow Qt.
Sonata No 1. 1956. 15'. vln, pno. CMC. RCI-194. Feb 13, 1957, Tor, CBC, Albert Pratz (vln), Mario Bernardi(pno).
String Quartet No 3 in E. 1959. 33'. CMC. Oct 9, 1959, Mtl, Mtl Str Qt, Hyman Bress (vln), Mildred Goodman(vln), Otto Joachim (vla), Walter Joachim(vlc).
Trio. 1960. 16'. fl, ob, hpschd or pno. CMC. RCA CC/CCS-1013; RCI-219. July 2, 1961, Mtl, CBC, Bar Trio Mtl, Mario Duschenes (fl), Melvin Berman(ob), Kelsey Jones (hpschd).
Two Fantasies for Cello and Piano. 1962 (rev 1970). 14'30". CMC. Feb 4, 1971, Tor, Tsuyoshi Tsutsumi(vlc), P Giron(pno).
Two Preludes. 1965 (rev 1972). 9'. vln, pno. CMC. July 31, 1969, Australian Broadcasting Commission, Ladislav Jasek(vln), Rhonda Vickers(pno).

PIANO

Sonata Tragica. 1945. 26'. ms. Mar 24, 1946, CBC, Oskar Morawetz.
Scherzo. 1947. 4'40". B & H, 1958. CBC BR SM-65/118; RCI-121. Apr 24, 1950, Tor, Rudolf Firkusny.
Fantasy in D Minor. 1948. 14'30". CMC. CBS-32110045/46; RCI-120. Jan 4, 1951, Tor, Glenn Gould.
Tarantelle. 1949. 5'. ms. Dec 7, 1949, Tor, Oskar Morawetz.
Ballade. 1950. 8'. CMC. 1951, Baltimore, Ray Dudley.
Fantasy on a Hebrew Theme. 1951. 14'10". CMC. RCI-133. Feb 28, 1952, Tor, Gordon Kushner.
Scherzino. 1953. 1'30". FH, 1955. RCI-121. 1957, Boris Roubakine.
Fantasy, Elegy and Toccata. 1958. 11'50". MCA, 1968. Jan 19, 1958, Tor, Oskar Morawetz.
Ten Preludes for Piano. 1966. 20'10". FH, 1966 (Nos 1 & 9).
Suite for Piano. 1968. 9'. MCA, 1971. Dec, 1969, Mtl, Anton Kuerti.

BIBLIOGRAPHY

See B-B; B65,71; Bec57,58,70; Bt; C63,66, 69,72; CrC(I); Esc; K; Lv; Wa.
'A Canadian Composer's Tribute to Anne Frank', *CanCo.* No. 53, Oct. 1970 (28–9, 32–3).
'J.F.K.'s Memory Inspires Composer', *CanCo.* No. 6, Feb. 1966 (10, 44).
'Oskar Morawetz: An International Success', *CanCo.* No. 16, Mar. 1967 (4–5, 44–5).
'Oskar Morawetz', *Time.* Vol. XCV, no. 23, June 8, 1970 (7–8).
'Oskar Morawetz – a portrait', *Mu.* No. 25, Dec. 1969 (8–9).
'Oskar Morawetz' Sinfonietta Wins Critics' Award', *CanCo.* No. 10, Sept. 1966 (34–5).
'The Poet, the Composer and the Artist', *CanCo.* No. 22, Oct. 1967 (20–1).
Schulman, Michael. 'Oskar Morawetz: Continuing to write in the "old" forms', *CanCo.* No. 90, Apr. 1974 (28–35, 46).

MOREL, FRANCOIS (b. Montreal, Que., 14 Mar. 1926). He is a member of the first generation of Quebec composers trained at the Conservatoire de Musique de la province de Québec (established in 1942), where he studied with Isabelle Delorme (harmony, counterpoint and fugue), Germaine Malépart (piano), and Claude CHAMPAGNE (composition). Unlike his contemporaries MERCURE, GARANT, PÉPIN, and MATTON who, on leaving the Conservatoire, continued their studies in Paris with Messiaen or Boulanger, Morel stayed in Montreal to pursue his own muse. At that time the CBC enlisted his collaboration to write songs and music for the theatre, etc. Recognition came on October 16, 1953, when *Antiphonie* (1953) was presented in Carnegie Hall, New York, in a concert of six Canadian works conducted by Leopold Stokowski. Determined to make known contemporary music, and new Quebec music in particular, Morel joined Serge Garant and Gilles TREMBLAY in organizing a concert (May 1, 1954) of works by Webern, Messiaen, Boulez, Tremblay, Garant, and Morel, which provoked violent reactions. In 1958, with the help of Otto JOACHIM and Jeanne Landry, Morel and Garant established 'Musique de notre temps', an organization devoted to the promotion of new music.

Several of Morel's works written during this period show the influence of his studies. Claude Champagne's teaching, for example, emphasized the construction of work built on well-known models; works of the great masters would be used as guides, the student composer being led to a freedom from formal elements – harmonic and rhythmic – by going beyond them. Thus *Esquisse* (1946), for orchestra, is suggested by Debussy's 'Images'. The *Quatre chants japonais* (1949), for voice and piano, recall Ravel. The music of Bartok and Stravinsky suggested to Morel directions in rhythmic explorations, as in the first *Quatuor à cordes* (1952). In 'borrowing' from the *Salve Regina*, Morel sought in *Antiphonie* a solution to the problem of melody, the source of musical continuity. A modal treatment evokes Gregorian plainchant. At the same time the alternations of psalm-form are reduced to an essential minimum; a debt to Messiaen is likewise evident. However, the rigidity of the theme within a spatial movement indicates the preoccupations that led Morel to his meeting with Varèse in the summer of 1958. The impact of this meeting is quite evident in *Rituel de l'espace* (1958–9) and *Boréal* (1959). Composed at the request of the CBC for l'Orchestre des Petites Symphonies, *Rituel de l'espace* is a symphonic poem in rondo form, extending into space a nostalgic cantilena (played by the English horn). Inspired by a poem by Wilfrid Lemoyne, Morel creates a static mood by means of large, slow-moving blocks of sound; change occurs without 'edges', almost imperceptibly. *Boréal* was written at the request of the Youth Committee of the Montreal Symphony Orchestra; a most eloquent witness to the influence of Varèse, it marks an important step in a search for control that hitherto had remained instinctive. In time this led further to the composing of *l'Etoile noire* (1962), a turning point in the composer's development.

It was after the slow, steady assimilation of the works of the Viennese, and principally of Schoenberg's works opus 11 – 22, that Morel came to adopt the fundamental principles of dodecaphonism. But their application was never to be total. In *l'Etoile noire* only the pitch is determined by a twelve-tone series, derived from the F major quartet of Beethoven, opus 135. This serial consciousness is developed in the course of the second *Quatuor à cordes* (1962–3; a 'mirror' series on B-A-C-H), in *Sinfonia for jazz-band* (1963; the series built on 'pivoting mirror' cells), *Nuvattuq* (1967; a work built on two series, the second a permutation of the first), and *Prismes-Anamorphoses* (1967; series built entirely of tones and half-tones forming invertible chromaticisms). On the formal plane Morel relaxed very cautiously the traditional structures before seeking new forms deriving from the series. *L'Etoile noire,* subtitled *Tombeau de Borduas,* pays homage to the great French-Canadian painter, 'l'homme des au-delà' ('the man from Beyond'); the composer has given it the emotion, the grandeur, and the violence of the Borduas painting, which is in black and white only. Just as the painter plays with colour, Morel plays with orchestral effect; the movement is made by a layering of intensities and by the juxtaposition of sound masses. *Nuvattuq* in its turn pays homage to Varèse; influenced by 'Densité 21.5', it employs the latter's main procedures. *Prismes-Anamorphoses* embodies an alternation of rule and freedom, achieved by fixed passages seen through 'windows' in the score, around which are quoted more relaxed, even non-serial passages. As a result of such new organization, on the level of language as much as of form, Morel deserted large ensembles in favour of chamber groups ranging from the string quartet with solo instrument to groups of fifteen to eighteen instruments. Winds and percussion take the place of the symphony orchestra, which does not reappear in his output until 1972 with *Radiance*. The single exception was *Trajectoire* (1967), a work commissioned by the CBC to accompany film images to texts by St-Exupéry for a special program marking the opening of Expo 67. Less radical than those that preceded it, this work is built nevertheless on a series based on the minor second, the major third, and the minor third; eleven sections make up a single movement, suggesting the eleven intervals contained in the twelve notes of the series. Each section treats the material differently without inhibiting the overall continual variation. And as with most of his work, Morel here underlines the play of colour rather than the elements of structure.

The three works *Départs* (1968, rev. 1969), *Iikkii* (1972), and *Radiance* (1956, final rev. 1972) seem to mark the beginning of a third period – not that Morel abandons the principles of serial organization but rather that he masters them in order to achieve freedom. *Départs* was written for the McGill Chamber Orchestra and, as its title indicates, it points to a new period, marked by a more personal style and less subject to the various influences emanating from his contemporaries. *Iikkii* offers confirmation of this development. In this score, inscribed with a text of Maurice Beaulieu (1958) – 'Verdure glaciaire et toi, toundra, vous m'êtes fraternelle' ('Icy greenery and thou, tundra, are to me as brothers') – Morel conveys the calm rigour of the Eskimo verses; the gravitation of its various sequences about the pivot-notes E and F accentuates the horizontal line, and through the concertante structure he sets up the play of colour among the eighteen instruments. *Radiance* marks a return to the symphony orchestra; 'windows' in the score and multiple series are built into a highly compact serial organization in which rhythms and relationships are derived from the intervals of the series, semi-tones and sixteenths providing the underlying unity.

Brought up in the French tradition, Morel has undergone a measured development within which every step is marked with the sign of exorcism. Of the thirty-odd works that figure in his catalogue, eight are for orchestra, fifteen are for groups in which woodwinds, brass and percussion predominate, two are for string quartet, and five are for solo instrument. Some forays into the field of electronic music have been rejected on the grounds that such fixed works could never evolve as society evolves. Morel will always feel a need for the remaking of music: such is his concept of continual evolution.

Morel is a member of the Canadian League of Composers and an affiliate of BMI Canada. LYSE RICHER-LORTIE

MUSICAL WORKS

ORCHESTRA

Esquisse, Op 1. 1946–7. 8'55". med orch. Ber, 1964. RCI-129. Oct 7, 1947, Mtl, CBC O, Alexander Brott(cond).

Antiphonie. 1953. 5'30". full orch. Ber, 1960. Louis LS-661. Oct 16, 1953, NY, Carnegie Hall, Leopold Stokowski(cond).

Rituel de l'espace. 1958–9. 19'. full orch. ms. RCI-213. Apr 6, 1960, Mtl, Little Symphonies Orch, Roland Leduc(cond).

Boréal. 1959. 13'. full orch. Ber, (in process). Apr 26, 1960, Mtl, MSO, Markevitch (cond).

L'Etoile noire (Tombeau de Borduas). 1962. 6'40". full orch. Ber, 1964. Col MS-6962. Mar 13, 1962, Mtl, MSO, Thomas Schippers (cond).

Trajectoire. 1967. 11'10". full orch. ms. Apr 20, 1967, Mtl, CBC (Fr TV net), CBC O, Morel(cond).

Radiance. 1970–2. 19'. small orch. Ric, 1974. RCI-367. Feb 8, 1971, Vanc, CBC O, Serge Garant(cond).

CHOIR WITH ORCHESTRA

Intrada. 1957. SATB, orch. ms.

CHOIR

Osmonde. 1963. SSAA. ms.

VOICE

Quatre chants japonais. 1949. 4'30". sop, pno. ms. May 1, 1954, Mtl, Josèphe Colle (sop), François Morel(pno).

Les Rivages perdus. 1954. 7'55". sop or ten, pno. ms. RCI-201. Apr 3, 1955, Mtl, Josèphe Colle(sop), François Morel(pno). Text: Wilfrid Lemoyne.

INSTRUMENTAL ENSEMBLE

Diptyque (orig *Suite pour petit orchestre*). 1948 (rev 1956). 9'. 23 inst (ww, brass, perc). ms. RCI-7 (orig version). Mar 11, 1949, youth orch, Fernand Graton(cond).

Quatuor No 1. 1952. 15'30". str qt. ms. Mar 2, 1955, Mtl, Mtl Str Qt (Bress, Goodman, O Joachim, W Joachim).

Cassation. 1954. 8′55″. ww septet. ms. RCI-128. 1955, Mtl, Roland Leduc(cond).
Litanies. 1956 (rev 1970). c 10′. ww, brass, hp, pno, cel, perc. ms.
Spirale. 1956. 10′. ww, brass, hp, cel, perc. ms. Dec 31, 1956, CBC Mtl, Otto-Werner Mueller(cond).
Symphonie pour cuivres. 1956. c 15′. brass, perc. ms. May 1956, CBC Mtl, Otto-Werner Mueller(cond).
Rythmologue. 1957 (rev 1970). 12′. 8 or 6 perc. ms. RCI-298. May 8, 1970, Mtl, RCI, François Morel(cond).
Le Mythe de la Roche percée. 1961. 16′. double ww, perc. ms. June 10, 1961, Pittsburgh, Amer Wind Symph Orch, Robert Austin Boudrau(cond).
Quintette No 1. 1962. 9′. 2tpt, hn, tbn, tba. CMC. CBC BR SM-216. Aug 15, 1962, Mtl, MBQ.
Quatuor No 2. 1963. 16′. str qt. ms. July 10, 1963, Tor, Can Str Qt.
Requiem for Winds. 1963. c 15′. ww, brass, hp, cel, perc. ms.
Sinfonia for jazz-band. 1963. c 10′. 5sax, 5tpt, 4hn, 4tbn, tba, hp, pno, perc, cb. ms.
Etude en forme de toccate. 1965. 1′45″. 2 perc. Ber, 1968. CBC Mtl, François Morel (cond).
Neumes d'Espace et Reliefs. 1967. 7′40″. ww, brass, hp, cel, perc. CMC. Oct 28, 1967, Ed'tn, ESO, Brian Priestman(cond).
Prismes-Anamorphoses. 1967. 10′15″. ww, brass, hp, pno, cel, perc. ms. RCI-292. June 26, 1968, Tor, CBC O, Jean Deslauriers (cond).
Départs. 1969. 10′. guit, hp, str, perc. ms. RCI-367. Mar 17, 1969, Mtl, McGill Ch O, Alexander Brott(cond).
Iikkii (Froidure). 1971. 16′25″. 18 inst soloists. Ric, 1974. RCI-367. Feb 3, 1972, Mtl, SMCQ Ens, Serge Garant(cond).

PIANO

Ronde Enfantine. 1949. 2′05″. Ber, 1953. RCI-135.
Deux Etudes de sonorité. 1952–4. 2′20″, 4′15″. Ber, 1966. RCI-251. May 1, 1954, Mtl, François Morel.

INSTRUMENTAL SOLO

Nuvattuq. 1967. 4′30″. alto fl. CMC. Nov 1968, CBC Tor, Robert Aitken.

ORGAN

Prière. 1954. 5′25″. Ber, 1965. Feb 8, 1954, Mtl, Bernard Lagacé.
Alleluia. 1964–8. c 9′. ms. Madr MA-408. July 3, 1968, Mtl, Bernard Lagacé.

BIBLIOGRAPHY

See B-B; B58,71; Bec57,70; CrC(II); D165; K; Lv; Wa.
Beckwith, John. 'Recent Orchestral Works by Champagne, Morel and Anhalt', *CMJ*. Vol. IV, no. 4, Summer 1960 (44–8).
Bisbrouck, Noel. 'François Morel', *Culture Information*. Vol. I, no. 1, Apr.-May 1969 (18–20).
Cowell, Henry. 'Current Chronicle: New York', *MQ*. Vol. XL, no. 1, Jan. 1954 (56–62).
'François Morel: Faire Sonner la Musique', *Musiques du Kébèk* (R. Duguay, ed.). Montreal: Editions du Jour, 1971 (129–33).
Frankenstein, Alfred. 'If this were the music of Canada, God Save the Queen and les Canadiens', *High Fidelity*. Vol. XVIII, no. 3, Mar. 1968 (84–6).
Lagacé, B. 'François Morel, musicien canadien', *Liberté*. Vol. LX, Jan.-Feb. 1960 (66–71).
Thériault, Jacques. 'François Morel', *MuSc*. No. 256, Nov.-Dec. 1970 (4–5).

LITERARY WORKS

ARTICLES

'Edgard Varèse ou la conscience du son et de l'espace', *Liberté*. Vol. LIX, Sept.-Oct. 1959 (287–92).
'Hyperprisme', *Liberté*. Vol. LX, May-June 1960 (222–3).
'Quintette à cuivres', *Musiques du Kébèk* (R. Duguay, ed.). Montreal: Editions du Jour, 1971 (134).

N

NAYLOR, BERNARD (b. Cambridge, England, 22 Nov. 1907). He was born into a family steeped in the music of the English ecclesiastical tradition. His father was a composer, Cambridge lecturer in music history, and organist at Emmanuel College, Cambridge, and his grandfather was organist and choirmaster at York Minster. Bernard Naylor's advanced formal training began in 1924 at the Royal College of Music where, as an open scholar in composition, he studied under Vaughan Williams, Holst, and Ireland. At Oxford from 1927 to 1931 he was organ scholar at Exeter College and gained practical experience conducting the Oxford University Opera Club. He came to Canada in 1932 and became conductor of the Winnipeg Philharmonic and Male Choirs and the Winnipeg Symphony Orchestra, but he returned to England in 1936 and was appointed organist and Director of Music at Queen's College, Oxford, a post he retained until 1939. Back in Canada by 1942, Bernard Naylor founded the Little Symphony Orchestra in Montreal and conducted it until 1947. He held two further teaching posts in England, at the Faculty of Music, Oxford, 1950–2, and as Lecturer in Music at Reading University, 1953–9. In England he received commissions from the BBC (Proms, Third Programme, etc.), from the Louis Halsey Singers, and from the Thames Concert Society.

In 1959 Bernard Naylor moved permanently to Canada and thereafter devoted himself entirely to composition. He has lived in Victoria, B.C., since 1968. In Canada he has received commissions from the CBC (*King Solomon's Prayer*, commissioned in honour of the coronation of Queen Elizabeth II in 1953), from the Winnipeg Choristers (*Missa da Camera*, 1966), and from the University of Manitoba Chamber Music Group, (*The Nymph Complaining for the Death of her Faun*, 1965), the latter two in honour of the centennial of Canada's confederation.

Although Naylor has written some instrumental compositions (*Variations for Small Orchestra*, 1960; *String Trio*, 1960), his principal works are vocal. In their emotional and imaginative range and their personally evolved harmonic and contrapuntal idiom, they make a distinguished contribution to the contemporary choral repertoire. The second of his *Three Latin Motets* (1948–9) illustrates aspects of his later choral style in gestation: sombre intonations of repeated chords respond to the 'Victimae Paschali' text, and depictive harmonic clashes result from stepwise part-writing. But it is the central dialogue between male soloists and four-part women's chorus that best shows Naylor's acute sensitivity to the poetic overtones of the words; in answer to the tenor soloist's urgent question, an ethereal point of imitation setting the words 'surrexit Christus spes mea' gradually merges into an unexpected seventh chord by a process entirely linear.

One of Bernard Naylor's best-known works is the cycle *Nine Motets* (1952) for five-part unaccompanied chorus, with texts taken from the lessons according to the lectionaries for the nine major Feast Days of the Church. The second of these motets, setting verses from the ninth chapter of *Isaiah*, exemplifies some of the composer's characteristic melodic turns: a rising pattern of a second followed by a third eloquently conveys the concluding words 'The Mighty God, the Everlasting Father, the Prince of Peace', and other melodic lines move stepwise within a narrow range or outline an arc of successive thirds. Echo effects and a skilful juxtaposition of textual phrases enhance the almost pictorial impression of this fine piece. Motet one, 'Come Ye and Let us Go up to the House of the Lord', and motet six for Easter Day are the liveliest and most dance-like in the cycle, and the repeating scriptural invitation of the former is an especially felicitous touch. The cycle was first performed by the Elizabethan Singers under Louis Halsey in 1959.

Later works explore a more austere emotional landscape represented by a more closely reasoned organization of melodic intervals. Chief among these are the *Six Poems from Miserere* (1960) and the *Stabat*

Mater (1961). The *Miserere* poems are by the British poet David Gascoyne and express a religious and almost inconsolable contemporary consciousness. Changes of style are immediately declared in the opening bars of this cycle. Whereas the seventh chords in the eighth of the *Nine Motets* seemed like a reversion to an older harmonic style, here in the *Miserere* motets they gain a new, strangely disembodied and poetic power; i.e. the governing intervals of a second and a third permeate the entire cycle, methods of intervallic organization taking both horizontal and vertical forms, as in the fourth motet 'Kyrie'. The pervasive four-note imitations and motivic mirrors in the third motet, 'De Profundis', even suggest Webern; but the unbroken seams of stepwise melodies and a basic dependence on the interval of a third, as well as the composer's temperament and intentions, are poles apart from any such influence.

This ordering rigour finds its most extreme instance in Bernard Naylor's setting of the *Stabat Mater* for women's double chorus, strings, and double woodwinds in which the device of contrary motion is strictly applied to two voices or two pairs of voices throughout much of the composition. Two different single-voice passages and a closely imitative passage in four parts provide the only contrasting textures. The attenuated orchestral accompaniment is often locked, as it were, in repeated or sustained chords and its movements are subjected to the same principles determining the lines of the voices. A ghostly chromatic flutter barely disturbs the numbed atmosphere. This severe lament is one of Naylor's most hermetic and powerful works. It was given its first performance at the Three Choirs Festival in 1964.

Naylor's secular settings, in lighter vein, are comparatively fewer in number. An appealing representative is the four-part *Herrick-Suite* (1952 and 1956) to four poems from the *Hesperides* collection by Robert Herrick. The second song, 'To Springs and Groves', shows how the composer's deft disposition of words and illustrative rhythms can sharpen the witty edge of Herrick's conceit.

Works for voice with piano, orchestral or chamber ensemble accompaniment initiated Naylor's output, and throughout his career the solo voice has been, next to the chorus, his principal medium. One of the earliest and most expressive examples is the cycle of four songs, *The Living Fountain* (1947), to poems by the seventeenth-century poet Rowland Watkyns. The simplicity of these verses is faithfully captured in settings characterized by tender but deliberately restrained vocal writing and economical instrumental support. An 'Alleluia' epilogue, written in 1963, now rounds off the cycle with fragments of an expansive phrase from the fourth song. The 'quietist' elements in this work are signs of the tone predominant in the music to follow. Naylor is not concerned with baroque display in his vocal music; the virtuoso element is egregiously absent. This predilection for understatement accounts for the occasional failure to realize the poem; instrumental thinness at the end of the cantata *Sing O My Love* (1963), for instance, cannot support the George Herbert utterance that precedes it.

The years since 1963 have seen a steady flow of some thirty works, most of them choral compositions to sacred texts; among these may be cited *Exultet Mundus Gaudio* (1969) and *The Morning Watch and the Evening Watch* (Vaughan) (1970). The as-yet-unpublished *Personal Landscape* (1971), a song cycle (commissioned by the Thames Concert Society) for soprano and chamber ensemble to poems by the Canadian poet P.K. Page, marks a departure in choice of texts from Naylor's preference for the metaphysical poets and should prove to be a setting of exceptional interest.

Naylor is a member of CAPAC.

WILLIAM AIDE

MUSICAL WORKS

SMALL ORCHESTRA

Variations for Small Orchestra. Mar 1960. 1961, WSO, Victor Feldbrill.

SOLOIST WITH ORCHESTRA

The Living Fountain. 1947–63. 15'. high vc, str orch. Novl, 1966. Text: Rowland Watkyns. 1950, London, Eng, New London Orch, Alec Sherman(cond), Eric Greene (ten).

CHOIR WITH ORCHESTRA

King Solomon's Prayer. 1953. 11'. sop,

SATB, chamb orch. UE, 1955. Text: Wisdom of Solomon. 1953, Wpg, CBC, Wpg Choristers, W H Anderson(cond) Wpg Orch, Eric Wild(cond), Frances James(sop).
Stabat Mater. 1961. 10'. SSAA, orch. Novl, 1964. 1964, England, Hereford Cathedral, Three Choirs Fest, Melville Cook.
Sing O My Love. 1963. 9'. bs, SATB, str orch. Novl, 1964. 1964, London, Eng, BBC Prom Conc, Thames Chamb Choir, BBC O, Louis Halsey(cond), John Shirley-Quirk(bs).
The Resurrection according to Saint Matthew. 1965. 15'. sop, bar, bs, spkrs, SATB, orch. Novl, 1967.
Missa da Camera. 1954–66. 12'. solo qt (semi SATB), SATB, chamb orch. Novl, 1970. Nov 23, 1967, Wpg, Wpg Choristers, orch conducted by Filmer Hubble.
Festal Te Deum. 1968. SATB, orch. ms. 1970, WSO, Phil Choir, Arthur Polson.
Scenes and Prophecies. 1968–9. sop, SATB, brass, perc. ms. 1971, England, BBC Prom Conc, Janet Price(sop).

CHOIR

Dull Soul Aspire. 1950. SSAATTBB. Novl, 1965. Text: John Collop. 1967, England, BBC, Thames Chamb Choir, Louis Halsey.
Three Motets. 1950. SATB. West, 1950. 1950, Chichester Cathedral, (South) London Bach Soc, Paul Steinitz.
Motet for the Circumcision. 1951. SSATB. Novl, 1965. Text: Deut 30 vv 4–6, 8.
Nine Motets. 1952. SATB. Novl, 1960, Argo ZRG-5426. 1959, London, Eng, Elizabethan Sgrs, Louis Halsey.
Herrick Suite. 1952–6. SATB. Novl, 1966. Text: Robert Herrick. 1956, England, Dartington Hall, Saltire Sgrs.
The Spacious Firmament on High. 1956. SATB. Novl, 1962. Text: Joseph Addison.
I Sing the Birth was Born Tonight. 1959. SSATB. Novl, 1962. Text: Ben Jonson. 1961, England, BBC, Cecilia Sgrs, Richard Sinton.
Kubla Khan. 1960. SSAA, pno. Novl, 1963. Text: S T Coleridge. Wpg, Oriana Sgrs, Berythe Birse.
Six Poems from Miserere. 1960. 2 sop, SSAATTBB. Rob, 1972. Text: David Gascoyne. 1963, London, Eng, Wigmore Hall, Elizabethan Sgrs, Louis Halsey.
Vain Wits and Eyes. Jan 1960. SATB. Novl, 1961. Text: Henry Vaughan. 1960, Bristol Madrigal Soc, Herbert Byard.
My Song is Love Unknown. 1962. sop, ten, bs, SAA. Novl, 1967. Text: Samuel Crossman.
Does the Day-Star Rise? 1964. SATB, org. Novl, 1964. Text: Richard Crashaw.
Magnificat & Nunc Dimittis. 1964. SATB. Novl, 1965. 1967, England, BBC, Thames Chamb Choir, Louis Halsey.
Of One That Is So Fair and Bright. 1964. 2 sop, alto, SSA. Novl, 1965. Text: anon (c1300).
Service and Strength. 1964. SATB, org. Novl, 1965. Text: Christina Rossetti.
Creator Spirit. 1966. SATB. Novl, 1967. Text: John Dryden.
O Be Joyful in the Lord. 1966. SATB, org. Novl, 1966. Text: Psalm 100.
Sonnet to the Trinity. 1966. SATB, org (opt). Novl, 1967. Text: John Davies. 1967, Aldeburgh Fest, Purcell Sgrs, Imogen Holst.
The Star Song; 'A Carol to the King'. 1966. sop, SATB. Novl, 1967. Text: Robert Herrick. England, York Univ Choir.
The Armour of Light. 1967. 15'. sop, SATB, org, pno. Novl, 1967. Dec 13, 1967, U of Man Choir, Robert Irwin.
Exultet Mundus Gaudio. 1969. sop, alto, ten, bs, SATB. Rob, 1972. 1970, London Eng, Queen Elizabeth Hall, Caldicott Schl Choir, Louis Halsey.
Invitation to Music. 1969. 5'. SATB, org. Rob, 1973. Text: Richard Crashaw.
Missa sine Credo. 1969. 8'. SATB. Rob, 1973.

VOICE(S)

A Child's Carol. 1947. med vc, pno. West, 1948. Text: Arthur L Salmon.
Dreams of the Sea. 1947. med vc, pno. West, 1950. Text: W H Davies. Wpg, Albert Trueman(bar).
The Ecstatic. 1947. med (high) vc, pno. West, 1949. Text: C Day Lewis.
The Fallen Poplar. 1947. med vc, pno. West, 1949. Text: Mary Webb.
Rose-Berries. 1947. med vc, pno. West, 1949. Text: Mary Webb.
Sleep, O Sleep. 1949. med vc, pno. Augener, 1952. Text: John Gay.
To Sleep. 1949. med vc, pno. Augener, 1952. Text: John Keats.

VOICE WITH INSTRUMENTAL ENSEMBLE

The Nymph complaining for the death of her Faun. 1965. 11'. mezz (alto), fl, ob (EH), cl, bsn, str qt. CMC. Text: Andrew Marvell. Nov 23, 1967, Wpg, Heather Ireland, Arthur Polson.

On Mrs Arabella Hunt Singing. 1970. sop, vla da gamba, hpschd. CMC. Text: William Congreve. Feb 1971, Tor, York U, Burton Aud, Mary Morrison(sop).

INSTRUMENTAL ENSEMBLE

String Trio. 1960. vln, vla, vlc. CMC. 1960, Wpg, Corydon Str Trio.

BIBLIOGRAPHY

Wa.

Morgan, Kit. 'A Word Portrait of Victoria Composer Bernard Naylor', *CanCo*. No. 57, Feb. 1971 (14–16).

NIMMONS, PHILIP (b. Kamloops, B.C., 3 June 1923). He moved to Vancouver at the age of seven and began his musical training on the piano and clarinet. He graduated from the University of British Columbia in 1944 with a Bachelor of Arts degree in pre-Meds, but then decided to take up music seriously. He played with the Ray Norris Quintet (CBC radio) from 1943 to 1948. He received scholarships to study at the Juilliard School of Music in New York (1945–8), then at the Royal Conservatory of Music in Toronto, studying composition with John WEINZWEIG, Richard JOHNSTON and Arnold WALTER (1948–50). After his formal studies Nimmons' compositions were largely devoted to the jazz idiom, his works being generally for large jazz bands. Since 1950 he has been active as composer and arranger for documentaries and drama productions for CBC radio and television. In 1953 he formed his own jazz ensemble, 'Nimmons and Nine', and later 'Nimmons and Nine Plus Six', appearing regularly on CBC broadcasts and telecasts. Other activities of the group have included film scores with music by Nimmons for two feature films (*A Dangerous Age*, 1957; *A Cool Sound from Hell*, 1959); participation in the Toronto Jazz Festival (1959); concerts and lectures for jazz societies, schools, and universities; several recordings, including 'The Canadian Scene' (1957), 'Take Ten' (1964), 'Mary Poppins Swings' (1965), and 'Strictly Nimmons' (1965); appearances on the CBC-TV series 'The Barris Beat' and other CBC-TV specials; and performances throughout Canada and at Canadian armed forces bases around the world. In 1960 – with Oscar Peterson, Ray Brown, and Ed Thigpen – Nimmons formed the Advanced School of Contemporary Music in Toronto, but the enterprise proved too demanding on their professional careers and was dissolved in 1963. In 1972 he assumed direction of a jazz workshop in the Faculty of Music, University of Toronto. He is a member of the Canadian League of Composers and is affiliated with BMI Canada.

MUSICAL WORKS

FILM

A Dangerous Age. 1957. Film: Sidney Furie.

A Cool Sound from Hell. 1959. Film: Sidney Furie.

Power by Proxy. 1961. Film: Paul Almond.

RADIO AND TELEVISION

Affectionately Jenny. 1950.

Dr Dogbody's Leg. 1951.

High Adventures. 1952.

The Fantastic Emperor. 1961.

Music for several CBC radio drama, documentary and jazz series, including: CBC Wednesday Night (CBC Sunday Night, CBC Tuesday Night, 1950–64); CBC Stage (1953); Jazz Workshop (1962–5); On Stage (1967); etc.

Music for several CBC-TV music and variety series, including: The Barris Beat (1958–9); Show Time (1959); Folio (1950–61); All Canadian Jazz Show (1960, 1961); etc.

ORCHESTRA

Scherzo. 1950.

Suite for Spring. 1951.

VOICE(S)

Summer Rain. 1948.

Parting. 1948.

A Little Black Man. 1948.

INSTRUMENTAL ENSEMBLE

Sonatina. 1948. fl, str qt.

String Quartet. 1950.

Interlude. 1951. vla, pno.

Opus UNB. 1969. str qt, pno, jazz qt.

Palette à deux. 1972. alto sax, 4trb, rhythm section.

87 works for Jazz Ensemble, including: *Humpy* (1953); *Blues for Meetin'* (1954); *Groove* (1957); *I See the Blues for Me* (1957); *Little Father* (1957); *Mr Big Blues* (1957); *Phil Not Bill* (1957); *The Thirty Years Blues* (1957); *Bass-ically Yours* (1958); *Blues for Someone* (1958); *Here They Are* (1958); *I Told You So* (1958);

In a Minor Mode (1958); *MJQ* (1958); *Mrs Big Blues* (1958); *One for Mr 'B'* (1958); *Real Kicklets* (1958); *Sku-Ba-Doo* (1958); *Sneaky* (1958); *Some Others* (1958); *Squits* (1958); *Two of a Kind* (1958); *Who Walks* (1958); *Dig* (1959); *Ed's Up* (1959); *Jasper* (1959); Something *Else* (1959); *Swing Softly* (1959); *Tipsy* (1959); *Asarully* (1960); *Bugaboo* (1960); *Gone with the Blues* (1960); *Maybe Baby* (1960); *Squatter's Rites* (1960); *Squeeze Play* (1960); *Walkin' Lovers* (1960); *Blues for Someone Else* (1962); *Fancy Dancy* (1962); *Howlin' Marsh* (1962); *On the Autobahn* (1962); *Swing Lovely* (1962); *Twooch* (1962); *Back on the Bus* (1963); *Carey Dance* (1963); *Did You Say* (1963); *Ed's Comp* (1963); *Holly Dance* (1963); *Not Soon Enough* (1963); *One 'O' Nine* (1963); *Peaches and Brandy* (1963); *Steve's Theme* (1963); *The Getaway* (1964); *Room at the Back* (1964); *Watch Out for the Little People* (1964); *Ballad No 1 – Untitled* (1965); *Brassly Speaking* (1965); *Go Trane* (1965); *I Love to Play* (1965); *It Sounds Like You* (1965); *Kicks* (1965); *Just Us, Just Fun, Just Kicks* (1965); *One More for Baby* (1965); *Nosey* (1965); *Step Right In* (1965); *Blues-Ex* (1966); *Just for Now* (1966); *New Kicks* (1966); *Night, Night, Smiley* (1966); *Sometime* (1966); *Room In the Front* (1966); *What's It* (1966); *Ballad No 2 – Thordis* (1967); *My Name, Who Cares?* (1967); *Somewhere Every Summer* (1967); *Footsteps* (1968); *Jades to Open* (1968); *Nufsicisum* (1968); *Build Up* (1969); *Come What May* (1969); *Chips and Gravey* (1969); *Horns a Plenty* (1969); *Mod's Mode* (1969); *Blues Blow* (1970); *Lip Flap* (1970); *Shadows* (1970); *What Doin'* (1970); *It's Up to You* (1971); *Rickshaw* (1971).

PIANO

Toccata. 1949.

RECORDINGS

The Canadian Scene. 1957. Verve MGV-8025.
Nimmons 'N' Nine. 1959. Verve MGV-8376.
Take Ten. 1964. RCA LCP/LCPS-1066.
Mary Poppins Swings. 1965. RCA PC/PCS-1005.
Strictly Nimmons. 1966. RCA PC/PCS-1047.
Nimmons Now. 1970. CBC IS LM-74.

BIBLIOGRAPHY

CrC(II); K.
'Canadian Jazz Night at the Stratford Festival', *CBC Times.* Vol. IX, no. 2, July 22–8, 1956 (2).
Crandell, Ev. 'Phil Nimmons', *MuSc.* No. 245, Jan.-Feb. 1969 (8).

O

O'NEILL, CHARLES (b. Duntocher, Scotland, 31 Aug. 1882; d. Toronto, Ont., Sept. 1964). He studied in England with A.L. Peace (organ) and Archibald Evans (harmony and counterpoint) and at the Royal Military School of Music (conducting and orchestration). In 1906 he came to Canada as solo cornetist with the Royal Canadian Artillery Band in Kingston, Ont. From the McGill Conservatorium he received his Bachelor of Music (1914) and Doctor of Music (1924) degrees. He also studied composition with Herbert Sanders in Ottawa. While in Montreal he was bandmaster and director of music of the Royal Canadian Artillery and later of the Royal 22nd Regiment. He was co-conductor of the CBC's Little Symphony Orchestra in Montreal. He held teaching positions in the music departments of the University of Wisconsin and the State Teachers' College in Potsdam, N.Y. (1937–47), returning to Canada in 1947 to join the teaching staff of the Royal Conservatory of Music in Toronto.

O'Neill's works for band have been his most successful compositions. Using for the most part a simple A B A form in a traditional tonal idiom, he produced many popular marches, including *The Emblem* (published 1930), *Nulli Secundus* (published 1931), and *Regimental March of the RCMP* (published 1960). He was president of the American Bandmasters' Association and vice-president of the Dominion College of Music. His estate is a member of CAPAC.

MUSICAL WORKS

ORCHESTRA

The Land of the Maple and Beaver (arr). 1918; B & H, 1918.
Remembrance (arr). c1935.
A Day in June. c1945.
Prelude and Fugue in G. 1945–6.
Suite of Four Numbers. 1948.
Air de Ballet (La Ballerina). 1949.
Irish Fantasy. 1958.
Irish Rhapsody. c1959.
Many arrangements of works by other composers.

BAND

In the Moonlight (Entr'acte). c1925; Wat, 1928.
The Emblem. c1930; Wat, 1930.
Souvenir de Québec (Fantasia). c1930; Fischer, 1930. RCA PC/PCS-1003.
Nulli Secundus. c1930; Wat, 1931.
Mademoiselle Coquette. c1930; Fischer, 1933.
The Silver Cord. c1930; G Schirm, 1934.
Tout à Vous. 1932. Fischer.
The Knights Errant. c1935; Rubank, 1939.
Remembrance (Symphonic Serenade). c1935; Fischer, 1935.
The Three Graces. c1935; Fox, 1939.
Builders of Youth. 1937. Fischer.
Aladdin's Lamp. 1940. Fischer.
Sunshine and Flowers. c1940; E B Marks, 1943.
Autumn Glory. 1943.
Festival (Overture). 1943.
Greghmount. 1943.
Nobility (Overture). 1943; Remick, 1948.
Strongheart. 1943.
Majesty (Overture). 1945; Remick, 1948.
Fidelity (Overture). 1947; Remick, 1948.
Sovereignty (Overture). 1949; Remick, 1949.
Chorales and Carols for Band. c1950; Wat, 1953.
Concert Overture in F minor. c1940.
Irish Rhapsody. c1950; Boston, 1954.
Starlight Fantasie. c1950; Boston, 1953.
Regimental March of the RCMP. 1953; FH, 1960. RCA PC/PCS-1004.
Marche du Royal 22e. Wat. RCA PC/PCS-1003.
Many arrangements of orchestral and operatic works of other composers.

SOLOISTS WITH BAND

An Old Style Trumpet Tune. 1943. 4tpts, band.

CHOIR WITH ORCHESTRA

The Ancient Mariner. c1940. SATB, orch. Text: Samuel Taylor Coleridge.
Sweet Echo. 1943. SSAA, orch. Text: John Milton.

CHOIR

I Will Extol Thee. c1940; Fischer, 1940. SATB. Text: Biblical.
O Sleep. c1940; G Schirm, 1942. SSA. Text: Samuel Taylor Coleridge.
Say Thou Dost Love Me. c1940; Fischer, 1940. SATB. Text: Elizabeth Barrett Browning.
All Through The Night (arr). c1950. SSA. Wat. Text: A P Graves.
Believe Me If All Those Endearing Young Charms (arr). c1950. SAT. Wat. Text: trad.
Bonnie Dundee (arr). c1950. SSA. Wat. Text: Sir Walter Scott.
Holy Night (arr of Franz Gruber). c1950. SSA. Text: Jane Montgomery Campbell.
A-Hunting We Will Go (arr). c1950. SATB. Wat. Text: trad.
Nunc Dimittis. c1950. SATB. Text: liturgical.

VOICE

Sun of my Soul. c1950. Wat. Text: John Keble.

INSTRUMENTAL ENSEMBLE

Spring Fancy. 1938; Fischer, 1938. tba, pno.
Autumn Tones. c1940; Mer, 1946. 3cor.
All Together. c1950. 3trb. Wat.
By the Fireside. c1950. brass qt. Wat.
Chums. c1950. cor, pno. Wat.
Clover Leaf. c1950. alto sax, cor, trb. Wat.
Evening Shadows. c1950; Wat, 1956. brass qt.
Evening Thoughts. c1950. cor, pno. Wat.
Lake Goodwill. c1950. 3cor.
Melody Phantasie. c1950. sax, pno. Wat.
Three Friends. c1950. 3cor, pno. Wat.

Valley of Roses. c1950. cor, trb (bar), pno. Wat.

Many other works for woodwinds and brass with piano accompaniment.

BIBLIOGRAPHY

See B-B; C63,66,69,72; CrC(II); K.

P

PANNELL, RAYMOND (b. London, Ont., 25 Jan. 1935). He studied at the Juilliard School of Music in New York. In 1962 he represented Canada as pianist in the Tchaikovsky Competition in Moscow. His *Concerto for Piano and Orchestra* (1966–7) was written on a commission from the London (Ontario) Symphony Orchestra. With grants from the Centennial Commission, the Canada Council, and the Ontario Arts Council, the Canadian Opera Company commissioned and produced in 1967 his opera *The Luck of Ginger Coffey* (1967). In 1968 he was appointed assistant musical director and resident composer of the Atlanta Municipal Theatre Company. In 1972 he returned to Toronto, where he has been active in elementary music-education projects at the Ontario Institute for Studies in Education. His stage piece *Exiles* was written for the 1973 season of the Stratford Festival. He is a member of CAPAC.

MUSICAL WORKS

STAGE

Aria da Capo (chamb opera). 1963. Libretto: Edna St Vincent Millay.

The Luck of Ginger Coffey (opera). 1966–7. Libretto: Ronald Hambleton, after Brian Moore's novel.

The Government Inspector. 1967. Text: Nicolai Gogol, Peter Raby.

The Three Musketeers. 1968. Text: Alexander Dumas, Peter Raby.

Measure for Measure. 1969. Text: William Shakespeare.

She Stoops to Conquer. 1972. Text: Oliver Goldsmith.

The Exiles (opera). 1973. Libretto: Beverly Pannell.

SOLOIST(S) WITH ORCHESTRA

Double Concerto for Piano, Voice and Orchestra No 1. 1957.

Concerto for Piano and Orchestra No 2. 1961.

Ballad for Piano and Orchestra. 1968.

CHOIR WITH ORCHESTRA

Give Us This Day. 1970. children's chorus, orch.

VOICE

Death of Autumn. 1961. Text: James Joyce.

Rain is Falling. 1962. Text: James Joyce.

Sleep Now. 1962. Text: James Joyce.

Jabberwocky. 1963. Text: Lewis Carroll.

Stand on the Edge of the Ending Earth. 1963. Text: e e cummings.

The Complete Misanthropist. 1963. Text: Edna St Vincent Millay.

Death be not Proud. 1970. Text: John Donne.

INSTRUMENTAL ENSEMBLE

String Quartet No 1. 1954.

Variations. 1955. vln, pno.

PIANO

Sonata for Piano, Op 1. 1952.

Suite for Piano. 1954.

Five Etudes for Piano. 1959.

INSTRUMENTAL SOLO

Elegy for Cello. 1962.

BIBLIOGRAPHY

Wa.

'Canadian Opera Company to Premiere "Ginger Coffey"', *CanCo*. No. 13, Dec. 1966 (20–1, 40–1).

Hambleton, Ronald. 'The Luck of Ginger Coffey: the Libretto', *Opera Canada*. Vol. VIII, Sept. 1967 (32).

'The Luck of Ginger Coffey', *Opera Canada*.

Vol. VIII, Sept. 1967 (6, 29–32).
Mercer, Ruby. 'Raymond Pannell', *Opera Canada.* Vol. v, no. 4, Dec. 1964 (17–18).

PAPINEAU-COUTURE, JEAN (b. Montreal, Que., 12 Nov. 1916).

'The aesthetics of each individual is evidently the result of his own reflections in the face of the attitudes of his own musical environment, and even of society as a whole towards music.'[1]

Jean Papineau-Couture's lively, impish eye and alert mind are always ready to introduce a few little tricks into a counterpoint or fugue subject for his students. As a student of Nadia Boulanger, he has not forgotten the lessons of the illustrious teacher. He knows how to cultivate the joy of understanding and also that of making himself understood. Music enters into a context of art larger than its own limits and Papineau-Couture has always been an apostle of the history of art in general, and indeed would subscribe to Claude CHAMPAGNE's view that 'Aesthetic pleasure increases in proportion to our knowledge and the acuteness of our sensory perception.'

Although his mother did not take charge of her son's musical education at an early age, he read through different pieces that she would play on the piano. Then, after a year of study with Claire Laurendeau, Papineau-Couture studied piano with Françoise d'Amour, whom he called 'ma maîtresse d'amour'. Through her, Papineau-Couture was introduced to harmony, sight-reading, and also history, a subject that absorbed him. Perhaps no other teaching was as decisive as these first lessons, although one must also note the influence of Nadia Boulanger in the development of his musical education. There can be no doubt also that teachers such as Léo-Pol Morin (piano) and Gabriel Cusson (theory) made a deep impression on his future musical convictions, as did his periods of study at the Collège St-Ignace and especially at the Collège Brébeuf, which he attended for secondary studies (1929–37). It was there that he tried his hand at composition, beginning with choral and organ music, Gregorian chant, and the ancient church modes. He also decided to set the Offices to less tonal accompaniments! This was a creative period in which a good musical foundation and a solid classical education combined to make of this young composer a man of cultivated and universal spirit.

From his stay in the United States (1940–5) Papineau-Couture retained in particular the marked influence of Nadia Boulanger. After obtaining a Bachelor's degree in music (1941) at the New England Conservatory of Music in Boston, he studied at the Longy School of Music in Cambridge, Mass.; he then went to California to pursue his studies with Boulanger. Under her guidance he familiarized himself with the major works of Stravinsky ('Les Noces', 'Histoire du Soldat', 'Perséphone', 'Symphony of Psalms', 'Ebony Concerto'); of French composers such as 'Les Six', Fauré, Debussy, and Ravel; and also of Prokofiev (1st violin concerto) and Hindemith (2nd string trio).

The influence of Stravinsky is marked in the work of Papineau-Couture. He acknowledges himself to have been an active 'Stravinskyist', affected by his music more than that of any other composer. He followed this master through all the ramifications, as well as the impasses, of his composition. Other composers exercise an influence on him, mainly through their theories: Hindemith, with his ideas of chromaticism; Lutoslawski and Varèse; and the dodecaphonists through the writings of Leibowitz. Beyond this is the music of past ages, such as the composers of the French Renaissance and even those of the twelfth and thirteenth centuries, such as Léonin and Pérotin. Papineau-Couture has never denied such influences and even recognizes those unperceived by other analysts.

Whether it be through Bach's 'Musical Offering', Beethoven's 'Kreutzer' sonata or the 'Grosse Fuge', or again through Mozart, Papineau-Couture is always an attentive analyst who, relishing contrapuntal combinations, unusual harmonic procedures, and melodic ornament and in full possession of his craft, directs all to the grand lines of his message.

In 1945, on his return to Montreal,

---

[1] Papineau-Couture, Jean. *The modern composer and his world,* Kasemets and Beckwith (eds). University of Toronto Press, 1961 (23).

Papineau-Couture devoted himself to teaching and composition. He was initially in charge of piano classes at the Collège Brébeuf, thus beginning a long teaching career. By then he already had some ten pieces to his credit, retained from numerous attempts of his youth. These works suggest the post-impressionist, or perhaps the formal neo-classicist already conforming to Hindemith's theories of tonal polarity. The *Suite pour piano* (1943), typical of the writing of that time, returns to a classical structure; motifs are born from an initial cell idea, varied, enlarged, developed; these form the limits of the structure and serve the formal aspect that is so important to order, precision, and clarity. As with Stravinsky, this type of contrapuntal writing, which was to remain with him in his later career, reflects his attachment to the piano (this early period is the most fertile for his piano literature). Horizontal combinations become outlines that recall the technique and ornamentation of the French harpsichord school. Groupings by tetrachords where the interval of the fourth dominates the melodic and harmonic fabric, oscillation between major and minor, tonalities of flats and sharps – all these elements lead towards a light-dark impressionism without which neither the *Suite pour piano* nor even the *Concerto Grosso* (1943, rev. 1955) surpasses the suggestion of colour and even sensuousness found in *Eglogues* (1942), *Quatrains* (1947), and *Suite pour flûte et piano* (1945).

One cannot divide Papineau-Couture's output into 'periods'. The evolution of his musical thought is unbroken, his output presenting a remarkable continuity. However, as Andrée Desautels has pointed out, Papineau-Couture confronts himself with problems that require solutions, especially since his music is, above all, structuralist. Form is the principal parameter; he has a polyphonic conception of harmony that does not ignore tonality (which is inevitable and natural) but polarizes it at points of anchorage. 'Total chromaticism', this use of 'poles' of sonority, is not a form of serial composition and is certainly not dodecaphony. Papineau-Couture has never used a pure series, although the *Suite pour violon seul* (1956) shows a partial foray into this domain. The few 'serial' works that he has written are in the same spirit as those of the great sixteenth-century polyphonic composers. In a certain sense the twentieth century is the retrogradation of various phases from the medieval to the eighteenth century, and the five *Pièces Concertantes* (1957 to 1963, collectively a turning point in the output of Papineau-Couture) show this most obviously.

From 1942 to 1957 the principal works to consider are, in the opinion of the composer, the *Eglogues* and in particular the third, *Aria pour violon seul* (1946), *Papotages* (1949), the *Concerto pour violon et orchestre de chambre* (1952), and the *Psaume 150* (1954).

Since the sixties Papineau-Couture has interested himself particularly in an investigation of timbres. This entry into the world of sonority begins vocally with *Viole d'amour* (1966) and instrumentally with the *Sextuor* (1967). *Contraste* (1970) demonstrates the acuteness of Papineau-Couture's sensitivity, never sacrificed for facile effect.

Papineau-Couture has written above all for chamber combinations. This predilection brings him to unite more closely his notions of timbre to other features of his style. Different colours and their 'alloys' born through various instrumental combinations are not, with harmony, the only components of this polyphonic style; rhythm too is an essential part of composition as a whole. His is rich and often mocking, mordant and expressive. (One regrets perhaps only the irrepressible tarantella of sixteenth notes that flaps about somewhat abusively in his early works.)

The solid framework of compositions, their musicality always controlled, confirms Papineau-Couture's mastery of his art. His entire output exists in the most practical sense – performers know and like it. His music is written for them.

His sensitivity to his environment and his social involvement with music and Canadian musicians has led Papineau-Couture to play a very active role at many different levels of administration and in many various professional associations: for example the Association des Professeurs de Musique du Québec, the Canadian Music Council (president 1967–8), the Canadian Music Centre (president 1973–4), Les Jeunesses Musicales du Canada, the Canadian League of Composers (president 1957–9, 1963–6), the Quebec Arts Council, the Académie de Musique du Québec, the Société de musique contemporaine de Québec (founding president, 1966–73). He was Dean of the Faculty of Music at the University of Montreal from 1968 to 1973.

The teaching of piano and theoretical subjects, particularly composition, has never ceased to benefit him and to enrich his thinking:

> 'To teach is to try to understand how the other thinks, and how the other thinks in turn influences one's own thinking; the search for solutions to the problems of others leads to an enlargement of technique, to an evaluation of one's own thought.'[2]

Professionally the life of Papineau-Couture may be divided into three segments that are always inter-related: teaching, composition, and administration. His social involvement has always been heavy and multifarious. It is therefore not without admiration that one counts some sixty works in the catalogue of his output.

Jean Papineau-Couture received a Canadian Music Council Medal in 1973. He is a member of the Canadian League of Composers and an affiliate of BMI Canada.

LOUISE BAIL-MILOT

MUSICAL WORKS

STAGE

Le plus rusé des hommes (puppet show). 1948. mezz, ten, pno. ms. May 30, 1948, Mtl, marionettes of Micheline Legendre.

Les voleurs volés (puppet show). 1958. pno. ms. prob. Dec 27, 1948, Mtl, marionettes of Micheline Legendre.

Papotages/Tittle-Tattle (ballet). 1949. 35'. full orch. CMC. Nov 20, 1950, Mtl, Roland Leduc(cond).

Marianne s'en va-t'au moulin (puppet show). 1952. cel, str. ms. 1952, Mtl, CBC, Pierre Petel(prod).

Sous la grande tente (puppet show). 1952. cl, tpt, perc, pno. ms. Nov 18, 1952, Mtl.

Eclosion (stage music for a mime by Marie Racine). 1961. 8'. pno, vln, tape. ms. Apr 1961, Andrée Brunet(pno), Gilles Papineau-Couture(vln).

Le Rossignol (puppet show). 1962. fl, vlc, pno. ms. May 14, 1962, Warsaw, marionettes of Micheline Legendre.

ORCHESTRA

Aria (orch'n of 3rd mov't of '*Suite pour piano*'), 1942 (orch'd 1949). 7'. full orch. Ber. Jan 22, 1960, VSO, Irwin Hoffman.

Symphonie No 1 en Do Majeur. 1948 (rev 1956). 26'. full orch. Ber. Feb 20, 1949, Mtl, CBC O, Jean-Marie Beaudet.

Marche de Guillaumet (orch'n of an excerpt from '*Les Voleurs volés*'). 1949 (orch'd 1952). 6'. med orch. CMC. 1952, Tor, CBC O, John Adaskin.

Poème. 1952. 8'. full orch. Ber. Jan 27, 1953, Mtl, MSO, Désiré Defauw.

Prélude. 1953. 7'30". full orch. Ber. May 25, 1953, Mtl, CBC O, Roland Leduc.

Trois Pièces. 1961. 11'. orch. CMC. Nov 25, 1962, S'tn, SSO, Jean Papineau-Couture.

Pièce concertante no 5; 'Miroirs'. 1963. 12'15". full orch. CMC. Sept 21, 1963, Mtl, Place des Arts, Opening of Salle Wilfrid Pelletier, MSO, Wilfrid Pelletier.

Suite Lapitsky. 1965. 13'20". full orch. CMC. Feb 2, 1966, Mtl, MSO, Pierre Hétu.

Oscillations. 1969. 23'. med orch. CMC. Sept 27, 1969, Vanc, CBC Vanc Ch O, John Avison.

SMALL ORCHESTRA

Concerto Grosso. 1943 (rev 1955). 22'10". Ber. RCI-156. Apr 10, 1957, Mtl, CLC conc, Wilfrid Pelletier.

STRING ORCHESTRA

Ostinato. 1952. 2'30". str, hp, pno. CMC.

SOLOIST(S) WITH ORCHESTRA

Concerto pour violon et orchestre de chambre. 1952. 21'. Ber, 1960. Feb 3, 1954, Mtl, CLC conc, Geoffrey Waddington (cond), Noël Brunet(vln).

Pièce concertante no 1; 'Repliement'. 1957. 13'. pno, str orch. Ber, 1961. Col ML-5685/MS-6285 (Can). Apr 6, 1957, Mtl, CBC TV, Jacques Beaudry(cond), Jeanne Landry (pno).

Pièce concertante no 2; 'Eventails'. 1959. 17'. vlc, chamb orch. CMC.

Pièce concertante no 3; 'Variations'. 1959. 17'. fl, cl, vln, vlc, hp, str orch. CMC. Mar 24, 1959, Mtl, MSO, Igor Markevich.

Pièce concertante no 4; 'Additions'. 1959. 6'10". ob, str orch. CMC. Aug 7, 1959, S'tn, Golden Jubilee Mus Fest, SSO, Roland

---

[2]Jean Papineau-Couture, in interview with Louise Bail-Milot, taped January 29, 1973.

Leduc(cond), Philip West(ob).
Concerto pour piano et orchestre. 1965. 17'. CMC. RCA CCS-1029. Feb 6, 1966, Tor, CBC, TS, Alexander Brott(cond), Gilles Manny (pno).
Contraste. 1970. 10'. sgr, orch. CMC. June 9, 1970, Mtl, Concours Int de Mtl, MSO, Mario Bernardi(cond), 12 finalists of the competition.

CHOIR

'A Jésus, mon roi, mon grand ami, mon frère'. 1960. 3'30". 2 soli, children's choir. ms. Text: Sr Alfred Marie. May 1960, Sisters of l'Immaculée Conception choir, Sr Monique d'Ostie(dir).
Viole d'amour. 1966. 6'30". SATB. CMC. Text: Rina Lasnier. 1968, Choeurs de la Radiodiffusion-Télévision Belge, René Mazy.

VOICE(S)

Pater Noster. 1944. 5'. med vc, org. ms. June 15, 1944, Mtl, Gabriel Cusson(bar), Marcelle Martin(org).
Ave Maria. 1945. 5'. med vc, org. ms. June 23, 1945, Mtl, Suzanne Clerk.
Complainte populaire. 1946. 1'30". sop, bar, pno. CMC. Text: anon. Mar 21, 1953, Mtl, Marthe Forget(sop), Jean-Pierre Hurteau(bar), Mado Roche(pno).
Quatrains. 1947. 8'. sop, pno. CMC. RCI-148. Text: Francis Jammes. May 14, 1948, Mtl, Madeleine Dyotte(sop), Jean Papineau-Couture(pno).
Offertoire; 'Père daignez recevoir'. 1949. 3'. ten, org (harm). ms. 1949, 1st Mass of Père A Paquet.
Mort. 1956. 3'30". alto, pno. CMC. Text: François Villon. Nov 15, 1956, Mtl, Maureen Forrester(alto), John Newmark (pno).
Te Mater. 1958. 45". 3vcs. ms. 1961, Mtl, Mtl-Cons Choir, Marcel Laurencelle(dir).

VOICE(S) WITH INSTRUMENTAL ENSEMBLE

Eglogues. 1942. 6'. alto, fl, pno. Amérique française, 1943. Allied ARCLP-4. Text: Pierre Baillargeon. Feb 23, 1943, Cambridge, Mass, Eunice Alberts(alto), Betty Wood(fl), Jean Papineau-Couture(pno).
Psaume 150. 1954. 20'. sop, ten, 2fl, bsn, 3tpt, 3trb, 1 or 2org, SATB. Ber, 1964. RCI-128. Apr 11, 1955, Mtl, Bach Choir and CBC O, George Little(cond), Marguerite Lavergne(sop), Jean-Paul Jeanotte(ten), Françoise Aubut-Pratt(org).
Paysage. 1968. 10'. 8spkrs, 8sgrs, fl, ob, cl, bsn, hn, 2vln, vla, vlc, cb, pno, hp, perc. CMC. Text: St-Denys-Garneau. May 9, 1969, Zagreb, Yugoslavia, choir and ensemble of Radio-Television Zagreb, Jgor Kuljeric(cond).
Chanson de Rahit. 1972. 12'. vc, cl, pno. CMC. Text: Han Suyin. Mar 3, 1973, Mtl, Marthe Forget(sop), Jean Laurendeau(cl), Bruce Mather(pno).

INSTRUMENTAL ENSEMBLE

Sonate en Sol. 1944 (rev 1953). 12'. vln, pno. CMC. RCI-92. Apr 1946, Mtl, Clan St-Jacques.
Suite pour flûte et piano. 1944–5. 18'. CMC. 1954, Mtl, CBC 'Premières', Johan Van Veen (fl), Jeanne Landry(pno).
Suite pour flûte, clarinette, basson, cor et piano. 1947. 14'45". CMC. Jan 31, 1955, Mtl, CBC 'Premières', Mario Duschenes(fl), Raffaele Masella(cl), Rodolfo Masella(bsn), Joseph Masella(hn), Charles Reiner(pno).
Rondo. 1953. 3'. 4rec (SATB). AMP, NY, 1957. 1954, Otter Lake, PQ, Mus camp ens, Mario Duschenes(cond).
Quatuor no 1. 1953. 10'. CMC. RCI-362. Dec 8, 1953, Tor, Spivak Qt.
Trois Caprices. 1962. 11'. vln, pno. Peer, 1971. RCI-243. July 5, 1962, Mount Orford, PQ, JMC Competition.
Fantaisie pour quintette à vent. 1963. 12' 15". Ber, 1968. JMC C-30. June 1963, Wpg, CBC, Dirk Keetbaas Plyrs.
Canons. 1964. 6'. brass qnt. CMC. Feb 23, 1964, Winooski, Vermont, St Michael's College, MBQ.
Dialogues. 1967. 15'. vln, pno. Peer, 1973. Aug 19, 1967, Mtl, Steven Staryk(vln), Lise Boucher(pno).
Sextuor. 1967. 17'. ob, cl, bsn, vln, vla, vlc. CMC. Aug 15, 1967, Mtl, TRO, Milton Barnes.
Quatuor no 2. 1967. 18'. CMC. RCI-363. June 24, 1970, Orford Arts Centre, Orford Str Qt.
Nocturnes. 1969. 14'. fl, cl, vln, vlc, hpschd, guit, perc. ms. Nov 28, 1969, Mtl, Univ de Mtl Conc des 'Nocturnales', Serge Garant (cond), Mario Duschenes(fl), Jean Laurendeau(cl), Jacques Verdon(vln), André Mignault(vlc), Mireille Lagacé(hpschd), Marie Prével(guit), Guy Lachapelle(perc).

PIANO

Mouvement perpétuel. 1943. 1'10". Ber, 1949. RCI-134. Feb 22, 1947, New York, Rose Goldblatt.
Suite pour piano. 1943. 13'35". Ber, 1959. RCI-251. June 1957, Mtl, Laure Fink.
Deux Valses. 1944. 1'25". FH, 1955. Feb 17, 1950, Mtl, Jeanne Landry.
Etude en si bémol mineur. 1945. 2'45". Peer, 1959. RCI-135; CBC BR SM-78 & 114. 1946, New York, Charlotte Martin.
Rondo. 1945. 4'30". pno 4 hands. Peer, 1960. 1945, Mtl, CBC, Marie-Thérèse Paquin & John Newmark.
Aria. 1960. 1'30". Ber, 1964. CCM-2.
Complémentarité. 1971. 22'. CMC. Jan 24, 1972, Tor, CBC Conc, Jean-Paul Sévilla.
Dyarchie. 1971. hpschd. CMC. Mar 30, 1971, Boston, Mireille Lagacé.

INSTRUMENTAL SOLO

Aria. 1946. 4'. vln. Ber, 1966. Bar BC 1851/2851. 1956, Mtl, CBC, Noël Brunet.
Suite pour violon seul. 1956. 8'15". vln. Peer, 1966. RCA CC/CCS-1016. 1958, Mexico, Henryk Szeryng.

BIBLIOGRAPHY

See B-B; Aum; B65,71; Bec56,57,58,70; Bt; C63,66,69,72; CrC(I); D157, 165; Esc; Gf; K; Lv; MGG; Mm; Wa.
Baillargeon, Pierre. 'Jean Papineau-Couture', *Amérique française.* No. 1, Montreal, 1948 (75–7).
Beckwith, John. 'Jean Papineau-Couture', *CMJ.* Vol. III, no. 2, 1958–9 (4–20).
'Canadian Music for Quebec's Holiday', *CBC Times.* June 19–25, 1955 (4).
Chailloux, Nicole. 'Jean Papineau-Couture'. Paper presented at a Musialogue, Faculty of Music, University of Montreal, 1972 (13 pp.).
'The Composer Speaks', *CBC Times.* Nov. 18–24, 1961 (3, 4, 31).
Denis, Clotilde. 'Cérébralisme et Lyricisme dans l'oeuvre de Jean Papineau-Couture'. Unpublished thesis, University of Montreal, 1972.
'Jean Papineau-Couture', *Musiques du Kébèk* (R. Duguay, ed.). Montreal: Editions du Jour, 1971 (145–51).
'Jean Papineau-Couture', pamphlet, BMI Canada Ltd, 1970.
'Jean Papineau-Couture – a portrait', *Mu.* No. 3, July 1967 (8–9).
Kendergi, Maryvonne. 'Musique canadienne ou compositeurs canadiens?', *Cimaise.* Paris, Nos 80–1, Apr.-July 1967 (43–4).
Potvin, Gilles. 'Seven Leading Composers Look at the Music of Today and its Public', *MuSc.* Sept.-Oct. 1967 (5).
Poulin, Roch. 'L'oeuvre vocale de Jean Papineau-Couture'. Unpublished thesis, University of Montreal, 1961.
Rivard, Yolande. 'Jean Papineau-Couture's Return to Tone Colour', *MuSc.* No. 254, July-Aug. 1970 (4).
Stone, Kurt. 'Review of Records', *MQ.* Vol. VIII, no. 3, July 1967 (440–52).

LITERARY WORKS

ARTICLES

'L'année musicale au Canada', *Le livre de l'année.* Grolier, Montreal, 1958 (220–4).
'L'année musicale', *Le livre de l'année.* Grolier, Montreal, 1959 (300–4).
'Canadian Compositions at Hartford', *CMJ.* Vol. IV, no. 2, 1959–60 (35).
Notes on 'Pièce Concertante No. 1 pour piano et orchestre à cordes', *Canadian Contemporary Music,* Study Course No. 1. Toronto: CMC, 1961 (1–7).
'Que sera la musique canadienne?', *Amérique française.* Vol. II, no. 2, Oct. 1942.
'The training of composers', *The Modern Composer and his World.* University of Toronto Press, Toronto, 1961 (20–4).

PEACOCK, KENNETH (b. Toronto, Ont., 7 Apr. 1922). He studied with Alma Cockburn, Mona Bates, Reginald Godden, and Leo SMITH at the Toronto Conservatory of Music and, in the Faculty of Music of the University of Toronto he studied composition with Healey WILLAN and John WEINZWEIG, obtaining his Bachelor of Music degree in 1942. Other teachers have included Michel Hirvy in Montreal and F.J. Cooke in Boston. His *String Quartet* won the McGill Chamber Music Competition in 1949. Widely known as a folklorist with extensive experience as a field researcher among the Indian, Anglo-Canadian (particularly Newfoundland), Acadian, and European ethnic cultures in Canada and as an editor and writer on the folk music of Canada, he was a former director of ethnic folk-music research at the National Museum of Man in Ottawa (1962–72). Reflecting his interest in folk music, his compositions have folk-like themes in a basically tonal style. He has written for orchestra, voice, instrumental ensembles, and piano, utilizing some folk elements in many of his scores, which include, for orchestra, *Rituals of Earth, Darkness and Fire* (1950) and *Essay on Newfoundland Themes* (1961); for voice, *Songs of the Cedar* (1950) for mezzo, flute, cello, double bass, piano; and for piano, *Idiom* (one of a series based on tribal and folk sources). He is a member of the Canadian League of Composers and is affiliated with BMI Canada.

BIBLIOGRAPHY

CrC(I); K; Wa.
'Doukhobor Music', *CBC Times.* Feb 16–22, 1963 (30).
Fowke, Edith. 'Anglo-Canadian Folksong: a Survey', *Ethnomusicology.* Vol. 16, 1972 (335–50).
'Indians: Strange Music', *Time.* Sept. 21, 1953.
'Kenneth Peacock – Biography', *BMI Canada Ltd.* pamphlet, Jan. 1950.
Martens, Helen. 'The Music of Some Religious Minorities in Canada', *Ethnomusicology.* Vol. 16, 1972 (360–71).

LITERARY WORKS

BOOKS

A Practical Guide for Folk Music Collectors. Ottawa: Canadian Folk Music Society, 1966.

ARTICLES

'Establishing Perimeters for Ethnomusicological Field Reseach in Canada: On-going Projects and Future Possibilities at the Canadian Centre for Folk Culture Studies', *Ethnomusicology.* Vol. XVI, no. 3, Sept. 1972 (329–34).
'Folk and Aboriginal Music', *Wa* (62–89).
'The Music of the Doukhobors', *Alphabet.* No. 10, Dec. 1965–Mar. 1966 (35–44).
'Newfoundland and its Folksongs', *Canadian Folk Music Society Bulletin.* Vol. II, no. 1, July 1967 (2–9).
'Nine Songs from Newfoundland', *Journal of American Folklore.* Vol. LXVII, 1954 (123–6).
A Survey of Ethnic Folk Music Across Western Canada. Ottawa: National Museum of Canada, Anthropology Paper No. 5, Nov. 1963 (1–13).

TRANSCRIPTIONS

A Garland of Rue (Lithuanian Folksongs of Love and Betrothal). Ottawa: National Museum of Canada, 1971.
The Native Songs of Newfoundland. Ottawa: National Museum of Canada, Contributions to Anthropology, pt. 2, Bulletin No. 190, 1960 (1–15).
Songs of the Doukhobors. Ottawa: National Museum of Canada, 1968.
Songs of the Newfoundland Outports (3 vols). Ottawa: National Museum of Canada, 1965.
Twenty Ethnic Songs from Western Canada. Ottawa: National Museum of Canada, Bulletin No. 211, 1966.

PEDERSEN, PAUL (b. Camrose, Alta, 28 Aug. 1935). He studied composition with Murray ADASKIN at the University of Saskatchewan and with John WEINZWEIG at the University of Toronto, receiving his Master of Music degree in composition (1961) and Doctor of Philosophy degree in musicology (1970), both from the University of Toronto. From 1962 to 1964 he was a music director of Camrose Lutheran College. Two early compositions by Pedersen (*Quintet*, 1959, and *Sonata for Violin and Piano*, 1960) are in a free atonal style with a contrapuntal texture. Since about 1964 his interests have centred more on electronic and computer music and multi-media works. In 1966 he joined the staff of the Faculty of Music of McGill University and in 1970 became head of its Electronic Music Studio and Chairman of the Department of Theory. He is a member of CAPAC.

MUSICAL WORKS

INSTRUMENTAL

7 works for chamber ensemble: 2 *Woodwind Trios* (1956 and 1957) fl, cl, bsn; *Chorale Prelude No 2* (1958) fl or ob or cl, str qt; *Ricercare* (1958) vln, cl; *Wind Quintet* (1959); *Sonata for Violin and Piano* (1960); *Serial Composition* (1965) vln, hn, bsn, hp.
Lament for Piano. 1958.
2 works for full orch: *Concerto for Orchestra* (1961); *Lament* (1962).

CHORAL

8 a cappella works: *Ecclesiastes XII* (1958); *Psalm 117* (1959); *Chorale: All Praise to Thee* (1960); *Built on a Rock* (1961);

Chorale: God Himself Is Present (1961); *O Darkest Woe* (1961); *Psalm 134* (1961); *On the Nativity of Christ* (1963).
Cantata and Narrative for Good Friday. 1972. SATB, org, narr, soli.

ELECTRONIC
5 works: *The Lone Tree* (1964); *Themes from the Old Testament* (1966); *Fantasie* (1967); *Origins* (1967); *For Margaret, Motherhood and Mendelssohn* (1971).

LITERARY WORKS

ARTICLES
'The Mel Scale', *Journal of Music Theory*. Vol. IX, no. 2, Winter 1965 (295).

PENTLAND, BARBARA (b. Winnipeg, Man., 2 Jan. 1912). Pentland showed an interest in music as a very young child, undeterred by a serious heart ailment that frequently kept her bedridden and isolated from other children. This solitude tended to develop her intellectual interests as well as her strength of character, traits that have remained with her. Parental disapproval of her desire to compose, constant during the many years she lived at home, proved to be a greater and more discouraging obstacle.

Pentland's initial attempts at composition came soon after her first piano lessons, which she began at the age of nine with a teacher at Rupert's Land College, the private school she was attending at the time. She remembers that her first piano teacher could not cope with a child who was out of the ordinary, and discouraged this creative activity. In spite of opposition from all sides, Pentland persisted; but she soon learned that if she were more secretive about composing there would be less upset at home.

She was an intelligent, contemplative child who read extensively, finding the world of books more interesting than the world around her. A fascination for the French Revolution, which developed as a result of her reading pursuits during her early teen years, augmented her growing interest in the works of Beethoven, whose influence can be seen clearly in Pentland's compositions around 1925, mainly for piano. Access to new music came only through touring artists, who played conservative programs consisting of works by Beethoven, Bach, Chopin, and Debussy. Winnipeg provided a flourishing, if limited, local musical environment in the 1920s, dominated by English organists and choir directors who encouraged performances of the works of such composers as Handel, Mendelssohn, Parry, Stanford, and Elgar.

At the age of fifteen Pentland was sent to a very strict boarding school in Montreal for two years (1927–9). During this time she studied piano and theory with Frederick Blair, who gave her much encouragement. Proceeding to a finishing school in Paris for one year (1929–30), and, having at last been given permission by her parents to study composition, Pentland became a pupil of Cécile Gauthiez. A professor at the Schola Cantorum, Gauthiez had studied with Vincent d'Indy and was a staunch follower of the Franck movement in composition. She taught Pentland in the contrapuntal French tradition, transmitting to her the thick texture, full chords, and chromatic harmonies that are evident in the music of Franck. These characteristics, appearing in Pentland's works until the late 1930s, can be seen in *Five Preludes* (1938), *Rhapsody* (1939), and the *Piano Quartet* (1939).

On her return to Winnipeg in 1930, Pentland continued studying with Gauthiez by correspondence for eighteen months, by which time it became evident that this method of study was not satisfactory. Among her activities in Winnipeg, where she remained until 1936, were studies in organ with Hugh BANCROFT and in piano with Eva Clare, then a prominent teacher. Pentland was performing frequently, both as part of a small group and as soloist; in addition she was constantly composing. At this time she won several local composition contests.

In 1936 she was awarded a fellowship in composition at the Juilliard Graduate School in New York, and subsequently attended the school for three years. During the first two years Pentland studied with Frederick Jacobi, who gave her a sound contrapuntal training and introduced her to the music of Palestrina. Eager to try new methods, she found Jacobi's conservative approach stifling, and, as a result, chose Bernard Wagenaar as her teacher for the final year. Wagenaar, who encouraged freedom of expression in his pupils, proved to be an aid to Pentland's search for an individual style.

Having had such limited access to contemporary music in Winnipeg, Pentland found that her exposure to many new works in New York expanded her musical scope considerably. Of special interest to her was the music of Paul Hindemith, his use of intervals providing a model for her increasing interest in a contrapuntal approach. Though not a lasting influence, this direction helped to free her from traditional harmonies, leading her more towards a pursuit of linear methods.

On her return to Winnipeg in 1939 Pentland was appointed a member of the Music Advisory Committee and examiner in theory for the University of Manitoba. During the summers of 1941 and 1942 she attended the Berkshire Music Center at Tanglewood, where she studied composition with Aaron Copland. His influence, which led her to a lighter, more lucid style, is shown most strikingly in her *Variations* (1942), similar in form, texture, and melodic treatment to Copland's 'Variations' (1930). Also contributing to a clearer texture in Pentland's music was a neoclassic trend that became a dominant feature of her style from the early 1940s until the mid-1950s.

Persuaded that her works would have greater chance for performance in a larger centre, Pentland moved to Toronto in 1942. The following year she joined the faculty of the Royal Conservatory of Music, Toronto, as a teacher in theory and composition. During the 1940s interest in Canadian composers was flourishing, with frequent concerts being supported by such organizations as the National Council for Canadian-Soviet Friendship. As a result, Pentland enjoyed greater recognition in Toronto, gaining a reputation as a headstrong member of the *avant-garde*.

Pentland's contrapuntal leanings, gradually directing her to a more serial approach, can be seen in *Sonata Fantasy* (1947), in which the material presented in the opening bars provides the basis for the entire work. This approach was supported by her first significant exposure to serial music in the summers of 1947 and 1948 at the MacDowell Colony in New Hampshire. Here Dika Newlin, who had been a student of Schoenberg, introduced Pentland to many of his compositions. Though not at ease with what was, in her opinion, the overly romantic and tortured line characteristic of Schoenberg's music, Pentland became interested in the use of the row itself, as evidenced in *Octet for Winds* (1948), her first consciously serial work.

In 1949 Pentland moved to Vancouver, where she joined the music department of the University of British Columbia. She taught theory and composition there until she resigned in 1963 as a result of an unresolved dispute with the administration of the department.

The most significant influence on Pentland's mature style was the music of Anton Webern, which she first heard on a trip to Europe in 1955. At the ISCM festival in Darmstadt she heard the works of many contemporary composers, including Boulez, Stockhausen, Nono, and Berio, in addition to Webern. During the following year Pentland took a leave of absence from her university duties and returned to Europe to hear her *String Quartet No. 2* (1953), which had been selected for performance at the ISCM festival in Stockholm in 1956.

In its compact form and transparent texture the *Symphony for Ten Parts* (1957) clearly demonstrates the influence of Webern on her style. The three tightly knit movements are built on melodic shapes and rhythms presented in the short introduction. A new interest in sonority, also generated by Webern, may be seen in Pentland's instrumental combinations, which include such pairings as xylophone and double bass, as well as in the alternation of dry, percussive sections with those that are more lyric.

In her later music Pentland works within concise forms and uses as few notes as possible, continually striving for economy. Now much more conscious of texture, she substitutes silence for the scale passages and arpeggios that previously appeared frequently. The twelve-tone system is not applied rigidly by Pentland, but rather as a means of control. The rows are treated quite freely after the initial statement, which is itself characterized by a delay in the presentation of the final notes. Almost invariably the importance of the first part of the row is stressed, while the remainder is obscured or omitted entirely. Another distinctive feature is a touch of humour, which occurs in the form of syncopated or jazz rhythms, light melodies, or perky staccatos. Her interest in the effects of retrograde on material is evident in her frequent use of the technique. An entire work, or a segment of it, is often concluded with an exact retrograde of the initial statement of the row, thus providing material for a coda or a recapitulation.

Several distinctive characteristics have appeared in Pentland's works in recent years, including the use of aleatoric zones and quarter tones. The aleatoric zones which appear in works such as *Trio con Alea* (1966), *String Quartet No. 3* (1969), *News* (completed 1970), and *Mutations* (1972), consist of improvisation which is confined to short sections, interspersed with larger sections in which the composer maintains control. In the aleatoric zones the performer is given the freedom of rhythmic variation, based on a given series of notes; he may repeat combinations of notes and use whatever technique he wishes to produce the given notes. The final aleatoric zone may take on the function of a cadenza when it appears towards the end of a work.

Quarter tones are found chiefly in the string parts, being used effectively as a decorative device. In the vocal line of *News,* quarter tones are used for colouring and expression.

Pedagogical works for piano represent a significant part of Pentland's music since 1960, this new emphasis being largely a result of the encouragement of Rachel Cavalho, a piano teacher in Toronto. The works for young pianists include many short pieces, as well as a series of three teaching books of increasing difficulty: *Music of Now* (1969–70). Pentland's approach is strictly linear and has few chordal implications, the tone row being employed much more simply than in her more advanced works. In *Music of Now* the student is gradually introduced to such difficulties as accidentals, tone clusters, changing rhythms and changing meters, while canons in inversion and retrograde encourage an independent use of the hands.

Married in 1958 to John Huberman, son of the late violinist Bronislaw Huberman, Pentland has been composing prolifically at their Vancouver home during the past ten years, though still hampered occasionally in this pursuit by ill health. While the emphasis in her output has been on piano works, she has written extensively in other genres, including chamber music, choral, vocal, orchestral with soloist, and orchestral. With her usual determination and energy, she will undoubtedly continue contributing generously to Canadian music.

Pentland has received many commissions from various sources, including the CBC (*Variations on a Boccherini Tune,* 1948), (*Trio for Violin, Cello and Piano,* 1963), the University of British Columbia (*Trio con Alea,* 1966), the Hugh McLean Consort (*Septet,* 1967), and the Purcell Quartet (*String Quartet No. 3,* 1969).

She is a member of the Canadian League of Composers and an affiliate of BMI Canada.

SHEILA EASTMAN

MUSICAL WORKS

STAGE

Beauty and the Beast (ballet pantomime). 1940. 2pno. ms. Jan 3, 1941, Wpg Bal Club, B Pentland, M Dillabough.

Payload (radio play). 1940. ms. Text: Anne Marriott. Nov 8, 1940, Mtl, CBC o, Jean-Marie Beaudet.

The Wind Our Enemy (score for radio-drama). 1941. Text: Anne Marriott.

Air-bridge to Asia (radio documentary). 1944. ms. 1944, Tor, CBC.

The Living Gallery (film score). 1947. ms. 1947, NFB.

The Lake (chamber opera in one act). 1952. 27'. sop, alto, ten, bs, small orch. CMC. Libretto: Dorothy Livesay. Mar 3, 1954, Vanc, CBC o, John Avison.

ORCHESTRA

Concert-Overture. 1935. ms.

Lament. 1939. 7'. full orch. ms. Aug 1940, Wpg, Summer Symphony, Geoffrey Waddington.

Arioso and Rondo. 1941. 10'. full orch. CMC. 1945, London, Eng, BBC o, Sir Adrian Boult.

Symphony No 1. 1945–8. 25'. full orch. CMC. Oct 14, 1947 (3rd mov't), Mtl, CBC o, Alexander Brott.

Variations on a Boccherini Tune. 1948. 12'.

full orch. CMC. June 30, 1948, Tor, CBC O, Samuel Hersenhoren.
Symphony No 2. 1950. 16′. full orch. CMC. Feb 9, 1953, Tor, CBCSO, Ettore Mazzoleni.
Ave Atque Vale. 1951. 7′30″. full orch. CMC. Nov 15, 1953, Vanc, VSO, Irwin Hoffman.
Symphony No 4. 1959. 20′. full orch. Ber. Feb 25, 1960, Wpg, WSO, Victor Feldbrill.

SMALL ORCHESTRA

Holiday Suite. 1941. 10′. chamb orch. ms. July 27, 1948, CBC, Vanc, John Avison.
Symphony for Ten Parts (No 3). 1957. 10′. Ber, 1961. RCA CC/CCS-1009; RCI-215. 1961, Vanc, CBC Ch O, John Avison.
Ciné scene. 1968. 8′. chamb orch. CMC.

STRING ORCHESTRA

Two Pieces for Strings. 1938. ms.
Holiday Suite. 1941 (arr for str 1947). ms. June 18, 1947, Tor, CBC Str O, Harold Sumberg.
Ricercar for Strings. 1955. 6′. CMC. Aug 14, 1958, Vanc Fest, CBC Ch O, Nicholas Goldschmidt.
Strata. 1964. 9′. CMC. Sept 15, 1968, Vanc, CBC Ch O, John Avison.

SOLOIST WITH ORCHESTRA

Concerto for Violin and Small Orchestra. 1942. 17′. CMC. Jan 29, 1945, (reduction for vln & pno) Tor, Harry Adaskin(vln), Frances Marr(pno).
Colony Music. 1947. 12′. pno, str. CMC. Feb 9, 1948, Tor, New World Orch, Samuel Hersenhoren.
Concerto for Organ and Strings. 1949. 15′. CMC. Apr 7, 1951, London, Ont, London Ch O, Ernest White(cond), Gordon Jeffery (org).
Cadenzas for Mozart Violin Concerto K 207. 1950. ms. 1950, Vanc, Vanc Art Gallery, Harry Adaskin(vln), Frances Marr (pno).
Concerto for Piano and String Orchestra. 1956. 15′15″. Ber. RCI-184. Mar 12, 1958, Tor, CLC conc, CBCSO, Victor Feldbrill (cond), Mario Bernardi(pno).
News. 1970. 26′. virtuoso vc, orch. CMC. Text: from news media. Ottawa, CBC, NAC, NACO, Mario Bernardi(cond), Phyllis Mailing(mezz).
Variations Concertantes. 1970. 8′. pno, orch. CMC. June 1971, Mtl, Int pno competition, MSO, Franz-Paul Decker(cond), Zola Shaulis(pno).

CHOIR

Ballad of Trees and the Master. 1937. SATB. ms. Text: Sidney Lanier. 1938, Wpg, 4-vc ens, Filmer Hubble.
Dirge for a Violet. 1939. SATB. ms. Text: Duncan Campbell Scott.
Epigrams and Epitaphs (rounds). 1952. 2, 3, 4 vcs, unaccomp. ms. Text: various.
Salutation of the Dawn. 1954. 4′. SATB. CMC. Text: from the Sanskrit.
What Is Man? 1954. 4′. SATB. CMC. Text: Ecclesiasticus XVIII.
Three Sung Songs. 1965. SATB. CMC. 1967 (no 3: *Spring Days Come Suddenly*), Mtl, Expo 67, Le Petit Ensemble Vocal, George Little.

VOICE

'A Lavender Lady' and 'Ruins (Ypres, 1917)'. 1932. vc, pno. ms. Text: George Herbert Clarke. Sept 21, 1936, Wpg, Royal Alexandra Hotel, Agnes Kelsey(sop), Anna Hovey(pno).
They Are Not Long. 1935. vc, pno. ms. Text: Ernest Dawson. 1936, Wpg, Agnes Kelsey(sop), Anna Hovey(pno).
Unvanquished. 1940. ten, pno. ms. Text: Dallas Kenmare.
Song Cycle. 1942–5. 11′. sop, pno. CMC. RCI-20. Text: Anne Marriott. Apr 17, 1947, Tor, Harbord Collegiate, Frances James (sop), Barbara Pentland(pno).
Three Sung Songs. 1964. 7′30″. med vc, pno. CMC. Text: Chinese, trans: Clara M Candlin.
Sung Songs Nos 4 & 5. 1971. 8′. med vc, pno. 1972, Vanc, CBC, Phyllis Mailing(sop), Derek Bampton(pno).

VOICE WITH INSTRUMENTAL ENSEMBLE

At Early Dawn. 1945. ten, fl, vlc. ms. Text: Hsiang Hao.

INSTRUMENTAL ENSEMBLE

The Devil Dances. 1939. cl, pno.
Quartet for Piano and Strings. 1939. 20′. ms. Mar 12, 1941, Wpg, Barbara Pentland (pno), Mary Gussin(vln), Mary Graham (vla), Bruno Schmidt(vlc).
Sonata for Cello and Piano. 1943. 15′. CMC. 1950, Vanc, Sympos of Can Music.
String Quartet No 1. 1945. 14′. CMC. Col ML-5764; RCI-141. Apr 20, 1949, Phila, Philadelphia Art Alliance, D Steiner(vln),

N Heaton(vln), S Crossum(vla), J Eppinoff (vlc).
Vista. 1945. 9′. vln, pno. Ber, 1951. Aug 10, 1948, Vanc, U of BC Summer Fest, Harry Adaskin(vln), Frances Marr(pno).
Sonata for Violin and Piano. 1946. 15′. CMC. May 15, 1948, Wpg, I Thorolfson (vln), Chester Duncan(pno).
Octet for Winds. 1948. 8′. fl, ob, cl, bsn, tpt, 2hn, trb. CMC. Jan 12, 1949, Tor, CBC, TS Wind Soli.
Weekend Overture for Resort Combo. 1949. cl, tpt, pno, perc. ms.
String Quartet No 2. 1953. 26′. CMC. June 8, 1956, Stockholm, ISCM World Fest, Grünfarb Qt.
Symphony for Ten Parts (No 3). 1957. 10′ 40″. fl, ob, hn, tpt, xyl, timp, vln, vla, vlc, cb. Ber, 1961. RCA CC/CCS-1009; RCI-215. 1959, Vanc, CBC O, Hugh McLean.
Duo for Viola and Piano. 1960. 17′. CMC. RCA CC/CCS-1017; RCI-223. 1960, Vanc, Harry Adaskin(vla), Frances Marr(pno).
Canzona. 1961. 6′. fl, ob, hpschd. CMC. 1962, Mtl, CBC, Distinguished Artists' Series, Bar Trio Mtl, Mario Duschenes(fl), Melvin Berman(ob), Kelsey Jones(hpschd).
Cavazzoni for Brass (transcription from 3 organ hymns by Girolamo Cavazzoni). 1961. brass qnt. ms.
Trio for Violin, Cello and Piano. 1963. 12′. CMC. RCI-242. 1964, Halifax, CBC, Halifax Trio, Francis Chaplin(vln), Edward Bisha (vlc), Gordon Macpherson(pno).
Trio con Alea. 1966. 25′. vln, vla, vlc. CMC. Feb 8, 1967, Vanc, U of BC, John Loban (vln), Hans-Karl Piltz(vla), Eugene Wilson (vlc).
Septet. 1967. 14′. hn, tpt, trb, org, vln, vla, vlc. CMC. Feb 20, 1968, Vanc, Hugh McLean Consort.
String Quartet No 3. 1969. 23′50″. CMC. RCI-353. June 25, 1970, Vanc, Vanc Art Gallery, Purcell Str Qt.
Interplay. 1972. 13′. free-bass accord, str qt.
Mutations. 1972. 16′. vlc, pno. Feb 22, 1972, Vanc, U of BC, Eugene Wilson(vlc), Robert Rogers(pno).

PIANO
Sonate, C♯ minor. 1930. ms.
Two Preludes. 1935. ms. Sept 21, 1936, Wpg, Royal Alexandra Hotel, Barbara Pentland.
Sonata (two mov'ts). 1936. ms. 1936 (1st mov't), Wpg, Barbara Pentland.
Little Scherzo for Clavichord. 1937. ms. 1938, Wpg, Snjolaug Sigurdson(pno).
Five Preludes. 1938. 8′. ms. Apr 12, 1939, New York, Carnegie Chamb Music Hall, Earle Voorhies.
Rhapsody 1939. 1939. 5′30″. CMC. 1941, Wpg, Barbara Pentland.
Six Pieces for Children. 1939. ms.
Promenade. 1940. ms.
Studies in Line. 1941. 5′50″. Ber, 1949. CCM-2; RCI-134. 1941, Wpg, M Dillabough (pno).
Variations. 1942. 7′. CMC. 1947, Wpg, Barbara Pentland.
Piano Sonata. 1945. 14′. CMC. July 26, 1947, Prague, Marie Knotkova.
From Long Ago (3 little pieces). 1946. CMC.
Sonata Fantasy. 1947. 13′. CMC. Mar 20, 1948, Tor, Harry Somers.
Dirge. 1948. 3′30″. Ber, 1961. 1953, Seattle, Barbara Pentland.
Sad Clown, Song of Sleep (2 pieces). 1949.
Sonatina No 1. 1951. 8′. CMC. Apr 5, 1954, Vanc, Barbara Pentland.
Sonatina No 2. 1951. 6′40″. CMC. Jan 15, 1953, Seattle, Barbara Pentland.
Mirror Study. 1952. ms.
Two-Piano Sonata. 1953. 10′. CMC. May 2, 1954, Cambridge, Mass, Harvard Univ, Paine Hall, Ellen Arrow, Colin Slim.
Aria. 1954. 2′45″. CMC. Feb 7, 1955, Vanc Art Gallery, Barbara Pentland.
Interlude. 1955. 2′10″. Wat, 1968. Feb 13, 1956, CBC Vanc, Barbara Pentland.
Toccata. 1958. 8′5″. Ber, 1961. CBC BR SM-162; RCI-242. July 17, 1958, CBC Vanc, Barbara Pentland.
Three Duets After Pictures by Paul Klee. 1959. 6′15″. pno 4 hands. CMC. RCI-242. Feb 8, 1961, Vanc, Barbara Pentland, Robert Rogers.
Ostinato and Dance for Harpsichord. 1962. 4′15″. CMC.
Fantasy. 1962. 6′40″. Ber, 1966. RCI-242. 1963, Vanc, Leonard Stein.
Freedom March. 1963. 1′20″. ms. pno 4 hands. CMC.
Two Canadian Folk Songs (arr). 1963. pno 4 hands. CMC.
Puppet-Show. 1964. 4′50″. Ber, 1966.
Echoes 1 and 2. 1964. Wat, 1968. CCM-2.
Maze/Labyrinthe, Casse-Tête/Puzzle. 1964, 1968. Wat, 1969.

Shadows/Ombres. 1964. 4'15". Wat, 1968. RCI-242. 1965, Vanc, CBC, Barbara Pentland.
Signs (4 pieces). 1964. CMC.
Three Pairs. 1964. Ber, 1966. CCM-2.
Caprice. 1965. 2'20". CMC. 1966, Vanc, Barbara Pentland.
Hands Across the C. 1965. Wat, 1968. CCM-2.
Suite Borealis. 1966. 20'. CMC. Mar 5, 1967, Vanc, RCMT Alum Assoc.
Space Studies. 1967. Wat, 1968. CCM-2.
Songs of Peace and Protest. 1968. CMC.
Music of Now, Books 1, 2, 3. 1969–70. Wat, 1970.
Arctica (4 pieces). 1971–3.
Vita Brevis. 1973.

INSTRUMENTAL SOLO

Solo Violin Sonata. 1950. 17'. CMC. June 14, 1955, Brussels, Le Club B P W de Bruxelles, Louis Thienpont.
Sonatina for Solo Flute. 1954. 6'. CMC. Feb 2, 1955, Vanc, Women's Musical Club, Jean Murphy.
Variations for Viola. 1965. 10'. CMC.
Reflections. 1971. 5'. free-bass accord.

ORGAN

Prelude, Chorale and Toccata. 1937. ms. May 9, 1958, New York, Juilliard Conc Hall, Ashley Miller.
Ostinato. 1938. ms.

BIBLIOGRAPHY

See B-B; B65,71; Bec57,70; Bt; CrC(1); D165; Esc; Gf; Ip; K; MGG; Mm; Wa.
'Barbara Pentland', *Northern Review*. Apr. 1950.
'Barbara Pentland In Dual Role', *CBC Times*. July 27-Aug. 2, 1963 (4).
'Barbara Pentland – a portrait', *Mu*. No. 21, July-Aug. 1969 (8–9).
Huse, Peter. 'Barbara Pentland', *MuSc*. July-Aug. 1968 (9).
'Ideas on a Keyboard', *Saturday Night*. Jan. 9, 1951 (8).
'"The Lake": a Canadian Chamber Opera', *CBC Times*. Feb. 28-Mar. 6, 1954 (3).
'Music of Today', *The Canadian Composer* (CBC documentary tape, host Harry Somers in Conversation with Barbara Pentland). Apr. 29, 1966.
Turner, Robert. 'Barbara Pentland', *CMJ*. Vol. II, no. 4, 1957–8 (15).

LITERARY WORKS

ARTICLES

'Canadian Music, 1950', *Northern Review*. Vol. III, Feb.-Mar. 1950. (43–6).
'An Experiment in Music', *Canadian Review of Music and Art*. Vol. II, no. 7–8, Aug.-Sept. 1943 (25–7).
'"The Lake": One-Act Chamber Opera; Libretto by Dorothy Livesay', *Canadian Forum*. Apr. 1954 (16).

PÉPIN, (JEAN-JOSEPHAT) CLERMONT (b. Saint-Georges-de-Beauce, Que., 15 May 1926). At the age of only eight, the young Pépin undertook the composition of a large symphony for piano four-hands. After studying piano and taking harmony lessons from Georgette Dionne, in 1937 he was presented by Wilfrid Pelletier to the matinée audiences of the Quebec and Montreal symphony orchestras as composer and orchestral conductor. Also at the age of eleven he was awarded a special prize from the Canadian Performing Right Society (CPRS, later CAPAC) and went to Montreal to study harmony and counterpoint with Claude CHAMPAGNE, and piano with Arthur Letondal. In 1941 he received a scholarship from the Curtis Institute in Philadelphia, where he studied with Rosario Scalero and piano with Jeanne Behrend; he received his diploma in 1945. Three successive scholarships from CAPAC allowed him to study for three years at the Royal Conservatory of Music, Toronto, where his teachers were Arnold WALTER in composition and Lubka Kolessa for piano. The principal works of this period – such as the *Symphonie no 1, en si mineur* (1948), the *Concerto no 1* (1946) for piano and orchestra, and the *Variations symphoniques* (1947) – are interesting in their preoccupation with form, although the instrumentation is quite traditional. Stylistically these works show an undoubted talent, though as yet little originality, following in the footsteps of Franck or Rachmaninov.

Pépin's stay in Paris from 1949 to 1955, as winner of the Prix d'Europe from the Académie de Musique de Québec, marks a decisive turning-point in his musical development. At the Conservatoire he studied composition with André Jolivet and Arthur Honegger and attended analysis courses with Olivier Messiaen, where his fellow students were Pierre Boulez, Karlheinz Stockhausen, Michel Fano, and the Canadians Serge GARANT and Sylvio Lacharité. At that time Pépin was not at first attracted to serial composition, but an analysis of some pieces by Schoenberg and Berg, as well as the 'Turangalîla-Symphonie' of Messiaen, deeply modified his writing, style, and aesthetic. Two symphonic poems from this period, *Guernica* (1952) and *Le Rite du soleil noir* (1955), use the serial technique in part. These works, like the *Symphonie no 2* (1957) and the *Quatuor à cordes no 2; 'Thème et Variations'* (1955–6, Pépin's first completely serial work), show a striving for conciseness, greater rhythmic variety, and a keen sense of contrast.

On his return from Paris in 1955 Pépin was appointed professor of composition at the Montreal Conservatoire, a post that he occupied till 1964; he became administrative adviser in 1959 and in the following year was made Director of Studies. His teaching has certainly borne results; among his students are André PRÉVOST, Jacques HÉTU, and Micheline Coulombe SAINT-MARCOUX. During this period the *Quatuor à cordes no 3; 'Adagio et fugue'* (1959) was quickly followed by the *Quatuor à cordes no 4; 'Hyperboles'* (1960), of which Pépin said 'this does not represent the end of my exploration of the serial technique, but rather the beginning'. From 1967 to 1972 he shaped the destiny of the Montreal Conservatoire as its Director.

Alongside his purely instrumental works, Pépin has also written for dance and theatre. A first score of the ballet *Les Portes de l'enfer* (1953) is known today only in a version for two pianos, unchoreographed. *L'Oiseau-Phénix* (1956) and *Le Porte-rêve* on the other hand have been danced, the former on stage (choreography by Ludmilla Chiriaeff) and the latter on television (choreography by Michel Conte). In 1956 and after Pépin also wrote several musical scores for plays produced by the Théâtre-Club and the Théâtre du Nouveau Monde. These works show a composer in full control of his craft, capable of writing with speed and flexibility.

The time devoted to teaching and administration seems scarcely to have impeded Pépin's creative activity. In 1960 he composed a cantata for tenor and orchestra (or piano): *Hymne au vent du nord* on a poem by Alfred DesRochers, his first vocal piece of importance since the seven songs of the *Cycle Eluard* (1949) for soprano and piano to poems from 'La Capitale de la douleur'. Although not always a grateful one for the singer, Pépin's vocal line always shows much care in conveying the poetic thought.

With *Nombres pour deux pianos et orchestre* (1962), Pépin goes still further in his use of contemporary techniques. The work is rigorously serial, using the procedures of Boulez, which enter into a game of mathematical formulas; the ensemble is divided into twelve groups, two being the pianos. Moreover the composer envisages the location of microphones so that the groups would seem to be placed in all parts of the hall, the listener then being 'completely surrounded with music . . .'.

A commission from the Montreal Symphony Orchestra, *Quasars* (*Symphonie no 3*) (1967), allowed Pépin to return to large forms. This is possibly Pépin's most imposing work to date, being half an hour in length, in six sections, and making use of full orchestra with piano, harp and ondes Martenot. Pépin's interest in astronomy, space, and light provided a source of inspiration for this work.

In 1964 he composed *Monade I* for string orchestra, borrowing the name from Leibnitz, who used it to designate a single active and indivisible substance; long sustained notes without vibrato suggest electronic sounds. For the present *Monade II*, also for strings, remains incomplete. *Monade III pour violon et orchestre* (1972) is distinguished by a very difficult part for the soloist, in conformity with its requirements as a competition 'pièce imposée'. *Monade IV; 'Réseaux'* and *Monade V* (both in progress) call for the alternating resources of the violin and piano in very short segments that are minutely organized, the sequential order being chosen by the performers.

In *Prismes et cristaux* (in progress) Pépin once again links himself with the classical tradition in associating this work for large string orchestra with the concept of the prelude and fugue. The traditional contrast between the parts is observed, the first slow and dramatic, the other in a constant state of motion.

Along with some of his musical colleagues, and with some sociologists and artists, Pépin founded in 1966 the Centre d'Etudes prospectives du Québec, whose work is to consider the future and its implications. An initial study, devoted to noise pollution, appeared in 1970. In 1969 Pépin succeeded Wilfrid Pelletier as national president of Jeunesses musicales du Canada, occupying this post for three years. In May 1970 the St-Jean-Baptiste Society of Montreal awarded him the annual Calixa Lavallée prize and the Bene Merenti medal for his compositions, and for his services to the cause of music in Quebec.

Pépin is a member of the Canadian League of Composers and of CAPAC, of which he was vice-president from 1966 to 1970. GILLES POTVIN

MUSICAL WORKS

STAGE

Les Portes de l'enfer (ballet). 1953. 20'. med orch. ms. 1953, Paris (2pno version), Cercle Paul Valéry, Clermont Pépin, Raymonde Gagnon-Pépin(pnos).

Le Malade imaginaire (incidental music). 1956. 8'. xyl, cel, vlc, perc. ms. 1956, Théâtre du Nouveau Monde.

Athalie (incidental music). 1956. ms. 1956, Mtl, Fest Mtl, George Little, J B Moreau, C Pépin.

L'Oiseau-Phénix (ballet). 1956. 22'. med orch. ms. Sept 1, 1956, Mtl, Mtl Fest, C Pépin(dir), Ludmilla Chiriaeff(chor), F Bernier, L Chiriaeff(scenario).

Le Porte-rêve (ballet). 1957–8. 26'. orch. ms. Jan 28, 1958, CBC, L'Heure du concert, Otto-Werner Mueller(cond), Michel Conte (chor), Eloi de Grandmont(scenario), Françoys Bernier(prod).

La Nuit des rois (incidental music). 1957. guit. ms. 1957, Mtl, Compagnie du Théâtre Club.

L'Heure éblouissante (incidental music). 1961. 12'. harm, vc. ms. 1961, Mtl, Compagnie du Théâtre Club.

Le Marchand de Venise (incidental music). 1964. fl, bsn, hpschd. ms. 1964, Mtl, Compagnie du Théâtre Club.

ORCHESTRA

Variations symphoniques. 1947. 12'. full orch. ms. May 1, 1948, Mtl, Salle du Gesù, Société des Concerts symphoniques de Mtl, Désiré Defauw(cond).

Symphonie no 1, en si mineur. 1948. 18'. full orch. ms. Aug 1949, Mtl, CBC, Jean Beaudet(cond).

Guernica (symphonic poem). 1952. 17'. full orch. CMC. Audat 477-4001. Dec 8, 1952, Quebec, Wilfrid Pelletier(cond).

Le Rite du soleil noir (symphonic poem). 1955. 10'. full orch. CMC. Sept 1955. Luxembourg, Orch Symphonique de Radio-Luxembourg, Henri Pensis(cond).

Symphonie no 2. 1957. 23'30". med orch. CMC. RCA CC/CCS-1007. Dec 22, 1957, Mtl, CBC, Orch des Petites Symphonies, Roland Leduc(cond).

Monologue. 1961. 16'. med orch. CMC. May 10, 1961, Mtl, CBC, Orch des Petites Symphonies, Roland Leduc(cond).

Quasars (Symphonie no 3). 1967. 25'. full orch. MCA. Select CC-15.101. Feb 7, 1967, Mtl, MSO, Franz-Paul Decker(cond).

Chroma. 1973. 12'. full orch. ms. May 5, 1973, Guelph Spring Fest, QSO, Pierre Dervaux(cond).

STRING ORCHESTRA

Variations. 1944. ms.

Adagio pour cordes. 1947–56. 6'. ms.

Ronde de l'Oiseau-Phénix. 1956. 4'. ms. Dec 22, 1957, CBC, Orch Petites Symphonies, Roland Leduc.

Fantaisie. 1957. ms.

Three Miniatures for Strings. 1963. 4'. OUP, 1966. 1963, Tor, schl orch.

Monade I. 1964. 9'40". ms. RCA LSC-3128, CRI SD-317. Apr 1, 1964, Mtl, McG Ch O, Alexander Brott.

Prismes et cristaux. 1974. 13'. ms. Apr 9, 1974, Mtl, MSO, Franz-Paul Decker.

SOLOIST(S) WITH ORCHESTRA

Concerto pour piano et orchestre no 1, en do dièse mineur. 1946. 22'. pno, orch. ms. 1946, Mtl, Plateau Hall, Orch symphonique des jeunes de Mtl, Fernand Graton (cond,) Clermont Pépin(pno).

Concerto pour piano et orchestre no 2. 1949. 12'. ms. 1949, Mtl, CBC Orch, J Beaudet(cond), Clermont Pépin(pno).

Nocturne. 1950–7. 6'. pno, str orch. ms.

Hymne au vent du nord (cantata). 1960. 9'. ten, orch (pno). ms. Text: Alfred DesRochers. 1960, Mont-Orford, Orch des JMC, Sir Ernest MacMillan(cond), Raoul Jobin(ten).

Nombres pour deux pianos et orchestre. 1962. 12′25″. CMC. Feb 6, 1963, Mtl, MSO, CLC Con, Victor Feldbrill(cond), Renée Morisset(pno,) Victor Bouchard(pno).
Monade III pour violon et orchestre. 1972. 11′30″. CMC. June 1972, Mtl, MSO, Franz-Paul Decker(cond). Violin compet'n, Internat'l Institute of Music of Canada.

CHOIR WITH ORCHESTRA

Cantique des Cantiques. 1950. 6′. SATB, str. ms. Text: Bible. 1951, Paris, Maison canadienne.
Fantaisie. 1957. 6′. ten, SATB, orch. ms. Text: French-Canadian folk songs. 1957, Mtl, CBC Orch, Wilfrid Pelletier(cond), Raoul Jobin (ten).
Mouvement. 1958. 7′. SATB, orch. ms. Text: French-Canadian folk songs. 1958, Quebec, QSO, F Bernier(cond), Laval University Choir.

VOICE

La Feuille d'un saule. 1940. 2′. sop & pno. ms. Text: Chinese poems.
Chanson d'automne. 1946. 3′. ten & pno. ms. Text: Paul Verlaine.
Les Ports. 1948. 3′. bar & pno. ms. Text: Chadourne.
Cycle Eluard (7 mélodies pour soprano et piano). 1949. 9′26″. sop & pno. CMC. RCI-148. Text: Paul Eluard. Boston, N Eng Cons, Composers' Symposium, Elizabeth Benson-Guy(sop), Clermont Pépin(pno).

VOICES WITH INSTRUMENTAL ENSEMBLE

Pièces de circonstance. 1967. 3′. children's choir, schl band. CMC. Text: Jean Tetreau. July 5, 1967, NAC opening, John Sutherland (cond), Peter Manley(band cond).

INSTRUMENTAL ENSEMBLE

Trois Menuets. 1944. str qt. ms.
Quatuor à cordes no 1. 1948. 17′30″. CMC. 1948, Rochester, NY, Eastman Schl of Mus Symp, RCMT.
Quatuor à cordes no 2 (Variations). 1955–6. 9′. MCA. RCI-295. 1957, Mtl, CBC, Mtl Str Qt, Hyman Bress(vln), Mildred Goodman (vln), Otto Joachim(vla), Walter Joachim (vlc).
Suite pour violon, violoncelle et piano. 1958. 13′. CMC. 1958, Ottawa, Natl Congress of JMC, Jean-Louis Rousseau(vln), Dorothy Bégin(vlc), Janine Lachance(pno).
Quatuor à cordes no 3 (Adagio et Fugue). 1959. 8′. CMC. 1959, S'tn, S'tn Summer Fest of Music, Can Str Qt.
Quatuor à cordes no 4 (Hyperboles). 1960. 9′. CMC. Apr 1, 1960, Mtl, Hermitage, Mtl Str Qt, Hyman Bress(vln), Mildred Goodman(vln), Otto Joachim(vla), Walter Joachim(vlc).
Séquences pour 5 instruments. 1972. 15′. fl, ob, vln, vla, vlc. ms. Dec 17, 1972, Mtl, Ens Pierre Rolland.
Monade IV – Réseaux. 1974. 23′. vln & pno. ms. Mtl, Redpath Hall, Otto Armin (vln), Marie-Paule Armin(pno).

PIANO

Andante. 1939. 4′. ms.
Short Etude no 1. 1940. 2′. West, 1948.
Thème et Variations. 1940. 6′. ms.
Pièce pour piano. 1943. 5′. ms.
Short Etude no 2. 1946. 2′. West, 1948.
Short Etude no 3. 1947. 2′. West, 1948.
Sonate en un mouvement pour piano. 1947. 9′. ms.
Thème et Variations. 1947. 10′. ms.
Toccata, Op 3. 1947. 4′. CMC.
Etude-Atlantique. 1950. 5′. ms.
Petite Etude no 4. 1950. 2′. ms.
Suite pour piano (Allegro leggiero – Fantaisie en hommage à Arthur Honegger – Danse frénétique). 1951 (rev 1955). 9′45″. MCA. RCA CC/CCS-1022 (*Danse frénétique*).
Three short pieces for the piano (*The Nose – Cradle Song – Gates of Hell*). 1953. 3′30″. FH, 1953. Dom S-69002 (*Gates of Hell*).
Deux Préludes pour piano. 1954. 4′. ms.
Petite Etude no 5. 1954. 3′10″. CMC.
Trois Pièces pour la Légende dorée (Prélude – Interlude – Toccata). 1956. 3′45″. hpschd (pno). MCA, 1971.
Ronde villageoise. 1956 (arr 1961). 3′55″. 2 pno. CMC. CBC BR SM-61.
Toccata no 3. 1961. 6′15″. CMC. 1962, Tor, CBC, John McKay.

INSTRUMENTAL SOLO

Quatre Monodies pour flûte seule. 1955. 6′ 10″. MCA, 1971. Dom S-69005. Apr 5, 1960, Mtl, CLC conc, Jean Morin.

ORGAN

Passacaglia. 1950. 8′. ms.

BIBLIOGRAPHY

See B-B; B65,71; Bec57,70; Bt; CrC(II); D165; Esc; K; Lv; T; Wa.
'Clermont Pépin – a portrait', *Mu.* No. 2, June 1967 (8–9).
'Clermont Pépin: Pour une décolonisation

de l'oreille', *Musiques du Kébèk* (R. Duguay, ed.). Montreal: Editions du Jour, 1971 (153–6).
Dix, E. 'Le P'tit Pépin', *Saturday Night*. May 14, 1937 (30–2).
'Music Notes: "Dream Charm" – an Original Canadian Ballet', *CBC Times*. Jan. 26–Feb. 1, 1958 (11).
Rudel-Tessier, J. 'The Many Activities of Clermont Pépin', *CanCo*. No. 11, Oct. 1966 (4–5, 40–1).
Sauvé, Wilfrid. 'A Meeting with Clermont Pépin', *CanCo*. No. 47, Feb. 1970 (14–17).

LITERARY WORKS

ARTICLES

'Concert de musique canadienne organisé par la Ligue Canadienne de Compositeurs', *Vie des Arts*. 1956 (29).
'La Semaine Internationale de Musique Actuelle', *CMJ*. Vol. VI, no. 1, 1961–2 (29).

PERRAULT, MICHEL (b. Montreal, Que., 20 July 1925). He studied at the McGill Conservatorium (timpani and theory) before 1943 and from 1943 to 1946 at the Montreal Conservatoire with Gabriel Cusson (harmony), Réal Gagnier (oboe), and Louis Decair (timpani). His later studies were at the Ecole Normale de Musique, Paris (1946–7), with Nadia Boulanger, Arthur Honegger, and Georges Dandelot. On his return to Montreal he became a pupil and disciple of Conrad Letendre. He was timpanist for the Montreal Symphony Orchestra (1944–6) and for Les Petites Symphonies (Montreal, 1945–6). As composer and conductor for the CBC (1949–50), he wrote incidental music for radio and television, receiving the Radio Monde award for radio music in 1950. He was percussionist and assistant conductor with the Montreal Symphony Orchestra (1957–60) and musical director of Les Grands Ballets Canadiens (1958–60). He is founder and musical director of La Société des Concerts de Musique de Chambre Noire, a jazz organization, and musical director of the Minute Opera Company. He also established his own music publishing house, Publications Bonart, in Montreal. Perrault's early compositions reveal a similarity to the style of Maurice Ravel. His *Les Fleurettes* (1957) and *Trio* (1954) are characterized by folk-like melodies in a light polyphonic texture. In *Sea Gallows* (1958) and *Centennial Homage* (1966) the resemblance to Ravel's style is still apparent, but there is greater dissonance and, at times, thicker textures. He has received commission from the CBC (*Quatuor pour saxophones*, 1953; *Trio*, 1954; and *Sextuor*, 1955), Les Grands Ballets Canadiens (*Suite canadienne*, 1965), and the Victoria Symphony Orchestra (*Centennial Homage*, 1966).

MUSICAL WORKS

STAGE

Incidental music for: *Antigone* (1949); *La Belle au Bois* (1949); *Le Voyage de Thésée* (1949); *Caligula* (1950); *Le Farce du perdu dépendu* (1950); *Huon de Bordeaux* (1950); *Le Voyageur sans Bagage* (1950).
3 ballet scores: *Commedia del arte* (1958); *Sea Gallows* (1958) med orch, Bonart; *Suite canadienne* (1965).

ORCHESTRA

Centennial Homage (an overture to the second century BC). 1966. full orch. Bonart, 1966.
13 works for small orch, including: *Les Aquarelles* (1946); *Les Fleurettes* (1947); *Promenade* (1954) Bonart; *Scherzo* (1954) Bonart; 8 arr of French-Canadian folk songs, publ by Bonart.
Monologues. 1954. str orch. Bonart.
17 works for soloists and orch, including: *Les Trois cones* (1949) vlc, orch; *La Belle Rose* (1952) vlc, orch, Bonart; *Fête et Parade* (1952) tpt, orch, Bonart; *Esquisses en Plein Air* (1954) sop, str, Bonart; *Margoton* (1954) hp, orch, Bonart; *Le Saucisson canadien* (1955) 4sax, str, Bonart; *Pastiche espagnol* (1956) tpt, orch, Bonart; *Pastiche tzigane* (1957) 2 tpt, orch, Bonart; *Berubée* (1959) pno, orch, Bonart; *Jeux de quartes* (1961) hp, orch; *Serenade per tre fratelli* (1962) 3hn, orch; *Concerto pour contrebasse* (1962); *Concerto pour cor* (1967) Bonart.

CHORAL

Anne de Bretagne. 1953. SSA. Bonart.

VOCAL

Plus matin que la lune. 1953. vc, hp.
Fontaines noires; Douces fontaines. 1956. ten, 2hp. Bonart.

INSTRUMENTAL

7 works for chamber ensemble: *Triangu-*

laire (Les Trois cones) (1945) cl, hp, str qt; *Les Aquarelles* (suite) (1946) vln, pno; *Sonata* (1946) vln, pno, Ber; *Solitude* (1948) vln, pno, Ber, 1951; *Saxophone Quartet* (1953), Bonart; *Trio* (1954) vln, vlc, pno, Bonart; *Sextet* (1955) cl, hp, str qt, Bonart.

7 works for jazz group, publ by Bonart: *Prélude et Fugue à l'Américaine* (1956); *Half and Half* (1957); *Real Gone* (1957); *Two Three-Part Fugues* (1957); *All Wet* (1959); *Blues Prelude and Fugue* (1959); *Three Shades* (Suite) (1959).

Monologues. 1951. vla.

BIBLIOGRAPHY

See B-B; Bt; CrC(I); K; Lv; Wa.

POLGAR, TIBOR (b. Budapest, Hungary, 11 Mar. 1907). He studied at the Liszt Academy of Music in Budapest with Zoltan Kodaly, graduating in 1925. From 1925 to 1950 he was conductor of the Radio Symphony Orchestra in Budapest, becoming head of the music department of the Hungarian Radio Network in 1945. He was twice awarded the Erkel Music Prize. During this time he wrote scores for many stage and radio plays and for more than 150 feature and documentary films. He was also the associate conductor of the Philharmonia Hungarica in Marl-Westphalen, Germany (1962–4). He came to Toronto in 1964 and was conductor of the University of Toronto Symphony Orchestra from 1965 to 1966. Since 1966 he has been a member of the musical staff of the opera department, Faculty of Music, University of Toronto, and of the Canadian Opera Company, and in 1969 he was associate music director of the touring series, Prologue to the Performing Arts. In 1966 he received a Canada Council Senior Arts Fellowship. He has composed music for CBC radio and television. He received a commission from Jan Rubes for the chamber opera, *A European Lover* (1965), which Rubes performed extensively throughout Canada. In both *Variations on a Hungarian Folk Song* (1969) for harp, strings, and timpani and *Notes on Hungary* (1971) for concert band, his command of instrumental colour produces effectively the flavour of his Hungarian homeland. Even in works such as *In Private* (1964) for violin and viola and *Rhapsody of Kálló* (1970) for violin and harp, Hungarian idioms are dominant. He is a member of CAPAC.

MUSICAL WORKS

STAGE

3 operas: *Kérök (The Suitors)* (1954); *A European Lover (Musical satire disguised as an opera)* (1965); *The Troublemaker* (comic opera in one act) (1968).

INSTRUMENTAL

Miniatures. 1927. pno (orch'd 1930).

5 works for chamber ensemble: *Improvisazione* (1962) 4hn; *In Private* (1964) vln, vla; *Ilona's Four Faces* (1970) sax, pno; *Rhapsody of Kálló* (1970) vln, hp; *Sonatina for Two Flutes* (1971).

Variations on a Hungarian Folk Song. 1969. hp, str, timp.

Variations on a Hungarian Folk Song. 1969. hp.

Notes on Hungary. 1971. band.

CHORAL

3 arr for children's choir and orch: *Lánc, Lánc eszterlánc* (1962); *Das Bienchen* (1962); *Ein Vogel wollte Hochzeit machen* (1962).

The Last Words of Louis Riel (cantata). 1966–7. alto, bs, SATB, orch.

VOCAL

8 works for vc and pno: *All Our Edens Are Lost and Never Regained* (1965); *Change* (1965); *Fisherman* (1965); *Four Stanzas on Autumn* (1965); *Song for Naomi* (1965); *Stopping by the Woods on a Snowy Evening* (1965); *Twelve O'Clock* (1965); *Lest We Forget the Last Chapter of Genesis* (1970).

POLSON, ARTHUR (b. Vancouver, B.C., 2 Mar. 1934). He began studying violin at the age of four. Later he studied violin with Gregori Garbovitsky (1948) and Louis Persinger in Santa Barbara (1953). He was deputy concertmaster of the Vancouver Symphony Orchestra (1953–62), concertmaster of the Victoria Symphony Orchestra (1962–3), and of the Stratford Festival Orchestra. He has also performed as a member of the Cassenti Players of Vancouver and the Canadian Festival String Quartet. From 1966 to 1970 he was concertmaster of the Winnipeg Symphony Orchestra, the CBC Winnipeg Orchestra, and conductor and musical director of the Winnipeg Youth Symphony. From 1970 to 1971 he was assistant professor at the School of Music of the University of Manitoba. His *Improvisation for Violin and Orchestra* (1958) is a rhapsodic piece in a conservative, tonal style. Continuing in the rhapsodic vein, he began employing dissonant atonal materials (*Fantasy, Dracula*, 1958; *Concerto for Bassoon and Strings*, 1965).

Polson has written extensively for orchestra, especially for violin solo and orchestra. His orchestral works include *Concertino for Violin and Strings* (1957) and *Tension No. II for Violin (or Flute) and Orchestra* (1958), as well as *Introduction and Scherzo for Cello and Orchestra* (1959) and *Concerto for Bassoon and Strings* (1965). He has written several chamber works for violin and piano (*Dream*, 1956; *Fantasy*, 1958; *Melody*, 1962), three *Duos for Two Violins* (1959, 1965), two *Trios* for violin, viola and cello (1961, 1965), as well as two works for string quartet, a piano quintet (1959), and several works for various combinations of instruments. He has also composed *The Susceptible Widow* (1957) for soprano and piano; *Romance* (1956) for soprano, two violins, cello and piano; *Six Little Piano Pieces* (1964); and *Sonata for Solo Violin* (1959). He is a member of CAPAC.

BIBLIOGRAPHY

'Arthur Polson', *CanCo*. No. 51, June 1970 (34).

PRÉVOST, ANDRÉ (b. Hawkesbury, Ont., 30 July 1934). Although born in Hawkesbury, André Prévost came of a family rooted in Quebec, his ancestors having been associated with the development of several muncipalities in the Laurentians north of Montreal. He grew up in Saint-Jérôme; at the age of fifteen he completed his classical studies in Montreal at the Collège Saint-Laurent. In 1951 he entered the Conservatoire in Montreal, where he studied under Georges Savaria (piano), Symon Kovar (bassoon), Isabelle Delorme and Jean PAPINEAU-COUTURE (harmony, fugue and counterpoint) and Clermont PÉPIN (composition). Graduating from the Conservatoire in 1960 he obtained the first prize in both composition and harmony; in 1959 he had won the Sarah Fischer Award in composition and the Chamber Music Award of the Fondation Les Amis de l'Art. By then his catalogue of works extended to a *Quatuor à cordes* (1958), several works for one or two instruments (*Pastorale pour deux harpes*, 1955; *Fantaisie pour violoncelle et piano*, 1956) and his first work for orchestra, *Poème de l'infini* (1960).

During this period his musical thought followed the precepts of his acknowledged masters, especially in the search for liberation from the bonds of tonality. Thus, in the quartet, a linear construction allowing many kinds of juxtapositions edges into the world of modality. The second movement of *Mobiles* (1959–60) constitutes a first venture into serial technique. *Poème de l'infini*, a large-scale orchestral fresco, marks a culmination of this period of his studies. Through the use of total chromaticism the composer here expresses the awe and anguish of Man before his Creator. 'Being persuaded that every work of art has basically a religious impulse, I have done no more than offer a prayer of thanksgiving.' Here he embodies a primary element of the human search through music, a search sometimes manifested in a 'program', sometimes in timbres, colour, and rhythm. The return to human sources of inspiration, to the primary instincts of man, to the tribal instinct, is a necessity. In this Prévost sees an assurance of universal communication.

Such a philosophical preoccupation must always be accompanied by a search for form. From any strong and simple idea will spring a host of other ideas, which the composer must put in order if he is to use them. Thus the *Sonate pour violon et piano* (1960) is structured on a twelve-tone series, although this material is not developed dodecaphonically; the three movements are linked without interruption and doublings are avoided in the continual confrontation of the new and the traditional. The *Préludes pour piano* (1961) are likewise constructed on a twelve-tone series, built upon intervals such as the augmented fourth and the minor third. The *Sonate pour violoncelle et piano* (1962) does not escape from this preoccupation but constitutes a sort of lyric hiatus in the composer's output. Even though Prévost makes use of several elements within the serialist framework, he is not imprisoned in the serial aesthetic and the message to the ear includes nothing of the pointillist. His developments often pivot on serial principles, but the language is always different. Prévost does not eschew repetition. On the contrary he insists that the continuity of a work be assured, whether through a rhythmic motif, a melodic cell, or a series of timbres. Such a continuity will be perceivable and the foundation further strengthened by contrapuntal writing. These three works, like the *Scherzo* (1960) for string orchestra, were written during a stay in Paris, a sojourn made possible by grants from the Canada Council and the government of Quebec. There he worked at the Conservatoire from 1960 to 1962, in analysis with Olivier Messiaen; during the second year, he studied composition at the Ecole Normale with Henri Dutilleux.

Prévost's return to Montreal in April 1962 marked the beginning of a greater preoccupation with large ensembles. More and more repelled by human stupidity Prévost wrote *Fantasmes* (1963), a symphonic movement describing 'the unwelcome and desperate vision of a nightmare ..., the logical and almost inevitable reaction more and more to the spectacle of man at grips with the impenetrable mystery of life. This work bears witness to the unique and cruel solitude of man and is a symbol of his terror.' First performed on November 22, 1963, it is now dedicated posthumously to John F. Kennedy. Hammered out in one repetitive hypnotic movement, the work embodies philosophical preoccupations already expressed in *Poème de l'infini*. These are further accentuated in *Terre des hommes* (1967) for full orchestra, three choirs and two narrators, on a poem of Michèle Lalonde and written for the Montreal concert that inaugurated Expo 67. Development along similar lines is seen in *Diallèle* (1968) for full orchestra; in *Psaume 148* (1971) for choir, brass and organ; and in *Chorégraphie I* (1973).

By its title *Diallèle* describes the vicious circle in which men are imprisoned, tormented, and destroyed by one another. This absurdity is realized by the progressive overlaying of instrumental textures and by the repetitious aggressiveness of the motivic and rhythmic elements. *Psaume 148* is set to a poem exalting all creation; following a movement that descends to the depths of an abyss, the poem again rises slowly to the heavens in an exhortation to the peoples of the earth to recapture a celestial purity. The music follows closely upon the text. *Chorégraphie I*, written just after the horror of the dramatic events in the Olympic Village at Munich in 1972, takes some of its themes from *Terre des hommes* and actually quotes from *Diallèle*. Its mood is sarcastic, demonic, and suggests intolerance and exasperation. It marks an apex in the composer's reaction to the world in which he finds himself. By contrast this work was followed by a *Missa De Profundis* (1973) expressing feelings of joy and hope.

Even though Prévost favours large ensembles in his writing, he has not forsaken the chamber group as is evident from his *Triptyque* (1962) for flute, oboe, and piano; *Geôles* (1963), three songs for mezzo-soprano and piano; and the *Quatuor à cordes no 2* (1972). This quartet was written on the eve of his departure for a year (June 1972 to June 1973) in Epalinges, close to Lausanne, Switzerland – a much-needed respite from the demands of his university career, begun in 1964. Torn between differing concepts of music education, Prévost is attempting a solution to the confrontation of two schools of thought: that which would build upon tradition and that which rejects it.

Prévost is a member of the Canadian League of Composers and is an affiliate of BMI Canada. LYSE RICHER-LORTIE

MUSICAL WORKS

STAGE

Electre. 1959. 15′. ob, perc. ms. Text: Sophocles. June 1959, Mtl, Cons d'art dramatique, P Valcour(stage dir).

Trois pièces irlandaises. 1961. 15′. guit, fl, ob, vln, vlc, pno. ms. Feb, 1962, Paris, Alliance Française, Compagnie Jacques Tourane.

Primordial (Vln-pno Sonate arr for ballet). 1968 (arr). 16′55″. ms. Nov 10, 1968, London, Ont, Talbot Coll Th, New Dance Gp of Canada.

ORCHESTRA

Poème de l'infini (poème symphonique). 1960. 17'. full orch. CMC. June 11, 1960, Mtl, Plateau Hall, Mtl-Cons O, Charles Houdret(cond).

Fantasmes. 1963. 9'6". full orch. Ber, 1970. RCA LSC-2980, Victrola VICS-1040. Nov 22, 1963, Mtl, MSO, Pierre Hétu(cond).

Célébration. 1966. 8'. med orch. CMC. July 30, 1966, Charlottetown Fest, Halifax SO, John Fenwick(cond).

Diallèle. 1968. 15'15". full orch. CMC. May 30, 1968, Tor, MacM Th, CBC Summer Fest, TS, Otto-Werner Mueller(cond).

Evanescence. 1970. 10'. med orch. Ric, 1971. RCA VCCS-1640. Apr 7, 1970, Ottawa, NACO, Mario Bernardi(cond).

STRING ORCHESTRA

Scherzo. 1960. 5'30". CMC. Mar 12, 1961, Mtl, JMC, Paul Kuentz Ch O.

Hommage. 1971. 12'. 14str. CMC. Apr 19, 1971, Mtl, McG Ch O, Alexander Brott.

SOLOIST WITH ORCHESTRA

Pyknon (pièce concertante pour violon et orchestre). 1966. 13'50". 1966, Mtl, Int'l Music Compet'n, MSO, Otto-Werner Mueller(cond), Roman Nodel(vln).

CHOIR WITH ORCHESTRA

Terre des hommes. 1967. 46'20". 2 narr, 3 choirs, full orch. CMC. Text: Michèle Lalonde. Apr 29, 1967, Opening of Expo 67, World Fest Chorus, Marcel Laurencelle (choirmaster), MSO, Pierre Hétu(cond), Michelle Rossignol and Albert Millaire (narrs).

CHOIR

Soleils couchants. 1953. 3'. SATB. CMC. Text: Paul Verlaine. 1954, Mtl, CBC, Mtl Bach Choir, George Little.

Psaume 148. 1971. 10'. SATB, brass, org. CMC. May 1, 1971, Guelph, Fest Sgrs, T Mend, Elmer Iseler.

VOICE

Musiques peintes. 1955. 8'45". high vc, pno. CMC. Text: Gatien Lapointe. 1957, Mtl, Mtl-Cons, George Coulombe(ten), Patricia Going(pno).

Trois Mélodies pour mezzo-soprano et piano. 1963. 8'20". CMC. Allied ARCLP-4. Text: Michèle Lalonde. 1963, Louise Myette(mezz), Josephte Dufresne(pno).

VOICE WITH INSTRUMENTAL ENSEMBLE

Ode au St Laurent. 1965. 40'15" (18' without narr). narr, str qt. CMC. Text: Gatien Lapointe. Mar 22, 1965, Mtl, Nicole Morin (narr), Yaela Hertz(vln), G Csaba(vln), J Csaba(vla), R Robitaille(vlc).

INSTRUMENTAL ENSEMBLE

Pastorale pour deux harpes. 1955. 10'. ms.

Quatuor no 1. 1958. 20'. CMC. Nov 2, 1959, Mtl, Sarah Fischer Conc, André Svilokos (vln), Maria Klanner(vln), Romain Desroches(vla), Hans Siegrist(vlc).

Mobiles. 1959–60. 15'. fl, vln, vla, vlc. CMC. Sept 1962, Paris, ORTF, Christian Lardé(fl), Pepito Sanchez(vln), Colette Lequien(vla), Pierre Dégesnes(vlc).

Sonate. 1961 (arr for ballet 1968). 16'55". vln, pno. Ber, 1968. BAR JAS-19002; CBC BR SM-172. July 1962, Mtl, CBC, Jacques Verdon(vln), Gilles Manny(pno).

Sonate pour violoncelle et piano. 1962 (arr vln and pno or ondes Martenot 1967). 15' 40". Ricordi 1973. VD/ 3035, RCI-356. Mar 1, 1962, Paris, Salle Marceau, Pierre Morin (vlc), Rachel Martel(pno).

Triptyque. 1962. 14'. fl, ob, pno. CMC. RCI-297. Mar 1, 1963, JMC tour, Trio Canadien, Gail Grimstead(fl), Jacques Simard(ob), Pierre Hétu(pno).

Mouvement pour quintette de cuivres. 1963. 6'. brass qnt. CMC. Apr 6, 1964, Quebec, MBQ, J Ranti(tpt), J L Chartel(tpt), A Lainess(hn), J Zuskin(trb), R Ryker(tba).

Suite pour quatuor à cordes. 1968. 19'. CMC. 1968, Tor, Orford Qt, Andrew Dawes(vln), Kenneth Perkins(vln), Terence Helmer (vla), Marcel St-Cyr(vlc).

Quatuor no 2; 'Ad Pacem'. 1972. 19'. CMC. June 1973, Tor, CBC, Purcell Qt.

PIANO

Préludes pour deux pianos. 1961. 12'. ms. July 11, 1961, Mtl, CBC, Victor Bouchard, Renée Morisset.

ORGAN

Cinq Variations sur un thème grégorien (Salve Regina). 1956. 10'. CMC. July 1968, Mtl, Lyse Thouin.

BIBLIOGRAPHY

CrC(II); Lv; Wa.

'L'Atonalisme naturel', *Musiques du Kébèc* (Raoul Duguay, ed.). Montreal: Editions du Jour, 1971 (167–71).

Germain, Jean-Claude. 'Choquer ne veut pas dire le public en maudit', *Le Petit Journal.* Montreal, Apr. 23, 1967.
Heller, Zelda, 'André Prévost', *MuSc.* Nov.-Dec. 1968 (10).
Lamoureux, Jacques. 'En musique il n'y a pas d'inspirations miraculeuses', *Vie Etudiante.* Montreal, Jan. 15, 1964.
Lefebvre, Marie-Claire. 'André Prévost', paper presented at Musialogue, Mar. 1972 (9 pp.).
Loranger, Pierre. 'André Prévost: "Evanescence" ', *CMB.* Vol. IV, Spring-Summer 1972 (169–72).

LITERARY WORKS

'Analyse de la sonate pour violon et piano', *Le Musicien Educateur.* FAMEQ, Vol. 5, no. 2 (29–38).
'Formulation et conséquences d'une hypothèse', *CMB.* Vol. I, Spring-Summer 1970 (67–80). Reprinted in *Musiques du Kébèc,* Montreal, Editions du Jour, 1971 (172–90).
'La musique de "Terre des hommes" ', concert program, opening of World Festival, Expo 67, Apr. 1967 (29–30).
'Propos sur la création', *Vie Musicale,* Quebec, Ministère des Affaires culturelles, No. 7, Oct. 1967 (14–18).

R

RAE, ALLAN (b. Blairmore, Alta, 3 July 1942). He graduated in composition and arranging from the Berklee School of Music in Boston (1965) and then became a composer and conductor of television variety shows and weekly radio programs for the CBC in Calgary (1966–70). His *String Quartet No. 1* won second prize in the Second-Century-Week Composition Competition at the University of Alberta (1967). In 1970 he began studying composition and electronic music with Samuel DOLIN at the Royal Conservatory of Music, Toronto. In 1971 he received a Canada Council Arts Bursary. Rae's compositions combine the exploitation of instrumental colours with the overlaying of several rhythmic units or tempi to create a highly active mass-structure form. He has written a number of works for orchestra, some of which use material from his incidental music for theatre productions, including *Trip* (1970; from '*Trip . . .*'), *Love Is Me* and *Two Thousand Years Ago* (1972; from '*Charles Manson AKA Jesus Christ*'), *The Hippopotamus* (1972), *Symphony No. 1* (1972). His works for chamber ensembles include *Autumn Colours* (1969) for woodwind quintet; *A Day in the Life of a Toad* (1970) for brass quintet; *Impressions* (1971) for woodwind quintet; *Sleep Whispering* (1971) for vibraphone, alto flute, and piano; and two *String Quartets* and *Wheel of Fortune* (1971) for woodwinds and strings.

Rae has composed musical scores on commission from Theatre Calgary (*You two stay here and the rest come with me,* 1968–9; *Trip,* 1969–70), the Vancouver Theatre Playhouse (*Beware the Quickly Who,* 1971; *Where are you when we need you Simon Fraser?,* 1971), and Theatre Passe Muraille, Toronto (*Charles Manson AKA Jesus Christ,* 1972). He was also commissioned to write music for jazz concerts at the Allied Arts Centre in Calgary. He is affiliated with BMI Canada.

RATHBURN, ELDON (b. Queenstown, N.B., 21 Apr. 1916). He began his early studies in piano in New Brunswick, later studying at the Toronto Conservatory with Healey WILLAN (composition), Charles Peaker (organ), and Reginald Godden (piano). In 1938 he won first prize in the Canadian Performing Right Society Competition (*To a Wandering Cloud; Silhouette*); his *Symphonette* won first prize in the Los Angeles Young Artists' Competition (1944). In Saint John, N.B., he was an organist and was active in musical programs for radio. He received commissions from John Adaskin for the CBC (*Nocturne,*

1953) and from the Halifax Symphony Orchestra (*Gray City*, 1960).

Anyone who has seen many National Film Board of Canada films will probably have heard of Eldon Rathburn. He has been a composer with the NFB since 1947 and has written scores for many internationally acclaimed films, including *Labyrinth*, the NFB's multi-screen extravaganza at Expo 67. Generally his music is light, with a predominance of wind instruments. In *Aspects of Railroads* (1969) his ability as orchestrator is evident. As befits a composer of film scores, he is concerned with building mood through tone-painting.

In 1972 Rathburn began teaching at the University of Ottawa. He is a member of the Canadian League of Composers and of CAPAC.

MUSICAL WORKS

FILM

To the Ladies (1947); *Family Circle* (1949); *Children's Concert* (1951); *The Romance of Transportation* (1952); *Who Will Teach Your Child* (1952); *City of Gold* (1957); *Universe* (1960); *Drylanders* (1963); *Pillar of Wisdom* (1968); *Labyrinth* (1967). film: Roman Kroiter for the NFB Pavilion at Expo '67. LAB-650 S; over 100 other films for NFB.

ORCHESTRA

Silhouette (arr) (1940); *Symphonette* (1943, rev 1946); *Cartoon No 1* (1944); *Cartoon No 2* (1946); *Parade* (1949); *Suite (Family Circle)* (1949); *Images of Childhood* (1950; Ber) CBC BR SM-119; *Suite (Children's Concert)* (1951); *Maritime Reel (Square Dance)* (1952); *Overture to a Hoss Opera* (1952); *Nocturne* (1953) pno, small orch; *Overture Burlesca* (1953); *Variations and Fugue on Alouette* (1953); *Milk Maid Polka* (1956); *Gray City* (1960); *City of Gold* (1967); *Aspects of Railroads* (1969).

CHOIR

Raftsmen (arr). c1960. TTBB. Text: trad.

VOICE(S)

To a Wandering Cloud. 1938.

A Ship, An Isle, A Sickle Moon. 1939. Text: James Elvoy Flicker.

Spring. 1939. Text: Andrew Lang.

Twilight. 1939. Text: Duncan Campbell Scott.

Mr Churchill Our Hats are Off to You. 1940. GVT, 1941. Text: Bruce E Holden, Dave Marion Jr.

INSTRUMENTAL ENSEMBLE

Andante. 1933. str qt.

Five Short Pieces. 1949.

Miniature. 1949. picc, ob, cl, bsn, 2tpt, hn, trb.

Parade. 1949. fl, picc, ob, cl, bsn, tpt, hn, trb, perc.

Pastorella. 1949. ob, vln, vla, vlc, cb.

Waltz for Winds. 1949 (rev 1956). ww qt.

Second Waltz for Winds. 1949. ww qt.

Conversation. 1956. 2cl. Jay.

In a Purple Mood. 1959. 5sax, 6brass, rhythm.

Bout. 1971. guit, cb.

The Metamorphic Ten. 1971. Ber. accord, mand, banj, guit, cb, hp, pno, cel, 3perc.

Two Interplays. 1972. sax qt.

Rhythmette. 2pno, rhythm band.

PIANO

Silhouette. 1936. 2pno.

Five Preludes. 1938–45.

Two Caricatures. 1946.

Valse. 1946.

Black and White. c1970. Wat, 1970.

MULTI-MEDIA

'Of Many People ...'. 1970. slides, film. Text: Gabrielle Roy.

BIBLIOGRAPHY

Bt; CrC(1); Esc; K; Mm; Wa.

'Eldon Rathburn', *Atlantic Advocate*. Vol. LIV, June 1964 (89).

'Music Can Often Communicate Better than Dialogue: a Profile of NFB's Eldon Rathburn', *CanCo*. No. 35, Dec. 1968 (4–7).

'Music from the Films', *CBC Times*. Apr. 28-May 4, 1962 (9).

LITERARY WORKS

ARTICLES

'My Most Successful Work: "Labyrinth"', *CanCo*. No. 30, June 1968 (8–9).

REA, JOHN (b. Toronto, Ont., 14 Jan. 1944). He studied composition at Wayne State University in Michigan, receiving his Bachelor of Music degree in 1967; he was an active member of the Wayne State University Improvisation Ensemble. He received fellowships from the University of Toronto and the Canada Council to study composition at the University of Toronto with John WEINZWEIG and Gustav CIAMAGA, obtaining his Master of Music degree in 1969. In the same year Princeton University awarded him a fellowship to begin doctoral studies in composition. He has received a BMI Student Composer Award (1968), a John Adaskin Memorial Award (*Anaphora*, 1969,) and third prize in an international competition for ballet music in Switzerland (*The Days,* 1969). Rea's compositions follow the post-Webern experimentation in serial technique, with an emphasis on form. In *Prologue, Scene and Movement* (1968) Rea has taken Latin palindromes and, using serial operations, has created a complex structure. In such works as *Anaphora II* (1971) for piano solo, where a repeated-note figure is used, the structure is built not only intellectually, but intuitively as well. In 1972 he was commissioned to compose a children's opera (*The Prisoners Play*) for the opera department, Faculty of Music, University of Toronto. He is affiliated with BMI Canada.

MUSICAL WORKS

STAGE
The Days (ballet). 1969.
The Prisoners Play (opera). 1972–3. Libretto: Paul Woodruff.

SMALL ORCHESTRA
Piece for Chamber Orchestra. 1967 (rev 1971).

VOICE
The Four Corners of the Year. 1968. Text: John Rea.

VOICE WITH INSTRUMENTAL ENSEMBLE
Prologue, Scene and Movement. 1968. sop, vla, 2pno. Text: Sotades Cinaedus.
Tempest. 1969. any comb of voice(s) and/or instruments. Text: John Rea.

INSTRUMENTAL ENSEMBLE
Two Short Pieces. 1964. fl, vln.
Sonatina. 1965. cl, pno.
Sestina. 1968. alto fl, cl, tpt, vlc, hpschd, perc.
Fantaisies and/et Allusions. 1969. sax qt, SD.
Anaphora. 1970. fl, cl, bsn, vln, vla, vlc, pno.

PIANO
What you will. 1971; Jay, 1971.
Anaphora II. 1971 (rev 1972).

ELECTRONIC MUSIC
S.P.I. 51. 1969. MMI MS 2211.
STER 1.3. 1969. MMI MS 2211.

RENAUD, EMILIANO (EMILIEN) (b. St-Jean-de-Matha, Que., 26 June 1875; d. Montreal, Que., 3 Oct. 1932). He took his first music lessons from his mother, later becoming a student of Dominique Ducharme and Paul Letondal. He was organist at Ste-Marie College in 1890, and at Church Point, N.S., in 1892. He returned to Montreal to pursue his studies until his departure for Europe in 1897 where he studied piano in Berlin and Vienna with Madame Varet-Stepanoff of the Leschetitsky school. In 1899 he returned to Montreal, where he became known as a piano virtuoso and composer. He accompanied the singer Emma Calvé on tour in the U.S. and lived in Boston and New York before settling permanently in Montreal in 1921, thereafter devoting himself to teaching and composition.

In April 1900 the Montreal Symphony Orchestra, conducted by J.-J. Coulet, performed Renaud's *Concertstück* for piano and orchestra with the composer as soloist. During the years following he gave a number of recitals in which he played many of his own works. Generally these pieces, such as the *Prélude, fugue et choral* dedicated to Paderewski, may be considered part of the 'grande tradition romantique'; likewise the polonaises, waltzes, and other various pieces were in keeping with the taste of the period. On February 17, 1930, a recital devoted entirely to his works was presented at the Ritz-Carlton Hotel in Montreal with the collaboration of the tenor Rodolphe Plamondon and the violinist Emile Taranto. Renaud composed some fifty songs for voice, of which a number were performed by well-known singers, such as the mezzo-soprano Sigrid Onegin. Mention should also be made of his religious music and an opéra comique, *Dymko,* for which he wrote his own libretto. Renaud's works were published in Europe and the United States by Borneman, Girod, Costallat, Péregally, Ditson, White Smith, and New Music Publishing. He also developed a piano-teaching method, presented on records, which received praise from both Paderewski and the critic James Gibbons Huneker.

GILLES POTVIN

BIBLIOGRAPHY

See B-B; CrC(II); K; Lv.

RIDOUT, GODFREY (b. Toronto, Ont., May 1918).'One thing I would like to make clear', said Godfrey Ridout for a 1964 CBC collection of thirty-four biographies of Canadian composers, 'it is harder to be a reactionary now than to be a revolutionary, because everybody is a revolutionary.' The point is gracefully made, and true if one accepts that everyone wearing the uniform of the army of revolution is a revolutionary: or that everyone rejecting the uniform – every 'conscientious objector' – is by definition a rugged individualist, creatively speaking. But music, when we get down to it, is never a matter of uniforms on or uniforms off, and Ridout oversimplifies his own extremely interesting case by declaring himself, with 'people like Oskar MORAWETZ and even Glenn Gould', a representative of 'a rather curious little island of reaction'.

To be sure, he cast himself early in the mould of conservatism. Born of an old Toronto family, he moved as such through his student years – piano with Weldon Kilburn, organ with Charles Peaker, harmony and orchestration with Ettore Mazzoleni, composition (1938) with Healey WILLAN – and on into a Toronto academic adulthood; teaching at the Toronto (now Royal) Conservatory off and on after 1939, lecturing at the University of Toronto Faculty of Music from 1948 onwards (assistant professor 1961, associate professor 1965, full professor 1971). He put in some time with the Canadian Militia (1938); composed for the National Film Board; composed, conducted and talked for the CBC; was assistant editor of two publications (*Canadian Music* 1940–1, *Canadian Review of Music and Art* 1942–3); and was musical director of Toronto's Eaton Operatic Society (1949–59). He is honorary vice-president of the Gilbert and Sullivan Society, Toronto branch, and in 1967 was awarded an honorary LL.D. from Queen's University.

Since the *Ballade* of 1938, with which Ridout won a year's scholarship for study with Willan, he has added steadily to the catalogue of his works. The *Festal Overture* of 1939 – which the composer has taken a disappointing but perhaps accountable decision to suppress – is a work of strange promise, combining Waltonesque brilliance and Shostakovian shadow in a tantalizing chiaroscuro. There is not the suavity of scoring we take for granted in later Ridout, but there is a rhythmic life more interesting than the square jazz and routine syncopations of Ridout in the sixties. He may have decided that he doesn't like the *Festal Overture* as it is, and that to polish it would spoil it, hence the urge to suppress it; it remains a testimonial to an extraordinary talent at odds with the conventions and conveniences of a middle-class background.

In the *Two Etudes* for string orchestra of 1946, the first – slow and melancholy – has a mordant lyricism, an emotional punch that suggests (again) Shostakovich or possibly Britten. The second *Etude* – fast and vigorous – has a brilliance that is more controlled, if also slightly more stereotyped, than that in the *Festal Overture*. There are lapses into the rather stilted syncopations that British-oriented composers tend to use when they are 'being rhythmic', but the string effects are splendid, idiomatic yet fresh.

Esther, for chorus, two soloists, and full orchestra (1952), is a setting of the biblical story as arranged by the Canadian writer and theatre director Herman Voaden. Styled a 'dramatic symphony' (a title reminiscent of Berlioz) rather than cantata or oratorio, it is held together effectively by recurrent chord progressions and short motifs, often in diatonic-seventh harmonies, and the chorus part, in clear block rhythms much of the time, breaks into strong unisons or sonorous imitative textures at key dramatic moments (such as the a-cappella conclusion to section 3 of the work's five sections).

In the 1953 *Cantiones Mysticae* – settings of Donne dedicated to Lois Marshall – the second, 'Thou Hast Made Me', begins like a Bach trio sonata, with soprano and violin gracefully entwined above a simple walking bass; but there are dark brushings of orchestra dramatizing the centre section, which deals with death, despair, and terror. The third song, 'At the Earth's Imagined Corners', looks to a lesser model than Bach for a stylistic point of rest, falling somewhere – though stylishly enough – between Parry and John Ireland.

The little *Ave Maria*, written in 1954 for St Joseph's College School, harks back to the Elizabethans and is quite lovely in itself, considered out of time and apart from environment.

Three Preludes on Scottish Tunes (1959) are pleasant, conventional organ stuff of good craft – like handknit pure wool scarves. The third of the group, the prelude on 'Martyrs', has a smooth and peppy charm prophetic of the urbane Ridout to come.

Music for a Young Prince (commissioned in 1959 by the CBC for a royal visit on the opening of the St Lawrence Seaway and dedicated to Prince Charles) comes across as a kind of Elgar sandwich with Morton Gould in the middle. It is a highly expert work and a natural for symphonic programs with guilt feelings about Canadian Content. The first of its four movements, 'Dreams', takes inspiration from a line of Dickens about the dreams of childhood and proceeds through a texture of easy tunes and soft instrumental upholstery. It is a kind of dilute Elgar 'Serenade for Strings', not inventive but utterly competent. The second movement, 'From the Caboose', is possibly the best train on any musical track, both for onomatopaeic verisimilitude and for the excitement of the ride. Ridout had fun with this, the fun inspiring his sheer ability as an orchestral craftsman. The third movement, 'The Cowboy and the Injun', is more of the same, a stunning genre piece commenting wryly but never cruelly and always stylishly on the Hollywood cowboy music many Canadians grew up with. With the final movement, 'Pageantry', we are back with Elgar, this time 'Pomp and Circumstance'.

In *The Dance* (1960), another CBC commission, setting for choir and orchestra a mannerly passage from John Aldington Symonds' translation of 'Carmina Burana', the Dionysian potential of the words is forgone in favour of a nostalgia that prints regret in terms of Parry. The same year's *Sainte Marguerite* is like a poignant morsel by Henry Wood, but it wins through by its modesty. The charming French-Canadian tune is touched softly, lightly, tastefully.

Fall Fair (1961) is a cheery, conservative work in which Ridout appears as Canada's answer to William Walton. It is lively, pictorial, conventionally effective, and not impossible for a good amateur orchestra to win applause with. It gets probably more performances than any other Canadian orchestral piece. Indeed, Canadian Content regulations would fall on stony ground if a few works like this did not permit orchestras to beg the question.

The Ascension (*Cantiones Mysticae No. 2*) (1962) was commissioned by Lois Marshall, and sets the Propers for the Feast Day of the Ascension and the Ascension Hymn by Bishop V. Fortunatus for soprano, trumpet and strings. The Propers are jauntily treated. The hymn has a measured, civil ecstasy, a loveliness not too eccentric.

In 1963 Ridout's craft came into useful play when he was commissioned by Ten Centuries Concerts to reconstruct *Colas et Colinette*, a comic opera by the eighteenth-century French Canadian Joseph Quesnel, of which only the voice parts and the 2nd violin parts were extant. He completed the job in 1964, also composing an overture for the opera, in the style of Quesnel and using his tunes. (A little over a decade later he transcribed some tunes from band compositions of the nineteenth-century Quebec musician Joseph Vézina into an orchestral suite, *Frivolités canadiennes*, as another skilful restoration of forgotten Canadian musical literature.)

In 1965 the CBC, commissioned *In Memoriam Anne Frank*, a work for soprano and orchestra, to a text arranged by Bruce Attridge. The work is subtitled 'A Song of Strength', and Ridout has concerned himself with the phenomenon of Anne Frank's hope for humanity rather than with her personal tragedy.

In the full-scale ballet, *La Prima Ballerina* (1966), the big orchestra is handsomely used: witness the fresh use of pizzicato in the second movement of the first suite. But Tchaikovsky (and Prokofiev) are never far out of mind, and the 'Tarantella' is like an addendum to 'Daphnis et Chloé'.

Partita Academica (1969) is a work for brass band in the tradition of another Ridout hero, Gustav Holst. It is certainly a worthy addition to the repertory and the composer thought enough of the middle movement to arrange it for organ under the title of *March*.

The Domage of the Wise, also of 1969, was commissioned by the CBC for the Tudor Singers of Montreal and is a choral treatment of 'clichés concerning time' assembled by Ronald Hambleton – the now-settled Ridout musing on 'Yesterday', 'Today', and 'Tomorrow'.

Ridout is a member of the Canadian League of Composers and of CAPAC, of which he has been a director since 1966.

KENNETH WINTERS

MUSICAL WORKS

STAGE

La Prima Ballerina (ballet). 1966. 70'. full orch. ms. Oct, 1967, Mtl, Expo '67, NatBalCo, H Heiden(choreog), MSO, George Crum (cond).

ORCHESTRA

Festal Overture. 1939. 6'30". full orch. CMC. RCI-41. 1943, Tor, CBC O, Sir Ernest MacMillan.

Comedy Overture. 1941. 5'. ms.

Dirge. 1943. 7'. ms.

Music for a Young Prince. 1959. 18'30". full orch. CMC. 1959, Tor, CBCSO, Geoffrey Waddington.

Fall Fair. 1961. 8'. full orch. GVT, 1966. Audat 477-4001. Oct 1961, New York, UN General Assembly, CBCSO, Sir Ernest MacMillan.

Overture to Colas et Colinette (opéra comique by Joseph Quesnel). 1964. 5'. med orch. GVT, 1971. Sel SC-12.160, Sel SSC-24.160. 1965, Mtl, CBC.

La Prima Ballerina (overture). 1967. 5'. full orch. CMC. Oct 1967, Mtl, MSO, George Crum.

La Prima Ballerina (Suite No 1). 1967. 15'. full orch. CMC. Aug 1, 1971, Tor, TS, Victor Feldbrill.

La Prima Ballerina (Suite No 2). 1967. 15'. full orch. CMC.

BAND

Partita Academica. 1969. 9'35". ms. Mar 16, 1969, Tor, U of T Concert Band.

STRING ORCHESTRA

Two Etudes. 1946 (rev 1951). 10'30". Chap, 1960. 1946, Tor, CBC O, Harold Sumberg.

SOLOIST(S) WITH ORCHESTRA

Ballade for Viola and String Orchestra. 1938. 9'. CMC. May 20, 1939, Tor, Melodic Str, Alexander Chuhaldin(cond), C Figelski (vla).

Cantiones Mysticae. 1953. 11'10". sop, orch (pno). FH, 1956. Text: John Donne. Oct 1952, New York, orch conducted by Leopold Stokowski, Lois Marshall(sop).

Holy Sonnets. 1953. vc, orch. ms.

The Ascension (Cantiones Mysticae No 2). 1962. 14'25". sop, tpt, str. FH, 1971. Text: Propers for the Feast of the Ascension and 'Ascension Day Hymn' by Bishop V Fortunatus (530–609). Dec 23, 1962, Tor, CBCSO, Victor Feldbrill(cond), Mary Morrison(sop), Joseph Umbrico(tpt).

In Memoriam Anne Frank. 1965. 8'. sop, full orch. ms. March 14, 1965, Tor, TS, Victor Feldbrill(cond), Mary Morrison (sop).

Folk Songs of Eastern Canada. 1967. 9'. sop, full orch (pno). GVT, 1970. July 11, 1967, Tor, Mario Bernardi(cond), Lois Marshall(sop).

CHOIR WITH ORCHESTRA

Esther (dramatic symphony). 1952. 60'. sop, bar, SATB, orch. ms. Text: H Voaden. 1952, Tor, RCMT, Ettore Mazzoleni.

Coronation Ode. 1953. SATB, orch. ms. Text: H Voaden.

The Dance. 1960. 10'. SATB, orch. Novl, 1964. Text: Carmina Burana CXXXVII. Trans: J A Symonds. 1960, Tor, CBC, CBC Youth Choir, Elmer Iseler, CBCSO, Mario Bernardi.

Pange Lingua. 1960. 10'35". SATB, orch. Wat, 1960. Text: St Thomas Aquinas. 1961, Buffalo, New York, St Paul's Cathedral, Three Choir Hymn Fest, Godfrey Ridout.

Four Sonnets. 1964. 18'. SATB, orch. GVT, Novl, 1964. Text: J E Ward. Mar 30, 1966, Tor, TS, T Mend, Elmer Iseler.

O Canada (arr). 1965. 4'. SATB, orch (band). GVT, 1965. Text: Stanley Weir.

When Age and Youth Unite. 1966. 8'. SATB, orch (band). GVT, 1966. Text: Claude Bissell. Mar 28, 1967, London, Ont, Convention of CMEA, North Tor Coll O, L MacDowell(cond).

Cantiones Mysticae No 3 (The Dream of

the Rood). 1972. 22′. bar (ten), SATB, orch, org. ms. 1972, Guelph, Bach-Elgar Choir, HPO, Charles Wilson(cond), Allan Monk (bar).

CHOIR

Come Rejoicing. 1952. SATB, org (pno). CMS, 1952.
Ave Maria. 1954. 2′05″. Poly 2917 009. 1954, choir of St Joseph's College Schl.
We'll Rant and We'll Roar (arr). 1958. SATB. Wat, 1958. Text: W H Le Messurier.
The Shepherds' Watch. 1959. SATB. Gray, 1961. Text: T Linsey Crossley.
The Blooming Bright Star of Belle Isle (arr). 1960. SSAATBB. Wat, 1960.
J'entends le moulin (arr). 1960. SATB. Wat, 1960.
Sainte Marguerite (arr). 2′. SATB. Wat, 1960. CMC BR SM-19.
Summer in Winter (from 'Two Christmas Carols') (arr). 1960. SSA. Wat, 1960. Text: Richard Crashaw. BSS Choir.
We Three Shepherds (arr) (from 'Two Christmas Carols'). 1960. SSA. Wat, 1960. BSS Choir.
A General Invitation to Praise God. 1964. SATB, org. GVT, 1964. Text: George Wither.
Star of the North. 1967. 3′. unis & SAB, 2 pno. ms. May 9, 1967, Tor.
The Domage of the Wise. 1969. 7′15″. SATB. ms. CBC BR SM-86. Text: Ronald Hambleton. 1969, Tor, Tudor Sgrs.
Choral Prelude on 'Martyrs'. 1′27″. ms.
Two Choral Preludes. 4′20″. ms.
Whence is This Fragrance? (arr). SSA. CMC. Text: trad. John Cozens. BSS Choir.

VOICE

Landscapes (two songs). 1939. 4′. sop, ob.
What Star Is This? 1941. 3′. vc, pno (org). GVT, 1942. Text: from Latin hymn 'Quae Stella Pulchrior'. Trans: A R Thompson.
Folk Songs of Eastern Canada. 1967. 9′. sop, pno (orch). GVT, 1970.

INSTRUMENTAL ENSEMBLE

Folk Song Fantasy. 1951. 6′. vln, vlc, pno.
Introduction and Allegro. 1968. vln, vlc, fl, ob, cl, hn, bsn. ms.

PIANO

Prelude in F. 1958. 3′. GVT, 1958.
Variation on a Canadian(?)Theme(??) (from 'Variations on Opening a Music Library'). 1967. 2pno. CMC. Dec 9, 1967, Tor, opening of TPML, Sheila Bluethner, L Kohlund(pnos).

ORGAN

Three Preludes on Scottish Tunes. 1959. 7′. GVT, 1960.
Prelude for Organ (from 'Four Sonnets' by Godfrey Ridout) arr F R C Clarke. 1968. 3′. GVT, 1968.
March (arr from *Partita Academica*). 1969. 7′45″. CMC.

BIBLIOGRAPHY

See B-B; B58,65,71; Bec57; Bt; CrC(II); Esc; K; Mm; T; Wa.
Cowell, Henry. 'Current Chronicle: New York', *MQ*. Vol. XL, no. 1, Jan. 1954 (61).
'Godfrey Ridout', *CanCo*. No. 45, Dec. 1969 (28–9).
'Godfrey Ridout – a portrait', *Mu*. No. 12, June-July 1968 (8–9).
Kidd, George. 'Godfrey Ridout: Distinguished Composer and Teacher', *CanCo*. No. 6, Feb. 1966 (4–5, 40–1).

LITERARY WORKS

ARTICLES

'Aspects of Arnold Walter', *CanCo*. No. 38, Mar. 1969 (14–15).
'Canadian Composing', *Here and Now*. Vol. I, Dec. 1947 (78–80).
'Elgar, the Angular Saxon', *CMJ*. Vol. I, no. 4, 1956–7 (33).
'Sir Ernest MacMillan: An Appraisal', *Canadian Music Educator*. Vol. VI, 1964–5 (39–48). Reprinted from *MAC*. Vol. I, no. 6, July-Aug. 1963 (30–4).
'Healey Willan', *CMJ*. Vol. III, no. 3, 1958–9 (4).
'Orpheus in Ecclesia, or The River Lute', *Canadian Journal of Theology*. Vol. XV, no. 3–4, 1969 (165–76).
'Two West Coast Composers', *Canadian Review of Music and Art*. Vol. III, no. 11–12, Dec.-Jan. 1945 (39–40).

ROBBINS, DAVID (b. Greensburg, Ind., 14 Aug. 1923). He studied theory, conducting, and brass instruments at the Cincinnati Conservatory of Music (summer sessions, 1939–41). He received a Bachelor of Science degree and a Secondary-Schools Teacher's Certificate (1943) from the Sam

Houston State Teachers' College, Texas, majoring in Music Education, and his Master of Science degree from the University of Southern California (1951).

He taught in Centerville, Texas, and directed the band and orchestra as well as the chorus and Boys Glee Club (1941–3). Serving in the U.S. Marine Corps from 1943 to 1946, he was leader of the Dance Orchestra and arranger for the U.S. Marine Band 'Halls of Montezuma' Radio Orchestra (San Diego, Calif.). Coming to Canada, he became a part-time secondary school teacher in Vancouver (1951), and later taught at the Vancouver City College and was lecturer-instructor in trombone at the University of British Columbia (1959–66). He was manager of the Instrumental Department of the Western Music Company (1954–6) and was founder and leader of the CBC (Vancouver) Jazz Workshop Orchestra (1956–66). He became a Canadian citizen in 1965. From 1962 to 1966 he played numerous public school concerts in and around Vancouver and on Vancouver Island and until 1969 was an instructor of theory at the Faculty of Education, University of British Columbia.

As composer and arranger he has been much involved in many CBC program series, including 'CBC Jazz Workshop', 'Parade', 'Sound of the Sixties', 'Music-Canada', and 'Variety Showcase'; as composer-conductor of the films 'Home Sweet Cedar' (1968) and 'Fisherman's Fall' (NFB, 1969); and as composer-conductor for the CBC 'Heritage' series. As performer he was with the Harry James orchestra as trombonist (1948–54) and toured with the orchestra through Great Britain and Europe (1971–2, 1972–3). He was a member of the Hollywood Bowl Symphony Orchestra (1946–8), principal trombonist for fourteen years with the Vancouver Symphony Orchestra, and performed with the CBC Chamber Orchestra for ten years. He is affiliated with BMI Canada.

BIBLIOGRAPHY

'Dave Robbins' Jazz', *CBC Times*. Mar. 10–16, 1962 (4).

ROGERS, WILLIAM KEITH (b. Charlottetown, P.E.I., 16 Mar. 1921). He studied with Arthur Newstead (piano) and Vittorio Giannini (composition) at the Juilliard School of Music in New York. In 1945 he received a fellowship in composition from the Juilliard Graduate School, where he studied with Frederick Jacobi, obtaining his Master of Music degree in 1948. From 1948 to 1950 he taught at the Hamilton Conservatory of Music and in 1950 was appointed musical director of radio station CFCY in Charlottetown. He continued to study composition with Nadia Boulanger in Paris (1954–5) and at the Berkshire Music Center with Ernst Toch (1954). In 1960 he moved to Montreal. Rogers' works are characterized by lyrical melodic writing in a conservative contrapuntal texture. His *String Quartet* (1947–8) is similar in style to the early tonal quartets of Arnold Schoenberg. His *Six Short Preludes on a Tone Row* (1963), although dissonant, are still lyrical. Rogers' relatively small output is diversified, with works for orchestra (for example, *A Coronation Tribute*, 1953); for choir (*Choral Episode from Antigone*, 1948, and *Three Songs from Emily Dickinson*, 1948); for solo voice (*At the Aquarium*, 1938, and *Clouds in Summer*, 1938); for chamber ensembles (*Narration*, 1947, for violin and piano, *Sonatina*, 1952, for viola and piano, and *Sonata*, 1942, for violin and piano); and for piano solo (*Ballade*, 1937, *Suite for Piano*, 1941, and *Sonatina*, 1946). He is affiliated with BMI Canada.

BIBLIOGRAPHY

See B-B; K; Mm; Wa.

S

SAINT-MARCOUX, MICHELINE COULOMBE (b. Notre Dame-de-la-Doré, Que., 9 Aug. 1938). She began her musical studies in composition with François BRASSARD in Jonquière, Que., and then in Montreal studied composition with Claude CHAMPAGNE at the Ecole Vincent-d'Indy and with Gilles TREMBLAY and Clermont PÉPIN at the Conservatoire, completing her baccalauréat at the Ecole Vincent-d'Indy in 1962. In 1967 she received first prize in composition from the Conservatoire and for *Modulaire* the Prix d'Europe in composition. In the summer of 1965 she studied composition with Tony Aubin in Nice and in 1969, on a bursary from the Canada Council, she was able to begin in Paris the study of electronic music with the Groupe de Recherches Musicales de l'O.R.T.F. (Pierre Schaeffer, François Bayle, Bernard Parmegiani), while continuing composition studies with Gilbert Amy and Jean-Pierre Guézec.

Her *Quatuor à cordes* (1966) is atonal and dissonant, although the development of small pitch and rhythm cells is generally traditional. This is also true of her orchestral piece *Modulaire*, where her attention has been drawn to exploitation of instrumental colour by combining different instruments – for example the bassoon with a bass clarinet an octave lower on the opening motif – and with the use of the ondes Martenot with the double-reed instruments. *Hétéromorphie* (1970), a commission from the Montreal Symphony Orchestra, may be a departure from her earlier works, following a style similar to Ligeti and Xenakis with the use of clusters, glissandi, random rhythms, and free semi-improvisational sections. In *Arksalalartôq* (1971), an electronic work, she uses vocal and instrumental as well as electronic source material, generating a sense of urgency by the use of violent scraping and explosive sounds.

She is a founding member of the Groupe International de Musique Electroacoustique de Paris (1969), a group of six young composers from different countries who performed several electronic music concerts. She has received commissions from the Groupe de Recherches Musicales (*Arksalalartôq*, 1971) and the Groupe de Musique Experimentale de Bourges (*Moustières*, 1971). She teaches at the Conservatoire in Montreal and is a member of CAPAC.

MUSICAL WORKS

ORCHESTRA

Modulaire (1967); *Hétéromorphie* (1970).

VOICE

Chanson d'Automne. 1963 (rev 1966). vc, pno. ms. Text: Paul Verlaine.

INSTRUMENTAL ENSEMBLE

Sonate pour flûte et piano (1964); *Quatuor à cordes* (1965–6); *Equation I* (1967), 2 guit; *Séquences* (1968), 2 ondes Martenot, perc; *Trakadie* (1970), tape, perc; *Makazoti* (1971), 8vcs, instr. Text: Noël Audet, Giles Marsolais; *Episodie II* (1972), 3 perc plyrs and audio mixer. ms.

PIANO

Kaléidoscope (left hand) (1964); *Assemblages* (1969); *Doréanes* (1969; GVT, 1969). Dom s-69002 ('Brouillard épais').

ELECTRONIC TAPE

Bernavir. 1970. Text inspiration: Noël Audet.
Arksalalartôq. 1971.
Contrastances. 1971.
Moustières. 1971.
Zones. 1972.

BIBLIOGRAPHY

'Coulombe Saint-Marcoux ... a young composer of great talent ...', *CanCo*. No. 51, June 1970 (30–3).
'News from Paris', *CanCo*. No. 49, Apr. 1970 (29).

LITERARY WORKS

ARTICLES

'Réflections d'une jeune compositeur', *Vie Musicale*. No. 8, 1968 (13–16). Reprinted in English in *CanCo*. No. 33, Oct. 1968 (30–3).

SCHAFER, R. MURRAY (b. Sarnia, Ont., 18 July 1933). Schafer may be considered one of Canada's most successful composers, one of a few with an international reputation. He also enjoys fame as an educator who has effectively sought to introduce ideas and means that would turn music learning into a living contemporary experience. But first and foremost he is a concerned citizen – a world citizen at that – who uses his considerable talents, insights, and expertise for socially significant and ecologically purposeful ends. It just may be that, no matter how significant his achievements as a composer and educator, Schafer's most important contribution to the culture of his time will be his visionary and sensitive research to evaluate the goods and ills of the world sound-environment. He has done a considerable amount of writing and speaking on the subject of the production, reduction, preservation, and elimination of sounds of diverse nature and origins. His most extensive essay on this topic, *The Music of the Environment*, was prepared for *The UNESCO Journal of World History*, and serves as a blueprint for Schafer's inventory of World Soundscapes, a large-scale undertaking for which he was awarded in 1972 a $39,000 Donner Foundation grant. Potentially of far-reaching consequences, this project aims for nothing less than bringing man into a totally revaluated relationship with his sonic environment.

Schafer studied at the Royal Conservatory in Toronto with Alberto Guerrero (piano) and John WEINZWEIG (composition). From 1956 to 1961 he lived in England and Europe working as a free-lance journalist and BBC interviewer. Among his activities there was the editing of Ezra Pound's opera 'Le Testament' for a BBC performance. On his return to Canada in 1961 he founded and became the first president of Ten Centuries Concerts, a Toronto musicians' collaborative organization promoting new and rarely heard older music. From 1963 to 1965 he was artist-in-residence at Memorial University in Newfoundland, and in 1965 he was appointed to the faculty of the newly founded Simon Fraser University in British Columbia. Schafer is the author of many essays in various professional journals, a series of educational booklets, and *British Composers in Interview* (1963, Faber and Faber).

Traditional methodology cannot be applied to the analysis of Schafer's creative work. A chronological study of his music would provide very little consequential insight into his work since the early 1960s: all his later work has a specific homogeneity about it so that its chronology becomes insignificant. Similarly an attempt to survey his works by genre would lead to quick confusion since, with a few exceptions, the borderlines between the categories are quite blurred. A comparative study of the musical style of Schafer and his contemporaries would also lead nowhere: although his idiom is unmistakably of the third quarter of the twentieth century, Schafer is too much his own man to borrow from any of the 'main streams'. His early roots may lie in serialism, but he never really adopted twelve-tone writing for his own purpose. His style is dissonant, but free from any strait jackets of systems and speculative abstractions. He also draws upon other mid-twentieth century concepts such as indeterminacy, stereophony, media mixing, etc., but here too it is his intuition and sensitivity rather than existing theories and practices that guide his decisions in the use of these devices.

Schafer's music is best approached, therefore, by looking at its totality and by understanding the relationships of individual works and their details in that light. It becomes immediately evident that much of his source material is of extramusical origin. European and non-European philosophy and literature of many ages, as well as modern psychology and communication theories, appear in many forms as foundations of his works. Mythology, symbolism and mysticism play a considerable part in almost all of his scores, and frequently his works contain elements of program music.

Does this establish Schafer as a confirmed custodian of the heritage of the romantic past? Perhaps, but there is a radical difference between Schafer and the many composers who never really left the nineteenth century. Unlike them, Schafer discovered the Romantic era as a completely new experience from the vantage point of the fifties and sixties, with the eyes, ears, and mind of a man who had been, or was soon to be, witness to the technological revolution and the moon probes.

When Schafer chooses texts in Sanskrit, Tibetan, Egyptian, Persian, and Greek for his solos, ensembles, and choruses, he does so with a twentieth-century man's understanding of and sensitivity to the many qualities and quantities of language. It is not only for the semantic and poetic contents that Schafer has chosen texts in languages generally unknown to Europeans and North Americans, but also for their musical characteristics. Since the western listener is unable to relate to the immediate meaning of the words, the sounds of the syllables and the inflection of the language assume the role of musical configurations, purely acoustical sensations. But Schafer's aim is not just the shifting of the focus from the content of the words to their physical properties. By setting up unusual communication situations, he attempts to dramatize such issues as man's relationship to man, his feelings of love and passion on one hand and loneliness and alienation on the other.

Schafer's original approach to language music and psychological drama is manifested on a grand scale in two substantial works for the stage, *Loving (Toi)* (1965) and *Patria* (work in progress with Parts I and II completed in 1972). *Loving*, which received its television première on CBC-TV Montreal in 1966, is about love between the sexes. The opera is plotless, the participating personae standing for what the composer-librettist calls 'attitudes' rather than characters. Three female voices represent Vanity, Ishtar, and Modesty, while a fourth in her concluding aria 'The Geography of Eros' fuses the separate 'attitudes' into one. The single male in the cast, too, has an alter ego in the form of an off-stage pre-recorded voice representing the Poet. In the TV version the man spoke French whereas the women's language was English. It is the composer's wish that in any subsequent performances the women's parts be sung always in English, whereas the male part ought to be presented in whatever language is mainly spoken where the work is being performed. It is through such devices as juxtaposing language as sense with language as sound, modulating straight speech into melismatic or electronically manipulated song, and contrasting fully intelligible words with unidentifiable fragments that Schafer dramatizes the various states of mind from the conscious to the unconscious and the diverse forms of love from the spiritual to the physical.

Patria is a trilogy, intended for performance on three consecutive nights. The common theme of the first two completed parts is loneliness – alienation of people who find themselves in hostile environments as either political exiles or mental patients. As in *Loving*, there is no linear plot in *Patria*. In Part I, 'The Characteristics Man', an immigrant finds himself in a country where everyone around him speaks foreign languages, all incomprehensible to him. Again as in *Loving*, the principal character performs in the common language of the audience, who thus can sympathize with him and share his frustrations. As many as forty different languages are used to set the scene for the drama about inability to establish lines of communications.

In Part II, *Requiems for the Party-Girl*, first performed in its fullest form in 1972 at the Stratford Festival (an earlier and shorter version dates from 1966), the central figure is a schizophrenic girl in a mental hospital where the doctors and nurses communicate in languages incomprehensible to the patients. Only the latter use the 'mother tongue', but remain often incoherent themselves owing to the unsettled state of their minds. Ariadne, the main character, is not any *one* girl but a composite of many. Sometimes she is a young girl, sometimes a dead soul looking at her body from another world, sometimes a child. Around her is a world of darkness, peopled with men and women who would like to help her but whom she cannot understand. It is here that Schafer makes the most of the possibilities of his brand of language music. Live and on tape, spoken and sung, singly and chorally, straight and modified, the timbres, pitches, and rhythms of ancient and modern languages of many cultures are woven into sequences and constellations of sounds that most effectively dramatize the conflicts of the hallucinating schizophrenic's mind.

While these two dramatic works hold centre stage among Schafer's oeuvre (several extensive excerpts, arias, and choruses from the two operas have had, sometimes under separate titles, independent careers on the concert stage), there are a number of other compositions where his personal approach towards musical and extramusical ideas and processes is manifested with interesting results.

For his Montreal Symphony Orchestra commission *Son of Heldenleben* (1968), Schafer invented a program that is half satire and half tribute, and introduced a new member to the family of Richard Strauss's hero. Direct and indirect quotations from the Strauss tone-poem make up the musical materials of Schafer's work, including two basic tone-rows derived from the opening theme of the 'father'-score.

Schafer's more formalistic interests are in evidence in his 1962 score for soprano and four flutes, *Five Studies on texts by Prudentius.* In this work Schafer not only explores the various possibilities of canonic writing but also delves into the issue of stereophony with a good understanding of movement in space. The four flutes are situated in the four corners of the performance area, while the singer is placed centre stage. The spatial movements of the flute canons form clearly defined patterns in each song, with certain symbolic relationships between the centrifugal, diagonal, and circular movements of the sounds and of the religious texts they accompany.

In *Threnody* for five young narrators, youth chorus, youth orchestra, and magnetic tapes (1966), Schafer evokes memories of the bombing of Nagasaki as recorded in the words of surviving Japanese children. Typically Schafer here relies again on the power of words, this time on their descriptive realism. Spoken by the age-mates of the eyewitnesses of the holocaust, the statements are of shattering directness that is enhanced by a most discreet but poignant use of the orchestral and choral forces.

Threnody is one of many works Schafer has composed specifically for use by young musicians, works that stand out from the general bulk of educational music in that they are unconcerned with any dogmas, theories, or skills but rather concentrate on the creative, sensory, and emotional aspects of music. Schafer's prime concern as music educator is with sounds – all sounds: sounds in and out of concert halls, sounds past and present, sounds of nature and sounds of urban civilization. In his four booklets – *The Composer in the Classroom, Ear Cleaning, The New Soundscape,* and *When Words Sing* – he does not provide methods and classroom routines, but rather information, inspiration, provocation, and guidance for concentrated sound studies and the expansion of one's sensory and mental awareness. It was this intense preoccupation with sounds as physical phenomena and their effects on men's ears and minds that led Schafer to explore the total sound environment in which twentieth-century man finds himself.

In addition to the Donner Foundation grant mentioned above, Schafer has received numerous other commissions and awards, among them two grants from the Canada Council (1961 and 1963), a Fromm Foundation Award (1968), and the annual medal of the Canadian Music Council (1972).

Schafer is a member of the Canadian League of Composers and is affiliated with BMI Canada. UDO KASEMETS

MUSICAL WORKS

STAGE

Loving (Toi) (opera for TV or stage). 1965. 70'. sop, 3 mezz, 2 or 3 spkrs, dancers, chamb orch, elec tape. CMC. Libretto: R Murray Schafer. Fr trans: Gabriel Charpentier. Feb 3, 1966, Mtl, CBC-TV, Serge Garant(cond), Pierre Mercure(prod).

Patria II. 1972. 80'. mezz, actors, chamb orch, elec tape. ms. Libretto: R Murray Schafer. Aug 23, 1972, Stratford, Ont, Third Stage.

ORCHESTRA

Canzoni for Prisoners. 1962. 19'. full orch. CMC. 1963, Mtl, MSO, Victor Feldbrill.

Statement in Blue. 1964. 4'15". youth orch. Ber, 1966; UE 1971. Melb SM LP-4017. 1965, Tor, Dufferin Heights Junior High Schl, Carol Burgar.

Son of Heldenleben. 1968. 10'35". full orch, elec tape. UE. Nov 13, 1968, Mtl, MSO, Franz-Paul Decker.

No Longer than Ten Minutes. 1970 (rev 1972). 10'. full orch. CMC. Feb 16, 1971, Tor, TS, Victor Feldbrill.

SMALL ORCHESTRA

Untitled Composition for Orchestra. 1963.

4′. CMC. Nov 3, 1966, Tor, CBC, TS, Jean-Marie Beaudet.
East. 1972. 8′15″. CMC. Text: from 'Isha-Upanishad'. May 1973, Bath, Eng, NACO, Mario Bernardi.

STRING ORCHESTRA
In Memoriam: Alberto Guerrero. 1959. 5′. CMC. 1962, Vanc, Vanc CBC Ch O, John Avison.

SOLOIST WITH ORCHESTRA
Concerto for Harpsichord and Eight Wind Instruments. 1954. 25′50″. CMC. RCI-193. Feb 1959, Mtl, CBC wind gp, Kelsey Jones (hpschd).
Protest and Incarceration. 1960. 12′30″. mezz, orch. ms.
Brébeuf (cantata). 1961. 26′. bar, orch. CMC. Nov 17, 1966, CBC TS, Ettore Mazzoleni(cond), Cornelis Opthof(bar).
Divan i Shams i Tabriz. 1969 (rev 1970). 23′. 7sgrs, full orch, elec tape. CMC. Text: Jalal al-Din Rumi. 1972, Tor, U of T Symph O, Victor Feldbrill.

SOLOIST(S) WITH ORCHESTRA
Arcana. 1972. 16′. vc, med orch. CMC. Text: R M Schafer; trans into Middle Egyptian hieroglyphs by D B Redford. 1973, Mtl, Concours Int de Montréal.

CHOIR WITH ORCHESTRA
Threnody. 1966 (rev 1967). 17′. 5 spkrs, youth choir, youth orch, elec tape. Ber, 1970. Melb SMLP-4017. June 11, 1967, Vanc, Vanc Y O, West Vanc Secondary Schl Choir, Simon Streatfeild.

CHOIR
Four Songs. 1962. 10′55″. sop, mezz, alto, SA. CMC. Text: Tagore.
Gita. 1967. 13′. SATB, brass, elec tape. UE. Text: Bhagavad Gita. Aug 1967, Tanglewood, Mass, Fest, The Tanglewood Choir, Brass Ens, Iva Dee Hiatt.
Epitaph for Moonlight. 1968. 4′10″. SATB, bells (opt). Ber, 1969; UE, 1971. Melb SMLP-4017.
From the Tibetan Book of the Dead. 1968. 8′. solo sop, SATB, alto fl (picc), cl, elec tape. UE. Text: from the Bardo Thödol. 1968, Vanc, CBC, U of BC Chamb Sgrs, Cortland Hultberg(dir), Phyllis Mailing(sop).
Yeow and Pax. 1969. 6′30″. SATB, org, elec tape. CMC. Text: Isaiah 13: 6–13, 60: 18–20.
In Search of Zoroaster. 1971. solo male vc, SATB, perc, org. CMC. Texts: from The Sacred Books of the East. May 1973, Dartmouth, NH, Dartmouth College Glee Club, Mario di Bonaventura(cond).
Miniwanka or The Moments of Water. 1971. 3′30″. SA or SATB. UE.
Tehillah. 1972. 9′. SATB, perc. CMC. Text: Psalm 148.

VOICE
Three Contemporaries. 1954–6. mezz, pno. ms.
Kinderlieder. 1958. 10′. mezz, pno. ms. Text: Bertolt Brecht. Jan 1959, CBC, Phyllis Mailing.
Dream Passage. 1969 (preliminary study for *Patria II*). mezz, elec music. ms. May 27, 1969, Vanc, CBC, Vanc Symph Chamb Plyrs, Norman Nelson(cond), U of BC Sgrs, Cortland Hultberg(dir), Phyllis Mailing(mezz).
Music for the Morning of the World. 1970. 34′. vc, 4-track prepared tape. UE. Text: Discourses; Divan i Shams i Tabriz; Masnavi; by Rûmi.

VOICE(S) WITH INSTRUMENTAL ENSEMBLE
Minnelieder. 1956. 28′30″. mezz, ww qnt. Ber, 1970. RCA CC/CCS-1012. Feb 1960, London, Eng, London Wind Mus Soc, Brian Fairfax(cond), Dorothy Dorrow(mezz).
Five Studies on texts by Prudentius. 1962. 9′. sop, 4fl. Ber, 1965. 1963, Tor, Faculty of Mus, U of T, Mary Morrison(sop), Robert Aitken(fl).
Modesty (aria from '*Loving*'). 1965. 6′30″. mezz, 15 instr. CMC. 1966, Mtl, CBC-TV, Instrumental gp under Serge Garant, Evelyn Maxwell(mezz).
The Geography of Eros (aria from '*Loving*'). 1963. 9′30″. sop, pno, hp, 6perc, recorded vcs. CMC. 1964, Tor, TCC, perc ens under Howard Cable, Mary Morrison(sop).
Air Ishtar (aria from '*Loving*'). 1965. 8′30″. sop, pno, cel, cb, 6perc, recorded vcs. CMC. 1966, Mtl, CBC-TV, Instrumental gp under Serge Garant, Margo MacKinnon(sop).
Vanity (aria from '*Loving*'). 1965. 11′. mezz, hp, hpschd, mand, vln, vlc, perc, guit (elec guit, banjo). CMC. 1966, Mtl, CBC-TV, Instrumental gp under Serge Garant, Huguette Tourangeau(mezz).
Requiems for the Party-Girl. 1966. 15′. mezz, fl, picc, cl, b cl, hn, pno, hp, vln, vla, vlc, perc. Ber, 1967. CRI SD-245. Nov 21, 1967, CBC Vanc, Vanc Symph Chamb Plyrs,

Phyllis Mailing(mezz).
Minimusic. 1969. any combination of instr or vcs. UE, 1971.
Sappho. 1970. mezz, hp, pno, guit, perc. ms. Oct 31, 1970, Washington, DC, Elizabeth Sprague Coolidge Foundation Fourteenth Fest of Chamb Mus.
Enchantress. 1971 (rev 1972). 12′25″. sop, fl, 8vlc. CMC. Text: from poems by Sappho.
Arcana. 1972. 16′. vc, fl (picc), cl (alto sax), tpt, trb, vln, vlc, cb, hp, pno (elec org), perc. CMC. Text: R M Schafer; trans into Middle Egyptian hieroglyphs by D B Redford.

INSTRUMENTAL ENSEMBLE

Sonatina for Flute and Harpsichord (or Piano). 1958. CMC.
String Quartet. 1970. 16′. UE. July 16, 1970, Vanc Art Gallery, Purcell Str Qt.

ELECTRONIC

Kaleidoscope. 1967. 12′. multi-track elec tape. Expo 67, Mtl, Pavilion of the Chemical Industries, 'Kadeidoscope'.
Okeanos. 1971. 80′. elec tape incl sounds of the sea & readings. Text: from Hesiod, Homer, Melville, Pound. Mar 14, 1972, Burnaby, BC, SFU Open House.

BIBLIOGRAPHY

B65,71; Bec70; CrC(II); Esc; Wa.
Ball, Suzanne. 'Murray Schafer: Composer, Teacher and Author', *MuSc.* May-June 1970 (7–8).
Bissell, Keith. 'R. M. Schafer's Books', *CMB.* Vol. II, Spring-Summer 1971 (192–4).
'Festival: "Loving" ', *CBC Times.* May 21–7, 1966 (4–5).
Kasemets, Udo. 'Threnody', *CMB.* Vol. V, Autumn-Winter 1972 (205–8).
Mather, Bruce. 'Notes sur "Requiems for the Party-Girl" ', *CMB.* Vol. I, Spring-Summer 1970 (91–7).
'Murray Schafer – a portrait', *Mu.* No. 23, Oct. 1969 (8–9).
'Music Personified', *Atlantic Advocate.* Vol. LV, Mar. 1965 (67–8).
'Provocateur in Sound', *Time.* Sept. 4, 1972 (11).
'R. Murray Schafer', pamphlet, BMI Canada Ltd, 1970.
Siskind, Jacob. 'R. M. Schafer: Youth Music', *CMB.* Vol. II, Spring-Summer 1971 (199–200).
Such, Peter. *Soundprints.* Toronto: Clarke, Irwin Ltd, 1971 (126–62).
The Times Educational Supplement (interview with Dulan Barber). June 18, 1971 (19–20).
Tremblay, Gilles. ' "The Book of Noise" ', *CMB.* Vol. II, Spring-Summer 1971 (187–8).

LITERARY WORKS

BOOKS AND BOOKLETS

The Book of Noise. Vancouver (privately published), 1970.
British Composers in Interview. London: Faber and Faber, 1963.
The Composer in the Classroom. Toronto: Ber, 1965; U.S. edition – New York: AMP, 1971; British edition – London: UE, 1972.
Ear Cleaning. Toronto: Ber, 1967; U.S. edition – New York: AMP, 1971; British edition – London: UE, 1972.
The New Soundscape. Toronto: Ber, 1969; U.S. edition – New York: AMP, 1971; British edition – London: UE, 1972.
L'oreille pense (French translation of *Ear Cleaning*). Ber, 1972.
The Public of the Music Theatre: Louis Riel – a Case Study. UE, 1972.
Die Schallwelt in der wir leben (German translation of *The New Soundscape*). UE, 1971.
Schoepferisches Musizieren (German translation of *The Composer in the Classroom*). UE, 1971.
Schule des Hoerens (German translation of *Ear Cleaning*). UE, 1972.
Wenn Worte Klingen (German translation of *When Words Sing*). UE, 1972.
When Words Sing. Ber, 1970; U.S. edition – New York: AMP, 1971; British edition – London: UE, 1972.

ARTICLES

'A Basic Course', *Source – Music of the Avant Garde.* No. 5, 1969 (44–7).
'Le Bruit: le pollution du monde moderne' (review article) *CMB.* Vol. II, Spring-Summer 1971 (181–6).
'The Canadian String Quartet', *CMJ.* Vol. VI, no. 3, 1961–2 (29).
'Cleaning the Lenses of Perception', *Arts Canada.* Vol. XXV, Oct.-Nov. 1968 (10–12).
'Discovering the World's Soul', *Music Educators Journal.* Vol. LVII, no. 1, 1970 (31–2).
'Ezra Pound and Music', *CMJ.* Vol. IV, no. 4, Summer 1961 (15). Anthologized in

Ezra Pound: Critical Essays (Murray Schafer, ed.). Englewood Cliffs, N.J.: Prentice-Hall, Inc., 1963; French edition – *Ezra Pound et la musique*. Paris: Editions L'Herne, 1966; German edition – *22 Versuche über einen Dichter*. Frankfurt-am-Main: Athenaum Verlag, 1967.
'The Future for Music in Canada', *Mu*. No. 7, July 1967 (10–13); reprinted in *Proceedings and Transactions of the Royal Society of Canada*. Vol. v, series 4, 1967 (37–43).
'Lärmflut – eine Montage', *Musik und Bildung*. July-Aug. 1971.
'The Limits of Nationalism in Canadian Music', *Tamarack Review*. Vol. XVIII, Winter 1961 (71–8).
'A Middle-East Sound Diary', *Focus on Musicecology*. No. 1, 1969 (20–5).
'Money and Music', *Canadian Forum*. Vol. XLIV, Dec. 1964.
'Music ... 1961/62 in Toronto', *Canadian Art*. Vol. XIX, July-Aug. 1962 (307).
'Music and Education', *MuSc*. Jan.-Feb., Mar.-Apr. 1968.
'Music and the Iron Curtain', *Queen's Quarterly*. Vol. LXVII, Autumn 1960 (407–14).
'The Philosophy of Stereophony', *West Coast Review*. Winter 1967.
'Thoughts on Music Education', *CMB*. Vol. II, Autumn-Winter 1971 (115–22); reprinted in *Australian Music Educators Journal*. Spring 1972.
'Threnody: A Religious Piece for our Time', *Music: AGO–RCCO Magazine*. Vol. IV, no. 5, May 1970 (33–5).
'Two Musicians in Fiction', *CMJ*. Vol. IV, no. 3, Spring 1960 (23).
'What is this Article About?', *Canadian Forum*. Vol. XLIV, Dec. 1964 (201–2.)

SCHUDEL, THOMAS (b. Defiance, Ohio, 8 Sept. 1937). He studied at Ohio State University (1955–9) with Dr George Wilson (bassoon) and Marshall Barnes (composition), receiving his Bachelor of Science degree in music education (1959). From 1959 to 1960 he studied bassoon with Bernard Garfield in Philadelphia and taught music at Morristown High School in New Jersey. He continued to study with Marshall Barnes, receiving his Master of Arts degree in music theory and composition from Ohio State University (1961). He served in the U.S. army (1961–3) before studying at the University of Michigan (1961–4; 1967–8) with Lewis Cooper (bassoon), Leslie Bassett and Ross Lee Finney (composition), and George B. Wilson (electronic music, 1967–8).

Schudel's music is generally atonal, with some emphasis on the exploitation of instrumental colour. His structures are derived from the organic development of small motifs or cells. His compositions are mainly for chamber ensembles, including *Divertimento No. 1* for flute, oboe, violin, cello, and percussion, *Set No. 2* for woodwind quintet and brass quintet, *Sonata* for violin and piano, and *String Quartet 1967*. In 1968 he received a commission from the First Baptist Church in Ann Arbor, Mich. (*Psalm 23*). He was principal bassoonist with the Regina Symphony Orchestra (1964–7; 1968–70), and assistant professor (1964–7) at the University of Saskatchewan, Regina Campus (now the University of Regina), where he has been associate professor since 1972. Receiving his Doctor of Musical Arts degree from the University of Michigan in 1971, he won first prize in the International Competition for a Symphonic Composition at Trieste, Italy, in 1972 (*Symphony No. 1*). He is affiliated with BMI Canada.

SMITH, JOSEPH LEOPOLD (b. Birmingham, England, 26 Nov. 1881; d. Toronto, Ont., 18 Apr. 1952). Leo Smith studied with Carl Fuchs (cello) and Henry Hiles (theory) at the Royal Manchester College of Music and Manchester University, from which he received a Bachelor of Music degree. He was cellist with the Hallé Orchestra and at the Royal Opera House, Covent Garden, before coming to Canada in 1910. In the fall of 1910 he joined the Toronto Symphony Orchestra as cellist under Welsman and was principal cellist in 1917–18 when that orchestra disbanded, continuing as principal cellist (1923–50) with the New Symphony Orchestra, which became the Toronto Symphony Orchestra in 1927. Smith's compositions – including *Tambourin* (pub. 1930) and *Three Pieces:* 'The Song Sparrow', 'From an Old Note Book' and 'Schumanesque' for piano (pub. 1937) – are tonal and light in character. His orchestral work, *A Summer Idyll*, recalls Delius.

Smith was a lecturer at the Conservatory in Toronto (1911–52), a professor at the Faculty of Music, University of Toronto (1927–50), and the author of several texts on musical history and theory. He was a member of the Toronto Conservatory Quartet, contributing editor of the *Toronto Conservatory Quarterly Review*, and music critic for the *Globe and Mail* (1950–2). He also served on the board of the Toronto Musicians' Association for many years. He was made a fellow of the Royal Manchester College of Music in 1925 and was a member of CAPAC.

MUSICAL WORKS

INSTRUMENTAL

Summer Idyll. full orch. also arr. small orch (cl, str).

3 works for orch: *Divertissements in Waltz Time* (also arr for pno); *Elegy for Small Orchestra*; *Little Pretty Nightingale.*

Occasion for Strings. str orch.

6 works for vlc and pno: *Father O'Flynn*; *Four Pieces in an Old English Style* (Schmidt, 1946); *Indian Romance* (1935); *Intermezzo*; *Jig*; *Sonata in E Minor* (1943).

2 works for vln, vlc, pno: *Celtic Trio* (last movement extant); *Three Ravens.*

2 works for vln, vlc, hp: *Border Ballad* (lost); *A Horse Race Ballad.*

3 works for str qt: *Men of Harlech*; *O Mistress Mine*; *Quartet in D* (1932).

Trio (Pavane). treb viol, gamb, hpschd.

Many arrangements, including: *Au clair de la lune* (arr of melody attr to Lully) vlc, pno (FH, 1935); *Elizabethan Songs* (1951?) vlc, pno; *Four Pieces from 'The Book of Irish Country Songs'* vlc, pno, priv publ, ed Herbert Hughes; *Shakespearean Music* 2treb viols, gamba (gamb, hpschd; or viol, gamb, hpschd); *Tambourin* (French-Canadian fiddle tune) vln, pno (FH, 1930); *Three Sketches for String Quartet* (on British folk melodies) (GVT, 1942); *Trochaios* (French-Canadian fiddle tune) vln, pno (FH, 1930); *Two Sketches for String Quartet* (on French-Canadian folk songs).

2 works for piano: *Suite for Piano*; *Three Pieces for Piano* (FH, 1937).

Several arrangements for piano, including: *Four Poems*; *Minuet and Trio* (from Haydn's 'Quartet in D Minor', Op 76, No 2); *Transcriptions, Arrangements and Pieces for Piano* (GVT, 1942).

CHORAL

3 works for men's vcs: *Beloved and Blest* (G Schirm, 1914) Text: Swinburne; *Night* (G Schirm, 1914) Text: Swinburne; *On Dante's Track* (G Schirm, 1914) Text: Swinburne.

6 works for women's vcs: *Fresh from the Dewy Hill* (Alexander & Cable, 1929) Text: William Blake; *Night Piece to Julia* Text: Robert Herrick; *A Roundel Is Wrought* Text: Swinburne; *Time Lost Past* Text: Shelley; *To Music* Text: Robert Herrick; *We Are the Music Makers* (Alexander & Cable, 1930) Text: O'Shaughnessy.

2 part songs: *Christmas Bells* (G Schirm, 1916) Text: Longfellow; *A Dream* Text: O'Shaughnessy.

Dedication of the Fireplace. c1912. SATB Text: unknown.

Arrangements, including: *Quam Pulchram Es ...* (Dunstable) solo vc, vcs, treb viol, alto viol; *Shakespeare Songs* chorus, soloists, instr.

VOCAL

28 works for vc, pno, including: *As I Walk Forth* (1946) Text: unknown; *Ballad of Dreamland* Text: Swinburne; *The Donkey* Text: G K Chesterton; *The Dressmaker* Text: Millicent Payne; *Echo* (seven songs in low or medium voice) Text: Duncan Campbell Scott; *Five Songs* (c1912) Text: Blake, Browning, Swinburne; *Four Songs* (G Schirm, 1914) Text: Leigh Hunt, Poe, Swinburne; *Fresh from the Dewy Hill (Songs of Innocence)* Text: William Blake; *The Heavenly Bay* Text: Swinburne; *The Lake* Text: Edgar Allan Poe; *Mad Song* (seven songs for low or medium voice) Text: William Blake; *Nine Songs* (FH, 1938) Text: unknown; *Song of the Past* (pre-1910) Text: Shelley; *Songs of Experience* (1941?) Text: William Blake; *Spring Night* Text: Duncan Campbell Scott; *Three Shadows* (pre-1910) Text: Christina Rossetti; *Three Songs* (FH, 1930) Text: Duncan Campbell Scott; *To One in Paradise* (c1924) Text: Edgar Allan Poe.

3 works for vc and instr: *Echo Song* sop, alto, bs, 3str Text: anon; *Four Trios* vc, vln, pno Text: unknown; *Old London Street Cries* 2vc, vlc, pno.

Many arrangements, including: *Arrangements of 13th Century Responsories* vcs, vla; *20 Arrangements of 16th and 17th Century Songs* vc, instr; 5 arr of French-Canadian folk songs; 6 arr of Elizabethan songs and ballads; several arr of Old English songs using Elizabethan instr.

BIBLIOGRAPHY

See B-B; Bec70; K; Wa.
McCarthy, Pearl. *Leo Smith: A Biographical Sketch.* Toronto: University of Toronto Press, 1956.

LITERARY WORKS

BOOKS

Elementary Part-Writing. FH, 1939.
Music of the Seventeenth and Eighteenth Centuries. London: J.M. Dent & Sons Ltd, 1931.
Musical Rudiments. Boston: Boston Music Co., 1920.

ARTICLES (selected)

'Competition Reveals Outstanding Talent', *Canadian Review of Music and Art.* Vol. II, no. 9–10, Oct.-Nov. 1943 (21).
'Competition Reveals Outstanding Talent', *Canadian Review of Music and Art.* Vol. II, no. 11–12, Dec.-Jan. 1944 (22).
'Competition Reveals Outstanding Talent', *Canadian Review of Music and Art.* Vol. III, no. 1–2, Feb.-Mar. 1944 (14–15).
'Competition Reveals Outstanding Talent', *Canadian Review of Music and Art.* Vol. III, no. 3–4, Apr.-May 1944 (21, 24).
'Editorial Comments' (Conservatory Operatic Company), *Conservatory Quarterly Review.* Vol. IX, Winter 1929 (41–2).
'Editorial Comments' (on Gluck's 'Orfeo' at Hart House and establishment of symphony orchestra under Von Kunits), *Conservatory Quarterly Review.* Vol. V, 1923 (101–5).
'Editorial Comments' (on Hector Charlesworth's address, 'History of Musical Development in Toronto'), *Conservatory Quarterly Review.* Vol. III, Nov. 1920 (4–5).
'Editorial Comments' (history of Toronto Symphony Orchestra), *Conservatory Quarterly Review.* Vol. XVII, Aug. 1935 (3).
'Mr. Hector Charlesworth', *Conservatory Quarterly Review.* Vol. VII, Summer 1926 (131).
'Music', *Encyclopedia of Canada* (W. Stewart Wallace, ed.). Vol. IV, Toronto, 1936 (363–72).
'On Having Photisms'; 'Coloured Music', *Canadian Journal of Music.* Vol. II, Sept. 1915 (72–3).
'The R.S. Williams' Collection of Rare Instruments at the Ontario Museum', *Conservatory Quarterly Review.* Vol. I, May 1919 (60–2).
'Sociological Influences', *Conservatory Quarterly Review.* Vol. III, Feb. 1921 (31–2).
'A Survey of Music in Canada', *British Association for the Advancement of Science Handbook of Canada.* Toronto: University of Toronto Press, 1924 (90–4).
'William Byrd: Instrumental Music', *Canadian Review of Music and Art.* Vol. II, no. 7–8, Aug.-Sept. 1943 (10–12).
'Winner of the 1943 Award', *Canadian Review of Music and Art.* Vol. III, no. 5–6, June-July 1944 (22).

SOMERS, HARRY (b. Toronto, Ont., 11 Sept. 1925). He began piano and theory lessons in Toronto with Dorothy Hornfelt (1939–41). At the Royal Conservatory of Music in Toronto, he studied piano with Reginald Godden (1941–3) and Weldon Kilburn (1946–9), and composition with John WEINZWEIG (1942–3; 1946–9), receiving scholarships in 1947 and 1949. During the summers of 1947 and 1948 he studied piano with E. Robert Schmitz in San Francisco and Denver. In 1949 he was awarded a Canadian Amateur Hockey Association scholarship that enabled him to study composition with Darius Milhaud in Paris (1949–50). Aside from brief periods of other incidental employment, he has earned his living as a free-lance composer and has also acted as commentator and/or pianist in numerous CBC radio and television productions.

Although generally considered an eclectic, Somers has been able to fuse the many discoveries of an open and curious mind (absorbing such diverse 'influences' as baroque contrapuntal techniques, Mahler, Ives, Bartok, electronic and chance music) into a language of striking originality. The emotional drive behind his music (and perhaps the basis of its communicative power) has been coupled with a high degree of intellectual control, a keen sensitivity to timbre, and the ability to organize material over extended time periods. An extremely versatile composer, while exploring and working with many facets of 'advanced' music of the past few decades he has crossed boundaries that many of his more dogmatic colleagues have avoided, and contributed a body of music accessible to a wider audience – in his words, 'music for use': for example *Sonata for Guitar* (1959) and *The Picasso Suite* (1964). It should also be noted that Somers' versatility as a composer is paralleled by his involvement over the years in many aspects of Canadian musical life: earlier as a pianist, and later as a radio and television commentator (host of CBC-AM's 'Music of Today' between 1965 and 1969) and participant in the John Adaskin Project ('new music in education').

Somers' earliest compositions (1939–42) are short descriptive piano pieces whose syntax and vertically oriented texture largely reflect the piano repertoire he was then exploring. These early works are chiefly notable for a marked predilection for parallel progressions of various chords, especially those built in fourths. One finds this trait throughout the works of the 1940s, for example, in the second and third movements of *North Country* (1948). However, an inability to develop material beyond repetition was quickly overcome during the early years of study with Weinzweig, between 1942 and 1949.

Weinzweig was probably the most crucial single factor in Somers' development. At least five important aspects of his influence can be seen in Somers' work during the late 1940s and early 1950s: (i) a highly flexible use of serial technique (the series on the whole controlling linear rather than vertical events), for instance repeating certain pitches that are rhythmically varied, as if examining them from a different viewpoint; (ii) an emphasis on a highly controlled and elegant long melodic line that bears the main weight of the musical argument; (iii) transparent, clear textures (in orchestral works there are rarely more than three or four voices); (iv) an awareness of instrumental colour; and (v) a dry wit, manifested in a play of short rhythmic ideas.

Both the *String Quartet No. 1* (1943) and the *First Piano Sonata* (*Testament of Youth,* 1945) show a growing ability to extend and transform short motivic cells through larger movements. In *Testament of Youth* – a passionate, romantic work making use of a wide range of piano colours and textures – an important element of Somers' musical thinking is already in evidence; that is, a long melodic line moving slowly by small intervals and accompanied by a driving, rapidly moving ostinato-like figure. Such a superimposition of layers moving at different speeds recurs constantly and in many guises throughout Somers' music; for example, in the first movement of *North Country,* in episodic sections of the fugue in *Passacaglia and Fugue* (1954), and in the first part of *Stereophony* (1963). Over the years the 'long line' (actually indicated as such in the scores of many works of the 1950s) undergoes many surface changes. But the basic dynamic contour remains in later works – a gradual build-up of tension (sometimes resolved); for example, in the long solos of Riel (at the end of Act I) and of Marguerite (at the beginning of Act III – Kuyas) in the opera *Louis Riel* (1967), or in the flute solo *Etching – The Vollard Suite* (1964).

Closely related to the development of the dynamic contour of the 'long line' is another component of Somers' mature style that emerges during the period 1948–50: a sustained sound (whether a vertical aggregate of two or more pitches, or a single pitch, isolated or prolonged in a melodic line) is infused with a dynamic envelope or shape of its own, becoming as it were an active living organism. In the early stages this trait may generally be seen at the beginning or end of a movement (as in the first movement of *North Country* or the *String Quartet No. 2,* 1950), but later it can pervade the musical fabric of an entire work (for instance, in the opening motif of the *String Quartet No. 3,* 1959 – borrowed from *The Fool,* 1953 – or in the last movement of *Five Concepts for Orchestra,* 1961, where it becomes the basic compositional premise). Furthermore, striking use is made of this technique through the juxtaposition of blocks of dynamically fluctuating sonorities, beginning with the *Fantasia for Orchestra* (1958) and *Louis Riel.* By extension the crescendo, a kind of archetypal contour for Somers, becomes the determining factor in the overall dynamic shape of a movement or work: it is either arc-like, with the point of greatest tension at the apex (as in the second movement of the *Fourth Piano Sonata*, 1950, or in *Stereophony*) or it builds continuously until the end (for example in the orchestral introduction to *Louis Riel* or in *Fantasia for Orchestra*). The carefully managed build-up of tension creates a sense of drama in many of the larger works. An offshoot of this trait occurs in melodic lines that are rhythmically activated towards the point of highest tension by the repetition of notes in a written-out accelerando. This becomes a motivic figure in its own right in *Stereophony*. Points of high tension are often associated with a terse falling semitone figure.

Although introduced to the concept of serialism as early as 1942, Somers did not make systematic use of the technique until about 1950, and he has rarely used the series in a strict manner. In a few works of the 1940s he deliberately used all twelve pitches in isolated melodic statements; for example, in the first movement of *Testament of Youth* and *Moon Haze* (1944). In slightly later works such as the *First Piano Concerto* (1947), the *Rhapsody* for violin and piano (1948), and the *Woodwind Quintet* (1948), a series is stated at the beginning as a theme, and certain motivic ideas are extracted from it. In subsequent works the expressive character of certain intervals in a given series, rather than a systematic application of the series itself, determines the choice of pitch. Even works of the 1940s that do not use a series are highly unified through the use of a three- or four-note interval cell (for instance, in the first movement of *North Country*). Early sketches of the *Suite for Harp and Chamber Orchestra* (1949) show that in the late 1940s Somers was experimenting with the strict application of a four-note series. From here it was a short step to the stricter use of a twelve-note series.

In stricter serial works of the 1950s and early 1960s the degree of rigidity in applying the series varies greatly among works and even within the same work. As well as the already mentioned technique of extracting intervallic cells from the series, pitches may be repeated 'out of place' or omitted, and the order of segments may be altered. Somers' treatment of the series, then, could be considered generally similar to that of Alban Berg. Rarely is the same series used for an entire work. For example, the series of the Prelude in the *Symphony for Woodwinds, Brass and Percussion* (1961) is chromatically altered for the slow movement, but the Scherzo and Finale use a different series. It is important to point out that even in works after 1950 that apply the series more strictly there are tonal references, either built into the melodic line (and inherent in the series) or else as points of vertical repose before or after a more dissonant climactic episode (as in the first section of the *Symphony No. 1*). Beginning with the *String Quartet No. 3* (1959), tonal references sometimes found in the serially organized works of the earlier years are avoided in their experimental counterparts of the early 1960s, as in *Five Concepts*, *Stereophony*, or *Twelve Miniatures* (1964).

During the 1950s Somers was occupied with two main areas of exploration: the use of fugue-related textures and devices and the juxtaposition of different musical 'styles' within the same work or even within the same movement. The use of fugue-related devices – an attempt, in Somers' words, to 'unify conceptions of the baroque ... within the high tensioned elements of our own time' – stretches from 1951 (*12 x 12: Fugues for Piano*) through approximately half of all the works composed during the decade 1951–61.

The Somers 'fugue' is strongly stamped by many of the characteristics mentioned above. It bears little resemblance to the academic notion of fugue. There are two general types of subject: (i) fragmented and rhythmic (*Passacaglia and Fugue*, the first subject of the double fugue in the *String Quartet No. 3*) or (ii) lyrical and sustained (the slow movement of the *Symphony for Woodwinds, Brass and Percussion*). The success of the fugal movements is due in part to the earlier-mentioned characteristic of superimposing several layers moving at different speeds; this is ideally suited to a contrapuntal texture. But above all the fugue is a highly credible vehicle in Somers' hands: he continually presents the subject in new perspectives by adding new strands of figuration in the surrounding voices or by re-casting the subject itself.

The juxtaposition of tonal and non-tonal 'styles' within the same work, with varying degrees of success (for example in *The Fool; Violin Sonata No. 1*, 1953; *Piano Concerto No. 2*, 1956; and *The Fisherman and his Soul*, 1956), was intended to create tension by upsetting the normal expectation pattern of the listener. The germ of this device can actually be traced back to the second movement of the *Suite for Harp and Chamber Orchestra*, although here the use of stylistic contrast is the result of indulgence in a 'gentle satire on neo-classicism'. In *Louis Riel* four types of stylistic 'approaches' are used with great effectiveness: 'original folk material, ... abstract atonal writing, straight diatonic writing, and the constant juxtaposition of all these various things' (in Somers' words). In addition at certain crucial points in the opera electronic sounds are introduced.

The orchestral works of the early 1960s, while developing and enlarging on various earlier characteristics, show increasing experimentation with non-thematic textures (*Five Concepts, Stereophony*) and with the spatial and visual aspects of the performing situation (*Movement for Orchestra* and *Stereophony* respectively). After composing the music for the ballet *House of Atreus* (1963), which is one of Somers' best orchestral scores, his interest shifted to writing for the voice. He had, of course, previously written a number of works for voice using traditional resources, notably the chamber opera *The Fool* and *Five Songs for Dark Voice* (1955). In *Twelve Miniatures, Evocations* (1966), and *Louis Riel* a certain number of new techniques are introduced within a traditional framework – glissandi, whispering, vowel singing, quarter-tones, and timbral inflections.

Since *Louis Riel* Somers has explored the areas of improvisation and musical theatre, not only for their own sake, as in *Improvisation* (1968), but in conjunction with an astonishing range of new voice techniques and colours that he himself first presented in a 'lecture' at McGill University in 1968. These techniques include unvoiced vowel sounds, unvoiced exhalations and inhalations, sibilants, and voiced colour tones. In *Voiceplay* (1971), which grew out of this demonstration, the performer must, within the framework of a non-semantic 'lecture', play four roles: lecturer, demonstrator, actor or actress, and singer. Through the performer's presentation of 'symbols of subjective and objective states', the audience's responses and expectations become an important compositional factor (as in the 'style' juxtaposition of the 1950s). The score is largely diagrammatic, thus making pitch, timing, and even basic concept quite flexible. This fits Somers' belief, which has developed in recent years, that the performer should be a creative collaborator with the composer.

Somers' compositions of the 1950s included works commissioned by the University of Toronto Faculty of Music Alumni Association (*Little Suite for String Orchestra on Canadian Folk Songs*, 1955), the Stratford Festival for Maureen Forrester (*Five Songs for Dark Voice*), the Toronto Guitar Society (*Sonata for Guitar*), and the Vancouver Festival Society for the Hungarian String Quartet (*String Quartet No. 3*). Numerous works for the CBC include *Abstract* (1961, subsequently published in 1962 as *Movement for Orchestra*); *The Crucifixion* (1966); *Evocations* (1966); and *Voiceplay* for Cathy Berberian. In 1967 he composed *Kuyas* as the obligatory test-piece for the international voice competition in Montreal; the piece is also an aria in the opera *Louis Riel*, commissioned for the Canadian Opera Company on a grant from the Floyd S. Chalmers Foundation. Somers has also received commissions from the Koussevitzky Foundation (*Lyric for Orchestra*, 1960), the Toronto Symphony Orchestra (*Stereophony*), and the National Ballet Company of Canada (*The Fisherman and His Soul*; *Ballad*, 1958; *House of Atreus*).

In 1960 Somers was awarded a senior arts fellowship from the Canada Council. His *Movement for Orchestra* won a special Critic's Award at the Cava dei Tirreni Summer Festival in Italy (1965). From 1969 to 1971 he lived in Italy on an $18,000 award from the Italian government. In 1972 he was named Companion of the Order of Canada.

Returning to Canada from his two-year stay in Rome, Somers spent three months travelling in the Far East to explore its music. No doubt this experience will make itself felt in his music in the near future.

Somers is a former member of the board of Ten Centuries Concerts, a member of the Canadian League of Composers, and an affiliate of BMI Canada.

BRIAN CHERNEY

MUSICAL WORKS

STAGE (OPERA)

The Fool. 1953. 50′. SATB soli, chamb orch (10 instr). CMC. RCA LSC-3094. Libretto: Michael Fram. Nov 15, 1956, Tor, Victor Feldbrill(cond), Herman Geiger-Torel(dir).

The Homeless Ones (operetta in 3 scenes). 1955. 12′. narr, vcs, orch. ms. Libretto: Michael Fram. 1956. Tor, CBC TV, Victor Feldbrill.

Louis Riel. 1967. 2 hrs 13′. 6 principals, 20 soli, SATB, full orch, tape. ms. Libretto: (in Eng, French & Cree) Mavor Moore, Jacques Languirand. Sept 23, 1967, Tor, COC, Victor Feldbrill(cond), Leon Major (dir).

STAGE (BALLET)

The Fisherman and His Soul. 1956. 28′. small orch. ms. Choreography: Grant Strate. Nov 5, 1956, Hamilton, NatBalCo, George Crum.

Ballad. Oct 29, 1958. 29′. small orch. ms. Choreography: Grant Strate. 1958, Ottawa, NatBalCo, George Crum.

The House of Atreus. 1963. 31′. ms. Choreography: Grant Strate. Jan 13, 1964, Tor, NatBalCo.

FILM AND TV MUSIC

Scores for many films & TV programs, including:

Rehearsal. NFB, 1953.

Faces of Canada. 1956. 25′. small orch. ms. 1956, Tor, CBC TV, Victor Feldbrill.

Saguenay. 1959. 15′. full orch. ms. Film maker: Christopher Chapman. 1959, Ottawa, Crawley Films.

Picasso. 1964. small inst. group. CBC TV, Vincent Tovell(producer).

The Gift (background music for film on Japan). 1965. 60′. ms. Nov 11, 1965, Tor, CBC TV, Ron Kelly(producer).

The Well Known Stranger. 1966. Electronic. CBC TV (for Intertel), Vincent Tovell (producer).

And. 1969. 40′. sop, mezz sop, ten, bar, fl, hp, pno, 4perc, dancers. ms. Text: phonetics (Harry Somers). Choreography: Bertram Ross. Jan 28, 1970, Tor, CBC TV, TDT John Coulson(producer).

Images of Canada. 1972–3. series of 1-hr programs. Feb, Mar, 1973, Tor, CBC TV, Vincent Tovell(producer).

ORCHESTRA

Sketches for Orchestra. 1946. 14′. full orch. ms. RCI-88. Mar 1947 ('Shadows' only), Tor, CBC, Bernard Heinze; 1948 ('Horizon' & 'West Wind'), Rochester, Eastman Schl, Howard Hanson.

The Case of the Wayward Woodwinds. 1950. 5′. full orch. ms. 1951, Tor, CBC, 'Opportunity Knocks', John Adaskin.

Lament and Primeval (orch'n of last two of *Three Sonnets for Piano*). 1951. 5′. full orch. CMC. 1952, Ottawa, NFB Orch, Louis Applebaum. Choreographed Aug 18, 1955, Tor, Joey Harris.

Symphony No 1. 1951. 28′. full orch. Ber. Apr 27, 1953, Tor, CBCSO, Victor Feldbrill.

Prelude and Fugue for Orchestra. 1952. 5′. ms. CBC O, John Adaskin.

Passacaglia and Fugue for Orchestra. 1954. 11′15″. full orch. Ber, 1958. Lou LS-661, RCI-180. 1954, Tor, CBCSO, Ettore Mazzoleni.

Fantasia for Orchestra. 1958. 12′. full orch. Ber, 1962. RCA LSC-2980. 1958, Mtl, MSO, Igor Markevich.

Lyric for Orchestra. 1960. 7′30″. full orch. Ber, 1963. Apr 1961, Washington, DC, Orquesta Sinfonica Nacional de Mexico, L H de la Fuente(cond).

Five Concepts for Orchestra. 1961. 23′. full orch. Ber, 1964. Feb 25, 1962, Tor, CBCSO, Geoffrey Waddington.

Movement for Orchestra (originally 'Abstract for Television'). 1962. 10′. full orch. Ric, 1964. Mar 4, 1962, Tor, CBC TV orch, Mario Bernardi.

Stereophony. 1963. 17′. full orch. Kerby, 1972. Mar 19, 1963, TS, Walter Susskind.

SMALL ORCHESTRA

Symphony for Woodwinds, Brass and Percussion. 1961. 17′45″. large wind orch. Peters. CBC BR SM-134. July 1, 1961 (last mov't only), Pittsburgh, Pittsburgh Wind Symph, Robert Boudreau.

The Picasso Suite. 1964. 19′15″. Ric, 1969. Feb 28, 1965, S'tn, SSO, David Kaplan.

STRING ORCHESTRA

Slow Movement for Strings. 1946. 5′. ms.

1946, Tor, CBC O, Harold Sumberg.
Scherzo for Strings. 1947. 5′. AMP, 1948. RCI-238, RCI-41. July 17, 1947, Tor, CBC O, Harold Sumberg.
North Country. 1948. 12′50″. Ber, 1960. RCI-154. Nov 10, 1948, Tor, CBC Str O, Geoffrey Waddington.
Little Suite for String Orchestra on Canadian Folk Songs. 1955. 7′. pno accomp opt. Ber, 1956. Apr 2, 1956, Tor, Bennington Heights Community Orch, Assen Kresteff.

SOLOIST WITH ORCHESTRA
First Piano Concerto. 1947. 25′. pno, orch. ms. 1949, Tor, RCMT O, Ettore Mazzoleni (cond), Harry Somers(pno).
Suite for Harp and Chamber Orchestra. 1949. 23′. Ber, 1959. Col ML-5685/MS-6285. 1952, Tor, CLC conc, Bernard Heinze (cond), Marie Iosch(hp).
Five Songs for Dark Voice. 1956. 11′50″. alto, orch. Ber, 1972. RCA LSC-3172, CBC BR SM-73, RCI-286. Text: Michael Fram. Aug 11, 1956, Stratford Fest, Maureen Forrester (alto).
Second Piano Concerto. 1954–6. 43′. pno, orch. Ber. Mar 12, 1956, Tor, CBCSO, Victor Feldbrill(cond), Reginald Godden(pno).

CHOIR WITH ENSEMBLE
Gloria. 1962. 2′57″. SATB, 2tpt, org. GVT, 1964. RCA LSC-3043, CBC BR SM-53. Dec 24, 1962, Choir St James' Cathedral, Tor, CBC TV, Vincent Tovell(producer).
Crucifixion. 1966. 6′. SATB, EH, tpts, perc. ms. Apr 8, 1966, Tor, Fest Sgrs, Iseler, CBC TV, Vincent Tovell(producer).
Kyrie. 1972. 25′. SATB soli, SATB, fl, ob, cl, vlc, 3tpt, pno, 6perc. *Exile.* Vol 1, no 3, 1973.

CHOIR
Where Do We Stand, O Lord (chorale & fugue). 1955. 8′25″. SATB. Ber, 1955. RCI-130. Text: Michael Fram. 1955, Tor, Collegium Musicum of Hamilton, Udo Kasemets(cond).
Two Songs for the Coming of Spring. 1955. 2′15″. SATB, Ber, 1957. RCI-206. Text: Michael Fram. 1957, Tor, OMEA Convention.
God, the Master of This Scene. 1962. 3′35″. SATB. GVT, 1964. Cap T/ST-6258. Text: adapted by Bruce Attridge from Jeremy Taylor. July 28, 1962, Choir St James' Cathedral, Tor.
The Wonder Song. 1964. 4′. SATB. Ber, 1964. CBC BR SM-19. Text: Harry Somers. Mar 5, 1965, Tor, EJB, John Adaskin Project Seminar, CMC.
Five Songs of the Newfoundland Outports (arr). 1969. 19′. SATB, pno. GVT, 1969. RCA LSC-3154. Songs collected by Kenneth Peacock. June 26, 1969, Tor, CBC, Fest Sgrs, Iseler.

VOICE
Stillness. 1942. 3′. sop, pno. ms. Text: Harry Somers.
Three Songs (*4th Song* (optional) added 1948). 1946. 6′20″. med vc, pno. CMC. Text: Walt Whitman. 1946, Tor, Frances James.
A Bunch of Rowan. 1947. 4′. med vc, pno. Ber, 1948. Text: Diana Skala. 1949, Budapest, World Youth Fest.
A Song of Joys. 1947. 4′. med vc, pno. ms.
Three Simple Songs. 1953. 6′. med vc, pno. CMC. Text: Michael Fram. 1954, Hamilton, CLC conc, Trudy Carlyle(mezz), Mario Bernardi(pno).
Conversation Piece. 1955. 2′30″. high vc, pno. Ber, 1957. Text: Michael Fram. 1956, Catherine Hindson.
Evocations. 1966. 15′15″. alto, pno. Ber, 1968. CBC BR SM-13 & 108. Text: Harry Somers. Jan 26, 1967, Tor, CBC, Patricia Rideout(alto), Harry Somers(pno).
Voiceplay. 1971. 15′-20′. sgr-actor (male or female any range). CMC. Nov 14, 1972, EJB, Cathy Berberian.

VOICE(S) WITH INSTRUMENTAL ENSEMBLE
At the Descent from the Cross (J S Bach, arr). 1962. bs, 2guit. CMC.
Twelve Miniatures. 1963. 15′. med vc, rec (fl), vla da gamba (vlc), spinet (pno). Ber, 1965. RCA CC/CCS-1011. Text: Japanese Haiku. Trans: Harold G Henderson. Feb 2, 1964, Tor, CBC, Mary Morrison(vc), Nicholas Fiore(fl), Walter Buczynski (spinet), Donald Whitton(vlc).
Kuyas (extract from 'Louis Riel'). 1967. 7′15″. sop, fl, sleigh bells, tom-tom, ten drum, BD. Ber, 1971. Text: Cree Indian, compiled by the composer. June 1967, Int'l Mus Inst compet, Mtl.
Improvisations. 1968. 10′. narr, sgrs, str, ww, perc, 2pno. Text: Shakespeare, W B Yeats. July 5, 1968, Mtl, CBC Fest, Roxolana Roslak(sop), Patricia Rideout(alto), David Astor(ten), Maurice Brown(bar),

Charles Reiner, Harry Somers(pno), chamb gp directed by Victor Feldbrill.

INSTRUMENTAL ENSEMBLE

Duo. 1943. 4′. 2vln. ms.

String Quartet No 1. 1943. 17′30″. CMC. 1945 (3 mov'ts only), Tor, RCMT.

Suite for Percussion. 1947. 8′. pno, 4drums (African Tom Toms). ms. 1947, Tor, Reginald Godden(pno), Harry Somers(perc).

Mime. 1948. 5′. vln, pno. ms. Tor, Morry Kernerman(vln).

Rhapsody. 1948. 9′. vln, pno. CMC. RCI-244. Nov 10, 1948, Tor, CBC, Morry Kernerman (vln), Harry Somers(pno).

Woodwind Quintet. 1948. 24′. ms.

String Quartet No 2. 1950. 25′20″. CMC. Mar 18, 1963, CBC, Tor, Can Str Qt.

Trio for Flute, Violin and Cello. 1950. 12′. CMC.

Sonata No 1. 1953. 24′. vln, pno. Ber, 1968. RCA CC/CCS-1015, RCI-221. 1955, Stratford Fest, Hyman Goodman(vln), Leo Barkin(pno).

Sonata No 2. 1955. 15′. vln, pno. Ber, 1968. RCA CC/CCS-1016, RCI-222. June 11, 1955, Tor, RCMT, Jacob Groob(vln), Harry Somers(pno).

Movement for Wind Quintet. 1957. 6′. ms.

String Quartet No 3. 1959. 22′. CMC. CBC BR SM-45. 1959, Vanc, Hungarian Str Qt.

Theme for Variations. 1964. 3′05″. any comb of instr. Ber, 1966. Mar 5, 1965, Tor, EJB, Seminar II, John Adaskin Project Seminar, CMC, Blythwood Public Schl, Scarborough Woodwind Ens.

PIANO

Strangeness of Heart. 1942. 3′25″. Ber, 1974. RCI-132. c1943, Tor, R Godden.

Etude. 1943. 2′. ms. 1945, Tor, R Godden.

Dark and Light. 1944. 1′20″. ms. 1945, Tor, R Godden.

Flights of Fancy. 1944. 8′. ms. 1945, Tor, R Godden.

A Fragment. 1944. 2′. ms. 1945, Tor, R Godden.

Moon Haze. c1944. ms. 1945, Tor, R Godden.

Testament of Youth (1st Piano Sonata). 1945. 12′20″. CMC. 1946, Tor, R Godden.

2nd Piano Sonata. 1946. 20′. CMC. 1948, Tor, RCMT, Harry Somers.

Three Sonnets for Piano. 1946. 9′. Ber, 1948. 1948, Tor, Harry Somers.

Solitudes. 1947. 10′. ms. 1948, Tor, Harry Somers.

Four Primitives. 1949. 9′. ms.

3rd Piano Sonata. 1950. 24′. CMC. RCI-251. 1957, Mtl, McGill, Samuel Levitan.

4th Piano Sonata. 1950. 15′. CMC. 1950, Paris, Eugene Gash.

12 x 12 (Fugues for Piano). 1951. 15′. FH, 1955 (*Fugue 1*), Ber, 1959 (all).

5th Piano Sonata. 1957. 15′. CMC. CBC BR SM-162 ('Lento' only).

INSTRUMENTAL SOLO

Sonata for Guitar. 1959. 10′30″. Kerby, 1972. 1964, Tor, CBC, Peter Acker.

Etching – The Vollard Suite (extract from 'The Picasso Suite'). 1964. 2′30″. fl. Ric, 1969. CBC BR SM-114.

Music for Solo Violin. 1974. 21′20″. ms. Apr 27, 1974. Guelph Fest, Yehudi Menuhin.

BIBLIOGRAPHY

See B-B; B65,71; Bec56,57,58,70; Bt; CrC (I); D165; Esc; K; Mm; Wa.

Arthur, F. 'Somers in Recital of Own Works', *Saturday Night*. Vol. LXIII, Mar. 20, 1948 (34).

Ferry, A. 'Harry Somers: a Composer, TV Teacher, Beachcomber on the Fringe of Art', *Maclean's*. Vol. LXXVI, June 1, 1963 (62).

'The Fool', *CBC Times*. Dec. 11–17, 1965 (11).

Graham, June. 'A Harry Somers Evening', *CBC Times*. Aug. 17–23, 1968 (4–5).

———. 'Louis Riel', *CBC Times*. Oct. 25–31, 1969 (2–6).

'Harry Somers' (CBC documentary tape). Apr. 14, 1972.

'Harry Somers', *MuSc*. Sept.-Oct. 1967 (7).

'Harry Somers', pamphlet, BMI Canada Ltd, 1970.

'Harry Somers – a portrait', *Mu*. No. 4, Sept. 1967 (8–9).

Hudson, Richard. 'Canadian Contrasts', *Ricordiana*. Vol. X, no. 4, Oct. 1965 (92–5).

Kraglund, John. 'Two Canadian Operas', *CMJ*. Vol. I, no. 2, 1957 (43).

Loranger, Pierre. 'Harry Somers: "The Picasso Suite"', *CMB*. Spring-Summer 1970 (145–52).

Lowe, J. M. 'Agony of Modern Music', *Canadian Forum*. Vol. XXXV, Sept. 1955 (137–8).

MacNiven, Elina. 'Louis Riel', *Opera Canada*. Vol. VIII, Sept. 1967 (42).
McLean, Eric. 'Harry Somers: "The Fool" ', *CMB*. Spring-Summer 1970 (157–60).
Moore, Mavor. 'Why Louis Riel', *Opera Canada*. Vol. VII, May 1966 (9).
Morey, Carl. 'Canadian Opera?', *Canadian Forum*. Vol. XLVIII, Dec. 1968 (206).
Olnick, Harvey J. 'Harry Somers', *CMJ*. Vol. III, no. 4, Summer 1959 (3–23); Corrections, Vol. IV, no. 1, Autumn 1959 (46–7).
Rosenthal, Harold. 'Harold Rosenthal Reports from Canada', *Opera*. London, Nov. 1967 (865–7).
Schafer, R. Murray. *The Public of the Music Theatre – Louis Riel: A Case Study*. Vienna: Universal Edition, 1972.
Such, Peter. *Soundprints*. Toronto: Clarke, Irwin Ltd, 1972 (30–53).
Wilson, M. 'Music Review', *Canadian Forum*. Vol. XXXVI, Apr. 1956 (15–16).

LITERARY WORKS

ARTICLES

'Analysis of "Suite for Harp and Chamber Orchestra" ', *Canadian Contemporary Music*, Study Course No. 1. Toronto: CMC, 1961 (1–10).
'Composer in the School: A Composer's View', *Mu*. No. 19, May 1969 (13–16).
'Harry Somers' Letter to Lee Hepner', *CMB*. Autumn-Winter 1971 (87–97).
'A Letter from Rome', *CMB*. Spring-Summer 1970 (105–8).
'Louis Riel: the Score', *Opera Canada*. Vol. VIII, Sept. 1967 (46).
'Stereophony for Orchestra', *MAC*. Mar. 1963 (26–8).

SOUTHAM, ANN (b. Winnipeg, Man., 4 Feb. 1937). She studied at the Royal Conservatory in Toronto with Pierre Souvairan (piano) and Samuel DOLIN (composition). She is an instructor in the electronic music studio of the Royal Conservatory and has long been associated with the New Dance Group, later renamed the Toronto Dance Theatre. Her instrumental works, particularly for piano, are atonal character pieces with lyrical contrapuntal lines (for example, *Altitude Lake* for piano solo and *A Rhapsodic Interlude for Violin Alone*). She composed *Momentum* (1967), *Against Sleep* (1969), *Boat, River, Moon* (1972), and many other dance scores on commission from the Toronto Dance Theatre. In many of these scores, for electronic tape, a lyrical quality still prevails. She has combined instruments with electronic tape in such works as *Counterparts* (1971) for full orchestra and tape and *Counterplay* for string quartet and tape. She is a member of the Canadian League of Composers and is affiliated with BMI Canada.

BIBLIOGRAPHY

Mitchell, J. C. 'Warmth a Characteristic of Ann Southam's Electronic Music', *MuSc*. No. 269, Jan.-Feb. 1973 (6).

SURDIN, MORRIS (b. Toronto, Ont., 8 May 1914). As a youngster Surdin taught himself piano, subsequently taking lessons on the violin, cello, trombone, and French horn, and in theory and harmony. He studied composition with Louis Gesensway in Philadelphia (1937) and Henry Brant in New York (1950) and conducting with César Borré in Toronto (1945). He formed his own dance band at the age of sixteen and later was a copyist for Ben Bernie and Horace Lapp. After two years as a music arranger for the CBC (1939–41), he became a free-lance arranger and conductor, working for five years with the CBS network in the U.S. with Ray Darby, Goodman Ace, and others (1949–54). He then returned to the CBC to collaborate on many programs with the playwright Len Peterson and to compose music for many programs, including a long series of radio plays by W.O. Mitchell. He was music director for the radio drama series 'CBC Stage' as produced by Esse W. Ljungh, J. Frank Willis, and others.

Surdin's compositional work is characterized by colouristic though uncomplicated orchestration with free thematic development in a generally dissonant neo-classical style. An example is his *A Spanish Tragedy* (1955), written originally as incidental music for the play 'The Love of Don Perlimplin and Donna Belisa in the Garden' by Frederico Garcia Lorca and produced by the CBC. Using traditional Spanish motifs, he shows his craft in evoking the colourful atmosphere of Spain. He was asked by the CBC to form a suite of the songs from the play as a concert work. Similarly in *The Remarkable Rocket* (1961), Surdin's command of orchestral colour is apparent. In the *Concerto for Mandolin and Strings* (1966) he again recalls the technique and style of Spanish music. Surdin is adaptable to any style of writing, whether in a background drama score or in a work for the concert hall. It is therefore difficult to discover among his many works any single unifying characteristic, although a fairly free structural base is usually apparent. With his experience in theatre it would be expected that he would undertake the writing of an opera and, in collaboration with W.O. Mitchell, Surdin completed *Wild Rose* in 1967 on a commission from the Centennial Commission. The story is about a prairie hamlet awaiting the arrival of the Royal train; again with his adaptable style, Surdin has captured the atmosphere of the Canadian prairies.

Surdin has received commissions from the National Ballet Company (*The Remarkable Rocket*), the Hart House Orchestra (*Concerto for Accordion and String Orchestra*, 1966), and the Shevchenko Ensemble (*Suite Canadienne*, 1970; *A Feast of Thunder*, 1972). He is a member of the Canadian League of Composers and of CAPAC.

MUSICAL WORKS

STAGE

Ring Around the Moon. 1953. Text: Jean Anouilh.
Petite Ballet. 1955.
The Remarkable Rocket (ballet). 1960–1. Col MS 6763 ML 6163.
Look Ahead (musical comedy). 1962. Lyrics & text: Len Peterson.
Wild Rose (musical). 1967. 'The Arithmetic of Love' Dom LP 1368s. Lyrics & text: W O Mitchell.
The Great Hunger. 1968. Lyrics & text: Len Peterson.

FILM

Irons in the Fire. 1951. Film: NFB.
Power-Town Story. 1952. Film: NFB.
The Settler. 1954. Film: NFB.
Jake and the Kid. 1958. Film: NFB.
The Hospital. 1971. Film. Arthur Hiller.

RADIO

Once Upon a Tune (39 musicals). 1946. Text: Ray Darby.
The Gallant Greenhorn (musical). 1949. Text: Ray Darby, Harry Boyle, Kimball McIlroy, Esse Ljungh.
Jake and the Kid (more than 150 scores). 1950–72. Text: W O Mitchell.
Top Level (musical comedy). 1958. Lyrics & text: Hugh Laming.
A Beach of Strangers. 1959. Text: John Reeves.
The Rookie (musical). 1954. Text: Kimball McIlroy.
Songs of the Old Contemptibles (musical). 1964. Text: Len Peterson, lyrics: Robert Service.
At the Back of the North Wind (mini-musical). 1969. Text: Len Peterson.
The Chimes. 1969. Lyrics & text: Len Peterson.
Numerous scores for CBC Stage (15 years), Theatre 10:30, etc, etc.

TELEVISION

The Dream of Peter Mann (musical). 1962. Text: Bernard Kopf.
The Devil's Instrument. 1962. Text: W O Mitchell.
Seaway. 1965–6. Film: Seaway Films.
Hatch's Mill. 1967. Text: George Salverson.
De Tocqueville's America. 1969. Film: Vince Duval.
Taming of the Canadian West. 1969. Film: Ray Purdy.
The Land God Gave to Kane. 1970.
MacKenzie the Firebrand. 1971. Text: Lister Sinclair.
Listen to the Children (musical). 1972. Lyrics & text: Adele Ward.

ORCHESTRA

Credo (1950); *Two Symphonic Hoedowns* (c1950); *Carol of the Bells* (1955); *Concert Ballet* (1955); *Kid Stuff (Fantasy)* (1955); *A Spanish Tragedy* (1955); *V'là le bon vent* (arr) (1958).

BAND

Trees of North (1962); *Formula Ia* (1968); *Formula II* (1969).

STRING ORCHESTRA

Four X Strings (1947); *Incident I* (1961); *Time* (1966); *Horizons* (1968); *Alteration II* (1970); *Serious IX* (arr) (1970); *Five Adagios*.

SOLOIST(S) WITH ORCHESTRA
Inheritance. 1951. ww qt, str.
Softly as the Flute Blows. 1954. fl, str.
A Spanish Tragedy. 1955. sop, orch. Text: Morris Surdin.
Concerto for Mandolin and Strings. 1961–6.
Five Shades of Brass. 1961. tpt, orch.
Concerto for Accordion and String Orchestra. 1966.
Two Solitudes. 1967. hn(EH), str.
Short!. 1969. pno, str.
Short! (#2). 1969. pno, ww qt, str.
Alteration I. 1970. picc, str.
Terminus. 1972. ob, bsn, str.

CHOIR WITH ORCHESTRA
Portrait of a River. c1955. Text: John Luceratti.
Suite Canadienne. 1970. TTBB, orch. Text: R S James, Len Peterson, Ray Darby, W O Mitchell.
Billie Carney-o. 1971. TTBB, orch. Text: R S James.
Sea Song. 1971. TTBB, orch. Text: R S James.
Feast of Thunder. 1972. soli, TTBB, orch. Text: George Ryga.

VOICE
Tugboat Danny. 1954. Lyrics & text: Ray Darby.
Two Bits. 1954. Lyrics & text: Ray Darby.
Two Songs. 1959. B & H, 1964. Text: R S James.
On Christmas Day. 1962. B & H, 1963. Text: Rita Greer Allen.
Storm Child. 1964. B & H, 1965. Text: R S James.
Prairie Boy. 1964. B & H, 1965. Text: W O Mitchell. Cap ST 6087.
Gentle as a Summer Rain. 1969. Text: Michael Cook.
The Snows of William Blake. 1970. Text: Miriam Waddington.

INSTRUMENTAL ENSEMBLE
Suite for Viola. 1954. vla, pno (str, pno).
Carol Fantasia for Brass. 1955.
Tuckett of Trumpets. 1958. brass ens.
A St-Malo (arr). 1960. brass ens.
Brave Wolfe (arr). 1960. brass ens.
Incident II. 1961. ww, hns, hp.
Mandolin & Guitar. 1961. mand, guit.
Elements. 1965. 2vln, cb, hpschd.
Matin. 1965. ww qt.
Arioso. 1966. 4vlc.
Quartet in G minor. 1966. str qt.
Two by Two. 1966. 2ww.
Takeoné to Duo-s-burg. 1968. fl, pno.
Trio for Saxes. 1968.
Piece for Woodwind Quintet. 1969.
Trinitas in Morte. 1973. 3ob, bsn, 3hn, timp, 8vlc, 2cb.

PIANO
Naiveté (6 pieces). 1962.
Chantal. 1963.
A Gentle Set. 1966.
Poco Giocoso Variation. 1966.
Mood. 1967.
3 Piano Pieces. 1968.
In Search of Form I, II. 1970.
Fragmentations I, II, III. 1972.

INSTRUMENTAL SOLO
Canadian Folk Songs. 1969. B & H, 1970. accord.
Serious I-VIII. 1969. B & H, 1970. accord.
Serious IX-XVI. 1973. accord.

BIBLIOGRAPHY

See B-B; K; Mm; Wa.
'Agostini and Surdin', *CanCo*. No. 38, Mar. 1969 (16–21).
'Canada's Music Ambassadors to the Ukraine', *CanCo*. No. 54, Nov. 1970 (24, 26).
Graham, June. 'Morris Surdin', *CBC Times*. Dec. 6–12, 1969 (11–14).
'Ljungh and Surdin', *CBC Times*. Vol. VIII, no. 26, Jan. 1953 (6–14).
'Morris Surdin Says: "the main difficulty in collaborating with a writer is trying to get inside his mind" ', *CanCo*. No. 48, Mar. 1970 (34, 35, 37).

LITERARY WORKS

ARTICLES
'A "How-To" Fantasy on Writing Music for Drama', *CanCo*. No. 6, Feb. 1966 (8–9, 42, 44).

SYMONDS, NORMAN (b. Nelson, B.C., 23 Dec. 1920). He taught himself clarinet while serving in the Royal Canadian Navy (1939–46) and played with a local jazz group in Halifax (in 1940 until he was sent overseas in 1941). From 1945 to 1947 he studied clarinet and piano at the Royal Conservatory of Music, Toronto, on grants from the Department of Veterans Affairs. He then entered the dance-band field as performer and arranger (1947–50), while continuing to study theory, harmony, and composition privately with Gordon DELAMONT. After 1950 an interest in the composition of 'non-jazz' music was coupled with his active participation in jazz ensembles, particularly his own jazz octet (1953–7).

Most of Symonds' compositions employ jazz idioms and he is a major proponent of Third Stream music. In *Concerto Grosso for Jazz Quintet and Symphony Orchestra* (1958) he uses a small jazz ensemble accompanied by an orchestral sound dominated by clusters. The same is true of *Tensions* (1964), in which the orchestra provides a kind of 'interference' against a constant stream of jazz. In *Democratic Concerto* (1967), a commission from the Winnipeg Symphony Orchestra, Symonds integrated the orchestra and jazz quartet by including some jazz idioms in the orchestral parts and by breaking the 'stream' of jazz with some aleatoric sections. Symonds does not call on jazz idioms all the time. *Pastel for String Orchestra* (1963), for example, employs the baroque chaconne form in a dissonant neo-classical style, and *Three Atmospheres* (1970), a commission from the Hamilton Philharmonic Orchestra, is primarily a mood piece using aleatoric techniques.

Symonds has written commissioned works for the George Shearing Quintet (*Fugue for Shearing*, 1957), Moe Koffman (*Shepherd's Lament*, 1959), R.W. Finlayson for the Toronto Symphony (*Impulse*, 1969), and two works in collaboration with the CBC radio producer and poet John Reeves (incidental music for W.H. Auden's *Age of Anxiety*, 1959; Reeves' *Autumn Nocturne*, 1960). Other commissions from the CBC include the *Concerto Grosso for Jazz Quintet and Symphony Orchestra* (1958), *Tensions* (1964), and *The Nameless Hour* (1966). He has also received commissions from Ten Centuries Concerts (*IInd Perspective*, 1967) and the Canadian Opera Company (*The Spirit of Fundy*, 1972). In 1968 he received a Canada Council senior fellowship and travelled across Canada for half a year in a Volkswagen bus, collecting musical and literary impressions for his work *Big Lonely*. He is a member of the Canadian League of Composers and of CAPAC.

MUSICAL WORKS

STAGE

'Charnisay Versus LaTour' A One Act Opera (or *The Spirit of Fundy*). 1972. Libretto: Norman A Symonds.

RADIO

Age of Anxiety. 1959. Text: W H Auden.
Autumn Nocturne. 1960. Text: John Reeves.
Opera for Six Voices. 1961. Libretto: John Reeves.

TELEVISION

Tensions (ballet). 1964. jazz qnt, orch.
The Story of a Wind (Concerto for TV). 1970. sgr, narr, jazz ens.
Canada, What's it to you Bob Stanfield. 1972. sgr, jazz qnt. Film: Allan King.
The Land (Concerto for TV). 1972–3. narr sgr, jazz ens.

ORCHESTRA

Impulse. 1969.
Three Atmospheres. 1970.

STRING ORCHESTRA

Overture. 1959.
Elegy for String Orchestra. 1962.
Pastel for String Orchestra. 1963. Kerby, 1973. CTL S-5030.

SOLOIST(S) WITH ORCHESTRA

Concerto Grosso for Jazz Quintet and Symphony Orchestra. 1958.
Autumn Nocturne. 1960. ten sax, str. Kerby.
The Nameless Hour. 1966. improv soloist, str. MCA, 1971. Dec. DL-75069 MPS 21 21704-3.
Democratic Concerto. 1967. jazz qt, orch.
Concerto for Flute and Others. 1971.

CHOIR

Boy Meets Girl. 1964. SATB, perc. Text: Norman A Symonds.

VOICE WITH INSTRUMENTAL ENSEMBLE

Lament. 1962. low vc, guit. Text: John Reeves.
... Deep Ground, Long Waters.... 1969. fl, vc, pno (or vc, pno). Kerby, 1972. Text: Norman A Symonds.

INSTRUMENTAL ENSEMBLE

Fugue for Reeds and Brass. 1952.
First Concerto for Jazz Octet. 1955.
Hamburg Suite. 1956. jazz octet.
Second Concerto for Jazz Octet. 1956.

The Cocktail Party. 1956. jazz octet.
Experiments for Improvising. 1957. jazz ens.
Bordello Ballad. 1957. jazz ens.
Fugue for Shearing. 1957. pno, vib, guit, cb, perc.
A Six Movement Suite for Ten Jazz Musicians, plus Four Songs and Incidental Music. 1959. vc, jazz tentet. Text: W H Auden's 'Age of Anxiety'.
Shepherd's Lament. 1959. jazz qt.
Perspectives (an essay for jazz octet). 1962.
Music for Interpreter. 1964. jazz octet.
Fair Wind. 1965. jazz ens. Dec DL 75069.
Duet for Violin and All the Percussion That Can be Carried Across Town by One Man – Blues. 1967.
IInd Perspective. 1967. jazz ens, elec tape.

MIXED MEDIA
She Gently Moves. 1959. jazz dancer, jazz qnt.
Little Hearts Ease. 1972–3.

BIBLIOGRAPHY

Bec70; Bt; CrC(II); Esc; Wa.
'Big Lonely: Work in Progress', *CanCo*. No. 57, Feb. 1971 (22–5).
'clJasAsiZcaZl = Third Stream Music', *CanCo*. No. 37, Feb. 1969 (4–7).
'A Conversation with Norm Symonds: "Third Stream" Jazz Composition', *CanCo*. No. 24, Dec. 1967 (16–17, 36–7, 42–3).
'The "Duke" Plays Canadian Works on Latest Jazz LP Release', *CanCo*. No. 32, Sept. 1968 (12–13, 42–3).
'Jazz in Concert', *MAC*. Feb. 1963 (18–21).
'Man, Inc, Multi-Media Co-Authorship', *CanCo*. No. 47, Feb. 1970 (33–5).
McNamara, Helen. 'Norman Symonds', *International Musician*. July 1970 (10, 17).
'Opera for Six Voices', *CBC Times*. Nov. 25–Dec. 1, 1961 (10–11).

LITERARY WORKS

ARTICLES
'Solving a Problem: How to Find a Good Libretto', *CanCo*. No. 68, Mar. 1972 (16–19).

T

TANGUAY, GEORGES-ÉMILE (b. Quebec City, Que., 5 June 1893; d. Quebec City, 24 Nov. 1964). He studied first in Quebec with Léon Dessane and Arthur Bernier, then in Montreal with Arthur Letondal and R.-O. Pelletier. During his first visit to Paris (1912–14) he studied organ with Louis Vierne and harmony with Félix Fourdrain. In 1920 he was again in Paris, this time studying organ with Edouard Mignan, harmony and counterpoint with Georges Caussade, and piano with Simone Plé. At the Schola Cantorum he took courses with Vincent d'Indy. In New York his teachers were Pietro Yon and Gaston Dethier. In 1925 he was appointed organist of the church of the Immaculate Conception in Montreal, a post he held for twenty years. A teacher of organ and harmony at the University of Montreal, he was also on the staff of the Montreal Conservatoire from its foundation in 1942. Among his students were the organists Marcelle Martin, André Mérineau, and Marcel Beaulieu. Tanguay's works are finely constructed in a conventional style that illustrates his devotion to the French school from which he comes.

MUSICAL WORKS

ORCHESTRA
Danseuses devant Aphrodite (arr). c1920; Rou, 1920.
Pavane (arr). 1925. med orch. CBC Album 2 PR 1010.
Lied (arr). 1947. str orch. CBC Album 3 PR 1148–9.

SOLOIST WITH ORCHESTRA
Romance. 1915. vln, orch.

CHOIR
Cor Jesu. 1912; Passe-Temps, 1912. SATB.

O Salutaris. 1912; Passe-Temps, 1912. bar, SATB.
Cor Jesu. SATB. L'AC.

INSTRUMENTAL ENSEMBLE
Souvenir. c1912. vlc, pno. Durand.
Romance. c1920. vln, pno.
Apaisement (arr). c1920; Rou, 1920. 2ww qnt, hp.
Hommage à Couperin (arr). c1920; Rou, 1920. cl, bsn, str qnt.
Lied (arr). c1930. str qt.

PIANO
L'Air de Ballet. c1912. Durand.
Causerie. c1912. Passe-Temps.
Gavotte et Musette. c1912. Passe-Temps.
Menuet. c1912. Durand.
Sarabande. c1912. Arch.
Scherzo-Valse. c1912. Durand.
Pavane. 1914; Ditson, 1914.
Trois Pièces Brèves. c1920; Rou, 1920.

ORGAN
Prière. 1915.
Lied. 1924.

BIBLIOGRAPHY
See B-B; D157; K; Lv; Mm; Wa.

TREMAIN, RONALD (b. Feilding, New Zealand, 9 Oct. 1923). He received his Bachelor of Music degree (1945) from the University of Canterbury, New Zealand, and his Bachelor (1951) and Doctor (1953) of Music degrees from the University of London. An Italian Government Bursary (1952–3) enabled him to study composition with Petrassi at the Conservatorio S. Cecilia in Rome; he later studied conducting at the Accademia Chigiana in Siena (1953–5). He was senior lecturer at the University of Auckland from 1957 to 1967. A Carnegie Scholar in 1963, he made a study tour of the United States, visiting several universities and conservatories. He was visiting professor (1967–8) at the School of Music of the University of Michigan and the following year was professor at the State University of New York, Buffalo. Over the years, especially in New Zealand, he presented in concert much new music of European, American, and New Zealand composers and, from 1965 to 1967, was president of the New Zealand Section of the International Society for Contemporary Music. In 1970 he immigrated to Canada to initiate a music program at Brock University, St Catharines, Ont., where he is now chairman of the newly established Music Department.

As with many prominent English composers of his generation, with whose music his own has a kinship, much of Tremain's music is for voice, his output for the most part being for small ensembles. He is a member of the Australasian Performing Right Association (APRA), of whose Advisory Council he has been a member.

MUSICAL WORKS

INCIDENTAL MUSIC
The Tempest. 1959. str, hpschd. Text: William Shakespeare.
Good Woman of Setzuan. 1960. ww trio, voices. Text: Bertolt Brecht.
Murder in the Cathedral. 1961. wind ens, male vcs. Text: T S Eliot.

STRING ORCHESTRA
Allegro for Strings. 1958; Wai-te-Ata, 1969. Kiwi SLD-16.
Symphony for Strings. 1959.
Five Epigrams for Twelve Solo Strings. 1964; Otago U Press, 1968. Kiwi SLD-16.
Music for Strings. 1967.

CHOIR
Mass for Choir and Organ. 1964.
Tenere Juventa. 1965. SATB, 2pno. Text: Carmina Burana. Kiwi.

VOICE WITH INSTRUMENTAL ENSEMBLE
Three Mystical Songs. 1952. Text: Thomas Traherne, Robert Herrick. Kiwi SLD-16.
Four Medieval Lyrics. 1965; Wai-te-Ata, 1969. mezz, str trio. Kiwi SLD-16. Text: anon.

VOICE
Four Chinese Lyrics for Soprano and Piano. 1951. Trans: Arthur Waley.
Three Songs for Mezzo Soprano. 1960. mezz, vla. Text: A R D Fairburn.
Three Songs for Tenor and Piano. 1960. Text: Ursula Bethell, Michael Joseph.

INSTRUMENTAL ENSEMBLE
Variations for Two Violins. 1952.
String Trio. 1958.
Nine Studies for Violin and Viola. 1960.

PIANO
Prelude, Aria and Variations for Piano. 1966.

Three Inventions for Piano. 1968; Wai-te-Ata, 1968. Kiwi SLD-16.

TREMBLAY, GILLES (b. Arvida, Que., 6 Sept. 1932). After private studies with Gabriel Cusson, Jean PAPINEAU-COUTURE, Edmond Trudel, and Isabelle Delorme he studied with Claude CHAMPAGNE (composition) and at the Conservatoire in Montreal (1949–54) with Germaine Malépart (piano); he also attended the lectures of Jean VALLERAND in the history of music at the Université de Montréal. In 1953 he received his Premier Prix in piano at the Montreal Conservatoire. In 1950, 1951, and 1953 he followed the summer courses of the Marlboro School of Music in Vermont, then under the direction of Rudolf Serkin, Marcel Moyse, and Adolf Busch. He was greatly influenced by his meeting with Varèse in 1952.

Arriving in Paris in 1954, he studied at the Conservatoire with Olivier Messiaen (analysis), Yvonne Loriod (piano), and later (1956) with Maurice Martenot (ondes Martenot). He received the Premier Prix in analysis in 1957 and the Première Médaille in ondes Martenot in 1958. He also studied counterpoint with Andrée Vaurabourg-Honegger at the Ecole Normale de Musique, receiving his diploma in 1958. He attended the Ferienkurse für neue Musik in Darmstadt in 1957, studying with Karlheinz Stockhausen, and again in 1960 on a scholarship from the Kranichsteiner Musikinstitut, studying with Pierre Boulez and Henri Pousseur. In 1959 he began working in electro-acoustics with the Groupe de Recherches Musicales de l'O.R.T.F. under Pierre Schaeffer. He received three Canada Council scholarships (between 1958 and 1961) and in 1968 was awarded the Prix Calixa Lavallée of the St-Jean-Baptiste Society of Quebec.

Returning to Canada in 1961, Tremblay started teaching analysis at the Conservatoire in Quebec City (until 1966) and at the summer courses of the Jeunesses Musicales of Canada at Mount Orford (1959 and 1961). In 1962 he collaborated with the poet Fernand Ouellette for the thirteen-week radio series 'Paroles de Poètes' on the CBC French network. Since 1962 he has been a professor at the Montreal Conservatoire, where he teaches analysis and composition. In 1972 he sojourned for several months in the Far East, especially in Bali, where he studied the music and artistic conceptions of the native musicians.

Tremblay's works have been performed extensively in North America and Europe and at major international festivals at Tanglewood, Avignon, Royan, Brussels. He has received commissions from the Société de Musique Contemporaine du Québec, the CBC, the Communauté Radiophonique de Langue Française, the National Arts Centre Orchestra, and the Stratford Festival.

Tremblay shows a definite preference for winds and percussion. Voices are used only in *Kékoba* (1965), where they appear towards the end of the work. Always present is a poetic symbolism. In *Champs II* (*Souffles*) (1968) this manifests itself in an opposition between 'souffle' (duration) and 'fulgurance' (the instant). The opening of the work illustrates the transition between wind and sound by instructing the players to breathe into their instruments, just touching the threshold of instrumental sound before returning to wind. More often than not the music is monodic, with an extreme development of rhythmic and timbral subtleties. Sometimes a very rarefied texture is used to facilitate perception of such subtleties as the pitch of cymbal resonance being echoed by the ondes Martenot. Formally it is often a mosaic with sharp contrasts of pitch, dynamics, and density – a dense improvised passage following an instrumental solo, for instance. Although static in detail, it is very mobile in the length and pacing of the various sections. The freer sections – where, within a total duration, one finds a network of pitches, choice of rhythmic cells, attacks, dynamics, and pauses – give birth to a definite and distinctive result. The 'réflex', another principle of co-ordination, forces one player to react to the musical signals of another. Notable in *Champs II* are instrumental solos in the spirit of plainchant, punctuated by staccato echoes, and a multi-layered structure with low chords (piano, double bass), a very soft chorale-like passage by muted brass in the middle register, and, on top, cascades of grace notes (xylophone, glockenspiel, piano).

Solstices or *'The days and seasons revolve'* (1971) is in twelve continuous fields paralleling the characteristics of the months of the year. 'Winter' features the horn and a music of silences, slow evolutions coloured by discreet metallic sounds; 'Spring' features the flute and a music of contrasts, melodies, awakening of life; 'Summer' features the clarinet, a music with torrents of percussion and insect sounds; 'Autumn' features the double bass and a music of filtered, decomposed sound, of storms and silences. The point of departure of the work is determined by the hour of the day at which it is performed, read on the same twenty-four-hour clock face that contains the twelve months of the year; the character of the work is determined by the season in which it is played, the overall form by the hour at which it begins. For instance, if it is played in the summer at 6 p.m. (i.e. at 1800 hours, corresponding to the beginning of the tenth month), one takes the order autumn, winter, spring, summer. The summer sections would be played as they are and in the other sections the supplementary pitch material (bracketed in the score) would be played with the rhythmic, melodic, and timbral characteristics of the summer music. In this work the principles of reflex and reaction become the main mode of interplay between the instruments.

Tremblay has created a very personal and original way of organizing events in time. In fact the allusions to natural phenomena in most of his works are not at all gratuitous programmatic elements. A parallel with Messiaen is obvious, because of the similar sources of inspiration and the preoccupation with monody, but Tremblay's music never sounds like that of Messiaen. Tremblay is a disciple in the best and most creative sense of the word; one who, inspired by the achievements and teachings of the master, creates a new expression.

Tremblay was awarded a Canadian Music Council Medal in 1973. He is a member of the Société de Musique Contemporaine du Québec and of the Canadian League of Composers, and is affiliated with BMI Canada. BRUCE MATHER

MUSICAL WORKS

STAGE

Dimension Soleils (music for film). 1970. 5′. elec tape. Mtl, NFB, film by Raymond Brousseau.

ORCHESTRA

Cantique de durées. 1960. 19′5″. full orch. CMC. Mar 24, 1963, Paris Domaine musical, Ernest Bour.

VOICE(S) WITH INSTRUMENTAL ENSEMBLE

Matines pour la Vierge. 1954. SATB, small instr gp. ms.

Kékoba. 1965 (rev 1967). 23′30″. sop, mezz, ten, perc (extensive), ondes Martenot. Ber, 1968. RCI-240. Feb 25, 1966, Mtl, CBC, Trio vocal de Mtl, Gilles Tremblay(cond), Josèphe Colle(sop), Fernande Chiocchio (mezz), Georges Morgan(ten), Guy Lachapelle(perc).

INSTRUMENTAL ENSEMBLE

Double quintette pour instruments à vent. 1950. ms.

Mobile. 1962. vln, pno. ms.

Champs I. 1965 (rev 1969). 10′. pno, 2 perc. Salabert. Feb 1965, Mtl, Ens de perc de Paris, Claude Raynaud(pno), Vincent Gémignani, Boris de Vinogradov(perc).

Souffles (Champs II). 1968. 15′. 2fl, ob, cl, hn, 2tpt, 2trb, 2perc, cb, pno. Salabert. RCI-370. Mar 21, 1968, Mtl, SMCQ, Serge Garant.

Vers (Champs III). 1969. 22′35″. 2fl, cl, tpt, hn, 3vln, cb, 3perc. Salabert. Aug 2, 1969, Stratford, Ont, Lawrence Smith.

'. . . le sifflement des vents porteurs de l'amour . . .' 1971. 10′. fl, perc. Mar 1, 1971, Ottawa, NAC, Robert Cram, Ian Bernard.

Solstices (ou Les jours et les saisons tournent). 1971. 10′–15′. fl, cl, hn, cb, 2perc. CMC. May 17, 1972, Mtl, Ermitage Studio, Gilles Tremblay.

PIANO

Trois Huit (Scherzo). 1950. 2′5″. CMC. RCI-135.

'Mouvement' pour deux pianos. 1954. ms. May 1, 1954, Mtl, Conserv, Salle St-Sulpice, Serge Garant, Gilles Tremblay.

Deux pièces pour piano: 'Phases', 'Réseaux'. 1956–8. 8′. CMC. RCA CC/CCS-1022; CBC BR SM-162 ('Phases' only). May, 1959, Cologne, Yvonne Loriod.

ELECTRONIC

Sonorisation du Pavillon du Québec (stereophony in 24 channels). 1967. 8′. elec tape. 1967, Mtl, Expo '67.

BIBLIOGRAPHY

See B-B; B65,71; Bec70, CrC(I); D165; K; Lv; Wa.

'Gilles Tremblay', *Musiques du Kébèc* (R. Duguay, ed.). Montreal: Editions du Jour, 1971 (267–71).

'Gilles Tremblay – a portrait', *Mu.* No. 24, Nov. 1969 (8–9).

Martin-Dubost, P. 'Le "Cantique de durées" de Gilles Tremblay', *Vie des Arts.* No. 31, Summer 1963 (45, 51).

Stone, Kurt. 'Review of Records', *MQ.* Vol. VIII, no. 3, July 1967 (440–52).

Thériault, Jacques. 'Gilles Tremblay', *MuSc.* Mar.-Apr. 1970 (6–7).

LITERARY WORKS

ARTICLES

The following articles have appeared in *Musiques du Kébèk* (R. Duguay, ed.). Montreal: Editions du Jour, 1971:

'Cantique de Durées' (276).

'Kékoba' (277).

'Notice (1967) pour "Phases" (1956) et "Réseaux" (1958)' (272–5). Reprinted from *Vie Musicale.* No. 7, 1967 (10–13).

'Notice pour "Souffles (Champs II)"' (281–2).

'Vers (Champs III) pour 12 exécutants' (283).

'Vers une nouvelle écoute' (284–8).

'Vie quotidienne et acte musical' (289).

'Hommage à Messiaen', *Melos.* Vol. XII, Dec. 1958 (392).

'Oiseau – nature – Messiaen – musique', *CMB.* Spring-Summer 1970 (15–40).

'R. Murray Schafer: The Book of Noise', *CMB,* Spring-Summer 1971 (187–8).

'Les sons en mouvement', *Liberté.* Vol. LIX, Sept.-Oct. 1959 (297–303).

TRUAX, BARRY (b. Chatham, Ont., 1947). He received his Bachelor of Science degree from Queen's University (1969), where he also studied music with Graham GEORGE and F.R.C. CLARKE. He studied composition with Cortland Hultberg at the University of British Columbia, receiving his Master of Music degree in 1971. Two Canada Council arts bursaries (1971–3) enabled him to study principally with G.M. Koenig and O.E. Laske at the Institute of Sonology, the Netherlands. He was appointed to the Centre for Communications, Simon Fraser University, Burnaby, B.C., in 1973.

Truax has written for piano solo, including *Hexachord Sonata* (1969) and *Two Dances* (1969); for cello and piano (*Theme and 12 Miniatures,* 1970); and for a vocal ensemble (*Moon Dreams,* 1971). However, he has concentrated on works involving electronic tape, including *Children* (1970) for soprano and tape (text by e.e. cummings); *From the Steppenwolf* (1970) for twelve singers and tape; *Hexameron* (1970) for flute, clarinet, horn, viola, piano, and 2 two-channel tapes; *Sonic Landscape No. 1* (1970) for solo horn and tape and *No. 2* (1971) for flute, piano, and tape; *The Little Prince* (1971), a dramatic story in ten scenes for singers and tape; and *Tapes from Gilgamesh* (1972–3) for twelve four-channel tapes. In 1972 he was commissioned by the CBC to write *She, A Solo.* He is affiliated with BMI Canada.

LITERARY WORKS

'The Computer Composition – Sound Synthesis Programs POD4, POD5 & POD6', *Sonological Reports No. 2,* 1973, Institute of Sonology, Utrecht.

'General Techniques of Computer Composition Programming', *Numus West,* No. 4. Fall 1973.

'Some Programs for Real-Time Computer Synthesis and Composition', *Interface.* Vol. II, Swets & Zeitlinger, Amsterdam.

TURNER, ROBERT (b. Montreal, Que., 6 June 1920). Turner began composing music in the popular idiom when he was thirteen. His earliest formal instruction in composition was received from Irvin Cooper, supervisor of music in Montreal schools, who encouraged him to continue his musical studies at McGill University. There he studied composition with Douglas CLARKE and harmony and counterpoint with Claude CHAMPAGNE, graduating with the Bachelor of Music degree in 1943. The next two years were spent in service with the R.C.A.F.

After the war Turner studied further with Clarke, and during the summer of 1947 in Colorado Springs with Roy Harris, who had a strong influence on his compositional style. During 1947–8 he studied composition with Herbert Howells and orchestration with Gordon Jacob on a scholarship at the Royal College of Music in London. He spent the years from 1948 to 1951 in the United States, where he studied composition, again with Harris, at the George Peabody College for Teachers at Nashville, Tenn. At Tanglewood, where he went in the summer of 1949 for study with Messiaen, a performance of his *String Quartet No. 1* (1949) brought high praise. The first movement of the Quartet is neo-modal in flavour and lyrical in character, blending aspects of Vaughan Williams and Debussy. A broadly arched fugato slowly unfolds at the beginning of the second movement, followed by a second, rhythmically more active fugato, these two subjects being then combined. The third and concluding movement is a scherzo. Turner has withdrawn all his compositions written prior to this Quartet, and some of his later works as well.

After teaching high school music in Kentucky (where his wife Sara was timpanist with the Louisville Orchestra), Turner returned to Canada to take up a similar post in Kelowna, B.C. Then, in 1952, he joined the CBC in Vancouver as music producer, a position he held for sixteen years. In 1954 he received a doctorate in music from McGill University for his *Canzona* (1950) and *Concerto for Chamber Orchestra* (1950). From 1955 to 1957, while still with the CBC, Turner taught at the University of British Columbia. He was awarded a Canada Council Arts Fellowship during 1966–7. He taught at Acadia University from 1968 to 1969 and since then at the University of Manitoba, where he holds the rank of Associate Professor of Music.

A conservative modern, Turner has been described as 'rather a shy, slow-spoken man'. A basic sincerity emanates both from him and from his music. Most of his output has been in response to numerous commissions, especially from the Canada Council and the CBC. 'I don't believe in that ivory tower idea of writing for posterity or yourself. The specific occasion is my inspiration'. The variety of his works attests to the different kinds of commissions he has received. One of his most-performed works is the overture *Opening Night*, commissioned by the Vancouver Symphony Orchestra in 1955. 'The work is meant to convey the general mood of excitement and glamour that surrounds an opening night in the theatre, whether the vehicle be a play, musical, ballet or an opera.' It begins with a syncopated fanfare in bright contemporary harmonies for brass, which is answered by a sharply punctuated pattern for timpani. The violins take up a running passage derived from the fanfare and given a jazzy twist. After a lyrical middle section, there is a return to the opening material to which Turner adds a snatch of 'From Leicester Square to Old Broadway', the theme song of the CBC Vancouver series of that name written by Harry Pryce and familiar to many radio listeners. The *Lyric Interlude* (1956), also commissioned by the Vancouver Symphony, is in quite a different mood. A long-breathed, rather liturgical melody in the Phrygian mode is harmonized by layered major triads that spread in contrary motion to bitonal combinations and converge again to triadic focus. After a climactic point the material is repeated with a quiet ending on a C major chord.

In marked contrast *Robbins Round* (1959) is a third-stream work in the form of a 'Concertino for Jazz Band', the subtitle provided by the composer. Dedicated to the Vancouver jazz musician, Dave ROBBINS, the piece allows for free improvisation by solo instruments mostly in slow-blues tempo, alternating with bright swing-style entries for large jazz orchestra.

Three Episodes (1963) is scored for a large orchestra including piano, harp, vibraphone, and celesta. The movements – titled Prelude, Interlude, and Finale – are intended to represent the exposition, crisis, and dénouement of a concise drama. The slow, atmospheric interlude based on the tonal centre of E is flanked by more vigorous and dramatically conceived outer movements with B flat as the tonal centre. Making use of twelve-tone technique in a diatonic context, each of the three movements has shattering climaxes, achieved mainly through rhythmic diminution. The music is evocative with a hobbled waltz tune, repeated 'weeping' chords, and contrasts between vigorous rhythmic activity and pensive lyricism.

For 1967, Canada's centennial year,

Turner was commissioned by the CBC to write a radio opera. *The Brideship* is based on an episode in British Columbia history (1862). The libretto, by George Woodcock, concerns a young lady named Rose, a passenger in a shipment of brides for B.C. miners and trappers. She falls in love on board with John Atkins, a corporal in the Royal Engineers, but they are forcibly separated when Atkins is arrested for this misdemeanor, and Rose, not expecting to see Atkins again, marries Jim Wilson, a lonely trapper and prospector. A year later, when Atkins appears at Wilson's cabin, a scuffle ensues and Wilson is accidentally killed. It cannot be said that the libretto serves the opera well – Wilson is painted in sympathetic tones, but Atkins remains an enigma – but despite the work's lack of dramatic power, Turner has provided a musical score combining dramatic realism and lyric beauty somewhat in the Menotti manner.

Turner considers his *Trio for Violin, Cello and Piano* (1969) important in the development of his style, and has subtitled the work 'Transition'. The first two movements make use of the twelve-tone technique but, as the composer points out, the third movement, a recapitulation of the first, treats the same material tonally. There is no dichotomy of harmonic concept however; the twelve-tone technique as used by Turner is oriented to a diatonic tonalism with the triad as the basic unit. Indeed the occasional use of bitonality and quartal harmonies is more ornamental than basic to Turner's harmonic language. In spite of canonic passages in inversion, retrograde, and retrograde inversion, the *Trio* has a Schumannesque spirit, representing a return to more traditional models and underscoring Turner's basically conservative and neo-Romantic allegiances.

Turner's ear for orchestral timbres is revealed in *Concerto for Two Pianos and Orchestra* (1971). The three movements use contrasting instrumentation: the first employs upper-range instruments (excepting piccolo) and percussion instruments of wood; the second uses the lower instruments (excepting tuba and basses) and metal percussion instruments; while the third uses full orchestra and 'skin' percussion. The soloists pluck or beat on the piano strings in the slow movement, and in the third their cadenza makes use of motifs from various other Turner works.

Robert Turner is a member of the Canadian League of Composers and is affiliated with BMI Canada. LEE HEPNER

MUSICAL WORKS

STAGE

Object Matrimony (CBC-TV play). 1958. 30'. chamb orch. ms.

The Pemberton Valley (CBC-TV docum). 1958. 60'. med orch. ms.

A Question of Principle (CBC radio play). 1959. 30'. chamb orch. ms.

Josef Drenters (sculptor) (CBC-TV docum). 1961. 30'. brass qnt. ms.

The Brideship (lyric drama). 1967. 54'. 8 voc soli, orch. Peer. Libretto: George Woodcock. Dec 12, 1967, Vanc, CBC, Hugh McLean.

ORCHESTRA

Canzona. 1950. 9'30". full orch. ms. 1956, Vic.

Opening Night (theatre overture). 1955. 9'. full orch. Ber, 1960. RCI-179; CBC BR SM-163. 1955, Vanc, VSO, Irwin Hoffman.

Lyric Interlude. 1956. 11'. full orch. CMC. 1956, Vanc, VSO, Irwin Hoffman.

Nocturne. 1956 (orch'd 1965). 10'30". med orch. Ber, 1972. CBC BR SM-63; Ace of Diamonds SDD-2121. 1966, Vanc, CBC, CBC Vanc Ch O, John Avison.

A Children's Overture. 1958. 8'. med orch. CMC. CBC BR SM-63; Ace of Diamonds SDD-2121. 1959, Vanc, CBC, Vanc Ch O, John Avison.

The Pemberton Valley (suite from film score). 1958. 30'. med orch. ms.

Three Episodes. 1963. 16'20". full orch. CMC. CBC BR SM-4. Feb 27, 1966, Tor, CBC, TS, Jean Deslauriers.

SMALL ORCHESTRA

Concerto for Chamber Orchestra. 1950. 11'30". ms. 1952, Vanc.

Sinfonia for Small Orchestra. 1953. 18'. ms. 1955, Vanc.

Eidolons (12 Images for Chamber Orchestra). 1972. 25'. CMC. Sept 12, 1972, Vanc, CBC Fest, CBC Ch O, John Avison.

STRING ORCHESTRA

Symphony for Strings. 1960. 27'. CMC. RCA CC/CCS-1008; RCI-214. Mar 27, 1960, Mtl, McGill Ch O, Alexander Brott.

SOLOIST(S) WITH ORCHESTRA

Four Songs. 1959 (orch'd 1969). 10'30". sop (ten), full orch or pno. CMC. Text: Wilfred Watson. 1959, (vc and pno version), Vanc Fest, Milla Andrew(sop), George Brough(pno).

Concerto for Two Pianos and Orchestra. 1971. 18'. CMC. 1972, Wpg, WSO, Piero Gamba(cond), Garth Beckett and Boyd McDonald(pno).

Johann's Gift to Christmas. 1972. 45'. narr, full orch. CMC. Text: Jack Richards. Dec 18, 1972. Vanc, VSO, Kazuyoshi Akiyama (cond), Eddie Albert(narr).

CHOIR WITH ORCHESTRA

The Third Day (an Easter cantata). 1962. 30'15". soli, SATB, med orch. CMC. Text selected from medieval & renaissance sources by Peter Haworth. 1962, Vanc, CBC-TV, Cantata Sgrs, Vanc Ch O, Hugh McLean (cond), Audrey Farnell(sop), Winona Denyes(sop), Katherine Fearn(alto), Victor Martens(ten), Donald Brown(bs).

CHOIR

Two Choral Pieces. 1952. 6'16". SATB. CMC. RCI-70 & 206. Text: Wallace Stevens, e e cummings.

Prophetic Song. 1961. 5'45". SSAA. Peer, 1971. Text: Percy Bysshe Shelley.

The House of Christmas. 1963. 20'50". SATB. CMC. Text: G K Chesterton.

VOICE

The Seasons (song cycle). 1954. 12'. sop, pno. ms. Text: Leroy Smith, May Sarton, Jay Smith, Mary E Osborn.

Thought for the Winter Season. 1954. 3'. sop, pno. CMC. Text: Mary E Osborn. 1954, Vanc, CBC, Natalie Minunzie(sop), Genevieve Carey(pno).

VOICE(S) WITH INSTRUMENTAL ENSEMBLE

Eclogue. 1958. 5'. sop, ob (fl or cl or vln), hpschd (pno). CMC. Text: Sir Walter Raleigh. 1958, Vanc, CBC, Hugh McLean Consort.

Pastoral Triptych. 1958. 13'. sop, ten, ob, trb, hpschd. ms. Text: Christopher Marlowe, Walter Raleigh, John Donne.

Four Songs. 1959 (orch'd 1969). 10'30". sop (ten), pno or full orch. CMC. Text: Wilfred Watson. 1959, (vc and pno version), Vanc Fest, Milla Andrew(sop), George Brough(pno).

Mobile. 1960. 5'. SATB, 7perc. CMC. Text: Elder Olson. 1962, Mtl, McGill, Mtl Bach Choir, George Little.

The Phoenix and the Turtle. 1964. 20'. mezz, fl, cl, b cl, vln, vla, vlc, cel, hp. CMC. Text: Shakespeare. 1964, Vanc, CBC Chamb Ens, Hugh McLean(cond), Winona Denyes (mezz).

Suite in Homage to Melville. 1966. 15'. sop, alto, vla, pno. CMC.

INSTRUMENTAL ENSEMBLE

String Quartet No 1. 1949. 23'. CMC. 1949, Tanglewood, Mass, Berkshire Mus Center.

Lament. 1951. 6'. fl, ob, cl, bsn, pno. CMC. Apr 8, 1960, Vanc, CBC, Cassenti Plyrs.

Sonatina for Oboe and Piano. 1951. 7'. CMC. 1957, Vanc, CBC, Roland Dufrane(ob), Carol Jutte(pno).

String Quartet No 2. 1954. 19'. Ber, 1963. 1965, Mtl, McGill, McGill Str Qt.

Sonata for Violin and Piano. 1956. 18'. CMC. RCI-194. 1956, Vanc, U of BC, Harry Adaskin(vln), Frances Marr(pno).

Robbins Round (Concertino for Jazz Band). 1959. 7'30". CMC. 1959, Vanc, CBC, 'Jazz Workshop', Dave Robbins.

Variations and Toccata. 1959. 12'. ww qnt, str qnt. Ber. RCA CC/CCS-1009; RCI-215. 1959, St'n, Fest Chamb Gp, Murray Adaskin.

Serenade for Woodwind Quintet. 1960. 9'. CMC. CBC BR SM-139. 1960, Vanc, CBC, Cassenti Plyrs, Kenneth Helm(fl), Ronald Dufrane(ob), John Arnot(cl), Robert Creech(hn), George Zukerman(bsn).

Four Fragments for Brass Quintet. 1961. 9'. Peer, 1972. 1962, Vanc, Vanc Art Gallery, Vanc Brass Ens.

Fantasia. 1962. 10'. org, brass qnt, timp. CMC. July 1963, Los Angeles, Calif, Amer Guild of Organists, Los Angeles Brass Gp and timpanist, Hugh McLean(org).

Diversities. 1967. 17'. vln, bsn, pno. CMC. RCI-239. 1967, Vanc, CBC Fest, Cassenti Plyrs.

Trio for Violin, Cello and Piano. 1969. 19'15". CMC. July 1969, Victoria Trio.

Nostalgia. 1972. 6'. sop sax, pno. CMC.

PIANO

Sonata Lyrica. 1955 (rev 1963). 25'20". CMC. 1956, Vanc, CBC, Marshall Sumner.

Nocturne. 1956. 8'. ms.

A Merry-mournful Mood. 1971. 1'. Wat.

INSTRUMENTAL SOLO

Little Suite for Harp. 1957. 10′. Peer, 1971. 1958, Vanc, CBC, Gertrude Graf.

Fantasy and Festivity. 1970. 18′. hp. CMC. CBC BR SM-188. June 21, 1971, Tor, AGO, Judy Loman.

ORGAN

Canon, Chorale and Fugue for Organ. 1957. 7′30″. ms.

Six Voluntaries. 1959. 18′. Ber, 1968. RCA CC/CCS-1020; RCI-226. 1959, Vanc, CBC, Hugh McLean.

BIBLIOGRAPHY

See B-B; B58,65,71; Bt; Cb; CrC(I); Esc; K; Lv; Wa.

'The Brideship', *CBC Times*. Dec. 9–15, 1967 (6–7).

Garvie, Peter. 'Robert Turner', *MuSc*. No. 245, Jan.-Feb. 1969 (9).

'Robert Turner – a portrait', *Mu*. No. 29, 1970 (10–11).

'Three Episodes for Orchestra', *CBC Times*. Feb. 26–Mar. 4, 1966 (6).

LITERARY WORKS

ARTICLES

'Barbara Pentland', *CMJ*. Vol. II, no. 4, 1957–8 (15).

TWA, ANDREW (b. Ellisboro, Sask., 13 Dec. 1919). He received his early musical training in Brandon, Man., and in 1945 began studies in composition with John WEINZWEIG at the Royal Conservatory in Toronto. In 1949 he received the McGill Chamber Music Society Award. He was violist in the Toronto Symphony Orchestra for a short time, teacher of viola at the Royal Conservatory, and conductor of an amateur orchestra in Scarborough, Ont. Twa generally uses rhythmic ostinato figures in a polytonal or chromatic, contrapuntal texture (*Prairies*, 1947; *Serenade for Clarinet and Strings*, 1948). Although his output has not been large, Twa has written mainly for orchestra, including *Symphony* (1955) and *Serenades Nos. 1 and 2* (1948 and 1951), and for chamber ensembles, including *String Quartet* (1948) and two *Sonatas* (1951), one for violin and piano and the other for viola and piano. He has also written a *Sonata for Solo Violin* (1948). Twa was general manager of Berandol Music (1970–1); a chartered accountant by profession, he has been in business independently since 1972. He is a former member of the Canadian League of Composers.

BIBLIOGRAPHY

See B-B; K.

'Andrew Twa – Biography', pamphlet, BMI Canada Ltd, Nov. 1949.

V

VALLERAND, JEAN (b. Montreal, Que., 24 Dec. 1915). He studied violin with Lucien Sicotte (1920–35) and composition with Claude CHAMPAGNE (1935–42). He has written and conducted many scores for CBC radio and television plays and has conducted performances for the Opera Guild of Montreal and the Montreal Symphony Orchestra. In 1940 he was awarded the Schumann trophy for composition in Quebec. He has been music critic for several Montreal newspapers, among them *Le Canada, Montréal-Matin, Le Devoir, Le Nouveau Journal,* and *La Presse,* and in addition was music columnist for the French edition of *Maclean's* magazine. He formerly taught at the Faculty of Music, University of Montreal, and was secretary of the Conservatoire in Montreal (1942–63).

Vallerand's early style, exemplified in *Sonata for Violin and Piano* (1950), is reminiscent of various styles of early-twentieth-century French music (e.g. Fauré and Poulenc). Vallerand says of the *Sonata* that it is 'a common denominator of all I knew about music at the time I wrote it!'. In the chamber opera *Le Magicien* (1961) he has followed a style closer to Poulenc, with the brittle quality typical of French neo-classicism.

In *Cordes en mouvement* (1961) Vallerand modified his style to exploit the possibilities of string writing. He has described the movements thus: 'The first movement (Allegro moderato) borrows its style from medieval organum – parallel fourths and fifths. The second movement (Adagio cantabile) is canonic in form, while the third (Allegro ben marcato) makes free use of a twelve-tone row. The fourth movement (Molto lento) exploits the particular sonority of harmonic "cross-relations". The fifth movement abandons itself in the accumulative general fun of a moto perpetuo. The sixth and last movement (Adagio – Allegro giusto) takes the open strings of violin, viola, cello, and contrabass as its structural point of departure, and ends by recalling the "organum" of the first movement.'

In *Etude concertante* (1969) Vallerand returned to his earlier drier style, using serial technique for a virtuoso work that was chosen as the obligatory test piece for the 1969 International Violin Competition in Montreal.

From 1963–6 Vallerand was director of music programs for the French Radio Network of the CBC. In 1966 he was appointed 'Conseiller culturel' to the Délégation générale du Québec in Paris, and in 1971 he became head of the Conservatoires de Musique du Québec and director of the Performing Arts Service of the Ministère des Affaires culturelles du Québec. In 1961 he received commissions from the Lapitsky Foundation (*Cordes en mouvement*) and the Jeunesses Musicales of Canada (*Le Magicien*). He is a member of CAPAC.

MUSICAL WORKS

STAGE AND RADIO

Le Magicien (chamb opera). 1961. sop, ten, bar, med orch. CMC. SM-42. Text: Jean Vallerand. Sept 2, 1961, JMC camp, Mount Orford.

Over 100 musical scores for radio plays produced by the CBC.

ORCHESTRA

Le Diable dans le beffroi. c1939. ms. RCI-41. 1942, Mtl, MSO, Désiré Defauw(cond).

Nocturne. 1947. ms.

Prélude pour orchestre. 1948. ms. RCI-116.

Réverbérations contractoires. 1961. ms. Mar 6, 1961, Mtl, Orch du Conservatoire, Charles Houdret(cond).

STRING ORCHESTRA

Cordes en mouvement/Strings in Motion. 1961. ms. RCA CC/CCS-1010. 1961, Mtl, McG Ch O, Alexander Brott(cond).

SOLOIST WITH ORCHESTRA

Concerto pour violon et orchestre (orch'd version of *Sonate*). 1951. ms.

Etude concertante. 1969. vln, med orch. CMC. 1969, Mtl, International Institute of Music of Canada vln compet'n.

CHOIR WITH ORCHESTRA

Deux Cantates. 1946. ten, choir, orch. ms. Texts: Gustave Lamarche and Rina Lasnier respectively. 1946, Ottawa, Congrès musical d'Ottawa.

VOICE

Les Roses à la mer. c1935. vc, pno, ms. Text: Marceline Desbordes-Valmore. Mtl, Marie-Thérèse Paquin, Jeanne Desjardins.

Quatres Poèmes de Saint-Denys Garneau. 1954. vc, pno. CMC. ARCLP-4. Mtl, Marguerite Lavergne(sop), John Newmark (pno).

INSTRUMENTAL ENSEMBLE

Sonate pour violon et piano. 1950. CMC. RCI-92, 1951, Mtl, Noël Brunet(vln), John Newmark(pno).

Quatuor à cordes. 1958. CMC. Col ML-5764. Mar 2, 1955, Mtl, Mtl Str Qt.

BIBLIOGRAPHY

See B-B; CrC(II); D157; K; Kh; Lv; Mm; Wa.

'Canadian Music Broadcast on French Radio Network', *CanCo.* Sept. 1967 (32).

LITERARY WORKS

BOOKS

Introduction à la musique, Montreal: Editions Chantecler, 1949 (269).

La Musique et les tout-petits. Montreal: Editions Chantecler, 1950.

ARTICLES

'Conquête de la forme: episode de la vie d'un compositeur', *Gants du Ciel.* Dec. 1943 (43–52).

'Le conservatoire dans la cité', *Culture vivante.* No. 11, Dec. 1968 (7–12.)

'La musique et la vie intérieure', *L'Action*

universitaire. Vol. XVI, Jan. 1950 (68–72).
'Pour que s'arrête le gaspillage du talent', *Vie Musicale.* No. 1, 1965 (9–11).
'Regards sur la musique au Québec', *Musical America.* Vol. LXXXIII, Sept. 1963 (18).
'Rencontre avec Varèse', *Liberté.* Vol. LXIX, Sept.-Oct. 1959 (304–6).

VAN DIJK, RUDI (b. The Hague, Holland, 27 Mar. 1932). He studied at the Royal Conservatory in The Hague with Leon Orthel (piano) and Hendrik Andriessen (1944–52). His *Sonatine for Piano* won first prize in the International Gaudeamus Composers' Competition in 1953. In the same year he came to Canada and served in the Canadian Army (1953–6), attending a summer course in composition in Toronto with Roy Harris (1955). From 1960 to 1964 he was a free-lance composer and pianist and in 1962 and 1963 he received the Ohio Arts Scholarship for Background Music. He was awarded a Canada Council Arts Scholarship to study composition with Max Deutsch in Paris (1964–5), and from 1965 to 1966 he worked for BBC television in London. From 1969 to 72 he was a teacher of piano and composition at the Royal Conservatory of Music in Toronto and since 1972 has been teaching composition, orchestration, and choral writing at Indiana University, Purdue, Ind. Van Dijk's style is reminiscent of early-twentieth-century English music (Delius, Vaughan Williams, for example). He uses small musical cells and treats them in a freely developed structure. Some examples are the B-A-C-H motif, making up the maerial in *Concertante for Flute and Orchestra* (1963), a commission from the Toronto Chamber Orchestra Society, and the 'Big Ben' motif in *Four Epigrams for Symphony Orchestra* (1962), a commission from the CBC. In 1971 he received a grant from the Canada Council to write *Four Lieder for Baritone and Orchestra* for Victor Braun. He is a member of the Canadian League of Composers and an affiliate of BMI Canada.

MUSICAL WORKS

INSTRUMENTAL

3 works for solo piano: *Sonatine* (1952); *Ballade* (1958); *Phantom*, Op 30B, No 1 (1969).
5 works for chamber ensemble: *Sonata for Clarinet and Piano* (1954); *Pastorale for Violin and Piano* (1955); *Sonata Movement* (1960) alto sax, pno; *Elegy for Violin and Piano* (1965); *Sonata for Violin and Piano* (lost).
March 'Homage for a Hero'. 1955. band.
2 works for solo and orchestra: *Symfonia Concertante for Piano and Orchestra* (1959); *Concertante for Flute and String Orchestra* (1963).
Four Epigrams for Symphony Orchestra, Op 16. 1962.

CHORAL

Christmas Cantata. 1967. children's choir, SATB, ten, orch.

VOCAL

Lieder for High Voice and Piano. 1959.
Four Lieder. 1971. bar, orch.
Immobile Eden. 1972. fl, sop, pno.

VIVIER, CLAUDE (b. Montreal, Que., 14 Apr. 1948). He studied composition with Gilles TREMBLAY and piano with Irving Heller at the Conservatoire in Montreal from 1967 to 1970, receiving a Jeunesses Musicales du Canada Award to study piano with Karl Engel (1968). Canada Council Arts bursaries (from 1971) enabled him to study composition and electronic music with G. Michael Koenig at the Institute of Sonology in Utrecht and composition with Paul Méfano in Paris (1971–2), and composition with Karlheinz Stockhausen, analysis with Richard Toop, and electronic music with Hans Ulrich Humpert in Cologne (from 1972).

Vivier's comparatively small output to date includes experimental aleatoric music, with aspects of theatre sometimes included (*Prolifération*, 1969; *Désintégration*, 1972). He has written mainly for chamber groups (*Ojikawa*, 1968; *Quatuor à cordes*, 1968; *Hiérophanie*, 1970; *Deva et Asura*, 1972) and electronic tape (*Hommage à un vieux corse triste*, 1972) and chorus (*Musik für das Ende*, 1971; *Chants*, 1972–3). Vivier is affiliated with BMI Canada.

LITERARY WORKS

ARTICLES

'L'Acte musical', *Musiques du Kébèk* (R. Duguay, ed.). Montreal: Editions du Jour, 1971 (291–7).

W

WALTER, ARNOLD (b. Hannsdorf, Moravia, 30 Aug. 1902; d. Toronto, Ont., 6 Oct. 1973). He received his doctorate in law from Prague University in 1926. In Berlin he studied musicology at the University and worked as a music journalist. Among his teachers were Bruno Weigl and Frederick Lamond. After an unsettling period in war-torn Spain (1933–6), he escaped to England and at length arrived in Canada in 1937, joining the teaching staff of Upper Canada College in Toronto.

Walter's *Trio for Violin, Cello and Piano* (1940), which won the Canadian Performing Right Society award in 1943, is in a traditional four-movement form with rigorous thematic development, including fugal treatment; stylistically it is in the tradition of Brahms' classical romanticism. His *Sonata for Piano* (1950) is atonal, built on a motif of an ascending augmented fourth and three descending semitones that appears throughout the work in various forms. This work is similar to the early atonal pieces of Hindemith. His *Concerto for Orchestra* (1958) is in a concerto-grosso form employing dissonant tonalities. This work is tumultuous with fragmented thematic treatment.

Walter was probably best known as teacher and administrator. From 1945 to 1952 he was director of the Royal Conservatory Senior School, during which time he founded the Opera School of the Conservatory (1946). From 1952 to 1968 he was director of the Faculty of Music, University of Toronto, later continuing as professor and special lecturer. He was president of the Canadian Music Council, the Canadian Music Centre, the International Society for Music Education, and the Inter-American Music Council of the Pan-American Union. He was chairman of the editorial board of the *Canadian Music Journal* (1956–62) and in 1965 he founded the Canadian Association of University Schools of Music, becoming its first president. He was a founding member of the board of trustees of the National Arts Centre in Ottawa. In 1967 he received an honorary Doctor of Music degree from Mount Allison University in New Brunswick. Other honours have included the Christian Culture Award from Assumption University (1945), the National Award in Music from the University of Alberta (1958), and the Award of Merit of the Corporation of the City of Toronto 'for distinguished public services' (1971). In 1971 he was created Companion of the Order of Canada. His estate is a member of CAPAC.

MUSICAL WORKS

RADIO

Several scores of music for radio plays.

ORCHESTRA

Music for Harpsichord and Strings. 1941.
Symphony in G minor. 1942.
Concerto for Orchestra. 1958.

CHOIR AND ORCHESTRA

For the Fallen. 1949. Text: Laurence Binyon.

VOICE WITH INSTRUMENTAL ENSEMBLE

Sacred Songs. 1941. sop, vln, vlc, pno. Texts: Anon, John Donne.

INSTRUMENTAL ENSEMBLE

Sonatina for Cello and Piano. 1940.
Trio for Violin, Cello and Piano. 1940.
Sonata for Violin and Piano. 1940.
Novelette. c1940. vln, pno.
Recitative and Aria. c1940. vlc, pno.
Pieces for Violin and Piano. c1940.

PIANO

Suite for Piano (1945; OUP, 1956); *Six Studies* (1946); *Toccata* (1947); *Naiad* (1947); *Sonata for Pianoforte* (1950; GVT, 1951); *Legend* (1962); *Etudes en émotions* (five studies in mood).

ELECTRONIC TAPE

Summer Idyll. 1960. Folkways FM 3436, collab with Myron Schaeffer, Harvey Olnick.
Project A. 1961. collab with Myron Schaeffer, Harvey Olnick.
Project TV. 1962.
Electronic Dance. 1963.
Becoming. 1963. collab with Myron Schaeffer, Harvey Olnick.
Indian Ballet. c1963.

BIBLIOGRAPHY

See B-B; B58,65,71; Bt; C63,66,69,72; Esc; K; T; Wa.

'Dr. Arnold Walter Retires as Music Faculty Director', *CanCo.* No. 26, Feb. 1968 (38–46).

Mercer, Ruby. 'Arnold Walter', *Opera Canada.* Vol. x, No. 2, May 1969 (12–13, 36–7).

Ridout, Godfrey. 'Aspects of Arnold Walter', *CanCo.* No. 38, Mar. 1969 (14–15).

Walter, Arnold. 'A composer's story', *CanCo.* No. 77, Feb. 1973 (4–13).

Weinzweig, Helen. 'Dr. Arnold Walter Honoured by Friends, Colleagues, Alumni', *CanCo.* No. 29, May 1968 (28, 46).

LITERARY WORKS

BOOKS

Aspects of Music in Canada (ed.). Toronto: University of Toronto Press, 1969. (*Aspects de la musique au Canada.* Montreal: Le Centre de Psychologie et de Pédagogie, 1970.)

ARTICLES

'Canadian Composition', Music Teachers National Association, *Volume of Proceedings.* Series 40, 1946.

'A Canadian Pattern', *CMJ.* Vol. I, no. 3, 1956–7 (33).

'Carl Orff', *CMJ.* Vol. I, no. 1, 1956–7 (55).

'A Composer's Story', *CanCo.* No. 77, Feb. 1973 (4–13).

'Education in Music', *Mm* (133–45).

'Elementary Music Education – The European Approach', *CMJ.* Vol. II, no. 3, 1957–8 (12).

'The International Society for Music Education', *CMJ.* Vol. II, no. 3, 1957–8 (35).

'In Memoriam: Edward Johnson', *CMJ.* Vol. III, no. 4, 1958–9 (38).

'Music Education on the North American Continent', *Food for Thought.* Vol. XIV, Feb. 1954 (31–5).

'Music and Electronics', *CMJ.* Vol. III, no. 4, 1958–9 (33).

'Music a Means to Unify Mankind', *Canadian Review of Music and Art.* Vol. III, no. 3–4, Apr.-May 1944 (19–20); Vol. III, no. 5–6, June-July 1944 (27–8, 31); Vol. III, no. 7–8, Aug.-Sept. 1944 (18–19, 30).

'Music in a Technological Age', *CMJ.* Vol. I, no. 3, 1956–7 (4).

'A Musical Journey to Japan', *CMJ.* Vol. VI, no. 1, 1961–2 (3).

'Problems of Patronage in a Democratic Society', *CMJ.* Vol. I, no. 3, 1956–7 (14).

'Toward Canadian Opera', *Here and Now.* Vol. I, May 1948 (79–81).

'What is Modern Music?', *Canadian Review of Music and Art.* Vol. I, no. 4, May 1942 (7–8, 17).

WEINZWEIG, JOHN (b. Toronto, Ont., 11 Mar. 1913). As the first Canadian composer to espouse the twelve-tone technique, John Weinzweig will always deserve a special place in the annals of Canadian composition. In addition, perhaps more than any other he has shaped the evolution of the Canadian school of composition that appeared after the Second World War, as a teacher of many of English-speaking Canada's most gifted composers, as a fighter for the status of the career composer in Canada, and as a composer ever evolving in style and idiom of expression.

He began his studies in piano and theory with Gertrude Anderson in 1927, later also studying mandolin, tuba, saxophone, and bass. In 1934 at the University of Toronto he studied with Leo SMITH (harmony), Healey WILLAN (counterpoint), Sir Ernest MAC MILLAN (orchestration), and Reginald Stewart (conducting), receiving his Bachelor of Music degree in 1937; in his freshman year he founded (and conducted) the University of Toronto Symphony Orchestra. In 1938 – having studied at the Eastman School of Music in Rochester, N.Y., under Bernard Rogers (orchestration and composition) and Paul White (conducting) – he received his Master of Music degree, and the following year he joined the teaching staff of the Toronto (now Royal) Conservatory of Music. He was the first composer (1941) to write incidental music for CBC radio dramas. Also during the war years he wrote for films (*Mackenzie River*, 1941; *West-Wind*, 1942; *The Great Canadian Shield*, 1945; *Turner Valley*, 1945). He served with the Royal Canadian Air Force from 1941 till 1943. In 1952 he was appointed to the Faculty of Music, University of Toronto. His many students have included Harry SOMERS, Samuel DOLIN, Murray ADASKIN, Harry FREEDMAN, Philip NIMMONS, R. Murray SCHAFER, John

BECKWITH, Norma BEECROFT, and Srul Irving GLICK.

It is difficult to imagine what contemporary Canadian composition would be like had it not been for John Weinzweig. As teacher of many of the English-speaking composers in this volume, he gave some of them their first glimpse of mainstream twentieth-century techniques and styles of composition. He fostered and encouraged individuality in his students while challenging them with the need for high standards and self-criticism. The diversity and quality of Canadian composition today attests to this country's debt to him in the arts.

Weinzweig has also been a primary motivating force in the establishment and success of most of the organizations that have promoted contemporary Canadian music during the past quarter of a century. His concern for quality in composition and his desire to increase the acceptance of contemporary music led to the establishment of the Canadian League of Composers in 1951. Much of his efforts on behalf of the League resulted in its becoming an enduring and truly national organization. To provide composers with a vehicle for making their works known on a wider scale among conductors and performers, Weinzweig played a key role in the conception and establishment of the Canadian Music Centre.

However, Weinzweig's efforts as a teacher and promoter of contemporary music would not have been nearly as effective had it not been for his integrity as an artist and for the high quality of his own compositions. If he had not believed so fully in his art, it is unlikely that he would have pressed so hard for the acceptance of unpopular stylistic features in a period of public antipathy towards them. Had his own music not been of such high quality, he would probably have been less convincing as a teacher and less tolerant of individuality in his students.

Throughout most of his music, Weinzweig's style is characterized by clear, often thin, textures and lucid form with strong motivic organization, usually serially derived. His music exhibits unrelenting rhythmic drive, frequent sharp dissonance, and a peripheral reliance on tonality. His melodies can be either angular or lyric. The general effect of his music can be either light and witty or warm and moving.

Weinzweig's music is almost entirely instrumental. The bulk of it is for orchestral and chamber ensembles. The size of his orchestra rarely exceeds that of Mozart. Five of his six divertimentos are for strings and one wind instrument. His *Concerto for Harp and Chamber Orchestra* (1967) utilizes an accompaniment of strings and single woodwinds. Only a few works, like *Wine of Peace* (1957) and the *Concerto for Piano and Orchestra* (1965), exceed this size.

Consistent, too, throughout Weinzweig's work is his affection for ensembles where one solo instrument is featured. However, in other respects Weinzweig's use of instruments has varied considerably throughout his thirty-five-year career as a professional composer. Since the mid-1960s he has become more interested in exploring and extending the extremes of the timbres and resources of such instruments as the harp, clarinet, and saxophone. Earlier he was content to use instruments in more traditional ways.

The music from the first decade of Weinzweig's career tends to be more richly orchestrated than that which follows. His general textures, although thin for the time, are relatively full in comparison with those in his works after the mid-1940s. From that time, regardless of the size of his orchestra, Weinzweig uses his instruments sparingly so that a chamber texture prevails. Melodies are often presented for several measures with little or no accompaniment. Phrases often change timbre by being passed from one instrument to another. Melodic doubling becomes almost entirely absent. Ensemble textures and accompaniments are usually divided among several sections so that the overall fabric is kaleidoscopic.

Another consistent feature throughout Weinzweig's melodies is the high degree of motivic organization. More often than not, this will have been derived from a twelve-note row. Much has been made of Weinzweig's use of this compositional procedure, since he is credited with having been the first Canadian composer to make use of it. However, his use of the twelve-note row has been overemphasized, particularly by those reviewers and performers who, in order to dispose of his music as 'cerebral', use the row's presence to excuse their own limited understanding of the more significant features of his music. In Weinzweig's early music particularly, the use of the row is frequently difficult to detect. *Dirgeling* (from the *Suite for Piano No. 1*, 1939), his first twelve-note composition, is not constructed in the systematic manner employed by the Viennese composers. Weinzweig's row is primarily a source for melodic invention, which is applied in such a way that it more resembles the baroque technique of 'Fortspinnung'. In early works, such as his *Violin Sonata* (1941) or his flute divertimento (*Divertimento No. 1*, 1946), he rarely derives his harmonies from the row, and he uses a different row for each movement.

However, Weinzweig's use of a row becomes more systematic as his career progresses. In his bassoon divertimento (*Divertimento No. 3*, 1959), or his *String Quartet No. 3* (1962), the same row generates all the movements. His harmonies and other accompaniments derive from it as well. Episodic passages not derived from the row are almost entirely absent. Still, his music does not resemble the traditional twelve-note approach. Weinzweig dwells on certain segments of the row to such an extent that the music almost becomes tonal. An entire section often consists of one exposition of a form of the row, as though it is the motif and not the row that is the primary concern of the composition. That the motif comes from a row serves to tie the work more neatly together.

The most engaging aspect of Weinzweig's work is his use of rhythm – rhythm almost entirely dependent on metre. Every work before 1970 has a time signature. In some pieces the time signature changes periodically, but a basic pulse is maintained throughout – for the listener through the frequent reference to groups of successive notes of equal duration. Weinzweig's rhythmic vitality stems from the manner in which he places motivic and textural material against this basic pulse. His most characteristic motivic material consists of short and fragmented units often only a beat or two long. These units usually contain few different pitches. Often the same note is played several times, either in rapid repetition or in alternation with one or several other notes. When a piece is derived from a tone row the motif is associated with a few adjacent notes from the row itself, which are in turn identified with a certain rhythm. In other places the pitches from the motif are played repeatedly but within a changing rhythmic pattern. Since the accents created by the successive entry of these motifs are rarely repeated successively in the same place within the metre, they create syncopations and counterpulses.

Weinzweig's distribution of these motifs among his instruments further reinforces the perception of accents and cross-accents. One or two isolated notes from a motivic figure are assigned to a single instrument. This may seem insignificant from the player's standpoint, but from the standpoint of the piece as a whole these notes form an integral part of the rhythmic fabric by accenting and drawing attention to specific moments. Occasionally this method of accent creation is shared among several players who must work together to make one rhythmic figure. Thus a sense of ensemble becomes critical in the intelligent performance of a Weinzweig composition.

The overall effect of Weinzweig's rhythm is one of energy and vitality. In his music before the 1950s the sense of constant forward propulsion that one receives comes closest to that of the music of Stravinsky. After that time – as in works such as *Divertimento No. 3*, *Divertimento No. 5* (1961), and the piano concerto – the rhythms come closer to swing or jazz. Since the *Concerto for Harp and Chamber Orchestra*, Weinzweig's rhythm, while still well organized, has a drive that is less immediately obvious. His use of metre is freer in such works as *Trialogue* (1971) and *Around the Stage in Twenty-five Minutes during which a Variety of Instruments are Struck* (1970).

These last two works are representative of his latest interest in the theatrical possibilities in music. They contain not only the usual musical indications but also instructions for lighting and stage action. If the past is any indication, Weinzweig will continue to explore thoroughly these possibilities and with characteristic self-discipline will refine his explorations into precise, coherent, and expressive works.

Weinzweig's numerous commissions include many works for the CBC: *Our Canada* (1943), *Edge of the World* (1946), *Round Dance* (1950), *Wine of Peace* (1957), *Concerto for Piano and Orchestra* (1965–6), *Divertimento No. 4 for Clarinet and Strings* (1968), *Dummiyah* (1969), *Around the Stage in Twenty-five Minutes during which a Variety of Instruments are Struck* (1970), and *Trialogue* (1971) for soprano, flute and piano. During the 1940s he also composed works for Temple Emmanuel, N.Y. (*Improvisation on an Indian tune*), the Forest Hill Community Centre (*Quartet No. 2*, 1946), and the Volkoff Canadian Ballet (*Red Ear of Corn*, 1949). *Am Yisrael Chai!* (1952) and *Dance of the Massadah* (1951) were commissioned by the Canadian Jewish Congress of Toronto. Weinzweig also received commissions from the Saskatoon Symphony Orchestra (*Symphonic Ode*, 1958), the Saskatchewan Music Festival (*Divertimento No. 3*), and the Canadian Music Centre for its John Adaskin (school music) Project (*Clarinet Quartet*, 1965); in 1967 he composed the *Concerto for Harp and Chamber Orchestra* on a Centennial commission from Judy Loman and the Toronto Repertory Ensemble. Under Canada Council grants he received commissions from the Canadian String Quartet (*String Quartet No. 3*, 1962) and from Paul Brodie for the Third World Saxophone Congress (*Divertimento No. 6 for Alto Saxophone and Strings*, 1972). His *Divertimento No. 1* received the highest award for chamber music at the London Cultural Olympics in 1948. In 1968 Weinzweig received a Canada Council Senior Arts Award and in 1969 an honorary Doctor of Music degree from the University of Ottawa and in 1974 was made an Officer of the Order of Canada.

Weinzweig is a member of the Boards of Directors of the Canadian Music Centre, of the Canadian League of Composers, and of CAPAC (President, 1973).

RICHARD HENNINGER

MUSICAL WORKS

STAGE

Red Ear of Corn (ballet in 2 acts). 1949. 30′. full orch. ms. Choreog: Boris Volkoff. 1949, Tor, Royal Alex Th, CBC O, Samuel Hersenhoren(cond).

FILMS

Mackenzie River. 1941.

West-Wind; 'Life and Art of Tom Thomson'. 1942.

The Great Canadian Shield. 1945.

Turner Valley. 1945.

RADIO

100 or so radio drama scores: Riel, Whiteoaks of Jalna, White Empire, etc.

ORCHESTRA

Legend. 1937. 5′. full orch. ms.

The Whirling Dwarf. 1937. 3′. med orch. ms. 1939, Tor, CBC, Samuel Hersenhoren.

The Enchanted Hill. 1938. 10′. full orch. ms. 1938, Rochester Civ O, Howard Hanson.

Suite. 1938. 7′. full orch. ms. 1938, Rochester Civ O, NBC, Howard Hanson.

Symphony. 1940. 30′. full orch. ms.

Rhapsody for Orchestra. 1941. 10′. full orch. CMC. 1957, Tor, CBCSO, Victor Feldbrill.

Our Canada. 1943. 11′. med orch. CMC. RCI-41. 1943, Tor, CBC O, Samuel Hersenhoren.

Edge of the World. 1946. 7′15″. med orch. MCA, 1967. CBC BR SM-163. 1946, Tor, CBC O, Geoffrey Waddington.

Red Ear of Corn (ballet suite). 1949. 17′10″. med orch. CMC. Dom 1372, Col ML-6163/MS-6763 (Barn Dance). 1951, Tor, Emil Gartner.

Round Dance. 1950. 2′15″. med orch. CMC. 1950, Tor, CBC O, John Adaskin.

Symphonic Ode. 1958. 9′. full orch. MCA, 1962. Mar 22, 1959, S'tn, SSO, John Weinzweig.

Dummiyah/Silence. 1969. 15′30″. full orch. CMC. July 4, 1969, Tor, EJB, CBC Fest O, Victor Feldbrill.

BAND

Band-Hut Sketches. 1944. 3′. ms. 1944, CBC, RCAF Rockcliffe, Central Band, John Weinzweig(cond).

Round Dance (arr by Howard Cable). 1950. 2′18″. full band. MCA, 1966. RCA PC/PCS-1004.

SMALL ORCHESTRA

Spectre. 1938. 7′. str orch, timp. ms. 1939, Tor, CBC, Alexander Chuhaldin.

STRING ORCHESTRA

Interlude in an Artist's Life. 1943. 7'. str orch. MCA, 1961. 1944, Tor, CBC O, Ettore Mazzoleni.

SOLOIST(S) WITH ORCHESTRA

A Tale of Tuamotu. 1939. 23'. bsn, full orch. ms.

Divertimento No 1. 1946. 10'30". fl, str orch. B & H, 1950. RCI-182, Dom S-69005/6. 1946, Vanc, CBC O, Albert Steinberg(cond), Nicholas Fiore(fl).

Divertimento No 2. 1948. 13'30". ob, str orch. B & H, 1951. RCI-86. 1948, Tor, CBC O, Harold Sumberg(cond), Perry Bauman(ob).

Violin Concerto. 1951–4. 27'. vln, orch. CMC. RCI-183. 1955, Tor, CBCSO, Ettore Mazzoleni(cond), Albert Pratz(vln).

Wine of Peace. 1957. 17'. sop, orch. CMC study score, 1957. RCI-182. Text: Pedro Calderon de la Barca, Anon. Trans: Arthur Symons, E Powys Mather. 1958, Tor, CBCSO, Walter Susskind(cond), Mary Simmons(sop).

Divertimento No 3. 1960. 17'30". bsn, str orch. MCA, 1966. CBC BR SM-15. 1959 (2nd mov't only), S'tn, S'tn Mus Fest O, John Weinzweig(cond), June Taylor(bsn); 1961, (complete work), Tor, CBCSO, Geoffrey Waddington(cond), Nicholas Kilburn(bsn).

Divertimento No 5. 1961. 12'30". tpt, trb, winds. MCA, 1969. RCI-292. 1961, Pittsburgh, 'Creative Spirit of Canada Festival', Amer Wind Symph O, Robert Boudreau.

Concerto for Piano and Orchestra. 1966. 18'20". CMC. CBC BR SM-34 & 104. Dec 15, 1966, Tor, CBC, TS, Victor Feldbrill(cond), Paul Helmer(pno).

Concerto for Harp and Chamber Orchestra. 1967. 17'30". MCA, 1969. CBC BR SM-55. Apr 30, 1967, Tor, TRE, Milton Barnes (cond), Judy Loman(hp).

Divertimento No 4. 1968. 13'. cl, str. CMC. CBC BR SM-134. Sept 22, 1968, Tor, CBC-FM, CBC Vanc O, John Avison(cond), R de Kant(cl).

Divertimento No 6. 1972. 13'. alto sax, str. CMC. Aug 21, 1972, Tor, EJB, World Saxophone Congress, John Weinzweig(cond), Paul Brodie(sax).

CHOIR

To the Lands Over Yonder. 1945. 5'. SATB. FH, 1953. 1946, Tor, CBC, Geoffrey Waddington.

Of Time, Rain and the World. 1947. 6'. vc, pno. ms. Text: John Weinzweig. 1948, Tor, Frances James(sop), Earle Moss(pno).

Dance of the Massadah. 1951. 4'. bar, pno. CMC. RCA LSC-3092. Text: Itzchak Lamdan. 1952, Tor, Harry L Felton(bar), Gordon Kushner(pno).

Am Yisrael Chai! (Israel Lives!). 1952. 5'30". SATB, pno. MCA, 1964. Text: Malka Lee; trans: John Weinzweig. 1953, Tor, Gordon Kushner.

INSTRUMENTAL ENSEMBLE

String Quartet No 1. 1937. 15'. CMC. RCI-12 (2nd mov't). 1938, Rochester, Eastman, Kilbourn Qt.

Sonata. 1941. 8'. vln, pno. OUP, 1953. 1942, Tor, Harry Adaskin, Frances Marr.

Fanfare. 1943. 2'15". 3tpt, 3trb, perc (opt). CMC. 1943, TSO, Sir Ernest MacMillan.

Intermissions. 1943. 10'35". fl, ob. South, 1964. 1949, Tor, CBC, Dirk Keetbaas(fl), Harry Freedman(ob).

String Quartet No 2. 1946. 10'. CMC. Col ML-5764/MS-6364. 1947, Tor, Forest Hill Community Centre conc, Parlow Str Qt.

Cello Sonata; 'Israel'. 1949. 15'30". vlc, pno. CMC. RCI-209. 1950, Tor, CBC, Isaac Mamott(vlc), Leo Barkin(pno).

String Quartet No 3. 1962. 29'. CMC. 1963, Tor, EJB, Can Str Qt, Albert Pratz(vln), Bernard Robbins(vln), David Mankovitz (vla), Laszlo Varga(vlc).

Woodwind Quintet. 1964. 11'. CMC. RCA-CC/CCS-1012; RCI-218. 1965, Tor, EJB, Ten Centuries Conc, TWQ, Nicholas Fiore(fl), Perry Bauman(ob), Stanley McCartney(cl), Eugene Rittich(hn), Nicholas Kilburn(bsn).

Clarinet Quartet. 1965. 8'. MCA, 1970. Dom S-69004. 1965, Tor, EJB, Seminar II (John Adaskin Schl Mus Project), Forest Hill Collegiate Inst student qt, supervised by Ben Steinberg.

Trialogue. 1971. 15'. sop, fl, pno. ms. Text: John Weinzweig. July 19, 1971, Tor, EJB, CBC Fest, LAT.

PIANO

Suite for Piano No 1. 1939. 10'. CMC & FH, 1955 (no 1). 1940, Tor, Sophie Cait.

Piano Sonata. 1950. 10'. CMC. CBC BR SM-162. 1951, Tor, CLC Conc, Reginald Godden.

Suite for Piano No 2. 1950. 5'15". Mov'ts 1 & 3, OUP 1965; Mov't 2, OUP, 1956. 1950, Tor, CBC, Neil Van Allen.

INSTRUMENTAL SOLO

Around the Stage in Twenty-five Minutes during which a Variety of Instruments are Struck. 1970. 25'. solo perc. CMC. June 1, 1970, Tor, Town Hall, St Lawrence Centre, CBC Fest, William Cahn.

ORGAN

Improvisation on an Indian Tune. 1942. 5'. ms. 1942, NY.

BIBLIOGRAPHY

See B-B; Aum; B58,65,71; Bec56,57,58,70; Bt; C63,66,69,72; CrC(II); D165; Esc; Ip; K; MGG; Mm; T; Wa.

'Good Reviews for a Canadian Composer', *Maclean's*. Vol. LXXVI, Mar. 1963 (65).

Graham, June. 'Exploring Silence at Popocatepetl', *CBC Times*. June 7–13, 1969 (10–11).

'John Weinzweig' (CBC documentary tape in honour of John Weinzweig's 60th Birthday). Nov. 1973.

'John Weinzweig – a portrait', *Mu*. No. 9, Mar. 1968 (8–9).

Kasemets, Udo. 'John Weinzweig', *CMJ*. Vol. IV, no. 4, Summer 1960 (4–18).

Littler, William. 'John Weinzweig: the CBC Birthday Concert', *CanCo*. No. 78, Mar. 1973 (24–5).

'Professor John Weinzweig: Important Musical Influence', *CanCo*. No. 14, Jan. 1967 (4–5, 40–1, 44–5).

Seay, Albert. 'Review of Concerto for Harp and Chamber Orchestra', *Notes*. Vol. XXVI, no. 3, Mar. 1970 (624).

Such, Peter. *Soundprints*. Toronto: Clarke, Irwin Ltd, 1972 (2–29).

'Tributes on Weinzweig's 60th Birthday', *CMB*. Spring-Summer 1973 (19–37).

Webb, Douglas John. *Serial Techniques in John Jacob Weinzweig's five Divertimentos and three Concertos*. Unpublished Ph.D. dissertation, University of Rochester, 1973.

'Weinzweig in Mexico', *CanCo*. No. 42, Sept. 1969 (30–2).

'Weinzweig's "Harp Concerto" Wins Critical Praise', *CanCo*. June 1967 (12–13).

Wilson, M. 'Music Review', *Canadian Forum*. Vol. XXXI, July 1951 (88).

LITERARY WORKS

ARTICLES

'A Composer looks at the teaching of Musical Theory', *Conservatory Bulletin*. Nov. 1949.

'The New Music', *Canadian Review of Music and Art*. Vol. V, no. 5, June 1942 (5–6, 16).

'Writings of John Weinzweig' (Richard Henninger, ed.), *CMB*. Spring-Summer 1973 (39–77).

WEISGARBER, ELLIOT (b. Pittsfield, Mass., 5 Dec. 1919). He studied with Bernard Rogers and Howard Hanson (composition) and Rufus M. Arey (clarinet) at the Eastman School of Music, University of Rochester, receiving his Bachelor (1942) and Master of Music (1943) degrees. He also studied composition with Nadia Boulanger (1952–3) in Paris and with Halsey Stevens (1958–9) in Los Angeles. The Canada Council awarded him two short-term grants (1966, 1967) and a Senior Fellowship (1968–9) to study in Japan with Tanaka Yuhdoh (shakuhachi master of the Kinko-ryuh, Kobe); Takafuji Emoh, at the Otana University in Kyoto); Tsuda Michiko (koto and shamisen genres, Kyoto); and Hayakawa Ikutada (Satsuma biwa, Japanese culture and aesthetics, Saga-Kyoto). He was associate professor of music at the Women's College of the University of North Carolina (1944–58), guest lecturer in composition at the University of California at Los Angeles (1958–9), and is professor of composition and Asian music at the University of British Columbia (1960–).

Weisgarber has received commissions from the CBC (scores for the radio series 'From the Mountains to the Sea', 1967; *Illahee Chanties* for the centennial of British Columbia), from Thor Johnson for the Chicago Little Symphony (*Sinfonia Pastorale*, 1960), the Philharmonic Music Club of Vancouver (*Sonata for Flute, Viola and Piano*, 1963) ,the First World Shakespeare Congress (*Of Love and Time*, 1971), Tsuda Michiko Jiuta-kai of Kyoto (*Yamato-no-haru, Sekisai, Omi Hakkei* and *Rokudan Henka-no-shirabe*, 1971), and from the Vancouver Chamber Choir (*Night*, an ode for lyric baritone, mixed voices and string quartet on the poem by Robinson Jeffers).

He is a member of the Canadian Folk Music Society, the Society for Ethnomusicology, and CAPAC.

MUSICAL WORKS

STAGE, RADIO, TELEVISION

The Good Woman of Sechuan (incidental music), 1960.

Trailing to Nazko (from CBC TV series 'This Land of Ours').

INSTRUMENTAL

7 works for chamber ens: *Sonata for Flute, Clarinet and Piano* (1953) Cor Editions; *Divertimento for Clarinet, Violin and Viola* (1956) Cor Editions; *Sonata for Viola and Piano* (1956); *Divertimento for Horn, Viola and Piano* (1959) Cor Editions; *Sonata for Flute and Piano* (1963); *Suite for Viola and Piano* (1964); *Sonata for Unaccompanied Violoncello* (1965).

3 works for orch: *Sinfonia Pastorale* (1961) small orch; *Kyoto Landscapes: Lyrical Evocations for Orchestra* (1970, rev 1972); *Illahee Chanties* (1971) chamb orch.

Sinfonia Concertante. 1962. ob, 2hn, str.

4 works for Japanese instr: *Henka-no-shirabe ('Changes')* (1965) shakuhachi, elec tape; *Yamoto-no-haru* (1971) kokyu, shamisen, koto; *Omi Hakkei* (1971) shakuhachi, shamisen, koto; *Rokudan Henko-no-shirabe* (1971) 2koto, 2shamisen.

2 works for piano: *Four Pieces in the Japanese Spirit* (1965) 2pno; *A Japanese Miscellany* (nine pieces for piano) (1969).

CHORAL

Num Mortuis Resurgent? (cantata). 1963. SATB. Text: Fr Dunstan Massey.

Night. 1973. bar, SATB, str qt. Text: Robinson Jeffers.

VOCAL

In Country Sleep. 1963. ten, chamb orch. Text: Dylan Thomas.

3 works to Japanese texts: *Fuyu-no-uta* (1969) sop, shamisen, shakuhachi, koto; *Of Love and Time* (1971) sop, fl, ob, str trio, hpschd Text: Shakespeare, trans by Tsubouchi Shoyo; *Sekisai* (1971) sop, shamisen, koto.

LITERARY WORKS

ARTICLES

'The Honkyoku of the Kinko-Ryu: Some Principles of its Organization', *Journal of the Society of Ethnomusicology*. Vol. XII, no. 3, Sept. 1968 (313–44).

'Mayonnaise on the Sashimi: Portrait of a Cultural Dilemma', *CanCo*. No. 44, Nov. 1969 (15, 17).

WHITEHEAD, ALFRED (b. Peterborough, England, 20 July 1887; d. 1 Apr. 1974). In England he studied organ with Haydn Keeton in Peterborough and Eaglefield Hull in Huddersfield, receiving an ARCO diploma in 1910. Immigrating to Canada in 1912, he obtained his FCCO diploma (1913), his Bachelor of Music degree from the University of Toronto (1916), his Doctor of Music degree from McGill University (1922), and his FRCO diploma (1924), receiving the Lafontaine prize for first place in the FRCO examinations. He also studied painting in Montreal from 1922 to 1947. He began his career as organist and choirmaster of Trinity Congregational Church in Peterborough, England (1905–12), and continued in Canada as organist of St Andrew's Presbyterian Church in Truro, N.S. (1912–13). From 1913 to 1915 he was a teacher and assistant director of the Mount Allison Conservatory in Sackville, N.B. He moved to Quebec, where he was organist at the Anglican Church in Sherbrooke (1915–22) and at Christ Church Cathedral (1922–47) in Montreal, where he founded and conducted the Cathedral Singers (1931–9). He was also instructor in organ and theory at the McGill Conservatory (1922–30). In 1947 he returned to Mount Allison Conservatory as dean and professor of organ and theory, becoming dean emeritus on his retirement in 1953. From 1953 to 1966 he was organist at Trinity St Stephen Church in Amherst, N.S.

Whitehead's compositions are mainly for choir and organ and follow in the same tradition as Healey WILLAN, excelling in rich tonal harmonies and intricate contrapuntal lines. He received many honours, including the Nova Scotia Society of Artists award (1955) and honorary Doctor of Laws degrees from Mount Allison (1958) and Queen's (1970) universities. He was a member of the Nova Scotia Society of Artists and of CAPAC.

MUSICAL WORKS

CHOIR

Bell Carol. Boston, 1928. SATB.

Bird Carol. Boston, 1928. SSATTBB.

Jesu, the Very Thought of Thee. 1930; Gray, 1931. SATB.
All Mankind Voices Raised. Boston, 1931.
All My Heart. Boston, 1931.
Jesu, Gentlest Saviour. Fischer, 1931. SATB.
When Caesar Augustus. Fischer, 1931. SATB.
Angels Holy. Boston, 1932.
Christ the Lord Is Risen. Gray, 1932. SATB, org.
Earth Today Rejoices. Boston, 1932. SATB.
The Echo Carol. Novl, 1932.
Good Christian Men Rejoice. 1932; Fischer, 1933. SATB.
Golden Grain, Harvest Bringing. Boston, 1932. SATB.
Into This World, This Day Did Come. Boston, 1932.
King of Heaven. 1932; Ditson, 1932. SSA, SSATTBB.
Love Unknown. 1932; Stainer & Bell, 1932. SATB.
Most Glorious Lord of Life. Gray, 1932. SATB, SATB.
Soldiers of Christ Arise. Boston, 1932. SATB, org.
When Morning Gilds the Sky. GVT, 1932. SATB, org.
Alleluia! Christ Is Risen. Boston, 1933. SATB.
Awake! The Morn Is Here. 1933; Gray, 1935. SATB, org.
Come, Sweet Guest. Boston, 1933. sop (ten), SATB, org.
Come Ye Faithful, Raise the Strain. Gray, 1933. SATB.
Eighteen Faux Bourdons and Descants. Fischer, 1933. SATB.
Lord of Our Life. Schmidt, 1933. anthem.
The Magi Journey Far. Novl, 1933.
Magnificat and Nunc Dimittis. Fischer, 1933. SATB, SATB, org.
Now Christmas Day Is Come. Fischer, 1933. SATB, org.
O Lord Support Us. Fischer, 1933. SSATB.
O Merciful God. Fischer, 1933. SATB.
Ye Choirs of New Jerusalem. Schmidt, 1933. SATB, org.
Almighty God, Whose Glory. Schmidt, 1934. SATB.
Grant Us Grace, Lord. Curwen, 1934. SSATB.
Hast Thou Not Known?. Curwen, 1934. SATB, org.
In Thee Is Gladness. Boston, 1934. SATB.
Light's Abode, Celestial Salem. Boston, 1934.
The Lord Is My Shepherd. 1934; Fischer, 1935. SSATB.
Now that the Sun Hath Veiled His Light. Boston, 1934.
O Light, Beyond our utmost light. Boston, 1934. SATB, org.
Watchman, from the height beholding. Boston, 1934. sop, bar, SATB, org.
The Chariots of the Lord Are Strong. Schmidt, 1935.
Early One Morning. Schmidt, 1935. SSA, pno.
Evening Hymn. Boston, 1932; 1935. SATB (SSA).
Mary's Farewell. Novl, 1935.
May the Strength of God. Boston, 1935. SATB, org.
The Seven Joys of Mary. Schmidt, 1935. sop, SATB.
Whither Shepherd, Haste Ye Now. Schmidt, 1935.
Benedicite, omnia opera. Gray, 1936. SATB, org.
O Mighty Soul of England. Curwen, 1936. SATB, org (pno).
At the Mid-Hour of Night. West, 1937.
The Christ-Child Smiles. West, 1937.
Come In, Dear Angels. West, 1937.
Dear Nightingale. West, 1937.
Farewell to Sliev Morna. West, 1937.
If Ye then Be Risen with Christ. Gray, 1937. sop, bar, SATB, org.
Jesus Bread of Life. West, 1937.
Ponder My Works, O Lord. Curwen, 1937. solo, SATB, org.
Praise Him, Ye that Fear Him. Gray, 1937. sop, alto, ten, bs, SATB, org.
O Blest Are They that Fear the Lord. West, 1937.
Saviour, Breathe an Evening Blessing. West, 1937.
Carol of the Good Thief. West, 1938.
Down in Demerary. West, 1938.
God Save the King (arr). West, 1938.
I Beheld a Great Multitude. Curwen, 1938. ten, SATB, org.
King Arthur. West, 1938.
Leezie Lindsay. West, 1938.
O Gay Is the Day We Sing. West, 1938.
O Little Christ Sweet. West, 1938.
Benedictus es, Domine. Galaxy, 1939.
As Bends the White Birch. Galaxy, 1940.
Early One Morning. Schmidt, 1940.

women's vcs (mixed vcs).
Have You Seen a Lady. Novl, 1940.
I Have Longed for Thy Saving Health (arr, Byrd). Gray, 1940. SATB.
Make Us to Love Thee, O Lord. Schmidt, 1940.
Now God Be with Us. Galaxy, 1940.
O Hearken Thou, O Lord. Galaxy, 1940.
Three Captains. Galaxy, 1940.
Through a Long Cloister. Galaxy, 1940.
The Hawthorne Tree. Galaxy, 1941.
I Wish I Were Where Helen Lies. Galaxy, 1941.
Of These I Sing. OUP, 1941. SATB.
Walking at Night. Galaxy, 1941.
Winter's End. Galaxy, 1941.
Gate of Life Stands Wide. Boston, 1943. SATB, org.
Nanette. Schmidt, 1943.
O Fly Little Swallow. Schmidt, 1943.
Eternal Ruler of the Ceaseless Round. Boston, 1944. SATB, org.
Sunday Morning in Norway. Novl ,1947.
Bread of the World. Ditson, 1948. SATB.
The Carol of the Messenger. Galaxy, 1950.
O Gladsome Light. Schmidt, 1950.
Challenge to Free Men. Galaxy, 1951.
Circus Parade. Schmidt, 1951. SAB (SA).
House to Let. FH, 1964. unis.
Come Holy Ghost In Love. FH, 1967. SATB, org.
Let All the World in Every Corner Sing. FH, 1967. SATB.
God of Mercy, God of Grace. FH, 1970. SATB, org.

Also arrangements of some
15 folk songs, Canadian and English (mostly Fischer, Boston).
14 carols, Christmas and Easter (mostly Ditson, Fischer).
6 anthems (Fischer, Curwen, Schmidt).

ORGAN

Christmas Slumber Song. Schmidt, 1932.
Prelude on 'Winchester Old' (Christmas Pastorale). Gray, 1937.
Prelude on a Theme by Orlando Gibbons (song). Gray, 1940.
The Westminster Suite (arr). OUP.

BIBLIOGRAPHY

See B-B; C63,66,69,72; CrC(I); K; Wa; Ww 62,69,72.
'Alfred Whitehead', *Atlantic Advocate*. Vol. LIV, July 1964 (88).
George, Graham. 'Alfred Whitehead: Doctor of Music', *Music: AGO–RCCO Magazine*. 1971 (60–6).
McRae, C. F. 'Alfred Whitehead', *CMJ*. Vol. v, no. 3, Spring 1961 (14–20).

WILLAN, HEALEY (b. Balham, England, 12 Oct. 1880; d. Toronto, Ont., 16 Feb. 1968). His early education was undertaken privately. At the age of eight he was enrolled in St Saviour's Choir School at Eastbourne, remaining there until 1895. After several positions as church organist in the London area (he received his FRCO in 1899), he was appointed to St John the Baptist, Holland Road. The years at this church saw his first published compositions – songs, partsongs, organ and church music. Several large-scale orchestral and choral works, many of them unfinished, also date from this period.

Willan's early style shows him to have been thoroughly immersed in the music of the late nineteenth century and he displayed great technical fluency. His admitted idols were Brahms and Wagner, while in his church music it is hard not to see the influence of Parry and Stanford. Typical of this period are two organ compositions: the *Prelude and Fugue in C minor* (1908) and its smaller companion, the *Prelude and Fugue in B minor* (1909). Showing clear signs of the late-Victorian church-music tradition are such works as the anthem *I looked, and behold, a white cloud* (1908) and a setting of the *Magnificat and Nunc Dimittis in B flat* (1906). His songs, some of which are still available in *Healey Willan Song Albums* (two volumes pub. 1925 and 1926) and *Ten Songs* (reissued in 1967), demonstrate a sure touch for vocal melody coupled with richly harmonic accompaniments. He wrote over a hundred songs and it is a pity that they are not better known.

In 1913 Willan moved to Canada to take up the position of head of the theory department of the Toronto Conservatory of Music; he was also appointed organist and choirmaster at St Paul's Church. In the next year he joined the staff of the University of Toronto. From 1919 until 1925 he was musical director of the Hart House Theatre, for which he composed fifteen sets of incidental music, the best known of which is *The Chester Mysteries* (1919). His most celebrated composition from this period is the *Introduction, Passacaglia and Fugue* of 1916. Cast in a heroic mould, it is a technically demanding work that shows in its development a fine sense of colour and spacing, as well as a fertile imagination. It represents the high point of Willan's earlier style in writing. Almost as impressive, though in a very different style, is the lengthy unaccompanied choral work *An Apostrophe to the heavenly hosts* (1921). Written for the Toronto Mendelssohn Choir, it shows interesting contrasts of deliberate simplicity, with an almost Russian opulence in many of its broader and more dignified passages.

Willan's appointment as precentor of the Church of St Mary Magdalene in 1921 contributed more than anything else to a severe pruning of this exuberance, at least in his smaller sacred works. He established there a High Church tradition, based musically on the use of Renaissance masses and motets together with Plainsong, which he adapted to the vernacular. To this he added works of his own in a compatible style. His knowledge and love of Plainsong dates from his earlier years in London when he had been a friend and associate of Francis Burgess, the founder of the Gregorian Association. The modality, rhythmic freedom (based mainly on verbal accentuation), and flowing melismas of Plainsong evoked a sympathetic response from Willan in his shorter liturgical works. Typical of this approach are the *Six Motets* of 1924, the eleven *Liturgical Motets* (1928 to 1937), fourteen settings of the *Missa Brevis* (1928 to 1963), and various sets of Evening canticles (Plainsong with fauxbourdons) that he wrote from 1928 onwards. It is likely that within these works is to be found Willan's most lasting contribution to church music. They display a terse but unhurried aptness and an idiomatic expression that is easily recognizable as Willan's. Both in the liturgy and in recital they make an instant and lasting impression.

Willan stayed at St Mary Magdalene's until his death and he naturally continued to write music for that church's use. At the same time, however, he became a 'public' composer. A variety of positions – he was vice-principal of the Conservatory between 1920 and 1936, professor at the University from 1936 until 1950, and University Organist from 1932 until 1964 – and his growing reputation as a composer attracted commissions and requests for choral and orchestral works. In these compositions he stayed closer to his earlier style. Such works as the *Te Deum in B flat* (1937) and the *Coronation Suite* of 1953 show the older, more obvious gift for melody clothed in spacious and warm harmonic dress, a style he deliberately avoided in the shorter liturgical works. Some large-scale anthems – such as *Sing we triumphant songs* (1951), *O Lord, our Governour*, written for the Coronation of Queen Elizabeth II in 1953, and *O sing unto the Lord* (1956) – show a similar and equally effective use of the ceremonial vein. *Gloria Deo per immensa saecula* (1950) is an exceptional work, both in its style, which is almost academic by comparison – it takes the form of a prelude and fugue – and in its stirring effectiveness.

A large number of smaller works, written in a more simple and direct vein, fall between the broad 'occasional' style and the mysticism of the St Mary Magdalene pieces. Prominent among these are sets of motets and anthems for the use of the Lutheran Church in the U.S.A., a large number of hymn-anthems and such things as collections of carols, both original and arranged, hymn-tunes and fauxbourdons, and miscellaneous liturgical works. Willan also wrote several pieces for children's choirs.

There is an interesting break in his output for the organ between 1916 and 1950. The style of the later works is considerably more dependent on contrapuntal techniques. The fugue of the *Passacaglia and Fugue No. 2 in E minor* (1959) is perhaps his finest essay in this form and shows a much greater command than any of the earlier fugues; the Passacaglia, however, lacks the teeming ideas and vitality and the sheer technique of the earlier one. Two sets of *Six Chorale Preludes* (1950), *Five Preludes on Plainchant Melodies* (1951), and three sets of *Ten Hymn Preludes* (1956) provide very useful music for the church organist, while *A Fugal Trilogy* (1958) and *Andante, Fugue and Chorale* (1965) seem unjustly neglected by recitalists.

An earlier interest in dramatic music was revitalized in the 1940s and commissions from the CBC led to such works as the radio opera *Transit through fire* (1942), the pageant *Brébeuf* (1943), and the opera *Deirdre* composed between 1943 and 1945. *Deirdre* is Willan's most ambitious undertaking. It was later revised and adapted for stage use and has had two successful productions in this form, by the Opera School of the University of Toronto in 1965 and by the Canadian Opera Company (its first production of a Canadian opera) in 1966. It is possibly a little too oppressed with Celtic gloom and musically too close to previous operatic composers to be a widely popular work, but it has made a strong appeal to the audiences that have heard it and it marks a milestone in the history of Canadian music.

Again a ripe romanticism remains as the hallmark of Willan's later orchestral works. Indeed, it is very difficult to date his orchestral compositions on the basis of style alone: passages in later works read very similarly to some in his earlier unfinished compositions. For the first movement of his *Symphony No. 1 in D minor* (1937, rev. 1948) is worked in this vein and is remarkable for a suave melodic touch, an easy harmonic movement, and steady development of ideas. The *Concerto in C minor for Piano and Orchestra* (1944) gives full opportunity for the soloist to show technical prowess while displaying the same virtues as the *Symphony* in its overall design. It is a work well worth revival.

It is disappointing that Willan never completed any of the string quartets that exist in fragmentary states among his manuscripts, although one movement did appear as *Poem for String Orchestra*. Two violin sonatas and a *Trio in B minor* (part of the score of the first movement unfortunately lost) make up the total of his chamber music, apart from some smaller pieces. A work for two pianists, *Variations and Epilogue on an original theme* (1915), is his only major piano composition. For the rest his piano music may be classified as for student use.

The quality and sheer quantity of Willan's compositions have given him a commanding place in the history of Canadian music. Of equal importance is his influence on church music, particularly in Canada and the U.S.A. It has been widespread in all types of churches and has undoubtedly helped to raise standards in many areas. The model for an Anglo-Catholic service that he perfected at the Church of St Mary Magdalene, while of course drawn by him from earlier sources and from his own experience, has often been an inspiration to others. His ideals of what was good and what was bad in church music, frequently and cogently expressed, have helped to banish some of the more meretricious music from some services. One must salute his championship of Plainsong in the vernacular, which bore public fruit in the *Canadian Psalter* (*Plainsong Edition*) (1963) and has encouraged a more extensive use of that unassuming form of church music. Willan introduced much Renaissance music to Canadian church choirs, and while this music would eventually have been heard in any case, his early example must be viewed as the work of a pioneer. Finally his performances with his choirs, both in and out of church, have been greatly admired, by ordinary listener and musician alike, for their careful attention to purity of tone, delicate shaping of phrases, and constant striving for the full meaning of the text.

Willan's work as a kindly guide to his many students encouraged many composers and performers of the next generation. The greatest gift he gave them was a sense of beauty in sound achieved by sure craftsmanship.

In 1967 Willan was made a Companion of the Order of Canada, the first musician to receive that honour. He was an honorary member of the Canadian League of Composers and an affiliate of BMI Canada.

GILES BRYANT

SUMMARY LIST OF WORKS

DRAMATIC

The Beggar's Opera ('Mr Gay's The Beggar's Opera with new symphonies and accompaniments arranged from the second edition, 1728'). 1927. vc, fl, cl, str. FH, 1928.

The Order of Good Cheer. 1928.

4 other ballad operas (2 lost).

Hymn for Those in the Air (incidental music). 1942. narr, small orch. Text: Duncan Campbell Scott.

Transit through Fire (opera). 1942. 6 soli, SATB, orch. Text: John Coulter.

Brébeuf (cantata). 1943 (rev 1947). 2narr, SATB, orch. Text: E J Pratt.
Deirdre (opera). 1945 (rev 1962, 1965). 9 vcs, SATB, orch. Text: John Coulter.
15 sets of incidental music for Hart House Theatre.
4 other sets of incidental music.

CHOIR WITH ORCHESTRA

Coronation Suite. 1952. SSATB, orch. Ber, 1953. Text: John Milton, James Edward Ward, scriptures. RCA LSC 3054, LSC 3043, CBC IS-118.
9 large works with chorus and orch.

ORCHESTRA AND BAND MUSIC

Symphony No 1 in D Minor. 1936. Ber. CBC PAT-41791.
Symphony No 2 in C Minor. 1941 (rev 1948). Ber. CBC BR SM-133.
Pianoforte Concerto. 1944 (rev 1949). Ber, 1960. RCA DM 1229.
Royce Hall Suite for concert band. 1949. Associated Music Publishers, 1952.
Overture to an Unwritten Comedy. 1951.
Three Fanfares. 1959. 4tpt, 3trb, timp.
5 *Marches*.
3 early works.

CHOIR (SACRED)

An Apostrophe to the Heavenly Hosts. 1921. SATB, SATB, Mystic chorus I SATB, II AAT Composer's Publication Society, 1921. FH, 1936, rev 1952. RCA LSC 3054, LSC 3043.
The Mystery of Bethlehem (cantata). Gray, c1923, c1951.
Six Motets. 1924. Gray, 1924. CMR 712–717.
Gloria Deo per immensa saecula. 1950. West, 1952. Cap ST 6248.
The Story of Bethlehem. 1955. Concord, 1955.
13 Introits for the Church Year. West, 1950; Mills Music, 1960.
Introits, Graduals and Responsories (Lutheran use). Concord, 1967.
We Praise Thee (junior choir) Vols 1 and 2. Concord, 1953 (Vol 1), 1962 (Vol. 2).
Canadian Psalter (Plainsong Edition) (ed by Willan). The Anglican Church of Canada, 1963.
Red Carol Book (40 carols ed by Willan). FH, 1930.
Carols for the Seasons (arr by Willan). Concord, 1959.
14 settings of the Missa Brevis. 1928 to 1963. various pubs.
10 settings of the Communion Service.
35 fauxbourdon settings of Canticles.
15 full settings of Canticles.
Liturgical Motets (11). 1928–37. OUP and C Fischer, 1928–37.
20 miscellaneous motets.
39 anthems.
31 hymn-anthems.
29 original carols.
31 hymn tunes.
29 fauxbourdons to hymn tunes.
Numerous arrangements of carols and hymn tunes.
Numerous Plainsong adaptations.

CHOIR (SECULAR)

15 partsongs.
14 folk-song arrangements.
Miscellaneous works.

SONGS

Over 100 original songs.
Numerous folk-song arrangements.

INSTRUMENTAL ENSEMBLE

Trio in B Minor. 1907. vln, vlc, pno.
2 *Violin Sonatas*.

ORGAN

Two Preludes and Fugues. 1908, 1909. Novl, 1909.
Introduction, Passacaglia and Fugue. 1916. G Schirm, 1919. Odeon CLP 1752, CSD 1550.
Rondino Elegy and Chaconne. 1956. Novl, 1957.
Fugal Trilogy. 1958. OUP, 1959. Col ML 6198, MS 6798.
Five Pieces for Organ. 1958. Ber, 1959. SR 101568.
Passacaglia and Fugue No 2 in E Minor. c1959. Peters, 1959. Col ML 6198, MS 6798.
Andante Fugue and Chorale. Peters, 1965.
97 *Choral Preludes*.
Numerous arrangements.

SUMMARY BIBLIOGRAPHY

See B-B; Aum; B65,71; Bec56,57,58,70; Bt; C63,66,69,72; CrC(II); D157,165; Esc; Gmu; Ip; K; Mce; MGG; Smh; Wa.
Beckwith, John. 'Healey Willan', *Canadian Forum*. Vol. LII, Dec. 1972 (32–4).
Bryant, Giles. *Healey Willan Catalogue*. Ottawa: National Library of Canada, 1972 (contains complete list of works and bibliography).
Bryant, Giles. 'Condensed List of Compositions'. *Mu*. Vol. IX, Mar. 1968.

Dobbs, Kildare. 'Canada's impish dean of composers'. *Star weekly magazine.* Dec. 22, 1962 (1–2, 5–6).
Ellinwood, Leonard W. *The history of American church music.* New York: Moorhouse-Gorham, 1953 (passim).
Giles, W. B. 'The organ music of Healey Willan', *Journal of church music.* Vol. 7, Sept. 1965 (12–14).
McCready, Louise G. *Famous musicians: MacMillan, Johnson, Pelletier, Willan.* Toronto: Clarke, Irwin Ltd, 1957 (103–34).
Marwick, William E. *The sacred choral music of Healey Willan.* Unpublished Ph.D. Thesis, Michigan State University, 1970.
Osborne, Stanley L. *The strain of praise.* Toronto: Ryerson, 1957 (passim).
Palk, Helen. *The book of Canadian achievement.* Toronto: Dent, 1951 (206–11).
Peaker, Charles. 'Works for organ by Healey Willan (review of 4 published works)', *CMJ.* Vol. 4, Winter 1960 (60–3).
Ridout, Godfrey. 'Healey Willan', *CMJ.* Vol. 3, Spring 1959 (4–14).
Telschow, Frederick H. *The sacred music of Healey Willan.* Unpublished Ph.D. Thesis, Eastman School of Music, University of Rochester, 1969.
Wagner, Jacob David. *Healey Willan, his life and organ literature.* Unpublished Ph.D. Thesis, Union Theological Seminary, New York, 1957.
Wyton, Alec. 'Healey Willan's musical London (interview)', *Music: AGO–RCCO Magazine.* Vol. 2, Jan. 1968 (32–3, 52–3).
Wyton, Alec. 'Reminiscences: Healey Willan in a conversation with Alec Wyton', *Music: the A.G.O. magazine.* Vol. 1, Dec. 1967 (24–7).

LITERARY WORKS

ARTICLES

'Canadian theme in a Queen's opera', *Saturday night.* Vol. 64, Dec. 18, 1948 (2).
'Carolling at Christmas', *Anglican.* Vol. 6, no. 11, Dec. 1963 (1).
'Church music in Canada'. London, Royal College of Organists. *Calendar*, 1936–7.
'Church music or music of the church'. Gregorian Association (Canada). 9th Annual Festival. *Order of service.* Toronto, 1959 (19).
'In quires and places where they sing', *Huron church news.* Vol. 7, Apr. 1, 1956 (1, 9).
'[Letters to the editor] Honour to whom honour is due', *Diapason.* Vol. 55, May 1964 (26).
'[Messages from Past Presidents] A message from Healey Willan to the C.C.O.', *Musical Canada.* Vol. 11, Oct. 1930 (23).
'On hymn playing', *Conservatory quarterly review.* Vol. 8, Spring 1926 (91).
'[On hymn tunes]', *Hamilton Spectator*, Sept. 8, 1956 (15).
'Organ playing in its proper relation to music in the church', *Diapason.* Vol. 29, Oct. 1937 (22–3).
'Plainsong, the earliest song of the church', *Canadian churchman.* Vol. 90, July-Aug. 1963 (15).
'Sir Ernest at 70', *Diapason.* Vol. 54, Nov. 1963 (6).
'Tribute to Farnam [text of an address]', *Diapason.* Vol. 23, Dec. 1, 1931 (14).
'The Tudor church music series, a review', *Music bulletin* (Oxford University Press, Toronto branch). No. 2, Feb. 28, 1941 (7–8).
'The use of plainsong in church worship', *Jubilate Deo.* Vol. 1, no. 6, Sept.-Oct. 1957 (94–5).
'A well-known and dear friend writes a revealing and inspiring letter [an autobiographical note]', *Flammerion newsletter.* Vol. 8, Jan. 1966 (1–2).
'What's wrong with church music in Canada', *Cap and gown.* 1959 (112–14).
'William Byrd (1543-1623): choral work', *Canadian review of music and art.* Vol. 2, Aug.-Sept. 1943 (8–9).

WILSON, CHARLES M. (b. Toronto, Ont., 8 May 1931). At the age of six he began piano lessons with Wilfred Powell and later, as a student at Lawrence Park Collegiate, Toronto, played piano and clarinet in the school orchestra, directed by Harvey Perrin. It was during this period that Wilson made his earliest attempts at musical composition. Perrin encouraged him to take instruction in theory and composition with Godfrey RIDOUT at the Royal Conservatory of Music, Toronto.

Although he had seriously considered architecture as a career, Wilson decided to enrol in the Bachelor of Music course at the University of Toronto. Meanwhile he continued to study privately with Ridout and his compositions began to attract attention. During the summers of 1950 and 1951 he went to the Berkshire Music School at Tanglewood, Mass., for study in composition with Lukas Foss the first year and with Carlos Chavez the next. He also studied conducting with Leonard Bernstein.

Wilson graduated with the Bachelor of Music degree in 1952 and immediately entered into study for a doctorate at the University of Toronto. A year later he passed all the required examinations with first class honours, an unusual achievement, and began work on the *Symphony in A* (1954) to fulfil the requirements for the degree. He spent the next year at the University of Saskatchewan in Saskatoon.

In 1954 he returned to Ontario, received the Doctor of Music degree, married, and took a post as organist-choirmaster at Chalmers United Church in Guelph, where he has continued to live, holding various positions as choir director and as a secondary-school music-teacher. He organized the Guelph Light Opera and Oratorio Choir with which he has presented annual productions of Broadway shows or operettas as well as choral concerts of more serious content. Since 1962 he has also been the conductor of the well-established Bach-Elgar Choir in Hamilton, driving the forty miles from Guelph for rehearsals and concerts. All these activities severely limited time for composition, creative work being relegated largely to the summer months at his cottage at Paudash Lake near Bancroft.

Wilson wrote very little music in the years following the *String Quartet No. 1* (1950) and the *Symphony in A*. Only after 1960, beginning with the *Sonata da chiesa* (1960), did a steady output of compositions begin. There was a marked increase in Wilson's creative activity as the 1960s progressed. This reached impressive proportions in the early 1970s: in 1973 no less than seven first performances were given, of which five were new compositions and one a major opera (*Heloïse and Abelard*). Electronic music, new spatial concepts, chance music, textural writing, multi-media presentation represented new techniques, new ways of thinking about music, and these have influenced the composer's style in recent works. His music has become increasingly diversified in its techniques and his expressive capacity has been much enriched. Never at home with atonality, Wilson has nevertheless made use of Schoenbergian techniques in the manipulation of musical material. The harmonic movement from dissonance to consonance (though the consonance may be another less-pungent dissonance) is basic to his sense of musical structure. The building up of tone clusters and their dissipation is a characteristic of his style.

Changes of metre are a feature of Wilson's scores but, like other aspects of his music, rhythm is derived from traditional usages. The music is lyrical in essence, with harmony playing a supporting role. Characteristic of the composer is a predilection for the use of cross-relation between major and minor modes. The melodic element is given a greater emotional charge by leaps of an octave, so that what is fundamentally a melodic movement by step takes on an exciting angularity. Bartokian is the chromatic alteration of notes in adjacent melodic modules that hover within the same tonal range. In spite of the dissonant effect, melodic lines within a thick contrapuntal texture are often quite simple in themselves. These elements – melody and harmony – are given a rich orchestral garb. Although he may call for unusual effects, Wilson's orchestration, in general, is quite within the bounds of historical practice. Scoring for the full orchestra from the start of work on a new composition, he possesses a thorough knowledge of the capabilities of the various instruments.

Based on medieval Latin lyrics, the *Three Madrigals* are evidence of Wilson's affinity for early polyphony. The second is based on a text by Pierre Abelard, the religious philosopher on whose life his opera is based. In the first of the *Madrigals,* Wilson deploys his skill in contrapuntal technique by writing a 4-in-2 canon. Soprano and alto are in canon at the fourth, while tenor and bass are in canon at the third. The tenor-bass subject is the inversion of the soprano-alto subject with slight modification.

The *Song Cycle* (1962) for soprano and piano is a series of five portraits of a girl growing through womanhood to old age. Tender lyricism and impressionistic harmony touched with dissonance lend an appealing character to the songs. Written in 1963, the *String Trio* makes use of the four-movement classical form. The third movement, however, is a waltz, and the second half of the concluding movement is a note-for-note retrograde version of the first half.

Angels of the Earth (1967), composed for Canada's Centennial, was Wilson's first large-scale work since the *Symphony* of 1954. This oratorio, lasting some two and a half hours, is a setting of a poem by the Canadian writer Wilson MacDonald. The text concerns a personal search for truth and beauty in the modern world. Wilson employs a large orchestra, choir, soprano and baritone soloists, and two narrators, one female and the other male. Music for each of the sixteen sections chosen by Wilson is evolved from one or two motifs that are treated in symphonic fashion. Although containing much fine music – the choral writing is excellent – *Angels of the Earth* is flawed by an over-long text that allows too little opportunity for expansion into purely musical expression.

The founding of the Guelph Spring Festival in 1968 brought new professional opportunities to Wilson, both as conductor and as composer, and he began to attract the attention of a larger audience. For its first season in 1968 the Festival commissioned *En Guise d'Orphée* for baritone and sixteen solo strings. His *String Quartet No. 2* (1968), played during the 1970 season, combines a somewhat free use of twelve-tone technique with aleatoric elements in places where two, three, or all four parts proceed independently. The composer employed textural writing extensively in *En Guise d'Orphée,* textural writing and aleatoric elements having become features of Wilson's compositional style.

The *Concerto 5 x 4 x 3* for string quintet, woodwind quartet, and brass trio (1970) allows freedom for the performers to decide the order of proceedings. Wilson first made a chart of the work with verbal instructions and then proceeded to its composition. It can be played by any one, two, or all three groups. The *Sinfonia* (1972) is a work for double chamber orchestra, each with its own harmonic and rhythmic material as well as tempo indications. They come together only in the closing section of the work.

Three operas were completed by him for performance in 1973. *The Selfish Giant,* an opera for children, is a setting of Oscar Wilde's story. *The Summoning of Everyman* is a church opera with a libretto adapted from the fourteenth-century morality play. Also based on a medieval topic is the opera *Heloïse and Abelard,* commissioned by the Canadian Opera Company for performance during its twenty-fifth season in the autumn of 1973. The libretto, written by Eugene Benson in close collaboration with the composer, is a biographical treatment of the lives of the two religious scholars and their tortured love for each other. Such elements as Latin religious ceremony, a troubador's song with medieval cadences, religious dogma and philosophical theory, and a bawdy drinking scene heighten the medieval colour of the musical presentation.

Wilson is a member of the Canadian League of Composers and of CAPAC.

LEE HEPNER

MUSICAL WORKS

STAGE

John Fibber (play for children). 1970. ms. Text: P J Spensley.

Heloïse and Abelard (full-length opera). 1972. 57′. ms. Libretto: Dr Eugene Benson. Sept 9, 1973, Tor, O'Keefe Centre, COC, Victor Feldbrill(cond), Heather Thomson, Allan Monk (title roles), Leon Major(dir).

The Selfish Giant (children's opera). 1972. ms. Text: Oscar Wilde.

The Summoning of Everyman (one-act church opera). 1972. ms.

Ballet Score (based on Can Indian legend). ms.

ORCHESTRA

Tone Poem. 1950. 12′. ms.

Symphony in A. 1954. 25′. full orch. ms.

Sinfonia for Double Orchestra. 1972. 12′45″. med orch. CMC. Mar 3, 1973, Tor, Eaton Aud, CBC Fest O, Lawrence Leonard.

Theme and Evolutions for Orchestra. full orch. ms.

SOLOIST WITH ORCHESTRA

Sonata da Chiesa for Oboe and Strings. 1960. 18′10″. CMC. 1961, Guelph, members of TS, Charles Wilson(cond), Perry Bauman (ob).

En Guise d'Orphée. 1968. 12′. bar, str orch. May 15, 1968, Guelph, Chalmers United Church, James Bechtel.

CHOIR WITH ORCHESTRA

Cantata; 'On the Morning of Christ's Nativity'. 1963. 25'. sop, ten, bar, SATB, small orch. CMC. 1967, Hamilton, Bach-Elgar Choir, HPO, Charles Wilson(cond), Carol-Ann Curry(sop), Glyn Evans(ten), James Bechtel(bs).

The Angels of the Earth (oratorio). 1966. 2hrs 15'. sop, bar, narrs, SATB, orch. CMC. Text: Wilson MacDonald. June 19, 1967, Guelph, Bach-Elgar Choir, Guelph Light Opera Co, TS plyrs, Mary Morrison(sop), James Bechtel(bs), J Horton, T Davies (narrs).

CHOIR

The Cherry Tree Carol Part II (arr). 1'25". SATB. Wat, 1953.

And Now Bless the God of All. 1965. SATB, org. Wat, 1965. Text: Sirach.

Three Madrigals on Latin Lyrics. SATB. CMC.

VOICE(S)

When I Set Out for Lyonesse. 1949. 5'. ms.

The Flute Player. 1950. 5'. vc, EH, fl. ms.

Six Songs. 1951. 10'. Text: R L Stevenson.

Songs (cycle on poems of William Blake). c1953. 8'.

Song Cycle. 1952. sop, pno. CMC.

VOICES WITH INSTRUMENTAL ENSEMBLE

Dona Nobis Pacem. 1970. 7'25". SATB, brass (org). CMC. GVT, 1972. Poly 2917 009. 1971, Hamilton, Bach-Elgar Choir, brass ens from HPO, Charles Wilson.

INSTRUMENTAL ENSEMBLE

String Quartet No. 1. 1950. 20'. CMC.

String Trio. 1963. vln, vla, vlc. CMC.

String Quartet No. 2. 1968. 20'35". CMC. May 11, 1970, Guelph, Spring Fest, Orford Qt.

Concerto 5 x 4 x 3. 1970. 12'10". str qnt or ww qt or brass trio or any combination of these ensembles. CMC. CBC BR SM-195.

MIXED MEDIA

Phrases from Orpheus. 1970. 25'. SATB, dancers. ms. Text. D G Jones. May 10, 1971, Guelph, Tor Dance Theatre, Guelph Oratorio Soc Chorus, Charles Wilson.

BIBLIOGRAPHY

See K.

Schulman, Michael. 'Heloise and Abelard – What Price Canadian Operas?' *PAC*. Vol X, no. 4, Winter 1973 (9–12).

WUENSCH, GERHARD (b. Vienna, Austria, 23 Dec. 1925). He studied musicology at the University of Vienna and obtained a Doctor of Philosophy degree in 1950. He received his Artist Diplomas in piano and composition from the State Academy for Music and the Dramatic Arts in Vienna in 1952. He was free-lance pianist and accompanist in Austria and Germany and was staff composer for the Austrian Radio Network RAVAG (1951–4). He was awarded a Fulbright Grant in 1954 for post-doctoral studies at the University of Texas, where he studied composition with Paul A. Pisk and Kent Kennan. From 1956 to 1963 he was a teacher at Butler University in Indianapolis and musical director of the German Choral Society and of Indianapolis theatre groups. He received the Benjamin Award for Restful Music in 1956 (*Nocturne for Orchestra in F Minor*) and in 1962 won first prize in the Syracuse Fine Arts Festival (*Mosaic*) and second prize from both the Los Angeles Horn Club and the American Guild of Organists (*Ricercare*). From 1964 to 1969 he was a member of the Faculty of Music, University of Toronto and from 1969 to 1973 he was with the music department of the University of Calgary. In 1973 he was appointed head of the department of theory and composition, Faculty of Music, University of Western Ontario, London, Ont.

Wuensch is one of Canada's more outspoken composers and, although at times he is quite biting in criticism of himself and others, his quips are always filled with wit that charms his listeners. In the program note for his *Trio for Clarinet, Bassoon and Piano* (1948), he writes: 'One of the greatest benefits derived from my musicological studies was the realization of the total insignificance of my talents as a composer'. Nevertheless he has continued to add to his large list of works. Although basically tonal, the *Trio* has sudden harmonic twists, resulting in an almost parodistic style reminiscent of Max Reger, the subject of Wuensch's doctoral thesis in musicology. Wuensch has written collections of educational piano pieces (*Spectrum, Opus 41*, 1969; *Twelve Glimpses into 20th Century Idioms*, 1969), in which he has utilized the principal techniques of twentieth-century music from polytonal to aleatoric and indeterminate idioms. His own personal style, as exemplified in *Symphonia Sacra, Opus 30* (1967), deals mainly in dissonant chromaticism. The *Symphonia* alternates between heroic brass sections and soft, lyrical sections with organ and harp. The choral writing is contrapuntal and, although relying on non-tonal material (whole-tone scales for example), it is more conservative than his instrumental writing.

In 1972, in collaboration with Keith MacMillan, he was commissioned by the Contemporary Music Showcase Association to write a work for high school students (*Six Guises*, for narrator and 26 wind instruments). In December 1972 he received a Research Fellowship from the Canada Council to enable him to complete a book on Max Reger. He is a member of the Pi Kappa Lambda Music Fraternity, the Phi Kappa Phi Honorary Society, and of CAPAC.

MUSICAL WORKS

STAGE

Labyrinth, Op 7 (ballet). 1957.

Il Pomo d'Oro, Op 9 (musical comedy). 1958. Libretto: Allegra Stewart.

ORCHESTRA

Nocturne for Orchestra in F minor, Op 6. 1956.

Variations on a Dorian Hexachord, Op 10. 1959.

Symphony No 1, Op 12. 1959.

BAND

Caribbean Rhapsody, Op 11. 1959.

Symphony in E flat, Op 14. 1960.

Symphony, Op 35. 1967. brass, perc.

SOLOIST WITH ORCHESTRA

Piano Concerto, Op 17. 1961.

Ballad for Trumpet and Orchestra, Op 19. 1962.

Concerto for Piano and Chamber Orchestra, Op 57. 1971.

Scherzo for Piano and Wind Ensemble, Op 58. 1971.

Six Guises, Op 62. 1972. narr, winds, perc. Text: Keith MacMillan.

CHOIR

Vexilla Regis Produent, Op 36. 1968; WIM, 1968. soli, SATB, org. Text: John Skelton.

Fragments: Beach, Op 63. 1972. SAB. Text: Margaret Atwood.

CHOIR WITH INSTRUMENTAL ENSEMBLE

Symphonia Sacra, Op 30. 1961. soli, SATB, brass, perc, org. Text: First Epistle of St John.

VOICE

The Apostles, Op 4. 1951. Text: Hans Nüchtern.

Five Vignettes, Op 50. 1970. Text: Richard du Wors.

VOICE WITH INSTRUMENTAL ENSEMBLE

Six Songs. 1970. vc, fl, accord. Text: Louis Dudek, Simone Rontier, Myra von Riedemann, Anne Hébert, Marjorie Pickthall, L A MacKay.

INSTRUMENTAL ENSEMBLE

Trio for Clarinet, Bassoon and Piano, Op 1. 1948.

Divertimento in G, Op 5. 1954. fl, pno.

String Quartet No 1 in D major, Op 8. 1955.

Mosaic, Op 13. 1959. brass qt.

Partita for Horn and Piano. 1961.

Sonatina for Viola and Piano, Op 15. 1963.

Lento and Vivace, Op 16. 1963; WIM, 1966. hn, pno.

String Quartet No 2, Op 18. 1963.

Ricercare, Op 21. 1963. 8hn, org.

Woodwind Quintet, Op 22. 1963.

Sonata for Horn and Piano, Op 24. 1964.

Music for Seven Brass Instruments, Op 27. 1966. WIM.

Sonata, Op 28. 1966. tpt, pno.

Sextet for Horns, Op 33. 1966.

Second Quintet, Op 34. 1967. ww qnt.

Sonatina, Op 43. 1969. cl, pno.

Music Without Pretensions, Op 45. 1969. accord, str qt. Wat.

Cameos, Op 46a. 1969; MCA, 1971. fl, pno.

Suite for Trumpet and Organ, Op 40. 1970; WIM, 1972.

Polysonics, Op 44. 1970. variable instr.

Music in 4 Dimensions, Op 49. 1970. brass, hp, perc.

Trio ('Three Conversations'), Op 51. 1971. vln, vlc, pno.

Variations, Op 52. 1971. cl, pno.

Six Duets, Op 53. 1971. fl, cl.

Prelude, Aria and Fugue, Op 54. 1971. accord, brass qt.

In Modo Antico. 1971. cl, pno.

Sonata, Op 59. 1971. sop sax (or ob), pno.

Aria and Fugue, Op 65. 1972. ob, org.

PIANO

Esquisse, Op 2. 1950 (rev 1970).

Sonatina, Op 3. 1951.
Canzona and Toccata, Op 20. 1963.
Six Serial Cereal Pieces, Op 32, 1966.
Mini Suite No 1. 1969; MCA, 1969. 'Voices from the Past' Dom s-69002.
Two Sonatinas, Op 38. 1969.
Spectrum, Op 41 (30 Studies in Contemporary Idioms). 1969; MCA, 1971.
Twelve Glimpses Into 20th Century Idioms, Op 37. 1969; MCA, 1969. 'The Big Leap Forward', 'Rain Clouds' Dom s-69002.
A Winter Foursome, Op 39. 1969; Wat, 1972.
Alberta Sketch Book, Op 56. 1971.
Valses Nostalgiques, Op 61. 1972. pno 4 hands.
Two Piano Pieces, Op 66. 1973; Wat, 1973.

INSTRUMENTAL SOLO
A Merry Suite for Harpsichord, Op 26. 1965; Wat, 1972.
Fantasy for Harp, Op 31. 1968.
Four Mini-Suites, Op 42. 1968; Wat, 1969. accord.
Sonatina for Unaccompanied Flute, Op 46b. 1970.
Sonata da Camera, Op 48. 1970; B & H, 1971. accord.
Three Pieces for Solo Flute. 1971.
Alberta Set, Op 55. 1971; B & H, 1972. accord.
Monologue, Op 60. 1972. accord.
Diversions, Op 64. 1972. accord.
Deux Sentiments, Op 67. 1973. accord.

ORGAN
Toccata Piccola, Op 23a. 1963; AV, 1963.
Sonata Breve, Op 25. 1963; AV, 1966.
Aria, Op 23b. 1964; AV, 1964.
Prelude and Fugue, Op 29. 1964.
Praeludium Secundi Toni. 1966; AV, 1966.

LITERARY WORKS

'The Programme Sonatas of J. L. Dusik', *CAUSM Journal*. Vol. 1, no. 2 (17–24).
'Spielformer in Regers Klaviermusik', *Mitteilungen des Max Reger Instituts, Bonn*. 18, Heft, July 1971 (16–29).
'Max Reger's Choralcantatas', *Music*. Vol. 6, no. 2, Feb. 1972 (32).

Z

ZUCKERT, LEON (b. Poltava, Russia, 4 May 1904). He studied with Boris Bordsky at the Imperial School of Music in Poltava (1916–18). He came to Canada in 1929 and studied conducting with Reginald Stewart in Toronto. As a composer he is mainly self-taught. From 1933 to 1942 he conducted many radio programs of his own compositions and arrangements. Such works as *Divertimento Orientale* (1962) and *My Paintings* (1969) evoke visual images within a generally conservative style; this is also true of his symphonic suite *Quetico* (1957), originally a film score for Chris Chapman's film of the same name. Zuckert has played violin or viola in several orchestras, including the Winnipeg (1932–4), Toronto (1951–6; 1961–3), Portland, Oregon (1958–9), Indianapolis (1959–61), and Montreal (1961) Symphony Orchestras, as well as others in South America, Mexico, and the United States. From 1963 to 1965 and from 1967 to 1969 he was principal violist and assistant conductor of the Halifax Symphony Orchestra. He is a member of CAPAC.

MUSICAL WORKS

INSTRUMENTAL
2 works for accord solo: *Gypsy (Buda) Memories* (1938); *Poltava Waltz* (1967).
6 works for orchestra: *My Canadian Travels* (1938); *Symphony No 1* (1948–50), *No 2* (1959–62); *Oriental Romance* (1960); *Impressions of Teneriffe* (1970).
18 works for chamber ensemble, including: 3 works for vln and pno; *Bonita* (1948), accord, pno; *Sisterly Love* (1963), vln, vla; *Preludio en modo antiguo* (1964), brass choir; 3 quartets for strings (1965, 1971, 1972); *Little Prince in Montreal* (1968), ww qnt; *Psychedelic Suite* (1968), brass qnt; *Little Spanish Dance* (1970), fl, pno.

Jar 1971 Dom s-69006.
Divertimento Orientale. 1965. ob, str.
2 works for str orch: *Two Moods in One* (1967–8); *My Paintings* (1969).
Nostalgia I and II. 1968. org.

CHORAL
Dniepr (cantata). 1961. 35′. SATB, orch. Text: Taras Schevchenko.

VOCAL
12 works for vc and pno, including: *Oifn Veg* (1948); *Autumn Wind* (1959); *Prayer* (1960); *Two Romances* (1961); *Five Philosophical Songs* (1970–1).
Song in Brass. 1964. sop, orch.
Quintet of the Moon and the Sea. 1972. vc, pno, str qt.

LITERARY WORKS

ARTICLES
'Musical Life on the Island of Teneriffe', *CanCo.* No. 51, June 1970 (16–19).